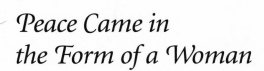

*Peace Came in
the Form of a Woman*

Peace Came in the Form of a Woman

Indians and Spaniards in the Texas Borderlands

JULIANA BARR

Published in Association
with The William P. Clements
Center for Southwest Studies,
Southern Methodist University,
by The University of North
Carolina Press ⟿ Chapel Hill

Designed by Heidi Perov
Set in Minion by Keystone Typesetting, Inc.
Manufactured in the United States of America

Publication of this book was aided by a grant from the Program for Cultural Cooperation between Spain's Ministry of Culture and United States Universities.

The paper in this book meets the guidelines for permanence and durability of the Committee on Production Guidelines for Book Longevity of the Council on Library Resources.

Library of Congress Cataloging-in-Publication Data
Barr, Juliana.
Peace came in the form of a woman : Indians and Spaniards in the Texas borderlands / Juliana Barr.
p. cm.
Includes bibliographical references and index.
ISBN-13: 978-0-8078-3082-6 (cloth: alk. paper)
ISBN-13: 978-0-8078-5790-8 (pbk.: alk. paper)
1. Indians of North America—Texas—History—18th century. 2. Indian captivities—Texas—History—18th century. 3. Spaniards—Texas—History—18th century. 4. Missions, Spanish—Texas—History—18th century. 5. Women and peace—Texas—History—18th century. 6. Women—Texas—Social conditions—18th century. 7. Diplomacy—Texas—History—18th century. 8. Texas—History—To 1846. I. William P. Clements Center for Southwest Studies. II. Title.
E78.T4B37 2007
976.4004'97—dc22   2006027686

Portions of this work appeared previously, in somewhat different form, as "Beyond Their Control: Spaniards in Native Texas," in *Choice, Persuasion, and Coercion: Social Control on Spain's North American Frontiers*, ed. Jesús F. de la Teja and Ross Frank (Albuquerque: University of New Mexico Press, 2005), 149–77; "A Diplomacy of Gender: Rituals of First Contact in the 'Land of the Tejas,' " *William and Mary Quarterly*, 3rd ser., 61 (July 2004): 393–434; and "From Captives to Slaves: Commodifying Indian Women in the Borderlands," *Journal of American History* 92 (June 2005): 19–46 and are reprinted here with permission of the publishers.

cloth   11 10 09 08 07   5 4 3 2 1
paper   11 10 09 08 07   5 4 3 2 1

contents

illustrations

acknowledgments

In writing this book, I have been the beneficiary of the aid and goodwill of numerous individuals and institutions. A Summerfield-Roberts Fellowship from the William P. Clements Center for Southwest Studies at Southern Methodist University got me off to a great beginning, as it provided the opportunity to exchange ideas with a group of scholars who also focus their work on the multicultural realms of the Southwest. The department of history and the Faculty of Arts and Sciences at Rutgers University and the department of history at the University of Florida granted sabbaticals that gave me sustained periods of time in which to revise much of the manuscript. A year spent as a faculty fellow at Rutgers' Institute for Research on Women in 2001–2 offered a collegial space within which to explore questions concerning the intersections of race and gender.

A veritable host of archivists have shown me unstinting generosity and knowledgeable direction as I completed research and later gathered maps and illustrations. I gratefully thank Ralph Elder, John Wheat, and Steven Williams at the Center for American History at the University of Texas at Austin, Kinga Perzynska and Susan Eason at the Catholic Archives of Texas, John Anderson at the Texas State Library and Archives, Susan Danforth and Leslie Tobias-Olsen at the John Carter Brown Library, Roy Goodman and Robert Cox at the American Philosophical Society, Carolyn Spock at the Texas Archeological Research Laboratory, Mary Linn Wernet at the Cammie G. Henry Research Center at the Eugene P. Watson Memorial Library on the campus of Northwestern State University, Patricia Mercado-Allinger at the Texas Historical Commission, Beth Standifird at the San Antonio Conservation Society, Amy Verheide and Cary McStay at the Fray Angélico Chávez Library and Photo Archives at the Palace of the Governors, John O'Neill at the Hispanic Society of America, and Shane Culpepper at the Gilcrease Museum. I thank Melissa Beaver at the *Journal of American History* for designing the four maps that appear in this book. I would also like to express my appreciation to Dan Flores, Jack Jackson, George Sabo, and Ron Tyler, who have kindly allowed me to include in this book maps or photographs of their own creation or from their own collections.

While working on this manuscript, I have inhabited different scholarly worlds—some focused on the history of women and gender, others on the history of the Spanish borderlands and early America. All of them offered me intellectually creative, supportive, and challenging atmospheres in which to work and to think. Long ago, it seems, I took my first steps as a historian within the stimulating realm of the U.S. women's history program at the University of Wisconsin and with the guidance and inspiration of Gerda Lerner, Jeanne Boydston, and Linda Gordon. I could not ask for better mentors and models. Charles Cohen kept me grounded in early America, spending hours turning my arguments inside out and then right side in, to my eternal betterment. Time at the University of North Carolina with Judith Bennett, Cynthia Herrup, and Barbara Harris expanded my intellectual horizons to include the analysis of women in medieval and early modern Europe, which enriched my understanding of early modern America in ways that I appreciated more with each page of this book I wrote. The Clements Center for Southwest Studies at Southern Methodist University gave me an intellectual home where I might try out different manifestations of my manuscript in the warm and spirited company of David J. Weber, Sherry L. Smith, William deBuys, Heather Trigg, John R. Chávez, and Ed Countryman. The collegiality of the history department at Rutgers University made for an awfully nice place to write and rewrite, with Alison Isenberg, Indrani Chatterjee, and Gail Triner helping me to keep my head above water. And now at the University of Florida, I thank Jon and Beverly Sensbach, who have been fun and supportive comrades during the final leg of the race.

If left only in my hands, this book would not have reached this point—thank goodness for the insightful scholars who have taken a hand in helping me to improve it in numerous and immeasurable ways. I have benefited from presenting aspects of this research at annual meetings of the American Historical Association, the Organization of American Historians, the American Society for Ethnohistory, the Berkshire Conference on the History of Women, the Avignon Conference on Slavery and Forced Labour, the Omohundro Institute of Early American History and Culture, the International Seminar on the History of the Atlantic World at Harvard University, the Western History Association, and the Southern Historical Association. At these presentations, I received perceptive commentary from Jennifer L. Baszile, Carol Devens, Patricia Galloway, Walter Johnson, Karen Ordahl Kupperman, James Merrell, Theda Perdue, Nancy Shoemaker, Pete Sigal, Alan Taylor, Tanis Thorne, and Neil L. Whitehead. In different forms, limited parts of the book have appeared previously as essays in the *William and Mary Quarterly*, the

Journal of American History and *Choice, Persuasion, and Coercion: Social Control on Spain's North American Frontiers*, edited by Jesús F. de la Teja and Ross Frank. Via comments on these essays, insights from Rudolph Bell, Indrani Chatterjee, Paul G. E. Clemens, Laura F. Edwards, Alan Gallay, Ramón A. Gutiérrez, Nancy A. Hewitt, Joseph C. Miller, Marla Miller, George Sabo, Nancy Shoemaker, and Jennifer M. Spear also made their way into the text. A stalwart few have read the manuscript from cover to cover at different times during the manuscript's maturation—James F. Brooks, Kathleen M. Brown, Light Townsend Cummins, Frank de la Teja, Gunlög Fur, Laura J. Moore, Christopher Morris, Nancy Shoemaker, Sherry L. Smith, and David J. Weber—and they all offered invaluable direction about its arguments, its prose, and its conceptual analysis.

I owe my thanks as well to the good people at the University of North Carolina Press. Katy O'Brien, Ron Maner, and John K. Wilson have been generous and patient in taking care of all the details, both little and large, in bringing this manuscript to its published form. Chuck Grench's warmth, kindness, and dogged encouragement saw me through to the end.

To Gunlög Fur, David H. Grace, Laura J. Moore, and Jennifer Spear, I give my thanks for friendships that have made me happier, saner, and smarter than I would have been without them around. To my parents, Alwyn and Nancy Barr, and my sister, Alicia Barr, I write what I hope they already know: that they have always been and always will be my terra firma upon which everything rests. To Sean Adams, I give my thanks for the spaces in our togetherness that he promised to me on a lovely day in July in Bernalillo, New Mexico. I have accomplished nothing that I do not owe to both that space and that togetherness.

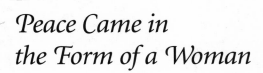

Peace Came in
the Form of a Woman

Introduction

On a crisp spring day in March 1772, a woman led a group of seven Comanches into the town of San Antonio de Béxar, Texas, carrying a white flag and a cross. Her approach was the initial step in a peace process between Comanche and Spanish peoples in a time of violent interaction. Since they had first come into contact thirty years before, Spaniards and Comanches in Texas had never known peace, much less friendly negotiation, with one another. Rather, hostility had ruled their relations. By 1772, the groups viewed each other with such deep suspicion that thirteen more years would pass before they completed a treaty agreement. Significantly, every time hostilities flared anew during those thirteen years, women stepped (or were pushed) forward as the chosen emissaries of truce.

It may perhaps seem strange that Comanches would send a woman at the head of this delegation. It certainly was not customary among Comanches to assign women to positions of diplomatic authority, any more than it was the custom of Spaniards to receive women in such capacities. Indeed, *this* woman did not travel as an authority in her own right. She was a former captive of Spaniards whom they had sent home thirty days before to win diplomatic favor with Comanche leaders. Comanche chiefs had promptly sent her back to the Spanish *villa* in order to retrieve other Comanches held captive by Spanish officials. Why, then, did Spanish and Comanche men choose this woman and so many others as political mediators in the eighteenth century? Because after decades of violence, it had become virtually impossible for an all-male party from either group to approach the other without being presumed hostile; the presence of women was the only way to signal peaceful intentions. This role was not a new one for women in the region, but rather one that had evolved over the eighteenth century as powerful and populous Indian nations negotiated economic and political relations with small numbers of European settlers and traders in the midst of mounting violence and enmity.

Peace Came in the Form of a Woman: Indians and Spaniards in the Texas Borderlands investigates the history behind moments such as this one in 1772.

To do so, it explores the stories of a range of Indian peoples—including Caddos, Apaches, Payayas, Ervipiames, Wichitas, and Comanches—and the varied relationships that they each formed with Spaniards at different moments in time from the 1690s, when Spaniards first attempted to settle in the region, through the 1780s, when Comanches decided a Spanish peace might be desirable—the last major native power in Texas to do so. More specifically, the book seeks to illuminate what lay beneath the surface of political ritual in order to show how those moments when women acted as mediators of peace did not simply signal cross-cultural rapport, but rather the predominance of native codes of peace and war.

The political symbols and acts of Spanish-Indian interaction in Texas must be understood as a diplomacy of gender. Hitherto, European-Indian interactions have been viewed primarily in the context of race relations. This in turn implicitly assumes that Europeans had all the power, since race was becoming the crucial component of European categories of social and political hierarchy. This book argues that Native American constructions of social order and of political and economic relationships—defined by gendered terms of kinship—were at the crux of Spanish-Indian politics in eighteenth-century Texas. In some ways, it is an old-fashioned insight that gender is about power, but in native worlds, where kinship provided the foundation for every institution of their societies, gender and power were inseparable. Once Spaniards arrived on the scene, they discovered that they too would have to operate within those terms if their relationships with Native Americans were to succeed.

Why would Europeans have to play by native rules? Despite well-entrenched myths of Spanish conquest, claims of imperial control made by Spanish officialdom did not reflect reality on the ground in much of the region they identified as the province of Texas. Indians—and the Spaniards who lived among them—recognized most of the region as Apachería, Comanchería, Wichita, and Caddo territories. In fact one Franciscan missionary explained in a 1750 report to the king that missions in the Spanish towns of San Antonio de Béxar and La Bahía lay outside the "Province of Texas"—in other words, Texas was the province in which lived Tejas Indians (as Spaniards began calling Hasinai Caddos in the 1690s), and Spaniards certainly did not control that. The reports of military expeditions sent to reconnoiter Spanish defensive capabilities in the region in 1727 and 1767 similarly referred to the region as the "Province of the Texas Indians," suggesting the Spaniards' awareness that they were living in or near Caddo lands at Caddo sufferance as long as a peace alliance held. In 1727, Pedro de Rivera in turn identified the "Tejas province" as stopping at the boundary of the Apache-controlled hill country he called "Lomería de los

Apaches." Thus, as provincial governor Tomás Felipe Winthuysen described to his superiors, San Antonio stood at the core of Apachería. By 1767, Spaniards recognized that the "true dominions" of Comanches had superseded those of Apaches. Thus, presidial soldiers spent several hours a day patrolling a semicircular path twelve miles out from San Antonio de Béxar, where lay "El Paso de los Comanches" and the many other *puertos* (gateways) into Comanchería that surrounded the Spanish villa. Indians, not Spaniards, expanded their territorial claims over the century.[1]

The marqués de Rubí, head of the 1767 expedition, drew pointed distinctions between the "real" and "imaginary" boundaries of the nominal Spanish province of Texas. After almost eighty years of a Spanish presence in the region, he called for the evacuation of the few Spaniards living in Caddo, Wichita, and Comanche lands—where "imaginary missions," empty of neophytes, huddled along "imaginary frontiers." Only when the territory claimed by Spain, "which we call with high impropriety 'Dominions of the King,'" was drawn back far to the south to constitute just the areas around the towns of San Antonio de Béxar and La Bahía could "those which are truly dominions of the King" (territories *south* of the Rio Grande) be defended against Indian *invasion*. Indians were the feared conquerors in Texas.[2]

Others agreed. In 1778, *fray* (friar) Juan Agustín Morfi recorded that "though we still call ourselves [the province's] masters, we do not exercise dominion over a foot of land beyond San Antonio." Nicolás de Lafora, a member of Rubí's 1767 expedition, wrote that Indians "have little respect for the Spanish and we are admitted only as friends, but without any authority." Tellingly, Lafora measured Spanish powerlessness through the story of one woman's fate in these lands. He recorded the expedition's galling discovery of a Spanish girl living as a "slave" of Hasinai Caddos—a girl whom neither "so-called" Spanish authority nor Spanish money could liberate, leaving Lafora to bewail how in Texas the "honorable forces of his Majesty" could be forced into "the shameful position of suppliants."[3]

Yet, suppliants they were, and Lafora's lament echoed two hundred years of Spanish experience in these lands. A much earlier chapter of Spanish subordination to Indian peoples of Texas had been written in the sixteenth century. In 1530, survivors of an expedition led by Pánfilo de Narváez had been stranded on the Texas coast after taking to the sea in flight from Indians in what would become Florida. At the end of six years living among Indian peoples of south-central Texas, only four men remained alive of the original four-hundred-man expedition. Alvar Núñez Cabeza de Vaca, Andrés Dorantes, Alonso del Castillo, and an enslaved Moor named Estevanico had negotiated themselves into positions as enslaved traders and emissaries among different Indian groups. Their survival may well have rested upon their

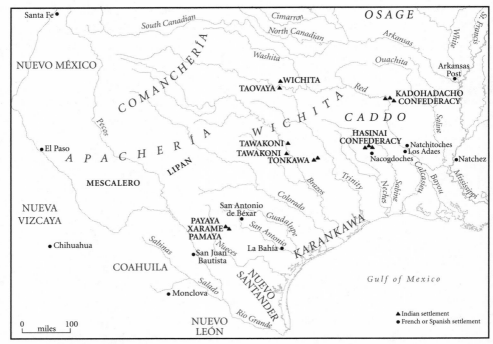

Indian and European settlements in the eighteenth-century Texas borderlands. Map drawn by Melissa Beaver.

ability to play intermediary roles usually associated with women by the region's native peoples, especially in acting as go-betweens among different groups. Though Cabeza de Vaca later, in his published narrative, put an ennobling spin on his experiences, at the time it surely represented a different but no less painful loss of male honor than that cited by Lafora.[4]

In the eighteenth century, when Spaniards came again to Texas, they sought permanent settlement among native peoples from whom they still earned no recognition as representatives of the most extensive, wealthy, and powerful European empire in the Americas. The Spanish state cast little shadow in these lands. To understand the world they entered, imagine present-day Texas divided into quadrants, three under native control, with Apaches in the west, Caddos in the east, and Comanches and Wichitas in the north. The fourth, the Spanish quadrant of Texas, consisted of the south-central areas of San Antonio de Béxar and La Bahía (and a tiny pocket of soldiers, Franciscans, and civilians who lived scattered among Caddo hamlets around the presidio and missions of Los Adaes). Within these islands of Spanish settlement, mission-presidio complexes served as the primary sites of

Spanish-Indian interaction, where Franciscan missionaries fought for Indian souls and soldiers fought for Spanish security—neither with much success. They had first thought to make the small settlement in the middle of Caddo territory the base for Spanish occupation. In the face of Caddo indifference and rejection by 1730, however, the area of southern, rather than eastern, Texas had emerged as the center of Spanish development. There, multiple and diverse Indian peoples, including Cantonas, Payayas, and Ervipiames began to put Spanish institutions and relationships to their own use.

Indian observers never saw Spaniards as a ruling power. Indians were the rulers in these lands. Outside of their very limited areas of settlement, in fact, Spaniards merited little native attention at all. There were no conquests and no attempts to subject Indians to tribute or labor systems as found elsewhere in Spanish America. A few missions and fewer presidios made up the Spanish landscape and aimed solely at defending the small, struggling Spanish population against superior Indian forces. The total population of Spanish Texas spread among the three areas of San Antonio, La Bahía, and Los Adaes never exceeded 3,200 people in the eighteenth century, and that number included those Indians who had chosen to enter mission settlements to live with Spaniards.[5] Many Indian villages and *rancherías* (Spaniards' term for native seasonal encampments) dwarfed those of Spaniards. Although the spread of epidemic disease diminished native population numbers as the century wore on, it did so unevenly, allowing some, like Comanches (who did not suffer their first smallpox outbreak until 1779), to avoid exposure for most of the century, while others implemented strategies to respond to population losses through adoption, intermarriage, and confederation with extended kin and allies.

In the eyes of Apaches, Comanches, Wichitas, and Caddos, Spaniards operated as just another collection of bands like themselves in an equal, if not weaker, position to compete for socioeconomic resources in the region. Throughout the century, different Indian groups made it clear that they viewed each Spanish settlement as an individual entity. At midcentury, allied Wichitas, Caddos, and Tonkawas maintained peace with Spaniards living at Los Adaes while making war against those at San Antonio de Béxar and the nearby mission-presidio complex at San Sabá. Karankawa peoples along the coast saw no conflict between keeping up a long-running war with the people of La Bahía while entertaining diplomatic negotiations with San Antonio officials. Conversely, coastal-dwelling Akokisas saw no reason to petition the governor of Texas for a mission while visiting San Antonio because they believed each Spanish settlement to govern itself independently and so queried authorities in La Bahía instead, since that was the settlement nearest their own.

The attenuated position of Spaniards in Texas was no mere fancy of Indian observers. Spaniards did indeed operate similarly to Indian bands, living in farming and ranching settlements, loosely allied so that their small contingents of soldiers came to one another's aid if and when able to do so in times of threat. Economically, they were often worse off than their Indian neighbors, as high risks and high costs of transporting imports over great distances stymied a reliable supply of goods from Veracruz. Exports also remained almost nonexistent due to the lack of production of domestic trade goods and the absence of mining. What little market economy emerged consisted of mission and civilian farms and ranches supplying food to the military. In turn, only presidio payrolls brought cash into Texas. Ranching did not take off until the 1770s and 1780s, when peace agreements with Wichitas and Comanches slowed the raiding of herds and market conditions in northern Mexico and Louisiana encouraged the Texas industry to expand beyond subsistence into cattle drive exports. Trade to the west with New Mexico required practically impossible passage across Comanchería, and thus routes, much less exchange, remained nonexistent until the end of the eighteenth century. Saltillo (south of the Rio Grande) emerged as the nearest market center for Texas residents, and even then, Texas Spaniards only began attending the annual trade fairs there regularly in the 1770s. Along the Texas-Louisiana border to the east, isolated Spaniards in Los Adaes and later Nacogdoches (est. 1779) depended upon exchange with Caddos and Frenchmen for their very survival (despite Spanish trade prohibitions that only periodically relaxed to allow for trade in food). All these problems reflected and refracted Spanish officials' failures to attract a growing population to Texas in the face of the ever-present threat of Indian neighbors—creating what David Weber has termed a common conundrum in much of the northern provinces: "there would be safety in numbers, but they could not raise the numbers without guarantees of safety."[6]

Spaniards in Texas therefore struggled to establish a presence among multiple native groups who had no need for mission salvation or welfare, no fear of Spanish military force, and no patience for the lack of Spanish markets or trade fairs (especially in comparison with those offered by Frenchmen in Louisiana and by Spaniards in New Mexico). The primary power relations were not European versus Indian, but relations among native peoples. At stake were regional networks and territories that could be used to the advantage of individual groups in order to protect and to expand their domestic political economies. Resource management, trade, and economic well-being determined territorial imperatives. When it came to Spaniards, Indian groups like Comanches and Wichitas had an easy choice: if they could not trade for Spanish guns and horses, they simply would take them by force. Thus, for much of the eighteenth century, Spanish settlements in Texas earned native attention only as targets for raids. As a result, Spanish-Indian contact long remained limited to an exchange of small-scale raids and attacks from which no stable structures of interchange developed. With little incentive to be in contact, much less to seek accommodation, Indians and Spaniards found that disorder and violence defined their relations in the region as much as, or more than, order and peace. In this particular "colonial" world, Indians not only retained control of the region but also asserted control over Spaniards themselves.[7]

Texas thus does not fit any of the usual categories posited in colonial and Native American historiography. No stories of Indian assimilation, accommodation, resistance, or perseverance here. Eighteenth-century Texas, instead, offers a story of Indian *dominance*. As such, Texas forces us to reconsider the expectations we bring to European-Indian encounters in early America. Our very term for the period, "colonial America," not only describes the relationship between colony and mother country but also presumes European political domination over the territories and peoples of this supposedly "New World." To paraphrase Daniel Richter (a bit out of context), "invasion" and "conquest" trip all too easily off our tongues because the "master narrative of early America remains essentially European-focused." That easy-if-lamentable conquest model triggers certain formulaic assumptions that are rarely questioned because it is so terribly difficult to reverse our perspectives—not only to reimagine the past from Indian frames of reference but to rid ourselves of 20/20 hindsight that tells us "how it all turned out": the United States in control of North America and much-reduced native populations living as semisovereign nations on reservations within the U.S. domain. No matter how determined the attempts to envision Indian perspectives or to champion Indian "agency," our foundational model always puts Indians on the defensive and Europeans on the offensive. But Texas was different. There, not even a "middle ground" emerged, because this was not a world where a military and political standoff could lead to a "search for accommodation and common meaning," as drawn so persuasively by Richard White for the Great Lakes region. In Texas, native peoples could and did gain their ends by dominant force.[8]

The first aim of this book, then, is to reframe the picture by visiting a world in which Indians dictated the rules and Europeans were the ones who had to accommodate, resist, and persevere. This story qualifies the narrative of "colonial America" by countering teleological visions of European invasion and Euroamerican manifest destiny leading inevitably to the creation of the United States. The first step is to invert our standard model. Studies of Spanish American borderlands, for instance, recognize so-called frontiers as "zones of constant conflict and negotiation over power," but only because such regions were "boundaries beyond the sphere of routine action of centrally located violence-producing enterprises" (i.e., those of the state). From a Spanish perspective, the frontiers and borderlands of New Spain's far northern provinces were indeed peripheries, far from the imperial core. And from this perspective, the question of control in these peripheries measured the extent or limit of New Spain's ability to exercise a "monopoly on violence" over Indian subjects, or potential subjects, far from its institutional center. Yet, it is impossible to understand Texas without recognizing it as a core of *native* political economies, a core within which Spaniards were the subjects, or potential subjects, of native institutions of control. Spanish authorities encountered already existent and ever-expanding native systems of trade, warfare, and alliance into which they had to seek entry. Control of the region's political economy (and with it, the "monopoly on violence") rested in the collective (though not united) hands of Apaches, Caddos, Comanches, and Wichitas. By extension, native raiding served geopolitical and economic purposes, not as a form of defensive resistance or revolt, but of offensive expansion and domination.[9]

In turn, the second aim of this book is to illustrate the ways in which Indians dictated the terms of contact, diplomacy, alliance, and enmity in their interactions with Spaniards. More specifically, I seek a means of expanding our understanding of Indian-European relations and how we might delineate expressions of Indian power in a period that offers no records written from that perspective. To pursue this perspective, we need to move away from the European constructions of power that are so familiar to us—those grounded in ideas of the state and of racial difference—and try to understand the world as Indians did—organized around kinship-based relationships. To understand the institutions and idioms of power within this Indian-dominated world, we then need to analyze the ways various participants used languages of gender to understand and misunderstand each other.

Because no one Indian group ruled the entire region, and because native polities did not resemble those of Europeans, native institutions of control were not expressions of power by a dominant state within a clearly bounded society. Instead, they were negotiations of power between separate societies and nations. Different groups wielded power in different ways vis-à-vis Spaniards. Still, the fluidity of native political configurations as individual or allied bands, tribes, or confederations organized around familial, cultural, and linguistic affinity does not negate their structural integrity or the aptness of categorizing them as "nations." A body of people, recognized as a *nación* by Spaniards, might represent both a cultural group of affiliated communities and a political entity controlling certain geographical territory. In turn, the vehicles of control through which native nations institutionalized their power over Europeans were not institutions like Spanish missions or presidios.[10]

Rather, networks of kinship provided the infrastructure for native political and economic systems and codified both domestic and foreign relations. "Kinship, society, politics, economics, religion," anthropologist Raymond DeMallie explains, "are not for Native American peoples differentiated into independent institutions." A certain holism prevails. At root, Indians used principles of kinship to classify people and their relationships with others. Such classifications determined peoples' attitudes, behaviors, rights, and obligations to one another in every aspect of life. Those principles shaped relationships outside of society as well. For Indian leaders in Texas, the Spaniards who sought access to their political and economic networks did so as "strangers" to kinship systems of familial relations and political-economic alliances. Kin designations were a prerequisite for interaction and thus were extended to Europeans (as they were to native strangers); social, political, and/or economic ties could not evolve otherwise. In response, Europeans were expected to abide by the expectations of that kin relationship. In this way, kinship ties were not simply metaphors but the very foundation of Spanish-Indian relations.[11]

As a relational model for native societies, kinship provided a certain system of categories that operated both socially and politically. Categories help people to establish a framework that makes sense of the world and the ordinary and extraordinary events of everyday life. People thereby use these categories "to comprehend the natural world and to organize the division of labor and the distribution of material goods, rights, obligations, status, honor, respect." Categories are relative to others and so often appear as paired or contrasting sets that oppose and balance one another—earth and sky, man and woman, human and supernatural, order and chaos. As such, they emphasize the importance of relationships to the welfare of the human community. Kinship systems, in turn, rely on categories of gender and age as the primary determinants of peoples' identity, status, and obligation vis-à-vis others.[12]

In contrast, by the eighteenth century, Europeans drew on categories of race and class to explain the social, economic, and political customs and laws governing all aspects of life. In colonial Latin America, for instance, a diversity of racial constructions (*sistema de castas*) developed over the sixteenth and seventeenth centuries as Indian and African peoples were incorporated into Spanish society. Believing the success of their earlier conquests in Central and South America to lie in the superiority of their Christian "civilization" over native pagan "savagery," Spaniards drew distinctions between Europeans and Indians, expanding the categories of conqueror and conquered into a caste system of sociocultural rankings. Categorizations that constituted differences of culture as differences of race reflected Spanish colonial domination. It was only with the establishment of hegemony and the ability to cast a relationship as one of subordinate and superior, however, that hierarchies of difference, constituted as race, developed. Thus, expressions of race became a signature of European power in cross-cultural relations.[13]

Because Spaniards never enjoyed such power in Texas, such a language of hierarchy rarely emerged outside of civil proceedings within its central town of San Antonio de Béxar. It was not that Spaniards did not think in racial terms, but they could rarely act upon them. The only Indians who fell into Spanish racialized caste systems meant to structure rank and order were those individuals who became a part of Spanish society. Indian peoples included in these social orders were those who had been officially "reduced" by the church and the state. Indian nations remaining outside the purview of Spanish society and government—the native majority in Texas—were not incorporated into such categorizations. In the upper echelons of Spanish imperial bureaucracy, officials might refer rhetorically to *indios bárbaros* or other generic groupings of Indians, yet even then the label was not used to convey a racial or cultural identity but rather a political one designating Indians independent of Spanish rule. Still, at the day-to-day level of provincial life in Texas, a man's survival might depend on his ability to distinguish between Apaches and Comanches, and Spaniards did not have the luxury of lumping all Indian peoples into a single category. They depended on the amity of some groups against the enmity of others for the safety and well-being of their own families and communities.[14]

While some Indian peoples in North America expressed awareness of European categories of race in the eighteenth century, gender was the organizing principle of kin-based social, economic, and political domains within and between native societies. Therefore, gendered language appears "in descriptions of kinship and in the metaphors used in diplomatic negotiations, it affects perceptions of power and authority, practices and beliefs surrounding rituals, cosmology and spirituality, as well as production, reproduction, life and death, numbers, and mediations." Groups in Texas related to one another as kin or as strangers, allies or enemies. Leading chiefs and warriors cast the bonds of military and trade alliances as "brotherhood" and the fictive kinship of male sodalities. Exchanges of women through marriage, captivity, and adoption provided further ties of both real and fictive kinship as different peoples became incorporated into one another's trade networks, political alliances, and settlements. Men and women were both makers of kin. In turn, such practices weighted political and economic interactions with gendered standards of honor associated with family, marriage, and social relations. Masculinity and femininity were not fixed or static categories but were defined and produced by the interactions and relationships between men and women, among men, and among women. For Indians, the prism of kinship thereby defined political as well as social and economic relationships within the terms and expectations of male and female behavior.[15]

Spaniards, of course, were no strangers to ideals and standards of manhood and womanhood. European societies used gender and honor systems to structure relations between and among men and women, to allocate power in their civil, economic, and political systems, and to structure racial caste systems. The majority of studies examining the intersections of Latin American kinship and honor systems within Spanish-Indian relations have done so primarily in terms of enslaved, missionized, or subjugated Indians who were incorporated into Spanish society. The influential works of James F. Brooks and Ramón A. Gutiérrez on New Spain's northern provinces document closely how Spanish society in New Mexico (where detribalized Indian captives and slaves made up almost one-third of that society) did or did not incorporate different native groups into systems of gendered honor and kinship, how kinship and honor in turn became bound up in class and race identity and hierarchy, and how native peoples within Spanish society sought to shape for themselves the codes governing their lives. Notably, Brooks draws a pointed comparison of Spaniards' more rigid racial codifications of the enslaved Indians held in their settlements versus native kinship systems, like those of Comanches and Kiowas, that opened up a range of identities and ranks for the captured women and children they incorporated into their communities.[16]

Because gender operates as a system of identity and representation based in performance—not what people are, but what people do through distinctive postures, gestures, clothing, ornamentation, and occupations—it functioned as a communication tool for the often nonverbal nature of cross-cultural interaction. Gendered codes of behavior could convey either peace or hostility, power (submission or domination), and strength (bravery or cowardice). In the face of multiple dialects and languages, Indian peoples in Texas relied upon sign language in trade and diplomacy to communicate with one another, and these signs offered a starting point for their communications with Europeans as well. Spanish missionaries in the earliest expeditions described Indians "so skillful in the use of their hands for speaking that the most eloquent orator would envy their gestures." Fray José de Solís asserted in 1767 that Indian sign language was common to all and that with it Indians could "converse for days at a time." Such communication appeared so crucial to Spaniards, Solís wrote, that newly arrived missionaries to Texas "lose no time in learning these signs, so as to understand so many different tribes and so as to make themselves understood by them." Without a shared spoken language, then, Europeans and Indians could use sign, object, appearance, gesture, action, ritual, and ceremony to express and interpret one another's intent and purpose. The presence of translators did not obviate the need for signs and actions. As late as 1781, Wichita and Spanish men in an unexpected encounter "looked each other over" and made "many kind gestures," even as a French interpreter stood by translating their words fluently.[17]

The often contentious tenor of relations encouraged Europeans and Indians to evaluate one another by visible dispositions, postures, and actions. In fact, transmissions of meaning were often made more powerful through visible demonstrations than through verbal declarations that could prove false, be misunderstood, or remain incomprehensible. For instance, one Spanish official worried about relations with Wichitas, fearing that "our lack of deeds cannot fail to estrange them, for words unaccompanied by acts do not suffice." It was a two-way street, however. During negotiations the same year, another diplomat pleaded with Wichita leaders to "refrain from moving their lips to invent excuses which sooner or later their deeds would belie." The Apache expletive "mouth of the enemy!" suggests the associations they made between enmity, speech, and lies. Quite simply, actions spoke louder than words. Thus, diplomacy's gift giving, titles of honor, and hospitality rituals and warfare's battlefield stances, trophy taking, and violent mutilation all became decipherable codes between men. The participation of women too—in rituals of respect, hospitality, and intermarriage or in hostage taking, ransom, and violence—gave expression to amity and enmity in gendered terms. In search of peace, Spaniards and Indians might find a seeming resonance across their gender practices—a common ground of meaning or cultural cognates—by which to relate to the other. Yet, as the term "cognate" suggests, Europeans and Indians did not always conceive of gender standards in the same way.[18]

Europeans and Indians alike measured military, and thereby political and economic, power in terms of warrior numbers and ability. The character of contact over the eighteenth century gave greater authority to certain kinds of masculinity associated with a military identity. Honor codes among multiple Indian peoples in the region were in the process of militarization as the spread of European horses, guns, and disease influenced hunting patterns, seasonal migrations, territorial and settlement locations, and balances of power—changes that increased the authority of war chiefs and warriors. The constancy of raiding and warfare also heightened concepts of militarized honor for the Spanish men who were called to defend against them, coloring their confrontations and negotiations with Indian nations. Dating back to the *reconquista* (reconquest) of Spain when Spaniards fought to reclaim Iberia from Moorish control after the Muslim invasion from North Africa in 711 (a struggle that finally ended successfully in 1492), Spanish society linked male honor with violence, warfare, and military occupation. Later Spanish conquests in the Americas only reinforced such associations. Spanish *machismo* had as much to do with exerting power—often violently—over other men as it did with exerting power over women. Indian and Spanish men thus interpreted and judged one another's actions by their respective male honor.[19]

As Spanish and Indian men in Texas defined hostile actions primarily as masculine endeavor, the involvement of Indian women in cross-cultural relations assumed specific importance of its own. This is not to say that women were incapable of violent acts and men of peaceful ones, but the power of elemental associations of masculinity and femininity held sway, especially in unstable times. Indian peoples in this region had long associated women with peace—Cabeza de Vaca's experiences in the sixteenth century indicated how native women moved freely across social and political boundaries as mediators and emissaries. The role of Indian women could equally serve more symbolic than active purposes when it came to political and economic diplomacy. Either way, relations with women opened up the potential of expressing peace rather than hostility, and alliance rather than enmity. While the presence of women offered the possibility of stabilization, however, the relative lack of women as actors on the Spanish side of the equation often brought an imbalance to these relations and meant that interactions remained only between sets of men. Women's absence often had an important, negative effect on Spanish-Indian negotiations, making it harder for Spanish groups to break the cycles of hostility and tension that so dominated their interactions with Indian nations. As was the case with the Comanche emissaries of 1772 with whom this introduction began, enmity might define the tone and idiom of even the most ardent Spanish efforts at peace. As the century progressed, then, coercion and violence increasingly shaped political interpretations of native femininity and the political realities of native female experience.

Although all these factors—the lack of a common language, the use of nonverbal signs, a seeming universality of gender categories, and unstable political relations—played a role in making gender so prevalent in Spanish-Indian diplomacy, the central reason was simple: Indians in Texas controlled their political and economic relations with Spaniards, so that their kinship systems for ordering and understanding relationships provided the structure for cross-cultural diplomacy. And just as race was a construction of European power in other areas of colonial America, gender emerged as a signature of Indian power in interactions with Europeans here. This was a world dominated by Indian nations and to enter that world meant that Europeans had to abide by the kinship categories that ordered it and gave it meaning. To ignore or transgress that system meant that one became a source of chaos and disorder, and Spaniards did so at their own risk.

The succeeding chapters roughly follow the chronological order in which different Indian peoples came into contact with Spaniards over the eighteenth century. The six chapters fall into three period groupings, and each of the three has its own introduction to set the time, place, and actors from an Indian perspective. Chapters 1 and 2 explore the first three decades of the century, during which Caddo chiefdoms established relations with Spaniards who sent expeditions to Caddo territories beginning in 1689. Small contingents of Spanish missionaries and soldiers tried to make allies of the powerful and populous Caddos as the only means of defending New Spain's northern provinces against feared French invasion. As both Frenchmen and Spaniards entered their lands, Caddos sought to ascertain their intentions and, if deemed potentially valuable allies, find a place for them in their economic and political networks. Through public rituals of greeting and hospitality, theocratic leaders of Caddo communities first incorporated visiting Europeans into their diplomatic ranks as men of recognizable status and honor. When Spaniards and Frenchmen expressed interest in settling in Caddo lands, Caddo conventions then required that they be assimilated as "kin" for permanent relationships to become possible. The different forms of French and Spanish incorporation into the Caddo world via female-informed practices of familial union illuminate the resourcefulness of Caddo social controls.

The third and fourth chapters turn to south-central Texas from the 1720s through the 1760s, when bands of Coahuilteco, Karankawa, and Tonkawa speakers used Spanish mission-presidio complexes to broker political and economic alliances. Within those complexes, Spanish and Indian peoples came together for subsistence, defense, and family building, and therein native standards of male and female identity and labor defined the form and practice of their political union. Apaches saw a different kind of political potential in the mission-presidio complexes, first subjecting them to raids as a new resource by which to expand the horse herds so valuable to their hunting and warfare needs. By midcentury, however, challenges from Wichita and Comanche competitors led Apaches to negotiate terms by which the Spanish complexes might become institutions of military alliance between European soldiers and Apache warriors, even as Apache leaders sought to keep their families separate and their women out of the reach of Spanish men.

The final two chapters explore Wichitas' and Comanches' economic and political transition from indifferent enemies to diplomatic neighbors of Spaniards in the 1770s and 1780s, when peace rather than war finally appeared to provide greater advantages to their communities. Spaniards responded eagerly, seeking to gain these fear-inspiring nations as new friends. Wichita and Comanche leaders used male honor codes to establish truces on terms that transformed military opponents into military "brothers." Hostility and violence had such a strong hold over Wichitas' and Comanches' contacts with Spaniards, however, that women emerged as crucial components of diplomatic efforts to ensure that a nominal truce became a permanent peace. Both the coercive trafficking in women through hostage taking and ransoming as well as the mediating involvement of women as symbolic and active emissaries of peace offered a key to solidifying amity between Spanish, Comanche, and Wichita peoples by the late 1780s.

Plunged into a world ruled by Indian politics, Spaniards found they could not assert control beyond the boundaries of south Texas and had trouble negotiating the native power relations outside those boundaries. Without the force to conquer or the finances to trade, Spaniards had to accommodate themselves to native systems of control if they wished to form viable relationships with Comanches, Apaches, Wichitas, Caddos, and others. Thus, it would take nearly the entire century for Spaniards to succeed in selling themselves as better allies than enemies, for native groups to find the terms by which they could tolerate if not benefit from the Spanish interlopers, and for a tenuous peace to finally emerge. The prevalence of gendered codes of rank, status, and identity forcefully demonstrated natives' power to make Spaniards accede to the concepts and rules governing native polities. As Spaniards struggled to play by those rules, the predominance of gender in their diplomacy served as a barometer of native power and European powerlessness.

PART ONE

Turn-of-the-Century Beginnings, 1680s–1720s

One day in the late spring, a Hasinai Caddo man hurriedly rode into his home town, bringing with him two men.[1] Like many men from the town, he had been out on a deer hunt with his wife and children since the spring planting of corn, beans, tobacco, and sunflowers had been completed. He had had a successful trip, but that was not what brought him home with such speed. Rather, he came to announce the approach of a group of twenty-four men who had entered Caddo hunting terri- tories and merited the hospitality of his community. He had found them carry- ing all their belongings on their backs while walking in the general direction of the Hasinai villages. They must have been far from home, because they were unknown to the man. Because they looked footsore and hungry, he had left one of his horses and some of the meat from his hunt with the man he could tell was a leader among the wanderers. After inviting them to visit his village, the man had gone ahead to alert village caddís *(headmen) of their approach while his wife and children remained with the strangers as a pledge of his return. He took two of the new- comers with him as an answering pledge—so he understood—from the strangers that they would await his return; they could not speak his language, nor he theirs, so he had to interpret their intentions as best he could. Such pledges were custom- ary gestures to him, but caution dictated that he not leave his family too long alone in the company of the strangers, despite indications of their goodwill. Oddly, no women traveled with the newcomers—an absence that normally would indicate a raiding party—so there was some room to wonder at his family's safety among them. Yet, at the same time, the strangers carried heavy bundles that seemed more indicative of trade supplies than of weaponry. He could only hope he had under- stood their signs and behavior correctly. It had taken him half a day to get home, and it would be another day before he could speak with village leaders and a greeting party could be assembled to return to the meeting place.*

In his account to Caddo caddís, *several factors may have shaped the Hasinai* man's reading of the newcomers' intent and purpose in Caddo lands. They bore no paint or decorations of war. Their clothes and belongings looked like those of traders displaying their wares. Members of the party wore dress similar to that worn by, and sometimes given to Caddos by, their Jumano trading partners to the west. Since Jumanos had acquired the accoutrements from settlements further west, perhaps these travelers came from those far western peoples. If Hasinai Caddos could obtain more from the newcomers, all the better. The new cloth and decorations made appealing additions to the turquoise and cotton cloth they already had gotten from those lands.[2] Yet, unlike Jumanos and others to the west, the travelers came on foot, and their lack of horses might indicate that they came from a less prosperous nation. Their horselessness could also mean they were from the east; the Hasinais' own well-established horse herds gave them an edge over their eastern neighbors who did not yet have them. Since the strangers had approached from a southwesterly direction, however, an origin nearer the Jumanos seemed more likely. Thus, although the strangers and their language were unknown to Caddos, aspects of their appearance gave the impression of a trading party like those they had hosted many times before. As it turned out, a Jumano trading party was at the Hasinai village when he arrived, so perhaps they could identify the newcomers if and when they were brought into town.

In response to the man's report, several Hasinai caddís rode out, accompanied by a small contingent of amayxoyas (noted warriors), bringing with them two more horses loaded with food provisions, as hospitable custom demanded and as the practicalities of travel required. Members of the party had dressed in fine deerskin clothes and feather adornments and carried with them a ceremonial pipe (also ornamented with feathers) for their greeting rituals. Once the party of strangers was found and the ritual pipe smoke shared, the Hasinai men escorted the wanderers back to town. There, a great concourse of people inspected and greeted the visitors as they wound through the many hamlets making up the settlement on their way to a ceremonial compound where they would meet the principal caddí at his home. The size and breadth of the settlement, stretching for over twenty leagues, seemed to overwhelm the strangers, another hint that their nation might not be so large or prosperous as that of the Hasinais. In accordance with Caddo custom, the Hasinai escort directed the leader of the trading party to lodging within the principal Hasinai caddí's household, while the rest of the party were told where they could camp outside the village for the four days that trading negotiations lasted. Regardless of this precaution, young Hasinai men stood guard in shifts day and night throughout the settlement.

Not surprisingly, given the poor condition of their party, the strangers wanted horses and food for the continuation of their journey, and since Hasinais could easily provide both, they offered five horses in addition to provisions and received some knives, axes, and ornaments in exchange. The visitors expressed equal interest in the Jumano traders already lodged at the Hasinai village, yet it was interest not in their goods but in the news they might have from the west. Contrary to what the Hasinais might have expected, the strangers knew neither the Jumanos nor the sign language that most nations in the region used to communicate during economic and political exchanges. Yet, the Jumanos certainly seemed to think they knew the strangers or people like them, so the Hasinai leaders let them take the lead in seeking to identify and communicate with the visitors.

The Jumano representatives thought one man in particular, an elder dressed in robes rather than the leggings of the others, might be able to communicate with them. They tried different signs, alternatively touching their chests in a pattern of motions with one hand, kneeling, and raising their arms to the skies. Finally, they drew an image on bark of a man being tortured on a post while a woman looked on weeping, an image that seemed to have some impact on the strangers. When the elder expressed excited recognition of these body movements—sign language, the Jumanos explained, that had been taught them by people in the west with whom they had been trading for quite some time, the strangers then indicated their desire to know the direction to those people. In response, the Jumanos drew a map on bark to indicate the region as a whole, rivers and landmarks, the location of neighboring nations, and a description of these particular people to the west.

Once the strangers learned the identity of the western-dwelling people, they seemed eager to disassociate themselves from them. Their leader began a long speech, with intermittent gestures at the sky (or was it the sun?—the Hasinai and Jumano onlookers were not sure), in which he seemed to recite mighty deeds of war. Although the stories remained indecipherable, the enmity he felt for the people in the west became clear. In response, the Jumanos tried to explain that the people of the west had recently angered them too. Just three years before, Jumano leaders had sent a delegation to the westerners' settlement to seek explanation for their failure to honor trade agreements. In return, they had gotten a half-hearted commitment of military alliance against their Canneci enemies that had proven ineffectual or unfulfilled within less than a year.[3] Now, they were considering a battle or raid against the western people and invited the newcomers to join them if they wished.

After five days, the strangers finally went on their way with what the Hasinais hoped would help their travels: five horses and a supply of maize, beans, and pumpkin seeds. A few days later, however, news arrived that did not surprise those in the Hasinai settlement. Under cover of night, four men from the trading party had reappeared at a neighboring Caddo village, that of Nasonis. Apparently not wishing to travel further, the men had left their leader and comrades and returned to the village to ask whether *they might stay among the Caddos. The Nasonis sympathized with their needy situation and offered them new homes, at least temporarily. To the Hasinais, the desertions may have bespoken a failure of leadership.[4] The strangers' party had not seemed well-equipped to survive; beyond their lack of supplies, many did not appear to have a warrior's strength and fortitude required for a long journey. Indeed, events a few months later confirmed these suspicions. Hasinais and Nasonis (in whose society domestic murder was unheard of) watched with shocked dismay as the strangers killed their* caddí *and then turned against one another, until the dissension ended in three more murders.*

This passage tells the story, from a Caddo perspective, of the first contacts between Caddos of the Hasinai confederacy (who would later be known as "Cenis" by Frenchmen and as "Tejas" by Spaniards) and René Robert Cavelier, Sieur de la Salle, and members of his 1685 expedition into the region that would memorialize Hasinais in its name: "Texas." The Frenchmen who arrived at the Hasinai villages that spring were survivors of an excursion sent to find, chart, and claim the Mississippi River for France. Failing to recognize the mouth of the Mississippi River, however, La Salle's ships had landed on the Texas coast in January 1685, where they established a settlement named Fort Saint Louis in or near Karankawa territories. La Salle had then sent parties inland in hope of finding an overland route to the Mississippi River and a way back to French settlements in Illinois and Canada, and their northward searches took them through Caddo lands.

Their Hasinai hosts were members of one of three affiliated confederacies among Caddoan peoples. Caddos had maintained a thriving culture in the region for over eight hundred years, with agriculturally based communities spread thickly over an area that encompassed hundreds of miles in parts of present-day Louisiana, Texas, Arkansas, and Oklahoma. Although their numbers had declined drastically from an estimated 250,000 people in 1520, they remained the dominant power in the region. The majority of the 8,500 to 12,675 people had coalesced, by 1690, into three confederacies, or chiefdoms, known as Hasinai, Kadohadacho, and Natchitoches.[5] Twenty member bands of these confederacies and at least three other independent Caddo bands now clustered in fertile river valleys of present-day northwestern Louisiana and northeastern Texas, along the Angelina, Neches, Sabine, and Red Rivers. As fray Isidro de Espinosa, a Franciscan missionary who lived among Hasinais from 1716 to 1722, described, the Hasinai nation "extends in each of the four principal directions for more than one hundred leagues."[6] The governance of the multicommunity chiefdoms remained quite similar to their earlier political systems. Town centers, surrounded by a multitude of temple mounds built by their ancestors up through the fourteenth century, still served as both the residence of paramount chiefs and the locus for public gatherings and ceremony. Kin-based hamlets located near agricultural fields radiated out from these centers. A balanced kinship system structured Caddo societies. Matrilineage defined the ranks and divisions within their communities, while hereditary hierarchies that passed power independently via a patrilineage governed the bands and confederacies. Caddo economies rested upon steadily intensifying agricultural production and a far-reaching commercial exchange system trading hides, salt, turquoise, copper, marine shells, bows, and ceramic pottery long distances into and out of the regions of New Mexico, the Gulf coast, and the Great Lakes.[7]

The effects of European contact had begun to reach Caddoan peoples long before these French visitors arrived at the end of the seventeenth century. Another straggling expedition, the exploratory party of Hernando de Soto, led by Luis Moscoso after Soto's death, had rampaged through their lands in 1542.[8] Almost one hundred and fifty years passed before La Salle's venture to Caddo lands, and no Caddos seemed to know about the earlier European visitors. Yet, the effects of the sixteenth-century contact—long-term population decline in response to the epidemic diseases that Soto's expedition had left in its wake—had certainly made its mark on Caddoan peoples. Though their dispersed settlement patterns had reduced the spread and severity of disease, smaller populations made the previously high number of independent agricultural communities more difficult to defend and encouraged the consolidation of Caddo bands into the confederacies that Frenchmen and later Spaniards encountered in the 1680s.

Despite that population decline, the Caddoan world remained impressive in size, breadth, and development. French priest Anastase Douay described his first sight of the great Hasinai settlement in 1686: "This village, that of the Cenis, is one of the largest and most populous that I have seen in America. It is at least twenty leagues long, not that it is constantly inhabited, but in hamlets of ten or twelve cabins, forming cantons, each with a different name. Their cabins are fine, forty or fifty feet high, of the shape of beehives." He concluded they were a people "that had nothing barbarous but the name."[9] Because of their confederacies' economic and political strength, Caddo leaders viewed European newcomers as insignificant. Yet, as increasing numbers of regular visitors replaced the early wanderers, these leaders saw that perhaps Spaniards and Frenchmen might be usefully incorporated into their already extensive political economies by carrying Caddo trade goods in new directions and bringing new ones back to them in return. Still, Europeans from the northeast and southwest entered Caddo orbits only as aspirants.[10]

In 1686, Caddos greeted the newly arrived Frenchmen hospitably, with little reason

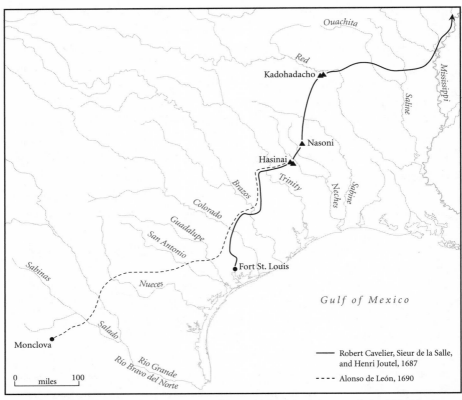

Routes of the earliest French and Spanish visitors to Caddo lands in the 1680s and 1690s. Map drawn by Melissa Beaver.

to associate them with past events or past foreigners. Caddo custom dictated the rituals offered to La Salle as leader of the visiting party—housing in one of the *caddís'* homes, presentations of food, pipe-smoking ceremonies, and diplomatic exchanges. For the French party, though these early exchanges were a success, the initial trip northward was a failure. La Salle was murdered by several of his own men on his second attempt to reach the Mississippi (just a few miles from the Hasinai settlements), but seven survivors eventually made it to Illinois posts in 1687. Meanwhile, in 1688, Karankawas destroyed the struggling settlement on the coast in response to repeated French thefts and harassment. As a result, Hasinais encountered more French deserters and survivors (eight of whom remained to live among them) while other Caddos to the northeast met rescuers from Illinois under the leadership of Henri de Tonti, who came in search of the lost French settlement. The friendliness of these early exchanges later convinced French officials in Illinois and France that

Caddos could be key to expanding their economic networks in Louisiana in pursuit of trade both with Native American peoples in the south and southwest and with Spaniards in New Mexico. Within the next fifteen years, trading outposts in Illinois and seaports in France would send more Frenchmen to Caddo lands.

Meanwhile, as reports of La Salle's venture filtered in from different sources in the Spanish empire, officials in New Spain began to spin out a quite different narrative of the events they believed to be taking place in the "land of the Tejas." In 1685, reports had reached viceregal officials in Mexico City and, eventually, the Council of the Indies in Madrid of a serious threat to Spain's colonial possessions in the Americas. All told, the reports indicated that a "Monsieur de Salaz" had gathered a maritime expedition made up of four ships carrying 250 people, including soldiers, craftsmen, missionaries, settlers, and at least four women, to establish a colony at a place called "Micipipi" along the coast of the Gulf of Mexico in Spanish territory. Well-provisioned with guns, tools, and merchandise for trade, the Frenchmen, it seemed, planned to build a fortress from which they could win over Indian allies and ultimately assert control over the rich mines they had been told lay within reach of the Mississippi. The Spaniards could only conclude that these mines were in fact their own and that the colonization plans represented a scheme to conquer the northern settlements of New Spain.[11]

Over the next four years, Spanish officials sent eleven different expeditions, five by land and six by water, in search of the rumored French colony. When in 1690 a party led by Alonso de León finally found La Salle's Fort Saint Louis on Matagorda Bay, it had been destroyed by disease and a Karankawa attack. Only a handful of French deserters and children living among and adopted by Caddos and Karankawas remained to tell Spaniards of the initial goals and ultimate fate of La Salle and his colony. It mattered not to Spanish officials that the expedition lay in ruins and the expedition leader himself had died at the hands of his own men, however. Protection against another attempted French intrusion had to be secured.[12]

Spanish state and church officials had been discussing the potential of trading posts and even presidial settlements for the region to the east of New Mexico for over fifty years, ever since the 1620s when Jumanos had first traveled west to initiate contact with Spaniards. Since 1650, Spaniards in the province of New Mexico had been sending scheduled trading expeditions, under military escort, to Jumano settlements at the confluence of the Nueces and Colorado Rivers to exchange Spanish products first for pearls (from river shells) and later for deerskins and bison hides. A growing eastern Apache presence in the region made the military escort a necessity, and the need for defense against Apaches had further encouraged some Jumanos' interest in a potential alliance with Spaniards. The increasing dangers in fact eventually stopped the Jumanos' visits to New Mexico and forced Spanish expeditions to come to them instead if they wanted to maintain contact. The continuing expeditions attest to Spanish interest not only in the Jumano peoples but also in their Caddo trading partners, whom the Jumanos had spoken about in glowing terms to Spanish officials.[13]

From Jumano reports, Spaniards in New Mexico gathered that the "Kingdom of the Tejas" was a populous and powerful nation, with a "king" or "great lord" who ruled with "lieutenants" over a people so numerous their cities extended for miles, so powerful that their warriors were feared by all neighboring groups, and so organized that they had a hierarchical governing system. Balancing "civilization" with strength, the Hasinais enjoyed an agricultural economy successful enough to produce surplus grain for their horse herds, worshiped a single omnipotent deity, and maintained a material trade that supported a well-dressed and well-housed people. As a result, Spanish officials thought they recognized in the Hasinai world social, political, and economic practices not too unlike their own, and in the Hasinai people, good candidates for alliance and religious conversion.[14]

At the same time, Jumano traders carried to the Hasinais both Spanish goods and their own impressions of Spanish soldiers. Viewing Spanish horses, ornamented swords, and items of personal adornment such as lace, silver, and military clothing and listening to stories of Spanish warfare, slave raiding, and missions, Hasinais too may have recognized attractive characteristics in Spaniards—a people with warriors as reputable and decorated as their own, riders of heralded horsemanship, and traders interested in mutually profitable exchange. The predominance of horses already in Caddo settlements (that Frenchmen had carefully noted) suggested that Caddos would view Spaniards as an invaluable trade source for expanding their horse herds. Yet, by the 1680s, Jumano reports to the Caddos also came with a warning: Spaniards had not proved reliable trading partners since the Pueblo Revolt of 1680 in New Mexico. Moreover, the revolt had completely removed a Spanish presence from the Pueblo region, pushing them back to a location along the Rio Grande, where they had established a new settlement called "El Paso del Norte." Not only had the revolt disrupted all political and economic relations that Spaniards had sought to maintain among several native populations, it had also suggested to native leaders a real weakness in Spanish military capabilities—all of which may have reduced the Spaniards' appeal as allies of any kind, be it for trade or diplomacy. That appeal had certainly declined in the Jumanos' opinion, but Caddos as yet had little reason to decide either way.[15]

Even as Spaniards struggled to find the means to reestablish a presence in New Mexico, they faced a new, French challenge from the east. Fortuitously, it seemed to viceregal officials, the search for La Salle's colony had fixed Spanish attention upon "Tejas" Indians. Alonso de León and fray Damián Mazanet, who headed the 1690 expedition that found the remains and the survivors of the ill-fated French colony, elaborated upon earlier Jumano reports of the advanced "civilization," commercial power, and political influence of the Hasinais and their many fellow Caddo allies along the Red River. Their reports encouraged Spanish officials to conclude that the Hasinais represented both promising converts to Christianity and important allies to be won against the French. Since La Salle's expedition had proved the Spaniards' vague fears of French expansionism to be real, Spanish officials quickly initiated plans to court a Hasinai alliance in earnest. Thus, Spaniards envisioned a bulwark against French aggressions created through settlement in the "land of the Tejas." Whether Hasinais would offer the same welcome to Spaniards that had comforted the French stragglers and survivors of La Salle's failed expedition, however, remained to be seen.

chapter one

Diplomatic Ritual in the "Land of the Tejas"

In the 1680s and the 1690s, multiple Caddo groups within the Natchitoches, Kadohadacho, and most notably the Hasinai confederacies began to give hearings to the various European aspirants who came to their lands, seeing in them the possibility of meeting ever-increasing political and economic needs for horses, guns, and military allies. Over time, Hasinai goals and Spanish and French ability and willingness to meet those goals determined the shape and form of eighteenth-century socioeconomic relations. Yet, in the last two decades of the seventeenth century, these Europeans and Indians struggled simply to establish contact with one another. The earliest meetings between Caddos and their French and Spanish visitors delineated what might be imagined as the outer rings of cross-cultural interaction. Their encounters skimmed the surface of Caddo and European societies by calling into action only the most public manifestations of male and female honor required by formal diplomatic ceremony.[1]

Caddo, rather than European, custom dictated the ceremonies followed in the first meetings of these peoples, making clear the Caddos' power over their European visitors. Unable to communicate well with each other through speech, Europeans and Caddos searched for other means to convey and interpret meaning—making object, appearance, expression, and action critical. They brought together their respective traditions of ceremony and protocol in efforts to establish diplomatic exchange. The Caddos' advantages of home ground, superior numbers, and force offset any presumed military superiority afforded by European technology and arms. Frenchmen and Spaniards arrived in such small numbers relative to their Caddo hosts that aggression on their part would have been foolhardy and self-destructive. The European newcomers thus followed the Caddos' lead in protocol.[2]

Caddo hospitality rituals conveyed and affirmed honor both domestically and diplomatically. Ceremonies of early contact included all members of Hasinai communities and reflected the civil and political dimensions of Hasinai identity, position, rank, and prestige. Welcoming rituals allotted to all persons a role commensurate with their position and contribution to the society and presented to observers the social value of each. Status position accorded by social order and hierarchies of age, lineage, and gender thereby determined individual and community roles in Caddo ritual performances. Caddo men and women of both elite and nonelite status had their parts to play. Europeans thus enjoyed a composite view of Caddo societies in their own villages, temples, and ceremonial centers—how adequately or poorly they interpreted what they saw was another matter entirely.[3]

In contrast, Caddos gained only a faint glimpse into Spanish or French cultures, their view being limited to the few men who wandered into and out of their lands in the 1680s and 1690s. They saw nothing of the Europeans' own communities and socioeconomic systems, and among the groups with whom they did interact, Caddos could make judgments only of the divisions and ranks structuring relations among Spanish and French men because the parties were all-male. The Frenchmen and Spaniards that Caddos met also presented quite contrasting pictures to them. In 1689, for example, Alonso de León's expedition included a military leader, about ten officers, eighty-five soldiers, two missionaries, one guide, one interpreter, and twenty-five muleteers, craftsmen, and laborers in charge of supplies, food stores, and manual chores. Those stores included seven hundred horses, two hundred head of cattle, and pack mules carrying eighty loads of flour, five hundred pounds of chocolate, and three loads of tobacco. In contrast, the French survivors and deserters from La Salle's Fort Saint Louis came on foot, carrying their supplies and what goods they hoped to trade on their backs, and they arrived in much smaller numbers; twenty-four men made up La Salle's first party and seventeen the second. At the beginning, then, cross-cultural understanding, if even possible, was inevitably uneven.

In the early stages of contact, when both the Europeans' and the Caddos' goals remained simply ascertaining a starting point for friendly relations, the key exchanges were those between elite men, mostly because of Caddo custom. Rituals reflected the sociopolitical categories of Caddo society, in which patrilineal descent of political and religious leadership existed within a larger matrilineal kinship system. Caddos lived in dispersed settlements, each of which consisted of multiple family farmsteads of generally equivalent status. These local communities allied together to form larger confederacies. *Caddís*, men of civil and religious authority, headed each village and were advised by councils of elders called *canahas*, while a *xinesí* functioned as a head priest at the level of the confederacy. These positions

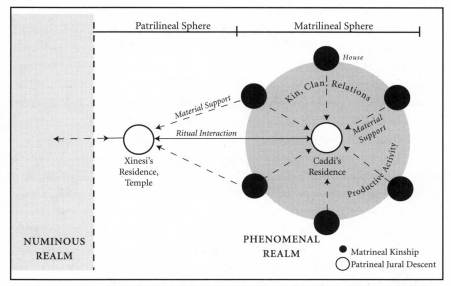

Diagrammatic representation of houses and ceremonial centers (caddís' *and* xinesís' *residences) as icons of matrilineal and patrilineal spheres, by George Sabo III, "The Structure of Caddo Leadership in the Colonial Era,"* in The Native History of the Caddo: Their Place in Southeastern Archeology and Ethnohistory, *ed. Timothy Perttula and James Bruseth, Studies in Archeology, no. 30 (Austin: Texas Archeological Research Laboratory, 1998). Courtesy of George Sabo III and the Texas Archeological Research Laboratory, University of Texas at Austin.*

were all hereditary offices, almost all male (Spanish and French records indicate two historical moments in which extraordinary circumstances put women into positions as *caddís*), and passed by descent through a male line but within the matrilineal kinship system—for example, from a man to his sister's son.[4]

Meanwhile, households under the authority of the matrilineal clan functioned as the basic social and economic unit of production. Women, as heads of clans, held primary authority in Caddo cultivation, organized divisions of farming labor, and controlled the agricultural produce. Caddo cosmology established the interdependence of patrilineal leaders and matrilineal clans in the origin story of Ayo-Caddí-Aymay, the Supreme Being, which fray Isidro de Espinosa recorded in the 1720s. In the beginning of the world, only one woman and her two daughters (one of whom was pregnant) existed, and one terrible day a demon in the form of a giant horned snake attacked and killed the pregnant daughter. A miracle saved the son she carried in her womb, and under the remaining women's care, he grew to adulthood in two nights and immediately avenged his mother's death by killing the demon with a bow and arrows crafted by his grandmother. The young man, accompanied by his grand-mother and aunt, then ascended into the sky, where he began governing the world as the Supreme Being. Thus, a founding matrilineage of three women restored "posi-tive conditions in the world by empowering male descendants to act on their be-half." The women ensured the youth's success in the male realm of warfare (and ultimately political leadership). Male skills, and the power they garnered, depended upon female skills in women's realm of production and sustenance.[5]

Reflecting those sociopolitical divisions, public ceremonial life in Caddo societies took place in gendered spaces to which Europeans—as men—did not have equal access. The ritual performances held at temples and ceremonial compounds, in which native and European foreigners were more likely to be included, highlighted the authority of male political and religious leaders—the *caddís*, *xinesí*, and *canahas*. Women took part in ceremonies at the compounds, but their authority was not the focus of that venue. Rituals performed in individual homes emphasized the matri-lineal structuring of clan, kinship, and socioeconomic units of production. Planting, first fruits, and harvesting ceremonies held in the home were public rituals reinforc-ing the social basis of kinship and women's productive contributions to both family and community. Europeans, however, were far less likely to witness these seasonal ceremonies in their initial visits to Caddo lands. In turn, the potential gender biases of European men, whose own societies had no similar balance of public authority for women as well as men, did not initially have much bearing on diplomatic proceedings.[6]

Thus, from the beginning, gender influenced what Europeans learned and did not learn about their hosts. Europeans did not have a chance to be surprised by Caddo women's power because they did not witness it, at first. The encounters recorded by Europeans between 1687 and 1693 make clear that Caddos welcomed Spaniards and Frenchmen only into the ceremonial compounds where male-defined rituals held sway. In these spaces, masculine power was the source of mutual understanding. As ethnohistorian George Sabo explains, "the ritual performances that were enacted in the context of encounters between Europeans and American Indians were staged . . . to convey those beliefs, values, or principles that one or the other (or sometimes both) of the participating groups considered appropriate or necessary for the situa-tion at hand." As symbolic communication, ritual performances "served, among other things, to define and categorize participants according to systems of social classification and to establish 'ground rules' for cross-cultural communication and interaction." Until Spanish and French male leaders had passed the tests set for them by their Caddo counterparts, only the male domain of Caddo polities would be open to them. Only later, after the rules had been laid out and accepted, might the locus of cross-cultural interaction expand to include the more female-influenced kinship rituals of alliance and settlement represented by the matrilineal household.[7]

What protocols did Caddos enact when Europeans entered the outer limits of their lands? La Salle's story provides some hints, but a more detailed accounting can be elicited from Spanish expedition records. Hasinais customarily met European parties a few miles outside their villages for the first round of greetings. Once lookouts sent word of Europeans' arrival in the vicinity of their villages, the *caddís* rode out to greet them, accompanied by men, women, and children in groups numbering anywhere from ten to fifty. When within eyesight of one another, both the Europeans and the Caddos halted to salute each other and then advanced in "military formation" according to rank, with all cavalry, arms, and munitions on display. Caddos entered the meeting ground in three files, with the central one led by the head *caddí*, followed by other *caddís* and leading men, and with the remainder of the people making up the two side lines. Echoing the Caddo formation, Spaniards advanced with the military expedition leader carrying the royal standard painted with the images of Christ and the Virgin of Guadalupe, while missionaries and soldiers filed in on either side. The military captain then passed the standard to the head missionary, knelt before it in veneration, kissed the images, and embraced the missionary or kissed his hand or habit. Spaniards sang the *Te Deum Laudamus* as they processed, and in response, Caddo men gave another salute.[8]

Upon exchanging initial courtesies and gifts, the *caddís* would escort visitors into their village. Europeans sometimes proffered gifts to the man they assumed to be "head chief," particularly gifts of clothes, so that he might carry or wear them into the village in symbolic recognition of the respect they had for him. As the Spaniards or Frenchmen entered settlements, entire bands of three to five hundred men, women, and children welcomed them. Entry to the village usually repeated the ranked processions for the benefit of the village audience, as all paraded to a public plaza where blanketed and adorned seats were set out. After more salutes (in early years, with hand gestures, but later with gunfire), Caddo men often took care to lay down their arms. Finally, before sitting, leading warriors and *caddís* embraced Spanish or French officers and missionaries, and the visitors then went through a purification ritual, often by having their faces washed or by smoking pipes.

During the formal meetings that followed, the leading men of both Caddo and European parties sat in a circle on special benches designated for them according to rank, and the people of the village ranged around the circle of dignitaries as audience. Caddo men brought out a pipe decorated with white feathers, and the *caddís* mixed their own tobacco with that given them by the visiting Spaniards or

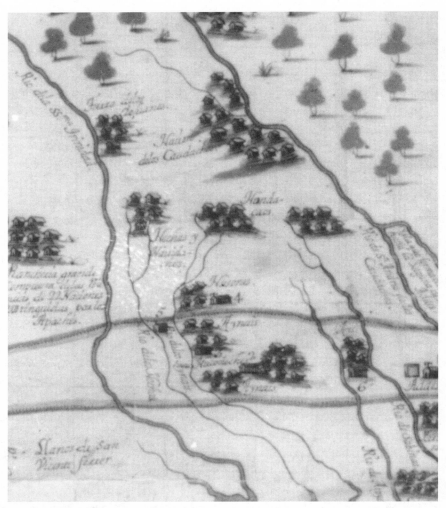

Detail showing the lands of the Tejas from the 1728 map drawn by Francisco Barreiro, the engineer who accompanied Inspector General Pedro de Rivera's 1724–28 inspection tour of the defensive capabilities of New Spain's northern provinces. Courtesy of The Hispanic Society of America, New York.

Frenchmen and blew smoke to the cardinal directions—east, west, north, south— and to the earth and the sky. Then they offered the pipe to their European counterparts and thereafter to all present, until it had passed through everyone's hands. Next, the European and Indian leaders addressed speeches to one another, using interpreters to translate as best they could. Caddo women then brought forward corn, watermelons, tamales, and beans for the feasts that followed. In exchange, Spaniards and Frenchmen usually offered gifts of clothes, flannel, blankets, hats, and

tobacco to be distributed among all the village inhabitants. European officers designated special gifts for the *caddís*, their wives, leading warriors, and any others
deemed to be in positions of authority. Frenchmen also gave guns and ammunition.
After these formalities, more feasts, dancing, singing, drumming, blowing of bugles
and horns, and firing of salutes created a festive atmosphere as celebrations continued through the night. *Caddís* then insisted that expedition leaders and missionaries stay with them in their own households. For several days, this pattern of
festivities continued, with groups from neighboring Caddo villages often coming to
meet the Europeans, or with Spaniards and Frenchmen going to their settlements to
enact similar rituals.

Through these rituals, Caddos, Spaniards, and Frenchmen sought to introduce
themselves, to convey friendship, and to evaluate one another as potential military
allies and trading partners. Europeans were not singled out for special treatment;
these were the same ceremonies Caddo leaders used when entertaining native foreign
embassies. As fray Espinosa later attested from firsthand observations, *caddís* received native ambassadors "with much honor," meeting them leagues outside of
villages with formal escorts, assigning them principal seats at meetings, and giving
presents, dances, and festivals during their visits. Such foreign policy receptions were
annual events among a number of different bands inside and outside the Caddo
confederacies. Hasinais, for instance, welcomed diplomatic parties from the Gulf
coast, "who are accustomed to come as allies of the Tejas in times of war . . . [thus]
they entertain them every year after harvest, which is the time when many families of
men and women visit the Hasinais," Espinosa explained. It was also "the time when
they trade with one another for those things lacking in their settlements."[9]

Notably, native visiting parties included women and children to emphasize the
diplomatic nature of the mission. Practical demonstrations of peace involved specific male and female behaviors. Europeans might focus on male actions, but for
Caddos and other Indian peoples across Texas, the clearest signal of intent lay in the
gendered makeup of visiting parties. For them, the inclusion of women and children
in traveling and trading parties communicated a peaceful demeanor, because customarily, female noncombatants and families rarely accompanied raiding or warring
parties. Thus, Caddo "welcome committees" sent out to greet visitors prominently
advertised the presence of women and children. If women did not attend the first
meeting, Indian leaders often insisted that Spanish and French expeditions return to
their villages to greet their women and children there. French priest Anastase Douay,
for example, recorded the "pressing" invitations of a *caddí* to visit his settlement and
thus his people. In similar spirit, neighboring Yojuanes entreated the 1709 expedition

of fray Isidro de Espinosa, fray Antonio de San Buenaventura y Olivares, and Captain Pedro de Aguirre to come with them to their settlement, arguing that their women and children would be "very sad and disconsolate" if they did not meet them. Caddo women's and children's involvement in visitor receptions served as marks of trust vested by Caddo hosts in their visitors. By presenting women and children, *caddís* acknowledged the visitors' peaceful intent and conferred honor on them by conveying the leaders' faith that the vulnerable or noncombatant members of their communities would be safe in the visitors' company.[10]

Ritualized touching provided a physical extension of these gestures of peace for many Texas Indian groups. The very gestures established a bond by transferring touch back and forth between people. Thus, fray Isidro de Espinosa compared Indian caresses to a "manner of anointing." Frenchmen of La Salle's expedition were embraced and caressed all along their path from the coast to Caddo settlements. When some of La Salle's men encountered Karankawas along the coast of Texas in 1685, the Indians approached as soon as the Frenchmen had disarmed at La Salle's command and "made friendly gestures in their own way; that is, they rubbed their hands on their chests and then rubbed them over our chests and arms." After this ritual, "they demonstrated friendship by putting their hands over their hearts which meant that they were glad to see us"—greetings that the Frenchmen returned "in as nearly like manner as we could." The Indians further inland also signaled friendliness, according to Joutel, by putting their hands over their hearts and, he believed, communicated a desire for alliance with the Frenchmen by hooking their fingers together. Upon reaching Caddo settlements, Hasinais too embraced them "one after another" to demonstrate their affection.[11]

The act of touching transformed a greeting into a personal bond because the proximity and intimacy required for the act conveyed both trust in the visitor and sincerity in the host. Symbolically expanding the welcome to include the whole community entailed the involvement of men, women, and children in these ritual gestures. Thus, gender again served as a central means of communication and, as it would turn out, miscommunication. Europeans like Anastase Douay often particularly noted women's participation in physical greetings, recording that Indians "received us with all possible friendship, even the women coming to embrace our men." Captain Domingo Ramón argued that, in the Hasinai ceremony, first the *caddí* and then all the warriors, women, and children in succession "threw their arms around" him and the missionaries—and thus the ceremony took more than an hour to complete—which he decided must be "significant of friendship." Fray Espinosa found that "there was not an Indian, man, woman, or child, who did not do his or her share of petting."[12]

Europeans quickly adapted to native practice, as a missionary in the 1718 Alarcón expedition, fray Francisco de Céliz, recorded: "we caressed them by embracing them," following their "customary signs of peace." But adaptation did not come easily for them. European notions of male self-mastery associated masculine strength with control of thought, emotion, and body. Religious custom, which Spaniards hoped to encourage Indians to imitate, allowed for kissing Franciscans' habits and sometimes their hands. Beyond that, however, they limited bodily contact to good friends and boon companions. When Indians made clear that their courtesies called for reciprocity, the struggles of Spaniards and Frenchmen to do so reflected their discomfort at this unfamiliar diplomatic requirement. Henri Joutel reported with seeming nonchalance an encounter with two women who "came to embrace us in their special way" and continued the gesture by "blowing against our ears." Yet when several men followed suit by greeting the Frenchmen "in the same way the women had done," Joutel and his companions broke out in nervous laughter.[13]

Since European expeditions precluded families, they had no women to offer the same assurances of peace. Not surprisingly, given the signal importance of women and children to regional Indian greetings, Caddo leaders noted with concern the "strange" absence of women among Spanish and French expeditions, an absence that potentially signaled hostile intentions on their part. Lacking a shared language or, for that matter, shared symbolism, European men had to find other gestures or actions with which to express an absence of hostility. Supplementing women's presence, Europeans noted, Caddo custom often dictated that men assume nonhostile stances. Europeans thus recorded Caddo men's ceremonial disarmings, laying down clubs, swords, bows, and lances. As Henri Joutel related, Hasinai men "indicat[ed] to us that they came in peace by putting their bows on the ground," and in combination with other "signs," such as dismounting from horseback, encouraged the Frenchmen of Joutel's party to approach. Sometimes, as observed by Domingo Terán de los Rios, they came forward to meet Spaniards visibly bearing no arms. Here were gestures Spaniards and Frenchmen could answer in kind.[14]

The all-male delegations of Frenchmen were so small that they rarely represented a likely threat, and French efforts to match Caddo salutes and disarmings sufficed to offset initial suspicions. Spaniards, however, came in more extended and well-equipped expeditionary parties and thus presented a more alarming semblance of force. Though they came with no women, however, an unwitting exchange of female symbolism unexpectedly got Spaniards in the metaphorical door of Hasinai diplomacy in the 1680s and 1690s. In early efforts to introduce themselves to the Hasinais, Spaniards gave center stage to religious images of the Virgin Mary and to stories of María de Jesús de Agreda.

Engraving of María de Jesús de Agreda, the "Lady in Blue," appearing before Indians to the east of New Mexico. Courtesy of the Catholic Archives of Texas, Austin.

According to legend, María de Jesús de Agreda was the first Spanish missionary to the Indian peoples of Texas, predating the Franciscans by almost one hundred years. According to historical record, she served as a major inspiration and catalyst for a missionary movement into the northern provinces of New Spain. In 1630, the *custodio* of the New Mexico missions, fray Alonso Benavides, informed the king of Spain and the Council of the Indies that God had marked the work of his Franciscan missionaries with special approval. Accounts had reached Benavides about a Franciscan nun, Agreda, living in Spain, who had traveled in spirit to the New World hundreds of times to instruct Indians in Christianity. Also recently, Indians to the east of New Mexico (later Texas) had approached his friars to request a mission for their people, telling of a "Lady in Blue" who had appeared in the sky and directed them to seek salvation from the missionaries. Benavides concluded that these events were miraculous.[15]

Nearly sixty years later, in 1689, when Spaniards pursued permanent settlement in the "land of the Tejas," they recalled stories of Agreda's prior visitations to the region and sought evidence of her that might serve as a touchstone for their own missionary efforts. Fray Damián Mazanet accompanied Alonso de León's 1689 and 1690 expeditions to Caddo lands, and while military forces searched for signs of La Salle, Mazanet looked for indications of Agreda's contact with the Caddos. Much to his delight, some Hasinais responded positively to his queries about her spiritual visits. Yes, he understood them to say, "they had been visited frequently by a very beautiful woman, who used to come down from the heights, dressed in blue garments, and that they wished to be like that woman." This mysterious female figure had appeared among them, not in living memory, but in the past, as one *caddí* attested, according to stories told by his mother and other elders. To Mazanet, it was "easily to be seen" that the Caddo leader referred to Madre María de Jesús de Agreda.[16]

How fully did the Spanish missionary and the Hasinai *caddí* understand one another in this exchange? Certainly, Mazanet's queries appeared to strike a chord; at the very least, the Hasinai leader heard the outlines of a story much like those told of one of his people's own deities. One Hasinai creation myth, recorded by Franciscans two years after the *caddí*'s exchange with Mazanet, told of a woman in heaven who daily gave birth to the sun, moon, water, frost, snow, corn, thunder, and lightning. Another Caddo oral tradition, reported in 1763, told of a female goddess called Zacado who appeared to their ancestors to teach them how to survive in the world and then disappeared once they learned how to hunt, fish, build homes, and dress. Perhaps the Hasinais responded affirmatively to the *familiarity* of the missionary's story of a spiritual apparition in female form who came to teach people how to live.

Like Benavides, they too could have found the story of Zacado on the lips of a Spaniard to be a miracle.[17]

The iconography surrounding the Virgin Mary held even more crucial significance for initial Spanish-Caddo symbolic exchanges. To Spaniards, the Virgin's image embodied who they were as a people, underscoring their religious identity as Catholics and their political and social identity as New World subjects of Spain. The Virgin served a multiplicity of roles as the patroness and protectress of the Church, the Franciscan order, the Franciscan colleges and missions of New Spain, New Spain itself, and all the people contained within it. More specifically in Texas, Spaniards proclaimed the Virgin—in her various manifestations as the Virgin of Guadalupe, Dolores, Luz, Refugio, Pilar, and Purísima Concepción—the source of spiritual guidance and protection for the members of all expeditions into the region during this period. In 1691, Domingo Terán de los Rios wrote that "the great power of our Lady of Guadalupe, the North Star and Protector of this undertaking, carried our weak efforts in this task to a successful ending." Accompanying the Aguayo expedition in 1721, Juan Antonio de la Peña concluded his account with the declaration that "Our guiding light in this enterprise has been Our Lady of Pilar whom the governor selected as guide and patroness. As a shield on the Texas frontier he left this Tower of David so that she might protect it just as she had done when the Most Holy Virgin left her image and column of Non Plus Ultra at Zaragoza, which was then the edge of the known world of the Spanish people."[18]

Spanish missionaries hoped that Our Lady of Pilar, whom they considered responsible for the conversion of old Spain, would work her old influence on the "edges" of New Spain as well. The Virgin Mary had earlier symbolized the conquest and conversion of non-Christian peoples during the Reconquest of Spain, when Spanish soldiers used her image to appropriate and transform mosques into churches. In the New World, the royal banner similarly flew as a sign of sovereignty over not only their encampments but also the territories they claimed in the name of the king. Yet, that message of conquest was not one meant for Indian observers but rather for rival Europeans who might otherwise challenge Spanish claims. When soldiers and missionaries marched into Caddo lands in the 1680s, the predominance of such banners also represented a shift in Spanish policy in response to the Crown's 1573 Order for New Discoveries that prohibited violent conquest and instead promoted the "pacification" of Indian lands, with missionaries at the head of exploration and settlement. Though Franciscans in New Spain eschewed syncretism of the Virgin Mary and indigenous deities in the worship of their mission neophytes, they used her image to extend a promise of peace and protection to "the most remote people who have been discovered in America by the Spaniards." When a Hasinai *caddí* inquired of a missionary the meaning of the sacred image on the Spanish altar, the Franciscan appealed to her identity as Christ's mother and her intercessory role in the Catholic Church, characterizing her to the *caddís* as the "mother of help and of the religion of all human kind."[19]

Spaniards displayed their religious icons to Indians because they believed there was no better image of peace (and, by extension, peaceful intent) than the cross and images of Christ, Mary, and the saints. In 1709, for instance, fray Espinosa used a cross fashioned out of paper and painted with ink as a calling card that was sent to the Hasinais when his expedition was unable to make it all the way to the eastern settlements. More important, though unaware of Caddos' symbolic association of women with peace, Spaniards gave center stage to religious images of the Virgin Mary as their chosen sign of peaceful intent. The Virgin's image was the focal point of Spanish self-presentation to Indians across the region—dominating as she did their rhetoric, prayers, banners, and rituals. Every Spanish expedition into Texas displayed the royal standard "bearing on one side the picture of Christ crucified, and on the other that of the Virgin of Guadalupe." Each day, expedition leaders like Domingo Terán de los Rios chronicled their expeditions as the movements of "our royal standard and camp." Routinely recording that "our royal standard went forward today," Spanish officers and missionaries transformed the standard into a pronoun for themselves. Spaniards then took possession of lands by "fixing the royal standard" or leaving crosses as symbolic claims to territory. Spaniards also made Indians an audience to the regular performance of daily masses, processions, and celebrations of feast days in the Virgin's honor before makeshift altars incorporating her image, thereby reinforcing the import of the Virgin's presence within their expeditions.[20]

Fray Damián Mazanet, for example, took special care in planning the Spanish entry into one Hasinai village in 1690. "My opinion was," he recorded, "that we four priests should go on foot, carrying our staffs, which bore a holy crucifix, and singing the Litany of Our Lady, and that a lay-brother who was with us should carry in front a picture on linen of the Blessed Virgin, bearing it high on his lance, after the fashion of a banner." Mazanet further reported that the royal standard with its double picture of Christ and the Virgin of Guadalupe waved over the dedication of the first Tejas mission in 1690 during mass, a procession of the holy sacrament, the firing of a royal salute, and the singing of the *Te Deum Laudamus* in thanksgiving.[21]

In response to such declarations and ritual enactments, Indian peoples in Texas quickly came to associate Marian iconography symbolizing a powerful peacemaker specifically with Spaniards. The Virgin was not associated with Catholic Frenchmen (who until the mid-eighteenth century had few priests of their own in Louisiana,

Image of the Virgin of Guadalupe printed on a pink silk banner, 1803. Courtesy of the John Carter Brown Library at Brown University, Providence, R.I.

much less missionaries seeking to convert Indians). An episode related by French missionary Anastase Douay, one of the survivors of La Salle's expedition, illustrates Caddo interpretations. Encountering a Hasinai man, Douay learned of the nearby presence of people who resembled Frenchmen and whom the man described by sketching "a painting that he had seen of a great lady, who was weeping because her son was upon a cross." Much later, in the 1760s, fray José de Solís reported the still-powerful symbolic association of the Virgin with Spaniards. He told of a man from an Ais village (another Caddo band) who rejected the Spanish missionary's preachings by asserting to Solís that "he loved and appreciated *Misurí* (who is the Devil), more than he did the Most Blessed among all those created, the Holy Mother Mary, Our Lady."[22]

Spaniards' prominent display of the Virgin's image did indeed succeed in giving signs of peaceful intent to Caddos, but not for reasons that Europeans would have understood. Caddos deemed Spaniards friendly because of the *female*, not the spiritual, embodiment of the figurative María. They, of course, did not understand Catholic iconography but instead translated it within the context of their own beliefs. Caddo responses indicate that they understood the Virgin's image, not as a Spanish assertion of political identity or religious intent, but as an effort by Spaniards to compensate for their lack of real women and thereby to offset any appearance of hostility. Pierre Talon, one of the French youths from the La Salle expedition living among Caddos in 1690, described the initial appearance of Spanish expeditions while standing on the Hasinai side of the encounter: it was an overwhelmingly martial vision as men on horseback rode up "armed with muskets or small harquebuses, pistols, and swords and all wearing coats of mail or iron wire made like nets of very small links." Though Talon did not make much of the banners emblazoned with a female figure, the Hasinai leaders did. In one of the earliest Spanish-Hasinai meetings, military commander Domingo Terán de los Rios reported what he believed to be the pacifying effect of the Virgin's image on Caddos. He wrote that when faced with the difficult task of persuading the Hasinais of the sincerity of Spanish efforts to capture and punish the Spanish murderer of one of their people, he believed the Virgin "calmed and soothed" them, perhaps helping to communicate the expedition's peaceful intentions in the face of such an act of violence.[23]

Most tellingly, Hasinais and other Indians directed customary renderings of welcome and honor to the figurative image of the Virgin Mary as they did to women of any visiting party. In the place of caresses reserved for real women, they might salute or kiss the standards bearing the Virgin's image. Another native practice also incorporated her image. Indians normally put on display gifts received from allies in past ceremonial exchanges as a signal of welcome when those allies returned for later visits. When they extended similar gestures to Spanish visitors, objects carrying the image of the Virgin Mary were their choice for display. Time and again, Spanish missionaries wrote excitedly about Indians greeting them with images of the Virgin upon arrival at their villages. In 1709, as the Espinosa, Aguirre, and Olivares expedition approached a village of Yojuanes, a small group came forward in single file, led by a man carrying a cross made of bamboo, who was "followed by three other Indians, each one with an image of Our Lady of Guadalupe, two of which were painted, and the other was an old engraving." As they processed forward, they bowed and made other manifestations of peace toward the icons before approaching the Spaniards for customary embraces. The Indian men then formally requested that the Spanish representatives in turn go to meet the women of their village. Caddo leaders made even more direct their veneration of the female icon. When the Ramón expedition reached the Hasinai settlements in June of 1716, all the *caddís* and leading men came forward and kissed the image of Our Lady of Guadalupe, "whom they all adored." The Hasinais further honored the female presence of the Virgin by attending a mass presided over by her image. Missionaries later endeavored, unsuccessfully, to build upon what they saw as signs of native interest in Christianity; their failure to convert gave further proof that these gestures were indeed the Caddos' efforts to recognize ceremonially a female presence among the Spaniards.[24]

Once both sides had established nonhostile intent, diplomatic protocols could get under way, calling upon each side to behave according to its customary, gendered notions of honor. For Caddos, initial meetings with foreigners involved only the establishing of acquaintance (alliance, trade, and relationships of any other kind were not yet being negotiated). At this point, they required primarily elite male leaders who stood for or embodied the community. Having vested authority in their leaders, Caddos established relations with other groups through these high-status individuals. Diplomatic rituals therefore linked together Caddo male elites with Spaniards and Frenchmen of analogous status in order to incorporate symbolically the foreigners into the Caddos' ranked social systems—giving them the status and position required for interaction with the Caddo *xinesí* and *caddís*. Meanwhile, Europeans tried to ascertain which men represented the Caddo villages, and even more important, the confederacies, or "kingdoms," and so had the authority to broker trade agreements and political alliances.[25]

    With these goals in mind, both European and Caddo men spent much of their time in early meetings trying to read one another's appearance, hospitality, and gift giving as indicators of status and power. Because Caddo ritual focused on linking together elite men from both sides of the cross-cultural encounter, efforts at communication reaped greatest success in contexts governed by rules of masculine conduct. The reception of foreign visitors offered a venue for conflated representations of national and male honor, especially when male elites vied to impress or outdo each other in display. The care Caddo men put into diplomatic ceremonies—

reflected in the elaborate nature of feasts, dances, festivals, presentations of gifts, customary gala attire, and formal "harangues"—conveyed the significance of any invitation to share in such ritual. Congruence emerged between Spanish, French, and Caddo norms of masculinity when similar customs of militarized dress, displays of strength, and rituals of respect helped to enact public communications of honor between men. These shared bases of male honor facilitated good relations even if Spanish, French, and Caddo men did not grasp the nuances of each other's behavior. As with the fortuitous misinterpretations of the Virgin Mary, in other words, each side appeared to conform to the other's expectations of proper deportment toward fellow men, even while not fully understanding how and why.[26]

Caddo men greeted their European visitors with well-defined ceremonies to which like-minded Spanish and French men easily adapted because, coincidentally, they resembled their own. Europeans too came from worlds with long traditions of ceremony and rites of political, spiritual, and social meaning. Much in the rituals marking Hasinai diplomatic events resonated with French and Spanish men accustomed to civic and royal pageantry; the pomp of public entries, audiences, and departures; and the gift giving and banquets that surrounded the reception of foreign embassies and ambassadors. Caddo ceremony inspired fray Francisco Casañas de Jesús María to credit them with demonstrating "courtesies that Christians are accustomed to observe," and he was particularly impressed with their deference to age. Twenty years later, fray Espinosa similarly asserted that Hasinais "most displayed their diplomatic policy in the embassies that they send to one another's settlements." Spaniards concluded from the formality of Caddo ceremony that any pledges given or taken would be strictly observed, while Frenchmen similarly read the ritual smoking of pipes (which they called "calumet" ceremonies) as a commitment of sincerity. From the symbolism inherent in many of these ceremonies, moreover, Europeans learned the protocols of respect due their native hosts. Arguing for the importance of these early meetings, one Spanish officer wrote that "much care is necessary, to the point that when the ways of the people are recognized, one arranges things to their taste." By taking part in such rituals, Spaniards and Frenchmen communicated their respect for their Indian hosts and their awareness that they too must earn respect.[27]

For all these groups, civic and national displays of power took the form of male displays in military musters, oath swearings, and processions. Because of the times in which they lived, these European and Indian societies bound their concepts of political authority to military identity and ability. Growing challenges from expanding Apache and Osage bands over the eighteenth century were increasing the authority of war chiefs in relationship to the theocratic rule of the *xinesí* and the *caddís* within the Caddo chiefdoms. Tellingly, the status of *amayxoyas* (a category of warriors who earned the honorific title in recognition of valorous deeds and from among whom war chiefs were elected) appeared to be on the rise in response to these increasing tensions. Spanish, French, and Hasinai men established male honor through their deeds and accomplishments and expected public recognition of that honor through public ritual. In turn, for both Europeans and Indians, encounters with new groups required that men provide militarized displays and demonstrations of male prowess. Such rites determined the authority each brought to the following negotiations by establishing mutual, rather than hierarchical, honor and respect.[28]

At all stages of their journeys through Texas, Spanish officers thereby kept in mind the possibility of Indian surveillance and directed their expeditions to move in "military formation" to inspire the awe of onlookers. Although ceremonial formations and processions were a regular part of daily military life for the presidial forces, Spanish commanders clearly manipulated displays to achieve certain effects before Indian audiences. Concerned with their "mode of entry" to Hasinai settlements, commanders decided that a "good example would be set by having the priests and officers march in a procession," followed by "all the cavalry, arms, munitions, and the necessary rear guard." The retinue of supplies, munitions, and horses came last in the ranked orders. Such organized fanfare was not simply defensive but aimed to impress without antagonizing native groups targeted for diplomacy. The Hasinais met them with their own processions as *caddís* assembled their people, arranged them in the typical three files, and advanced to meet the Spaniards outside their villages.[29]

Next came the exchange of salutes. In the earliest meetings, Caddo men saluted by raising their arms and yelling in unison before approaching visiting Europeans. When survivors from La Salle's party arrived at one Hasinai village in 1687, a dozen *caddís* and elders marched out in procession with warriors and youths "in the wings," all wearing ceremonial dress. As soon as they drew near, Henri Joutel recorded, they all "raised their hands above their heads and came straight toward us uttering a certain unanimous howl." By the 1710s, when French trade had increased the number of arms among Caddos, discharging guns replaced the yells as an imposing salute. In return, Spanish cavalry units discharged volleys, beat drums, and blew bugles. Both peoples endowed these exchanges of firepower with a dual purpose—as a literal "salute" of respectful greeting and as a figurative display of military strength. Fray Mazanet recorded that soldiers of the 1690 León expedition "had been given leave to fire as many salutes as they could during the procession, at the elevation, and at the close of mass." The number of shots reinforced both the force and extent of the Spanish military power. Over time, greetings increased in intensity. As fray Francisco de Céliz described in 1718, "all the Indians came in marching order, firing their muskets with such precision that it seemed that they had been well disciplined in the militia; and as was noticed by all, the governor [Martín de Alarcón] was received with shots from more muskets than the said governor had on his side." As early as 1718, then, Hasinais had closed the technological gap, and Spaniards found themselves outgunned. By 1721, the marqués de San Miguel de Aguayo felt compelled to bring out the big guns—quite literally—in order to outdo Caddo leaders. He divided his battalion into eight companies arranged in three files, placed cannons between them and fired three general salutes, and delightedly had his diarist record that the firing of the artillery and the companies' volleys in concert had finally "created substantial wonder" among the watching Hasinai men.[30]

Once inside the Hasinai villages, both sides continued their displays of military presence and prowess unabated. *Caddís* stationed warriors as guards day and night as long as visitors remained present. Spanish expedition leaders similarly called officers and soldiers into military assembly to stand as an audience to ritual and rhetorical exchanges in the course of meetings. According to fray Espinosa, Hasinai men "do not yield a point in proving themselves warlike and valiant." Guns only became available to the Caddos in the 1700s with the French trade, but because of trade with the Jumanos from the west, horses were well-established as a marker of male status by the time Europeans arrived in the 1680s, their value reflected by Caddo warriors' choice to include their steeds among their prized burial goods at death. In later years, Caddo men thus chose their manner of display based upon their trade advantages in either guns or horses, Espinosa continued, and "make a show of wielding their guns with dexterity and racing their horses at great speed." In the 1760s, a French traveler, Pierre Marie François de Pagès, related a strikingly similar performance by Hasinai men. In an encounter with a party on horseback, he recorded, Caddo men

> were eager to display with much ostentation the swiftness and agility of their
> horses, as well as their own skill and dexterity in the art of riding; and it is but
> doing them justice to say, that the most noble and graceful object I have ever
> seen was one of those savages mounted and running at full speed. The broad
> Herculean trunk of his body, his gun leaning over the left arm, and his plaid
> or blanket thrown carelessly across his naked shoulders, and streaming in the
> wind, was such an appearance as I could only compare to some of the finest
> equestrian statues of antiquity.[31]

Responding in kind to such demonstrations, Spaniards mounted their own displays of armed cavalry performances to affirm their standing as formidable warriors and as men. In 1716, the Ramón expedition had to stop for a day of rest on their way to the Hasinai villages because cavalrymen—including Captain Ramón himself—had been racing and attempting stunts from horseback with such recklessness that several had suffered injurious falls. The 1721 expedition of the marqués de Aguayo, of all the Spanish *entradas* to Caddo lands, was the one most designed to impart Spanish power, with its five hundred men marching in eight companies. Expedition diarist Juan Antonio de la Peña recorded that the size of the army—as well as the train of cargo and livestock—did appear to impress Hasinai leaders. Beginning with meetings with a *caddí* named Cheocas, who was known to have a "great following," and at each subsequent meeting with different Caddo groups, Aguayo repeated a scenario of putting his troops through their paces and having them pass in formal review before Caddo leaders and warriors.[32]

Orchestrated display shifted to the individual level when Caddos and Europeans had to identify elites. Spaniards, Frenchmen, and Hasinais based initial impressions on appearance, so dress and adornment held considerable importance. Using dress as a marker of identity was not always so simple, however. Europeans recorded instances when they failed to recognize Caddos at all, mistaking them because of clothing and manner as either French or Spanish. Henri Joutel made such an error in perception in 1687. One afternoon, he explained,

> we saw three men, one of whom was on horseback. They were coming from
> the direction of the Cenis' village and consequently straight to us. When they
> came close, I noticed that one was dressed in the Spanish manner, wearing a
> short jacket or doublet, the body of which was blue with white sleeves as if
> embroidered on a kind of fustian; he was wearing small, tight breeches, white
> stockings, woolen garters, and a Spanish hat that was broad and flat in shape.
> His hair was long, straight, and black, and he had a swarthy face. I therefore
> did not have much difficulty persuading myself that he was a Spaniard.

Joutel did not realize his mistake until the man responded to his attempts to speak "in a broken Spanish or Italian" by saying "*Coussiqua,*" which Joutel understood to be a Hasinai expression for "I have none of it," or "I don't understand it."[33]

Indians too used dress and appearance to distinguish among foreigners, whether European or native. The vast array of different hair styles, clothing, tattoos, and body paint of Indian peoples in the region, noted carefully by Europeans, testified to the importance of distinct markers of identity. Yojuanes, Simonos, and Tusonibis told fray Espinosa that they recognized Spaniards by the red waistcoat worn by one of the officers. In interactions with Frenchmen, Hasinais referred to Spaniards by "depicting" their clothing. Similarly, Paloma Indians, perhaps trying to smooth over an unintended offense, once assured Frenchmen that they "did not look like Spaniards." Not surprisingly, but much to the consternation of Europeans, however, Indians in the early period of contact often could not differentiate between Frenchmen and Spaniards. Since they used clothing as identity markers, they found Europeans much alike. The marqués de Aguayo explained to Viceroy Casafuerte that because "the Indians of all those nations [in the Texas province] do not distinguish between us," they sometimes called both Spaniards and Frenchmen by the same term.[34]

European and Indian societies nevertheless similarly invested dress with significations of individual honor as well as social, political, and military rank, and so clothing emerged as a useful means of communication. Caddos reserved "gala attire" particularly for diplomatic feasts and celebrations in which "neither the men nor the women lack articles of adornment for their festivities." "When the day arrives," described fray Espinosa, "they get out all the best woolen clothing they have, which they reserve for this purpose, along with very soft chamois edged with little white beads, some very black chamois covered with the same beads, bracelets, and necklaces, which they wear only on this and other feast days." Because these ceremonies revealed each person's contributions to society and highlighted social and political authority and rank, dress took on significance as a symbolic extension of that status.[35]

In addition to the swords, clubs, and later guns carried by leading warriors as emblematic of their elite rank, European observers remarked that dress was an arena of particular male display and subsequently laid great import upon it in judging character. To Alonso de León, for instance, a Hasinai *caddí* he met was clearly a man of ability, because his appearance and comportment outweighed his "barbarian" identity. Jean Cavelier, La Salle's brother, judged Hasinais to be the "most polished" of Indians based on appearance, arguing that "From the layout of their village and the style of their houses, from the cloth of bird feathers and hair of animals, they seem to be more intelligent and more clever than all the other nations we met."[36]

What was so remarkable about the dress and decor of Caddo men? Hasinai men especially, explained fray Francisco Casañas de Jesús María, "pride themselves on coming out as gallants," and some costumes were "of so hideous a form that they look like demons," since some "go so far as to put deer horns on their heads." Men displayed rank and occupation by choosing among elaborately decorated bison skins, feathers, jewelry, and battle trophies. Henri Joutel wrote that, when all the elders of one Hasinai community came out to greet French visitors, they appeared dressed in their finery which consisted of some dressed skins in several colors which they wore across their shoulders like scarves and also wore as skirts. On their heads, they wore a few clusters of feathers fashioned like turbans, also painted different colors. Seven or eight of them had sword blades with clusters of feathers on the hilt. . . . they also had several large bells which made a noise like a mule bell. With regard to arms, some Indians carried their bows with a few arrows, while others carried tomahawks and had smeared their faces, some with black and others with white and red.

Painting their faces with vermilion (red pigment) and bear's grease made their faces red and slick, according to Spanish observers. Feathers served as particular signs of prestige for men. Fray Espinosa wrote that "when they see the feathers of the chickens from Spain which we raise they do not stop until they have collected the prettiest colored ones," saving them "to wear at their brightest." Among the spiritual elites, feathers marked the personal insignia and ritual tools of Hasinai shamans, a predominantly, but not exclusively, male group. And at the highest level of all, as fray Espinosa described it, were the chests in the house of the *cononicis* (revered child spirits who acted as intermediaries between the *xinesí* and the Supreme Being, Ayo-Caddí-Aymay), which were filled with "many feathers of all sizes and colors, handfuls of wild turkey feathers, a white breast knot, some bundles of feather ornaments, crowns made of skins and feathers, and a headdress of the same"—all to be used by the *xinesí* in domestic and diplomatic rituals.[37]

Spanish and French men accurately assessed markers of Caddo male status when it came to warrior strength and valor (observations that Caddo male display often left little room to doubt). "In appearance," fray Espinosa wrote of Hasinai men, "they are well built, burly, agile, and strong; always ready for war expeditions and of great courage." Domingo Terán de los Rios similarly assumed Hasinai appearance to be indicative of warrior demeanor, because after watching their movements and expressions, he "concluded that [Hasinai men] were very brave, haughty and numerous." Describing a ceremony he compared to a knighting, Frenchman Henri Joutel recognized the significance of clothing to a Hasinai male youth's assumption of adult male position and status. Once a young man reached the age of becoming a warrior, he recorded, elders assembled an outfit and equipage for him, consisting of a garment made of tanned hide and a bow, quiver, and arrows over which was chanted a blessing. Tattoos also offered a visible record of male status and honor. Adult men's body decorations focused on "Figures of living creatures, like birds and animals," to reflect their role as hunters. Martial images depicted individual accomplishments in war. Hasinai warriors further carried as "arms and banners" the skins and scalps of defeated enemies. According to fray Francisco Hidalgo, they "wear the scalps of their enemies at their belts as trophies and hang them from reeds at the entry to their doors as signs of triumph." Displays conveyed rank *among* men as well, when entire hanging heads and skulls marked the residence of the grand *xinesí*—trophies brought him by the warriors he commanded.[38]

Spanish and French officers and soldiers sought to impress Caddo men too with an appearance of courage and strength to win respect that could later be built upon to forge trust and alliance. Of first importance to Europeans was communicating to Indians that they met as equals and that it was not in the Indians' interest to fight them. Europeans wished to convey that they were there as representatives of nations capable of offering military aid and alliance. The composition of the earliest expeditionary forces reinforced their efforts to appear powerful. With missionaries, officers, soldiers, and traders the sole members of the initial groups visiting Caddo lands, Spaniards and Frenchmen could not help but communicate a primarily militarized image of male strength. Officers and soldiers always dressed in full regalia, sporting military coats and hats, chain mail, and an assortment of armaments. One Spanish expedition leader delayed the departure of his forces for over a month while awaiting the delivery of new uniforms for the soldiers.[39]

If Caddos used their own theocratic hierarchies of male leadership to aid them in discerning the ranks among Spanish and French men, however, they likely concluded that no one within the visiting parties occupied the elite level of their *xinesí* or perhaps even their *caddís*. A *xinesí* was both a religious and a political leader, who did not hunt because his household was supported through gifts of food and meat from the surrounding communities; in fact, fray Casañas explained that "all of the Indians give him portions of what they have so as to dress and clothe him." He maintained perpetually the sacred fire at the temple complex and mediated between the spiritual and human worlds. In turn, this mediation informed the guidance he offered the *caddís* and *canahas* as they assembled to make decisions about the welfare of their communities. Thus, the *xinesí's* complex functioned as the center of both spiritual and political power, uniting the surrounding communities. Neither *xinesí* nor *caddís* carried weapons to mark their status, because although they held authority in military decisions, they were not warriors or war chiefs (a different political category with different symbols). Spanish military commanders, in contrast, did wear their arms as emblems of rank, and though their authority over soldiers was clear, by such appearance they were most analogous in standing to the Caddo war chiefs. The separation of religious and military leaders within Spanish expeditions and the subordinate status of missionaries to military commanders further prevented any association of the spiritual vocation of missionaries with that of the *xinesís,* leaving them analogous in rank to the *connas* (shaman priests) among the lower orders of Caddo nongoverning elites. During diplomatic meetings with Spaniards, then, *caddís* might oversee the rituals and ceremonies, but Spanish commanders and missionaries primarily shared status with the lower orders of governing and nongoverning elites—*canahas, amayxoyas,* and *connas.*[40]

After sussing out personal appearance and rank, rules of male precedence ordered Caddo hospitality customs of pipe-smoking and the seating, housing, and feeding of guests. Spaniards observed that each Hasinai household set aside a special seat for only the *caddí* to use when he visited, and that offers of hospitality served as payments of respect to leaders. In the *caddís'* households, fray Mazanet and fray Casañas quickly learned not to approach, much less sit upon, a particular wooden bench in front of the fire; to do so constituted a breach of etiquette that might result in supernatural death because the seats were reserved for the *xinesí* alone. At a nonelite home that Terán de los Rios visited in the company of a *caddí,* the military commander noted that the *caddí* was offered a seat as soon as he crossed the threshold, "deference" that was shown to no others in the party. Caddos also provided leaders with special feasts, and rituals required the people of each household to present *caddís* and the *xinesí* with food and supplies on a regular basis. In public ceremonies, seating arrangements and orders of ritual always affirmed rank and prestige among the Hasinais.

Just as Caddos showed deference to their leaders, shamans, and *caddís* in civil ceremonies, so in turn did they reserve markers of prestige for respected visitors, seeking to unite host and guest in bonds of shared honor. Spaniards and Frenchmen recorded with appreciation that ritualized gestures and privileges that leading Caddo men and principal warriors enjoyed were ceremonially extended to their own leaders. At each visit, for instance, Hasinais accorded missionaries and officers the honor of staying within a *caddí's* residential complex. At meetings, Hasinai leaders orchestrated the design and arrangement of seats to reaffirm and accord honor. Carpets of mats and blankets, roofs of tree boughs, and benches covered with bison skins decorated reception areas. Juan Bautista Chapa described the special benches brought forward by Hasinais when the León expedition first visited in 1689 and again in 1690 as a "civility that greatly surprised our troops." The importance of such rituals was clearly borne home to Europeans, as evidenced by their efforts to match such hospitality when Caddos visited Spanish encampments away from their villages. When Spanish officers found themselves in the position of host, they carefully imitated Caddo custom in setting up similar housing and seating arrangements commensurate with the rank and status of the various members of the visiting group. As Captain Domingo Ramón made his first approach toward the Caddo villages in 1716, he knew that a welcoming party would be sent out to greet him, so he had his men build a structure of tree branches covered with blankets, with all the packsaddles available arranged around to serve as seats to allow him to greet Hasinai leaders in the appropriate fashion.[41]

The housing of visiting dignitaries held particular significance, indicating their honorary but probationary status within Hasinai settlements. Military commanders and missionaries thus found themselves housed in *caddís'* ceremonial compounds, where "there was room for all," explained one *caddí* to fray Mazanet. And room there was. Located near the geographic center of each Caddo community, but separated from the surrounding hamlets and farmsteads, the complex included the *caddí's* residence, a building for public gatherings, and a residential building to house *canahas* when called into meetings by the *caddí*, all three built around a central plaza with a cane-covered arbor nearby—a two- to three-acre site altogether. The residence itself was the largest of the three—a circular pole-framed house with a thatched grass roof twenty *varas* in height (fifty-five feet), within which the focal point was a hearth fire "fed by four logs forming a cross oriented to the cardinal directions" and lit by embers brought from the sacred fire at the *xinesí's* temple complex. "Ranged around one-half of the house, inside, are ten beds, which consist of a rug made of reeds, laid on four forked sticks," described Mazanet. "Over the rug they spread buffalo skins, on which they sleep. At the head and foot of the bed is attached another carpet forming a sort of arch, which, lined with a very brilliantly colored piece of reed matting, makes what bears some resemblance to a very pretty alcove." The other half of the house provided shelves upon shelves of storage as well as working areas for the ten women who oversaw the day-to-day functioning of the compound and prepared the feasts offered as part of the *caddí's* hospitality. "Skillfully fashioned" wooden benches brought out into a patio fronting the plaza served as the dining area for guests.[42]

Visiting European and native diplomats became temporary residents of the compound like *canahas*, the ranking elders who left their own homes to take up temporary residence in the building designated for them when *caddís* called them to council duty. Both groups of men, whether domestic or foreign, were recognized as men of standing—secondary to *caddís*—who gathered at this site to take part in public ceremonies and rituals. Yet, the temporary housing of European visitors reflected not just the official nature of their visit but also their separation from the surrounding community. As George Sabo explains, "rituals performed in temples or at ceremonial centers emphasized the hierarchical priority of leaders as representatives of their communities," thus distinguishing them as discrete from the rituals performed in individual houses throughout the Caddo community that reflected kinship, clan membership, and the matrilineages of those homesteads. To house (and confine) visitors at the *caddí*'s compound emphasized their standing as men of rank while at the same time keeping them distant from the Caddo community itself. The Caddos' response to Spanish leaders who failed to abide by the rules indicates how important this separation was. Commander Domingo Terán de los Rios, for instance, managed to offend more than one *caddí* during his 1691 travels through Hasinai territory. One leader, who quickly developed hostile relations with Spaniards, never opened his home to Terán, leaving him to remain in the camp his men had pitched at a distance from the Hasinai villages. When the expedition moved on to another village, the *caddí* there offered his house as shelter to the military commander because of the bad weather but was displeased when Terán left the compound, "displeasure" that necessitated Terán's hasty return to the complex. Telling as well, when the two men together visited another village across the river the next day, Terán noted that only the *caddí* was offered a seat by their host.[43]

When Europeans learned and obeyed the rules governing visits to Hasinai villages, they then participated in other ceremonies that reinforced shared male honors and prestige. Smoking ceremonial, or "calumet," pipes—usually made of stone (but later sometimes brass), with a stem more than one *vara* (2¾ feet) in length, with numerous white feathers attached from one end of the stem to the other—held a central place in publicly joining together Caddo and European men of stature. Spanish officials interpreted the mixing of Caddo and European tobacco and the shared smoking of a pipe as signaling friendship, a "unity of their wills," and mutual "compliments." In French observances, the singing or chanting of the calumet similarly translated as a "mark of alliance" or promise of "good union." While everyone in a Caddo community took part in the ceremony—reflecting the Caddo presumption that everyone had an investment in the union and spirit represented by the ritual—the order of smoking itself reconfirmed the position and power of governing male elites. The *caddí* prepared the tobacco on a "curious and elaborately painted deerskin," lit the pipe, and blew the first smoke, before passing the pipe to their leading warriors, then to guests of analogous prominence, and eventually to all others. Although Caddo women and children took part in pipe ceremonies, they did not actually smoke the pipe, and the performance of the smoking ceremony aimed primarily at validating the honor and position of Caddo and European male leaders.[44]

Once status was clearly established, European men had to go through purification rituals that would admit them into Caddo male ranks, a diplomatic formality necessary before any kind of negotiation for trade or alliance could begin. Washing was one form of purification for strangers, as when some Caddos brought water and cleaned Henri Tonti's face with such care that he concluded it must be a particular ceremony among them. Henri Joutel wrote that they actually wanted to bathe the Frenchmen entirely, but because of their unfamiliar clothing, elders chose only to apply fresh water to the visitors' brows. Perhaps to make up for that limitation, one Caddo village farther north in present-day Arkansas made abbé Jean Cavelier part of a far more elaborate transformation or adoption ceremony. There, village leaders identified Cavelier as the "chief" of the party, to be honored in a calumet ceremony —reinforcing the impression that the Caddos had difficulty discerning leaders of equivalent status to their own. Elders accompanied by young men and women sang before the dwelling where Cavelier and other Frenchmen were housed, then led Cavelier outside to a prepared location, put a large handful of grass under his feet while two others brought out an earthen dish filled with clear water with which they washed his face. After this cleansing, he found himself seated on a specially prepared bison skin with a calumet pipe laid before him on a dressed bison skin and white deerskin, which were stretched over three forked pieces of wood, all dyed red. Surrounded by elders and men and women singing and shaking gourd rattles, a Caddo man stood directly behind Cavelier to support him and made him "rock and swing from side to side in rhythm with the choir." Worse still from Cavelier's perspective, two young women then came forward with a necklace and an otter skin to be placed on either side of the calumet and, with matching symmetry, placed themselves on either side of the Frenchman, facing one another with their legs extended forward and intertwined so that Cavelier's legs could then be arranged across theirs. The ceremony wound on until Cavelier—reeling with exhausted embarrassment "to see himself in this position between the two girls"—signaled to his French companions (who were highly amused by his predicament) to extract him. The smoking of the pipe had to await the morning and the recovery of Cavelier's dignity.[45]

Spanish expedition leader Martín de Alarcón's experience in 1718 further illustrates the ritual elaborations by which Caddos consecrated foreign men of stature as dignitaries. As soon as Alarcón arrived in one Hasinai village, men came forward to take him from his horse, a *caddí* removed his sword and guns, and two warriors picked him up, one by the shoulders and the other by the feet, and carried him to the door of the house where he was to stay. Standing him on his feet, "they washed his face and hands gently and dried them with a cloth." Again picking him up, they carried him inside and placed him on a special bench alongside several *caddís* with whom he "reciprocally performed" a pipe ceremony. Only after this ceremonial cleansing, followed by presentation into the company of Caddo leaders, did Caddo men formally "give him to understand how greatly they enjoyed his coming." Smoking a pipe as well as washing thus appeared to be part of the induction rituals.[46]

Spanish and French officers sometimes received titles reflecting their new status among Caddos as diplomats and traders. At the close of purification rituals for Alarcón, one group of Hasinais declared that "they received him as their chief," while another chose to address him as "*Cadi A Ymat.*" Observing the rituals as they took place, fray Espinosa, who had been living among Caddos for three years, explained that "this is the ceremony with which they declare someone a *capitán general* among them." Hasinai leaders meant these titles to confer symbolic inclusion or membership among a community of leading men and warriors. Europeans appreciated but often did not fully understand this honor. Time and again, Europeans conflated titles conferred on them with the authority held by *caddís*, failing because of language barriers or ego to recognize the complexities of Caddo leadership hierarchies and their own subordinate status within them. Spaniards in particular often hoped that such ceremonies indicated Caddo acceptance of nominal Spanish rule—quite a leap of imagination in the absence of military conquest. Without being aware of European flights of fancy, however, Caddos used such titles to their own advantage. In response to French trader Jean Baptiste Bénard de la Harpe's proposal to establish a trading post in their village, a Caddo band of Nasonis rewarded the Frenchman with a title of "calumet chief." He soon discovered to his dismay that the title came with more obligations than privileges. In recognition of his newly conferred position—a position demanding displays of "chiefly" largesse and generosity—Nasoni leaders called upon him to supply them with gifts rather than simply the trade he had come seeking.[47]

To accompany such titles, Caddo leaders also presented Spanish and French men with dress and insignia reflecting native male rank and honor. After Jean Cavelier's purification in Arkansas, Caddo elders tied up his hair and placed a dyed feather at the back of his head and, following the completion of the smoking ceremony, gathered the pipe and the red-dyed sticks upon which it had rested into a deerskin pouch and presented it to Cavelier as a token of peace, which he could use as a passport to other Caddo villages. *Caddís* placed on the head of Martín de Alarcón "some feathers from the breasts of white ducks and on his forehead a strip of black cloth which fell to his cheeks." At about the same time that Alarcón was with the Hasinais, Bénard de la Harpe had moved on from the Nasoni villages to those of allied Wichita bands, where he received a grand reception. A Tawakoni chief recognized him by giving him "a crown of eagle feathers, decorated with small birds of all colors, with two Calumet feathers, one for war and the other for peace, the most respectable present that these warriors may give." Ritual exchange continued the next day when the warriors painted Bénard de la Harpe's face ultramarine blue and presented him with many bison robes. In the three ceremonies, feathers, which Europeans had noted to be signifiers of elite male status, appeared as a central decoration in the insignia offered foreign dignitaries.[48]

Once visiting leaders had been inducted into Caddo ranks, the entire community then welcomed them, and here women took center stage to emphasize the newcomers' inclusion. Whether Spanish and French expeditions encountered Caddos along the roads or within villages, feasts and food items were always part of what Europeans understood as native "gifts" of hospitality. Away from villages, food was a key feature in the Caddos' welcome committee greetings. When ninety-six Hasinais met the Ramón expedition several leagues outside of their villages in 1716, "gifts of ears of green corn, tamales, and beans cooked with corn and nuts" followed quickly upon the smoking of the calumet pipe at the impromptu feasting site. Once meetings moved to the more formal complexes of the *caddís*, women's prominence in hosting the rituals clearly reflected that the bounty of feasts rested upon their successful direction of agricultural cultivation within the community. Fray Francisco de Céliz recorded that Caddo women "came from all the houses, offering their baskets of meal and other edible things . . . which was all that they had at that time." As women brought ears of green corn, watermelon, beans, and tamales for the feasts, each woman designated for expedition leaders "a small gift of the food that they themselves eat." Thus, domestic economies intertwined with political diplomacy to accord women (and the matrilineal households they represented) a place of honor in hospitality ceremonies. Nevertheless, European visitors remained within ceremonial compounds to which each household's contribution was brought; they were not yet invited into the community itself.[49]

The honors implicit in Caddo leaders' demonstrations of hospitality obligated a reciprocal "favor" from their Spanish and French guests, generally in the form of diplomatic gifts. Each side interpreted gift giving according to their own gendered view of what was necessary to maintain order. Gifts answered the debt incurred by partaking of the bounty of the *caddís*' villages. As Bénard de la Harpe recorded, whenever a group honored him with the calumet ceremony, it "obliged" or "induced" him to reciprocate with gifts. Gift giving, hospitality, and reciprocity figured prominently in Spanish and French culture as well, rooted in ideals of the obligations of public and familial patriarchs, and were basic to European male honor. So gift giving was another custom that could promote cross-cultural communication while, yet again, not being fully understood by either side. Every expedition sent by the Spanish Crown to visit Indian nations carried with it "the stock and the supplies designated for use in gaining the friendship of the Indians and winning their affections." While European representatives sought to impress with shows of generosity and the material benefits of their nations, however, Hasinais and other Caddo peoples accepted and interpreted these gifts according to their own definitions and beliefs regarding political courtesy.[50]

Just as Caddos showed deference and honor to their *xinesí* by giving items of value, and just as they exchanged similar items with neighboring Caddo allies, they also recognized European gifts as marks of honor, but not in quite the way Europeans expected. *Caddís* controlled all European gifts, as it was through their authority that items were redistributed to all others in Caddo communities. Bénard de la Harpe noted that when various Caddo bands celebrated the calumet, they "cast off all the clothes that they might have on" to give to others. Fray Francisco Hidalgo similarly remarked that despite Hasinais' love of clothes, "what His Majesty has given them has been of but little use to them because they immediately divide it with their friends." When Hasinai women piled foodstuffs at the center of an assembly of Caddo leaders and representatives of the Ramón expedition, Captain Ramón ordered an analogous stack of one hundred yards of cloth, forty blankets, thirty hats, and twelve packages of tobacco to be furnished for the Hasinai leaders to divide among their assembled peoples. The Spanish commander noted that once all had been distributed by the principal leaders, they had nothing for themselves—and "they were as happy as if they had received all of the goods themselves." "Happy," perhaps, because giving away, rather than amassing, wealth was how they established and reinforced their right to be honored and listened to by the rest of the community. In this way, they expanded the honor of the gifts to the entire community while at the same time reinforcing their own authority and the deference reserved for Caddo leadership.[51]

Spaniards and Frenchmen certainly did not grasp all that they observed in the Caddo ceremonies, especially the deeper social and political significance it held for the Caddo community. But their recognition of Caddo political hierarchies focusing on identifiable male elites at least helped them manage to pay respect where it was expected and to provide the right types of gifts. Previous encounters with Indians in other regions of the Americas led Frenchmen to anticipate Caddo men's practical desire for firearms, yet increasing militarization in the region made weapons not only the tools but also the emblems of masculine ability. Meanwhile, gifts of clothing predominated among Spanish presents to male leaders. Spaniards themselves saw such gifts as a means of "civilizing" Indians by dressing them in European clothing. Pointedly, when the 1690 expedition led by Alonso de León met Hasinais for the first time, León gave the *caddí* special garments "in order that he might enter his village clothed, so that his people might see how highly we thought of him." Domingo Ramón similarly recognized a "Captain General" of one Hasinai settlement with the gift of "one of my best jackets to improve his appearance." Later, Spanish expedition leaders made even grander efforts to transform Caddos into Europeans through their dress. In 1718 and 1719, Martín de Alarcón gave clothing to the leaders of twenty-three nations, regularly asking *caddís* to assemble their people so that he could distribute clothing to each man, woman, and child. During the Aguayo expedition three years later, the marqués de Aguayo followed the same procedures, giving clothes to the *caddís* with whom he met and all those who assembled with them. Juan Antonio de la Peña reported that on multiple occasions he "completely clothed" over four hundred Caddos "in cloth, baize, coarse woolen cloth, *quexquémiles*, and ribbons."[52]

The supposed transformative aspect of these gifts translated quite differently for Caddos, however—beauty (or value) is indeed in the eye of the beholder. Spaniards might have wished that clothes "civilized" Indians and that the Caddos' acceptance of such gifts signaled subordination to Spanish superiority, if not yet rule—just as they wanted the Hasinais' respect for the Virgin's image to mean that they were ready to convert. Such interpretations may have made sense from a Spanish perspective, with their faith in the power of Christian civilizations, but Hasinais could have had no idea what was on their new friends' minds and probably would not have cared. Hasinai men incorporated Spanish gifts into a native system of customary diplomatic favor, as they did "ornaments they have secured from other nations, such as glass beads, bells, and other things of a similar nature which are not to be found in this country." Hasinai leaders likely viewed gifts of clothing as a form of tribute signaling appropriate European deference.[53]

When Spanish officers distinguished *caddís* from others by offering gifts of hats with braid, plumes, or galloons, ornamented shirts and jackets, military coats often of red cloth, epaulets, and medals, the gifts resonated with Caddo status markers. The marqués de Aguayo outfitted each *caddí* with an "entire suit" of "distinctive apparel in the Spanish style," generally consisting of a military overcoat, jacket, and woolen breeches. He singled out Cheocas, a principal *caddí* among the Hasinais in 1721, with "the best clothing he had, made of blue fabric embroidered with much gold, and with a waistcoat of gold and silver fabric and everything else needed to be completely dressed." Spanish gifts may have looked even more like tribute when combined with gestures recognizing the *caddís'* civil and political power. In his 1690 visit, Alonso de León's gifts accompanied a formal presentation to a Hasinai *caddí* of a cross-headed staff in recognition of his "title of governor of all his people." Expedition leaders who came after León regularly offered Caddo leaders silver-headed batons as "emblems of authority" and "tokens of royal protection."[54]

To Spaniards and Frenchmen, military dress and ceremonial staffs and batons honored Caddo leaders by incorporating them into European governing hierarchies as allies, if not subalterns. Hasinais and other Caddo peoples viewed the situation from the other side of the looking glass, seeing ceremonies by which Spaniards proved their honor and worthiness prior to becoming subalterns or allies within Caddo hierarchies. Gifts and titles did not constitute political ties or pledges. To Caddos, ritual offerings from Europeans replicated the gifts and labors they themselves gave to the *xinesí* and *caddís* in tribute to their leadership. Such cross-cultural misunderstanding was, at this point, lucky for both sides and actually, ironically, fostered communication, since the actions themselves served to maintain each group's perceptions of mutual respect among their leaders. In short, attention to male diplomatic protocols mediated early contacts, even though neither side completely understood the other's meanings.

Late seventeenth-century encounters came to quite different ends, however, for Spaniards and for Frenchmen. Within only a few years of passing Caddo settlements en route to French posts in Illinois, the survivors of La Salle's expedition spread word of the commercial potential to be found among Caddoan peoples. By the 1690s, trade contacts opened between Caddos and Henri de Tonti's post at Fort Saint Louis, at the juncture of the Illinois and Mississippi Rivers, and by 1700, both French officials and traders began to arrive in the region to set up permanent outposts. In 1693, Spaniard fray Mazanet remarked with chagrin the "fine French garment" worn by a *caddí* and the material importance of a growing number of French muskets carried by Hasinai warriors—both brought to the land of the Tejas through the Caddos' extensive trade networks. Caddo leaders' overtures to those early Frenchmen had rapidly begun to reap economic benefits. As yet, though, the Frenchmen with whom the Caddos traded remained at a distance.[55]

The Hasinais were more concerned about dealing with Spaniards who quickly set up camp among their hamlets. Between 1691 and 1693, Alonso de León, Domingo Terán de los Rios, and fray Mazanet had brought eighteen people—four missionaries, three lay brothers, eight soldiers, two young boys, and one servant—to man two missions, San Francisco de los Tejas and Santísimo Nombre de María, near villages of Nabedaches, Neches, Hainais, and Naconos within the Hasinai confederacy. They certainly did not represent a portentous number, but even a very few proved capable of creating enough problems for Caddo leaders that they banished the Spaniards from their lands after only three years. What caused the breakdown of diplomacy?

Contrary to what one might expect, it was not religion. The Franciscans were indeed set on changing Caddo spirituality and, in that context, Spanish behaviors were meant to be disrespectful of Caddo social and religious practices. Thus, even in the midst of negotiating the establishment of relations, Spaniards who should have known better nevertheless acted in culturally chauvinistic ways. Fray Casañas seemed the worst. He first tried to establish residence in the *xinesí*'s compound and was sent packing. He then interfered with the healing rituals of the *connas*, "hurling exorcisms" to challenge their power. Most insulting of all, the foolhardy missionary one day darted into the temple of the sacred fire and attempted to throw the icons representing the two sacred *cononicis* into the fire in a bid to replace them with two little images of Christian saints. The apoplectic response of the *xinesí* immediately sent Casañas into appeasement mode. No matter how much the Franciscan maintained a regular patter to his superiors about Caddo spiritual "liars," "impostors," and "enchanters," however, the Caddos could easily ignore him. Mazanet soon had to confess complete missionary failure and explained to the viceroy that "the Indians' love for the Spaniards is due to the things your excellency has sent them and not to any desire to leave their witchcraft, superstitions, and deceits of the devil."[56]

In the Caddos' opinion, a handful of foreign men who offered little beyond the annoyances of proselytizing did not have much to recommend them. Certainly, Hasinai *caddís* had allowed the small Spanish presence among them, thinking to extend trade alliances on the heels of successful preliminary meetings with Spanish leaders. Yet, the two tiny missions instead functioned merely as semiautonomous farmsteads under the guardianship of the confederacy's *xinesí.* Moreover, when Spaniards proved unable to abide by the social rules and responsibilities of inclusion within Caddo dominions, tensions began to mount. The first critical blow to the Spaniards' standing among the Caddos came in the spring of 1691, when a smallpox epidemic swept through Caddo villages. Many Caddos blamed the devastation on Spaniards. Hasinai leaders firmly denied missionaries' requests to bury victims of the epidemic—who they claimed to have baptized on their deathbeds—in what the Spaniards deemed "consecrated ground." Even those who accepted the Franciscans' prayers on their behalf insisted that "they wanted to be buried in the country, in accordance with their ceremonies and superstitions of placing food and other things that they use in the grave," Mazanet complained. In disbelief, he recorded their claims of a Caddo afterlife where "they go to another world, in body as well as soul."[57]

When Hasinais in the vicinity of Mission Santísimo Nombre de María lost between three and four hundred people, they concluded that the Spaniards "had killed them," and in response, "some of them tried to kill us," wrote fray Casañas. *Connas* urged their followers not to take baptism, arguing that the water was deadly. Following customary routes of male authority, Casañas quickly went to confer with *canaha* elders and other leaders at the house of the nearby *caddí*. He tried to argue that since a missionary had also died, it was not a scourge sent by Spaniards against Caddos, but instead God's will, one that clearly did not distinguish between Caddos and Spaniards. The leaders seemed to find his point persuasive and spread the word to others. Casañas believed that those who blamed the Spaniards for the epidemic were only a few, primarily the village *connas* and, countering their claims, pushed the idea that baptismal waters might help the sick. Seeming to lend weight to his argument, Casañas recorded that a time came when a *caddí* fell sick and, fearing that he was dying, allowed Casañas to baptize him on what he believed to be his deathbed. When he recovered (seemingly against all expectation), the *caddí* praised the healing power of the holy water—as medicine, though, not as a means of spiritual conversion. In August of 1691, as Casañas wrote a report to the viceroy, peace appeared to be restored through ties among male elites. Disease threatened the Caddo-Spanish alliance, but it did not cause the Spaniards' expulsion from Caddo territory two years later.[58]

The problem instead was Spaniards' desecration of women. The cultural misunderstandings that had enabled communication among men broke down when Spaniards moved from male ceremonial spaces to spaces controlled by matrilineal clans, where they misinterpreted women's status and prestige. As it became clear that the small number of Spaniards planned to live permanently among them (the missions having been interpreted as independent households by the Caddos), Hasinai leaders began to express concern over the continued absence of Spanish women. When fray Casañas had first arrived among the Hasinais, he had read to the *caddís* and *canahas* the letter he carried with him outlining the people who were on their way to settle in Texas. "The first thing they noticed in the letter was that the men were coming without their wives," he recorded. Casañas therefore in 1691 repeated to the viceroy the concern that Caddo leaders were clearly reiterating to him: "Every day these Indians ask me whether the Spaniards are going to bring their wives with them when they come back." Even the *caddí* whose life Casañas had supposedly saved declared that "he likes the Spaniards and that he would be glad if many of them were here, but under the condition that they should bring their wives along." In fact, Casañas concluded, Caddo leaders were no longer expressing curiosity but were clarifying demands. "They tell me I must write to Your Excellency," explained Casañas, "and tell you in this missive that they want to be friends, but if the Spaniards want to live among them it must be under such conditions that no harm will be done their Indians by the Spaniards if they do come without their wives, but if the Spaniards bring their wives, the Indians will be satisfied." What had happened to sharpen Caddo doubts regarding Spaniards?[59]

Just as women had been crucial figures in first establishing peaceful contact between Caddos and Spaniards, women were also the key to those contacts collapsing into hostility. Spanish failures to meet the Hasinais' requirement that women be included in a settlement spelled doom for the two missions and their inhabitants. In terms of long-lasting relationships, the Spaniards gave no indication of establishing family homesteads capable of meeting the socioeconomic obligations of membership within Caddo communities (which will be the focus of Chapter 2). More significantly, even their inability—or refusal—to uphold the responsibilities that Caddos demanded of short-term guests soon became all too clear. Requisite in the Caddos' welcome of foreigners into their society had been the promise that newcomers honor the women and children of Caddo communities and make good on the trust invested in them through the ceremonies linking elite male leaders together in reciprocal status. When women and children had accompanied *caddís*, elders, and warriors in welcome committees and greeting rituals, when they had served as witnesses to pipe ceremonies, and when they had presented the bounty of their fields in feasts for Spanish and French dignitaries, their presence exacted a commitment of respect and safety from those foreigners.

Yet, respect for Caddo women was a more complicated diplomatic task for the Spaniards than they realized. Commanders had duly recognized the women identified as wives of *caddís*, *canahas*, and *amayxoyas* with special gifts in appreciation for their hospitality, and gifts might have been sufficient in the short run while proceedings remained within the ceremonial complex. That such offerings from the Spanish elite recognized those women only as extensions of their husbands need never have been revealed. But the longer soldiers and missionaries remained, with men camped outside the villages but dependent on daily exchanges for food and supplies from their Caddo hosts, the greater the danger of contacts outside that diplomatic realm—exchanges that by Caddo custom were controlled by the women in homesteads spread widely around village centers. In turn, the danger increased that Spaniards' misunderstanding of Caddo rituals involving women would provoke explosive breaches with the very people they were courting as allies and converts.

In the early meetings that had made the Virgin Mary's iconography so important to Spanish greetings, the only actual women involved were Hasinai. Caddo society structured women's honor and socioeconomic position in ways unfamiliar to Spaniards. Spanish society, like that of all of western Europe in the early modern period, conceived of women's honor as resting upon sexual virtue expressed in modesty and chastity. Both the attainment and expression of female honor remained private in nature, associated with intimate bodily functions, and dependent upon the protection of enclosure. Distinctions between "good" and "bad" women relied upon appearance rather than acts or deeds. Modest dress and behavior marked the honorable woman, with clothes fully covering the flesh and manners avoiding notice and attention to signal sexual unavailability. Gender codes further structured a woman's honor or dishonor as not only her own but also her husband's. His honor depended upon the control or protection of her virtue. The only public markers of prestige Spaniards recognized for women were ones associated with their husbands, fathers, sons, and brothers, and these in turn reflected the man's position in his community's sociopolitical hierarchy.[60]

In Hasinai society, sexual behavior did not translate into a measurement of honor for women. Nor, by extension, did physical appearance. Hasinai women's honor relied not on passivity or sexual abstinence, but on active contributions to food production and distribution. Hasinai ceremonies revolved around seasonal and annual cycles based on crop cultivation, with planting and harvesting celebrations focusing the community's attention and ritual appreciation on the arena of Hasinai sustenance, which was controlled by women. Annual planting ceremonies, for instance, called upon women and girls of all ages to gather together and weave strips of cane into mats to be presented to the *caddí* or *xinesí*, who in turn offered them to the sacred temple fire to ensure good crops and, in the process, consecrated women's work as a critical, indeed sacred, element of community life. Such ceremonies recognized women's contributions and thereby their position within Hasinai society. Hence, food production was as much a social and political matter as an economic one in the organization of Hasinai society, serving as a critical medium for structuring the status of women in complementary relationship to that of men.[61]

Hasinai men's honor was linked to that of their wives, but women's socioeconomic labors for family and community, not sexuality, provided the link. The family of women into which a man married ranked alongside hunting and battle glory as essential for securing male honor. Through a system of bride service, a man had to establish his ability to protect (warrior skills) and support (hunting skills) a woman and her family. Thus, successful courtships rested upon the measure of a man's contributions and provisions to the extended family matrilineage. In turn, Caddo men's honor, defined as the ability to demonstrate hospitality, depended on the horticultural work of women. A *caddí* relied upon the women of his village to present visitors with feasts, and the men of a matrilineal, extended-family household relied upon their wives, sisters, mothers, and mothers-in-law to provide the same courtesies to visiting *canahas* or *caddís*. Thus, when fray Casañas wrote that

Hasinai men prayed for "a great deal of corn, good health, fleetness in chasing the deer and the buffalo, great strength for fighting their enemies, and many women to serve them all," he in fact illustrated women's central economic, social, and political importance. Early missionaries noted that these roles found expression in the recognition of senior women as heads of household, reflecting both matrilineal family structure and women's power within it.[62]

It is difficult to ascertain what most European men saw, or thought they saw, when they entered this Hasinai world and interacted with Hasinai women. The recorded responses and observations of military officers and missionaries provide only faint clues to the thoughts of their subordinates. Spaniards clearly made their first mistakes when they misinterpreted Hasinai women's dress and appearance. Hasinai women used adornment to reflect their rank according to age and socioeconomic contributions to the community. Decoration marked the transitions through a woman's life cycle and reflected sexual experience only as it related to marriage and childbirth. Both men and women used body paint and tattoos to communicate rank and status. Women "painted themselves with great care" from the waist up in various colors, concentrating decoration on their breasts. The faces of young women displayed a narrow line painted from the forehead, over their nose and mouth, down to their chin. Once women married, the lines on the face increased, and body decoration extended from the shoulders to their chests in swirling floral and leaf designs. The extent of female adornment thus reflected the different stages of women's life cycles. The horticultural designs of women's tattoos likely symbolized their role in cultivation and food production.[63]

Although European men had recognized as familiar the Hasinai men's efforts to appear strong and to convey military ability, their cultural matrix led them to interpret Hasinai women's adornment solely within European notions of sexual virtue. In short, immodest dress indicated immodest behavior to them. While dismissing with little concern the "laxity" of male clothing, they condemned Hasinai women who seemed to make such "show" of their breasts. Where body tattoos represented stages of the life cycle, Spaniards saw promiscuity. The location of the tattoos on women's breasts so distracted them from the possible significance of the decoration itself that they saw only a display of flesh endowed with sexual meaning. The men interpreted the limited facial paint of younger women as a sign of virginity and the elaborate decoration of mature women as a sign of sexual "corruption."[64]

Spaniards also responded uneasily to Hasinais' use of touch, especially that of women. The embrace by unknown Indian men elicited mostly discomfort at the presumption of intimacy. Europeans greeted the physical aspect of Indian greetings with dismay and awkwardness, but if Indian men seemed unduly emotional, women seemed downright lewd. Early modern Europeans believed all women to be ruled by their bodies, which by "nature" made them spiritually and emotionally weak. Such weakness in turn meant women had no control over their actions and particularly their sexuality. Thus, the experience of scantily clad Hasinai women "embracing" and "caressing" European men reverberated with mythological visions of heathen worlds run amuck with licentiousness. French missionary Anastase Douay stressed particularly Caddo women's attentions when he wrote that they "received us with all possible friendship, even the women coming to embrace our men," though his careful designation of "our men" rather than "us" seemed to imply that he had managed to elude the women's grasp.[65]

European prejudice and misunderstanding of Hasinai women's touch and appearance (and what that might mean about their roles in hospitality rituals) led to a confusing range of interpretations regarding Hasinai sexuality, all carrying the common theme of female "promiscuity." To European eyes, polygyny, divorce, and serial monogamy meant that Hasinai men enjoyed the ready availability and sharing of women—practices that, in contrast, scholars today interpret as indications of egalitarianism in native cultures and of women's and men's freedom to make choices. Fray Casañas claimed that only among the "noblest" families were Caddo men's wives deemed inviolate and never to be touched by other men, because only in those circles was marriage considered binding. Seemingly for all others, licentiousness was the rule, and men could take their pick. Because fray Espinosa believed that Hasinai customs did not punish infidelity, he concluded that most men merely turned a blind eye if their wives slept with other men. Louis Juchereau de St. Denis reported that "with regard to the wives, these are not communal, since they are married in their style to the Indian men. But the spinsters are."[66]

No evidence directly links the misperceptions recorded in the journals of officers and missionaries with the events that came to a head in 1693, but the actions of Spanish soldiers seemed to reflect sentiments similar to those of their superiors. Violence erupted almost immediately in 1690. According to fray Mazanet, the military forces had been a troublesome and hostile group throughout the expedition, and "in this year '90 there hardly passed a day without someone fighting, or else the officers stabbing soldiers, so that a lay-brother who had come with me was generally kept busy tending the wounded." Once they arrived in the Hasinai villages, "Evidently some of them [soldiers and officers] thought they were to be made rulers of the Tejas," Mazanet recorded, and he "hardly knew them for the same persons after we were in the village." Many soldiers asserted their supposed "rule" through sexual violence. Mazanet reported that some Spanish soldiers entered Hasinai homes, attacking any women they found, including the attempted rape of the wife of one *caddí*'s brother. León's lack of a punitive response to his soldiers' crimes exacerbated hostilities further. In his own report, Mazanet angrily wrote that the soldiers went unpunished and Hasinai rage went unanswered by León. "I urged that conduct like this, which would not be tolerated even among the Moors or heretics, should be the more severely reproved because we had come among these heathen people in order to give an example of right living," argued Mazanet, but "León did not say a word—perhaps because he feared exposure."[67]

In the wake of the violence, the expedition quickly departed, having been there only ten days. Juan Bautista Chapa, a Spanish officer under León, stated that Caddo leaders allowed few others to remain because they "objected that the Spaniards would be without women to attend them, which would cause them to harass the Indian women." León had hoped to leave a forty- to fifty-man garrison in Caddo lands, but instead could only assign three soldiers to stay with three missionaries, fray Francisco Casañas de Jesús María, Miguel de Fontcuberta, and Antonio Bordoy. Two months after the arrival of a letter from León attempting to exonerate himself, another letter reached the viceroy from Mazanet offering warnings but also solutions for the future. "In the province of the Tejas it is not worthwhile to send soldiers to settle or to man presidios," Mazanet wrote. "What I believe would be advisable is to send some tradesmen—carpenters, masons, and others—to build dwellings and churches, as well as to teach the Indians. . . . I beseech your excellency, and request on behalf of the wounds and passion of Christ, our life, that the soldiers sent to Tejas neither enter the settlement nor arrive at the homes of the Tejas, due to what happened on the last trip."[68]

The following summer (1691), when Domingo Terán de los Rios led another expedition to renew diplomatic contacts with the Hasinai leadership and to bring back fray Mazanet along with eight other missionaries who came in hopes of building seven more missions, order broke down again. Mazanet's report perhaps had made an impression upon officials in the Spanish government, because clearly stated in Terán's instructions for a successful *entrada* were directions that the military commander as well as his corporals and soldiers "must avoid all carelessness in conduct and example," "must be anxious to prove their honesty, their religious faith, and their charity by their acts," "must not cause the Indians any trouble, either in persons and property," and, most clearly, "shall not arouse their anger by interfering with their women." Yet their arrival in Tejas following on the heels of the smallpox epidemic that spring did not leave Caddo leaders well disposed to allow more Spaniards in their midst, most particularly when violence against Caddo women reoccurred.[69]

In yet another letter to the viceroy, Mazanet reported that an officer left in command of ten soldiers among the Hasinais (while Terán took the expedition to meet with Kadohadachos to the east) threatened Caddos, raped "all the Indian women whom he took a fancy to," and then ran off after stealing all the horses (presumably of the mission and presidial force). Before that, a servant of Terán's had raped two Hasinai women and then accompanied the commander to the Kadohadacho settlements, where he repeated his crime. When Kadohadacho warriors captured him and brought him before Terán, "he was given no punishment whatsoever." Once it became clear that Terán would not punish such violence, Mazanet reported, soldiers felt emboldened to invade Hasinai homes and attack any women who could not escape their clutches. As a final ironic symbol of the Spaniards' breach of honor with the Caddo leadership, the night before Mazanet had written the letter, soldiers had broken into one *caddí*'s home and stolen the baton that had been a gift from the viceroy. Meanwhile, enemy hostilities elsewhere required Caddo leaders to send out a war party, and as they departed, one *caddí* told the missionaries not to be there when he returned.[70]

In a very short time, the imprudent lawlessness of a few men had wrought untold damage to Spanish political and spiritual goals. Terán had to leave, taking all but eight soldiers with him—along with six of the nine missionaries whose dreams of an additional seven missions lay in ruins. For the handful who stayed behind, prospects were dim as the situation devolved into a seeming war of attrition. A flood washed away Mission Santísimo Nombre de María on the banks of the Neches River, all eighteen Spaniards crowded into San Francisco de los Tejas, drought wiped out their crops, and angry Hasinai men stole their horses and ran off their livestock, forcing the missionaries to buy back what animals they could. When soldiers continued to fight Hasinai men "over any trifle [in order to get] their wives," the Hasinai men threatened the Spaniards themselves. Periodically, meetings were called to debate whether the simplest solution would be to kill them.[71]

After a small expedition, led by Gregorio de Salinas Verona and sent to resupply the struggling missions, departed in 1693 without taking the rest of the unwelcome Spanish guests with it, word reached the missionaries that a Hasinai *caddí* was summoning warriors from surrounding villages, as well as Frenchmen, to help attack and kill the Spaniards. Events in the following two months lent strength to the rumors. The *caddí* repeatedly urged the Spaniards to leave his lands and warned them of the dangers of not heeding his demand. Meanwhile, warriors intimidated soldiers and missionaries alike with a steady barrage of hostility. Spanish alarm grew apace as a swelling number of warriors arrived from other villages, and Hasinai men slowly but surely killed off the Spaniards' horses and cattle. Notably, they could have taken the animals for their own needs, but the symbolism of the extermination outweighed such practicalities, because they destroyed what the Spaniards relied upon for food. When Mazanet finally got up the nerve to ask the *caddí* directly whether the rumors of a concerted attack against the Spaniards were true, the Hasinai leader answered "tauntingly" that yes, they were, because "his people had told him many times to throw [the Spaniards] off their land."[72]

And this he did. In October of 1693, a large contingent of Caddo warriors hounded the small group of Spanish missionaries and soldiers out of their lands, following them for many days and for a distance well beyond the boundaries of their territory. Communicating the finality of the intruders' expulsion every morning, the warriors burned the campsite where the Spaniards had slept the night before until the party reached the Colorado River, four hundred miles away from the Hasinai villages. After wandering without direction for over a month, the Spaniards found temporary sanctuary among Cantona Indians. In an explanation to his superiors, Mazanet reported that one of the Hasinai men had told him that the greatest enemies to the success of the Spanish mission were to be found among the Spaniards themselves —soldiers who dishonored Caddo women and men alike with their continued assaults.[73]

Facing barriers of language, custom, and worldview that might have appeared to defy translation at the end of the seventeenth century, Caddo leaders had welcomed Spanish and French visitors into their lands and treated them to a series of protocols meant to vet them as potential allies. Caddos invested both spiritual and political authority in their male elites to protect and maintain the well-being of the community. From such positions, the *xinesí*, *caddís*, and *canahas* took the lead in initial meetings and ritual exchanges with the leaders of European groups. As a prerequisite for negotiations of political, military, or economic alliance, these leading Caddo men sought to incorporate European leaders into Caddo social systems as men of honor within their own elite ranks. Because Europeans and Caddos came to their meetings in Texas with similar rituals for asserting strength in order to garner the respect of other nations, Spaniards and Frenchmen successfully negotiated Caddo ceremonial displays of male prowess and prestige.

In the Caddo view of the human social order, disorder resulted when people failed to maintain categories of rank and relationship. Rituals offered the means to protect or restore order against possible disturbance. Yet, by 1693, Spanish leaders proved themselves unable to restore the disorder created by disease, divisions within their own military and religious ranks, and, especially, violent abuse of the women who had symbolized the peaceful intent and community of spirit with which Caddos had welcomed Spaniards to their lands. Though Spaniards had realized an initial accord with Caddos in their efforts to communicate peaceful intent through female religious icons (more by luck than perspicacity) and through similar performances of male honor, violence directed at Caddo women had destroyed it. The inability to work within Caddo cultural and political systems culminated in the Spaniards' expulsion from Caddo territories.

As the eighteenth century began, greeting ceremonies continued as the preamble to diplomatic negotiations when Frenchmen returned to renew the promise of their meetings with Caddos in the 1680s and again when Spaniards returned to rectify the disastrous conflicts of the 1690s. Caddo political relations with Europeans took new forms, though, as Spanish and French residents near or within Caddo villages created bonds with the family members of matrilineal households that now took the lead in cross-cultural relations. Most important, different tacks taken by Spaniards and Frenchmen to work within the parameters of Caddo cultural systems—again centering on women as mediators of peaceful relations—determined the extent of their ability to establish settlement and achieve socioeconomic success as aspirants in the lands of the Tejas.

chapter two

Political Kinship through Settlement and Marriage

In the 1680s and 1690s, Caddoan greeting ceremonies had welcomed, purified, and honored Europeans; rituals had remained public in scope; and exchanges had been those of elite men who were deemed, during the course of meetings, to be within the ranks of the Caddo leaders who greeted them. Caddo conventions of interaction shifted, however, when relations moved beyond initial visits to political and economic alliance. Simply put, when European peoples expressed interest in living permanently in or near Caddo settlements, the rules shifted to a different arena of Caddo politics. Between 1700 and 1730, handfuls of Europeans came and went from Caddo lands as two very small populations, one Spanish and the other French, established a long-term presence there. Throughout that time period, there was no question of who held the power to determine the terms by which the two groups would remain in the region—that power resided in the hands of Caddoan leaders and their people.

In order for Caddoan peoples to broker permanent relationships with Europeans, they had to incorporate the strangers as "kin." At that point, the kinship system structuring Caddo society came into play, and the locus of interaction expanded to include that of individual, family, and household. Moreover, because that kinship system was matrilineal, except at the highest levels of leadership, relations grew beyond those of only the elite men who made up leadership ranks and began to involve Caddo women. Matrilineal kinship defined the basic social unit of Caddo communities and also relations of production, trade, and diplomatic alliance. Marriage and kinship thus functioned as a "meta-institution" that "underpinned the organization of economics, politics, religion" among Caddoan peoples. Principles of dual realms, or "paired categories or contrast sets," structured not only the symbolism of rituals, cosmological beliefs, and mytho-historical traditions but also kinship and clan organization and the spatial relationship of individual homesteads and ceremonial centers. These contrasting pairs included order/chaos, phenomenal (human)/numinous (spiritual), inside/outside, junior/senior, and male/female. In turn, "the well-being of the human community depended on the maintenance of positive (orderly) relationships between the two realms." These dual realms would necessarily help to determine the relationships Caddos formed with Europeans.[1]

The Europeans who bid for permanent residence among Caddoan peoples would be evaluated as individuals or families rather than as representatives of foreign nations, because each would assume a place in the order of the Caddos' world. Caddo leaders' demands that Spaniards bring women with them to Caddo lands did not simply reflect a desire to protect Caddo women from abuse. It also meant that they expected those who settled among them and became part of Caddo societies to be properly equipped to contribute to those societies. All members of expedition—now settlement—parties fell under the Caddos' scrutiny, and the focus also tightened on individual leaders who in initial contact situations had been identified as men of like rank with Caddo leading men. Would they be true to the pacts agreed to in those early meetings, and could they sustain their people's commitment to the mutual obligations of those pacts? In the Caddos' eyes, those leaders who visited only briefly and then departed had far less significance than those who remained to live in Caddo territory. If the settlers or traders who proposed to live among Caddos were predominantly single men (and among both Spaniards and Frenchmen, they were), they had to be given some kind of kinship affiliation. The easiest way to accomplish that was through marriage. Thus, at this stage, Caddos put their association of women with peace to work politically through their kinship practices.

Spanish and French imperial goals of settlement reinforced the Caddoan locus of negotiation on the household, since French agents pursued relations primarily with individual hunters and traders, while Spanish missionaries focused their efforts of conversion on individuals and their families. As well, whether or not they fully realized it, Spaniards and Frenchmen used the gender identity of women to resolve the fine lines between expressing peace rather than hostility, and strength rather than aggression in their relations with Caddos. For the predominantly male European groups who moved into Caddo territory, women represented the key element needed to solidify relationships with Caddoan peoples. Settlement and marriage served as demonstrable acts of commitment. The presence of wives and the children they bore signaled European men's ties to a location and their determination to settle, maintain, and defend it. That tie in turn helped ensure alliance. Women might also bind men to one another through the kinship relations formed in marriage. Intermarriage established a permanent basis for relationships that informed economic and political behaviors outside the familial and social domain of the relationship itself. It linked peoples as well as families together in networks of interaction and reciprocity.

Yet, different French and Spanish diplomatic strategies distinguished the ways in which each group was willing to integrate itself into the kinship-based organization demanded by Caddos. Spaniards' mission-presidio diplomacy, though seemingly offering a kind of joint settlement and alliance, envisioned and demanded fundamental changes of their Caddo allies and did not allow their different socioeconomic and political visions to be ignored. Frenchmen, on the other hand, shared many compatible habits with Caddos when it came to family-based settlement and alliance, because it served their purposes of trade. As will be seen, Frenchmen established the province of Louisiana for purposes of commerce, which tied locales of French settlement closely to Caddos and other native trading partners. The gender relations of marriage in turn provided Frenchmen with immediate entry into Caddo social and economic networks. Frenchmen's unions with Caddo women made real the fictive kin relationships forged by trade in hides, horses, and captive women. Through intermarriage, Frenchmen regularly entered Caddo systems of bride service with their attendant designations of sociopolitical honor and status. In the act of seeking wives, French traders and officials unknowingly deferred to Caddo custom and presented themselves to be ranked as men by Indian families and leaders. Ties of settlement, marriage, and trade provided untold diplomatic and economic advantages to the Frenchmen of western Louisiana as they competed with the Spaniards in Texas for the loyalty of powerful Caddo allies.

Meanwhile, Spaniards struggled to redeem themselves, seeking ways to erase memories of the violation of Caddo women and to build new relations focused around six mission and two presidio communities scattered among Caddo hamlets. It quickly became clear, however, that Caddo and Spanish ideas about the relationship between their communities diverged considerably. Both wanted the other as an ally, but Caddos sought to achieve that end by making Spaniards into kin through trade and marriage, while Spanish officers and missionaries envisioned Christian conversion as the means to achieve the "civilization" of Caddos. Both wanted to convert the other. At the heart of missionary goals lay the requirement that converted Indians become members of Spanish society, but the reverse was unthinkable —that Spaniards might enter Caddo society and live by their terms. Thus, both Caddo and Spanish leaders failed in their initial designs. The Hasinai Caddos' rejection of Spanish mission projects in their lands and the Spanish rejection of any notion of intermarriage as a political tool in relations with "heathen" Caddos soon became clear. Spanish and Caddo emphases then gradually reoriented to affirming the common needs and ties of their neighboring civil settlements, especially as families increasingly made up the Spanish population in the region and the presence of Spanish women and children stabilized relations. Only then did Spaniards find a route, different from that of Frenchmen, into the realms of Caddo acceptance and extended-kinship status.

In order to more fully understand the Caddos' perspectives that informed their relations with Spaniards in the early 1700s, it is instructive to look at French experiences in the land of the Tejas, in a sense looking down the road not taken by Spaniards. In the stories of Frenchmen may be seen the Caddos' designs for relating to other peoples and nations through kinship—designs that did not work with Spaniards. Spanish officials and missionaries spent much of their time bemoaning the success of their French competitors, and thus the Caddos' relationships with Frenchmen provide an illuminating context within which to explore comparative Spanish failures. To do so, we must first flash back to the 1680s when the handful of survivors and deserters from La Salle's expedition found homes and families in Caddo villages. Just as the earliest contacts between Spaniards and Hasinais presaged the difficulties Spaniards would have in later years, so too did the experiences of French deserters foreshadow the better fit French cultural categories would have with Caddo polities. Though these Frenchmen did not, in the end, remain among Caddos permanently (four of them stayed four years), their experiences as recorded in the journal of Henri Joutel and in the interrogations of Pierre Talon offer detailed accounting of Caddo customs of inclusion via kinship.

A few months before the deserters and survivors first took up residence in Caddo lands in 1687, La Salle had left ten-year-old Pierre Talon to live among the Hasinais, hoping that the boy would learn their language and be able to act as translator for the Frenchmen. La Salle also may have intended to make a political gesture to the Caddos, since French experience had shown that some native societies exchanged children as a way of strengthening alliances. Indeed, ceremonial traditions among Caddoan peoples indicate that they may have exchanged children with other bands, each adopting the other's children into their communities in reflection of a political alliance. In a "Baby Dance" practiced by twentieth-century Wichitas (relatives of the Caddos), participants dress a boy and a girl from another native group in Wichita clothing and symbolically adopt them as Wichitas in a ceremony, thus making the birth and adoptive parents ritual friends. Such practices suggest that Caddos may well have viewed La Salle's actions in leaving Pierre with them as a signal of his wish for long-term relations of peace.[2]

Talon lived among the Hasinais for three years before the León expedition captured him and another French youth, Pierre Meunier, in 1691. Pierre Talon and his brother Jean Baptiste, who was found living among Karankawas along the coast, eventually testified before Spanish and later French officials about those experiences. In turn, the Talons would play a significant part in Frenchmen's return into the good graces of Caddo leaders in the 1710s. Information gained from French officials' interrogations of the two Talon boys convinced Louis de Pontchartrain and Pierre Le Moyne d'Iberville that the boys could serve as passports into the Caddos' realm. The Talon brothers accompanied d'Iberville's second expedition to Louisiana in 1699, when the region was officially claimed as a province for France, and d'Iberville most likely sent them with his brother, Jean Baptiste Le Moyne Bienville, to explore trade possibilities among Caddos in 1701 (one of the first priorities of the officials of the new province). The brothers assuredly played a role in introducing Louis Juchereau de St. Denis, the founder of the first French trading post in Caddo lands, to Hasinai and Natchitoches peoples in 1714.[3]

In the thirteen years that had passed since Pierre Talon's childhood years among the Hasinais, he had lost much of what had been his "perfect" knowledge of the Caddo language—though we may speculate that some of it surely returned once he was back among the people who had cared for him during a critical period of his youth. He had certainly cared for them, since he had tried so hard to resist the Spaniards who took him from his Caddo home back then: when word had come to the Hasinai village of the approach of the Spaniards in 1690, Talon and Meunier had tried unsuccessfully to flee to a nearby Tonkawa settlement in hopes of eluding capture, but Spanish troops discovered them en route. When Pierre Talon returned to the Caddos in the 1710s, he greeted them with the sign language that they had taught him. Perhaps more important, his tattoos identified the grown man as the boy they had adopted so many years before. Though French officials valued Pierre's knowledge of the geography and the language, to Caddos, Pierre's identity as kin— adoption having made him a Caddo—was crucial. By sending Pierre back to the Hasinai villages, French officials returned to them a lost son taken away by the Spaniards.[4]

Pierre's earlier testimony about Caddoan peoples had illuminated the importance of kinship within the Caddos' world. Pierre described the setting in which the boys found themselves among "the most gentle and the most civil of all the nations," with settlements "divided into families" that lived in clusters reflecting the clan divisions, each with its own fields. Moreover, the ties formed through kinship meant that the "people of the same nation live among themselves in a marvelous union." A *caddí* had chosen to adopt Talon, and the boy spent all his time at the side of him and the *caddí*'s father, a leading community elder. Talon remembered the home he and

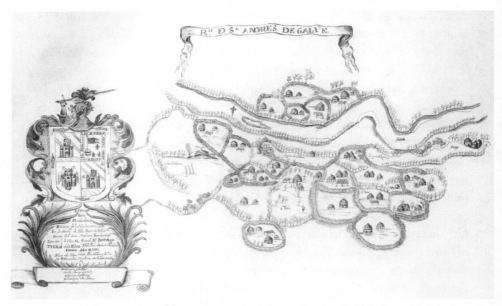

Map of 1691 of Caddo settlement patterns along the Red River, based upon the findings of the expedition led by Domingo Terán de los Rios in 1691–92. Hand copy of the original located in the Archivo General de Indias. Map collection, CN 00920, The Center for American History, University of Texas at Austin.

Meunier shared as one in which their new family "loved them tenderly and appeared to be very angry when anyone displeased them in any way and took their part on these occasions, even against their own children." The boys had quickly been transformed into kin to make their inclusion in the community permanent. Because Caddos were "so desirous that others imitate and resemble them in everything," they dressed and tattooed the two boys as their own. Thus, Talon and Meunier received tattoos "on the face, the hands, the arms, and in several other places on their bodies as they do on themselves," with black dye made of charcoal and water inserted into the skin with thorns. The markings provided overt testimony of their adoption and tribal identification as Caddos.[5]

The boys then had to be taught the bearing and abilities of Caddo males. Their adopted fathers and brothers trained them to run and swim for strength and fleetness of foot, to shoot arrows for the hunt, and to fight in battle alongside their elders. Talon testified to the "brotherhood" implicit in men's joint battle experiences when he told French superiors that "an unfailing means, other than small gifts that the Europeans still have of winning the friendship of the nations whose alliance could help them the most in their settlements, is to take part in the wars that they often wage against others." Though the warriors valued the addition of European firearms among their weaponry, Talon cautioned that he and Meunier "do not think that they ever showed veneration for them." Indeed, as will be seen, the standing given the adult French deserters who fought alongside Caddo warriors against Apache foes proved Talon's claim. Instead, the gifts that Hasinais "love passionately" had to be "useful or ornamental," seemingly to be worn as status markers in reflection of honor and rank or to be passed along to others, "since they give voluntarily of what they have," as obligated by ties of reciprocity.[6]

The experiences of the French deserters who joined the two young Pierres to live among the Caddo settlements offered an adult version of the Caddos' efforts to incorporate male strangers into their communal midst. Two different traveling parties from La Salle's coastal Fort St. Louis visited Caddoan peoples, first in the summer of 1686 and then in the spring of 1687, during attempts to reach French settlements in Illinois and then Canada. During and after those visits, five French deserters—Jacques Grollet, Jean L'Archevêque, two known only as Rutre and La Provençal, and one unnamed man who died shortly—found not only sanctuary but also new lives among Hainai and Nasoni members of the Hasinai confederacy. In response to the Frenchmen's supplications—they had arrived sick, exhausted, and clearly in needy condition—Nasoni leaders took them into their communities. As La Provençal attested, the Nasonis "had been very solicitous and taken very good care of him during his illness and had shown him friendship." The observations of other Frenchmen and Spaniards who later witnessed the deserters' relations with the Caddo communities provide a portrait of their adoptions.[7]

Once four of their French charges had recovered, Caddo leaders endeavored to transform the men so that they could find a place in their society, as had the two boys. First, they dressed the men. Henri Joutel, who passed through in 1687 on his way to Illinois, described seeing Rutre in "a paltry covering that the Indians of the area make with turkey feathers, joined together very neatly with small strings," giving him what Joutel thought was the "naked and barefoot" appearance of having lived with the Caddos for ten years. "As a result, there was almost nothing about him that was unlike them except that he was not as agile"; in fact, upon their meeting, Joutel initially failed to recognize him as a fellow Frenchman. Beyond clothing, the men displayed body decorations—the same birds, animals, and zigzag patterns that marked and identified the faces and bodies of Caddo men. The tattoos signaled their status as men (that is, hunters) and also provided them with markings that would identify them as members of a Caddo society—tattoos that served as both passport and protection into and out of that society.[8]

Caddos further marked the Frenchmen's acceptance into their community by providing them with shelter and dwellings. La Provençal lived in the home of a Hasinai *caddí* that, like most Caddo households of sixty feet in diameter with divided living areas, housed eight to ten families; Rutre and Jacques Grollet lived in the home of a Nasoni *caddí* in a neighboring settlement. By the time of Alonso de León's 1689 expedition in search of La Salle's colony, Spaniards found Grollet and L'Archevêque living in the company of a Hasinai *caddí* who was "keeping them with great care." Like Joutel, Spaniards repeatedly commented about how the two Frenchmen were "streaked with paint after the fashion of the Indians, and covered with antelope and buffalo hides." When Spanish officials later interrogated the two men back in Mexico City as to why they had allowed themselves to be so painted, L'Archevêque explained that, having been "importuned" by Caddo men and women, the Frenchmen had "thought it necessary to do this in order to please the Indians who were caring for them and supporting them."[9]

Although the *caddís* clearly had made the decision to incorporate the men into the Caddo community, the adopted Frenchmen seemed well aware of the matrilineal and matrilocal organization of Caddo kinship and economy that put women at the head of families and households. They took special care to pay equal respect to the ranking women who had authority over the households within which they lived as they did to the *caddís* and *canahas* who had first welcomed them into the villages. Rutre, for example, in meeting with Joutel, asked him for "some strands of glass beads to make a present of them to the women of the hut." The beads were not pretty baubles for girls, but signified a gift obligated by the rules of reciprocity. Joutel matched such deference to senior women whom he regularly referred to as "women of the hut." Perhaps he followed the deserters' direction, but he also noted for himself the authority the women exerted over the divisions of household and agricultural labor. While staying among Nasonis, before the Canada-bound party left on their journey north, Joutel recognized that there was a "mistress of women" who "had supremacy over the provision and distribution of food to each person even though there were several families in one hut." A quick learner, "I took care to always give her something as well, sometimes this was a knife, another time beads or some rings and needles, and also some necklaces of false amber of which I had a number." The Frenchmen appeared to have learned the everyday rhythms of Caddo reciprocity as well as the balance of power and honor between Caddo men and women.[10]

The deserters reached another level of kinship through marriages with Caddo women. La Provençal reported being "given a wife," presumably as a means of providing him with family relations within the settlement. Though Joutel made specific reference only to La Provençal's Hasinai wife, whom he met personally, he described the other Frenchmen as "addicted to the wantonness of the women who already displayed toward them a certain attachment," indicating some kind of relationships, even if in his view they were not permanent or proper unions. Years later, Pierre Talon recorded that Rutre "had changed [wives] seven or eight times and left two children by one of these women, following in this, as in all the rest, the custom of the savages, who have in truth only one wife at a time, but who change them whenever they want to, which is to say often." Just as Joutel framed his interpretation of Caddo women through a European lens that cast the women in an illicitly sexual light, Talon likely exaggerated his depiction of Caddo practices of serial monogamy. Nevertheless, reading between the sexualized European lines, both observations indicate that unions with Caddo women were key to the incorporation of the Frenchmen into not only Caddo society but also the kin relationships that gave a man standing and identity within the matrilineal society.[11]

Gender and kinship worked in tandem to determine people's roles in Caddo society. A story Jean-Bernard Bossu later recorded of having met the "half-blood" son of Rutre during his own travels in 1751 points to another key to the Frenchmen's acceptance among Hasinais and Nasonis: their fighting ability. Bossu claimed that the son told him how "his father had been found and adopted by the Caddo Indians." "He was made a warrior and was given an Indian girl as his wife," Bossu continued, "because he had frightened and routed the enemies of the Caddos by using his rifle, which was still an unknown weapon among them at that time." Joutel similarly related that the four French deserters were "cherished by the Indians because they had gone to war with them." Not only that, they had succeeded in killing one of their enemies, "quite opportunely with one shot of a pistol or musket," which had "won them trust and a reputation among the Indians." Another time, during Joutel's visit to the Hasinai settlements, the Frenchmen went off to fight side by side with Caddo men in a battle against an unnamed enemy, in the course of which they and the warriors killed or captured forty-eight of the enemy, again with the help of French muskets, which killed several and forced others to flee.[12]

Hasinai and Nasoni leaders' interactions with Joutel himself cast further light upon the ways in which Caddos incorporated strangers into their world. From the time he arrived, Hasinai elders "often visited to exhort" him to join their men as a fellow warrior, one time pointedly telling him that "I should be like [Rutre] and go with them to war." Joutel doggedly refused, however, offering instead that once he reached Canada, he would gather more men and return to fight alongside them. Yet, the calls on Joutel to join Hasinai warriors in battle did not bespeak a need for military aid (as many Europeans assumed) as much as a call for him to prove his worthiness to join the ranks of Caddo men. His refusal must have baffled the Caddo men, especially when Rutre told them that, among the Frenchmen, Joutel was a high-ranking man, if not a *caddí* at least a "captain." Thus, when they continued their exhortations, they addressed him as "*cadi capita*." In the Caddo leaders' view, Joutel's refusals to fight eventually seemed to place him in a separate category of manhood. When the other Frenchmen went off to battle, Joutel and the two priests, Jean Cavelier (La Salle's brother) and Anastase Douay, remained behind "with the women and several old men who were not able to go to war." When word reached the settlement that the warriors were returning victorious, Joutel joined the Caddo women who sent out food for their husbands and sons by including his own offering to the fighting Frenchmen. For a week following their return, Joutel saw the French-men and warriors only at public victory celebrations; otherwise, the fighting men spent all their time together in discussions and "amusement" to which Joutel clearly was not invited—surely signaling his exclusion from Caddo military ranks and thus manhood.[13]

Joutel also joined the two French priests in refusing unions with Caddo women, unions that Caddo leaders tried to broker. One morning, as Joutel was hard at work sewing into shoes some antelope skin he had gained in trade, an elder who had repeatedly urged Joutel to go to war with them "brought me a girl whom he made sit near me and told me to give her the shoes to sew." Joutel could not explain how, but "he indicated to me in some way that he was giving her to me as a wife." It seems possible that if the elder had failed to convince Joutel to fight (one way to form a bond with Caddo men), perhaps he viewed this as a different means of giving him standing within a Caddo kin group, or at least some kind of connection. But Joutel again resisted, and after he talked only halfheartedly to the woman, "she realized that I was not recognizing her presence and went away."[14]

Senior Caddo women (Joutel's "women of the huts") echoed the sentiments of their *caddís* with solicitations that Joutel and the two priests go to war and with promises that "they would give us wives and build us a hut" if the Frenchmen wished to stay and live with them. Notably, father Anastase Douay had received no such offers of women during the first French party's visit to the Hasinais a few months earlier—when the French party had made it clear they were only stopping to trade for supplies needed for their trip northward to Illinois. But after the deserters from this first party returned seeking residence in the Caddo villages, Caddo leaders may have assumed the later visitors of Joutel's party to be seeking a permanent presence in the "land of the Tejas" as well. The implication behind the repeated exhortations about a wife seemed clear: if the foreigners were to remain among Caddos, they had to have the kinship ties of home and marriage necessary within Caddo society.[15]

These men's experiences indicated that dress and tattoos may have marked the

Frenchmen as adoptees of Caddo society and that fighting together may have made them "brothers" with fellow Caddo warriors, but it was unions with Caddo women that gave them a home, identity, and the kinship connections that were key to finding a place in the Caddoan realm. Caddo leaders and male elites readily formed alliances with strangers without bringing them into Caddo society, but the assimilation of strangers into their communities required the participation of women and took place at the level of individual household and family. Meanwhile, the political significance of the Frenchmen's adoption into Caddo society was sufficient for the news to travel through native transregional networks. In January 1689, some Jumanos carried reports to New Mexico that, even though La Salle's colony had been destroyed by neighboring Karankawas, as many as four or five strangers were living among the Hasinais, trading hatchets, knives, and beads to them, assisting them in their wars, and promising to be "brothers" or "relatives" with them in league against Spaniards "who were not good people."[16]

In the long run, the adoption and attempted adoption of these few men into Caddo society in the 1680s bore little connection to the Caddo-French relationships that would develop almost thirty years later in the early eighteenth century. None of the men were to be found in Caddo villages when the first formal French post was established in 1716 among neighboring bands of the Natchitoches confederacy. When Spanish expeditions led by Alonso de León and fray Damián Mazanet went in search of La Salle, they found and captured Jacques Grollet and Jean L'Archevêque on the first trip in 1689 and the two boys Pierre Meunier and Pierre Talon on the second trip in 1690 (as well as three more Talon siblings living among Karankawan peoples along the Gulf coast). Rutre had died before the Spanish expeditions arrived, and Caddo men showed his grave and that of the fifth unnamed Frenchman to the Spaniards. The fate of La Provençal remains unknown. The four found living among Caddo communities along with the three children from the Karankawa settlement were taken first to Mexico City and then to Spain to be interrogated about all they knew of French imperial designs in the region. While Pierre and Jean Baptiste Talon eventually made it back to France and then Louisiana, Grollet and L'Archevêque spent thirty months in a prison in Spain before returning to North America, where they spent the remainder of their lives as settler-soldiers in Spanish New Mexico. Their experiences during those early years among Caddos do, however, offer a blueprint for the ways in which Caddos would accept and build kin ties with later French traders in the eighteenth century.[17]

Continuing along the road-not-taken by Spaniards, Frenchmen led trade expeditions to the Caddo and Wichita bands spread throughout the areas of present-day western Louisiana, northeastern Texas, and the lower Southern Plains after the founding of the province of Louisiana in 1699. When these new French traders came calling at the beginning of the eighteenth century, Caddo custom determined the form and meaning of exchange relationships, and that custom depended upon two types of exchanges of women, one via intermarriage and the other via an emerging trade in captive Indians. Again, an examination of the experiences of Frenchmen offers a contrasting perspective on how Spaniards failed to respond in the same spirit to Caddo overtures of union and alliance.

In 1700, a key commission of the first governor of Louisiana, Pierre Le Moyne d'Iberville, had been to send his younger brother Jean-Baptiste Le Moyne de Bienville to promote trade among Caddoan peoples, but fourteen years elapsed before permanent posts and settlements began to spring up along the Red River. Having identified the numerous and prosperous Caddo settlements as crucial for entry into extensive native trade networks as well as a point from which to initiate expeditions to Spanish posts in New Mexico, Frenchmen established a military post named Fort St. Jean Baptiste aux Natchitoches, near a village of Natchitoches Indians in 1716, along with a subsidiary trading post farther upriver among the Nasonis in 1719 (followed later by Rapides, Avoyelles, Ouachita, Opelousas, and Atakapas posts along the Red River as well). A 1720 report to the French government, addressing the commercial potential of the Natchitoches post and its hinterlands, asserted that the most profitable trade with the Caddoan peoples of the area was in horses, hides, and Indian slaves. As Pierre Talon had testified twenty years before, the Caddos had so many horses that they both caught and raised (valuable to Frenchmen who had no other source for mules, horses, or cattle) that they would exchange them "for a single hatchet or a single knife."[18]

At Natchitoches, permanent French settlement first took the form of a trading warehouse that gradually expanded to include a small military post and civil settlement. In the early eighteenth century, private trading companies rather than the French government directed much colonial development. Imperial officials licensed trading companies to oversee internal and external trade within the new French colony, thus giving the companies the power to form alliances in the king's name, to build garrisons, to raise troops, and to appoint governors, majors, and officers for defense. Such licenses transformed individual traders who developed economic relationships with native peoples into representatives of the French government, putting them on a par with military and diplomatic officers of the Spanish government when it came to Caddo politics. As a result, French-Caddo relations along the Red River continued to take a more personal form at the level of the individ-

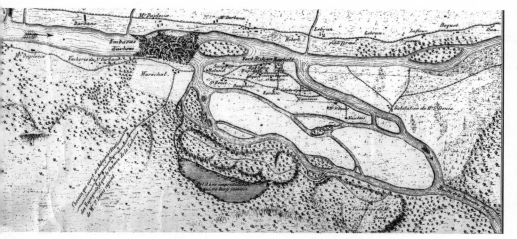

St. Jean Baptiste aux Natchitoches, c. 1722. In 1716, Frenchmen established this military and trading post near a village of Natchitoches Caddos. The map indicates the locations of leading traders' homes. Map by J. F. Broutin. Courtesy of the Cammie G. Henry Research Center, Watson Memorial Library, Northwestern State University of Louisiana, Natchitoches.

ual. At the same time, the Caddos' incorporation of French newcomers into their network of kin relationships took place on a broader scale in the 1710s than it had in the 1680s.[19]

Intermarriage had long served Caddos as a strategy for forming and solidifying political alliance. In the sixteenth and seventeenth centuries, marriage and family linkages had brought together the three Caddo confederacies as well as unified villages and settlements. Europeans observed the power of these bonds in linking together numerous Caddoan polities and peoples. Jean Baptiste Bénard de la Harpe noted that though Caddos lived in different villages, they nevertheless "formed together" a united nation. Juan Agustín Morfi argued that shared friendships, relationships, and intermarriage had joined and made kin "under the general name Texas" remnants of the "Texas, Asinais, Nabedachos, Nacogdoches, Nacogdochitos, Nadocoges, Ahipitos, Cadogdachos, and Nasonis." They had also allied bands of Caddos and Wichitas. Thus, to Caddos, intermarriage seemed an obvious and practical means of forming political ties and trade relations with Europeans as well.[20]

When Caddos sought to transform the Frenchmen who arrived in the 1700s into military allies and trading partners, they offered marriage. And Frenchmen accepted their proposals. French settlers and traders by and large came from Canada, where they already enjoyed a social and cultural heritage of intimate association with

Indian peoples. Unions with women of allied nations, and later with captive Indian women they acquired from those nations for sexual exploitation, were not new to the Frenchmen who emigrated to Louisiana. Because single male traders and agents, who often lived among their native trading partners, originally predominated in the French occupation of Louisiana, Frenchmen needed to intermarry if they were to have wives and families at all. Abbé Gillaume Thomas François Raynal, writing in the 1770s and looking back over the century, argued that the French had brought to Louisiana "the custom of living with the savages, which they had adopted in Canada," and which often involved marrying Indian women with the "happiest results." "There was never observed the least coolness in the friendship between these two so diverse nations whom matrimony had united," Raynal continued, because "they have lived in this intercourse and reciprocity of mutual good-will, which made up for the vicissitudes of events brought by the passage of time." French demographic and settlement patterns made social and familial intermixing almost inevitable as they built their trading and military posts in or near native villages. Consequently, Frenchmen joined with native peoples not only for trade but also for subsistence, family building, and daily life. In settlements such as Fort St. Jean Baptiste aux Natchitoches, community ties brought Frenchmen into the heart of Caddo political economies and offered foundations for long-lasting alliances.[21]

By forming unions with Caddo women, Frenchmen who pursued trade among Caddoan peoples took part in bride-service customs that incorporated them into Caddo systems of male status and honor—whether the Frenchmen realized it or not. In the Caddo system of bride service, marriage was a negotiation between a suitor and a woman's kin. As fray Francisco Casañas de Jesús María described, "If a [Hasinai] man wants a certain woman for his wife who he knows is a maiden, he takes her some of the very best things he has; and if her father and mother give their permissions for her to receive the gift, the answer is that they consent to the marriage." Fray Isidro de Espinosa similarly observed that a man spent more time courting a woman's kin than the woman herself, arguing that a man must "gain the goodwill of the fathers and brothers of his proposed bride by bringing them some deer or stag which he leaves at the door of their home without a word; if they accept and eat the meat, it is a sure sign of their consent [to the union]." Over the course of that negotiation, a man provided goods that demonstrated his ability as a hunter and warrior to defend and provide for a woman's extended family. Services to a woman's family continued after marriage to maintain the man's relationship and status within the woman's family and the greater clan-based community. Bridal goods thereby served as symbols of the man's personal prowess. The goods a French trader had for exchange ably substituted for products of the hunt, and the promise of their continued availability brought a different kind of "income" to the clan.[22]

Membership in a clan in turn gave a man standing in the larger community. Having Caddo wives enabled Frenchmen to participate in customary male exchanges of hospitality and gift giving beyond those of the more formal diplomacy between nations. Marriage in a bride-service society was a key determinant of male rank. A married man, as opposed to a bachelor, had the benefit of a wife (and by extension, her relatives) who fed and cared for the family, who provided a home through her kin or by building shelters herself, and who provided him with sexual intimacy. More important, marriage in a bride-service society allowed a man "to become a political actor—an initiator of relations through generosity," because "A man who has a wife and a hearth can offer hospitality to other men." Thus, marriage elevated male status. In this way, initial French-Caddo bonds took place at the level of the family and household rather than at formal levels of diplomacy.[23]

Over the century, Caddo settlements accepted resident traders into their midst whose status, while not contingent upon intermarriage with a Caddo woman, could certainly be enhanced and strengthened by such a bond. Such relations increased as the number of traders operating directly out of native villages, often as independent entrepreneurs rather than officially licensed agents, grew in response to French commercial expansion. As Athanase de Mézières explained to the viceroy in 1778, every resident merchant sent from Natchitoches was a man "well-versed in writing, skilled in the language of the Indians with whom he deals, acceptable to them, and the best fitted obtainable to inculcate in them the love and respect which it is desired that they should have for us." Resident traders, but especially "creoles," De Mézières continued, learned native idioms and, having lived or been reared in Indian villages, knew "how to gain their good-will" and how to "maintain the general union."[24]

The post at Natchitoches emerged as the focal point of French relations among the Caddo confederacies and their allies in western Louisiana and eastern Texas, serving as a nucleus of Louisiana's trade for the remainder of the century. Two traders, Pierre Largen and Jean Legros, were among the first Frenchmen to settle in the Natchitoches area as members of St. Denis's 1714 expedition, and both formed unions with Ais women (an independent Caddo nation located west of Natchitoches, with whom the Frenchmen lived). Their wives accompanied Largen and Legros as they traded extensively among different Caddoan peoples and must have aided in Legros's establishment of a trading post among a Caddo band of Yatasis in 1722. Two other figures from Natchitoches's early years, François Dion Deprez Derbanne and Jacques Guedon, brought wives with them to Natchitoches,

Jeanne de la Grand Terre and Marie Anne de la Grand Terre, who were former Chitimacha slaves captured near Mobile in the 1710s. Although not related by marriage to Caddo families, the two couples lived among their trading partners for much of the year. Baptismal records identify their children as residents of Caddo villages, indicating their close ties to Caddos. For example, Louise Marguerite Guedon (daughter of Jacques and Marie Anne) appeared in church records as "a native of the Cadeaux." Jacques Guedon held responsibility for establishing a subsidiary post at Bayou Pierre in 1723, which soon became known for its multiethnic population. The Derbanne family's relationship with Natchitoches Indians earned François Derbanne a reputation among provincial officials as "a man reliable, faithful and necessary for the trade in the things that we need among the Indians."[25]

Historical knowledge of French-Caddo unions rests upon French sacramental and notarial records, which unfortunately document only those couples who chose to confirm their marriages or the baptisms of their children in the Catholic Church or French courts. Such records tell us nothing of those couples who chose not to seek out such French institutions. Yet, the few who did left tantalizing hints about these relationships. A soldier named Jean Baptiste Brevel married a Natchitoches woman, "Anne of the Caddoes," in 1736 and with her had two children, Jean Baptiste and Marie Louise, whom they raised "at the Caddoes." Although their daughter married a Frenchman, as had her mother, their son spent much of his life with fellow Caddo and Wichita men, rounding up wild horses for trade in Louisiana. Other Frenchmen, such as Pierre Sebastien Prudhomme and Barthelemy Le Court, did not solemnize their marriages to Caddo women in the church but testified to the relationships by having their children baptized in the Natchitoches church, even as they and their families continued to live in Caddo villages. Thus, for example, Marie Ursulle of the Caddo nation agreed to Le Court's wish to baptize their five children, though she herself never submitted to such sacraments. The children of these unions furthered the connections between Caddo and French families through their own marriages. Alexis Grappe, for instance, married Louise Marguerite Guedon, and he and his son, François, became two of the best-known Caddoan agents chosen to represent them in political and economic negotiations with French, Spanish, and later Anglo-American governments.[26]

In addition to brokering unions between women of their own nation and Frenchmen, Caddo leaders found that European newcomers also showed interest in enemy women, primarily Apaches whom Caddo warriors took captive in war. Prior to the arrival of Europeans at the end of the seventeenth century, Caddoan peoples did not use enemy captives as a source of labor but did capture a small number of women and children in warfare to avenge or replace their dead through adoption. Caddo contacts with Frenchmen soon diverted these captive women and children to Louisiana and began to change the nature of Indian captivity.

Unlike settlers in the British colonies and New France (Canada), those in French Louisiana made little systematic attempt to exploit enslaved Indians as a labor force. Louisiana colonists did hold as slaves some Indians whom French forces had defeated in wars—notably the Chitimachas in the 1710s and the Natchez in the 1730s—but such enslavement was an isolated practice belonging to the early period of French invasion and colonization. In fact, as early as 1706, French officials in Louisiana began lobbying their imperial superiors for permission to trade those Indian slaves for enslaved Africans from the French West Indies. A 1726 Louisiana census listed enslaved Africans as outnumbering enslaved Indians, 1,385 to 159, and this ratio continued to skew due to an ever-increasing African population. Yet, despite the growth in the enslaved African population, the number of enslaved Indians held steady, indicating that the size of the two populations bore little relation to one other. The explanation lay, instead, in gender differences. Even as the imported African slave laborers replaced Indian slaves on plantations and in larger settlements like New Orleans, enslaved Indian women remained fixtures of Indian trade and French family life in western outpost settlements. The minimal use of Indian slaves in the establishment of French plantation agriculture and the French preference for enslaved Africans as a servile labor force indicate that the Indian slave trade remained important primarily in serving male domestic demands in the hinterlands of French settlement. The value to French buyers of enslaved Indians lay in the fact that most of them were female.[27]

In other words, Frenchmen at posts such as Fort St. Jean Baptiste aux Natchitoches formed marital unions with their Caddo trading partners and sexual unions with the captive Apache women who were often the objects of French-Caddo trade. The slave trade played a crucial role in supplementing the female population at Natchitoches and other posts throughout the eighteenth century. Both licit and illicit relationships became notable enough to inspire heated complaints from French government and ecclesiastical officials that fueled escalating demands for the immigration of Frenchwomen and for official surveillance of interracial sex and cohabitation. Despite such concerns at the imperial and provincial levels, however, the proportion of Apache women among enslaved populations and in Louisiana households steadily increased as trade networks in hides, horses, and captives grew between the French and the Caddos and, through the Caddos, later extended to Wichitas and Comanches.[28]

Even though captive women could not be used to constitute affinal kinship, their exchange supplemented French-Caddo ties of settlement and family. To its Caddo participants, the slave trade that developed represented two sides of native conventions of reciprocity. Caddos attained their trade goods from a range of sources: the hides came from hunting, the horses from Wichita and Comanche trading partners who raided Spanish settlements in Texas, and the captives from warfare with Apache enemies. One aspect of native conventions dictated that they take captives primarily from those designated as enemies or as strangers to systems of kinship and political alliance—thus, they took captives only in the context of war. On the flip side, once captive women became desirable commodities in Louisiana, their trade served to bind Caddo and French men together.[29]

Reciprocal relations both required and created kinship affiliation. Participation in exchanges made groups less likely to engage in confrontation and violence and brought them into metaphorical, if not real, relations of kinship. Caddo men cast trade alliances in terms of fictive kinship categories of "brotherhood." Unlike with marriage, the women who were the objects of exchange did not create the tie of personal or economic obligation; the exchange process itself did so, binding men to each other in the act of giving and receiving. Kinship moved far beyond biological relationships, economic ties could not be separated from political ones, and trading partners were also military and political allies. Meanwhile, the number of "Cannecis" (Apaches) among the enslaved Indian population in Louisiana became so predominant that the provincial governor, Louis Billouart de Kerlérec, argued in 1753 that trade was impossible with the Apache nations. Through intermarriage, adoption, reciprocity, and symbolic kinship relations, the French had become a subsidiary of the Caddos. They were family to the Caddos and enemies to the Caddos' enemies.[30]

Returning to the starting point of Spanish-Caddo relations at the end of the seventeenth century, then, one can well imagine that Spaniards had not progressed beyond a Caddoan category of stranger, if not enemy, following their ruinous first contacts. French experiences in Canada, where the success of French trade goals had rested upon their adaptation to native customs, made them better prepared to negotiate Caddo politics. Spaniards in the northern provinces of New Spain had much less frequently dealt with Indian peoples on their terms. Although the Pueblo Revolt had driven all Spaniards out of New Mexico just eight years before the first Spanish *entrada* to Caddo lands, more commonly, the native peoples encountered by Spanish officers and missionaries had been conquered militarily or devastated by European disease, and Spanish misunderstanding of Indian customs had little consequence for the outcome of interactions where their domination was already assured. Experiences in eighteenth-century Texas proved quite different. When they met a people as powerful as the Hasinais, Spaniards entered negotiations on equal or lesser footing with Indians whom they had to persuade to form an alliance, and with whom misunderstandings could have fatal repercussions.

The events of 1690–93, when the rape of Caddo women by Spanish men brutally violated the sanctity of matrilineal households, heralded the difficulties Spaniards faced in meeting the Caddos' terms in the wider realm of kin-defined politics. To the dismay of Spanish officials and missionaries, they could only watch from afar as French-Caddo relations grew over the first two decades of the eighteenth century. Monitoring the French presence in Caddo lands as best they could from the distance of Mexico City and the mission-presidio complex of San Juan Bautista along the Rio Grande (which, in the 1710s, represented the northernmost reaches of Spanish settlement), Spaniards had good reason to fear they would never regain a toehold in the good graces of the Caddoan peoples. Over those same years, missionaries who had lived oh-so-briefly among the Caddos kept up a steady barrage of requests to return and repair the damage that had so grievously destroyed their hopes of converting Caddos in the 1690s. But it was not until 1716 that an expedition finally set out for Caddo lands and began the process of rebuilding the missions that Hasinais had forced them to desert in 1693.[31]

Once back among the Caddos, Spaniards found Frenchmen well-established in Caddoan trading networks, exchanging French guns, clothes, and manufactured goods for animal skins, corn, horses, livestock, and Indian captives. Spanish observers noted first the trade and then the Frenchmen's relationships with Caddo women. During his expedition to Caddo lands in 1718, Martín de Alarcón reported two Frenchmen living among Kadohadachos "who are the ones through whose hands the French acquire slaves and other things of that land from the Indians." In 1722, fray Antonio Margil de Jesús, one of the missionaries sent to work among the Hasinais, reported that neighboring Frenchmen "mingle freely with the Indians who live there and some of them are marrying Indian women." Fray Isidro de Espinosa even recorded that he baptized the son of a Hasinai woman and a Frenchman.[32]

In seeking to explain the Caddos' devotion to the Frenchmen living among them, Spanish officials found a clear answer in the French influence secured by traders' customs of marrying Indian women. The governor of Texas, Jacinto de Barrios y Jáuregui, asserted that the French "regard the Indians so highly that civilized persons marry the Indian women without incurring blame, for the French find their greatest glory in that which is most profitable to them." Furthermore, missionary fray José de Calahorra y Sáenz had assured the governor "that it is the greatest vanity of the principal Indians to offer their women for the incontinent appetite of the French; to such a point reaches their unbridled passion for the French." The commercial profit realized by Frenchmen was obvious, Governor Barrios concluded: "As a result [of these unions], no Caudachos, Nacodoches, San Pedro, or Texas Indian is to be seen who does not wear his mirror, epaulets, and breech-clout—all French goods." Moreover, Spanish officials feared that residence among Caddo communities allowed Frenchmen to spy on Spaniards, "reconnoitering . . . all of this land and the posts that are in it" and "seeking the opportune moment in which to advise his fellow countrymen to send a troop of soldiers." And of course, in such an attack, family linkages through marriage would ensure for Frenchmen the military help and alliance of the numerous and powerful Caddo bands.[33]

Most Spaniards remained blind to the Caddos' initiative in these unions. Civic officials criticized the unions as a French tactic to gain Caddo alliance and trade, when it was really vice versa, while missionaries focused their condemnation on the Frenchmen's lack of effort to teach Christianity to Caddos. Missionaries' spiritual concerns found confirmation in the fact that many relationships lacked the sanctity of marriage, implying French deference to "heathen" Caddo practices. To many Spaniards, it was a toss-up who was most at risk of corruption—Frenchmen or Caddos. French acceptance and approval of "heathen" Caddo lifestyles, made implicit by their intermarriage and adoption of Indian customs, demonstrated a lack of concern for Caddo souls and encouraged the Indians' "heedlessness of religion" with their own. Ambitious Frenchmen, José Antonio Pichardo explained, "corrupt [Indians] with their unbelief and execrable habits, abuse all the persons of the other sex that they can, dress themselves á la Indian—that is to say, they go about unclothed as the Indians do, paint themselves, and live like them." Spaniards thus differentiated themselves from Frenchmen, and the French model—the road not taken—remained a subject only for Spanish denigration.[34]

Although fearfully aware of the economic and political gains of Frenchmen's receptivity to intermarriage, Spaniards did not emulate their imperial rivals, rejecting Caddos' overtures of intermarriage. Why? Intermarriage with Indians was not uncommon in Spanish America. Such unions and the mestizo population that resulted reflected the inclusive character of intimate Spanish-Indian relations across New Spain. Conversely, the absence of Spanish-Caddo intermarriage marked the Spaniards' *exclusion* from Caddoan political economies. The explanation rests both in Spanish and Caddoan determinations of acceptable behavior inside and outside the boundaries of society. In most parts of Spanish America, Spanish-Indian sexual relations and intermarriage took place within Spanish society. More specifically, it involved Indian populations who were members of conquered groups subject to the Spanish church and state. In other areas of Texas, such as the later villa of San Antonio de Béxar, Spaniards did form unions with Indians who had entered the

Caddo Indians dressed and decorated in trade items obtained from their Euro-American allies. Watercolor by Lino Sánchez y Tapia after the original sketch by José María Sánchez y Tapia, an artist-cartographer who traveled through Texas as a member of a Mexican boundary and scientific expedition in the years 1828–31. Courtesy of the Gilcrease Museum, Tulsa, Oklahoma.

missions there and converted to Christianity. But intermarriage with peoples of independent Indian nations had not been a tool of Spanish diplomacy beyond the first generation of *conquistadores* in the sixteenth century. Rather, it occurred only after Indians had been incorporated into Spanish society. Spaniards in Texas therefore rejected Caddos, despite the political and economic costs of rejection, because these nations represented so-called *indios bárbaros*, outsiders to Spanish society, religion, and authority. In the Texas borderlands where Spaniards were far from conquering any group, however, Spanish conditions upon intermarriage ensured their exclusion from Caddo kinship systems and thus from sociopolitical networks that would have proved advantageous to Spanish imperial goals.[35]

So what did Spaniards attempt instead to satisfy the Caddos' terms for accepting them back into their lands? Fortuitously for Spanish missionaries and officials, their return in 1716 was in fact aided by one of the Frenchmen already well-respected by Caddo leaders. In an effort to extend French trading networks into Spanish markets, Louis Juchereau de St. Denis—accompanied by twenty-five Hasinais and three Frenchmen—mounted an expedition to San Juan Bautista (along the Rio Grande) in 1714 and stunned the Spaniards there who greeted them. He came, he explained, in response to the bidding of fray Francisco Hidalgo, who had written Louisiana governor Antoine de La Mothe Cadillac in 1710 asking for French aid in reestablishing Spanish missions among the Hasinais. St. Denis further argued, seemingly on a side note, that this also seemed a good opportunity for Frenchmen and Spaniards to open trade with one another. Offering them reentry into Caddo territories, St. Denis's appearance at San Juan Bautista energized Spanish officials. In response, in 1716 a Spanish expedition, under the leadership of the military commander at San Juan Bautista, Domingo Ramón, but guided by St. Denis, found welcome in Caddo lands. Hasinai, Adaes, and Ais Caddos allowed them to return, presumably in hopes that if, as it appeared, Spaniards were now in league with Frenchmen, then they would change their practices in such ways as would accord with Caddo customs.

The greetings with which the Hasinais welcomed the Spaniards to their villages twenty-three years after their eviction revealed that a Spanish presence there would now be shaped by the Caddos' relationships with their new French kin. Upon entering Caddo lands, the expedition encountered Hasinai family parties out hunting who greeted them as usual with embraces and food, and one man led them to his hamlet, where more than twenty men and women welcomed the Spanish party with a feast. The next day, St. Denis went ahead to meet with the nearest Hasinai *caddí* to alert him of their approach; meanwhile, the Spaniards dawdled, traveling slowly and camping for two days in one spot and then another, to give the Frenchman sufficient time for his errand. Word finally arrived at the Spanish camp six days later that it was time to prepare for the arrival of the *caddí* and his attendants. At this point, the greeting ritual departed from what the Spaniards had expected. Thirty-four Hasinais approached, several releasing salutes with bows and arrows, before more men came on horseback, one by one in a single file, led by several *caddís* in the center and with St. Denis placed prominently within their ranks. Ramón was also quick to note nine muskets of French make carried by the Hasinai cavalrymen. The Spanish commander knew what was expected and promptly ordered his men into line to greet the Hasinais in matching single-file formation. Ramón himself carried the banner of the Virgin of Guadalupe, and he marched forward with soldiers on either side of him and missionaries behind. In the pipe ceremony, speeches, and feasts that followed, with everyone ranged around by rank in seats laid out by the Spaniards, St. Denis continued to act alongside the Hasinai leaders, translating their words to the Spaniards because he "understands and speaks their language quite well."[36]

In the days that followed, the Spaniards were reminded repeatedly of St. Denis's standing among the Caddos as they moved to new campgrounds and as increasingly larger groups of Hasinais arrived and asked the Frenchman to join their formations in greeting ceremonies. As they processed through the Hasinai villages, St. Denis again paced in ranked order within the three customary Hasinai columns, joining the *caddís* and leading men in the middle, while the Spaniards marched separately on their own. St. Denis even led them in kneeling to venerate the Virgin's icon, now a religious symbol of peace that Frenchmen and Spaniards shared. Hasinai warriors continued to salute with French guns and, to top it all off, *caddís* on the third day brought out a calumet pipe made of brass (surely a product of French trade) to celebrate the proceedings. By that third day as well, the Franciscans were trying to write down some of the Hasinai language, using St. Denis as their interpreter and instructor. What else might they need to do to ingratiate themselves into a Hasinai network newly configured with French members?

By the time the second and third expeditions, in 1718 and 1721, came to settle Spaniards in Caddo lands, the French overshadowed their Spanish rivals all the more. Spaniards had established a presidio-mission complex and small villa at San Antonio de Béxar in 1718, but it was approximately four hundred miles from the political and economic centers of the Caddo confederacies. In 1721, the marqués de Aguayo's approach to Caddo villages was greeted by repeated messengers notifying him that St. Denis had summoned convocations of Indians from multiple Caddo villages and neighboring native encampments to meet prior to the Spaniards' arrival. Between San Antonio de Béxar and the westernmost Caddo communities, a united settlement of Bidais, Akokisas, and multiple others responded to Aguayo's unfurling of the royal standard by unfurling one of their own: a white silk banner with blue stripes given them by Frenchmen. When on August 1 Aguayo finally met with St. Denis to confirm that the truce agreed to by France and Spain following the War of the Quadruple Alliance would be honored along the proclaimed Texas-Louisiana border, St. Denis rode over from his home in Natchitoches to hold the meeting among his Hasinai comrades. By this time, the French government had made St. Denis commander of the Natchitoches post and its surrounding population of French traders and their French and Indian wives, and from the Caddos, he had gained a title of honor translating roughly as "Big Leg." Because of the location of the French stronghold amidst the powerful Caddoan peoples, the Spanish government threw down a gauntlet: in 1721, they designated the easternmost mission-presidio complex at Los Adaes the capital of the Texas province. The complex (also in the midst of Caddo lands) was built a mere seven leagues (seventeen miles) from Natchitoches.[37]

There were no gauntlets for Caddos, however, as Spaniards did their best to identify the demands of Caddo leaders and to devise plans that would meet them. Citing past violent crimes as the cause for the 1693 Spanish eviction, officials repeatedly expressed the hope that the presence of soldiers' wives and families would ensure there was no repeat of the earlier abuses. Viceroy marqués de Valero ordered that only men with families be sent to Caddo lands because "the Indians find it strange that the soldiers do not bring women." The presence of women and children promised the soldiers' determination to join Caddo warriors in defense of the region as well as to avoid becoming a threat themselves. "The ties of matrimony," *auditor de guerra* (judge advocate) Juan de Oliván Rebolledo argued, "will cause them to take root more firmly wherever they may be assigned on military duty; they will be able to fill their presidio with the children their wives will bear them; thus they will not vex either Indian women who have recently adopted Catholicism or gentile Indian women." Oliván clearly knew that blame for the first missionary efforts' failure among the Caddos rested entirely with the soldiers' rape of Hasinai women. "This kind of disturbance caused much resentment among the Asinaiz that, with Roman tactics, . . . [Hasinai warriors] compelled them [Spaniards] to leave their lands." In later recommendations, he further directed that the number of soldiers and missionaries be subject to the Hasinai *caddís'* approval.[38]

Having seen the love that Hasinais had lavished on Pierre Talon and Pierre Meunier "as if they were their own," fray Damián Mazanet had made his own proposal back in 1690, suggesting that Spanish children be taken to the Hasinais to be raised among them while remaining under the instruction of missionaries living there too. Thus, the children "would have a great love for the land"—and presumably remain as settlers—and Hasinais "would love them deeply"—and thus extend loving welcome to other Spaniards. Although no one followed up on that idea in the 1710s, both Spanish officials and Franciscans did emphasize that families, not just women, should make up significant portions of the groups sent to Caddo lands. Moreover, the settlement of families was to be focused around missions and presidios to offset the predominantly male population at each kind of Spanish institution.[39]

Spanish officials felt so strongly about women's inclusion in settler groups that they were willing to invest money securing it. Fray Espinosa proposed paying and provisioning women independently of their husbands to encourage their participation in the settlement of Texas. Juan de Oliván Rebolledo made detailed plans for the viceroy, in a series of recommendations suggesting that a colony of Spanish families, each with an annual supplement of 300 pesos, and a colony of Tlaxcalan families (Indians from central Mexico), each with an annual supplement of 200 pesos, be paid and provisioned for ten years, each family receiving plots of land large enough to support themselves with farming and herding. In fact, twenty-five or thirty Indian families could be moved from Parras (at that time in the province of Nueva Vizcaya) to Texas, he argued, since they "are capable both in cultivating fields and in handling weapons," while the Spanish families could be relocated from Saltillo (also in Nueva Vizcaya at that time) or the kingdom of León. Soldiers too needed to be married, dexterous with arms, and capable of farming, and they could earn an annual salary of 400 pesos (with 50 pesos taken out to pay for the transportation of their families to the land of the Tejas). Colonization plans even suggested that male and female vagrants, "persons of both sexes . . . without a trade," and "any women taken into custody by court action" be sent as settlers and laborers. Clearly, the identity or status of the women mattered not; their physical presence within settlement groups was the whole point. Spaniards meant the presence of women and families to send a message of permanent residence and, by extension, imperial claim to the French as well. Despite all the plotting and planning, however, none of these settlement schemes ever materialized, as will be seen.[40]

Surveillance of French demographic patterns had brought Spaniards' awareness of the significance of women within settlement projects into even clearer focus. Since the 1680s, Spanish officials had estimated French colonial expansion, strength, and permanence in the region upon the presence or absence of women. Such monitoring took an unexpected turn when Caddo leaders intervened in Spanish-French politics. When trader Louis Juchereau de St. Denis traveled from Natchitoches to San Juan Bautista for a second time in 1717, officials sent him to Mexico City, where he was imprisoned for contraband trade and forced to answer questions regarding the intent and destination of French frigates reportedly carrying "families, militia, and missionaries" to Texas. To the surprise of the Spaniards, even this far from Caddo lands, his Indian brethren were able to exert their power and intervene on his behalf. During his first trip to San Juan Bautista in 1716, St. Denis had married Manuela Sánchez Navarro, the granddaughter of Domingo Ramón, and the Hasinai *caddís* used the union to manipulate Spanish officials. When word reached Caddo lands in 1717 that St. Denis had been imprisoned in Mexico City, Caddo leaders promptly demanded of fray Francisco Hidalgo that Spanish authorities release the Frenchman. The Caddo leaders cagily promised to congregate in missions, Hidalgo reported to the viceroy, but only if and when St. Denis returned to their lands *with his wife* (who had not yet left her family at San Juan Bautista to join him in Natchitoches).[41]

Beyond manipulating Spanish authorities to win the release of their French trading partner, Caddos expressed their belief that the presence of St. Denis's wife would be a sign of his permanent return from Spanish lands as well as his commitment to residing among them and, not incidentally, continuing to supply them with trade goods. In 1718, *auditor* Oliván forwarded to the king more documents, among which he cited a letter from fray José Diez (another missionary living near the Caddo villages) requesting that the trade goods confiscated from St. Denis at San Juan Bautista be restored "because he has married a Spanish woman" and that he be sent back to the Hasinai villages "because the love of the Indians for him is so great that if they lose him, there is danger of a general uprising." The Spaniards rejected these Hasinai maneuvers, at first. St. Denis finally escaped confinement in Mexico City and returned to Louisiana in 1717, but without his new wife. Fray Espinosa and fray Margil de Jesús then sent a third round of letters from the heart of Caddo lands, this time to ask that Manuela be allowed to join him at Natchitoches, and finally she did. This tale of diplomatic intrigue revealed the power of Caddo kinship ties; Caddo leaders used their influence to make the Spanish imperial bureaucracy unite a Spanish wife and a French husband who was their trading "brother."[42]

Although the highest levels of Spanish bureaucracy wanted to avoid a repeat of past abuses of the Caddos and to make viable a Spanish claim to Texas through a large female contingent among the settlers sent to Caddo lands, in practice, it proved difficult to find settler families for a post so distant from Spanish settlement and supply depots. In 1716, nine missionaries, twenty-five soldiers and officers, three Frenchmen (including St. Denis), sixteen laborers and servants, two Indian guides, and only eight women (wives of soldiers) and two children (for a total of sixty-five people) made up the members of the Ramón expedition. Alarcón's expedition in 1718–19 brought seventy-two people to the province, including thirty-four soldiers, but only seven families, many of whom remained along the San Antonio River to establish the villa of San Antonio de Béxar instead of traveling all the way to Caddo territory. The final foundational expedition of this early period, that of the marqués de Aguayo in 1721–22, was by far the largest, with five hundred men in eight companies—a contingent that "astonished" the Hasinais—yet, nevertheless, of the one hundred soldiers Aguayo left to garrison the two presidios built in the midst of the Caddo hamlets, only thirty-one had families with them.[43]

Many of the Spaniards who remained in the land of the Tejas were therefore bachelors like their neighboring Frenchmen. And in Caddoan terms, men who lacked their own families and were unwilling to marry Caddo women meant trouble. Even in the absence of violence, the men, whether soldiers or missionaries, represented a group of individuals without essential kin ties and thus lacked the identity, stability, and commitment to the bonds of alliance they claimed to want with Caddoan peoples. In the initial years of settlement, physical separation added to the Spaniards' social separation, as they isolated themselves in presidios and missions. In 1716, Spanish Franciscans and military officials established six missions (Nuestro Padre San Francisco de los Tejas, Nuestra Señora de la Purísima Concepción de los Hainais, Nuestra Señora de Guadalupe de los Nacogdoches, San José de los Nazonis, Nuestra Señora de los Dolores de los Ais, and San Miguel de Linares de los Adaes) and two presidios (Nuestra Señora del Pilar de los Adaes and Nuestra Señora de los Dolores de los Tejas) spread throughout Caddo lands from the Neches River to present-day Robeline, Louisiana. Missionaries and military officers must be held responsible for the Spaniards' separation from Caddo communities. Both groups tried to prevent abuses by keeping soldiers away from Caddo women. The Franciscans also demanded that if joint Caddo-Spanish communities were to be created, it would be only on Spanish terms—insisting that Caddos come into the missions as Christian neophytes and maintain a distance from those who chose to remain "heathens."

Caddo leaders repeatedly refused the overtures of Spanish missionaries, politely citing their inability to leave their cornfields, their homes, and the obligations of the hunt—in sum, all that made up their kinship responsibilities. Yet, missionaries noted, Caddos regularly traveled for their own spiritual ceremonies at "houses of worship" where they had "a perpetual fire which they never let die out." A *xinesí* served at each temple (fray Espinosa referred to them as a "parish church or cathedral" of the Caddos), which was a large, thatched structure containing an altar and a fire "always made of four large, heavy logs laid to face in the four principal directions." One temple served Neches and Hasinais, while another was the gathering site of Nacogdoches and Nasoni worshipers, each located within traveling distance of their congregations. Just as Franciscans told Caddos about Christianity, Caddo leaders and priests shared their creation story, showing the Spanish religious men their temples and reciting their rites and beliefs. If not in words, then in actions, Caddos communicated that they were not looking to be incorporated into Spanish religion or society. As Franciscans repeatedly recorded, these "good-humored," "joyous," "pleasant," and "intelligent" people had no need or desire for change. On the other hand, if the Spaniards wished to live among the Caddos, they were welcome to maintain their own spiritual beliefs. In fact, Hasinais argued that just as Spaniards had their heaven and Caddos their own, so too did each have their own god: the Spaniards' god "gives them clothing, knives, hatchets, hoes, and everything else that they have seen among the Spaniards," while the Hasinais' god gives them "corn, beans, nuts, acorns, and other things from the land, with water for planting." Each to his own. What Hasinai leaders did require was that the Spaniards abide by the conventions and customs that maintained balance, order, and reciprocity. The Spaniards were their supplicants, after all, not the other way around.[44]

Yet, Spanish efforts to maintain order and reciprocity proved difficult in the early years, especially in comparison with the stability of the neighboring French settlements. St. Denis commanded the Natchitoches post for forty-four years, offering significant continuity to Caddo-French relations, while Spanish presidial commanders came and went in a regular and frequent turnover. More important, St. Denis, and the French traders scattered throughout the Caddo villages, maintained personal contact, whereas Spanish expedition leaders with whom the Hasinai *caddís* forged pacts in ceremonies of 1716, 1718, and 1721–22 never remained to oversee their obligations of reciprocity and alliance, much less to relocate their wives and families. So, what did happen when these three Spanish expeditions requested residence among the Caddos without establishing a stable friendship?

An examination of housing—central to both Caddo rituals of incorporation and Spanish goals for alliance and conversion—reveals much about the disconnect between the two peoples. That the Caddos allowed missions and presidios to be erected does not indicate that they sought either Christian conversion or Spanish rule, which they clearly did not. Rather, the Caddos' understanding of the purpose of the Spanish structures must be found within the bounds of their own customs and practices.

Housing had played a key role in hospitality rituals for visitors, and so too did it provide a focus for conventions marking the inclusion of newcomers within Caddo societies. "A Caddo house was more than an abode," and "houses (or, more specifically, the households represented by the houses) were regarded as constituent elements of matrilineally organized communities." In Caddo villages and hamlets, house building represented a communal effort, a house's dimensions reflected the rank of its inhabitants and the organizing principles of the community, and a house's location in proximity to temple fires, other homes, and the complexes of the *caddís* reinforced the interconnectedness of families and villages. Thus, in 1716, 1718, and 1721, when *caddís* offered Spanish leaders homes of their own rather than hosting them in their households, they were inviting them to become members of the Caddo realm.[45]

When someone needed a new home, village *caddís* called on the community to come together and help build it. The *caddís*' first task was to send out *tanmas* (or *tammas*, their administrative assistants) by horseback to notify all families in the surrounding hamlets that their help would be needed to build a new home on a certain date. Carrying as many little sticks as there were to be poles in the house, a *tanma* left one or more sticks at each home to tell the family how many poles the men of their household were to cut, trim, carry to the construction site, and set into the hole designated for them on the appointed day. Others might be assigned to bring a crosspiece, lath poles, or bark cords. Women from each home provided bundles of long grass for the thatched walls. A *tanma*'s final duty was to sleep at the new homesite on the eve of building, staying until the *caddí* arrived at daybreak to take his seat on a special bench from which he would oversee construction. That morning, at a signal from the *tanma*, each man came forward with his pole to a circle of holes carefully measured out by the *connas*, and the work began. To erect the distinctive beehive structures that ranged up to fifty-five feet high, the men had "cut full-length trees as thick around as a thigh" and then set them upright in the ground in a circle, bringing them together at the top with crosswise laths tied together with bark cords. Once the framework was set, women came forward to thatch all the outer walls from bottom to top with long grass reeds. Upon completion, they placed "some kind of fanciful crown likewise made of grass" atop the roof, perhaps symbolizing social or political rank or matrilineal clan affiliation. The daylong event culminated with blessings upon the house from the *conna* and a feast made of foods brought by all participants. By the end of the choreographed day, the village's communal ethos, the gendered division of labor within the participating matrilineal households, the ranked hierarchy ruled by the *caddí*, and the spiritual blessings of the *conna* together rendered the new home and its residents a part of the community. Thus, home building marked as yet another ceremony that could make strangers kin.[46]

Thus, when Spaniards expressed the desire to live among the Caddos—that is, in the Caddos' perspective, to move from roles as allied foreigners to community members—the *caddís* insisted that they had to have their own homes. Back in 1690, for example, fray Mazanet recorded that the *caddí* instructed him that they must "build the house in the most suitable place, that he would show us the village, and that I might choose the spot." For his part, the Franciscan might well picture a church and priests' dwellings as a separate Spanish complex, even if physically near the village (near enough to attract neophytes). For the *caddí*'s part, the Spanish missionaries and officers could have no separate complex conveying special standing or equivalent residence to rival his own; they would live *in the village*, just as did *canahas*, *connas*, and *amayxoyas*. Spatial arrangements reflected everyone's place in the social order. In due fashion, Hasinai leaders called on their people in 1716 and again in 1718 to build thatched living quarters for military commanders Domingo Ramón and Martín de Alarcón as well as for the individual missionaries who accompanied their expeditions. Caddo men accompanied the Spaniards to select sites for presidios and missions and then divided up the responsibilities for building the different structures. Ramón at least appreciated the speed and precision of the Caddo system of building, noting that "they were well suited for this work."[47]

Notably, it was only after Alarcón requested a house in which he could live among them that the Caddo leaders held ceremonies by which they declared him a "*capitán general*" among their people. After two days during which Hasinai men and women built the commander's home "in accordance with their custom," the work came to an end with the usual feasts and festivities around a "great bonfire" at the new house. Alarcón's induction began as soon as several *caddís* and leading men arrived at the new home. After washing his face as ritual purification, the men put a headdress made of white duck feathers on Alarcón's head and a strip of black cloth across his forehead (perhaps to signify, if only temporarily, tribal tattoos), put a peace pipe in his mouth to smoke, and began to sing and dance. A leading warrior then interrupted the singing to announce that "thenceforward their friendship and relations would be closer, and that since he had permitted to let himself be received according to their custom, they no longer looked upon him as a stranger but as if born among them." Another group of Caddos also gave him a title and declared that they now "looked upon him as if they had created him."[48] Yet Alarcón did not remain.

So when the marqués de Aguayo arrived three years later, the Caddos appeared more aware of the ephemeral nature of Spanish commanders' commitment to them. Aguayo asked for no home of his own, nor did any Caddo village build one for him or ritually adopt him. Instead, he made camp with his men as he moved from one Caddo village to another. The only way he earned Caddo appreciation was by ensuring that his five hundred troops did not trample or encamp in the cornfields during their migrations between settlements. *Caddís* among the Hasinais, Neches, Naconos, Nasonis, Nacogdoches, and Adaes all met with him, smoked calumet pipes, and made promises of friendship, but no more. For his part, Aguayo undermined the spirit of each meeting by his staunch refusal to accept anything that might appear to be a gift from Caddo leaders. His stated intent was to offer a contrast to the French in order to convince the Caddoan peoples that Spaniards asked nothing in return for their "gift"—the promise of spiritual salvation.[49]

Yet, from the Caddos' perspective, Aguayo gave every appearance of avoiding the obligations of reciprocity requisite of Caddo diplomacy, much less that requisite of a joint settlement. Even if he did not know a thing about Caddo gift-exchange standards, he had some sense of the costs of exchange, as his chronicler recorded: "The governor had not wanted to receive even one tanned hide, that there might not be the slightest obligation of recompense." Perhaps even more disquieting, Aguayo chose his own sites for the six missions and two presidios that he was charged with reestablishing after their retreat was forced by the French in 1719, during the War of the Quadruple Alliance. Reinforcing the sense of Spanish disconnectedness, even though the structures were to be built among the villages of Hasinais, Hainais,

Nacogdoches, Nasonis, Ais, and Adaes peoples, he put detachments of soldiers in charge of constructing each mission and presidio as well as the living quarters of missionaries, again slighting his Caddo hosts.[50]

Spaniards understood little of Caddo civic authority or the insults implicit in these actions. When Caddos used house building to incorporate Spaniards into Caddo lines of authority and kinship, Spanish missionaries believed that prospective Caddo neophytes were building houses for priests in mission compounds to which Caddo families would soon move to join them. Military commanders saw themselves as being honored by subalterns who demonstrated their deference to their new Spanish rulers by such construction. To both groups of Spaniards, the Caddos' acceptance of Spanish presidios and missions conveyed the absorption of Caddo villages into the Spanish domain. They called it the "province of the Tejas Indians," knew they had conquered no one, knew in point of fact that they could well be evicted again (for a third time). Yet, at some level, they were unable to discern fully what it meant that they were on Caddo soil, living there on Caddo sufferance.

Needless to say, to the Caddos' eyes, the rules governing a Spanish presence among their villages were quite different from those envisioned by Spaniards. Franciscans would live among them as *connas*, and soldiers and military officers as warriors and *canahas*, each in their own customary Caddo-designed homes, the mission and presidio complexes. Even when Spaniards tried to impose their own marks upon these dwellings (in the 1721 construction), the Spanish rituals seemed familiar to the watching Caddos. Crosses atop churches resembled the grass crowns placed on Caddo homes; Franciscan blessings at the dedication of each mission echoed those of *connas* at the celebration of a new Caddo homestead. It was when missionaries and military commanders repeatedly directed the Hasinais and their neighbors to "congregate at the missions" that the disconnects really became evident. Spaniards heard resistance, stubbornness, truculence, or pagan disregard in Caddo "excuses" not to follow such Spanish dictates. More likely, it was bafflement that colored the Caddos' responses. In practical terms, they repeatedly explained that they had responsibilities and obligations to meet, that harvests, bison hunts, and the everyday responsibilities of life were ongoing and required their presence in their own homes, fields, and hamlets. Only blindly and blithely could Juan Antonio de la Peña conclude, as Aguayo left 6 missionaries, 125 men, and 31 women and their children living amidst 12,000 Caddoan peoples, "Thus was concluded the conquest, or recovery, of the entire province"![51]

Beyond the intermittent exchanges in response to the missionaries' queries about when the Caddos would come to the missions, everyday life went on, and the exigencies of that life brought other conflicts that had to be negotiated by Caddos and Spaniards. If one imagines the six missions and two presidios from a Caddo viewpoint as extended households scattered throughout their villages—the presidio of Los Adaes the only one large enough to equate with a Caddo hamlet by itself—the missions presented the greater obstacle to fitting into Caddo cultural categories. But that challenge was over and above the differences of religion. The Franciscans confounded the Caddo leaders' attempts to incorporate them into their communities, because missionaries did not fit neatly into any category reserved for nongoverning elite men within Caddo ranks.

The Hasinais had not initially recognized Spanish missionaries as priests in the 1690s. Fray Damián Mazanet wrote that Hasinais assumed that Spaniards were there only because of the "desirability [of their land], which [they think] is the best in the world," and thus their expectations of Spaniards were no different than they would have been for any men who wished to join their settlements. Because they "see no difference between the religious and laymen," Mazanet recorded, "many times they have told us [the missionaries] that if we will not go with them to war and to kill their enemies, then we should go back to our land." For Spaniards who had chosen to settle and live in Hasinai villages to refuse to uphold a key societal practice of men was to deny their gendered responsibilities. And if the Spaniards would not fight with them, then in return Hasinai men saw no reason to help the missionaries defend their horse and cattle herds when coastal "Guatsa" Indians raided them. At other times, Caddo leaders acknowledged Franciscans' claims of spiritual power and treated them as they would their own *connas*. When Mazanet and the other missionaries appeared to bring death to the Caddos with baptisms in the midst of the 1691 smallpox epidemic, Hasinais threatened to kill them, just as they might have done to their own priestly healers. Custom dictated that *connas* could be beaten to death by village or family members who lost a relative to sickness while under their care. Nevertheless, even when the Caddos understood Franciscans to be men of faith, the problem remained that the missionaries did not match the communal, much less spiritual, expectations Caddos had of their *connas*.[52]

What most complicated Spanish missionaries' standing within Caddo communities was the fact that they did not bring wives of their own, nor did they show any interest in unions with Caddo women. Elsewhere, as in New Mexico, other native peoples seem to have interpreted missionary celibacy as a sign of power, associating it with their customs of sexual abstinence preceding rituals of spirituality or warfare that were meant to concentrate male strength. But within Caddo society, sexual avoidance taboos did not exist, and a man's rank and honor were measured through bride service, his affinal relations, and his ability to offer hospitality, something a man could not do without a wife. These standards applied equally to Caddo

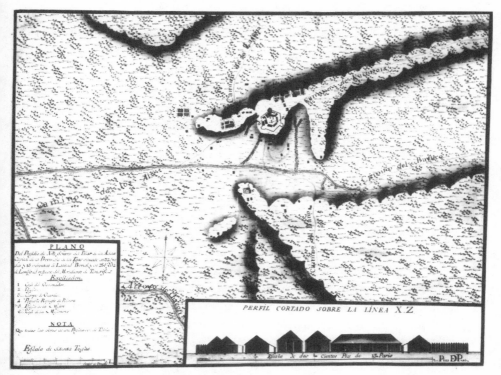

Plan of the Presidio Nuestra Señora del Pilar de los Adaes, which stood in the midst of Caddo territory until 1773, drawn by José de Urrutia, 1767. Courtesy of the Palace of the Governors (MNM/DCA), Santa Fe, New Mexico, neg. no. 15051.

religious elites, the *xinesís* and *connas*. In fact, the wives of *xinesís* held a special status of their own marked by the title "*aquidau*." In short, adult men without wives or female kin relations in Caddo society had no status among their matrilineally based clans. Celibate Spanish priests were in a helpless situation.[53]

In a Caddo world in which women controlled household and communal agricultural production, missionaries who lacked wives did not simply lack the ability to show other men hospitality, to offer feasts, or to contribute to communal celebrations and customary tributes owed to *xinesís*. Without any clan connection— available only through women—they also could not (and would not) practice the rituals so crucial to maintaining reciprocity and order with the spiritual world, such as the first fruits ceremony, that were performed within the household in honor of a clan's matrilineal kinship and the productivity of women's labor. In socioeconomic terms, the Franciscans became a drain on a community if their households (of missionaries and lay brothers) could not sustain themselves and relied on the generosity of others—that is, if they only took from, without contributing to, communal stores. Such seeming selfishness did not accord with Caddo conventions of mutual support and obligation that existed within the smaller clan villages and among different Caddo bands. Caddos customarily planted communal crops, along with those of individual households or clans, and gathered annually to plant crops for the *xinesí* and the principal *caddís*. Only *xinesís* and *caddís* merited such tribute, however, and for missionaries to ask it for themselves was to presume above their station.

Having failed to convince any Caddos to enter the mission as neophytes and thus provide the missions with a labor force, as happened in other areas of Spanish America, the Franciscans had no one but themselves and a few unwilling soldiers to work their fields. Without steady supplies from Mexico, missionaries had little to eat and, as fray Espinosa bemoaned, "abstinence commenced the first day" of arrival in Caddo lands. What little they did have came from Caddo charity, he continued, as "once in a while the Indians would give us a little corn, beans of a certain kind, and some wild fruits, which served to distract rather than to appease our hunger." "These Tejas Indians do not give us any help," fray Francisco Hidalgo similarly wrote with resignation. "They are content merely to visit us. The lack of necessities we suffer from, both food and assistance, we leave with God, who has thus decreed it." It was not the Caddos' rejection of Christianity, as missionaries imagined it to be, but their unwillingness to accord any special status to the newcomers, who were expected to be self-sufficient and contribute to the common weal just like everyone else. In a sense, that was the way to assume full-fledged membership within the villages. And it was impossible to be self-sufficient in Caddo society without women, who provided kin-based identity and agricultural productivity.[54]

In another twist, missionary labors often represented a reversal of gender roles in terms of Caddoan socioeconomics. Hasinai men periodically denigrated missionaries for performing women's work, mocking them outright when they saw friars tending herds of cattle, goats, and sheep; making adobe and building houses; and sowing maize, beans, and pumpkins. As one missionary explained, Hasinai men "did not esteem the padres as they ought to have done because, among themselves, all these menial household tasks are performed entirely by the women and children." Venerable fray Antonio Margil de Jesús, who worked among the Caddos during this period, also compared the work of missionaries in east Texas to that of women, saying that "they performed the duties of the women in New Spain by making corn cakes, usually called tortillas." Hasinai men, however, did not see the sphere of women's work as "menial" (that was the term used by missionaries); they directed their scorn not at the labor but at the overturning of the divisions between men and women, a sacred duality crucial to maintaining balance and order as ordained by their gods and laid out in their origin stories. In that world, Franciscans became sources, or potential sources, of cosmic disorder.[55]

Meanwhile, Spanish settlers often seemed no better off than the wifeless missionaries. Supplies came rarely, and fields proved more difficult to cultivate than anticipated. From Mission Concepción, fray Margil de Jesús pleaded to the viceroy in 1719, asking him to consider the lamentable image of "boy soldiers on foot, naked, and without arms, [which] causes them to be a laughingstock of the Indians themselves." The pitiable portrait he drew was the product of a lack of supplies in food, clothes, and arms—"not even a single musket" for three years—while the French by comparison distributed "hundreds" of guns in Caddo villages. In another bad supply season several years later, José González, the commander at the Los Adaes presidio, wrote to the provincial governor asking for relief for his soldiers' "wretched condition," dressed as they all were in only deerskins. To strengthen his plea, González went on to explain that "what grieves them most is seeing their wives and their children naked." "Some of the wives do not even go to church," he lamented, "because of their understandable embarrassment and shame." In times such as these, both the Franciscans at the missions and the soldiers and their families at the presidios needed whatever corn and agricultural produce that Caddoan peoples were willing to share.[56]

Caddo leaders might have expected the residents of the Spanish missions and presidios as a whole, or as individual homesteads, to act as a member village in the region. Each year, different Caddo bands came together after annual harvests to renew friendships and alliances. At these gatherings, each household made liberal contributions to the feasts that all would share, and each village provided goods that they might trade with others—ensuring that, in the exchange, everyone had an opportunity to acquire what their own settlements lacked. Yet, in the early years, Spaniards were often unable to be contributing participants in this system of communal feasting and exchange. Thus, in the Caddos' view, Spaniards brought little but disorder and imbalance. If they could not maintain their reciprocal obligations through trade or their own labors, they were, as a group, essentially the same as male individuals who, without wife or kin, became dependent upon society.[57]

Spaniards meanwhile measured the failure of their mission-presidio complexes by the complete absence of Hasinai conversions. Diplomatic strategists had imagined spiritual conversion to be a primary means of achieving the Caddos' alliance. Missionaries had been particularly encouraged in their aims by stories of the high level of Caddo "civilization"—marked by fields of cultivated crops, a well-developed culture, and a sedentary and productive population. To them, Hasinais already resembled Spaniards and so should convert all the more readily. In direct contradiction to such expectations, however, records indicate that the only baptisms took place *in articulo mortis* (at death); no healthy Hasinai chose to become a Christian. Some Franciscans recognized that the very characteristics that attracted them to Caddoan peoples were responsible for the missions' abysmal track record. Fray Ignacio Antonio Ciprián explained to his superiors in 1749 that the Hasinais' independent means of subsistence, trade with both Frenchmen and Spaniards, enough French firearms for defense, and dispersed settlement patterns, along with the absence of a Spanish force of arms to subject them to civil rule, meant the Caddos could stubbornly refuse to be "reduced" to mission life. Other missionaries explained their failures in east Texas in more culturally loaded terms, arguing that Caddos were "tied down by the cords of their superstition, ensnared in their lascivious lust," so that "they remain in voluntary blindness without deciding to open their eyes in the midst of the bright light which the apostolic doctrine opens up for them."[58]

Hasinais had no need for Spaniards as religious mentors, thereby confounding Spanish hopes and expectations. As measured by conversion numbers, the missions' failure was undeniable. In 1724–28, the viceroy sent an inspection team to assess the defensive needs and capabilities across New Spain's northern frontier, including the utility of its new mission-presidio complexes established among the Caddos. In the aftermath of his tour of the region, Inspector General Pedro de Rivera recommended that Presidio Nuestra Señora de los Dolores de los Tejas (located among the Hasinais) be "extinguished" and three of the missions (Nuestra Señora de la Purísima Concepción de los Hainais, Nuestro Padre San Francisco de los Neches—formerly "de los Tejas"—and San José de los Nazonis) be moved to the San Antonio area, where they might stand some chance of attracting neophytes. Almost fifteen years later, when Governor Tomás Felipe Winthuysen in 1744 surveyed the three missions that remained among the Caddos, he reported to Viceroy conde de Fuenclara that each and every one of them still "does not have and never has had a single Indian reduced to the mission." Clearly, he concluded, Caddos were "irreducible" to rule by the Spanish state or church; "since every effort that has been made to this end has failed, it is now considered an impossible undertaking."[59]

Yet, in a striking but subtle turnabout somewhere along the way in the 1720s and 1730s, these seeming failures ended up saving the Spanish settlement among the Hasinai confederacy. Once Spaniards let go of what they were supposed to be doing there—missionizing Indians and guarding against French encroachments—they could move in the right direction in Caddo terms of reciprocity, community, and interconnectedness. Not that anyone made a conscious conversion to the Caddo worldview, but they had little choice about the changes they had to make simply to survive. No neophytes (and thus no laborers) were ever going to materialize from among the Caddo populace. The sites of their missions and presidios, so carefully chosen by Aguayo, proved difficult landscapes in which to farm successfully, as corn crops failed year after year. High transportation costs and endangered supply routes from Coahuila all too often meant little material support from Mexico. Thus, Spanish settlers, soldiers, and missionaries did the only thing they could: they slowly but surely became participants in a "normative French-Caddoan symbiosis." In the process of adopting the socioeconomic changes necessary for survival, they implicitly recognized who was the real power in the region, adapted to the outlines of Caddo custom, and at last found acceptance in their lands.[60]

This transformative process began when Spanish residents de-emphasized agriculture as their primary subsistence economy and gave more attention to herding cattle, mules, horses, and sheep. As small-scale ranching developed, their homes spread out from Los Adaes into a dispersed settlement pattern much resembling that of their Caddo neighbors, with small ranches mixing with Caddo hamlets. Even some of the missions had their own ranches, including San Miguel de los Adaes's El Baño. One governor said the Los Adaes presidio reminded him more of a cattle pen than a military stockade because of its ranching orientation. In turn, individual as well as mission and presidio residents used the cattle and horses to trade with their Caddo and French neighbors for food staples. Annually, Natchitoches traders alone sold 200 barrels of corn, 60 barrels of beans, and 300 pounds of tobacco to Spaniards in the Los Adaes region. The more numerous Caddos likely traded even greater amounts to the Spaniards. Material goods too were forthcoming when Caddos traded hides and pelts and Frenchmen offered cloth, wine, and faience (enameled earthenware) in exchange for Spanish livestock.[61]

Spanish reorientation toward the Caddos' socioeconomic system was so complete that, during his 1727 inspection, Pedro de Rivera judged Spanish missions and presidios wholly unacceptable and declared that they merited removal or extinction according to his *Reglamento de 1729*. At the Presidio de los Tejas, which "consists of only a few huts of sticks and grass," he found all the soldiers "had been retired from guard duty for quite some time" and instead assigned to "cultivate the land, care for the few horses, and assist with the missions that pertained to the presidio because the missions lacked Indians [to do that labor]." Much was the same at Los Adaes, where because of the "calm nature" of the Caddos, one hundred men did little but guard the herds and assist the missions. Thus, Rivera recommended cutting the number of soldiers at Los Adaes by half and extinguishing the Tejas presidio entirely. When flipped on its head, however, the picture drawn by Rivera tells another story entirely. If there were no military jobs to be done there, Spaniards by 1727 were living in peace with both Caddos and Frenchmen. The presidios looked more like extended family homesteads by Caddo standards, not least because the Tejas presidio was built by Caddo construction—those "huts of sticks and grass"—but also because they now combined subsistence farming with raising horses and cattle for trade. Moreover, when Franciscans from the nearby missions petitioned against the suppression of the Presidio de los Tejas, they did not mention needing the protection of the soldiers' arms. Rather, they wanted the soldiers to aid them "with their example" by clearing fields, drawing water from streams for irrigation, and building their homes all together—an example of a self-sufficient household by any Caddo estimation.[62]

The small civilian and presidial population of Los Adaes that remained after 1730 became absorbed into Caddo-French trading networks, albeit unofficially, as Spanish law prohibited trade with French Louisiana. In 1730 and again in 1740, governors of Texas made official pleas to their superiors asking that, in view of the hardships of trade and the prohibitive cost of transporting goods from Saltillo, the decrees against the French trade be rescinded. Both times, viceregal officials agreed to allow commerce with Natchitoches but specified that the Adaesanos could purchase only corn, beans, and other foodstuffs. Not surprisingly, given the remoteness of the settlement, contraband as well as licit trade continued apace between Los Adaes and Natchitoches. The number of investigations of illegal trading by Spanish settlers— up to and including several governors of the province, whose official seat of government remained in Los Adaes until 1773—reflected the incorporation of Spaniards into the economic world of the Caddo villages surrounding them and the French traders who lived and worked there. In the resulting three-way relationship lay the salvation of Spanish standing among Caddoan peoples. Striking too, rather than the migration of Native Americans to, and concentration around, European trading posts seen in other areas of eighteenth-century North America, French and Spanish settlement patterns made clear that Caddo villages were the nuclei of their dependent populations, relying on the well-established Caddoan trade networks to maintain and extend their economic ventures.[63]

Missionaries too crafted roles for themselves among the Spanish, French, and Caddo villages. If they could not have families of their own at the missions, they each had two soldiers with their wives and children to live with them. Defending themselves against complaints from church superiors, Franciscans gently pointed out that the Holy Gospel did not command them to convert but only to preach. To do that, they learned two Caddoan languages and spent their days and weeks traveling through Caddo hamlets, most often during times of illness, so that they might care for the sick and baptize those who accepted the Christian sacrament at death (more than half of whom were children). After the removal of three missions in 1731, the Franciscans traveled even farther, going ten, fourteen, and twenty leagues at a time to make their visits. Caddos came to their homes to see them too, according to Franciscan reports, and during these visits listened to the missionaries without "displeasure," even as they remained true to their own beliefs. Some Caddos came to believe that baptism might be a curative for restoring health and absorbed it into Caddo spiritual understandings. In this way, missionaries did become a version of *connas* among the Caddos, emphasizing the healing elements of their mission and prayers. Even they recognized that they had earned this role in Caddo villages. Knowing as they did that death might await a *conna* who failed to heal, missionaries recorded that it was a sign of divine providence that no Franciscans had died at Caddo hands over the years. By midcentury, they viewed their work as a success and reason enough not to leave, despite still empty missions, concluding that "we have won them with love." Having won Caddo friendship, they had not lost them completely to the French—a much down-scaled version of their original goals. Spanish missionaries too married, baptized, and buried the French as well as Spanish residents of Natchitoches and Los Adaes through the 1760s. In that way, they tied themselves to those families and in their own way built bridges between the two communities.[64]

Local French-Spanish ties might also extend to military aid, even if not to alliance, which in a roundabout way solidified Spanish standing in the Caddos' minds. In 1731, for instance, the Natchitoches post found itself one of the targets of attack by Natchez warriors during a large-scale war later known as the Natchez Uprising. French and Natchitoches families from the surrounding hamlets crowded into the fort in such numbers that St. Denis emptied out the storehouse, requisitioned habitants' harvests, and killed all his oxen and cattle to feed the women and children. Responding to the call of Natchitoches warriors and of St. Denis, Hasinai warriors from multiple villages and Spanish soldiers from Los Adaes arrived to aid the fort's defense during the twenty-two-day siege. At the battle's conclusion, St. Denis sought to extend the bounty of the French-Caddo captive-slave trade to Spaniards and sent Governor Juan Antonio Bustillo y Ceballos a gift of several captive Natchez women. Again, an exchange of women sealed a bond of brotherhood.[65]

Even if Spaniards and Caddos did not intermarry, moreover, marital unions between members of the Spanish and French communities became increasingly common. Perhaps in the Caddos' eyes, such unions extended the kin status of their French allies to Spaniards. If Spaniards did not rank as true "brothers," they might be considered brothers-in-law. Given the importance Caddos placed on marriage ties, St. Denis's marriage to Manuela Sánchez Navarro back in 1716 proved the first of several politically significant unions between Spanish and French individuals that further united the two European communities and their Caddo hosts. In 1736, Jean Baptiste Derbanne (who had grown up among Caddos as the métis son of François Derbanne and Chitimacha Jeanne de la Grande Terre) eloped with Victoire Marguerite González, the daughter of the Spanish post commander at Los Adaes, José González. Marie des Neges de St. Denis, the daughter of St. Denis and Manuela Sánchez Navarro, married Spanish trader Manuel Antonio de Soto Bermúdez, who moved to Natchitoches and, with French partners, maintained commerce with Akokisa bands south of the Caddos' territory. Sacramental records for Natchitoches show growing numbers of such unions as the century progressed.[66]

From these well-placed unions to others involving soldiers, traders, and civilians, kinship increasingly tied the Spanish and French populations together and in turn contributed to the acceptance of the small Spanish population into Caddo orbits as fictive or extended kin. Meanwhile, a majority of Spanish civil, church, and military officials refocused their energy south to a new settlement region. By 1731, southern rather than eastern Texas had emerged as the center of Spanish-Indian relations focused on mission-presidio developments. In that year, the transfer of the three missions from Caddo lands to San Antonio de Béxar—renamed Missions Nuestra Señora de la Purísima Concepción de Acuña, San Juan de Capistrano, and San Francisco de la Espada—joined Missions San José y San Miguel de Aguayo and San Antonio de Valero and Presidio San Antonio de Béxar to make that focus a material reality. Both Caddo rejection of the missions in their own lands and diplomatic overtures of Indian peoples in the southern parts of the region led to this Spanish shift to the valleys along the San Antonio River. This settlement center would be the only part of the region where Spaniards could realistically claim some measure of control, but that assertion would rely upon the alliance with numerous Indian peoples who, over the course of the eighteenth century, made up the majority of the population, both inside and outside Spanish mission-presidio complexes.

PART TWO

From Contact to Conversion:
Bridging Religion and Politics, 1720s–1760s

The spring of 1709 offered a bounty of bison for groups of Cantonas, Yojuanes, Simaomos, Tusonibis, Emets, Cavas, Sanas, Tohahas, Tohos, Payayas, and many other peoples who moved seasonally through the lands around a central Texas river later known as the Colorado.[1] In fact, there were so many bison herds on both sides of the river that about two thousand people had gathered together into one en-campment while they pursued their hunting. The combined numbers allowed them to hunt more effectively while at the same time maintaining defensive safe-guards for their children and elders against Apache raiders who might contest the hunting territory. No time lacked hardship, and mourning rituals following the death of four community members had recently required moving the extensive camp ten miles in order to put distance between the living and the site of the burials. Yet, wood for the temporary housing was plentiful, and they had quickly rebuilt 150 large, solid, and circular jacales (thatched grass huts) into yet another ranchería, or seasonal encampment, in the customary shape of a half moon. Prospects looked good for a spring and summer free of hunger, following the herds on their slow and meandering progression northward with the shifting growing season of regional grasslands.

Not ten days after the deaths, however, peace was again disrupted when two youths came rushing into camp one morning to tell their seniors of a possible threat south of the river. While out scouting the day before, they had seen copious amounts of smoke—clearly from people making no attempt to hide their presence—and had quickly gone to investigate. They had followed the direction of the smoke and by nightfall had arrived near an encampment. They kept a cautious distance, since they feared it might be a camp of Apache raiders from the northwest, who in recent years increasingly menaced their peoples' hunting territories. Proudly the two boys explained that they had watched for movements at the camp, gradually approaching until they recognized—still at a safe distance—the distinctive military dress of a Spanish war leader. Once they had ascertained the identity and number of the newcomers, perhaps ten to fifteen men, they raced the twelve miles home to report their discovery.

Spaniards were preferable to Apaches, but recent conflicts over native refugees who had fled from Spanish religious settlements in the south to join relatives among the loosely united groups meant that peaceful interaction was not assured. Two years before, a Spanish war party had come to retake some of these refugees and "recruit" others by force, and thus relations were tenuous. Many in the encampment could have told stories of past encounters with the strangers. It had been almost ten years since a Spanish warrior, José de Urrutia, had left them after spending seven years in their camps. He had come to them wounded, and after nursing him back to health, they had taught him their languages, and he had chosen to live among them. Fighting side by side with their warriors against Apaches, he had proved an invaluable source for better understanding the foreigners to the south. He might be gone, but several principal men now had personal knowledge and experience with Spaniards and could act as interpreters. They chose one in particular, a Cantona leader, to head a delegation of seventy-seven Cantonas, Yojuanes, Simaomos, and Tusonibis quickly assembled to greet the Spanish party and discover what purpose had brought them so far north.

In the morning, they prepared to depart by gathering together gifts given them in the past by Spaniards—carvings, paintings, and banners—that they could display to signal peace and assuage possible Spanish fears about such a large group approaching the small camp. An early start ensured that they would cover the twelve miles in good time to arrive at the camp in the morning. The Cantona leader rode a horse while the others paced around and behind him on foot. Once they were in sight of the camp, those in the lead formed a single line, with the Spanish gifts held aloft and in clear sight—first, a bamboo cross, and then, two painted images and one engraving, all of a Spanish female deity in blue with light radiating out all around her. To complete the greetings, they approached the Spanish men—only seven or eight of them were there—and embraced them and touched their faces. Addressed simply as "Cantona" by the Spaniards, the party leader soon ascertained that the spiritual and war leaders of the Spaniards were away from camp but were expected to return by the end of the day. Forty delegation members chose to await their return in order to speak with them, and the other thirty-seven returned home to report events to their colleagues and families.

After dark, the missing Spaniards finally stumbled into camp. They had apparently gotten lost in the forest but happily had enjoyed a successful hunt, bringing back six bison carcasses with them, enough for a feast for themselves and their guests. Cantona and his colleagues embraced the newcomers in greeting, and the Spaniards honored them in return with gifts of tobacco, according to hospitable custom. Cantona received something further—a silvered-headed cane in recognition of his position of authority. Since night had fallen, the Indian delegation decided to stay at the Spanish camp until morning, using the time in between to talk with three Spanish officials: war leader Pedro de Aguirre and priests Isidro de Espinosa and Antonio de Olivares. Over the course of discussions, the Spaniards quickly made clear that they came not in search of more refugees but of news of Hasinais to the northeast, information the delegation could ably provide. Cantona explained that, no, the rumors about Hasinai migrations southward were false. No Hasinais had even joined them for the hunt this year, as they often had in the past, and they remained in the same villages they had occupied for untold years. Additionally, he felt obligated by his ties to Hasinai allies to tell the Spaniards that neither they nor any other Spanish people would find themselves welcome if they were to attempt to visit the Hasinai villages. Hasinai leaders well remembered the Spanish insults and conflicts of sixteen years before.

The news seemed to disappoint the Spaniards, and in the morning they announced plans to return south. Cantona and his colleagues quickly pointed out that the Spanish party had not yet visited their ranchería—where women, elders, and children as well as men awaited their appearance, as custom required. Recalled to their diplomatic obligations, the three Spanish leaders agreed to accompany the delegation home while seven of the soldiers remained behind to begin packing up the camp. Continuing to use the cross and three images of the female deity as a signal of the peaceful endeavor of the now combined party of Indians and Spaniards, they traveled across the country, following Cantona's mounted lead. Another horseman, watching for their return, rode up as soon as they came within sight of the ranchería to confirm their identity before returning to the village to alert everyone of their arrival. People poured forth from the jacales, men leaving all arms behind and raising their hands in the air as both a greeting and an assurance of disarmament for the foreign men, who appeared intimidated by the size of the ranchería and the number coming forward to meet them. Men, women, and children soon surrounded the visitors, shouting their welcome, embracing them, caressing their faces and arms and then their own, making sure to include the faces of babies and infants in the exchange of caresses. The women then graciously accepted gifts of tobacco from their courteous guests, while allowing their children to take sweets from the strangers, now acknowledged as friends.

Unable to stay long, the Spaniards soon decided to return to their camp, and, when asked, delegation leaders agreed to accompany them in order to conclude their diplomatic discussions. Cantona soon discovered that the Spaniards wished him to take a message and a gift to Hasinai leaders in the form of one of their customary icons. The two priests quickly assembled a cross out of paper and then decorated and painted it, asking Cantona to pass it along to Hasinai caddís. They wished him to extend an *invitation to Caddo leaders to come enjoy the hospitality of their rancherías to the south. They seemed to hope Cantona's influence might carry weight with the* caddís, *since they asked him further to show them the silver-headed cane he had accepted as a gift from them. Since he and his people would meet with some Hasinais after the hunting season to trade bison meat and hides in exchange for agricultural produce, such a request could easily be met, so Cantona agreed. He had warned the Spaniards of his Hasinai allies' lack of receptivity to their overtures, so he assumed they understood the likelihood of yet another rejection. Cantona and the other leaders were more interested in maintaining peaceful relations with the Spaniards, because if Apache raiders continued to cause them problems, one day soon they might need all the allies they could get. Spaniards, though few in number, at least came with guns and horses. Their Apache foes did not have guns, so those were less crucial, but horses were becoming increasingly important, and at present, they had only a few. Yes, the possibility of Spanish alliance bore consideration. . . .*

This story takes us back in time to 1709, just before the Caddos allowed Spaniards to return to their lands, in order to introduce early exchanges between some of the Indian peoples living in the area of present-day central Texas and some of the Spaniards marching to and from Caddo lands. Following their eviction from Hasinai villages, Spaniards had fallen back to the Rio Grande, where they built a presidio and three missions: the Presidio de San Juan Bautista and the Missions San Juan Bautista, San Francisco Solano, and San Bernardo. That location provided a base for Spanish expeditions into Texas for the next twenty years. In the 1710s, as Spanish expeditions renewed their treks into Caddo lands to challenge French claims to Caddo alliance, their routes took them through the territories of Cantonas, Payayas, and many others in and around joint settlements that the Spaniards referred to as "Ranchería Grande." These native peoples were tied into far-ranging, multiethnic coalitions made up of small subset populations of mobile hunting and gathering bands, who together controlled chosen geographic regions and resources. The information networks that stretched throughout those coalitions were as attractive to Spanish officials as their souls were to Franciscan missionaries.[2]

"*Ranchería grande*" was at first a general Spanish term for the kind of confederated, semisedentary encampments they found in that area of Texas. But they soon came to use it to specify certain bands of Indians they encountered time and again encamped at different sites between the Colorado and Brazos Rivers as they traveled more frequently through the region after 1709. As a result of those encounters, a series of negotiations began between Spaniards and affiliated Indian peoples that eventually led to the establishment of three shared settlements of Spaniards and

Indians based around San Antonio de Béxar. The choices made by these native peoples illustrate a new way that Indian families determined mission-presidio complexes to be of use to their survival. They meant the settlements founded with Spaniards to be a means of formalizing an alliance, not of declaring subordination to Spanish rule. As fray Benito Fernández de Santa Ana explained to his superiors, the Indians of the region who joined mission settlements "want no subjection to royalty. . . . Their first interest is in temporal comfort." So, why did their response to Spanish missions, tempered though it was, differ so much from that of the Hasinais?[3]

Different communal and social patterns as well as more recent demographic decline and increasing threats from Apache encroachment set the stage for native peoples of central Texas to view Spanish diplomatic overtures in a new light. Like the Caddos, they had suffered population losses, but theirs had been more recent and more destructive. Indian bands living in southern and central Texas in the 1700s had also coalesced into confederacies for greater strength, subsistence, and defense. Yet, unlike Caddoan peoples, their socioeconomic systems had resulted in political structures less centralized and less hierarchical than the three Caddo confederacies. Most striking of all, the experiences of many of the Indians (such as Cantonas and Payayas) reflected the impact their societies had already sustained from a Spanish presence south of the Rio Grande during the seventeenth century.[4]

The rituals enacted in the 1709 meeting hint at their prior experiences with Spaniards. The carefully orchestrated use of a cross and the iconography of the Virgin of Guadalupe by Cantonas, Yojuanes, Simaomos, and Tusonibis might appear to echo the early contacts of Caddos and Spaniards, but in fact a different political context put a different spin on the use of Spanish symbols. Like the Hasinais, these native leaders had their own uses for the icons and rosaries given to them by previous Spanish expeditions. In this native world, it was not the female gender of the Virgin's image that connoted peace. Instead, the iconography represented former gifts that had been given and accepted by male leaders in friendly exchange and now served as mnemonic icons of that previous, peaceful encounter. The more loosely structured confederations of these hunting and gathering bands— who coalesced and dispersed seasonally over the year—required that "groups and individuals maintain a vast network of friendly contacts, that individuals be easily identified while traveling, and that people abide by recognized and expected behavioral rules." With such expectations, the crosses carried by Spaniards became a kind of passport in that native region.[5]

Spaniards thus found crosses, rather than the standard and its image of the Virgin, to hold greater meaning for native leaders of central Texas. In 1691, Spaniards traveling on their way to the Hasinai villages had passed through a Payaya encampment where a tall wooden cross had been erected in the midst of their jacales. The inhabitants explained that they knew Spaniards put crosses in their houses and settlements in order to please or appease their gods, so they hoped similar spiritual benefits might accrue to their community if they did the same.[6] Perhaps they endowed the talisman from the south with power in order to deal with dangers from the south—disease and marauding Spanish soldiers. More often, crosses became symbols of diplomacy. In 1716, five hundred Payayas, Cantonas, Pamayas, Erviamames, Xarames, Sijames, and Mescales took Spanish missionaries to a *ranchería grande*, shared food and traded with them, and marked the site of the peaceful exchange with a wooden cross.[7] The Spaniards responded in kind, using crosses to announce their passage through the region. In 1719, Spaniards recorded that "Some crosses were left on the trees for the Indians as a sign, and on them some leaves of tobacco were hung, in order that, coming to reconnoiter, they would see that we were Spaniards."[8]

Why the later preference for crosses over images of the Virgin? As opposed to Spanish-Caddo contacts that had begun in peace and then were interrupted by violence, Indians of south and central Texas had had only violent encounters with Spaniards in the seventeenth century. For them, peace had to be forged in an atmosphere of distrust and suspicion. Cantonas, Payayas, and their multiple allies never had the chance to read (or misread) the Virgin Mary as a female symbol of greeting. Their earliest exposure to the Spanish standard had been in war—war waged by Spanish raiders or militias who, throughout the seventeenth century, crossed the Rio Grande bent on capturing Indian men, women, and children and imprisoning them for work camps or missions, two indistinguishable institutions from an Indian perspective. If they had singled out the Virgin, she would have resonated more with sixteenth-century Spanish imagery of *La Conquistadora*. When these Indian peoples later zeroed in on the cross as a diplomatic symbol to use with Spaniards, they did not choose the iconography of a male Jesus over a female Mary. Rather, they chose crosses based on their own diplomatic protocols. Crosses were the gifts received from more recent, and more peaceful, Spaniards, and their protocols called for a display of past exchange items if and when such peaceful visitors returned.[9]

These Indians peoples, their parents, and their grandparents had suffered at the hands of Spaniards long before this new round of contacts began in the eighteenth century. The advance of the Spanish frontier northward into present-day Nueva Vizcaya, Coahuila, and Nuevo León over the sixteenth and seventeenth centuries had gradually pushed Indian peoples northward. Yet, it was not Spanish settlement but the spread of European diseases and the intrusion of slave-raiding expeditions seeking forced labor for Spanish mines and ranches—inexorable forces that preceded much of the colonization of those northern regions—that put native peoples in flight. Epidemics that began in the 1550s had, by the 1700s, decimated native populations across northern regions of Mexico, scything their numbers by 90 percent.[10] Over the same period, Spanish demands for labor in their farms, ranches, and mines brought its own brand of annihilation. By 1600, trafficking in enslaved Indians had become an established way of life in Nuevo León. Then, once the Spanish population had killed off all the nearby Indian peoples by congregating them in crowded, unsanitary work camps where they died from disease or overwork, the Spaniards extended the relentless reach of their slave raids northward.[11]

To escape that reach, remnants of multiple bands who had lost family and community to death or enslavement gradually moved northward in search of new lands, new hunting territories, and new consolidations of kin and alliance. Although they had originally lived in regions far different and distant from one another—some native to the region, others migrants from lands ranging across present-day northeastern Mexico—multiple groups had coalesced in shared, mobile encampments in northeastern Coahuila and south Texas. By the end of the seventeenth century, south Texas provided sanctuary for an impressively diverse if ravaged congregation of native peoples and displaced refugees. Yet, their northward progression put them in the path of another danger: newly mounted Apaches from farther northwest, whose own hunting and raiding economy brought them south, following the migrations of bison herds and the lure of Spanish horses. In response, natives and refugees increasingly consolidated their numbers for communal shelter, subsistence, and defense in south and central Texas.

The resultant hunting and gathering groups tended to live in small, family-based bands, moving regularly in response to seasonal subsistence patterns in specific territorial areas. The small size and geographical dispersion required by their socioeconomic systems limited their social and political organization, yet many groups maintained both smaller camps made up of individual ethnic groups and, at other times, larger shared settlements where two or more groups came together for purposes of hunting and defense. Archaeological evidence indicates that both types of settlement existed during the precontact period, but shared encampments became notably more frequent during the late seventeenth and early eighteenth centuries, reflecting the upheavals caused by Spanish and Apache invasions.[12]

These shared encampments and shifting group associations have made identifying the linguistic and cultural affiliations of many of these peoples difficult and often impossible. The language and ethnic origins of the Cantona groups encountered by the Espinosa-Olivares-Aguirre expedition in 1709, for example, are a mystery. From 1690 onward, they shared settlements variously with Caynaaya, Cholomé, Cíbola, and Jumano peoples from western Texas, with Coahuilteco speakers such as Payayas, Xarames, Mescales, and Ervipiames who had migrated from northeastern Mexico, with Tonkawa speakers such as Cavas, Emets, Sanas, and Tohahas from north-central Texas, and with Wichita speakers such as Yojuanes who had migrated from north of the Red River in Oklahoma.[13] Such relationships among so many different peoples leave scholars to guess at the parties with whom Cantonas may have shared the closest ties.[14]

For a long time, many scholars erroneously referred to *all* hunting and gathering peoples of northeastern Mexico and south Texas—those most noted in association with Spanish missions at San Juan Bautista, Coahuila, and at San Antonio, Texas—as "Coahuiltecans," implying a linguistic and cultural relationship unifying untold numbers of people merely by their regional location and periodic residence in the missions there. Recent research, however, has shown that in fact this myriad of native peoples represented hundreds of small, autonomous bands who may have shared certain general traits but whose local and regional variations differenti-ated them quite distinctly. Most notably, at least seven different language groups—Coahuilteco, Karankawa, Comecrudo, Cotoname, Solano, Tonkawa, and Aranama—can be distinguished in Spanish records. Part of the scholarly confusion arose because the ties that developed among these peoples—begun in their shared en-campments and continued in the missions—eventually led to the use of Coahuilteco as the lingua franca by the late eighteenth century. Yet, beyond consideration either as a broad regional categorization or as a language group, the term "Coahuiltecan" cannot be used accurately to define a single group of people. As one archaeologist asserts, "We know a little about many of the Coahuiltecan groups but not much about any one of them—or any one aspect of their lifeway." Such a quandary testifies not only to the tragic consequences of European disease but also to the success of native confederations.[15]

In addition to the multiple allies and neighbors of Cantonas and Payayas in south and central Texas, coastal-dwelling Indian peoples also established on-again, off-again relations with Spanish Franciscans. These were marine-adapted hunting and gathering groups who lived along the present-day Gulf coast of Texas: Akokisas, Aranamas, Atakapas, Bidais, and Karankawas (who included Cocos, Copanes, Cu-janes, Coapites, and Karankawas proper). Similar to the Indian groups of south Texas, these peoples lived in small, kin-based bands moving strategically between the mainland, coast, and barrier islands to take advantage of a variety of key re-sources when and where they were most abundant. They spent the spring and

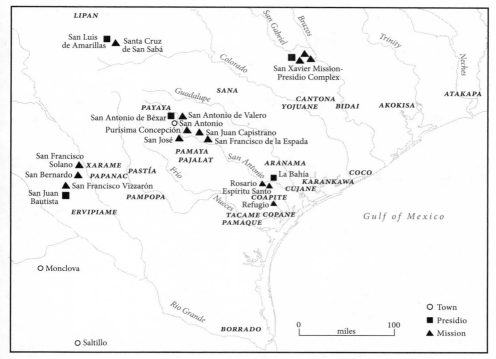

Territories and locations of Indian peoples who used the Spanish missions at San Juan Bautista, San Antonio de Béxar, and La Bahía as joint settlements. Map drawn by Melissa Beaver.

summer months dispersed for seasonal subsistence rounds in the salt marshes and upland prairies of the coastal plains, where they hunted bison, deer, and small animals and gathered nuts, roots, fruits, and greens. In the harsher months of fall and winter, though, they congregated together in estuarine bays, lagoons, and a narrow chain of barrier islands along the coast to form large fishing encampments focused on saltwater fish and shellfish. The islands also offered invaluable defensive positions for confederated settlements against native and European enemies alike. Unlike others, they did not feel the full brunt of Apache expansion into the south-central regions of Texas.[16]

The strategy of seeking safety in shared settlements may have encouraged many of the central and coastal native peoples to consider Spaniards possible partners or allies in a new form of mutual encampment via mission-presidio complexes. It can be no coincidence that the heart of Spanish missionary settlements in Texas took hold at a site long used for shared encampment, shelter, hunting, and defense—a site that natives called "Yanaguana" and Spaniards would come to call "San Antonio de

Béxar." It was in the mid-eighteenth century that crosses became political tools of truce and later symbols marking the sites of diplomatic alliance between Spaniards and Indian peoples. Yet, that transformation—sought by the joint efforts of Spanish and Indian leaders alike—was never complete. The early battles against European disease and Spanish raiding parties colored the eighteenth-century struggles of Indian men and women as they sought to maintain not only the physical but also the social and cultural integrity of their families from within the fortifications of missions. Although we tend to assume missions were European-directed spaces in which Indians could only "resist," the power relations within mission-presidio complexes of south and central Texas clarify how Indians could, in fact, exert control over the terms by which they lived together with Spaniards. In this setting, a different kind of tightrope bridged Spanish and Indian visions of male and female behaviors to define their carefully negotiated steps toward peaceful coexistence at midcentury.

chapter three

Civil Alliance and "Civility"
in Mission-Presidio Complexes

The exigencies of daily life in south-central Texas—a world fundamentally shaped by the regular occurrence of epidemic diseases and Apache raiders—led Spanish and Indian peoples to join forces for survival and defense beginning in the 1720s. Mission-presidio complexes provided the locus of such alliances. Once they had all been brought together, the five missions, presidio, and Spanish villa along the San Antonio River "form[ed] one community," fray Benito Fernández de Santa Ana claimed in 1740. Another community of Spanish and Indian settlers developed around the missions and presidio of La Bahía, closer to the coast. From the perspective of Spanish record keepers, these locales looked like familiar sites of religious conversion and regional defense as set up throughout New Spain. From the perspective of semipermanent native residents, the communities looked equally familiar, but as sites for socioeconomic alliance and communal ritual that existed across southern Texas and northern Coahuila. Though known by their Spanish names and with architecture outwardly reflecting the form of Spanish institutions, the native use of the community complexes resembled far more the joint settlements and confederated encampments that had been customary in the region long before the arrival of Europeans.

Indian peoples of southern and coastal Texas were no more inclined to forsake their settlement and subsistence patterns than the Caddos, but their socioeconomic systems allowed them to integrate part-time residence at missions into their seasonal calendars. From the 1720s through the 1760s, many never joined Spaniards in their settlements, however, and most made only periodic visits to the complexes as part of their annual subsistence cycles. For those who did visit, Spanish missions suited a different kind of settlement-as-alliance strategy, as Spanish and Indian men agreed to bring their wives and children together in shared communities. The transitory residence of south-central natives and the greater vulnerability to Apache raids felt equally by

Indians and Spaniards gave Indian peoples the power to exert control over their relations with Spaniards—power that would be grounded in the gendered terms by which they would live together.[1]

Over the middle years of the eighteenth century, Coahuilteco-, Tonkawa-, and Karankawa-speaking peoples incorporated the sites of Spanish missions into an old pattern of subsistence, seasonal migration, settlement, and alliance. Indian families sought a semisedentary encampment where they could gather to acquire food, shelter, and defense. By their own custom, aggregate settlements were the locations for annual or biannual practices that served to renew alliances through communal rituals of healing and spirituality, exchange, joint hunting expeditions, and feasts. These gatherings also offered the opportunity for courtship and intermarriage that extended economic and political relations into the realm of kinship. Indians brought similar expectations to the settlements established with Spaniards, but they were not always met. Constant problems with the supply of material goods and foodstuffs promised by missionaries, the encroachment of ranches and farms into traditional hunting territories, the growing threat of Apache raiders attracted by Spanish cattle and horse herds, and the far more deadly threat of European diseases all fatally detracted from the initial appeal of mission-presidio complexes. Spaniards also put conditions on the exchanges they were willing to make with their new Indian allies. They tried to assert that their own practices and ceremonies take precedence over native ones within the confines of the settlements.

Spaniards thus fundamentally challenged native notions as to the form that joint settlements should take. Franciscans who came to Texas in the eighteenth century saw the "civilization," or what historians have referred to as "hispanization," of Indians as crucial to the process of Christian conversion. Their mission was twofold: first, teaching the fundamentals of Christian worship and administering the holy sacraments; second, the more temporal task of instructing Indians in how to live as Christians, or more aptly, as Spaniards. The hispanization program endeavored to instill conditions in the lives of Indians that would encourage a "virtuous" life: recognition and respect for royal government and law; life in a communal, town setting; Euroamerican material accoutrements, such as dress and housing; and Euroamerican familial and sexual practices, particularly monogamy formalized through a marriage ceremony. The temporal training of Indians, fray Mariano de los Dolores y Viana explained, would teach them "to live the common and civilized life," a necessary lesson, because "without the human strength the spiritual would not be gained." Similar to their opposition to syncretism in religious concepts or rituals, missionaries did not imagine it possible to interweave Indian and Spanish social practice.

Instead, they believed that Indians' "savage" lifeways had to be destroyed and replaced with Euroamerican customs congruent with Christian ethics and morals.[2]

Yet, the contest between differing visions of social organization took place within an unstable demographic and geopolitical setting that limited both the Spaniards' ability to assert their demands and the degree to which any Indians would commit to joint settlements with them. This period was marked by disease repeatedly cycling through Spanish settlements, hitting native residents the hardest, and economic instability caused by fitful Spanish supply routes and Apache raids disrupting efforts at agriculture, ranching, and trade with other Spanish provinces to the south. Disease exacted the greatest devastation, as Indian populations faced epidemics in the region at least once every decade. When that was combined with low fertility rates, high infant mortality, and high female mortality in childbirth, records indicate that, until the 1780s, only the recruitment of new residents maintained a "nominal stability" in Indian populations living in San Antonio. When the Spanish alliance did not meet their material needs or set terms that they were unwilling to meet, many Indians left to rejoin relatives and allies in settlements elsewhere. Most kept their visits to the missions brief and while present expressed but a superficial and temporary adherence to Spanish practices. Thus, missions functioned solely as a temporary seasonal base at which individuals and family bands could meet periodically to marshal resources, intermarry, and regroup socially and culturally. With families moving in and out of the missions on a constant basis, Franciscans negotiated their hoped-for reforms with peoples who could and did remain closely tied to their own customs and belief systems. Equally important, when Indians were in residence, the subsistence and defense needs of the mission populace continued to rely upon native socioeconomic and military knowledge and skills. Although Franciscans urged Indian men and women to abandon their customary norms and behaviors as a step toward "civilization," the survival of Spanish and Indian populations in and around the missions often depended precisely upon the maintenance of native gender conventions.[3]

Constructions of masculinity and femininity lay at the heart of Spanish "civilization," while gender was equally important to Indian conceptions of who they were as peoples and cultures. As a result, the customs that missionaries most sought to change were the ones that Indians most sought to maintain. Thus, the struggle over the terms governing their joint settlements more often than not drew its battle lines along contrasting notions of manhood and womanhood. Still, the realities of a world defined by European disease and Apache raids meant that the battles of eighteenth-century daily life did not end up waged over competing concepts of civilization (or God); they were fights for safety and subsistence. In that contest, native-dictated patterns of domestic and diplomatic alliance were crucial to both Spanish and Indian survival and thereby proved to carry the day.

On August 16, 1727, two days after recording that they had crossed the "creek of Los Payayas, named for a nation of Indians who live much of their lives on it," Pedro de Rivera and his inspection team rode up to the Presidio San Antonio de Béxar. Two "small pueblos" of Indians each stood about a mile away, one to the northeast, the other to the southwest, both inhabited by Mesquites, Payayas, and Aguastayas. Each was associated with a different mission: one with San Antonio de Valero, the other with San José y San Miguel de Aguayo. Yet, to observer Rivera, it was not two missions but two Indian settlements that stood in company with the presidio. In similar language four years later, fray Benito Fernández de Santa Ana recorded the transfer of three nominal missions from Caddo lands as the addition of three "Indian villages" side by side with the newly named Spanish villa of San Fernando de Béxar along the river.[4]

Indian names as well as settlements dominated the landscape, marking the land as theirs. Located in the "best position of any [he] had seen," Rivera remarked upon San Antonio's potential for farming and ranching but found that fifty-three soldiers, a captain, and two lieutenants at the presidio spent all their time on military patrols and convoys aimed at holding off Apache raiders from "*la Lomería*," the hill country to the northwest of the settlement. Rivera's emphasis on the predominance of soldiers among the Spaniards, the lack of a civilian population, the location of the presidio situated to contain the "*Apaches de la Lomería*," and the soldiers' constant occupation in patrols and convoys indicated that the joint settlement looked most like a defensive fortification. Moreover, he noted in his report the *potential* rather than present use of the land for farming and ranching as well as the need for "people to work the land." Apparently, the Spanish and Indian settlers did not yet have significant crops or cattle under cultivation, and the Indians were not providing the labor force expected by the Spaniards. Tellingly, Rivera observed, the countryside and its rivers offered an abundance of wild animals, particularly bison and deer, but also bears, turkeys, and catfish, suggesting that the actual sources of subsistence were hunting and fishing. Along with the military men's wives and children and four civil residents, Governor Fernando Pérez de Almazán estimated the total Spanish population to be about 200 by 1726. Six years before, Juan Antonio de la Peña had recorded that the two Indian settlements at Valero and San José had 240 and 227 residents, respectively (and that number did not include the neighboring Indian settlement at Ranchería Grande); thus, the Indian population, when present, was more than twice the size of its Spanish neighbors. Pointedly, when Rivera discovered that the presidial captain had stationed two soldiers at each mission settlement to assist in defense, he deemed this protection unnecessary, given the presence of able Indian warriors among the residents. Altogether, the picture Rivera painted was one of Spanish and Indian settlements side by side, living in close proximity in a mutually dependent relationship of subsistence and defense.[5]

How had those allied but still separate Spanish and Indian communities come into being in the nine years preceding Rivera's visit? Individual negotiations between officials of the Spanish church and state and the male heads of different family bands had created the settlements one by one. The first mission-presidio complex in this area of Texas officially appeared in 1718, when Franciscans transferred Mission San Francisco Solano, originally established in northeastern Coahuila in 1700, to a site called "Yanaguana" by Xarames, Payayas, and Pamayas. The community there would be known as Mission San Antonio de Valero by Spaniards. Ten Spanish soldiers and their families along with seventy members of the Xarame, Sijame, and Payaya confederation moved together from Coahuila. Though Payayas represented one of the more numerically dominant groups in the regions surrounding both the Coahuila and Texas sites, only Marcela, a twenty-five-year-old woman, and Antonio, a young man of unknown age, actually moved from Coahuila. No one came from the Yanaguana area at all, and it took two months for the Coahuila migrants to persuade some of their Payaya and Pamaya allies and relatives to join the settlement. Slow beginnings indeed.[6]

Strikingly, although Spanish political ritual and nomenclature—as conveyed through Spanish records of events—colored this diplomacy, native conventions of male-led family bands determined the structure of the joint settlement. Payaya, Pamaya, and Xarame headmen at the new Valero pueblo divided up among themselves the titles of *gobernador* (governor), *mayordomo* (superintendent), *justicia* (judge), *regimiento* (town council), and *alcaldes* (magistrates) to reflect balances of power and obligation among the three groups' leaders. Spaniards further recognized the men with special clothes, gifts, and batons of command, thereby acknowledging the headmen's political standing within the new settlement and in the day-to-day functioning of the mission communities. Martín de Alarcón might claim to have instituted such offices "so that thus they [the Indians] might enter better into the art of government," but the "choices" of recognized leaders suggest deference to native hierarchies of authority and governance.[7]

Families of Pampopas, Pastías, and Sulujams established a second settlement in the San Antonio area known as San José y San Miguel de Aguayo. Three of their headmen, one from each of the groups, had met with fray Antonio Margil de Jesús in 1719 to discuss the possibility of establishing an allied village with the Spaniards but had made clear that they desired one separate from the Payaya-dominated community at Valero. Margil, in commenting on both their large numbers and the respect they instilled in other area Indians, emphasized that Pampopas, Pastías, and Sulujams operated from a position of power when demanding that Spaniards ally with them separately. In their turn, Xarame and Payaya leaders at Valero tried to ensure that this second proposed settlement did not infringe upon their territory. Fray Antonio de Olivares joined the Valero council in presenting a formal request to Juan Valdéz, captain of the Béxar presidio and judge of the commission delegated by the provincial governor to establish San José, that he enforce Spanish law requiring a minimum of three leagues between frontier settlements. Thus did Spaniards comply with the demands of the two native confederations.[8]

On February 23, 1720, Captain Valdéz stood in for the absent marqués de Aguayo in formalizing a settlement site three leagues from Valero for Pampopa, Pastía, and Sulujam family bands. In ceremonial recognition of their possession of the site, Valdéz grasped hands with native leaders, accompanied them on an inspection tour of the boundaries and water resources, and watched as the men ritually pulled up grass, threw rocks, and sliced branches from the brush to signal that land clearing would soon begin. As with the Payaya confederation, in recognition of their civil and criminal jurisdiction, Captain Valdéz gave insignias of office to Pampopa headman Juan, who would serve as *gobernador* of the settlement; to Sulujam headman Nicolás, who would be *alcalde*; to Pastía headman Alonso, as *alguacil* (sheriff); and to a Pampopa named Francisco and a Sulujam named Antonio, who would serve as *regidores* (councilmen). Valdéz provided Spanish ritual to the occasion when he exhorted Indian leaders that they govern, set up a watch, maintain good conduct, construct homes and beds so as to sleep off the ground, raise chickens, promote the progress of their village, follow the guidance of the missionaries, and have their families do so as well "for the service of God." The directives' content, translated for the Indians by Captain Lorenzo García as best he could, reflected Spanish goals of conversion, but the ceremonies nevertheless made clear that political, civil, and diplomatic authority resided with Pampopa, Pastía, and Sulujam leaders, leaving missionaries to act as a new kind of shaman in native, if not Spanish, eyes.[9]

A third set of negotiations had begun shortly before, in 1719, between Spaniards and the Indian residents of the Ranchería Grande, although they took much longer to come to fruition. That year, Alarcón formally recognized the authority and leadership of an Ervipiame named "El Cuilón" ("Juan Rodríguez" to Spaniards) with a gift of a "baton of command." Rodríguez was then about forty years old, had been born in Coahuila, and passed time at the mission established in 1698 for Ervipiames, before they abandoned the Spaniards in 1700. Since then, he, his wife, Margarita (an Iman Indian), and their children, Ana María, Miguel Ramón, and Francisco, had been living among their relatives in Texas and, with them, had joined the Ranchería Grande. Spaniards clearly depended upon the aid and diplomacy of this group, since the 1719 Alarcón expedition remained stranded in San Antonio until a Payaya and a Muruame from the Ranchería Grande agreed to guide them to the Caddo villages in the east.[10]

Spanish diplomatic exchanges with Ranchería Grande leaders only turned into an alliance when the marqués de Aguayo met with Juan Rodríguez and fifty families in 1721, exchanged gifts, and discussed erecting a third, separate settlement within the Yanaguana area. Interestingly, these negotiations may have been rooted in the Spaniards' need for Rodríguez's aid in their diplomacy with the Caddos. Rodríguez and other leaders from Ranchería Grande had gathered information for their own ends about Indian bands—many of whom came from the Ranchería Grande itself—who had met in convocation with the Frenchman Louis Juchereau de St. Denis that year. When Aguayo went east to meet with the Caddos and to confront St. Denis, Rodríguez agreed to accompany him on the trip. Spaniards needed the alliance of the large confederation not only for overtures to the Caddos but because they also feared losing Ranchería Grande residents to a French alliance. This concern had been made all too apparent when confederated Ranchería Grande leaders greeted Aguayo by unfurling a French flag when he arrived at an encampment on the road to the Caddo villages. All Aguayo could do was request that the Spanish standard be added to their flagpole along with the one given them by Frenchmen—he had no power to displace it. Gifts of tobacco, cattle, food, and clothes followed as Aguayo worked to win them over. In similar spirit to his diplomatic ploys with Caddo leaders days later, Aguayo called his men into a square battalion formation with a trumpet call "so that the [Ranchería Grande] Indians would be loyal to the Spaniards out of love and fear." Adding to the display, his men urged him "to ride his horse in the Spanish manner, to impress the Indians with the advantages of a horsemanship that they had never seen." Aguayo thereby "maneuvered [his horse] masterfully with all the different turns and styles that are customary" before assuming his place at the head of the battalion and leading the soldiers in a ranked procession. Thus did he woo the Ervipiame leader Rodríguez and his colleagues with advertisements of the advantages offered by a Spanish alliance—numerous fellow warriors, guns, and horses.[11]

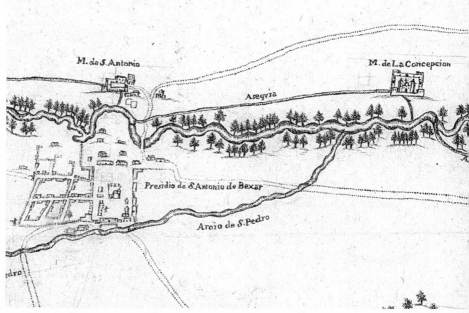

The five missions, military presidio, and civilian villa of San Antonio de Béxar, all located along the San Antonio River. Map drawn by the presidio commander, Luis Antonio Menchaca, in 1764. Courtesy of the John Carter Brown Library at Brown University, Providence, R.I.

The following year, 1722, Rodríguez and several families from the Ranchería Grande finally accepted the Spanish invitation to form a settlement called "San Francisco Xavier de Nájera." As in their earlier negotiations, military ceremony continued to make clear that this was an alliance being brokered between Indians represented by Rodríguez and Spaniards represented by Aguayo. The officer corps of Aguayo's battalion attended the ceremonies and stood witness to the presentation of "an entire suit of English cloth in the Spanish style" to Rodríguez, again emphasizing Spanish recognition of his authority. Spanish officials well understood the military and diplomatic gains to be made through alliance with leaders such as Rodríguez and confederations like that of the Ranchería Grande. In the Yanaguana/San Antonio area, these men would be crucial to Spaniards in the concerted defense needed to curtail the ever-expanding raiding territories of Apaches. Although the Nájera settlement soon disappeared, new ones sprang up along the river when three missions were transferred from east to central Texas in 1731 under new names—San José de los Nazonis became San Juan de Capistrano, San Francisco de los Neches became San Francisco de la Espada, and Nuestra Señora de la Purísima Concepción

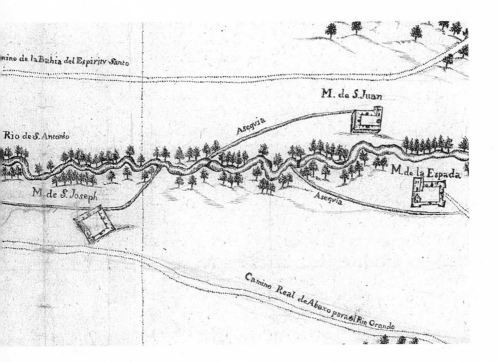

Camino de la Bahia del Espiritv Santo

M. de S.Juan

Rio de S. Antonio

Asegvia

M. de la Espada

M. de S. Joseph

Asegvia

Camino Real de Abaxo para el Rio Grande

replaced "de los Hainais" with "de Acuña." Defense needs grew apace, as the now five Indian villages, one Spanish villa, and one presidio gained still more unwanted Apache attention.[12]

The spirit and form of mission-presidio complexes reflected their function as shared settlements of Spaniards and Indians coming together for defense and subsistence, even as individual communities—the Spanish villa of Béxar and the five native mission settlements—governed themselves independently. Just as the Spanish families of Béxar had their own *gobernador*, *alcaldes*, *justicia*, and *regimiento*, so too did each Indian community. Spanish-designated positions for decision making within the new mission settlements resonated with precontact practices. When groups dispersed into individual bands (usually constituting an extended family) for summer hunting and gathering, whoever was deemed the male head of the family led them, and it was only at encampments of multiple congregated bands that "headmen" or "chiefs" assumed leadership. Though Spanish government officials and Franciscan missionaries superimposed Spanish titles of office over already existing lines of native authority, in effect they simply gave notice of their own awareness of interband diplomatic alliances. At San José, for instance, the Spanish meanings of individual titles held by Pampopa headman Juan, Sulujam headman Nicolás, and Pastía headman Alonso meant little; what was important was that the three men continued to share the leadership of their united family bands. The confederated settlement at the mission thereby gave physical form to political alliance.[13]

Far from mere formalities, the titles and offices accorded male officeholders continued through the century and marked mission governance with the customary kinship organization that had long structured the hierarchy of family bands. Offices tended to remain in the control of certain "old families," with Xarames dominating at Valero, and positions of *gobernador* and *alcalde* alternating annually between Pajalats and Tacames at Concepción. The mix of civic and military officials ensured that Indian leadership ranks would "exercise military and political jurisdiction, and their tribunals impose penalties without shedding blood." Special clothes for office-holders became commonplace in mission supplies. For instance, Nicolás Cortés, the Xarame *mayordomo*, and Hermenegildo Puente, the Papanac *fiscal* (an official in charge of maintaining mission lands), at Valero were singled out with cloaks made of Querétaran fabric, shag garments lined with Rouen linen, and shirts of the same fabric. Guidelines for the missions directed that each year *gobernadors* would receive new Spanish coats and *alcaldes* new capes and designated special benches for the men's use. Such men also remained exempt from obligations of manual labor within the missions, a mark of prestige legally recognized even after mission secularization in 1794.[14]

Mission and presidio architecture also reflected the coming together of Indian and Spanish cultures. All original buildings—chapels, Spanish and Indian quarters, granaries, and nearby civilian homes and military barracks—were of jacal construction, thatched huts that could be made variously of straw, mud, and adobe. Only over several decades were they gradually replaced with the stone preferred by Spaniards. The jacales, with poles set into the ground and interlaced with flexible straw or grass, plastered with mud or adobe, and roofed with thatch, closely resembled the structures erected by many of the native groups of the region. Native housing in southern Texas usually consisted of round huts built around a hearth area and covered with cane or grass, depending on available construction materials. Further south, in the Rio Grande delta area, groups chose various structures, again depending on their environment, including brush arbors called "*ramadas*" consisting of support poles and a flat roof made of leafy tree branches, huts built of palm fronds called "*toritos*," and houses covered by mats and thatch that were easily transportable. Along the coast, houses were also built around a pole in a circular style and covered with mats or hides—all materials chosen for easy set up, dismantling, and transportation by canoe. Since native construction focused on temporary structures made from locally available materials, it is not surprising that their housing styles predominated at settlement sites where the need for shelter and defense was immediate but residency was not year-round. In the early days, too, Spanish soldiers and missionaries lived just as did the Indians, with presidios following the same patterns as jacal mission settlements, reflecting their own jacal tradition that had been brought with them from the interior of Mexico and that represented a hybrid of Old and New World construction techniques.[15]

Notably, even as stone gradually replaced jacal construction in church buildings and in missionary and soldier quarters, most Indian quarters remained jacales. Stone construction for Spaniards was a sign of affluence as much as preference, so it is difficult to disentangle native influence on housing from a lack of financial and material resources available to mission residents. The advantage of adobe and stone was greater protection in the case of enemy raids and greater security in the event of fire. At the same time, however, because jacal construction was meant to be temporary, its continued use may have signaled the transitory nature of native residency in San Antonio. Indeed, if natives used the missions in a seasonal manner similar to the way they used their other joint encampments, then only jacal housing would be necessary. It was not until 1749 that fray Ignacio Antonio Ciprián reported that San José Mesquites and Pastías had "houses of stone built with such skill that the mission is a fort." Xarames, Payayas, Sanas, and others at Valero had stone quarters in 1762, but only by 1772 did all resident Pajalats, Sanipaos, Manos de Perro, Pacaos, and Borrados at Concepción live in stone houses built along the outside wall. Yet, that same year, stone housing had only begun to be built at San Juan de Capistrano and San Francisco de la Espada and would never be completed for all resident Indians. At Nuestra Señora del Rosario and Nuestra Señora del Refugio along the coast, jacales remained the only shelter ever used by Karankawas, Cocos, Copanes, Cujanes, and Coapites during their periodic visits. That Ciprián used "fort" to describe San José houses might well explain the shift to stone as defensive strategy rather than Spanish preference.[16]

Stone came to dominate, but mission settlements maintained the physical feeling of native encampments and living spaces—even the church structures. As stone chapels arose under the direction of Franciscans, Indian residents influenced their decoration. Though the major forms and symbols found in the architecture, carvings, and decor of mission chapels remained Spanish, the Pampopa, Xarame, Tilpacopal, Pamaque-Piguique, Payaya, Ervipiame, and Pajalat men listed among the recorded masons, carpenters, and blacksmiths interpreted them as they built.

Painted decorations in the form of birds, flowers, chevrons, circles, simple waves, and continuous, vinelike lines attributed to Indian workmanship that adorn the walls of the chapel (now confessional room) at Mission Nuestra Señora de la Purísima Concepción de Acuña. Courtesy of the Texas Historical Commission, Austin, Texas.

Carvings at Valero, Concepción, and San José reflected a "fusion of Spanish and Indian tradition," with "Christian symbols or the classic orders of Greco-Roman buildings" transformed by native artisans. Multicolored murals painted in the original church at Rosario exhibited a free-flowing design of "scored half circles or lunettes" and flora resembling yucca plants found within Karankawan coastal territories, expressing the natives' imaginations reproducing images taken from environments they knew so well.[17]

Although Spaniards controlled much of the structure for this new form of settlement, native usage followed precontact patterns. Just as they had moved between shared and unshared encampments of their own, so too did they come and go from Spanish missions in accordance with subsistence needs, diplomatic alliances, and kinship obligations. The same loosely allied bands that gathered together at confederated settlements did so at missions. From San Juan Bautista in northern Coahuila to San Antonio de Béxar in Texas, native families joined missions nearest their hunting ranges and long-used encampment sites. Often a mission represented one or more particular confederacies, as allied families entered missions in both Coahuila and Texas as groups. In turn, missionaries identified and named each affiliation after the group who had numerical dominance within it, such as the Terocodame and Xarame confederacies of Coahuilteco speakers at San Francisco Solano, the Sana confederacy of Tonkawa speakers at San Antonio de Valero, and the Pajalat confederacy of Coahuilteco speakers at Nuestra Señora de la Purísima Concepción.[18]

At the same time, the independence of kinship groups, even under the leadership of confederation headmen, also remained intact. When families made the decision to join native or mission settlements, they did so in family units. Missionary reports regularly recorded that headmen came to the various missions bringing with them their wives and children or even larger family groups. Once they were inside the mission settlements, housing patterns seem to have reflected these extended family groupings, such as the eight larger units divided by band at San José. One Tacame family group tried out several missions, shifting from San José to Espada to a native settlement on the Colorado River and then back to San Antonio at Valero before finally settling at Concepción, where they became a leading family in mission governance. Others knew what they wanted ahead of time. When allied groups of Mayeyes, Yojuanes, Deadoses, and Bidais first discussed joining a mission, fray Mariano de los Dolores y Viana asked them to visit San Antonio, but they explained that the Indians there "were not related to them, nor did they come from their locality, and for that reason they could not live with them." Insisting instead on a mission settlement within their own territories, they said that "they could not move so far away from their relatives . . . nor could they leave their neighboring and allied nations because they were all intermingled and had intermarried." The power of kin-based requirements resulted in the establishment of the San Xavier missions in the 1740s in their lands along the present-day San Gabriel River, east of San Antonio.[19]

Just as Indians came to missions in family groups, so too did they leave that way. As fray José Francisco López reported, "one after another they have followed their kin." Thus, the Spanish settlements held no more sway than other settlements visited during seasonal migrations around San Antonio and among relatives and allies spread throughout hunting territories all the way down to Coahuila. Fray Antonio Margil and fray Isidro de Espinosa lamented that too many Indians "live on their ranches and do as they wish. . . . There is no force able to subdue them and oblige them to live in a pueblo under Christian management." In a 1737 report, fray Benito Fernández de Santa Ana had to admit that in the month of August Mission Espada had "very few" present, Mission San Juan de Capistrano stood "abandoned," and Mission Concepción "runaways" had fallen victim to Apache raiders during their migrations. Three years later, writing another report on the state of the missions, Fernández de Santa Ana lamented, "It is the exception who does not flee to the wilderness two or three times and so far away that sometimes they go so far as 100 leagues away." What missionaries often characterized as "running away" represented customary migrations between encampments of kin groups living in much the way they always had.

Ironically, after judging Indians to be without a sense of "family," missionaries confronted undeniable family cohesion as families united in acceptance or rejection of mission residence. In 1753, five families of Pamaques, Paguacanes, and Piguiques left San Juan de Capistrano to rejoin relatives at Mission San Francisco de Vizarrón near the Rio Grande in Coahuila. They soon intermarried with several Vizarrón residents, and the increased kin ties strengthened the families' refusal to return to Capistrano when the two missions began fighting over jurisdiction of the family groups. Thus, they successfully used the unions to stay together and to remain at the settlement of their own choosing. In turn, the extended nature of these families often represented kin ties of intermarriage rather than multigenerations of long duration. When fray Jesús Garavito conducted a census of Indians at Refugio before they left for their winter camps on the coast, he listed three groups—Karankawas from Rosario, Cocos from Rosario, and Karankawas from Refugio, each with its own "captain," respectively Manuel Zertuche, Pedro José, and Diego—representing three extended families. A Rosario census from the year previous listed Manuel Zertuche as a twenty-five-year-old captain with a twenty-year-old wife, María, and their four children: Margarita, seven; Ysabel, four; José Guadalupe, three; and José María del Pilár, one. The youth of these families showcased the hardships of subsistence, raids, and disease shaping their lives. Not surprisingly, as Rosario collapsed in the early nineteenth century, many resident Indian families chose to move to Refugio "in order to be with those they are related to by marriage."[20]

Family bands' coherence also had the power to destabilize mission settlements. The encampment at San Francisco Xavier de Nájera lasted for only four years, and it was known during that brief period as the Ervipiame "barrio." The number willing to stay year-round steadily languished over those years, and by 1726, the twelve remaining residents, including Juan Rodríguez, Margarita, and their children, moved to Valero. San Francisco Xavier de Nájera shut down. But Ranchería Grande did not. Mayeyes, Yojuanes, and various other Tonkawa speakers maintained their shared encampments and continued to be known as the Ranchería Grande. In turn, it continued to serve as a destination for independent families, refugees who left missions, and those who moved between the two kinds of settlements—native and Spanish—according to the seasons of the year. Ervipiames, Payayas, Cocos, and Mayeyes all appear on lists of "fugitives" from Valero, and missionaries attributed the nearby presence of the Ranchería Grande as both a constant lure and an asylum for any Indians who wearied of mission regimens or short supplies. As early as 1727, when Pedro de Rivera passed through the region, he recognized the Ranchería Grande as a "republic" that offered safe haven to Indians from other mission settlements, especially as the "republic" refused to give up "escaped" Indians to the Spaniards who came to encourage or coerce their return to San Antonio.[21]

Three later missions established along the San Gabriel River in the 1740s attempted unsuccessfully to draw the Ranchería Grande residents, as well as the Bidais and Akokisas, into an alliance, but they failed within ten years. Keeping a focus on Akokisas in the 1750s, Spaniards built another complex along the Trinity River, with the Presidio San Agustín de Ahumada and the Mission Nuestra Señora de la Luz (together called "El Orcoquisac," from "Orcoquizas," another name for Akokisas). Spanish officials hoped an Akokisa alliance might help to forestall intrusions of illicit French traders among Indian bands living along the lower Neches, Trinity, and Brazos Rivers. To offset French trade, Spaniards thereby wooed Akokisas and, by extension, their Atakapa allies and kinsmen with promises of weekly supplies of beef and corn. Yet, when Spanish transportation lines proved unreliable, the Akokisas and Atakapas simply cut visits to the missions from their customary seasonal movements between fall/winter aggregations on the coast and spring/summer dispersals inland. When the marqués de Rubí traveled through the province on his 1766–68 inspection tour, he added the mission to his "empty and abandoned" list, while noting populations of Aranamas, Cocos, Mayeyes, Bidais, and Akokisas living in shared and independent encampments in numbers far greater than those ever counted in mission censuses.[22]

Along the coast, families of Karankawas, Akokisas, Atakapas, Bidais, and Aranamas found the least reason of any Indians to reside with Spaniards during their customary seasonal migrations. Early on in 1719, Martín de Alarcón reported that "proud" Aranamas rejected Spanish overtures, saying that they were "as brave as the Spaniards," thereby implying that they did not see any need for alliance with the intrusive Europeans. The security of their encampments in coastal marshes and barrier islands—rather than a valor differential—set these groups apart from those in the San Antonio area. That left only supplementary subsistence resources to attract coastal natives into contact with Spaniards—which was not often enough. In

1723, at the complex of Mission Espíritu Santo de Zúñiga and Presidio Nuestra Señora de Loreto (together known as "La Bahía"), the native community collapsed after only a two-year existence due to a complete Karankawa desertion. Spaniards attempted another coastal venture at Mission Nuestra Señora del Rosario in the 1750s, but all too soon it ended in failure as well. In 1767, Rubí declared that any number he might attempt to offer as a count of the Cocos, Cujanes, Karankawas, and Aranamas reputedly resident again at Mission Espíritu Santo was "less certain, for they frequently desert and flee to the coast." Moreover, he implied, the count of converts was zero, since "it is evident that the mission is composed mostly of pagans."[23]

Most missionaries' understanding of Karankawa movements between mission and coast remained limited to responses to conditions at the mission—food shortages, conflicts with soldiers, or sheer stubbornness. Yet, visits and periodic residence at missions did not represent "random or haphazard events," as the missionaries believed, but rather strategically designated times in seasonal rounds when mission offerings would be most useful. Since missions like Espíritu Santo, Rosario, and later Refugio were built on sites of the Indians' spring and summer hunting camps in the coastal plains and prairies, periodic visits to the Spanish institutions fit naturally into old subsistence patterns. Fray José Francisco Mariano Garza, for instance, wrote to Governor Manuel Muñoz one summer that as Karankawa family bands began to shift inland to spend the season at their prairie camps, they dropped by Refugio, received a supply of tobacco, and promptly left to gather prickly pear at Copano Bay and along the Aransas River. Karankawa family bands stayed to hunt in the vicinity of the missions during those months and then returned to their fishing camps along the coast in the fall and winter. Missions functioned within their regular subsistence patterns as just another ecological resource. Before bringing their families to the missions, headmen and warriors even made preliminary inspection visits to ensure sufficient food supplies were on hand. "All of them, and especially the chief referred to [Fresada Pinta]," Garza complained, "have come with the selfish intention of seeing if the provisions of foodstuffs and clothing which they say Your Lordship promised them are in the mission yet." Equally, though, the missions seem to have been mere camping sites, as archaeological remains of whitetail deer, alligators, turtles, ducks, herons, turkeys, beavers, fish, and freshwater mussels as well as wild plants, such as mesquite beans, seeds, and pecans, demonstrate the variety of foods that coastal Indians brought into Rosario, Espíritu Santo, and Refugio themselves. It was only in the 1790s that missionaries seemed to accustom themselves somewhat to Karankawa movements and simply kept track of Indian families at Rosario and Refugio, taking censuses before they departed each year.[24]

The ravages of European diseases also encouraged regular residential and subsistence movements of Indian families. As happened throughout the Americas, once native peoples congregated in or near Spanish settlements, they put themselves in reach of epidemics that could strike in particularly pulverizing fashion, returning every decade to decimate new resident populations. Indians lost the isolation and thus protection afforded by the small size and mobility of hunting and gathering bands when they joined others in settlements where diseases swept through with all-encompassing and thus devastating effect. Epidemics in turn precipitated flight back to native settlements far from the specter of death. Newcomers from regions increasingly distant from Spanish contact then arrived and became the next group to fall victim to the next wave of disease.[25]

In San Antonio, epidemic outbreaks occurred in 1728, 1736, 1739, 1743, 1748, 1749, 1751, 1759, 1763, and 1786. Thus, although mission counts indicated fairly steady population numbers at the San Antonio missions from 1720 to 1772—sometimes listing an annual total of over one thousand people for all five missions between 1745 and 1772—it was only an appearance of stability. The numbers did not reflect the continuity of a self-reproducing community (through steady birthrates and/or declining death rates) but rather the constant recruitment of new residents by Spanish church and state officials. Exacerbating the losses from disease, infant mortality and female mortality in childbirth were so high that two-thirds of children born in the missions died before reaching three years of age. Life spans shortened by disease and ill health further decreased fertility rates. The mean age of Indian populations in the San Antonio missions was roughly twenty-six years old. It was not until the 1780s that an increase of children in the population, a decrease in the number of widows and widowers, and an increase in the median size of families from 2.7 to 3.5 heralded gradual stabilization of Indian populations associated with the Spanish community.[26]

Such demographic factors meant that native populations in San Antonio consisted of a constantly shifting and predominantly young population for whom daily life was fraught with instability due to high mortality for all ages. As late as 1789, fray José Francisco López recorded that despite the age of the missions, the Indian residents were mostly children of "uncivilized" Indians. Thus, a majority of those Indians who interacted with missionaries over the century did not begin life in mission settlements, maintained the ties and communal practices of the families into which they had been born, and viewed relations with Spaniards as a new and unfamiliar experience.[27]

Within that destabilized setting, where daily survival was a struggle for Spaniards and Indians alike, mutual need served to maintain a balance of power, and day-to-day subsistence and defense earned the greatest attention from Indian headmen and Spanish leaders. The need was clear even to officials in Mexico City. In 1733, judge advocate Juan de Oliván Rebolledo advised the viceroy that an alliance with the Indian peoples of central Texas, who could augment Spanish forces with their own, would be essential if Apaches were to be compelled to make peace. Spanish and Indian peoples thereby each played a role in the security and subsistence of the community—Indian warriors with their skills of hunting and defensive combat, and their Spanish counterparts with material supplies as well as fortifications, guns, and ammunition that supplemented the warriors' lances and bows and arrows. And security came first, as Apaches stepped up their raids against San Antonio communities in often unrelenting fashion from the 1720s until the 1750s.[28]

Spanish contributions to fortifying their communities indicated that joint Indian-Spanish settlement represented first and foremost a defensive alliance for mutual protection. Citing the vulnerability of the San Antonio area to Apache attack, the marqués de Aguayo was the first to order fortifications built in the form of a presidio, "with four baluartes [bastions] proportioned for a company of fifty-four men." Yet, in the eyes of missionaries and Indian residents, the presence of a presidio did not provide sufficient defense for the individual mission settlements surrounding it, because as the missions took form, their own defensive architecture and armaments competed for importance with chapels and church furnishings within the mission grounds. Stone walls to enclose and protect jacal housing always came before the building of stone churches.[29]

By midcentury, San José's outer wall boasted parapets, battlements, and tower bastions at all four gateways, from which sentinels kept guard. A granary and well were located inside the walls in case of siege, and the trees and brush that stood outside the walls were cut down to safeguard against surprise attacks. In addition, fray Juan Agustín Morfi noted that loopholes had been made through the outer walls into the adjoining Indian quarters so that warriors could fire guns from cover if the mission were stormed. The San José armory held guns, bows and arrows, and lances with which to equip the warriors, and a *plaza de armas* (military plaza) provided space for the warriors' military drills as well as bow and arrow and musket practice. On Saturdays, during processions of the Feasts of Christ and of the Virgin Mary, armed warriors stood guard and sentinels on horseback stationed themselves outside the ramparts to ensure security.[30]

Meanwhile, just a league and a half away, San Antonio de Valero had stone walls, fortified doors, and a watchtower with loopholes for three swivel guns (cannons), along with muskets, shotguns, powder, and ammunition for the warriors who defended the mission community. Concepción, Capistrano, and Espada between them

Aerial view of Mission San José y San Miguel de Aguayo, c. 1944, indicating both the size and defensive structure of the mission. Courtesy of the San Antonio Conservation Society Foundation, San Antonio, Texas.

had an assortment of cannons at each gate, swivel guns, "slingers," and general arms and ammunition to aid warriors in defense of their walls as well. Despite missionary claims for the primacy of religious conversion and social "hispanization," these were in fact embattled settlements marshalling the strengths of all inhabitants for a united defense.[31]

That is not to say that Franciscans did not attempt to use the labor demands within mission communities for "civilizing" purposes. Missionaries had a threefold purpose in trying to divide labors between Indian men and women residents at missions. First, although missions received financial support from the Crown, each had to be largely self-sustaining. Second, self-containment of the mission community aimed to keep Indian peoples safe from what Franciscans believed to be the potentially detrimental influences of "unsavory" Spanish settlers. Maintaining a distance from the presidial and civil populations of nearby settlements required that missions provide their own skills, crafts, and services. Thus, the native workforce had to be capable of providing their families with food and sustenance. Third, Franciscans hoped that in the process of securing the mission communities' subsistence, they could teach Indian residents labors that ideally would serve them well once the missions were secularized and the Indians became citizens of Spanish society. "To make this method work," fray Mariano de los Dolores y Viana wrote, the Indians must "work their own fields, open up their irrigation ditches, build their houses and churches, breed cattle, protect and maintain them; eat and dress themselves and have the necessities for civil and rational style of living." Attaining these skills and industry would make them "gather more readily in the new Pueblos, embracing our Religion and becoming subjects of His Majesty," according to Commandant General Pedro de Nava. Instruction in work roles commensurate with Christian living, church and state officials asserted, would enable Indian men to provide for themselves and their families and teach them to be respectable, contributing—and manly—members of Spanish society.[32]

Because of agriculture's social and cultural importance within Spanish society as well as its economic importance to the mission's food supply, farming was key to the ideology and mores that were to be taught Indians—particularly Indian men— through labor. Both Old and New World Spanish societies based their socio- economic systems on land ownership and cultivation. Land tenure formed the principal basis of wealth, prestige, social hierarchies, and political rights among Spanish men. In the attempt to make native labor practices conform to Spanish norms, Franciscans wanted to structure labor systems at the missions around clear divisions of gender that located men in the fields and women within the confines of mission living quarters.

These divisions' importance rested in both the spatial location of male and female labor and the meaning of the work itself. For men, gendered divisions of labor reflected what Spaniards understood to be the proper distribution of authority and power within a family. Thus, to the missionaries, women's seclusion and men's control of farming would firmly establish Indian men as patriarchal heads of house- hold and family providers. In the ceremonies surrounding the initial establishment of mission settlements, Spanish officials ritually called upon Indian men to assume new labor routines and to pass them down to their sons in accordance with divine law and patriarchal custom. Captain Juan Valdéz's description of the formal prom- ises elicited from Pampopa, Pastía, and Sulujam male leaders at the 1720 founding of the San José mission outlined this commitment: "Not only did they agree to dig their irrigation ditches and cultivate their lands, but also promised to teach their sons to do the same, insisting that they want to obey the law of God." In this spirit, missionaries, or more likely civilian and military overseers, sought to teach Indian men "how to plant, how to cultivate the crops, and how to harvest them." A diversity of tasks associated with running mission farms and ranches also fell to Indian men, including irrigating, weeding, gathering in seeds, tilling and plowing fields, mending fences, burning cane, working fruit orchards, herding and branding the mission cattle, horses, and oxen, and herding and shearing sheep.[33]

While men were to work in agricultural fields, women were to learn to remain secluded from them. The Spanish emphasis on the domestic seclusion of women in the home concerned control of female sexuality. Early modern European ideas about women's "natural" susceptibility to sinful temptation led many in Counter-Reformation Spain and New Spain to believe the "enclosure" of women to be a protective measure for ensuring female chastity and family *limpieza de sangre* (purity of bloodlines). Conceptions of male honor thus depended upon the supervision of female sexuality. In this way, the household became a "sacred" *male* domain where the property of men—wives, daughters, sisters, and mothers—needed to be protected. Within the home, men ideally guarded the purity of their female family members and, in turn, the honor of their name and lineage. Keeping Indian women out of the fields reinforced not only women's sexual seclusion but also, simultaneously, men's role as family patriarch and provider. As one mission manual explained, "the women should be in their homes grinding grain and preparing the meals for their husbands and not be going through the fields doing men's work."[34]

The necessities of daily life regularly thwarted missionary ideals, however. Resident male populations rarely could meet all the labor needs required by mission farms and ranches, and women labored side by side with their husbands, brothers, and sons, even though missionaries wrote reassuringly to their superiors that women did so "only when necessity demands it because of the scarcity of men." Claims concerning "proper" gender divisions of labor among mission Indians, especially protections for women, reportedly reached the highest levels of Spanish bureaucracy. In 1768, for example, a military captain at La Bahía found himself caught in the middle of struggles between presidio and mission personnel at Espíritu Santo over the work assignments of Indian men and women as well as over Indian complaints of excessive work demands. In his attempt to sort out the controversy, Francisco de Tovar cited viceregal authority, asserting that "His Excellency [the viceroy] does not want the [Indian] women to work on those occupations not proper for women."[35]

If they could not always keep women out of the fields, Franciscans tried to emphasize that their labor within mission quarters was the primary and most identifiable work of women. Missionaries tried to structure women's labor by designating certain tools and provisions "for women," locating their work within the living quarters of the missions, and even determining the foods that Indian women might cook. At Mission San José, each home in the Indian quarters came supplied with stones for grinding corn (*metates*), grills for making tortillas, water jars, and adjoining patio areas with ovens "reserved for the private use of the Indian women." Inventories show that every mission supplied women of Indian families with pots, earthenware pans, griddles, kettles, dippers, and various other "domestic utensils." The material limitations of mission supplies might sometimes require the women to cook together communally but still allowed the construction of an ideological domain of female labor and activity in service to their husbands and children. Mission dictates further determined that it would be the women who assembled regularly to receive rations of salt, fruit, beans, vegetables, and meat, marking their responsibility for food preparation even as they were nominally prohibited from its cultivation.[36]

Mission plans also purported to train Indian men and women in distinctly gendered skilled labors and crafts. Inventories documented that every mission in the San Antonio area included rooms with spinning wheels where Indian women spent hours cleaning, drying, carding, combing, and spinning cotton and wool. Then, once male weavers who were hired from the nearby Spanish villa had woven the cloth, all the members of a family received their ration so that their wives or mothers could sew clothes for them. Beyond spinning and sewing, all other skilled labors were supposedly reserved for men, who were to learn mechanical trades such as blacksmithing, carpentry, and masonry work. Yet, it was not until the 1770s that Indian men began to appear on lists of trade specialists in mission records and that fray Juan Agustín Morfi could write that Pampopa and Mesquite men of San José "know how to work very well at their mechanical trades." For most of the century, Spanish citizens from the nearby villa assumed all skilled positions of blacksmith, carpenter, stonemason, tailor, shoemaker, candlemaker, *cañero* (in charge of San José's sugar mill), and *vasiero* (in charge of breed herds of sheep and goats). This time lag likely reflected the rarity of those skills and the lack of demand for them among the Spanish as well as Indian populations.[37]

These labor guidelines illuminate what Franciscans envisioned for their missions but reveal little of the day-to-day reality in the San Antonio communities. Petitions asking that at least one soldier be stationed at each mission—not as a defender but as an overseer, "so that respect for him will make the Indians do the work necessary for maintaining civilized life and the holy Faith"—indicates the futility of missionary efforts to require Indian residents to pursue work not of their own choosing. That appeared particularly true when the work challenged native gender divisions of labor. Many men and women simply left, traveling back to the community life and work they had known previously. "Returning then to their old means of sustenance," fray Dolores y Viana bitterly wrote, Indians "leave the missions and gladly live in the woods as before." Upon arrival back in native settlements, Toribio de Urrutia feared, many "runaways" told family and friends that in the missions they had been made servants of Spaniards.[38]

Many others did not abandon mission settlements, but neither did they accept labors charged them by Franciscans. Fray Dolores y Viana noted that Indian men in the fields worked so carelessly "with the usual slowness, characteristic of their innate indolence," that "it is necessary always that some Spaniard direct them; what could be done by one person is usually not done by four." Men also simply left for short periods of time as a break from work. In fact, Indian men proved to be such "enemies of work" that "on many occasions they arm themselves in order not to be forced to do anything for long periods of time." Franciscans read the Indian men's refusal to carry out the labors requested of them as signs of "laziness." As fray Manuel de Silva explained, "It takes great effort to make the Indians work, for idleness pleases them much more. But this is contrary to civilized life, and little by little I manage to get them to work moderately."[39]

Missionaries ignored or were incapable of perceiving the gendered meanings behind Indians' labor choices, however. Despite their own observations, they remained blind to the fact that Indian men refused to do only certain kinds of work. As one Franciscan recorded, "any work, *other than hunting and fishing*, was excessive to the Indian male," while another argued that they wanted nothing more than to hunt wild game and wage war. Indeed, men did work, but it was work consistent with their own communal patterns. Indian peoples of southern and coastal Texas who made up the majority of mission populations generally practiced little if any plant cultivation, living instead by hunting, fishing, and gathering. For Indian men, missionary labor demands cut into the time necessary for the appropriate male labors of hunting and fishing. Presumably, too, they might have asked: did not agricultural production represent one of the contributions that *Spaniards* were supposed to bring to the mission-presidio complex alliance?[40]

While Indians' very conception of maleness rested in hunting skills, women's work had customarily been tied to plant-based subsistence and craft production, which apparently translated more readily into Spanish labor roles. "The women are given more to work than the men," fray Manuel de Silva asserted, "and are most always busy" spinning cotton and wool, making pots, earthen pans, and other items of clay, which they traded or sold to Spanish women living nearby. Tellingly, in comparison to men, women's work skills and responsibilities within the divisions of labor of family and band matched those of missionary ideals. The mortars and pestles of native cultures closely resembled in form and use the *metates* and *manos* given to women to grind corn in the mission complexes. Harvesting agricultural crops may have echoed the gathering of berries, roots, and other plant foods customarily done by women. Similarly, native economies already assigned women responsibility for making clothes from animal skins, so women simply added cloth to their supplies of chamois and bison hides. Cloth did not replace them, though. Fray José de Solís noted that bison hides still shared space with cotton and wool blankets on beds in the Indian quarters of San José in 1767. Even lessons in weaving cloth would have been familiar to Karankawan women who erected and moved the portable dwellings that often included woven reed or grass mats. Thus, the domestic chores that missionaries believed they were teaching in accordance with "civilized" life differed little from the work roles Indian women brought with them to mission settlements.[41]

Native gender patterns predominated, whether the Spaniards fought them or encouraged them. In addition to crossovers between Indian and Spanish work regimens, traditionally defined native labors also played a crucial role in day-to-day subsistence within mission communities. The product of men's hunting and women's gathering continued to enliven both their living spaces and their diets. Disappearances called "flight" by missionaries in reality reflected the freedom with which Indians came and went from the missions in pursuit of their own socioeconomic activities. Though mission crops and cattle herds offered steady food supplies in San Antonio (though not at Espíritu Santo, Rosario, or Refugio along the coast), Indians continued their own subsistence technologies throughout the eighteenth century. In doing so, they not only supplemented and diversified the foods from mission farms and ranches but also maintained familiar gendered work roles and statuses. Indians left the San Antonio missions in the summer so that women could collect prickly pear fruit and men hunt deer and bison. Women at Concepción had a "habit of leaving the mission toward evening to eat tunas [prickly pears], dewberries, *cuacomites*, sour berries (*agritos*), nuts, sweet potatoes (*camotitos*), and other fruit and roots from the field." Faunal remains at San Antonio mission sites highlight Indian preference for diets of indigenous wild game, birds, fish, reptiles, and amphibians (despite ready supplies of beef cattle)—proof that choice, not necessity, guided their selection of the bounty of men's hunts. At San Juan de Capistrano, archaeological evidence of the diets of Pajalats, Pitalacs, Orejones, Pamaques, Piguiques, Chayopins, Pasnacans, and Malaguitas provide further indication of intermittent residence at the mission and continued reliance on coastal foodstuffs.[42]

More evidence of the prevalence of native gendered divisions of labor in mission communities lies in Spanish complaints about the difficulty in cultivating gardens and orchards because Indian women kept "gathering" fruit before it had ripened. And Indian men, even when they relied on mission cattle herds for their meat, transferred native butchering techniques to the domesticated animals. In similar spirit, in the coastal missions that depended not on agriculture but on cattle ranching for mission food supplies, missionaries recorded that Karankawa men—with better horses and arms than the Spanish *vaqueros* hired to care for the herds—arrived in bands of ten to twelve to "hunt" the cattle during the spring and summer. Such Karankawan hunting expeditions used mission cattle as a primary substitute for diminishing bison herds. As fray Antonio Garavito at Rosario lamented, "I fear that if the Indians from Rosario do not have enough to eat in their mission, they will wander about doing damage. . . . the cattle will be destroyed, the herds driven off, the tame horses taken, and nothing will remain that they will not steal." On the other hand, missionaries increasingly visited Karankawa bands in their hunting camps at intervals over the summer, and after enjoying their hospitality, one named fray José María Sáenz regularly brought back wild game and fruit to Refugio to liven up even the missionaries' diets. In 1805, Francisco Viana, the commander of La Bahía presidio, reported that local Indian populations continued to spend most of the year in their own territory, coming in periodically to receive blankets and other gifts from the missionaries and to trade the products of their hunting and gathering—such as nuts and bear lard—at the presidio. In support of their independent economic pursuits, Indian warriors even received musket balls and gunpowder from the Franciscans. In short, Karankawas and others used the Spanish institutions as a resource and buffer attuned to their own economic needs and gendered work customs.[43]

Archaeological finds at mission sites also include a profusion of arrow points, stone tools, and pottery—testifying to the native technologies and gendered divisions of labor that defined work there. The presence of arrow points shows the continued pursuit of traditional hunting skills by Indian men concurrent with their adoption of guns. Warriors appear to have preferred lithic arrow points and projectile points, though they sometimes incorporated metal and glass into their manufacture as well. A gradual shift from Perdiz to Guerrero points indicates that shared encampments with new Indian (as well as Spanish) neighbors influenced adaptations among diverse native manufactures. At the same time, they also transformed chert chips and flakes into gun flints, adapting their own manufactures to Spanish muskets. The presence of lithic blades and scrapers demonstrates that women too continued to choose chipped stone tools for processing animal and plant materials hunted and gathered by their family members.[44]

Indian preference for their own crafts and technologies ensured the persistence of the gendered divisions of labor that had long produced them. In the San Antonio missions, men hunted with bows and lithic arrow points made by women, while women tanned the hides from that hunt and made ceramic bowls, candlesticks, pots, jars, pipes, and whistles with animal bones marked by native decoration. Native manufacture of ceramic pottery in San Antonio—usually a craft production of women—continued virtually unchanged with bone-tempering, coil manufacture, clay and paint colors, polishing and burnishing with river pebbles, and water-proofing methods characteristic of precontact technologies. Ceramics found in mission contexts called "Goliad" ware did not differ from pottery at late pre-Hispanic sites identified as "Leon Plain" ware. Meanwhile, untempered or shell-tempered ceramics made of sandy clay with asphaltum decoration found at Rosario and Refugio and called "Rockport" ware reflected coastal workmanship like that of the Karankawas. Women also continued to make ornaments and beads from shell and bone or used trade beads given them by missionaries or other Indians to fashion into their own jewelry. Interestingly, archaeological digs have uncovered examples of Indian-interpreted rosaries made from trade beads restrung in combination with crucifixes.[45]

Unlike their contrasting notions of the sexual division of labor, Spanish and native ideas of manliness meshed when it came to defending their communities in the San Antonio area. The need for fighting men enhanced Indian men's responsibilities and made them essential to the survival of all residents. Within the context of escalating warfare brought about by the dual invasions of Spaniards and Apaches since the seventeenth century, fighting had served as primary employment for men, structured social and economic hierarchies, and provided the grounds for choosing both civil and military headmen. These functions continued unchanged within the mission-presidio complexes. Over the eighteenth century, the San Antonio presidial company, like many across the northern provinces of New Spain, suffered debilitating shortages in men and armaments and thus joined forces with civil as well as mission populations for offensive and defensive measures against enemies.[46]

In fact, Indian men by far made up the greatest percentage of fighting men in San Antonio, giving them plenty of opportunity to meet customary standards of manhood. As discussed earlier, church officials in the San Antonio and La Bahía areas kept armories at the missions with guns, ammunition, lances, bows, and arrows ready in case of attack. Many Indian men became trained *fusileros* (fusiliers). During a 1767 inspection tour of the Texas missions, fray José de Solís paid strict attention to each community's defensive readiness, counting 110 warriors among the population of 350 at San José, 45 of whom used guns while the remainder still preferred bows and arrows, spears, and other native-made weapons. The military force at San José alone outnumbered the San Antonio de Béxar presidio force more than two to one. Similarly, at Mission Espíritu Santo, Solís found 65 warriors, 30 armed with guns, and 35 armed with bows and arrows, spears, and boomerangs. Farther south, fray Juan de Dios María Camberos counted 400 Cujane, Coapite, and Copane men at Rosario able to bear arms, and to that number, he argued, could readily be added those warriors among the Karankawa proper. During that 1767 inspection tour, fray José de Solís noted in detail the military parades of Indian warriors through *plazas de armas* that took pride of place in welcoming ceremonies put on by each mission. At Espíritu Santo, Indian men twice provided formal displays of their defensive capabilities in honor of Solís's visit. In these instances, 40 armed Indian horsemen assembled to parade in double file and then continued their demonstrations with symbolic battle skirmishes. Such military drills confirmed the importance and status of Indian warriors within mission communities. Fray Solís gained personal appreciation of their valor when two warriors from Espíritu Santo who were escorting him on to the next mission saved his life when Aranamas attacked the party.[47]

Defensive demands increased in importance as horse and cattle herds at missions, presidios, and private ranches grew and in turn attracted Apache and later Wichita and Comanche raiding parties. Fray Dolores y Viana recorded that it was only the presence of Indian warriors from the mission settlements that ensured Apache raids were repelled in 1731. "They were the ones who up till now in all the campaigns and uprisings have come out against the Apache tribe, followed their tracks and spied upon their ranches with great loyalty and such manly spirit that without them not even the Spaniards would have entered," Dolores y Viana argued, "and even if [the soldiers] had, they would not have been victorious or saved their lives; they would have retreated in shame." On June 30, 1745, over 100 Indian warriors from Concepción and Valero routed the largest raiding party ever seen in San Antonio, 350 Lipan and Natage Apaches. When a Spanish lieutenant ordered soldiers and warriors to turn back after pursuing Apache raiders into their own lands without overtaking them, an Indian leader protested, reputedly saying, "Sir, you go back to watch the presidio, for I will go with my men to look for the Apaches." Failing to spur the Spaniard to action, the Indian governor and his men returned with the soldiers "much ruffled" at neither gaining their objective against Apaches nor receiving the credit due them "after they had saved the presidio and the villages from complete destruction, as all acknowledged."[48]

Increasingly, Indian warriors also offered their services as military escorts for cargo trains to and from Coahuila as Apache raiding routes shifted southward. In 1750, officials at the newly established missions in east-central Texas along the San Gabriel River were thrown into serious disarray in the midst of a series of Apache raids. Skilled Bidai, Akokisa, and Deadose horsemen and riflemen chose to leave Mission San Ildefonso, taking their families with them, when they were exhorted by an allied confederacy of Ais, Hasinais, Kadohadachos, Nabedaches, Yojuanes, Tawakonis, Yatasis, Kichais, Naconis, and Tonkawas to join a general campaign against Apaches. Despite promises to return in two months, the warriors and their families remained absent almost eighteen months while the men's military commitments took precedence over settlement ones.[49]

When the Indians of south-central Texas agreed to cast their lot with Spaniards in joint mission settlements, Spanish officials and missionaries alike often portrayed them as men who checked their valor at the mission door. The idea of missions as institutions through which to "conquer," "subdue," "pacify," and "subjugate" Indians was so firmly locked in their imaginations that they refused to acknowledge the reality of their situation. Despite such stereotypes (more often found at higher levels of administration), in day-to-day life the warriors at the San Antonio missions were crucial to the defense of the mission-presidio complexes, and the Spaniards knew it. In a 1744 letter to Viceroy conde de Fuenclara, Governor Tomás Felipe Winthuysen praised the Indian men at Valero, describing them as "among the most warlike and skillful in shooting arrows." As a member of the 1766–68 Rubí inspection team sent to evaluate defensive capabilities across the northern provinces, Nicolás de Lafora argued that presidial guards stationed at the San Antonio missions were unnecessary because the one hundred "bow and arrow men" living there put the missions "beyond reach of any local or outside attack." When Hugo O'Conor, the commandant inspector of presidios for the northern frontier, requested assessments of the province of Texas's capability to muster forces against a feared invasion by allied Wichitas and Comanches in the 1770s, three different military officials—Rafael Martínez Pacheco (twenty-year veteran and commandant of the El Orcoquisac presidio), Luis Antonio Menchaca (thirty-year veteran and commandant of the Béxar presidio), and Roque de Medina (adjutant-inspector of the interior presidios)—all counted mission Indian warriors as critical components of the "forces of the province." O'Conor responded with directives that Indian men at the five San Antonio missions receive 132 pounds of gunpowder, the same provisions allocated to the Béxar presidial company.[50]

Although the necessities of daily life kept Spaniards and Indians alike focused on subsistence and defense and ensured the continued value of native-defined divisions of labor, another potential arena for conflict between Spanish and Indian communal patterns emerged from Franciscan efforts to use the mission settlements to achieve the social "civilization" of Indian residents. Their attempted reforms centered on family and sexuality as they endeavored to make Indian men and women conform to Franciscans' definitions of Christian morals and Spanish mores. Here, they confronted the power of different patterns of kinship, which with constitutive relations and behaviors for men and women, were the central organizing principles of Indian communities in south and central Texas. With bands that each represented an extended family, kin relations defined not merely social units but political units, economic divisions of labor, and leadership and authority hierarchies. Therefore, when missionaries sought to influence Indian conceptions of "family" and its corresponding roles for men and women, they challenged constructs fundamental to their cultures and polities, constructs that natives sought to revitalize through joint settlement. Once again, such meddling on the part of relatively powerless Spaniards was largely doomed.

Indians who periodically joined mission communities constructed family units in various ways, which did, on the surface, resemble missionary ideals of a nuclear family composed of a husband, wife, and children. Indeed, the nuclear family formed a key social unit for them, but Spanish ideas posited these as patriarchal households, whereas native families were grounded in separate but complementary gender roles in extended kin networks. Most of the bands of southern and coastal Texas lived in consanguineous units constituted as extended family households or family bands within which nuclear families were subsumed. Whole villages or camps might represent one lineage, or when disease took its toll, remnants of families formed new ties and new villages through intermarriage. As fray Vicente Santa María argued of Indian bands in the area that became Nuevo Santander, "that which among themselves and by us are designated *nación* is nothing other than an aggregate of families." Levirate and sororal polygyny as well as matrilineal and bilateral kinship and matrilocal and bilocal residence often further differentiated Indian ideas of "family" from those of Spaniards. "Levirate" refers to the marriage of a man to his brother's widow (in addition to his own wife), and "sororal polygyny" is the marriage of one man to two or more sisters at the same time. "Matrilineality" traces kinship from mother to daughter, and "bilateral kinship" traces family lineages through both parents equally. "Matrilocal residence" means that when a couple is married they live with the woman's family, while "bilocal" practices give the couple a choice of residence with either the wife's or the husband's kin. Extended family settings further diffused the possibility of hierarchies between men and women, with age rather than gender serving as the more important basis of authority. Courtship and marriage practices also lessened potential imbalances in male-female power relations. Early marriage age, scarcity of unattached adults, and high rates of remarriage indicated Indians' recognition that it was hard to survive without the contributions of a spouse and that men and women merited equal value in their respective labors. Practices of sororal and levirate polygyny, birth control, and easy divorce limited male authority further by giving women more freedom within family units.[51]

Missionaries recognized that Indians formed marital unions, even if they did so without church sacraments—what Spaniards referred to as "natural marriage contracts" made "in the forest." Yet, because missionaries assumed women could not control themselves and because they could not see women's agency in such patterns, these unions seemed fragile, lasting only as long as the two people found it satisfactory. More important, from a Spanish worldview, they connoted male powerlessness and female promiscuity, because Franciscans interpreted Indian divorce as the exchange or sharing of women among men. Fray José de Solís believed such customs allowed men to sell or trade women for horses, guns, powder, bullets, and beads. Fray Juan Agustín Morfi condemned Karankawas in particular, claiming the men "barter one [wife] for another with the greatest facility, granting or requesting a bonus (*ribete*) in consideration of the advantage that they bring with them." Yet, a factor that equally disturbed missionaries was the gender equality of divorce, with women just as likely as men to end relationships, often simply by walking out of their home in a husband's absence. Because Christian moralists had long associated paganism with illicit sexuality, Franciscans may have been primed with misconceptions of the sexual mores they would find among Indian "pagans," thus distorting their readings of native marital customs. Therefore, they labeled Indian gender practices "evil," associated such "perversions" with other savage customs like cannibalism and witchcraft, and spoke of "hurling exorcisms" in response.[52]

Much of what informed Franciscan views of the sexual and familial life of southern and central Texas Indians originated more in their imaginations than in observed fact, but what most energized their concerns was the overturning of what the missionaries identified as the "natural" order between men and women. Added to Indian family and economic structures that Spaniards believed gave inordinate authority to women at the expense of men, Indian women expressed, in the missionaries' eyes, a freedom of sexuality in equal measure to that of men. Men were not only exchanging women, but women were exchanging men. By the Spaniards' reckoning, the power to divorce and to seek new partners meant that Indian women were not merely sexually licentious but also uncontrolled. Spaniards' early modern ideas of women as morally weak, sexually insatiable, and naturally sinful meant that, to them, the expression and exercise of women's sexuality acted as a dangerous source for moral and social disorder. In early modern Spanish society, two prominent symbols of social disorder were the broken sword (representing dishonored manhood) and the wandering woman (representing uncontrolled and thus shameful womanhood). Spaniards thus had a concept of social order posited on male honor that, in turn, depended upon the control of women, particularly their sexuality.[53]

In response, Franciscans sought every opportunity to "civilize" Indian sexuality and to order family life while Indians were resident at mission settlements, yet their "successes" came only at a superficial level. One area of seeming influence that Indians often agreed to change was dress. Spaniards came from a society with mandated sumptuary laws that distinguished people's social and economic class through their clothing and endowed those distinctions with judgments of sexual respectability, particularly for women. Ordinances, for instance, specified dress codes to identify and differentiate prostitutes, concubines, and "kept" women from respectable women. Most Indians did not earn missionary approval, because the heat and humidity of southern and coastal regions dictated limited covering except for mud and herbal mixtures rubbed on the skin to protect it from insect bites. Unlike Europeans, Indians did not automatically associate exposed bodies with sex or sexuality. Along the coast in particular, missionaries bemoaned that "Indians should come into the church, be present at the sacrosanct sacrifice of the Mass, and receive the Holy Sacraments in their barbarous disarray and as naked as they live in their primitive heathendom." Franciscans in northern Coahuila argued that Indian residents at San Bernardo "were so lax in their attitude toward dressing that married couples were prone to dispense with clothing altogether in their homes, so that the ministers found it necessary to take boys from the age of seven into the monastery."[54]

In terms of the connections between sexuality and dress (or the lack thereof), the male sexual appetite found expression, so the friars believed, in Indian men's minimal coverage with a "breech-clout" and tattoos on their faces, arms, chests, and necks, sometimes in imitation of a necklace. In the San Antonio area, where tanned and painted deerskins made up both male and female apparel, missionaries noted "some laxity in the dress among men" but greeted with pleasure the women who covered their entire bodies "from head to foot." Fray Espinosa especially praised women's "decorous" dress "even when nursing the young" (no bared breasts here). Fray Antonio de Olivares asserted that when women covered themselves "in all modesty down to their feet," it was a "trait to be admired for they are a people without the light of the Gospel."[55]

Indian men and women in the San Antonio communities readily adapted Spanish goods to their own use, and clothing was no exception. And why not? They had little reason to reject supplies of clothing, and Indian peoples likely interpreted the clothes given by Franciscans within their own understanding of the purpose of joint settlement, namely alliance and trade, both of which required ritual gift exchange to function properly. Their appreciation of dress and decoration meant that Spanish garments could be esteemed equally with their own. In fact, one governor at mid-century complained, "All the mission Indians: men, women and children, are well clothed even better than their station warrants." Mission inventories indicate that men received a shirt, breeches, a long, heavy wool pullover, a hat, shoes, a knife, and a rosary to wear. Women received a blouse, woolen and flannel skirts, ready-made underskirts and camisoles, shawls, shoes, earrings, strings of beads, necklaces, ribbons, and rosaries. The extensive nature and detail of these supplies indicate the thoroughness with which the Franciscans tried to cover Indian bodies and tattoos.[56]

Debates over how Indian men and women expressed themselves with their clothed bodies, in contrast, remained unresolved to the missionaries' satisfaction. Native dances, called "*mitotes*" by Spaniards, particularly garnered Franciscan attention. Dances ranged from "festive and happy" to "funereal and sad" in commemoration of the beginning or end of communal hunting or fishing expeditions, war victories and losses, and ritual or spiritual occasions. Yet, to Franciscans, they bespoke sinful sexuality. Missionaries such as fray Dolores y Viana feared the detrimental effects of letting mission residents mix with their "heathen" relatives, because such reunions encouraged them to engage in "diabolical rites observed by these savages in their dances and gyrations." More specifically, they believed that dances became "occasions for the Indian women to go to excess and fail in their moral standards." Franciscans had no power to stop the *mitotes*, however, even those held at mission settlements; a point they glossed over by arguing that permissiveness in this instance was necessary, "as we permit evil lest worse things happen." Missionary guidelines at San Antonio argued that the friars had to make allowances as long as the dances were not done with "any sinful motive." At Missions Espíritu Santo, Rosario, and San José, missionaries introduced Spanish and Mexican dances as a means of making the dancing more acceptable in their view. Franciscan complaints that mission residents regularly went off into the woods to hold their own "pagan dances and diabolical mitotes" show that Indians were the ones who chose when and with whom to dance.[57]

With an equal lack of success, missionaries hoped to use the confessional as a means of reform. Fray Bartholomé García's manual for administering church sacraments in a Coahuilteco dialect aimed to enable missionaries to communicate better through the confessional as well as in catechism, penance, matrimony, and extreme unction. It also clarified how central sexual behaviors were to the sins Franciscans most imagined Indian men and women falling prey to (though these may not have differed much from what they would have warned Spaniards against as well). Questions regarding violations of the fourth commandment—respect to parents—quickly elided into asking if parents had had sex or women had committed "immodest" acts with men in front of their children. The fifth commandment—about murder—elicited questions about whether the supplicant had beaten or killed anyone, eaten human flesh, used peyote or mescal, gotten drunk, danced *mitotes,* or practiced abortion.[58]

Fray García broke down the sixth commandment—on adultery—into different interrogations for men and for women. Missionaries were to ask both men and women whether they had engaged in sex; if so, with whom; whether the person was single, married, or a relative; and whether they had sex while other people watched. If a man or woman was living "in sin" with someone, they could not be confessed until they had moved out; an injunction that presumably applied to couples married by native custom but not church ceremony. Men were to be asked how many times a week they had sex or whether they had sex with animals—and how many times with any one animal. If they had engaged in sex with another man, fray García specified that the confessor had to ask whether they were the agent or recipient in the act. Questions asked only of women focused on intimate acts other than intercourse—whether they had allowed men to embrace or kiss them or to touch their breasts or genitals. The only inquiries about masturbation were to be asked of women, and missionaries were also to ask women whether they had engaged in sex with another woman. In the end, however, these questions reveal a great deal about missionary concerns and nothing about actual Indian sexuality. Nor do we have records of Indian reactions to such inquiries. What is known is that private confession took place only once a year, and it appeared that Indians who remained long enough to take part in the annual ritual quickly devised rote answers with which to avert missionary surveillance of their private lives.[59]

Franciscans expended the most energy seeking to institutionalize marriage between Indian men and women, identifying that relationship as the foundation of "family." Missionaries particularly latched onto an image of native women burdened with an inordinate amount of work but simultaneously rewarded with an inordinate amount of authority. Egalitarian relations between native men and women confounded Spaniards' notions of male familial authority, as when a Coco headman explained to Governor Rafael Martínez Pacheco that, even though he himself was a Christian, his wife's determination to remain "heathen" meant that he would not enter a mission because he simply would not leave her behind. To the missionaries, such perceived imbalances of power between men and women had to be corrected in order for Indians to act as Christian families.[60]

Franciscans therefore tried to use the day-to-day functioning of mission settlements to inculcate patriarchal customs in Indian family life, especially by directing Indian men in how to assume their "proper" place as head of the household. Their efforts to reorient gendered divisions of labor, as already discussed, aimed to help instruct men in their obligations and authority as fathers and husbands. Missionaries linked agricultural and technical/mechanical crafts directly to men's ability to support their families. In a decree conveyed to Indian residents at San José, Commandant General Pedro de Nava argued that Indian men must "apply themselves to daily service or work so as to earn the wherewithal to maintain and support their families." According to missionary teachings, the role of provider would then put men in a dominant position within the family, with women and children as dependents. This message remained a constant refrain through the eighteenth century as missionaries like Dolores y Viana reiterated the need to teach Indian men to look after their "temporal welfare" and "to manage affairs and support themselves and their wives and children."[61]

In their quest to meet church and viceregal expectations that they instill a "concept of the family" in Indian communities, Franciscans used not only mission management but also religious lessons to emphasize patriarchal relations within a nuclear unit of husband, wife, and children. The Holy Family, composed of Mary, Joseph, and the child Jesus, for instance, dominated Franciscan typology of the domestic life and relations in a Christian family, particularly in illustrating "proper" male and female roles within the family and women's "proper" submissiveness and modesty. This choice was not only doctrinal but also a practical one. Without families of their own, missionaries themselves offered no role model. They also turned to local Spanish men and women in the San Antonio community to help out by acting as godparents to Indian children at their baptisms (in the process perhaps attaining status as fictive kin in natives' eyes). Fray Isidro de Espinosa explained that "each child selected his padrino or madrina [godparents] from among the Spanish soldiers and their wives who were in attendance and entrusted to him, or her, the name of the saint he had chosen for his baptism. To help make it a festive occasion, the padrino took as much care in dressing and 'cherishing' his god children as his circumstances permitted."[62]

Franciscans used *saetas*, instructive verses that followed devotional hymns, as constant reinforcement of social as well as religious lessons. A *saeta* written by fray

Antonio Margil de Jesús entitled "As the Father, So the Son" reinforced patriarchal teachings for Indian men.

Food and dress and wise instruction
You must give your children,
Lead them to conform their conduct
To the holy law of God.

As you do, so they will do,
All your children, all your kin;
And your daily way of life
They will make their very own.

Keep in mind and know for certain,
T'is the ordinary course
And the sequence of events:
As the father, so the son.[63]

Franciscans also instituted patrilineal ethnic identification in census records by assigning children to their father's ethnic group and ignoring that of the mother. This manner of renaming may not have obscured the egalitarian status of native women as much as missionaries intended though. Studies of surviving examples of the Sanan language and patterns of group names at one of the San Antonio missions hint at the survival of social practices. Some Sanan group appellations contain recognizable female names, like "Ocava" and "Cocom," suggesting their derivation from the personal names of high-ranking people—in this case women. In turn, if groups took their names from female clan leaders, that would seem to indicate the continued prestigious place of women in descent and kinship systems among the Sanas at San Antonio de Valero.[64]

Balancing out their lessons in patriarchy for Indian men, the Franciscans also hoped Indian women would take the Virgin Mary as their exemplar, an ideal of womanhood regularly reinforced in catechisms of faith, viaticums to the sick, iconography of the church, weekly processions every Saturday, and feast days, masses, hymns, and verses in celebration of Mary. Even missionary gifts of rosaries as prayer aids might reinforce such emulation because the rosary offered an outward symbol of veneration toward Mary consisting of five or ten decades of beads (Hail Marys) broken up by a single bead (Our Father) through which the Mysteries of the Virgin were recited. Marian imagery and worship promoted the Virgin as a prescriptive model of female sexual and moral purity, as belief in Mary's Immaculate Conception, in addition to her stainless virginity, was at its height in Spain and its American colonies at this time. As missionaries baptized Indians, they named them after female and male saints, but the names Joseph (José) and Mary (María) from the Holy Family predominated, particularly in the case of women.[65]

Marriage rites were one of the central sacraments of the Catholic Church, so solemnizing Indian marriages through religious ceremony held the utmost importance in missionary plans to institute a "concept of family" in the lives of Indians. Prohibitions against baptizing the children of unions not solemnized by the church meant that marriage also became crucial to missionary efforts to convert children. When Mission Valero was established at San Antonio with Xarames from northern Coahuila, headman Santiago Ximenes became the first governor of the settlement and remarried his wife Juana María by church ceremony (their union was already at least three years old, as they had a two-year-old daughter with them when they moved to San Antonio in 1718). In the case of polygynous families, church law required that Indian men choose one among their wives with whom to commit themselves in marriages *in facie Ecclesiae* (by church ceremony; literally, "in front of the church"). As fray Dolores y Viana asserted, "for those who have married in the forest, the natural marriage contract is ratified (allowing only one wife to those who bring several)." Salvador, a Chaguane Indian at Valero, testified that even the governor of Texas, Juan Antonio de Bustillo y Ceballos, took part in the campaign against polygyny by attempting to take wives away from men with more than one. Intriguingly, however, missionaries interpreted practices of levirate polygyny—when a man took his brother's widow as a second wife—as miraculous due to its resemblance to the law of levirate found in the Bible. They therefore saw the native custom as indicative of the "greatest light exhibited by these savages in their pagan state" and as evidence that "there is something (a Being) that is the author of all things."[66]

No matter the argument, however, Indians sternly refused missionary demands that they renounce polygyny. Such calls represented an attack on a custom by which many Indian groups marked male prestige. Polygyny was generally limited to warriors, chiefs, and shamans. Among some Indian groups, for instance, fray Ignacio Antonio Ciprián found that only one-third of the men had two or three wives. Karankawa society allowed only shamans the distinction of multiple wives. Ciprián might proudly proclaim that Mesquites and Pastías willingly gave up polygyny, for whom it was "very common," by having their marriages with one wife blessed, but many more who accepted baptism nevertheless drew the line at changing their marriage customs. When compared to baptism statistics over the course of the eighteenth century, those for marriages solemnized in the church offer a striking contrast, consistently lagging far behind. In reports ranging from 1756 to 1767, at the high point of mission population counts, both secular and church reports found that rates of marriage amounted to only one-sixth to one-fourth those of baptism. Further, baptism rates may have been inflated in part because of the high number done *in articulo mortis* (at death) when epidemics swept through the missions every decade.[67]

As late as the 1790s, a Karankawa convert named Manuel Alegre left the Rosario mission with the woman considered his wife because he refused to marry by church sacrament, saying "he would rather die than go through with it." More interesting still, Manuel Alegre's marriage to María del Rosario may well have represented the practice of levirate, because María was the widow of Karankawa leader José María, and Manuel appears to have been his brother. Other men simply continued to practice polygyny even after their unions with one woman had been solemnized. That Indians who willingly accepted baptism still refused to change their marriage customs vividly indicates that, for them, accepting Christianity did not entail accepting Spanish gender systems. Even more important, it reflects natives' commitment to their own constructions of marriage and family, and the Franciscans' powerlessness to change them.[68]

In fact, native individuals and families used mission sites as gathering places where they might rebuild and reconstitute family bands through new kinship ties of intermarriage on their own terms. The seasonal migrations that brought Indian groups to mission settlements represented not only efforts at meeting subsistence needs but also the need to maintain and renew kinship ties. The movement itself reflected the independence of family band headmen to make decisions for their kin and to move them as they saw fit, according to their needs. Family bands in large, confederated groups could better preserve their customs, particularly those that determined the positions of men and women via kinship systems. For instance, the fall and winter fishing camps where Karankawa bands joined together along the coast appear to have been the location for rituals confirming family ties among bands and for courtship. The social function of these shared encampments became even more important as disease reduced population numbers and bands decreased in size, often melding together. Notably, however, for Karankawas and other coastal peoples, it was the shared settlements away from Spanish eyes that continued to serve the needs and interests of kinship and courtship practices. Indians of southern and central Texas did not enjoy the same isolation from disease as those on the coast, so they increasingly represented only the remnants of groups and came to mission settlements in small numbers to find other kin. They were not the last of their peoples, however, and the presence of relatives and friends living in settlements independent of Spanish mission-presidio complexes alternately meant that mission residents had other places to go if and when mission life became untenable. For those groups who faced even more drastic population declines, the mission settlements may have provided a place for individuals to seek new ties of kinship through adoption and intermarriage.[69]

Marriages strengthened alliances that were begun before the mission settlements existed. Members of a Pajalat confederacy, for instance, concentrated their settlement at Concepción, and intermarriage reinforced their alliances and united power within certain leading families. One of the first leaders to join the settlement was José Flores, a Patumaca "*Capitán de los Pajalats, Siquipiles, Tilpacopoales, y otros,*" and the first *gobernador* of Concepción. His wife, Efigenia, was a Pajalat whom he remarried in a church ceremony in 1733. Three of their four children went on to hold office or marry men who became officeholders over the next thirty years. It is likely their marriages to members of other groups helped to solidify the authority that kept family members in office. José and Efigenia's daughter Margarita, for instance, married a Pujan named Alberto Palacios, who served as *gobernador* in 1753; their son Juan Nicolás, who held multiple offices, married a Tilpacopal woman named Serafina Micheas; and their other daughter, Martha, had two different husbands, Fernando de Soto and Nicolás, who were both Tilpacopal *gobernadors*. Perhaps further consolidating bilineal kinship lines—and maintaining native customs of egalitarian authority between men and women—fray José Francisco López noted that during mission elections, if settlements lacked a sufficient number of men for a vote, married women were added to the voting register.[70]

By the 1770s, records at Valero show intermarriage constituted new and old alliances among Xarames, Sanas, Papanacs, Payayas, Lipan Apaches, and Muruames. Of the eleven married couples present in 1772, only three were not mixed marriages. The adoption of Coahuilteco as a lingua franca by the second half of the century also reflects the mixing of families and cultures within mission settlements in San Antonio. In 1740, Toribio de Urrutia noted that although many languages were spoken in the five missions, four had begun to predominate in common usage. By 1760, fray Bartholomé García had written his manual for the sacraments using a Coahuilteco dialect for administering to eighteen different groups (though not all the groups he listed were in fact Coahuilteco speakers). In 1789, fray José Francisco López reported that very different nations used one language, which through common usage had become "uniform in meaning."[71]

Intermarriage also helped to maintain ties between groups inside and outside mission settlements. Along the San Gabriel River, for example, fray Benito Fernández de Santa Ana had hopes of Akokisas joining Mission San Francisco Xavier because individual Akokisa women who had married Bidai and Deadose men among

the mission residents still maintained communication and contact with their relatives outside the mission. Similar ties existed along the coast at Refugio, where one-
fourth of the baptisms in the first two decades of the nineteenth century recorded
mixed Indian parentage among Karankawa, Piguique, Copane, Coapite, Pamaque,
Malaguita, Pajalat, Tobosa, and Coco peoples—groups known to have been allies
throughout much of the eighteenth century.[72]

Ultimately, the very ethnic complexity of mission settlement populations indicated the success of kinship networking. On the one hand, we know that Sanan
speakers appear to have been able to marry individuals of their own bands or
members of other Sanan-speaking bands because the language survived in the names
of multiple small social groups and hundreds of individuals belonging to these
groups. In response to spreading disease and warfare since the seventeenth century,
however, many other groups had increasingly formalized alliances through intermarriage. This practice may have developed out of older customs, at least among
bands of the same ethnic group, who married exogamously when individual bands
lacked potential spouses or band members were close consanguines and thus not
marriageable. For many others, intermarriage became a necessity only within mission settlements, as cycling epidemics and declining populations hurt their chances
of finding a mate within individual ethnic groups. Thus, for instance, Payayas
eventually intermarried with at least twenty-five other groups inside and outside
Valero over a seventy-year period, choosing whenever possible groups that had long
been their closest neighbors.[73]

Later, Indian peoples incorporated their Spanish neighbors into intermarriage
practices when mission residence began to include Spanish civil settlers and the
communities merged together. In the 1770s and 1780s, retired soldiers began to rent
land from the missions, while townspeople rented rooms at the missions. Others
came from as far as Nuevo León, Coahuila, New Mexico, Chihuahua, Oaxaca, San
Luis Potosí, and Mexico City to settle on mission lands. Ties inevitably developed as
families lived and farmed together. Between 1775 and 1790, reports from the missions
indicate that missionaries increasingly performed marriages uniting Indian and
Spanish peoples, so that by 1790 only one union took place between Indians; all
others were exogamic. Church and state officials used the Spanish-Indian unions to
support secularization of the missions, asserting that such relationships proved
that conversion had been successful and the missions could now become parish
churches. "It can therefore be inferred," fray José Francisco López concluded, "that
this mission cannot be called a mission of Indians but a gathering of Spanish
people." Yet, the mixed caste category of people in San Antonio did not reflect that
Indians had changed as much as "*mestizaje* had changed the complexion of the

community." The missions therefore offered an ideal way station for people to reunite with lost kin, to form new kinship ties, and to find cohesion through traditional customs of family building adapted to a new setting.[74]

By the 1760s, Franciscans were conceding that Texas was not one of their more successful mission fields, most often charging their failure to the supposed indolence, recalcitrance, innate savagery, and vices of Indians. Franciscans more specifically lamented the extremes of an "unnatural" native world of overturned gender relations. When missionaries could not attract or keep native peoples within the mission complexes, they blamed the attractions of the sexually charged world in which they believed Indians lived. It was the "continual seduction of the heathen" that repeatedly made mission Indians forget their newfound religion. Indians, they argued, rejected the mission life because they "prefer to suffer hunger, nakedness and the inclemencies of the weather provided they be left free to live indolent in the wilds or along the seashore, where they give themselves over to all kinds of excesses, especially to lust, theft and dancing."[75]

From a native perspective, missionary goals were often irrelevant to the political events and social processes taking place on the ground. Mutual needs brought Spanish and Indian peoples together in shared settlements and a new form of "confederation" by midcentury, and both found the means to stabilize their populations and maintain their families and societies. In this spirit, a memorial concerning military defense and economic subsistence published by the *cabildo* (city council) of San Antonio proudly referred to its joint constituency as "this community of mission Indians and residents of this *villa* and presidio." Geopolitical considerations had led Spanish and Indian leaders to interweave their communities, and mutual material accommodation allowed them to continue independent ways of social and family life, even as they defended that life from outside threats. In contrast, Apaches, long the impetus for the confederation between Spanish and Indian settlers in the San Antonio area, would follow a far different and more violent path in seeking political advantage in Spanish mission-presidio complexes.[76]

chapter four

Negotiating Fear with Violence:
Apaches and Spaniards at Midcentury

In July 1767, as the marqués de Rubí inspected the defensive capabilities of the northern provinces, riding up from Coahuila toward the Presidio San Sabá northwest of San Antonio, he passed through the Nueces River valley, where he found the remains of two missions, San Lorenzo de la Santa Cruz and Nuestra Señora de la Candelaria del Cañón, established for Apaches a mere six years earlier. In the eight days it had taken him to travel from Presidio Santa Rosa (in Coahuila) to the missions, his expedition had passed numerous Apache rancherías, some in which the Indians were farming along the Rio Grande, others in which they were traveling to trade with Coahuila residents and soldiers. The farther north he moved into Texas, though, the fewer he had seen, finding instead abandoned encampments alongside the sad stubble of crops from years past. Upon reaching the river valley known as El Cañón where the missions had stood, he camped at the "unpopulated ruins" of Candelaria— consisting of only a house with a small chapel and a large hut—before proceeding on to inspect the twenty-one soldiers (from Presidio San Luis de las Amarillas far to the north along the San Sabá River) who were garrisoned at Mission San Lorenzo, a place he also found "to be without a single Indian." He concluded that they could only be called "the imaginary mission[s] of El Cañón," while the Apaches were a "never-realized congregation." How had the project come to such an ignominious end in so little time?[1]

To associate Apaches with Spanish missions might seem rather strange. At midcentury, Spaniards and Apaches had been combatants far longer than allies. By the time Spaniards moved into Texas permanently in the 1710s, long experience in New Mexico had established in Spanish imaginations that Apache men were such fierce warriors that "in the end, they dominate all the other Indians." Viceregal authorities had initially identified Apaches as such a powerful nation that the Spanish government needed to form with them a "perpetual and firm confederation." They hoped that such an Apache alliance would serve as the equivalent of a northern cordon of armed garrisons protecting Spanish dominions from French aggressions. Yet, in Texas their attempts to ally with Caddos automatically put Spaniards into a hostile position vis-à-vis Apaches. The Spanish expeditions sent to Caddo lands and the missions and presidios that Spaniards erected there made a Spanish-Caddo alliance clear to Apaches. When native groups pledged alliance with each other, they simultaneously pledged their enmity against one another's enemies. No possibility of dual allegiance existed. Neither did they draw lines among economic, civil, political, and military relations—an alliance in one area meant alliance in all others. Thus, Spaniards became enemies of Apaches without even meeting them. The Spaniards' joint settlement in the mission-presidio complex at San Antonio with Indian bands of central Texas such as Payayas and Ervipiames (who also counted Apaches among their foes) only strengthened this enmity further.[2]

By the beginning of the eighteenth century, moreover, the spread of Spanish horses and French arms was reorienting native power relations across Texas and the Southern Plains, a development that did not bode well for Spaniards in Texas. Though now less well-known than their western relatives, Lipan Apaches represented a widespread and formidable power at this time. Eastern Apaches living in what is now Texas—primarily Lipan Apaches but also some Mescaleros, Natages (a division of Mescaleros), and Faraones (a division of Jicarillas)—had gained an early advantage there when they acquired horses in the seventeenth century through trading and raiding in New Mexico. By the 1740s, "Lipan" had become the designation used by Spaniards to refer to the easternmost Plains Apache groups variously identified as Ypandes, Ysandis, Chentis, and Pelones. Like their multiple Apache relatives to the west (Chiricahuas, Mescaleros, Jicarillas, and Navajos), Lipans spoke dialects of the southern branch of the Athapaskan language group. Their economy centered on hunting and raiding for bison and horses, which did not allow for permanent settlement, although they did practice semicultivation.[3]

Consisting of matrilocal extended families but often named after strong male leaders, Lipan social units farmed and hunted in individual rancherías that might cluster together for defense and ceremonial ritual. Usually numbering around four hundred people, such units aggregated ten to thirty extended families related by blood or marriage that periodically joined together for horse raids, bison hunts, and coordinated military action. No central leadership existed, and group leaders made decisions in consultation with extended-family headmen, but unity of language, dress, and customs maintained their collective identity and internal peace. An estimated twelve groups of Lipan Apaches, each incorporating several rancherías, lived in central Texas and used horses to expand their control over bison territories and to better secure their individual rancherías from attack during the agricultural cycles that alternated with bison hunting over the year. As horses' importance rose, so too did the raiding that maintained Lipan herds and sustained their economy.

Yet, the acquisition of horses by the oft-allied Comanches, Wichitas, and Caddos to their north and east soon neutralized the Apaches' advantage. More important, this triumvirate was the first to gain European arms through French trade to the east, while they simultaneously cut off the Lipans from trading posts in Louisiana that might have provided them with guns. By the 1720s, Apaches in Texas began to experience new pressures, caught as they were between Spanish settlements to their south that allied with their Caddo-, Tonkawa-, and Coahuilteco-speaking enemies and Comanche and Wichita bands to their north who were moving into hunting territories that Apaches claimed as their own. As the security and defense of their families became even more linked to the ability to move quickly, a regular supply of horses became all the more critical to Apaches' survival. The horse herds of Spanish missions, presidios, and settlements proved irresistible to increasingly vulnerable Apaches.

Apache domestic economies and power relations together became more defined by warfare. Lipan Apaches oriented their subsistence into seasonal patterns that allowed them to plant crops in the early spring and then move their entire bands through bison areas for extended periods of hunting in spring and fall, returning only after the hunting season ended to harvest crops. But farming was on the decline in the eighteenth century as economic activities that were centered on the care of horse herds and the production of saddles, bridles, and leather armor for both horses and warriors expanded along with increased hide processing. Band life thus became even more focused on the acquisition of horses and bison. Increased prestige for the warriors who supplied both followed apace as the reputations won or lost in raids and hunts became more central components to internal social, economic, and political relations and hierarchies. Women who practiced limited horticulture also gathered plant foods and traded with other native groups for agricultural products. At the same time, the larger size of raiding and hunting parties meant that women and children traveled with warriors, assisting men in maintaining camps, processing hides, and even making arrows. As they hunted in family bands, women might even participate directly in hunting deer, antelope, and rabbits.[4]

Apache adaptations of kin-based gender roles to these historical changes, however, could have unintended and deleterious effects. Women's presence in raiding and hunting parties put them in the line of hostile fire and capture by Spanish forces seeking retaliation for raids that were gutting their herds. For Spanish

Lipan Apaches north of the Rio Grande. The man has a painted buffalo robe draped over his shoulder, and the woman wears a fringed chamois skirt, poncho, leggings, and moccasins. Watercolor by Lino Sánchez y Tapia after the original sketch by José María Sánchez y Tapia, an artist-cartographer who traveled through Texas as a member of a Mexican boundary and scientific expedition in the years 1828–31. Courtesy of the Gilcrease Museum, Tulsa, Oklahoma.

observers, Apache socioeconomics seemed to mute or disguise gender divisions of labor, though it was not always clear whether they could not or chose not to recognize them. Either way, Spaniards had little understanding of Apache women as noncombatants and thus made little association of those women with peace. Indeed, at times, Spanish authorities officially categorized Apache women as a "regular reserve corps" of Apache military forces. Attitudes such as these put Apache women squarely in harm's way when it came to Spanish hostility and battlefield violence.[5]

But for Lipan Apaches, their mobile lifestyle kept inviolate their kin-based definitions of gender and the accompanying social and political roles for men and women. Though they traced their lineage bilaterally (through both parents), they organized their family bands by matrilocal residence. In a sense, female-defined households balanced male-defined raiding and hunting economies. The origin or emergence myth for Lipan people sanctified this order in the story of a divine heroine, Changing Woman, and her son, culture hero Killer of Enemies, who together created the world. Under his mother's guidance and direction, Killer of Enemies slew monsters who threatened the people, persuaded horses, antelope, and buffalo to provide for the people, and then taught the people how to raid and war. Once he had established peace and equipped the people for life on their own, Killer of Enemies returned to live in Changing Woman's home. From there, the two deities offered supernatural aid as well as a continued model of a matrilocal household and male-centered political economy. Thus, Spaniards not only refused to recognize divisions between Apache men and women. When they attacked kin-based rancherías and took women captive, Spaniards also struck at the peaceful order and gender balance within Apache polities.[6]

Apache raids and Spanish reprisals sparked a cycle of violence that lasted thirty years. If Apaches extended kin classifications to all with whom they interacted, then Spaniards represented the negation of brothers. Strangers were only potentially dangerous; enemies were a proven commodity. And Spaniards were clearly enemies. Raiding did not always signal war; it could be merely an alternative to trade. But in the case of Spaniards in the first half of the century, Apache raiding was an instrument of both economic gain and political competition. Yet, if Spanish-Apache relations were the antithesis of kin, even that relationship came with prescribed ritual and behavior. From the 1720s through 1740s, Spanish violence against Apache women via captivity and enslavement alternated with Apache violence against Spanish men via bloodshed and humiliation, as both groups became increasingly demoralized by the other. Spanish soldiers could not prevent Apache raids or bring about their complete defeat, despite numerous efforts to chase down Apache raiders and challenge them in battle. So, instead, they exploited the only vulnerability they could find in such an invincible foe: women and children. In the wake of daybreak attacks on their villages, Apache men answered the loss of family members at Spanish hands by cutting off those hands, often literally, with rare but potent displays of combat and mutilation on the battlefield.

At midcentury, however, when Spanish and Apache men came to realize that a far greater threat to both their women and families appeared with expanding Comanche and Wichita bands, they saw reason to make amends and then form an alliance for the first time. Past conflict inevitably shaped their first peace accord, nevertheless, and Spaniards and Apaches opened their diplomacy with handicaps when they pursued a relationship through bonds of fictive and real kinship. Mission-presidio complexes again became a focus of such efforts. Taking a more martial tone than that found in the San Antonio region, however, Spanish-Apache negotiations established these sites to ally Apache warriors and Spanish soldiers in defense rather than as an alliance of families joined in settlement. If the diplomatic pendulum had first swung far in the direction of male violence in the first half of the century, its swing in the opposite direction toward female mediation was a slow one. Replacing enmity with peaceful alliance did not prove easy, and Spaniards and Apaches spent the next twenty years (1750s and 1760s) sparring over how they might achieve that goal as Apache women asserted a more pacific role in diplomatic gambits.

Apache men's need to defend the women of their families and communities, on the one hand, and Spanish men's coercive use of those same women to manipulate Apache men, on the other, often put women at the center of violence and diplomacy. By a not too circuitous route, Spanish men's fear first led to Apache women's captivity. Construction on settlements at San Antonio had barely broken ground when Apaches declared war by planting arrows with red cloth flying from their shafts like small flags near the presidio site. As Apaches mounted raids on the horse herds of San Antonio missions, civilian ranches, and the presidio beginning in the 1720s, frustration escalated into terror among Spanish settlers, soldiers, and officials. The idea of Apaches as inveterate raiders became so fixed in Spanish minds that they attributed any attack by unknown raiders in the San Antonio area to them. Presidial forces' inability to stop the warriors' relentless attacks transformed simple horse raids into what Spaniards believed to be signs of a "war of extermination" against them. Thus, the tacticians of raids so profitable they took hundreds of horses became, in the Spanish telling, "enemies of humanity" terrorizing civilian populations of women and children. By such constructions, Spaniards transformed their soldiers and officers into chivalrous defenders of "civilization" while reducing Apache warriors to "unmanly" cowards preying on the "most defenseless of innocents."[7]

Death counts to the contrary, military and diplomatic officials labeled Apache warriors barbaric killers of women and thus characterized them as men without honor. Whenever Spanish officers and soldiers found themselves in a weak situation, they cast blame outward by projecting upon Apache men a "savage" nature that could not be answered in kind. It was no coincidence that the Apache bands who posed the greatest challenge to Spanish authority figured prominently in Spanish images of Indian warriors so cruel they "killed regardless of sex and age." Spanish officials stubbornly turned a blind eye to the economic considerations behind Apache men's raiding and instead ascribed only motivations of irrational bloodthirstiness to their actions.

Despite Spanish claims, however, horses were the attraction for Apache raids, and generally the only people injured or killed were ranch hands or soldiers trying to prevent the theft of animals. The burial records of Mission Valero, for instance, indicate that out of 1,088 deaths recorded between 1718 and 1782, only 15 people died at the hands of hostile Apache, Comanche, or Coco raiders (1.3 percent)—and Apaches did not even bear sole responsibility for the deaths. Moreover, the danger of injury rested outside the settlements, primarily where horse herds were maintained at nearby ranches or presidio corrals, away from the arenas and activities of women and children. Fray Benito Fernández de Santa Ana noted that although enemy Apaches "can travel through the land as they please," it was the "shepherd Indians" who were the most endangered. Fray Ignacio Antonio Ciprián similarly pointed out in the 1740s that "although [mission Indians] are in constant danger of attack by the Apaches (a very bold enemy who has dared to enter the presidio even in day time and roam the streets), they have never entered this mission grounds." Apaches only once approached the San Antonio community itself, and that, as will be discussed later, was an unheralded response to Spanish slave raids on Apache rancherías.[8]

Indeed, it was actually Apache women who became the primary targets of violence. In a series of retaliatory strikes after horse raids, Spanish forces aimed at the capture of Apache women and children. Echoing policies adopted late in the sixteenth century against Chichimecas who fought to keep Spanish invaders out of their lands in north-central Mexico, officials in Texas sought to use offensive raids on Apache encampments to exterminate or enslave as many as possible in order to "pacify" the regions nearest their settlements. Technically, any Indians captured in a "just war" were to be sentenced as criminals to a finite term of enslavement, but perpetual servitude was touted as the only means of achieving peace. The language used to describe the Apache threat bore a striking resemblance to what had been said over one hundred years earlier of Chichimecas, as Spaniards writing from a siege mentality rhetorically denounced Apaches as "barbarous enemies of humankind," while strategizing that the opportunity to gain Indian slaves would be sufficient incentive to motivate soldiers and civilians to take up arms for the state. Their repeated decisions to attack rancherías while the Apache men were gone on bison hunts made it clear that the Spaniards were not in search of peace but of women and children to enslave.[9]

In turn, Spaniards rationalized their decision to keep these captives in bondage as necessary for defense and, by sleight of interpretation, deemed Apache women and children captured by Spanish forces not *cautivos* but *prisioneros* (prisoners of war). By taking Apache women out of the category of noncombatants, Spaniards deprived them of the consideration and protection that Spanish codes of war dictated for women—in effect, a denial of their identity as women eligible for the privileges of respectful Spanish womanhood. They believed that if violence against Apache women helped to protect Spanish women by providing officials with pawns with which to manipulate Apache men, then so be it. In turn, Lipan oral traditions would later declare that raids on Lipan encampments by enemies who attacked women and children as they stood right by their homes were "not the way men fight."[10]

Telling incidents reveal the process by which captive Apache women and children became political capital. Spanish captive-taking began within five years of the establishment of the San Antonio de Béxar presidio, when Spanish military officials decided something had to be done about Apache raids. Following a raid by five Apache warriors that netted fifty horses early in 1722, Captain Nicolás Flores took ten men in pursuit of the raiders and retrieved all the horses. The Spaniards also marked the success of their punitive expedition by triumphantly bringing back to San Antonio four of the Apache men's heads as trophies. Within a month, Flores had received a promotion in his commission at the presidio. But still the raiders came. The next year, when Apaches showed up Spanish forces by carrying off eighty horses from the presidial herds despite the presence of ten soldiers guarding the gates, Flores opted for a more drastic plan to thwart the Apache men. After he and his soldiers had pursued the raiders for twelve hours without catching them, they returned to the presidio for reinforcements so that they could take living trophies—wives and children—from Apache rancherías.[11]

Following signs that the Apache raiding party had divided into five groups, going off in as many directions (suggesting that warriors from five bands took part in the raid), Flores, thirty soldiers, and thirty-three Indians from mission communities chose to follow only one. For thirty-six days, they tracked what they believed to be the raiders' path until they reached a ranchería of eight to nine hundred Apaches, more than a hundred leagues away from San Antonio. The combined presidio and mission forces made a surprise attack and fought Apache warriors for six hours before claiming to have killed thirty-four warriors, including one chief. Reports—including the testimony of four soldiers present at the battle—indicated that in fact Flores's forces had attacked an Apache band innocent of the raids, had shot men in the back as they covered the retreat of their families, and had killed and captured women and children as they tried to escape. From the belongings left at the ranchería by fleeing Apache families, Flores's men also plundered 120 horses, saddles, bridles, knives, and spears. Yet, their more significant war booty was twenty women and children.[12]

Upon their return to San Antonio, conflict immediately flared between military and church officials over the fate of the captives. Objecting to the tactics that had won Flores his human prizes, Franciscan fray Joseph González, one of the missionaries at San Antonio de Valero, demanded that, rather than dividing them up among the men along with the rest of the booty as planned, the captives be repatriated in order to reestablish peace. One Apache woman emerged as both pawn and agent in negotiations when fray González determined that if sent back to her village as a diplomatic overture, she "could be the most opportune means of bringing about peace with Apaches and the safety of the presidio." As a mark of goodwill, and perhaps as advertisement of the benefits of conversion, the missionary dressed her "after the Spanish fashion" as best he could, using a petticoat, blouse, white embroidered hose, ribboned hat, and green skirt borrowed from soldiers' wives. To mark the peaceful spirit of her mission, he presented her with "an inlaid cross, which was very beautiful and which she should wear on her neck, with an embossed ribbon which Father took with great faith, since it had served as the ribbon to the key of the depository [of the mission's sacred vessels]." With a flint and a rock for making fires along the way, she left for home with a group of soldiers to escort her out of town.[13]

Twenty-two days later, the captive woman returned to San Antonio accompanying a principal Apache man with his wife at his side and three warriors at his back. With no translator, communication was reduced to symbolic gestures. When greeted by Spanish officers, the Apache leader presented Flores with both a baton of command (as a sign of his chief's political authority) and a bison hide painted with the image of the sun (as a sign of Apache deities' spiritual power). The Spaniards interpreted them simply as "a sign of peace" sent by Apache leadership. Meanwhile, the captive woman greeted fray González with gestures of joy and, when introduced to the missionary, the principal man too placed his hand on his chest to convey his pleasure at meeting the man who had emancipated her. González and other missionaries then conducted the Apache delegation to Valero, where the Franciscans quickly donned formal vestments and had the church bells rung and mass celebrated in thanksgiving for the Apaches' arrival.[14]

The delegation tarried for three days, housed variously in Mission Valero and in the homes of soldiers. Nothing, however, could alter the fact that even as the female emissary had traveled home with González's peace commission, Flores and his soldiers had divided the remaining nineteen women and children among themselves, some of them being taken to the Bahía presidio, while others were deported to lands even more distant. In the end, the delegation departed with only gifts scrounged up by Valero missionaries: five rosaries and five knives for Apache chiefs, two bunches of glass beads, earrings, tobacco, brown sugar candy, and ground corn. Two months later, when thirty Apaches came again for their lost family members, a chief endeavored to end Flores's stonewalling about the captives' fate by offering four Apache men as hostages if the Spanish commander would at least free the children. Flores flatly refused. Four soldiers later testified that as Flores spoke heatedly, the Apaches gathered their belongings to depart the meeting room, and one chief took the hand of one of the little girls held captive, turned with her to face Flores, and gestured as if to say, " 'This is what you want, not peace.' "[15]

The experiences of Cabellos Colorados's family band a decade later illustrates most poignantly the devastation that could be wrought by Spanish military policy. In December 1737, the chief and his party approached San Antonio seeking trade with Spanish residents, as members of his band had done intermittently in past years. The equal number of men and women in the party suggested their peaceful intent, yet Spanish forces were looking for someone to nab for recent horse raids, and the Apache group's arrival appeared too providential to pass up. When twenty-eight armed soldiers rode out, Cabellos Colorados and his men clearly did not expect a fight and thereby were quickly surrounded and captured. As an indication that the Spaniards had no evidence that the men in this group were actually raiders, they insisted on hearings in order to gather proof.

In June of 1738, Governor Prudencio de Orobio y Basterra thus proceeded to solicit testimony on the "infidelity of Apaches"—implicitly deeming them all one united group—although Cabellos Colorados and his people were the designated targets on hand. In the end, the "evidence" against them amounted to assertions based on coincidence, rumor, and prejudice. First, Spaniards saw as suspicious that Cabellos Colorados's ranchería, of all the Apache rancherías known to them, was located closest to San Antonio. Second, various soldiers testified that no "assaults" had taken place since their capture, so the raiders must be the ones in jail. Third, presidio commander José de Urrutia identified Cabellos Colorados as a man of standing and reputation among Apaches—so much so that he claimed to have heard rumors that the leader had bragged to a nonexistent entity, a fictional *capitán grande* of the Apache nation, that he would raid all the presidial horse herds of San Antonio, Coahuila, San Juan Bautista, and Sacramento and then slaughter all the inhabitants. Such rhetoric implied that Cabellos Colorados was a powerful man whose downfall might strongly enhance the reputation of the Spaniard who brought it about.

Last but not least, the Spaniards recognized Cabellos Colorados's wife to be one of three women who had earlier come with a man to trade in San Antonio, and by roundabout logic, they argued that her presence among those arrested meant that she had been a part of a surveillance party sent to scout troop movements. In turn, if the four Apaches had been there to scout troop movements, the Spaniards surmised, then the family band must be guilty of the later raids. Since Spanish battlefield tactics omitted Apache women from the category of noncombatants meriting exemption from harm and instead viewed them as targets for enslavement, unsurprisingly, Spanish officials ignored the fact that warriors would not allocate the male-defined task of warfare to women and that a party of three women was most likely simply there to trade. In the end, Cabellos Colorados and the sixteen men and women were held responsible not just for one raid but for all the crimes of the preceding years.[16]

In the meantime, Cabellos Colorados tried to negotiate with his captors, relying on female hostages as mediators, by requesting that Spaniards allow one of the women to return to his ranchería to get horses with which to buy their freedom. Over several months between the December capture and the June hearings, Apache women traveled back and forth between Apache and Spanish settlements, trying to exchange horses for the captives. A subsequent attack on their ranchería by Hasinai Caddos killed twelve, captured two boys, and stole all their horses, however, severely limiting the Apaches' ability to produce enough horses to appease Spanish officials. In the meantime, the women brought bison meat for their captive kinsmen and bison hides as gifts of goodwill for Spanish officials. In August, an elderly man accompanied the women and brought news that, although they could not supply any horses, he had visited with all the Apache bands and asked them to stop all raids, and he now offered this peace agreement to the officials in exchange for the captives. Governor Orobio refused him. The elderly man then tried to exchange a horse and a mule in an effort to free his elderly wife who was among the captives. The governor rebuffed him again.

No peace offering could offset Spanish desire to punish someone for the deeds of Apache raiders who had long made a mockery of their presidial forces. Ultimately, Orobio consigned Cabellos Colorados and his entire family to exile and enslavement. In his order of February 16, 1739, he refused to spare the women and even went so far as to specify the inclusion of a baby girl in the punishment, declaring that "the thirteen Indian men and women prisoners in the said presidio, [shall be taken] tied to each other, from jurisdiction to jurisdiction, to the prison of the capital in Mexico City, and that the two-year-old daughter of chief Cabellos Colorados, María Guadalupe, shall be treated in the same manner." The *collera* (chain gang; literally, "horse collar") of Apache prisoners—seven men, six women, and one infant—left on February 18, escorted by a mixed guard of soldiers and civilians.[17]

They traveled for 102 days on foot—the men shackled each night in leg irons, stocks, manacles, or ropes—before reaching Mexico City in late May, where they were incarcerated in the viceregal prison, the Real Carcel de la Corte (the "Acordada"). Two of the fourteen died en route to Mexico City, and fewer than six months later, seven more had succumbed in the disease-ridden prison or workhouses. Whether any of the other five survived is unknown; the last records say only that prison officials sent two men to a hospital, while two women, although very ill, went into servitude in prominent Spaniards' private homes. Little María Guadalupe was left without her mother, and later efforts to reunite them failed when the appointed "guardian" absconded with Cabellos Colorados's wife. This family would not be the last to suffer such a fate.[18]

Taking the legal distinction between *cautivos* and *prisioneros* as a free pass for wartime enslavements, soldiers and civilians gradually but inexorably ravaged Apache family bands for their kinswomen and children in the 1730s and 1740s. The Apache women and children who served as human trophies of war were parceled out among soldiers and citizens to be used in their homes as slaves or sold for profit to Mexican mining districts or West Indian labor camps. Spanish military men might proclaim their capture as proof of the reassertion of Spanish honor, but in practice, expeditions reputedly sent to "punish" Apaches amounted to little more than slave-raiding parties. A 1787 memorial from the San Antonio *cabildo*, or city council, proudly promoted the deeds of the "flower of our ancestry" who had fought a "glorious war" in the 1730s and 1740s by seeking out Apaches in their own lands, where they "killed them, destroyed them, routed them, and drove them off." "They conquered them and formed chains of prisoners," it continued, "and spared the lives only of those captives who were likely to be converted to the faith, and the children, whom they brought back to increase the missions and the *villa*."[19]

The immediate baptism of captured Apache children further indicates that their Spanish captors had no intention of using the children to barter for peace. Rather, it signaled their new status as slaves of Spanish owners. Texas colonists, like their New Mexico neighbors, called enslaved children "*criados*" (literally, "those raised up") to signify that, in return for their rearing, these children owed a labor debt to their saviors. In this way, the trade in Apache children also circumvented legal prohibitions against Indian slavery. Franciscan missionaries did not accept this subterfuge and offered harsh criticism of the military's tactics. Fray Benito Fernández de Santa Ana argued that nothing was gained by the raids except increasing the Apaches' hatred, and that it was "ridiculous" that soldiers and citizens who pledged their service to the king in fact sought only their own gain through the "capture of horses, hides, and Indian men and women to serve them." With such vile intentions, their actions would result in an equally vile outcome, he concluded.[20]

Vile outcomes did indeed follow. Apache warriors responded to Spanish slave raids with their own carefully chosen violent expressions. Evolving European and Indian practices of mutilation and trophy taking held a crucial place in Spanish-Apache warfare. Spaniards severed the heads of Apache men before taking their wives. Similarly, Apaches took scalps from the heads of fallen foes as well as the military dress and decoration that marked them as warriors. Native fighting men in Texas displayed their war records in body painting, headdresses, and specially decorated spears or lances, and they recognized that Spanish uniforms and devices served the same purpose. Stripping a dead foe of the dress and markers of valor he had earned as a warrior or soldier stripped him of that identity.[21]

With such deeds, Spanish soldiers and Apache warriors inscribed expressions of valor and emasculation onto their warfare. Lipan Apache oral traditions directed that warriors in battle were to "keep it up till they find out who are the best fighters." Pointedly, a 1719 expedition diary recounted some soldiers' encounter with Apache men along the Arkansas River who fired insults at the Spaniards, calling them "*mujeres criconas*" (female genitalia). By extension, Spanish officials interpreted Apache raids as "insults" indicative of the Indian men's "insolence" and "haughtiness." Any chance to defeat them was the chance to "beat down their pride." Espousing such sentiment, Commandant Inspector Hugo O'Conor declared that, after various expeditions against Apaches, he and his men had "made evident to the barbarians what the arms of the King were like when there were serious attempts to make them glorious," thereby "reestablishing the honor of the King's arms."[22]

Spanish-Apache exchanges of vicious retaliations began in March 1724, less than three months after failed negotiations with Flores over the return of the first group of Apache captives held in San Antonio. Apache men attacked two Spanish military couriers fifteen leagues outside of the town who were bringing dispatches from the San Juan Bautista presidio on the Rio Grande. One man escaped and brought soldiers from the Béxar presidio back to the site of the attack, where they discovered soldier Antonio González's nude body mutilated with arrows in the stomach and back, a spear wound, flesh torn from one calf, and scalp taken. The discovery of his hat and shield a short distance away, in addition to the removal of his uniform, attested to his attackers' intent to strip him of warrior trappings. But then they found all of it—González's scalp, clothes, hat, and shield—abandoned a short distance away, perhaps left behind as a sign that Apaches did not even deem them worth taking as trophies.[23]

Warriors extended their scorn to an entire unit of Spanish soldiers in 1731. That year, an Apache raid that took sixty horses from the San Antonio presidio in broad daylight came to a crushing end for the Spanish military when the six soldiers who had been guarding the corrals decided to pursue the raiders, followed close behind by nineteen more men. When the reinforcements caught up with the six soldiers, they found them losing a fight with forty Apache warriors, and—to make matters worse—a reputed five hundred Apache warriors riding up (the number likely an exaggeration meant to excuse the Spaniards' defeat). "They attacked us with the greatest audacity," Captain Juan Antonio Pérez de Almazán reported of the ensuing two-hour battle, explaining, "They advanced in a crescent, pressing our center as vigorously as they did both wings, but because my men were so few we could not defend all sides at once." The Lipans accomplished all this armed with bows and arrows, while Spanish guns proved ineffective against mounted warriors who protected themselves and their horses with what the Spaniards could only describe as "armor" made of bison hides. The Apaches used the crescent-shaped line to surround the twenty-five overmatched Spaniards at the foot of a tree, whereupon "the enemy, for no apparent reason, took off at top speed and disappeared." A Spanish officer who judged victory in the number of dead left on a battlefield could not see the reasoning behind the Apache warriors' actions: for warriors who did not count victory in the number of enemy dead, two soldiers killed, seventeen more wounded, including the commander, and the complete dominance over them all established quite clearly the Apaches' superiority.[24]

Other Spaniards seemed to have reached the same conclusion about the Apaches' successful assertion of superiority, as Governor Juan Antonio de Bustillo y Ceballos soon set out to respond in kind with an expeditionary force made up of 175 Spaniards, 60 mission Indian warriors, 140 pack loads of supplies, and 900 horses and mules—an expeditionary force large enough to ensure the reestablishment of the "honor of the king's arms." They marched for six weeks, winding their way, and perhaps periodically losing their way, over two hundred leagues through Apachería before locating four separate Lipan and Mescalero Apache rancherías, with an estimated population of 2,000 men, women, and children spread out for a league along the San Sabá River. A majority of the men, some 500 warriors, were away hunting bison, so prospects for an easy victory appeared within the Spaniards' grasp.[25]

Spanish forces launched a daybreak attack, which the reduced number of warriors held off for five hours. Then, Apache men covered the retreat of their families as Spaniards captured 700 horses, 100 mule loads of peltry, and 30 women and children. The next morning, Spanish forces awoke in camp to see armed Apache warriors watching them from vantage points all over the surrounding hills. The surveillance continued as they made their slow way home over the course of fifteen days, with warriors tracking them the entire way to San Antonio and ensuring their departure from Apache lands with the loss of as many horses as could be taken each day in payment for the abuses they had suffered. The captured women and children remained under guard and beyond retrieval.[26]

Upon their return, Governor Bustillo and many others seemed more cowed than bolstered by their deeds on the San Sabá River. A petition of the *cabildo* stressed the need to strengthen defenses in anticipation of an invasion by Apache warriors aimed at liberating their kinswomen. Soldiers, perhaps in mute recognition of the Apache men's grief, wished to move their own families out of harm's way—beyond the Rio Grande. The threat of Apache attack overshadowed even everyday labors in the town. Spanish and Indian *vaqueros* refused to go to outlying mission ranches to guard cattle. Soldiers charged with defending the San Antonio community became increasingly desperate, judging from an escalating rate of desertion and their own raids on mission livestock and cattle to fulfill subsistence needs.[27]

After seeing firsthand the extent of Apache bands living northwest of San Antonio, military veterans did not doubt the Apaches' capability for revenge and within two days of their return petitioned the governor to negotiate with them, arguing that "Otherwise, this Presidio, with its town and Missions, will be exposed to total destruction by this host of enemies." Citizen settlers who had previously clamored for Apache slaves now pleaded with Bustillo to prohibit distributing the most recent captives and instead hold them as hostages to negotiate a truce—a failed plan. When one Mescalero and one Lipan woman were freed with letters of truce from the governor, Apache warriors sent a clear message in response by ambushing Spanish soldiers. Accounts of the event variously attested to the bodies of dead soldiers "marked with fury and impiety," "flayed" with pikes and arrows, and "inhumanly cut to pieces." And so the bloody exchange of manly retribution continued, back and forth through the 1740s.[28]

Then, Spanish slaving campaigns in 1745 finally ignited *concerted* violence by Apache men. In an unprecedented move, Apache leaders sent four women to San Antonio first to warn the missionaries at Concepción (notably, fray Fernández de Santa Ana, who had been one of the few in the San Antonio community to work with them for their wives' and children's emancipation). Next, the women notified presidial officials that only Mission Concepción would be spared their vengeance. Over the following three weeks, Apache raiders killed nine people and subjected presidial, mission, and civilian herds—all except those at Concepción—to relentless raids. Fernández de Santa Ana claimed later that Apache warriors "made war more cruelly than I have ever experienced in the province." San Antonio paid in lost lives and horses for the Apache women and children they had killed and enslaved over twenty-five years.[29]

Yet, the real measure of Apache fury came in a direct attack upon the presidio itself that same year—another unprecedented act in Apache warfare. Three hundred and fifty Lipan and Natage Apaches entered San Antonio at night and began their attack. As fighting broke out, an Apache captive held at one of the missions escaped to join the other Apache warriors. Once he was among them, a Natage chief immediately asked after the fate of his seven-year-old daughter taken captive two months before. The Spaniards in fact held not only the chief's daughter but also her cousin and a woman in her twenties with two children—all from the chief's family. Upon hearing that the captives were all well and in the missions, the Natage leader consulted with other band chiefs, and they called off their warriors. The attack's impetus must have been the men's belief that, like most of the captives before, their wives and children had already been sold away or deported, which required bloody revenge. The news that they were not lost to them was sufficient to stop the attack.[30]

Although Apache warriors took more Spanish horses and Spanish forces took more Apache captives before a truce was finally achieved, the fate of that Natage chief's seven-year-old daughter ultimately helped to bring about the first peace accord between Spaniards and Apaches. From 1745 through 1749, a stream of women, both captive and free, moved between San Antonio and Apache rancherías as a human line of communication. The process began in August 1745, when the Natage father sent a woman bearing a cross to San Antonio, accompanied only by a small boy, to offer gifts to presidial commander Toribio de Urrutia as a pledge of Apache goodwill. Other Apache rancherías sent women along the same path. The Spaniards responded with freed Apache women who left San Antonio carrying Spanish pledges to release hostages from previous campaigns in return for peace. All the while, presidial commander Urrutia fought long battles to force San Antonio residents to relinquish Apache women and children held as slaves in their homes— reputedly risking death threats from some enraged citizens. Under orders from the viceroy, even Governor Pedro del Barrio y Espriella released two Apache girls and one boy whom he had spirited off to the capital at Los Adaes, sending them home with promises of freedom for all captives.[31]

Diplomatic overtures begun by Apache women ended with the meeting of Spanish and Apache headmen to hammer out a truce. Militarized pomp and protocols ratified the peace that finally came in the summer of 1749. In San Antonio, presidial, state, and church officials greeted delegations led by four Apache chiefs while Spanish troops lined up in formation. At a meeting hall built especially for the occasion, feasts were prepared, and Apache chiefs and leading warriors were lodged in the presidio and missions in deference to their rank. Spaniards freed the 137 women and children taken captive that spring (the fate of those captured in past years remained to be decided). Ceremonies celebrating the treaty culminated in the burial of items chosen especially to signify a mutual pledge to end the war between Spanish soldiers and Apache warriors. With Spanish soldiers, missionaries, and civilians lining one side of a plaza and Apache chiefs, warriors, and newly freed captives the other, male representatives of both groups worked together to bury a live horse, a hatchet, a lance, and six arrows in a large hole dug for the occasion. At the end, Spanish officers joined hands with the four visiting chiefs, and each promised to regard the other as "brothers" from then onward.[32]

It was not pure chance that led Apache and Spanish men to look more favorably upon one another's peace overtures at the very time that Wichitas and Comanches were for the first time uniting in an alliance against which both Apaches and Spaniards would need all the help they could muster to defend their respective territories. By midcentury, Apaches were suffering high attrition rates due to years of hostility with Spaniards as well as intensifying conflicts with allied bands of Comanches, Wichitas, Caddos, and Tonkawas, a group that Spaniards began to identify collectively as "*Norteños*" (Nations of the North; literally, "notherners"). Spaniards meanwhile quailed at the notion that foes even more intimidating than Apaches were headed their way.

As Lipan-Spanish negotiations shifted toward institutionalizing the new alliance, Apache women continued to command center stage. The Spaniards' refusal or inability to return captives who had been enslaved, deported, or sold long distances away remained a sticking point in Spanish-Apache relations, and Apache efforts may very well have reflected their belief that since the women would never return, family reunions had to be secured by other means. When women were not liberated, at least one Apache family simply chose to move to San Antonio to be near their lost relatives in lieu of an interminable and perhaps hopeless wait for Spanish policy to change. Chief Boca Comida went to San Antonio "without other escort than his relatives and household" in November 1749 and, after a formal meeting with the presidial commander, requested that housing near Mission Valero be established for his family band. He and his family thereby remained at Valero rather than return to Apachería, putting him on the spot for continued negotiations with Spanish officials. Baptism records ten years later list a twenty-year-old Lipan Apache named Pedro as son of " 'old captain Boca Comida,' " indicating that at age ten he had come to Valero with his father and mother (both of whom were identified as still unconverted to Christianity in 1759). The choices made by Boca Comida and his wife seem to reflect a strategy in the face of unyielding Spanish captive diplomacy. The couple might have joined the Spanish community and offered their son for baptism (perhaps as a political gesture), but they nevertheless remained true to their own belief systems. Boca Comida then sought to establish kinship ties for generations when he suggested that "the maidens of their nation should marry the Indians from the missions, and the young men should marry their daughters, for with these ties peace would be assured."[33]

If the two sides were to build a relationship of peace, then Spaniards had to be made kin, and women of the Apache family bands stepped forward in a multitude of ways to pledge that alliance. As part of the 1749 peace treaty, Lipan leaders like Boca Comida proposed marrying some of their single women to mission Indian men at Valero. They did not seek unions with Spaniards, although whether they chose not to or the Spaniards rejected such proposals is unknown. The Apache headmen proposed the marriages as a means of creating kinship ties that would both solidify the alliance and perhaps win a measure of security and standing for Apache women within Spanish settlements. Pointedly, the young women involved in these political marriages were the very ones who had been held in the San Antonio missions for years as hostages. One of the girls was Chief Boca Comida's niece, which surely added even greater weight to the suggested unions.[34]

The marriage proposals served as political investments in Spanish-Apache alliance. Records confirm twenty-three baptisms and at least ten marriages of Apache women at Mission Valero between 1749 and 1753. Several of the women married men of status within the mission communities; for instance, Clemencia, a Lipan woman, married Roque de los Santos, a Xarame man who was the Valero governor for nine years. Lipan children, too, often quickly rose to prominence, such as Benito and Anselmo Cuevas, who were captured as small boys in 1745, grew up at Valero, and became a *fiscal* (official in charge of maintaining mission lands) and an *alcalde* (magistrate) as adults. In letters to both provincial authorities as well as the viceroy, fray Mariano de los Dolores y Viana stressed the political importance of these unions and baptisms. He reported that he had baptized and married several Apache women to native men of the Valero pueblo, while other mission residents apparently were courting women in Apache encampments outside of town. He concluded that Apache headmen "demonstrated their stability and firmness, significant of the union they desire in having agreed that some Indian women marry those of Mission San Antonio [de Valero]."[35]

In response to the Apache marriage policy, Spanish captive policies shifted to using the ransom and redemption of female Apache hostages to communicate their own commitment to peace. Perhaps to make amends for the captives they themselves were unwilling or unable to regain from fellow Spaniards, officials focused on preventing other Indian bands from attacking Apaches and, when they could not stop them, "redeeming" captives for return to their families. In 1750, for example, when Caddo bands and their allies appeared at the San Gabriel mission-presidio complex seeking to recruit Bidai, Coco, Mayeye, and Akokisa warriors to accompany them in a massive campaign against Apaches, missionaries tried to persuade Caddo leaders to call off their plans. When that tactic did not succeed, presidial captain Felipe de Rábago y Terán ransomed two Apache women whom the Caddos had captured during a raid in the hope that restoring the women to their families would reinforce the Spanish-Apache accord. Governor Jacinto de Barrios y Jáuregui later commended Rábago y Terán's efforts for bringing about "a better union."[36]

Bolstering the ties created by exchanges of women, the 1749 treaty also declared Spanish and Apache men "brothers." Thus, with treaty in hand, the next step for each was to make the other act upon the military alliance represented by the fictive kinship term. To do so, both Apaches and Spaniards saw a mission-presidio complex as a means of institutionalizing that alliance. Apache leaders hoped to gain European arms and a military supplement of presidial soldiers for their warriors and required that the complex be built in their own lands to the northwest of San Antonio. Provincial and viceregal officials rightly doubted that Apache interest in a mission complex would offer Franciscan missionaries much chance to convert them but instead recognized the opportunity to cement an alliance and what they hoped would be the "pacification" of the Apaches. The potential payoff lay not only in neutralizing the Apache threat. Admittance to Apachería also tempted them with the opportunity to explore for mineral wealth and to establish a trade route to Santa Fe—neither of which Spaniards had yet been able to pursue because of Apache animosity.[37]

For Apache men, it may have seemed eminently logical to appeal to a religious institution for political and military purposes. Their years of combat against Spaniards provided the primary context within which to interpret Christian symbols and institutions. They knew that missions often had more soldiers than priests and served as fortresses of defense. Spanish military men carried rosaries and medallions into battle that became amulets of personal male power, or "medicine" in Apache understanding. In turn, by midcentury, Apache leaders had already put crosses to diplomatic use, as evidenced by the number of Apache women traversing the countryside with only handmade crosses to identify them as emissaries of peace. Indeed, throughout negotiations for a mission in Apachería, fray Benito Fernández de Santa Ana preserved two very well made crosses brought to him by such women.[38]

In the late 1750s, a mission-presidio complex in Apachería gave literal form to Spanish-Apache efforts at allied brotherhood, and it did so on Apache terms. Missionaries seemed to realize that they would play second fiddle to military men in interactions with Apache leaders, repeatedly admitting that an "authority of arms" would be essential to maintaining the respect of Apache warriors. Fray Fernández de Santa Ana argued that Apaches would never be pacified or converted if the mission "lacks the respect commanded by a presidio"; only military men—fellow warriors—garnered the esteem of Apache men. The defensive capabilities of Mission Santa

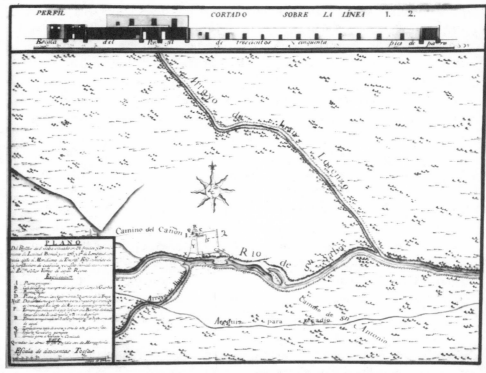

Plan of the Presidio San Luis de las Amarillas at San Sabá, drawn by José de Urrutia, 1767. The Mission Santa Cruz de San Sabá, built for Lipan Apaches in 1757, the same year as the presidio, was located roughly four miles to the east on the opposite (south) side of the San Sabá River before it was destroyed by allied Norteños in 1758. Courtesy of the Palace of the Governors (MNM/DCA), Santa Fe, New Mexico, neg. no. 15049.

Cruz de San Sabá seemingly provided a welcome sight to Apache observers. A log stockade surrounded the mission, with only one gate as entry, secured with iron bars, and buildings that cut into the outer wall with loopholes through which defenders could shoot guns or arrows. Across the river and three miles away, Presidio San Luis de las Amarillas had room enough for three to four hundred soldiers and their families—seemingly a permanent commitment to joining Apache warriors in confrontations with Comanche and Wichita foes.[39]

Yet, as the complex went up during the spring, "no Apaches had been seen." Mission superiors chose fray Benito Varela, because of the "special zeal he had displayed for their pacification," to go in search of the wayward Apaches, and soon he had an explanation for their absence. After traveling for days without a sign of Apaches, he arrived at a small encampment along the San Marcos River, where he encountered an Apache woman who told him of her capture and escape from a raiding party made up of Hasinais and four apostate warriors from the San Antonio missions. The party had attacked the family band of Apache chief Casa Blanca's brother, killing him, his wife, and their two children, before taking her, another woman, and two children captive. She later had escaped, bringing with her one of the little girls, who had been wounded by a bullet. Soon after, several Lipan bands, altogether numbering around three thousand, did appear at San Sabá and set up encampments, but in meetings that followed with Spanish military and religious officials, Apache leaders explained why this would be only a temporary visit.[40]

Avenging the loss or death of women and securing the safety of others determined the Apaches' decision making, allowing little role for their as-yet-unproven Spanish brothers—especially when it was other native Spanish allies who had attacked them. Two chiefs, Chico and Casa Blanca, alternately pledged their continued friendship but hedged on the arrival date of all their peoples. In meetings with the commander of the new presidio, Colonel Diego Ortiz Parrilla, the headmen found it hard to settle on an explanation that would satisfy, without alienating, the Spanish missionaries and officers. Angered by the death of Casa Blanca's brother and his family and the capture of his female relatives on the Colorado River, they demanded that the Spaniards bring the guilty mission Indians to San Sabá to be punished before Apache eyes. After Parrilla seemed to respond positively to their requests, they left and in three days returned with their families. Tellingly, however, they chose to pitch their tents not at the mission, but at the presidio where the colonel and his men were encamped.[41]

Despite Spanish gifts of tobacco and three head of cattle to "soothe his wrath" and "comfort" his grief, Casa Blanca brusquely concluded that "neither he nor his people would settle in a mission because that was not their choice." More immediately, they had to leave to join other Apaches in a war against their Norteño enemies. Vengeance and the recovery of lost family members were required. Though Casa Blanca was firm in his rejection of settlement at the complex, Chico tried to be more conciliatory, resting his inability to settle with the Spaniards upon his responsibilities as male head of his family and his band. He and his men "need to go and lay in a supply of buffalo meat," he explained, "and, not being able to deny his people what they asked of him on account of the love he felt for them, he had to accompany them." Chico went on to say that as long as those hunts remained necessary, they had to keep their families together for fear of a Norteño attack.[42]

Meanwhile, the deaths of Chico's brother and sister, who suddenly had fallen ill, cemented the Apache leaders' determination to depart. Apache beliefs regarding death and the proper rituals of mourning required that family members and their community leave the site of death immediately. The Spanish missionaries noted how the deaths "terrified and stunned the mind and spirit of Chief Chico." In speaking to fray Diego Jiménez after he and his people had concluded mourning ceremonies, Chico said simply that obligations of honor demanded that he aid the other Apache leaders who "had asked him with tears in their eyes not to abandon them at a time when they had decided on a campaign against the Comanches." The Apache men further rejected fray Jiménez's suggestion that they leave their women and children behind at the mission during the campaign. The tracks of Norteño foes could be seen everywhere, and the Apache leaders struggled to make clear to the Spaniards the danger of remaining in the area—implicitly indicating their lack of faith in the promise of safety heralded by the complex.[43]

Spanish officers and missionaries failed to register the meaning behind the actions of the Apaches who would be their allies, even as they recorded them in careful detail. Several small groups of Lipan warriors passed through in the fall of 1757, stopping only overnight at the mission, their fears manifest in their hurry to move onward in a southerly direction. Apache warriors proceeded to safer ground, distant from their Spanish allies and Norteño enemies, and sequestered their women and families far away from San Sabá. Meanwhile, rumors over the winter filtered into San Sabá that Norteños were massing to destroy Apaches, but well knowing that no Apaches could be found at the mission or the presidio, Spaniards dismissed the idea that the complex might be a target of attack. Rumor became reality when at midnight on February 25, 1758, warriors later identified as Comanches and Wichitas announced their presence by stampeding the presidio horse herd and driving off sixty animals. Although commanding officers sent fourteen soldiers in pursuit, twelve days of tracking garnered the patrol the recovery of only one animal and a disturbing new awareness that the countryside was full of unidentified warriors. Several days later, another squad sent to escort a supply train as it approached the complex fell under the attack of twenty-six Tonkawa, Bidai, and Yojuane warriors. And still the Spaniards failed to anticipate what was coming.[44]

At dawn on March 16, a united band of an estimated two thousand Comanches, Wichitas, Caddos, Bidais, Tonkawas, Yojuanes, and others (twelve different Indian nations in all) surrounded the mission. As soldiers reported it, the echoes of shouts, the nearby firing of guns, the puffs of powder smoke, and the pounding of horse hooves broadcast the sheer number of approaching Indians "until the country was covered with them as far as the eye could reach." In the subsequent attack on the Spanish complex, the Norteños pillaged mission stores and herds, burned mission buildings to the ground, and killed Spaniards, including two missionaries who would go down in Catholic record books as martyrs in the cause of saving Apache souls. Spaniards took pointed note of the fact that the attacking Indians rode Spanish horses and carried European arms and ammunition, which they could only assume were the profits of raids on Spanish settlements and of trade in the French markets of Louisiana.[45]

The Norteños' political economies in fact did guide their actions that day. With the bounty of raids against Lipans—Spanish horses and Apache captives—Comanches, Wichitas, Caddos, and Tonkawas maintained lucrative trade alliances with Frenchmen in Louisiana, gaining guns and ammunition in exchange. Comanches and Wichitas had not given Spaniards in Texas much attention (though Spaniards and Comanches had come into regular and unfriendly contact in New Mexico), but by midcentury, hostilities with Lipans had eventually brought them south to the fringes of Spanish settlement. As early as 1743, Comanches had pursued Apache raiders to the San Antonio area, and the Apaches' destination alerted Comanche warriors to a possible association between them. The solid form of the San Sabá mission-presidio complex now confirmed that possibility. Signs of economic, military, and civil alliance were there for any to see. To Norteños' eyes, the presidio conveyed the joining of Spanish soldiers with Apache warriors, while the mission represented material succor with its domesticated animals, agricultural fields, and regular supply of goods. Adding to Norteño suspicions of Spanish collusion in attacks on Comanche and Wichita rancherías, they had found Spanish goods carried by Apache raiders at the sites of raids. The complex, then, was a supply depot not merely for Apache settlers but also for Apache raiders. Thus, the same presidio-mission complex that Spaniards and Apaches, for different reasons, hoped would spell brotherly alliance transformed Spaniards from strangers to enemies in the eyes of Norteños who had watched its construction from a distance. With one turn of the political wheel, an alliance with one group again had begotten the enmity of another for the hapless Spaniards. The destruction of the San Sabá mission was the concerted Norteño response.[46]

So, what should be made of the Norteño attack at San Sabá? The first thing to note was that, despite clear numerical advantage, the Norteño allies never sought to engage the presidial forces in battle. The reputed 2,000 warriors did not once approach the presidio, located only three miles away and manned by only 59 soldiers. As a result, despite Spanish rhetoric that the attackers intended to "murder us all, including our wives and children," all 237 of those women and children remained unthreatened and unharmed within the presidio walls—they were not the Indians' target. During the three days it took to destroy the mission, Norteño warriors "were seen in the tree tops and on hillsides" around the presidio and clearly wanted their presence known since they "let themselves be seen." Such a watch would have alerted them to the fact that 41 of the 100 soldiers assigned to the presidio were absent. Rather than attack, however, the warriors instead allowed the presidial forces to bring their herds into the presidio stockade, to send a squad of 14 soldiers and 3 Indians to spy out the "state of affairs" at the mission, and then, after reporting back to Colonel Parrilla, to continue along the road toward San Antonio to meet a supply train headed for San Sabá and even escort it safely into the presidio walls. Telling as well, the majority of the mission's inhabitants—seven soldiers, one missionary, two soldiers' wives, eight soldiers' sons, three mission Indians, one Indian interpreter and his wife, one unnamed youth, and even two Apaches—safely traversed the ground between mission and presidio under the watchful gaze of Norteño lookouts, gaining the sanctuary of the presidio unchallenged. For three days, ultimately, Norteños kept the presidio waiting for an attack that never came.[47]

Meanwhile at the mission, the Norteños explained to the Franciscans who greeted them that they intended no harm to the Spaniards and sought only Apaches guilty of recent raids on their rancherías. The Spanish missionaries allowed the Norteños entry to the mission after interpreting their signs and gestures as ones of peaceful intent, although they actually indicated hostility with their war dress and decoration and their rejection of customary gifts of tobacco offered by the missionaries. Survivor fray Miguel de Molina described how he was "filled with amazement and fear when I saw nothing but Indians on every hand, armed with guns and arrayed in the most horrible attire. Besides the paint on their faces, red and black, they were adorned with the pelts and tails of wild beasts, wrapped around them or hanging down from their heads, as well as deer horns. Some were disguised as various kinds of animals, and some wore feather headdresses." Soldiers, in contrast, recognized native battle dress and knew they were looking at a group bent on a fight. Juan Leal observed that "most of the enemy carried firearms, ammunition in large powder horns and pouches, swords, lances, and cutlasses, while some of the youths had bows and arrows." "All wore battle dress and had their faces painted," he continued, while "many had helmets, and many had leather jerkins, or breastplates like those of the French."[48]

The missionaries' statements and the evidence of their eyes told Norteño warriors that Apaches were not present (the few still there were hidden). Yet, they must have found plenty to enrage them even without Apaches. The mission and the nearby presidio were proof positive of the Spanish alliance with Apaches. Adding insult to injury, the Franciscans endeavored to mollify the visitors with gifts—gifts that surely advertised better still the goods that provisioned Apache raiding parties against Comanche and Wichita villages. In the absence of Apaches, then, the Norteño warriors instead set about to destroy all objects and structures signaling Spanish-Apache alliance.

Although often referred to as a "massacre" by Spanish contemporaries and historians alike, only 8 people died during the three days of ransacking and demolition that followed at San Sabá mission—6 out of the 31 people at the mission, and 8 out of the 368 at both the mission and the presidio. The fact that so few died offers insight into Norteño perspectives and intentions. As mentioned, the majority of the mission's inhabitants—women, children, youths, several soldiers stationed to protect it, and two Apaches who were nominally the aim of the warrior party—were all allowed to escape. Half of the victims (4), including one of the missionaries, fray Alonso Giraldo de Terreros, fell in an initial rifle volley that cleared the mission grounds and allowed the attackers access to mission stores and supplies. Norteño warriors then set about destroying the mission itself, a systematic destruction that took many hours. Strikingly, they took very little for themselves, leaving smoldering remains to be found by the Spaniards, including "bales of tobacco, boxes of chocolate, barrels of flour, and boxes of soap, broken apart and burning." Razing, not raiding, was their aim. In all that time, the Norteños made no effort to locate, much less kill, the hiding Spaniards and Apaches who had taken refuge in one of the buildings. Too, that building was the only one they did not set afire.[49]

Notable as well, the eight people killed at San Sabá were all men. Although Sergeant Joseph Antonio Flores attested that "our forces had endured much suffering and many deaths at the hands of the savage barbarians, who did not spare the lives of the religious, or those of women and children," all the women and children at both the mission and the presidio escaped unharmed. One woman, the wife of mission servant Juan Antonio Gutiérrez, did momentarily fall prey to the attackers when they stripped her of her clothes (perhaps an act of plunder as much as humiliation—remember the different Indian and European understandings of nudity), but though surely terrorized, she was not injured bodily. The raiders saw no value in physically hurting Gutiérrez's wife or any of the other women in the mission.[50]

The only individuals violently attacked after the first shooting were ones who interfered with the raiders. More interesting still, despite the arsenal of French guns that so exercised Spanish imaginations, Norteño warriors primarily chose beating as their means of attack. One missionary, fray José Santiesteban, upon fleeing the mission yard, unfortunately chose a storage room in which to hide. When the attackers entered in search of plunder and found him there, they "killed him with blows," stripped him of his clothes, and beheaded him. Santiesteban's decapitation was long remembered by Spaniards as a particular moment of infamy, especially when his head was found casually tossed aside outside the mission walls. Spaniards found a statue of St. Francis similarly beheaded, its head also left discarded on the ground. Outside the mission grounds, two warriors gave one of the mission guards, Juan Leal, a "sound beating with the handles of their lances," stripped him of his clothes, but then stopped short of killing him at the urging of one of their Caddo allies. After the Caddo warrior had "protected him from the blows of the others" and patiently "took him by the hand and led him toward the Mission," Leal later was among those who escaped to the presidio. Finally, when nine soldiers rode over from the nearby presidio, Norteños met them outside the mission, shot two, and sent six fleeing back to the fort unharmed. The last of the nine, Joseph Vasquez, received the only individual attention of the group, being "badly battered" with pikes or lances, stripped of his clothes, and left for dead. After regaining consciousness, Vasquez dragged himself into the mission grounds where, being discovered a second time by those busy with their demolition, again did not merit death but was casually picked up and tossed aside by the raiders. He too later escaped to the presidio.[51]

Violence is rarely arbitrary but, indeed, a means of communication, so what do these beatings say about the Norteños' intent regarding their newly classified Spanish enemies? On the battlefield, Comanches, Wichitas, Caddos, and their allies recognized certain protocols of warfare based in concepts of male rank and honor. For a contest to be meaningful, opponents had to be equally matched, and fighting represented a duel. Victories were not measured by the number of dead but rather by "grades" of martial deeds demonstrative of a warrior's prowess. Comanche men, for instance, defined a "coup" as an exploit in battle that involved direct contact with the enemy and that public opinion recognized as worthy of distinction. According to Comanche belief, "it required more bravery to hit an adversary with a spear or a war club than to pierce him at a distance with an arrow or a bullet." The inherent risk involved in putting oneself in the proximity of an enemy was key to this code of coup honors, not the violence inflicted on the opponent. Moreover, the honor of coup did not require the death of an enemy.[52]

Thus, a warrior's mode of combat communicated his estimation of the enemy he struck down. Spaniards, in fact, shared a similar honor-bound ideology. One Spanish official called upon a Latin saying, "*Dolus, an virtus, quis in hoste requirat*" (Whether it be craft or valor, who would ask in dealing with a foe?), as precedent for his argument that Spanish soldiers did not have to demonstrate or maintain valor against "inhuman" foes like Indians. For both Europeans and Indians, ritualized acts of coup or demeaning modes of attack could assert the honor of the aggressor, while at the same time impugning that of the victim. Actions that fell outside customary fighting tactics thus took on a significance of their own. In this case, Norteños appear to have deemed beating appropriate treatment for an ignoble enemy—a punishment befitting criminals, not battlefield opponents, in their societies. Tellingly, at San Sabá (and later at El Cañón, as will be seen), Norteño allies rejected all possible battle trophies of Spaniards. They scalped no one except for the mission steward Juan Antonio Gutiérrez, who did not escape with the others, and left the heads of fray Santiesteban (and St. Francis's statue) where they fell, unscalped.[53]

As already mentioned, complicated systems of belief subtly linked together Spanish soldiers and Indian warriors across the region's battlefields and found expression in trophy taking. Both took goods from fallen enemies, though they often chose only men who had distinguished themselves in battle, the choice denoting their belief that trophies served to transfer courage and strength from one bearer to another. Trophy taking took literal form in bodily mutilation, especially in the taking of scalps and sometimes entire heads, associated as they were with political rituals that identified the head as a site for conferring honor. For the victim, mutilation underscored trophy taking as desecration, but the victor's incorporation of the scalp into his battle decorations transformed it into an emblem of his own bravery. Trophies also became focal points of elaborate rituals binding the enemy dead to the victor's living community. Caddos buried the skulls and bones of an enemy killed in battle in the ashes of their sacred fire, over which the *xinesí* watched at all times, because they believed that if the fire went out, the Caddo people would die out too. Caddo ritual thus united the enemy dead with their own strength and destiny. Similarly, Spaniards compared the solemnity with which Wichita bands observed scalp rituals to "a religion that takes the form of sacrificing the scalps of their enemies and the first of their own fruits." The ceremonial combination of trophies of war with products of cultivation recognized the equal importance of military and agricultural success to the survival of Wichita peoples. Despite the range of cultural differences, then, these groups seemed to share a similar warfare culture. Yet, Spaniards did not appear to rank within it.[54]

In sum, the Norteños at San Sabá never sought a fight with presidial soldiers; when forced to fight, they often stripped their opponents of clothes; they took no trophies; they chose beating as their form of attack; and upon leaving the area, they taunted the soldiers at the presidio who never came out to offer a fight. Combined with the number of people allowed to escape, the individual treatment of Spaniards seems to imply that the allied party of Comanches, Caddos, Tonkawas, and Wichitas did not view Spaniards as worthy of a fight, much less honorable warrior deaths. Rather than killing soldiers with customary weapons of arrow, lance, or gun, warriors beat Spaniards after having removed their battle dress and equipment, thus

La Destrucción de la Misión de San Sabá, *oil on canvas, 83 × 115 inches, c. 1763, Museo Nacional de Arte, Mexico City. Courtesy of Ron Tyler. Reproduction authorized by the Instituto Nacional de Antropología e Historia, Mexico City.*

stripping them of their identity and rank as warriors. Obviously not a soldier, fray Santiesteban would automatically be discounted from such ranks, since opponents had to be warriors of equal skill, but the soldiers received the same ignominious assault. Except for the nine soldiers sent over by the presidio, the presidial forces (quite sensibly, given the odds) mounted no defense of the mission. That left the thirty-one mission inhabitants on their own to offer what feeble defense they could. The situation was not one to inspire the Norteños' respect for a people already allied with their enemy. If the Spanish soldiers could not fulfill the part of warriors, they would not be treated as such. Every indication implies that once Norteños assumed cowardice and inferiority on the part of their foe, the violence handed out communicated derision and insult.[55]

Meanwhile, the dominating appearance of this army of Indians had quite the opposite effect on Spaniards, sending shock waves of fear all the way down to Mexico City. It was one thing for leather-armored soldiers to fight Indians armed with bows and arrows; it was quite another to face a force united across multiple nations and armed with guns as good if not better than those of Spanish soldiers. Fray Miguel de Molina noted that one Comanche chief wore a well-decorated red jacket "after the manner of French uniforms." "Never before," one of the mission

Petroglyphs from Cowhead Mesa at the head of Double Mountain Fork Canyon, in the heart of Comanchería in west Texas, believed to reveal a Comanche perspective on the 1758 destruction of San Sabá mission. Carved into the sandstone are multiple images of mission buildings in flames; men, perhaps missionaries, with their arms raised in the air; and scenes of personal combat. Photograph by and courtesy of Dan Flores.

guards argued, "had he seen so many barbarians together, armed with guns and handling them so skillfully." Colonel Parrilla concluded that the Spanish military in Texas faced a fearful native challenge, in sharp contrast to the "wretched, naked, and totally defenseless Indians of Nuevo León, Nueva Vizcaya, and Sonora." "The heathen of the north are innumerable and rich," he argued. "They enjoy the protection and commerce of the French; they dress well, breed horses, handle firearms with the greatest skill, and obtain ample supplies of meat from the animals they call *cíbolos* [bison]. From their intercourse with the French and with some of our people they have picked up a great deal of knowledge and understanding, and in these respects they are far superior to the Indians of other parts of these Kingdoms."[56]

The threat of French alliance with such nations, implicit in their weaponry, also struck terror (as well as fury) into many a Spanish heart. Spaniards already well knew Frenchmen's skills at ingratiating themselves into native systems of trade, alliance, and kinship. If the Norteños "wanted to kill them all" *and* they were armed with European weapons, then rumors of "wild hordes" in a "league of extermina-

Negotiating Fear with Violence ⮜ 187

tion" poised to descend upon Spaniards, savagely slaughtering women and children, seemed all the more ominously true to them. The Norteños' overwhelming domination at San Sabá, Parrilla warned the viceroy, "will encourage the barbarians to still greater boldness and audacity, for they will consider themselves capable of scattering our settlements and blocking our troops from advancing." Not only would they menace Spanish people, they also seemed capable of an unheard-of feat: the conquest of Spanish lands and the confounding of Spanish imperial power. "It is also quite probable," Parrilla concluded miserably, "that [they] might undertake the occupation of more territory, thus doing great harm to our settlements." In the face of native dominion, alarm spread rapidly from San Antonio to other Texas settlements and from there to Coahuila and Nuevo León farther south.[57]

In the months following the March attack, the "insults" mounted as raiders from various Comanche, Wichita, and Caddo strongholds took 750 more horses from San Sabá. In the spring of 1759, tensions drove soldiers stationed there to request moving the presidio southward to safer (Spanish) territory, all the while casting their fears in terms of concern for their wives and children. In response to the unprecedented insubordination signaled in the petitions of his men, Parrilla warned his superiors that he feared mutiny or desertion, agreeing with the men that if ordered to remain at San Sabá, they would be reduced to "bait for the cruel and bloodthirsty heathen." Provincial and viceregal authorities stood firm, however, asserting that Spanish honor forbade the abandonment of San Sabá as "ignominious and shameful," and that the same honor had to be avenged if they were to "impose respect on the heathens." If Norteño "insolence" went unanswered, "it would be natural that the offending Indians would assume that the fear among the Spaniards of another attack was what had occasioned the change and this very notion might encourage them to start it." Moreover, Apaches could not be given an impression of Spanish impotence because, if they were, continued truce and alliance might collapse.[58]

Apaches had not escaped being attacked either. Three months following the San Sabá debacle, Chico and his band found themselves completely surrounded by Comanches while hunting bison along the Concho River. Heavily outnumbered and burdened with wives and children needing protection, Apache warriors' only recourse was to flee, leaving behind tents, belongings, horses, and arms. The attackers captured nineteen Apaches and killed several more. The survivors slowly made their way by different paths to the San Sabá presidio, where they took refuge. Other Apache families poured into San Antonio, specifically to Valero, as the men pledged themselves to its defense. Apache warriors expressed grief at the missionaries' deaths at San Sabá, scouted the surrounding land for signs of attack, and offered to accompany a punitive expedition sent in response. Asked instead about whether they ever intended to join the missions, Chico and other Apache leaders responded with perplexity to the Spaniards' anger that it was "high time" to fulfill their promises in that regard. Yes, the Apache men replied, they fully intended to build a fortified settlement with Spaniards, but with honor at stake, surely vengeance must come first in the form of a campaign that would put an end to their enemies' harassment.[59]

Martial brotherhood won out, and in August of 1759, a punitive expedition of 600 men—380 presidial soldiers from Coahuila, Nuevo León, Saltillo, and Texas, 90 mission Indians called up as auxiliaries, and 134 Apache warriors—set out for the Red River, where they believed the Norteño foes to be massed. Nominally under the leadership of Colonel Parrilla, the expedition made real a Spanish-Apache military alliance. Along the way, the Spanish forces attacked a Yojuane village, killing 55 and taking 149 women and children captives. Many of these prisoners died in a smallpox epidemic that hit San Antonio in December 1759 while they were held in a chain gang; others were sold into slavery in distant lands. This proved to be their only "victory." Spaniards justified the deaths and enslavement with claims that evidence had been discovered in the village connecting Yojuanes to the San Sabá attack. Upon finally reaching settlements along the Red River, Parrilla's forces found Comanches and others waiting for them at a fortified Wichita village. Again, their opponents confounded expectation. Rather than being found "in rancherías *like Indians*," the Norteños presented an imposing sight, with a village fortified by a surrounding stockade and moat, warriors armed with French muskets, and pointedly, a French flag flying over the settlement. Far more demoralizing for the Spaniards, in the skirmishes that followed, 52 soldiers were killed, men quickly began to desert, two swivel cannons were lost to their foes, and finally, once the expedition deemed retreat the only option, they were pursued all the way back to San Sabá by unrelenting Norteño warriors. Apache warriors fared better, fighting on Parrilla's left flank during the Red River battle and escaping with no casualties. While Spanish officials lamented the defeat of the expedition as further "disgrace and dishonor to the honor of the king's arms," the Apache men did not stay at the San Sabá presidio with the remainder of Spanish forces but continued south to confederated encampments of Natages and Mescaleros, where they had left their families in safekeeping, in order to consult on their next move.[60]

Daunted but not yet defeated, Spanish and Apache leaders regrouped for one last attempt at joint battlement behind mission walls. In 1761, Apache leaders met with Spanish church and state officials at the Presidio San Sabá and demanded that new mission settlements for Apaches be moved away from the site of destruction at San Sabá. A principal chief named El Gran Cabezón said his aims "were only for the defense and security of his people" and promoted the Nueces River valley (which would come to be referred to as "El Cañón") as a promising location due to the natural defenses it would afford the settlement. Apaches had long used El Cañón as a safe shelter, located as it was in the midst of a mountain range accessible only by narrow passes. Lipan leaders assured the missionaries that they represented the wishes of ten other chiefs and their people, and that once they had become settled in the missions, allied Apache bands of Natages, Pelones, and Mescaleros—who were related to them via intermarriage—would congregate there as well.[61]

Although the Spaniards wanted the Apaches' verbal commitment to religious conversion in the new missions, the militarized diplomacy of their negotiations indicate they continued to bow to Apache visions that the site would be an alliance of Apache and Spanish fighting men. The new commander at San Sabá, Felipe de Rábago y Terán, claimed credit for persuading them to consider a mission settlement by pointing out that Comanches had now taken their lands and their bison (as if they did not know this quite well already). El Gran Cabezón promptly put the commander's offers to the test. The principal chief formally accepted missions on the Nueces River, contingent upon three stipulations, the primary one being the return of the daughter of one of his kinsmen, a Natage chief, held captive by Spaniards in Nuevo León. This recurrence of Apache captive diplomacy accompanied two other demands regarding bonds of brotherhood requisite in Spanish-Apache alliance: that soldiers accompany Apache warriors as guards during a great bison hunt and as allies in a campaign against Comanches prior to their encampment at the missions. Though Rábago y Terán could not agree to the last demand, fearing that another offensive campaign would only risk repeating Parrilla's failure, he agreed to the first two, recording that on five occasions he had already given them men to accompany their hunts as a means of obligating the Apache leaders to Spaniards.[62]

At the two new sites the following year, rituals of possession were carried out with much militarized pomp, in deference to Apache leaders El Gran Cabezón at San Lorenzo de la Santa Cruz and El Turnio at Nuestra Señora de la Candelaria del Cañón. After fray Jiménez blessed the sites marked by adorned crosses, Rábago y Terán recognized each of the two Apache men as "governor" as well as "war chief," and gifts and supplies suited to Apache horse culture followed. At varying times, though, headmen of six additional rancherías—Bordado, Boruca, Cojo, El Lumen, Panocha, and Teja—came and went with their bands as well. Adding to their numbers, Rábago y Terán stationed one-third of the San Sabá garrison at the two mission settlements to join Apache warriors in defending the complex.[63]

The new missions' construction again reflected their defensive—rather than religious—purpose. A protective stockade enclosed all the buildings, horse stable, and an interior plaza, overlooked by three stone bulwarks, two stone throwers, and four cannons, with access through only one gate. Apache leaders had chosen the site well, considering that the valley lay in the heart of a mountain range almost one hundred miles across, with hills surrounding the valley on four sides that were "difficult to traverse on account of dense forests, underbrush, and brambles and more so because they are stony and cut by deep gorges that make them impassable." Meanwhile, back at San Sabá, Rábago y Terán strengthened the presidio, replacing the wooden stockade with one of stone, with bastions in every corner and a stone blockhouse. Soldiers built stone rooms around the interior plaza to replace log cabins, and they dug two moats, or trenches, that ran from the presidio to the river and protected the horse corrals. Apache and Spanish men chose natural and man-made battlements with care.[64]

Still, their defensive brotherhood would be tested and found wanting. From 1762 through 1766, various war parties from Comanche, Wichita, Caddo, and Tonkawa bands attacked Apache rancherías in canyons near the missions, killing people and stealing horses. Slowly they hacked away at any sense of security Apaches might have felt in their mountain retreats. News of these attacks regularly filtered into the mission settlements, along with escaped female captives taken by the raiders who brought reports that the Norteño allies kept regular watch on Apache movements. Yet, it was not until 1766 that massing Comanche, Caddo, Tonkawa, and Wichita warriors launched an attack against the El Cañón missions themselves.[65]

Displays of honor and dishonor colored the various battles of 1766 and 1767. In October 1766, an estimated three hundred warriors attacked with such force that they almost reached the walls of San Lorenzo before the fire from two cannons on the bastions forced them back. In contrast, the Norteños had only fired guns into the air and shot arrows without stone tips during the charge, perhaps as insults directed at unworthy opponents. The attackers dominated the scene so completely that mounted warriors left their horses behind to attack on foot, firing constantly from the cover of trees and ravines around the mission from morning until midday, when rains finally led them to withdraw, taking with them a herd of Spanish mares. One month later, they returned, catching the mission population at a vulnerable time when many Apache men were away. In desperation, the lieutenant in charge of the mission guard costumed Apache women in soldiers' overcoats and hats and placed them along the walls with guns. In scornful response to the seemingly well-manned mission defenses, one Comanche warrior carried out an impressive coup in which he rode to within pistol-shot of the mission plaza, circled it three times (all the while dodging bullets), and then made a leisurely return to cover. Assaults near the mission came to a head in December, when Comanches followed the tracks of an Apache bison hunting party, attacked, captured more than thirty women and children and one thousand horses, and then paraded their spoils before the mission walls as they left the canyon, taunting the Apache and Spanish men inside with proof of their victory.[66]

Having left the mission populace demoralized over the winter, allied Norteños shifted their focus to the presidio at San Sabá and kept the garrison under siege for months as they wore down both Spanish numbers and military honor. It began when a Spanish force of forty soldiers went in pursuit of the Comanches who had ambushed the Apache hunting party, hoping to retrieve the captives and horses. But the warriors easily surrounded the Spaniards, killed eight, "ridiculed the cannon indecently" (which the soldiers had brought as part of their arms), and "practiced barbarous excesses with the dead." In a February 1767 assault on San Sabá, soldier-interpreter José Antonio de Trujillo died outside the presidio walls from three blows to the chest—blows so hard that soldiers could not tell initially whether they were stabbing or beating wounds. Norteño warriors next ambushed twenty-three soldiers cutting hay two weeks later, killing three, one of whom was found scalped. Another had been scalped, stripped of flesh, and decapitated, yet Spanish soldiers found his hairless head tossed aside as if it were of no value as a trophy of war. A month later, three soldiers sent earlier to carry dispatches to and from Mexico City returned by stealth and on foot to the presidio. They had wandered for almost a month in the countryside between Mission San Lorenzo and the presidio trying to elude enemy warriors, during which time they had escaped capture or detection four times, two horses had died of exhaustion, and another had been abandoned with their possessions so they could approach the presidio without being seen. In short, the Norteños had a firm grip on the region. By the time the marqués de Rubí rode through in July on his inspection tour (with which this chapter began), the vengeance parties had succeeded in emptying San Lorenzo and Candelaria of all residents. Spanish authorities extinguished the impotent presidio at San Sabá three years later.[67]

Most Apache leaders and their families, however, had departed long before the final indignities of 1766 and 1767. Deadly threats from the outside had only exacerbated internal disagreements at El Cañón, as Apache women became a focal point for Spanish-Apache tensions erupting within the complex. Over the years 1762–66, Lipan men had regularly left on requisite bison hunting expeditions while the women and children usually remained within the safety of mission walls, partly to reinforce the men's promise of return. As time passed, though, leading Apaches questioned how safe their women were in the company of Spanish soldiers and, in turn, used this concern to reject settlement at the missions. Even the missionaries shared their doubts. Fray Juan Domingo Arricivita reported that at San Lorenzo de la Santa Cruz missionaries felt it their duty to "exhort the women in the church to repentance and confession of their sins and to implore divine mercy, so that He would not permit them to fall into the hands of such ferocious beasts [Norteño raiders]." Suspicions among Spanish and Apache men were on the rise as escalating attacks of enemy warriors proved their military alliance ineffective. When officials requested that fray Jiménez explain the missionaries' difficulty in persuading Lipans to join the missions established for them, he replied that the chiefs increasingly had expressed "their unwillingness to leave their women and children in our care" while the men were away on campaigns and hunts. Jiménez did not say whether the Apache men believed that Spanish forces could not adequately defend the women and children from Comanche attack or whether, instead, they believed that the soldiers themselves menaced their women. Later Apache testimony clarified: they feared both.[68]

In 1763, a nightmare suffered by chief El Lumen while out with his men on a bison hunting expedition touched off an outpouring of suspicion, accusation, and hostility. What he saw in his dream brought the entire hunting party thundering back to San Lorenzo mission. As he told fray Diego Jiménez and fray Manuel Antonio de Cuevas later, he had dreamed that the Spaniards had taken advantage of the Apache men's absence to kidnap their women and children, suggesting the depth of Apache fears about the likelihood of Spanish captivity and enslavement of women. When the Lipan men arrived to find the dream untrue, El Lumen turned his anger on the women, accusing his own wife and the wives of his men of having sex with Spanish soldiers and mission Indians brought to El Cañón from the Rio Grande.

The missionaries had supernatural explanations for this incident, attributing El Lumen's visions to the devil, who, they believed, had spread rumors among Apaches while "assuming a human figure in their likeness." In that same report, fray Jiménez mentioned that the devil had also aided Apache sorcerers to ignite a nativistic movement among Lipans—a religious revival expressed in intriguingly gendered form. Apache men and women told of seeing an old man or woman who appeared and disappeared in different settings, always carrying the same message: baptism meant death, and immortality was to be gained only by fighting both Spaniards and Norteños. When it was an old man, the apparition appeared in battle, where he died and then later reappeared, encouraging Apache warriors to believe that they too would enjoy life after death when all Apaches were reunited. Changing to female form, the spirit appeared to Apache women in an equally inspirational (though unidentified) setting to that of the battlefield for Apache men. The apparition suggested to another chief that Spaniards only wanted them all to gather at the mission complex in order to kill them. Influenced by these fears, El Lumen and his leading warriors removed their women and children from the mission and did not return. El Turnio's band soon followed. Three years later, when fray Jiménez searched for explanations for the missions' collapse, he indicated that El Lumen's dream reflected a common fear among Apache men that "once they are in the mission our soldiers will take their women, steal what they have, and kill them"— considering past experience, a not irrational concern. Lipan men thus cast political tensions with Spaniards in terms of threats of rape or enslavement, using women's vulnerability as a medium through which to negotiate with or to renounce Spaniards. Even before the Norteño denouement, the brotherhood had collapsed upon itself.[69]

The devastating attacks on the San Sabá and El Cañón missions and the ignominious defeat of Parrilla's forces at the Red River heralded the Wichita and Comanche bands' entrance onto the battlefields of Spanish-Apache interchange. Fear and suspicion between the Spanish and Apache allies—often expressed through women's potential victimization—then sundered their fledgling brotherhood. The defeats warned Apaches that Spanish forces were too few and too weak to aid in the defense of their lands. The Spaniards, moreover, clearly did not hold Apaches in sufficient esteem to listen to them as equals, as would be required for a successful alliance. Although Apaches had concentrated their rancherías along the San Sabá, Llano, and Pedernales Rivers for as long as they had been in contact with Spaniards, they now began to shift southward, spreading from the Nueces and Medina Rivers to the Pecos and Rio Grande and on into Coahuila. Even rock art throughout the Pecos region—into which Apaches now found themselves driven—suggests their disillusionment. The paintings depict an association of Spaniards with missions throughout the eighteenth century, but with a "creeping hostility" over time. One pictograph in particular shows an anthropomorphized church as a missionary whose upraised arms serve as its towers, and whose hands are its crosses, but whose body is pierced by a spear or an arrow. The painting is one of several providing an iconographic representation of what Apaches "often wanted to do and occasionally did do" to Spaniards.[70]

Failing to understand the enmities in which they had entangled themselves, Spanish officers and soldiers struggled to explain the failures at San Sabá, the Red River, and El Cañón. Simplistic images of Norteño "savagery" and "barbarism" indicate Spanish panic as well as blindness to the forces guiding native regional political economies. If they could attribute the guns, palisaded village, and fighting tactics to French aid (because these things were too sophisticated for "savages"), if they could

Pictograph from Rattlesnake Canyon in the lower Pecos River country of southwest Texas believed to represent Apache hostility toward Spanish missions and missionaries, copied in 1936 by artist Forrest Kirkland. Courtesy of the Texas Archeological Research Laboratory, University of Texas at Austin.

point to, if not exaggerate, the numbers stacked against them (two thousand versus two hundred), and if they could hold Frenchmen responsible for inciting the attack on San Sabá, then they could reinterpret those events not as signs of Spanish inferiority and Indian invincibility but of French duplicity and military direction of "savage" Indians.

At higher levels, viceregal authorities chose to blame the alliance's failure on Apaches, judging their desertion and disinterest indicative of a "fickle" and "faithless" nature. "When [Apaches'] forces are inferior or they are overwhelmed by our victories, they profess a desire for peace," stated the *Reglamento de 1772*, outlining new guidelines for the defense of the northern provinces, but "afterwards, they abused our clemency at the first opportunity, interpreting as weakness the kind treatment they were given." More to the point for most officials at all levels, any plans for the northward expansion of Spanish settlement came to a halt in the face of Comanche and Wichita advances southward, and Spanish presidial forces struggled even to defend lands they already occupied against raids. They blamed Apaches for bringing the wrath of Norteños down upon them, casting their former allies as "infidel Lipanes" who had merely been "spoonfeeding us with their deceitful friendship and supposed desire to be reduced and made into a never-realized congregation." Such a situation would require a reassessment of diplomatic priorities.[71]

Policy shifts in relation to the Apaches in Texas found momentum in the late 1770s due to administrative changes in the governing structure of the far northern provinces of New Spain that removed them from the jurisdiction of the viceroy and made them into a semiautonomous unit—a *comandancia general* called the "Provincias Internas" (Interior Provinces) governed by a military commander. Once the military policy of Texas was tied to those of Coahuila, Nueva Vizcaya, New Mexico, Sonora, Sinaloa, and Baja and Alta California, so too were Lipan Apaches and their eastern Apache kinsmen lumped with all Apache peoples spread westward across those provinces, as officials pursued a policy that would deal with all of them at once. "Their dreaded name," one said of Apaches, "extends from the post of Chihuahua, as far as the Gila River on the west, and toward the north to Moqui, Nuevo México and the provinces of Texas and Coahuila." From this broad perspective, reports of three *junta de guerras* (councils of war) held in 1777 and 1778 in Coahuila, Texas, and Chihuahua concluded that Apache "experts at the operations of war" had to be stopped because "these fertile provinces are being converted into the most horrendous deserts." These "deserts" in turn would become an open door through which the Apaches, if not contained, "may be introduced within very few years even into the immediate regions of the capital of New Spain." They argued, furthermore, that only a general military campaign uniting a requisite three thousand soldiers across the three provinces would provide a solution; diplomacy could not. Apache warriors interpreted Spanish diplomatic overtures as signs of weakness, officials believed, proving by default the ineffectiveness of peace efforts and the necessity of war.[72]

Despite illusory diplomatic achievements of peace (often resting on the shoulders of Apache women), years of mutual hostility had made the task of finding common ground for peace among Spanish and Apache men nearly impossible. Idioms of male valor involving military prowess and violence against women defined both their hostile and peaceful interactions. Diplomacy had evolved only in the wake of war for Spanish and Apache nations in Texas, and violence generated over horses, territory, and, most important, women had been honed into a form of expression, negotiating relations of honor in the absence of established venues of interchange. The resulting environment of mistrust and martial tradition in turn made diplomacy, when finally pursued, difficult to establish and preserve. Spaniards had the chance after more than thirty years of hostility to achieve peace and alliance with Lipan Apaches, but they could not understand the situation and needs of Lipan bands and could not earn their respect. Their decision to pursue seemingly stronger native allies in Comanches, Wichitas, and, again, Caddos would spell temporary ruin for the Apaches in Texas in the 1770s and 1780s.

New Codes of War and Peace, 1760s–1780s

In July of 1765, Taovaya leader Eyasiquiche led a small, weary party of Wichita men to a Spanish mission named for the Nacogdoches Caddos among whom it stood. Having traveled far to the east of their own lands, he and his men had been riding for some days since leaving their Red River villages. They had stopped along the way at Tawakoni-Iscani villages only long enough to add two Iscanis to the party who could act as mediators with the Spaniards Eyasiquiche was going to see. It had to be a quick trip because allied Wichita warriors, gathering for an expedition against enemy Osages, awaited Eyasiquiche's return. The Taovaya leader came in search of Franciscan missionary fray José de Calahorra y Sáenz, one of the few Spaniards with whom he had had contact—peaceful contact, that is.

Eyasiquiche and his people—along with neighboring Tawakonis, Iscanis, Flechazos, and Wichitas—had not had much to do with Spanish people to the south; they had little need or desire to. French traders from the east regularly visited their villages and kept them supplied with European goods in exchange for Spanish horses brought to the Wichitas by Comanches and for the hides of bison and deer they hunted themselves. In fact, the Taovayas had moved to the Red River area precisely to position themselves better to participate in trade networks stretching from Louisiana to New Mexico (as well as to distance themselves from Osages). Although they preferred Frenchmen as trading partners, Eyasiquiche knew that various Caddo groups traded with the small Spanish community at Los Adaes as well as with Frenchmen at Natchitoches, and they seemed to maintain good relations with them both. At the urging of Hasinai Caddos, Tawakoni and Iscani leaders living in villages closer to Caddo territory had intermittently exchanged visits with fray Calahorra and other Spaniards settled nearby.[1] Those leaders in turn had sought to include their other Wichita relatives and allies, but Eyasiquiche and his men had had to focus on defensive measures against Apache and Osage enemies who raided their villages. Moreover, the Spaniards whom Eyasiquiche was most familiar with were allied with Apaches, making them enemies.

But here he was now, riding to seek out Spaniards—at least some eastern-dwelling ones. Events had conspired to change Eyasiquiche's view of them. Back in December, he and forty-seven Taovaya warriors with other allies had attacked the San Sabá presidio where their Lipan Apache enemies had found sanctuary and supplies, using it as a base from which to launch raids against Wichita villages. While keeping the presidio under surveillance, they had also witnessed Spanish warriors accompanying Lipan Apache men on buffalo hunts. To Eyasiquiche, the joint ventures further proved the friendly relations uniting Spaniards with their Lipan enemies. And so he and his warriors had raided them. As it turned out, one party they attacked was made up of only Spaniards, four men and a woman. After the first Spanish man had fallen and a second fled, one of the remaining two had killed the woman with two shots of his gun before the Taovaya warriors could stop him, so they in turn dispatched him. Yet, the determined stand made by the fourth man in the face of superior numbers had earned Eyasiquiche's attention. Eyasiquiche ordered his warriors to spare him because of the valor he demonstrated in defending himself against forty-seven men, even after he received four bullet and two lance wounds.[2]

At first, Eyasiquiche had thought to add the man to his warrior ranks—permeable ranks that could always use more brave men to help counter Apache and Osage hostilities.[3] So, he had brought the injured man home with him to the fortified villages along the Red River that had withstood an assault by Spanish and Apache forces six years before. Eyasiquiche's new ward was the first Spaniard ever welcomed beyond the high earthen ramparts and deeply dug trenches protecting Taovaya homes. Eyasiquiche thus tried to ensure the man's reception and security by sending word ahead of the bravery he had shown on the battlefield. Once home, though, the chief discovered that if the battle feat had won the Spaniard his life, what earned him the acceptance of Eyasiquiche's relatives and comrades was the knowledge they soon gained that he came from the Spanish village at Los Adaes in Caddo territory rather than from San Sabá, where he had been captured. This discovery made sense to Eyasiquiche because the man's courage proved he could not be "one of those from San Sabá" who always fled like cowards as soon as they saw a war party.[4]

Eyasiquiche had his Spanish adoptee's wounds tended, and, over the following months, as they healed, so too did Eyasiquiche's perception of his enemies change. By summertime, "Despite the great and extreme love everyone felt for him [the Spaniard]," Eyasiquiche decided to send him back to his own home and people as a gesture of friendship. So, they rode east to Mission Nacogdoches, the Spaniard looking like a Taovaya, dressed as he was in their clothes and accoutrements. His transformation back into a Spaniard could await their arrival. There were not many to receive them at the mission—

fray Calahorra lived there with two soldiers and their families and some young farm-workers, though Nacogdoches, Nabedache, Hasinai, and Nasoni hamlets lay close by.[5]

Upon meeting the priest whom his Caddo friends so admired, Eyasiquiche sought to communicate his position with care, explaining via the translations of two Hasinai caddís named Sanches and Canos that this goodwill gesture extended only to the Spaniards "in this part of the country," that is, those living in and around the Los Adaes presidio and Nacogdoches mission. Eyasiquiche and the Taovayas he represented did not, and could not, seek peace with the Spaniards to the south at the San Sabá presidio and nearby San Antonio de Béxar as long as they continued to associate with Lipan Apaches. Emphasizing this distinction further, Eyasiquiche offered to give the eastern-dwelling Spaniards two cannons left behind by the other, southern Spaniards after the failed attack on his village. He was willing as well to send five other Spanish adoptees, all women and members of his village for a long time, to live instead among the Nacogdoches and Los Adaes Spaniards. Again, though, he would not release them to Spaniards from the south but would deliver them only into the hands of any from Los Adaes who would come for them. When Calahorra asked him why he and his warriors "did not keep the peace with all Spaniards," Eyasiquiche reiterated that as long as the Spaniards of San Sabá protected and defended Apaches who were his "mortal enemies" and who dared to attack Wichita villages, steal their horses, and capture their women and children, then Taovaya men "could do no less than carry out on those Spaniards all of the hostilities for which there was an opportunity."[6] Although his love and admiration for the adopted Spanish warrior had softened his opinion of Spaniards, Eyasiquiche was going to wait for the Spaniards of San Sabá and San Antonio de Béxar to prove themselves before changing his mind about them.[7]

The unofficial negotiations between Eyasiquiche and fray José de Calahorra brought about by presidial soldier Antonio Treviño's brave stand in battle provide a unique glimpse of how some Indian peoples perceived power relations within the region. Eyasiquiche's decision to differentiate between those Spaniards to the east at Los Adaes and at the Mission of Nuestra Señora de Guadalupe at Nacogdoches—who maintained good relations with their Caddo allies—and those Spaniards to the south at San Sabá and San Antonio, who allied with Apaches, suggests that Wichitas and their Norteño allies believed Spaniards to live in bands similar to their own. To their eyes, Spaniards might speak the same language, wear the same clothes, and share the same culture but have individual political identities and affiliations, as did many Indian peoples. And they were not far wrong. The state of the Los Adaes presidio in the 1760s attested to the fact that the small Spanish community existed in a world far distant from the conflicts and hostilities of San Antonio de Béxar and San Sabá. Norteño enmity never descended upon it, and peaceful relations had allowed the garrison to lapse into somnolent disrepair. Indeed, after his 1766–68 inspection, the marques de Rubí recommended that viceregal authorities extinguish the Los Adaes presidio as "worthless" to the defense of New Spain's northern provinces, a judgment they carried out in 1773.[8]

From various contacts in the 1760s, Spaniards gained new perspectives on Wichitas as well. Fray Calahorra had brought back the first reports of unstinting Wichita hospitality following a 1760 visit to the Tawakoni-Iscani villages along the Sabine River. There, four chiefs (two from each group) took turns honoring the visiting dignitary with bounteous feasts in their homes over the course of eight days. The hospitality reflected their economic prosperity, evident in abundant fields surrounding the two towns where they pastured fine breeding horses and cultivated maize, beans, and squash. The missionary praised Wichita communal agricultural labor and the equal division of their products at harvest. To protect such "riches of the land," Calahorra noted, they were building a defensive fort with subterranean chambers similar to that at the Taovayas' Red River settlement. Meeting with another Taovaya leader who traveled with twenty men and six women to talk with the missionary at the Tawakoni-Iscani villages, Calahorra also learned that they could add at least another 600 warriors to the 250 he estimated lived in the Sabine River towns. This knowledge further solidified Spanish views of the Wichitas as a military force to be reckoned with. On subsequent trips, Calahorra learned more about the Wichitas' close ties to French traders, noting that a French flag regularly flew over the Tawakoni-Iscani towns and that five French traders from the Arkansas post lived near villages of Taovayas, Iscanis, and Wichitas proper along the Red River.[9]

Antonio Treviño—the brave soldier saved by Eyasiquiche—offered an even more compelling description of the powerful position Wichitas occupied in the economic and political relations of northern Texas and the Southern Plains. Eyasiquiche had allowed Treviño to participate in all aspects of male village life. Thus, the soldier could provide an insider's perspective on the military defenses that had humiliated Colonel Diego Ortiz Parrilla's forces in 1759. Questioned closely by Spanish officials, Treviño described in detail the fortress with its subterranean apartments, within which all the women, children, and elderly could take sanctuary during an attack; the split-log picket surrounding the fort through which men could fire their rifles; the four-foot earthen ramparts that ran outside the palisade as the second line of defense; and the four-foot-deep and twelve-foot-wide trench offering a third and final barrier, designed to keep mounted attackers at a distance. The steady stream of French traders Treviño witnessed there testified to the central place the Taovaya towns held in the region's trade networks. Frenchmen from Louisiana brought to the Taovayas rifles, ammunition, cloth, French apparel, and material goods in exchange for bison hides and deerskins produced from the hunt, captive Apache women and children taken in war, and horses and mules raided from Spanish settlements to the south. Close ties with neighboring Wichitas and Iscanis meant that their three Red River communities alone could field five hundred warriors. The inner view of Wichita life impressed Treviño (and the Spanish officials who read his reports) with the military and economic power of Eyasiquiche's world just as much as Treviño's war deeds had impressed the Taovaya leader with the man's valor.[10]

Wichita-speaking peoples had begun a southward migration from the area of present-day Kansas late in the seventeenth century in response to pressure from Osages to the east, who were newly armed with French and British guns, and from Comanches to the west, who were newly mounted on Spanish horses. The Wichitas' acquisition of horses and guns accompanied their geographical movement and evolved more out of defensive needs than for hunting purposes. Wichita bands with a total population estimated between 10,000 and 30,000 at midcentury established fifteen to twenty consolidated, often palisaded, villages scattered across the northern regions of present-day Texas, concentrating particularly in fertile lands along rivers where they could successfully farm without jeopardizing their defensive capabilities. Although each village remained independent, leaders from larger settlements often exerted influence over others, and a loose confederation linked the scattered towns together, whether they were Taovaya, Tawakoni, Iscani, Kichai, Flechazo, or Wichita proper. Agriculture played a central role in Wichita socioeconomics and tied them to their matrilineal and matrilocal grass-lodge villages for much of the year while women farmed, but they spent the fall and winter in mobile camps when men hunted deer and bison. Yet, it was Wichita trade connections developed over the first half of the eighteenth century with Frenchmen and Caddos to the east and with newly allied Comanches to the west that secured a steady supply of guns and horses as well as critical alliances needed to defend these populous and productive communities against Osage and Apache raids.[11]

Their Comanche allies represented a branch of the northern Shoshones of the Great Basin region, whose acquisition of horses had led to their rapid evolution into a mounted, mobile military power. During the seventeenth century, they had first moved into the plains of eastern Colorado and western Kansas and then turned south, pushed by Blackfeet and Crows and pulled by abundant bison herds and Spanish horses. Much like the Wichitas, bands of Yamparicas, Jupes, and Kotsotekas had moved into the Southern Plains by the early eighteenth century, operating as independent, kin-based hunting and gathering groups loosely tied to one another in defensive and economic alliances. Yamparicas and Jupes focused their trading and raiding activities in New Mexico, while Kotsoteka bands lived to the east and interacted more with the native peoples of Texas.

By midcentury, these eastern Comanche bands had formed mutually beneficial relationships with Wichitas, allying militarily against common Apache and Osage foes and establishing trade ties that brought Louisiana material goods, Plains hides, and Spanish horses together for exchange. The trade secured both Wichita agricultural products and French guns and ammunition for Comanche communities, while sending a stream of horses and captives taken in New Mexico eastward to Louisiana markets.[12] By 1770, Natchitoches diplomat Athanase de Mézières summed up the dominant position of Comanches in the region: "They are so skillful in horsemanship that they have no equal; so daring that they never ask for or grant truces; and in possession of such a territory that, finding in it an abundance of pasturage for their horses and an incredible number of [bison] which furnish them raiment, food, and shelter, they only just fall short of possessing all of the conveniences of the earth."[13]

The lucrative political and economic ties among Comanche, Wichita, Caddo, and French traders had developed far from Spanish activity and observation. From 1758 onward, however, these ties commanded Spanish attention. In the wake of Mission San Sabá's destruction in 1758, Parrilla's ignominious defeat in 1759, and the ruin of the besieged El Cañón missions by 1767, Spaniards across the province feared for their lives, believing the Norteño allies' "great acts of audacity and boldness" would accelerate because of evident Spanish weakness.[14] And why not? When united, bands of Comanches, Wichitas, Caddos, and Tonkawas could field an estimated total of 10,000 men in comparison to Spanish forces that numbered between 150 and 200 men for the entire province.[15] Taovaya and Tawakoni forts offered better fortifications and defenses for Wichita peoples than the leading presidio of Texas, at San Antonio de Béxar, did for Spaniards—a presidio that in 1778 was described by fray Juan Agustín Morfi as "surrounded by a poor stockade on which are mounted a few swivel guns, without shelter or defense, that can be used only for firing a salvo." Three years later, even the paltry stockade had been destroyed in a storm.[16]

Echoing the worries within Texas, viceregal officials in Mexico City feared the loss of the entire province. "We shall have, it is undeniable, one day the Nations of the North as neighbors; they already are approaching us now," wrote the marqués de Rubí in 1768. Not only did he concede that Spaniards could not expand further northward into the "true dominions" of Comanches and Wichitas, he also proposed drawing back Spanish borders with the evacuation of the San Sabá and Los Adaes presidios. In designing a cordon of fifteen presidios to protect New Spain's dominions—which he located below the Rio Grande—he wanted to locate each fort no more than one hundred miles away from the next one, and the line of presidios was to stretch across the entire length of New Spain's northern provinces, from Texas westward through New Mexico and Sonora. Rubí only reluctantly stopped short of calling for the abandonment of San Antonio de Béxar and the entire Texas province. Spanish officials also feared British threats to their claims to the Pacific coast of North America, claims they would soon confront by extending settlements there. If won over as allies, Spaniards speculated, perhaps the Norteños could aid Spain in slowing or stopping the British advancement across the Plains. At midcentury, Spanish civil and military officials thereby decided their best option for saving the province was to seek a truce and then diplomatic relations with the formidable Comanche and Wichita nations.[17]

With new diplomatic goals vis-à-vis the nations of the Norteño alliance, Spanish officials completely reversed their portrayal of Comanche and Wichita men. Warriors feared as barbarous and cruel enemies across a battlefield became men of bravery and valor when sought as allies across the negotiating table. Rubí was one of the first to voice the dual perceptions attached to warrior reputations when he wrote hopefully that the "warlike" Comanches and Wichitas, "whose generosity and bravery make them quite worthy of being our enemies, perhaps will not be . . . [since] they have what is necessary to know how to observe [amicable relations]."[18] The ability to crush Spaniards in battle earned Comanche and Wichita warriors the respect of Spanish soldiers and officers. Many Spanish officials in turn envisioned an alliance with the seemingly indestructible Norteños against Apaches as the solution to all their problems. In one swoop, they would transform Comanche, Wichita, and Caddo enemies into allies while destroying Lipan Apaches entirely. Yet, winning over these powerful Indian nations would not be easy.

Local imperatives in the 1770s and 1780s eventually would encourage Wichitas and Comanches to consider Spanish overtures of peace emanating from San Antonio de Béxar. In the aftermath of the Seven Years' War, Louisiana formally shifted from French to Spanish rule, and the Spanish assumption of control there in 1769, together with stringent new trade policies, began to hamper the steady economic and defensive supplies previously enjoyed by Comanches and Wichitas. Regulations passed that year by interim Louisiana governor Alexandro O'Reilly aimed at cutting off trade in the upper Red River valley that put guns into the hands of native groups in Texas. This policy did not simply represent the extension of New Spain's general prohibitions against trading guns to Indians, however, but specifically targeted Comanches, Wichitas, and others identified as members of the Norteño alliance whom the Spanish government deemed "hostile."[19]

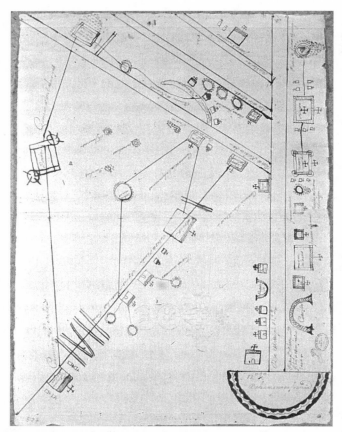

*Presidio de San Sabá hasta Adaes, 1763. Diagrammatic map made by
Frenchman Pierre Tamoineau for Spanish military commander Felipe de
Rábago y Terán at San Sabá in 1763 showing the locations and potential
threats of the allied Norteño nations who had been threatening Spaniards
since 1758. With a base point at New Orleans, the map indicates the
direction and distances of Caddo, Wichita, Yojuane, and Tonkawa
settlements in relation to the three Spanish presidios of San Sabá, San
Antonio, and Los Adaes and the Taovaya fort on the Red River, where
Spanish forces were defeated in 1759. Courtesy of the Texas State Library
and Archives Commission.*

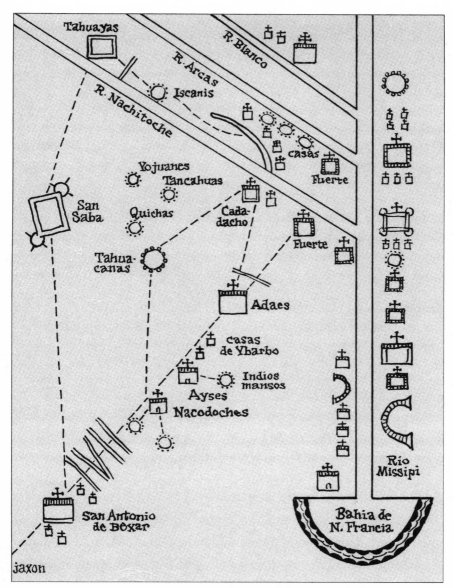

Modern rendering of the Tamoineau map of 1763. Tracing by and courtesy of Jack Jackson, from Shooting the Sun: Cartographic Results of Military Activities in Texas, 1689–1829 *(Austin: Book Club of Texas, 1998).*

Trade prohibitions also slowed the eastward flow of hides, horses, mules, and Apache slaves from Texas that had proven so profitable for Comanche and Wichita warriors. In accordance with O'Reilly's directives, officials in Natchitoches not only forbade trade but recalled all licensed French traders, hunters, and illicit "vagabonds" from their subposts or homes among "hostile" Indians. Spanish officials in Texas counted on the ban to weaken the economic networks of formidable Comanche and Wichita bands whose raids had been devastating horse herds in civil and mission settlements across the province. With such an opening, Texas officials hoped to offer native leaders Spanish gifts and diplomacy in the place of French trade and thus win some breathing space for the province.

In their turn, Comanches and Wichitas faced limited prospects in seeking replacements for the decline in French trade goods. Continued raids on Spanish settlements in Texas to fulfill their horse supply could not fill the gap in arms and material goods formerly provided by Louisiana markets. While French traders associated with the Natchitoches and Arkansas posts remained active covertly and soon British traders began pushing into the region, the trade potential of Spaniards in Texas still began to appeal to Comanches and Wichitas. To build peace out of past hostilities, however, proved a longer and more difficult task than anticipated. Two more years would pass after Eyasiquiche's 1765 visit before allied Norteños finished off the El Cañón missions, six more years before the first Wichita-Spanish treaty agreement, and twenty years before the first Comanche-Spanish peace accord.

chapter five

Contests and Alliances of Norteño Manhood:
The Road to Truce and Treaty

The power of the Comanche and Wichita military presence and their trade ties with Caddos and Frenchmen momentarily had led desperate Spaniards and Apaches to seek one another's aid against this united foe in the 1750s and 1760s. The strength of their foe, however, had just as quickly torn apart that tenuous alliance when Spanish officials decided to abandon the Lipan Apaches and negotiate with Comanche and Wichita bands instead. From the Comanche and Wichita perspective, Spanish communities in Texas had held little relevance before their relationship with the Lipan Apaches brought the Spaniards to their attention as new enemies and thus new targets for raids. When, in the 1770s and 1780s, some reason to establish peace arose, their hostile history would make efforts to replace enmity with diplomacy that much harder.

When the Spaniards approached this new set of potential native allies, Caddo, Wichita, and Comanche standards of diplomacy set the rules, as had those of previous groups. Male-dominated rituals shaped through militarization increasingly defined politics in the province as well as regional European and Indian economies, governing systems, social hierarchies, and ceremonial lives. In ranked societies like those of the Comanches and the Wichitas, prestige circumscribed men's social status. Through war deeds, raiding coups, generosity, and medicine power (what Comanches called "*puha*"), men gained honor that in turn translated into authority, access to status positions, and standing in their relations with other men. *Puha* and generosity were intrinsically tied to a man's achievements in raids and war, since those activities supplied the goods, horses, or captives by whose distribution he demonstrated his generosity, while medicine power was requisite for and reflected by war honors. Men's generosity not only tied people and families to each other; it enhanced the men's standing and that of their kin in the eyes of others. By extension, personal or medicine power was the foundation of rank and relations between men. As Athanase de

Mézières wrote of Wichita leaders, "they pride themselves on owning nothing, and, as they are not recognized as chiefs except in recognition of their deeds, the most able and successful warrior is the one who commands, authority falling to him who best uses it in the defense of his compatriots." Among Caddos over the eighteenth century, men's war deeds came to hold more sway within the cultural categories determining male rank and status, as horses and guns offered new routes to social distinction for men and as the basis of status positions shifted from sacred to secular authority and from heredity to individual achievement. Though Spaniards at the beginning of the century had imagined Caddos primarily as peaceful agriculturalists, Caddo men inspired one Anglo-American agent at the end of the century to compare their martial spirit to that of the Knights of Malta.[1]

During this period, Spanish government structures also reflected the region's increasing orientation toward war. Inspections of Spanish defensive capabilities across the far northern frontier in the 1760s led to the designation of the two Californias, Sonora, New Mexico, Nueva Vizcaya, Texas, and Coahuila as the "Interior Provinces" in 1776, all placed under the command of a military governor (entitled "commandant general"). Within Texas, as in other northern provinces, governors came from the military, ensuring that judicial, civil, and military authority rested in the hands of officers of the rank of colonel or lieutenant colonel. This culture of militarism led even Spanish missionaries to cast their work as manly and virile, arguing that religious conquest was itself a battle and a martyr's death as heroic and valorous as that of a soldier in war. But missionaries would not be called upon anymore. During the 1770s and 1780s, officials secularized New Spain's "Indian policy"; the state would no longer rely on missionaries or religious considerations to determine the course of negotiations with Indian nations. The takeover of Louisiana influenced these policy shifts in the northern provinces, as Spanish officials tried to emulate their successful French rivals by reversing former prohibitions denying guns and ammunition to Indians, by making it standard practice to employ French traders as mediators and translators for all negotiations with Indian leaders, and by instituting formal gift and trade supply lines to allied Indian nations.[2]

Because of these transformations within Spanish and Indian leadership ranks, individual men could exert significant influence over diplomacy—a certain power of personality prevailed. Consensual politics among Comanche, Wichita, and Apache bands demanded that leaders demonstrate not only bravery and fighting prowess but also the foresight, wisdom, and charisma reflective of personal *puha*, or medicine power. The capacity of individuals to determine the success or failure of diplomatic endeavors was even more critical to Spaniards, given their weak position vis-à-vis their Comanche, Wichita, and Apache counterparts. War or peace might hinge on certain men's ability to relate to Indian leaders, to convey respect, and to solicit trust. In the 1770s and 1780s, Athanase de Mézières, Juan María Ripperdá, Domingo Cabello, and Rafael Martínez Pacheco, for better or worse, swayed the political pendulum by their very personalities. Ripperdá and Cabello were both outsiders—formal military men for whom Texas was an undesirable posting. Yet, while Cabello's old-school military mind-set made him cautious and deeply suspicious of Indian diplomats, Ripperdá's internationalist outlook meant that he was far more open to working with French officials in Louisiana as well as with Caddo and Wichita leaders. Mézières and Martínez Pacheco were products of the borderlands, having lived and worked closely with numerous Indian peoples in a variety of settings in Louisiana and Texas, respectively. Mézières had such singular standing among Caddo and Wichita leaders that his death in 1779 nearly derailed the diplomacy of both provinces. In the years that followed, San Antonio officials struggled to fill his place by bringing a number of former French traders and translators into the Spanish diplomatic core—just to replace one man. The evaluation of individual male interactions—across negotiating tables rather than battlefields—thus became all the more personal in these later years.[3]

In a sense, Spaniards were back at square one by 1770—seeking first contacts with which to begin building diplomatic relations—though they did not enjoy the clean slate of 1690, but a bloodied one, stained by mutual violence. When representatives of the Spanish, Comanche, and Wichita nations met, they entered negotiations with grievances or demands that flowed from earlier raids and battles. Recognizing past Spanish misdeeds, the San Antonio *cabildo* worried about the lack of a foundation upon which to build peace in the 1760s, arguing that many of the Indian nations with whom Spaniards had warred "are naturally prone to break relations and are persuaded to do this by the merest breeze that brings to their remembrance the death or captivity of some son, mate, or parent that will stimulate that lust for vengeance to which they have such inclination and propensity." And Spaniards too had their own grievances. The only common ground therefore was one of shared tension and mistrust.[4]

The language of diplomacy used by Comanche and Wichita leaders rested upon highly masculine and militarized terms of warfare to an even greater degree than that used by Apaches. By symbol and rhetoric, protocols had to establish a mood and a situation in which men would open themselves to the negotiation itself. Rituals of respect functioned as the redemptive erasures of past slurs on the battlefield. Turning truce into alliance in this hostile situation meant diplomacy took its most powerful form in military commitments. Thus, pledges to fight jointly against common enemies (primarily Apaches) dominated diplomatic discussions among

Spaniards, Caddos, Wichitas, and Comanches. Rituals and gifts that followed lent a further martial air to negotiations, transforming fellow warriors into comrades and brothers. To forge bonds that could join rather than separate men on the battlefield, Comanches and Wichitas also appealed to a language of military titles and male kinship. Warrior prestige found expression in titles of "captain," "medal chief," and "*capitán grande*" as Spaniards and native men endeavored to extend respect to each other. Such exchanges often occurred with little shared understanding of the meanings each group read into them, however, and ignorance yet again could work to everyone's benefit. Each man could interpret the exchange as he was wont to do and walk away pleased.

Many times over the 1770s and 1780s, Spaniards feared their willingness to discuss peace might appear to be a sign of weakness or cowardice, particularly when they themselves viewed valor as synonymous with a "disposition to carry on offensive warfare and to defend [oneself]." Diplomat Athanase de Mézières questioned orders to seek peace with "haughty" Comanche warriors, writing, "Why should I go? . . . To fondle and protect barbarians whose crude understanding would ascribe our conduct to fear?" Yet, fear did define Spanish views of Apaches, Comanches, and Wichitas, as well as their view of the future of the province. In 1777, the commandant inspector of the interior presidios, Hugo O'Conor, argued that, of all of New Spain's northern provinces, Texas held the greatest strategic importance as the sole bastion against the French and the British, but that it had also been the most costly, of least use, and "produced the most hostilities." Apaches, he explained, were "every one of them enemies of our provinces" and thus the "most feared," Comanches ruled as "lords of the wide land," and Wichitas had been provoked repeatedly into war by Spanish mistreatment. Thus, as Teodoro de Croix expressed it, provincial officials had to use diplomacy as a means of "gentle persuasion which they [Native Americans] could never attribute to our weakness." Or, as Mézières put it, a diplomatic alliance with Indian leaders should function "to obtain from their aid the benefit promised, without giving them reason to think that we depend too much upon it."[5]

Meanwhile, Caddo, Wichita, and Comanche men still did not have much reason to seek out Spaniards as allies—they had little to gain from them, and so they set the bar high for Spanish proofs of commitment and value as "brothers." More often than not, as Spaniards tried to walk the fine line set for them by these dominant Indian nations, they erred by not paying due attention to the rules of a diplomacy in which they had little say. Because war so overshadowed the negotiations, honor was at risk, and peace remained contingent upon the precarious expressions of respect and reciprocity fundamental to native systems of alliance. Negotiators maintained a constant vigilance against perceived insult in the behavior or words of others. As a result, diplomatic relations that were difficult to achieve proved even harder to maintain, and a return to the battlefield often seemed likely. In such a context, Spanish failures to understand native codes of honor could very easily become acts of war. The actions of men therefore had to bring Wichitas and Comanches to a negotiating table with Spaniards, but as will be seen in Chapter 6, women provided the seal by which they did or did not cement the agreements made at those tables. Thus, Chapters 5 and 6 each take up a different half of the gendered politics that ruled the diplomacy of the 1770s and 1780s.

At the end of 1769, Caddos took the lead among their Norteño allies in establishing the terms by which newly established Spanish representatives from Natchitoches might assume the standing previously enjoyed by French officials within Caddo economic and political networks. At the diplomatic level, Spanish officials hoped to gain new kinship roles among Caddo leaders using political gifts and commercial trade. That is, they wanted the ties that Caddos had formed at the local level with their Spanish neighbors around Los Adaes and the nearby missions to be extended to the entire province of Texas. Although the strengths such ties provided at the local level were clear, Spanish officials did not always see the evidence for what it was. In the midst of critical reports on the state of Spanish institutions in east Texas, commandant inspector Hugo O'Conor noted that "the land [around Los Adaes] is one of those on which the Lipan, Natages, and other Apache Indians have never set foot either in time of peace or in war," and Nicolás de Lafora observed that the "savage tribes . . . are troublesome only at San Antonio de Béjar. . . . They never molest the presidio of Los Adaes." Why not? Because the Spanish soldiers and settlers there enjoyed the alliance and protection of Caddo warriors. Officials did not need to worry about defending the Spanish settlement there, because Caddos took care of it. Inspectors might complain that the Los Adaes presidio lacked operable arms, with its mere two cannons in total disrepair and only two rifles, seven swords, and six shields for sixty-one soldiers; that the men wore nothing resembling a military uniform and were without the proper hats, coats, shirts, and shoes; and that the company lacked "everything necessary to carry out its obligations." But Spaniards' obligations at that villa and presidio did not lie in defense; instead, they maintained obligations of trade and alliance with Caddos and, in circuitous fashion, gained needed defense in return.[6]

Echoing Wichita distinctions among different Spanish communities, Caddos' relations with Los Adaes residents had remained firm, but they viewed those at San Antonio with suspicion because of their Apache alliance. After the Louisiana cession, then, Caddo leaders chose not to approach Texas officials but instead worked through those at Natchitoches to convey their understanding of the shift in governance among their European trade allies. In effect, they were able to negotiate treaties with the new Spanish government of Louisiana that strengthened trade ties despite the new restrictions established by Governor O'Reilly. Although Caddos had participated in the raids against Apaches and the attack on San Sabá, the Spanish governments of Texas and Louisiana knew they could not enforce the trade prohibitions against "hostile" Wichitas and Comanches without Caddo aid.

The new commandant at Natchitoches, Athanase de Mézières, could ill afford to alienate Caddo leaders—their trade alliance was too important to the economies of both the Natchitoches post and the Louisiana colony, and their political alliance was crucial to the maintenance of peace in the region. He moved quickly to maintain diplomatic goodwill and the exchange of deerskins, bison hides, and bear fat for European material goods. This two-pronged strategy required two different lists of goods, one of the annual gifts that would be given to different Caddo confederations, the other of goods that licensed traders would contract to exchange in Caddo villages throughout the year. The two inventories shared many things in common, listing muskets, powder, musket balls, and gun flints to keep Caddo arms well supplied—notably, 89 muskets, 834 pounds of powder, 1,868 pounds of balls, and 2,000 flints. They also both included tools of daily life such as hatchets, knives, awls, kettles, mirrors, blankets, and red and blue Limburg cloth. Yet, other specialized goods designated on the "annual present" lists clearly targeted the need to solidify relations of honor between Caddo and Spanish leaders. Although much of the highly structured ceremonialism required by Caddo custom in their contacts with Europeans at the beginning of the eighteenth century had waned, the reciprocity of gift exchange had not. The gifts too reflected the militarization of Caddo leadership ranks: the theocratic position of the *xinesí* had disappeared, and the criteria for selection of *caddís* had shifted to battlefield strength and valor. Gifts of clothes marking male rank had become more elaborate so that *caddís* now received military uniforms, including hats trimmed with feathers and galloons (lace, embroidery, or braids of metallic thread), ornamented and laced shirts, flags, and ribbon with which to wear honorary medals.[7]

To convey that the Caddos accepted Spain's assumption of France's political obligations—that is, annual presents and the provision of licensed traders—Tinhioüen, a principal *caddí* of the Kadohadachos, and Cocay, a principal *caddí* of the Yatasis, traveled to Natchitoches in April 1770. Upon arrival, Tinhioüen and Cocay were feted in a solemn ceremony before an assemblage of Spanish officials, during which they received the king's "royal emblem [a flag] and his august medal with the very greatest veneration"—each silver medal had on one side a portrait of the king with the legend "Carlos III, King of Spain and emperor of the Indies," and on the other the words "In Merit," surrounded by laurels.[8]

Key to the Caddos' acceptance of such formalities, however, was that many of the assembled representatives of the Spanish government were the same Frenchmen they had long known and deemed kin. Mézières, a French soldier and trader now appointed commandant at Natchitoches, had married the daughter of Louis Juchereau de St. Denis, the French founder of Natchitoches back in 1716. Mézières enjoyed not only the benefits of inclusion within the powerful French family but also, by extension, their standing among Caddos as adopted kin. Indicating the central role these Caddo-related Frenchmen would play, Alexis Grappe stood beside the two Caddo leaders as their interpreter at the ceremony. Grappe was a trader and translator who had long lived among Kadohadachos at Fort St. Louis de Cadodacho, a trading post established at their central village along the Red River, with his wife, Louise Marguerite Guedon (daughter of Frenchman Jacques Guedon and Chitimacha Marie Anne de la Grand Terre), and their children. In addition to Grappe, Pierre Dupin (one of the other Frenchmen licensed to trade among Caddo villages) and Juan Piseros (the merchant who supplied traders in exchange for the products of Caddo hunters) also attended, representing the continuity of economic relations that bound the Caddo-Natchitoches communities together.[9]

In the ceremonial exchanges, Tinhioüen and Cocay promised that their men would continue "to employ themselves peacefully in their hunting," while the leaders would turn over any illicit traders to Spanish officials. They thus assured those same French merchants and traders that valuable bison hides, bear fat, and most important, deerskins would continue to flow into Natchitoches warehouses. More critically, the two Caddo leaders "engaged to aid with their good offices and their persuasion, in maintaining the peace." Tellingly, one of the ways in which Natchitoches officials requested the aid of Tinhioüen and Cocay was by asking them to curtail the arms trade with their Wichita and Comanche allies until the Texas government could forge a truce with them. Spanish officials clearly recognized that such a pact would not be achieved without Caddo help, and fewer than six months later, when Tinhioüen had put a peace process with the Wichitas in motion, Mézières attested to his superiors that indeed the "great loyalty of its inhabitants and the importance of their territory" made Caddos the "master-key of New Spain." As key mediators in brokering an accord between Spain and the numerous and powerful Wichita bands, Tinhioüen, Cocay, and later, Hasinai *caddí* Bigotes increased their leverage and status even further.[10]

Some ritualized ceremonies could not so easily accomplish the transition from French to Spanish diplomacy, however. If Spaniards failed to follow native dictates previously accepted by Frenchmen in day-to-day interactions, Caddo leaders willingly resorted to threats or acts of violence to enforce their economic and political authority. In 1768, for example, when soldiers under the new commandant inspector of presidios based at Los Adaes sought to arrest a Frenchman named Du Buche while on his way from Natchitoches with merchandise for Yatasis, principal men of the village reacted vigorously. Du Buche had lived and traded among them for years, and they were not about to lose a man they deemed a valuable trader and a kinsman who had long maintained his obligations. A *caddí* named Guakan quickly assembled his warriors to attack Los Adaes in response to this Spanish affront to relations of honor. Only the intervention of another Frenchman, Louis de St. Denis (son of Louis Juchereau de St. Denis) forestalled the planned assault. Luckily for the Spaniards, Guakan went to St. Denis's home, perhaps calling on him as kinsman to join the gathering warriors, and St. Denis instead dissuaded him from war, healing the diplomatic breach with presents to restore a reciprocal balance to the disrupted exchange.[11]

A life-and-death drama played out two years later when Kadohadachos tried to win the freedom of an adopted kinsman, thirty-five-year-old armorer and gunsmith François Morvant, who had lived among them for seven years. In 1770, Morvant responded to the official recall of all Frenchmen living in native villages but, upon reaching the Natchitoches post, was arrested for murder. Ten years before, in a heated altercation, he had killed the leader of an infamous band of illegal hunters and trappers based north of the Arkansas post. Fleeing for his life out of fear of the band's revenge, he had wandered for three years along the Arkansas River, until Kadohadachos found him so ill and near death that they took the young Frenchman back to their village to care for him. As he regained his health, Morvant also gained the status of adopted kin and, though his presence at the principal Kadohadacho village was known to French officials, none tried to arrest him due to the protection he enjoyed there. When Tinhioüen and the principal men of the village learned that Morvant's good-faith effort to abide by the recall in 1770—a decision they had urged him to take out of respect for the diplomatic agreements with their newly accepted Spanish allies—had threatened his life, they promptly went to negotiate his case with Mézières. Tinhioüen laid siege to Mézières and with great insistence pledged not to leave his side until Morvant was given his freedom. Clearly, his authority mattered, as Mézières and a council of Natchitoches officials decided after long meetings that they could ill afford to "displease an Indian of such good parts and distinguished services." Mézières released Morvant back "under the protection" of Tinhioüen, a decision his superiors found a "very strange" contradiction of Spanish laws. Indeed, a top-down view of Spanish policy misses on-the-ground necessities within the kin-based world in which the Spaniards had only a tenuous place.[12]

The first meeting of Spanish and Wichita leaders, organized by Tinhioüen in the fall of 1770, clarified the Spanish government's diplomatic dependence on the bonds of kinship formed between Caddo and French men. The Spaniards had no means of approaching Wichita peoples; no banner of the Virgin of Guadalupe or inclusion of women in a traveling party would suffice to convey peaceful intent after decades-long enmity. So, the Spaniards relied on the aid of male mediators, as Caddo leaders helped them to gain a hearing with the Wichitas. Tinhioüen had assiduously traveled to meet with his Wichita counterparts, leading men from different bands of Taovayas, Tawakonis, Kichais, and Iscanis, to propose meetings with the Spaniards. He offered as neutral ground his own Kadohadacho settlement for the site of such talks. Once he had persuaded them to hear the Spaniards out, Tinhioüen summoned Mézières and sent three leading men to escort him from Natchitoches to join seven leaders from different Wichita bands who had already assembled at Fort St. Louis de Cadodacho in his village. Mézières went at his bidding without waiting for the permission of his superiors, sure in the knowledge that if he failed to attend, the Wichitas and Caddos "will become disgusted, attributing [the nonappearance] to fickleness and lack of courage on my part . . . making difficult and even impossible their congregation and conquest in the future."[13]

Of first importance was that Natchitoches officials incorporate Spaniards into the Caddo-French kin ties that had long bound Caddos and Frenchmen in relations of honor. The language of European treaty-making lent itself to Caddo appeal, as officials asserted the "sacred ties of consanguinity" that now united Frenchmen and Spaniards under the (Bourbon) family compact. Mézières carefully selected the members of his traveling party to convey symbolically to Wichita and Caddo men a new "brotherhood" between Spaniards of Texas and Frenchmen of Louisiana. A sergeant and four soldiers from the Los Adaes presidio as well as a Spanish missionary joined a sublieutenant and five people from the Natchitoches post in the trip to Tinhioüen's village. At the October conference, Mézières pointed to the Spanish flag flying above the proceedings, using the symbolic object to assert that Wichita leaders "could not doubt, in view of that respectable flag which they saw hoisted, that we [the French] had become naturalized as Spaniards." To establish the Spanish king as a man and ruler worthy of the alliance they had previously maintained with the French king, Mézières assured them of the "immense power" of the Spanish king, a man who wished them to become "brothers" of his other subjects. In his most potent statement, Mézières insisted to the listening Wichitas—listening through the translations of Alexis Grappe, because they too spoke the Kadohadacho dialect—that they could not have peace with Natchitoches and war with San Antonio. Taking the hand of each of the Spaniards standing near him, Mézières asserted that "the very name of Frenchman had been erased and forgotten" and that "we were Spaniards, and, as such, sensitive to the outrages committed [referring to San Sabá and El Cañón] as we would be interested in avenging them as soon as they might be resumed."[14]

Yet, as Wichita leaders gravely explained in the Kadohadacho language, the Spaniards' proven alliance with Apaches had made them targets of their hostility; it had nothing to do with Spanish-French relations. They had been attempting to make this point clear to Texas Spaniards since 1760. In fact, they pointedly asserted, their warriors had long known the location of the numerous horse and cattle herds of Spanish ranches, villages, and presidios and had never raided them until the Spaniards made themselves enemies through their aid to the Apaches. Concluding simply, the Wichita spokesmen avowed that they put their confidence in their ancient protectors, the French. Ritual behaviors surrounding the proceedings echoed this sentiment. Fray Miguel Santa María y Silva complained to superiors that he found it significant that as the calumet pipe repeatedly went around the circle of dignitaries—a pipe he knew to be "the chief symbol and the surest sign by which these people signify peace and show the tranquility and love of their hearts"—it bypassed him and the other Spaniards, despite his position beside Mézières and the others' positions mixed in with the Frenchmen from Natchitoches. Even when they traveled through allied Caddo settlements where they were greeted with the Spanish flag, Caddo leaders regularly welcomed the Frenchmen with "much friendliness," while displaying little but "an indifference which I cannot express" for him and his fellow Spaniards.[15]

In turn, Mézières exacerbated the Wichita headmen's frustration by asking that they go to San Antonio de Béxar in order to "humble yourselves in the presence of a chief of greatest power who resides there [the governor of Texas]," if they wished to ratify a peace agreement. Essentially, he attempted to shame the Wichita men. Mézières compared them unfavorably to the Kadohadachos, who had demonstrated their bravery by repelling the Natchez attack on Natchitoches in 1731. In contrast, the Wichitas' hands were stained with Spanish-French blood (which was now the same), having "exultantly beheaded" a helpless missionary at San Sabá. To give "full evidence of humility and repentance," then, was the only answer for the "insults, robberies, and homicides" committed by Wichita warriors in the San Antonio vicinity. Not surprisingly, the chiefs "refused entirely to comply." They would not even accompany Mézières to Los Adaes as a demonstration of good faith to Spaniards. Although their immediate explanations for the refusal ranged from a lack of horses for travel to the lateness of the season, their politeness could not disguise that the Wichita men clearly were not going to sacrifice their honor on an altar of Spanish pride. Mézières tried to tempt them with the presents that awaited their acceptance of peace, and again the leaders "unanimously and without perturbation" said no. Finally, as a last resort, Mézières tried to cow them with the threat that their refusal "would bring upon themselves the imponderable weight of [the king's] arms," but considering the categorical defeats already suffered by those arms at Wichita hands, such claims were wishful thinking at best.[16]

To Spanish officials, the Wichita leaders' reluctance to accede to their wishes conveyed a dishonorable failure "to make any true sign of peace." Although Luis Unzaga y Amezaga, the governor of Louisiana, wrote that Spaniards could not expect Wichita men ever to approach them in good faith, "because our lack of deeds cannot fail to estrange them, for words unaccompanied by acts do not suffice," he still saw a threat to Spanish political standing in the region if they gave in to the Wichitas. Thus, when Mézières proposed to follow up by visiting Wichita leaders in their own villages with diplomatic gifts, the governor forbade it, because "this favor may not be conferred without strong proofs of fidelity and merit, lest the dignity of our nation be exposed to outrage." Mézières repeated his request to visit the Wichita villages five months later, and again Unzaga y Amezaga refused him. Negotiations over male honor were derailing political discussion.[17]

Spaniards had not heard the last from Wichita leaders, however. In the spring, they sought to reopen talks, sending overtures through their Caddo allies to contact the Frenchmen representing the Spanish government in Natchitoches. Hasinai *caddí* Bigotes arrived at the Louisiana post in the late spring of 1771, bringing two painted bison hides conveying a peace message from Wichita leaders. They had painted one of the hides entirely white to symbolize the end of war, so "that the roads [between Wichitas and Spaniards] were open and free of blood." The other they had painted with crosses, one for each of the bands of Taovayas, Tawakonis, Iscanis, Kichais, and Wichitas proper, having chosen the symbol of a cross because they knew it to be an "object of greatest veneration" among Spaniards. The two skins cast the Wichita and Spanish nations as equals in their truce without bowing to the Spanish desire for deference. Mézières recognized the hide treaty to have the "force of a contract" and called on the principal citizens of Natchitoches to attend a public reception in honor of Bigotes, the "considerable following of friendly Indians" accompanying him, and the welcome news they brought.[18]

Tawakoni couriers followed Bigotes to Natchitoches, and leading Taovayas working with Tinhioüen arrived at the post a month later with a diplomatic solution to the quandary facing the Wichita men. Since acts of violence had initiated Wichita-Spanish contact, they offered to disown the trophies from that violence as a codification of peace. Rather than humble themselves before the Texas governor, the Taovaya men offered to return two infamous trophies of war to the Spanish government: the cannons seized from Parrilla at the Red River in 1759. They had been offering them as a goodwill gesture off and on since 1760, but no one as yet had accepted. Now the Wichita men transformed the return of trophies of war into a gesture of alliance in the belief that their retrieval could redeem the dishonor their loss had meant for the Spaniards. Such thinking resonated with the Spanish men. Unbeknownst to Wichita leaders, Spanish officials for years had suffered angst over the retrieval of the cannons—not out of practical consideration for the Taovayas' potential use of them as weapons, but rather because of the cannons' symbolic importance to injured Spanish pride. Provincial officials wrote of Parrilla's expedition as a "shame to our nation" and "disgrace to our arms." Atonement might indeed be found in the restitution of these symbols of Spanish ignominy. And, as it turned out, in the formal treaty that finally emerged, the return of the cannons held equal place with the return of Spanish women still believed to be living in Taovaya villages.[19]

Nevertheless, the treaty negotiations that followed still hinged on the tensions of warriors seeking a means to maintain valor away from the battlefield. The peace could not require the sacrifice of warrior identity by either Spanish or Wichita men. Taovaya warriors promised to check in at the San Antonio de Béxar presidio if they passed that way in pursuit of Apache raiders, both to give notice of their intentions and to enjoy Spanish hospitality and entertainment. A Spanish flag given to them as a passport would ensure their welcome. In return, the Spanish military alliance would come in the form of a presidio built in Wichita lands—a proposition Taovaya leaders viewed as having some merit, since a presidio might bring arms and men that could supplement their forces against Osage raids. The final treaty stipulation promoted the idea of warriors no longer separated by war but united as allies by declaring that "as visible evidence of the reliability of their word, the war hatchet shall at once be buried by their hands in sight of the whole village, and that he who again uses it shall die." To enact such ritual language, Spanish soldiers and Wichita warriors each buried a hatchet, one at the site of the meeting in Natchitoches and another six months later in San Antonio.[20]

Although Wichita headmen had willingly met with Mézières in Natchitoches to draw up the treaty, it was Hasinai *caddí* Bigotes who first went to San Antonio as their proxy representative carrying messages of peace for Governor Ripperdá. So, it was to Bigotes that Ripperdá extended the first military honors from the Texas government. In order to thank him for his invaluable aid as mediator and to tie the chief to Spanish Texas, Ripperdá "named him and armed him" as a *capitán grande*, decorated him with yet another royal medal and a military uniform, and did it all "in the presence of the portrait of the king, the troops under arms, and the principal personages, ecclesiastical and secular, the act being solemnized as well as was possible." The Caddos appeared to respect these Spanish rituals of manly honor.[21]

Yet, acceptance of Spanish ritual could not be mistaken for acquiescence to Spanish power. Rather, honors were the means by which the groups could understand each other, whether in war or peace—at least well enough for now. More Wichita protocols followed as well. First, five Taovaya men with two chiefs traveled to San Antonio the following spring of 1772, carrying a Spanish flag emblazoned with the cross of Burgundy (given them in Natchitoches) to get them safely into the Spanish capital. Chief Quirotaches and Governor Ripperdá formally buried a war hatchet and exchanged diplomatic presents. Two months later, five chiefs and many principal men from Kichai, Iscani, Tawakoni, and Taovaya bands arrived to assert a balance of authority between their nations and that of Spaniards through Wichita rituals. In a public meeting formalized by an audience of four missionaries, two presidial captains, and San Antonio's *cabildo*, the five headmen recognized Ripperdá as a fellow "chief" by performing a sacred feather dance, reciting prayers, and calling on the "creator of all things" to bless their Spanish counterpart and the peace he had just sworn with them. Like earlier French traders and diplomats had experienced, Governor Ripperdá found himself wrapped in feathers and bison hides to symbolize his new status among Wichitas. Such physical decoration held political import among Wichita men, who used it extensively to denote honors attained through the course of life, from tattoos on their hands that marked their first hunting achievements as boys to ones across their chests and arms that commemorated acts of valor. Thus, Ripperdá entered the dispersion of leadership within Wichita bands.[22]

Meanwhile, Spanish officials used a language of military titles to recognize the Wichita headmen as *capitanes grandes*. Some Spaniards wished to believe that such ceremonies authorized them to choose native leaders and command the selected leader's subordination to the Spanish government through oaths of allegiance. From the perspective of Caddo, Wichita, and (later) Comanche men, however, the Spanish practice of handing out titles may have fused instead with two separate but interlinked native customs—one distinguishing men of battle valor with special names and another rewarding those same men with titles and positions of leadership. Comanche and Wichita men adopted names signifying war deeds by which they had earned reputations as men of valor. Comanches also chose names to reflect the qualities associated with male honor. Among Caddo bands, noted warriors who had achieved distinction in war earned the name *amayxoya*, translated as "great man," and war chiefs were chosen among men distinguished for their acts of bravery. In other words, men from these bands likely viewed Spanish titling ceremonies as expressions of due respect. They also judged Spanish protocol by French precedents, and Frenchmen in western Louisiana had long offered similar deferential titles, such as "captain," without claiming any form of authority over them.[23]

Spanish officials also began to accept diplomatic protocols of male kinship that Caddos and Wichitas had used with the French. To establish any kind of meaningful relationship—be it social, economic, or political—Caddo and Wichita leaders extended kin designations to those with whom they interacted. Appealing to obligations of kin, for instance, Wichita men often addressed the Spanish governor's relationship to a band as that of a "father." Spaniards wistfully envisioned the role of "father" as one of patriarchal authority to discipline, accompanied by the Wichitas' filial responsibility to obey. Spanish officials therefore referred to the governor's or king's affection for "his children," asked Wichitas to be "obedient sons," and couched their exhortations and directives as those of a loving or true "father." Athanase de Mézières, for instance, wrote of the achievement of peace as the transformation of Wichitas into "children" of the Spanish king.[24]

Wichita and Caddo men, in contrast, held a different understanding of the obligations invoked by familial metaphors. The forms of address that had worked with their French trading partners in Louisiana were not quite so simple or direct in meaning as Spaniards might have hoped. Frenchmen's assertion of the title and role of "father" often did not carry with it much influence, because many of the native groups with whom they maintained relations had matrilineal kinship systems in which the role of father had little authority. The Caddos and Wichitas were just such matrilineal societies, with the primary male authority figure in the family being the eldest maternal uncle rather than the father, so the paternal role assumed by a Spanish governor came with little power. In fact, the very absence of authority may have made such French designations appropriate. Europeans might become kin, but only in related, not direct, lines of influence.[25]

In contrast to Spanish officials' expressions, Caddo and Wichita men never referred to themselves by the diminutive term "children," even when designating the Spanish governor a "father." In a 1780 letter to Commandant General Bernardo de Gálvez, for example, Taovaya chief Qui Te Sain repeatedly addressed the commandant as "my father," but the only ones identified as his "child" and "children" were the Spanish representative sent to Qui Te Sain's village and the Spaniards of Texas, respectively. It was not for rule, direction, or dominion that Wichita chiefs looked to Spanish governors and commandants as "fathers," but for more practical needs of economic trade and military alliance—needs which firmly established Spaniards in a role of reciprocal yet distant male standing—in a sense, as fictive members of a father's clan.[26]

When metaphors of family bonds expressed diplomatic ties, Wichita and Caddo men more often called upon a language of "brotherhood," particularly between soldiers and warriors. Yet, again they meant "brothers" in a distinctly native understanding of that male relationship. Spanish observers noted that men among Nacogdoches, Hasinais, Nasonis, and other groups making up Caddo confederacies "treat one another as brothers and relatives," thus "they are always united in treaties of peace, or declarations of war." Among Caddos, two men who fought side by side in battle might afterward consider one another in a special category of friend, "*tesha*," which carried connotations of brotherhood. In similar fashion, "brother" conveyed bonds tying together various networks among men of Taovaya, Tawakoni, Kichai, and Iscani bands as well. By providing Spaniards with such kin designations, Caddos and Wichitas also provided the framework of terms and conditions within which they expected Spaniards to operate. The key seemed to be that family metaphors functioned well as false cognates. Both groups could use a language of kinship in ways that fit their own needs while unknowingly pleasing the other. Spaniards linked kinship to deference, dependence, and patriarchal hierarchy, while Caddos and Wichitas linked kinship to ideas of a balance between obligation and autonomy, with authority deriving from generosity and talent. But as long as Spaniards appeared to conform to native protocols, diplomacy worked.[27]

Honors, titles, and treaties meant little if the symbolic alliance was not confirmed by actions in accordance with the obligations of brotherhood, however, and in the years following the accords of the early 1770s, relations between Wichitas and Spaniards faltered. Negotiations over the terms of their alliance focused on three obligations Spaniards seemed unwilling or unable to fulfill: a presidio and settlement in Wichita lands, gifts and trade, and a military alliance against Apaches. Spanish officials had promised to institutionalize gift giving in annual ceremonies and to provide villages with resident licensed traders to replace former French trade networks. The "gifts" that concerned the principal men among Caddo and Wichita bands were not prestige items or medals but critical supplies of arms and ammunition. Yet, the Spanish government's financial woes, turnovers in Spanish officials, and thus unstable diplomatic policies meant that these promises often went unmet in the 1770s and 1780s. In turn, Wichita and Caddo leaders understood the failure to uphold gift and trade obligations not only as diplomatic slurs but also as threats to their economic well-being and military survival.

Wichitas had first wrangled for a presidio that they hoped would ensure military provisions and economic trade. If, as Wichita leaders proposed, Spanish citizens also settled nearby, then the Spanish government would be even more compelled to guarantee that defensive and trade supplies regularly flowed into the area. Spanish diplomatic gift giving and economic trade networks were to replace not only French goods but also what Wichita men had previously taken as booty in raids on Texas ranches and presidios. Daily exigencies determined their choice between trade and raids, and if Spanish leaders could not uphold promises of the former, then Wichita leaders would have a difficult time restraining their warriors from returning to the latter. Raiding did not signal a declaration of hostility or war; it was simply an economic alternative to trade. They needed arms and ammunition if they were to face the increasing pressure of Osage raids from the north. At the same time, the *contrabandista* traders from Louisiana and growing numbers of English traders (who were also arming their Osage enemies) wished to trade with Wichitas, and their presence ensured that an exchange could be had for raided Spanish horses and mules.[28]

Local Spanish officials tried to comply with the Wichitas' wishes, seeing in a presidio an answer to their needs as well. In Natchitoches, Mézières repeatedly pressed the advantages of such a plan, arguing that New Spain needed to fulfill the desires "unanimously" expressed by Taovaya, Tawakoni, Kichai, and Iscani leaders. A presidio, moreover, would provide a crucial Spanish base amidst Wichita villages that he hoped to unite into a northern cordon to protect the provinces of New Mexico and Texas from the invasion of "notorious" traders from the English colonies. If Comanches could be won over to the alliance, the cordon would stretch into the mountains of New Mexico. In San Antonio, Ripperdá seconded this call and proposed that Louis de St. Denis be made the commandant of the projected presidio. St. Denis's standing among Wichita men as well as his extensive knowledge of their languages and of the intricacies of their diplomatic customs was invaluable, because good relations could be "disconcerted at the slightest cause when their mode of intercourse is ignored." In other words, regional Spanish officials knew that diplomacy would take place on Wichita terms or not at all.[29]

Yet, the presidio did not materialize, a failure exacerbated by disconnects between Texas and Mexico City bureaucrats that made it even more difficult for local officials to meet military obligations by providing guns and ammunition to their new Norteño allies. Viceroy Antonio María de Bucareli y Ursúa angrily asked Governor Ripperdá what assurances he had that Wichitas would not change their "variable moods," destroy the province of Texas using the arms supplied them, and then proceed south to attack towns like Saltillo and San Luis Potosí. Trade restrictions set by the viceroy drew no distinction between hostile Comanches and the now peaceful Wichita bands. Wichita leaders learned of this mistake when a 1773 military escort of twenty-two soldiers led by Antonio Treviño accompanied a Taovaya party home from a visit to San Antonio de Béxar and passed through the Wichita villages to distribute gifts but were strictly prohibited from giving or exchanging "arms or warlike stores" while doing so. To compound this problem, the viceroy stopped all diplomatic communication between San Antonio and Natchitoches and curtailed all trade between the two provinces, even to the point that traders sent into Texas with trade licenses from the Louisiana government were subject to arrest. Spanish policy in Texas thus gave little indication of unity with their so-called Spanish brothers in Louisiana, much less their Wichita and Caddo brothers closer to home. Officials in Mexico City seemed unable to let go of their earlier awe and dread of the Norteños of San Sabá infamy, worrying even that a Texas governor's decision to give some Wichitas a passport to Mexico City had enabled them to learn the routes into Coahuila and the state of Spanish defenses all the way to the capital.[30]

When Spaniards did not act as brothers according to Wichita expectations, Wichita men appealed to kin obligations in Louisiana and reverted to raiding in Texas. Two French traders' experiences while on a diplomatic expedition to Wichita villages on behalf of the Spanish government highlighted these strategies. Throughout the mission, the agents' dependence upon Wichitas for escort, hospitality, and safety gave Wichita men repeated opportunities to extract goods from the Spanish representatives at the same time that it pointed up the failure of Spanish trade obligations. During the month it took to escort the two men to Taovaya villages, one of them named Gaignard recorded that principal men and warriors "make me give them booty" and "obliged me to give them each a Limbourg blanket." Once they arrived, a Taovaya chief called a council, praised Natchitoches officials for sending him a flag to make peace with Spaniards, promised to "love them like the French," but concluded by saying a "small present for his young men" was necessary. He at once garnered for his warriors eight pounds of powder, sixteen pounds of shot, twenty-four hunting knives, tobacco, and more from Gaignard and the other trader, Nicolas Layssard (Mézières's nephew). Gaignard sought to emphasize French-Spanish unity, arguing that "it is the same mouth which speaks; it is the same heart and the same blood," so he urged the leaders to recommend that their warriors not steal more horses and mules from Spaniards in Texas. Almost as though they got the idea from him, Gaignard learned a week later that warriors were about to go on just such a raid. The price for stopping them, explained the head chief, would be a letter written by Gaignard to the governor of Texas asking him to "send presents to stop the warriors." This time, the Taovaya leader demanded horses, bridles, and sabers for his men. Again, Gaignard responded promptly, though tellingly he sent a messenger not to San Antonio but to Natchitoches to explain the chief's requirements.[31]

The costs of French and Spanish "oneness" rose even higher during the following two months, as Wichita men used—to their benefit—evidence of both Texas officials' aid to enemy Apaches and Louisiana officials' failure to stop illicit French trade with Osages. First, some warriors insisted Gaignard pay them for the scalp of an Osage enemy if he truly wished to prove Osages were a shared enemy of Wichitas and Frenchmen. Then, when a group of Comanches arrived to report that in a recent fight Apaches had carried Spanish guns, Taovaya leaders argued that only more presents would heal the French betrayal and Spanish lies and "make their hearts content." Next came contraband traders from the Arkansas River, presenting the Taovaya chief with another opportunity to emphasize to Gaignard the failings of Spanish trade. The headman pointedly explained that these newly arrived traders still accepted horses, mules, and war captives in exchange for the arms and goods needed by Wichitas. That same month, Gaignard's complaints that his hosts refused to feed or even sell him food indicated that the representatives of the Spanish government no longer merited the ritual obligations of Wichita hospitality. The lengthy visit ended only when Louisiana officials sent more traders with more goods, at which point Gaignard and Layssard made their way—without guide or escort—back to Natchitoches.[32]

In other situations, principal men from various Wichita bands adeptly manipulated a political language of kinship as well as former diplomatic gifts and prestige objects given them by Spaniards to meet their political and economic needs. Two incidents illustrate how they manipulated such titles and objects with Spaniards and Frenchmen to quite different effect. In 1780, Taovaya chief Qui Te Sain welcomed Louis de Blanc de Villenuefve (St. Denis's grandson) to his village as a representative of Louisiana governor Bernardo de Gálvez, seeking to expand the trade supplies coming out of that province. Referring to Gálvez as "my father," Qui Te Sain first directed De Blanc to convey his thanks to the governor for sending his "child" (De Blanc) to him. He wished a reciprocal visit to New Orleans were possible, the Taovaya leader continued, but "the road from your village to mine is too obstructed to enable me to go and taste of your drink and tobacco." Osage raids required that he remain to defend his people and his village, but he asserted his trust in Gálvez, "offering you my hand, as do all the people of my village." His trust would not be betrayed, Qui Te Sain was sure; Gálvez would aid them with supplies and a blacksmith, which they needed because they had "neither hatchets, nor picks, nor rifles, nor powder, nor bullets with which to defend ourselves from our enemies."[33]

Village of the Pawnee Picts [Wichitas], *by George Catlin, 1834–35. Courtesy of the Gilcrease Museum, Tulsa, Oklahoma.*

Quite a different tone was struck when disputes erupted between Spaniards in Texas and Frenchmen in Louisiana over trading privileges with the Wichitas, and Wichita leaders used diplomatic language and objects masterfully to play the two provinces' traders against one another. In one instance, Wichita leaders confronted Spaniard Antonio Gil Ibarvo over the higher prices and woeful stores he offered them in comparison with Frenchmen in Natchitoches by "destroying at every step my flags, staff of command, and medals, saying that they cannot live on the luster of these," Ibarvo recorded. Two years later, another conflict began when Ibarvo tried to extend his trading jurisdiction from Kichai villages on the Trinity River to those along the Red River near the Kadohadachos by declaring that Frenchmen from Natchitoches were unlicensed to trade there. Kichai men simply refused to recognize Spanish dictates about trading partners and challenged Ibarvo directly when he traveled to their village to demand explanation for their continued trade with Louis de Blanc Villenuefve and his cousin Bouet Laffitte (also of the St. Denis family). They explained that the two Frenchmen gave them ten musket balls for each deer-skin, as opposed to the five offered by Ibarvo. In a tidy twist—unknown to Ibarvo—

Kadohadacho chief Tinhioüen had used the vying trade to make French officials at Natchitoches adhere to the same price of ten balls and ten shots of powder for their hides just two months before.[34]

Kichai men had far more to say in response to Ibarvo's attempt to undercut them. To communicate why "they had always traded with the French" and "would always trade with them, even a small child, and not with the people of Nacogdoches," Chief Nicotaouenanan devoted some time explaining to Ibarvo the kin relations between French and Kichai men that underlay his village's economic ties to De Blanc and Laffitte. He first asserted that the two men always opened their homes to Kichais, where they were treated and fed well, and that they had maintained the trade even during times of scarcity. They thus met the obligations of generosity required of any respected kinsman. Most important, the Kichai leader continued, the "real chief for them was the chief with the big leg [De Blanc's grandfather, Louis Juchereau de St. Denis] . . . who had first opened the trails in all their nations . . . who had provided all manner of help to them," and though he had died, "he had left one of his descendants, and that it was him whom they regarded as their chief and that they would similarly look upon all his descendants, as long as there would be some." How could Ibarvo or any Spaniards compete with kin ties so close that they reached down through a family lineage to maintain the standing of each generation of St. Denis men within Wichita ranks? To express the finality of their rejection of Spaniards, Nicotaouenanan called for an end to all ritual hospitality, declaring that Ibarvo "must never come to their house, as they wouldn't go to his house either," and taking the Spanish medal hanging around his neck, hurled it away from him.[35]

Meanwhile, Wichita men used raids to rein in their defaulting Spanish allies in San Antonio. Raiding that began in the winter of 1783 brought Spaniards back to the negotiating table by the summer of 1784. The first hints of trouble came in the winter of 1783–84 when, despite a blistering snowstorm, horses tied to their owners' doors throughout San Antonio vanished. Pursuers tracked them through the snow with no success. The following spring, Spaniards from San Antonio rounding up wild cattle out by the Guadalupe River suddenly found themselves challenged by young warriors. They fled in fear, returning later to find many of the beeves slaughtered and eaten. The next month, the governor's own household was struck. Warriors broke through a neighboring building, found access to the stables of the governor's residence, took his two best horses along with two servants' horses, and made their way out through the governor's garden, where they wreaked havoc in the beds of melons, squash, and corn. In pursuit of this last raiding party, Spanish soldiers finally learned the culprits' identity—not because they overtook them, but because an escaped captive, a Spanish youth from New Mexico named Francisco Xavier Chaves, turned up with an account of the recent events.[36]

It turned out that, with little reason to respect their leaders' claims of Spanish alliance when Spaniards themselves ignored them, young Taovaya and Wichita warriors had spent the year in and about the San Antonio region on a coup-gathering venture. In May, the young men had broken off from a larger campaign of allied Wichita warriors seeking revenge for recent attacks by Lipan Apaches to look for their own raiding targets. Thus, while senior Wichita warriors met with presidial commander Luis Cazorla at the Bahía presidio to explain that the aim of their party was a fight with Apaches, not Spaniards—as a diplomatic courtesy in exchange for his hospitality—the younger men defiantly went off to prove otherwise. And impressive coups they indeed earned—taking horses from the midst of a sleeping settlement, especially horses of a man of rank like the governor, at the risk of death if they were caught.[37]

Brought together again by the raids of the young Wichita men, Spanish and Taovaya leaders pursued new means to reassert a truce through diplomatic rituals of mutual respect. The governor of Texas, Domingo Cabello, turned to a Frenchman to make his overtures for him. He sent Jean Baptiste Bousquet, a trader who had once lived in a Taovaya village, to pay special respect to Taovaya leaders Gransot and Quiscat. Along the way, though, he was also to carry goodwill messages from the governor to leaders at Iscani, Flechazo, and Tawakoni villages. Upon arrival at the Taovaya settlements, Bousquet discovered that Chief Gransot had recently died and the Taovayas had chosen a leading man named Guersec as his successor. The turn-over in leadership offered both Taovayas and Spaniards a serendipitous opening to mend their breach through the political ceremonies surrounding Guersec's succession. After pledging to redirect his young men's military energies to maintaining an active war against enemies whom Wichitas now shared with Spaniards, Guersec ordered four of his men to accompany Bousquet to San Antonio to renew relations with the Texas government through the formalities attendant on Spanish recognition of Guersec's new rank. Notably, Guersec did not go in person to meet with Cabello but delegated that duty to other, lesser, men.

From a Spanish perspective, the investiture of Guersec was a perfect opportunity to extend Spanish hospitality to Wichita leaders for the first time in a long while, and Bousquet readily grabbed at the chance to escort Guersec's chosen emissaries to San Antonio. The formal recognition of Guersec's succession further provided Governor Cabello the means by which to send the Taovaya leader diplomatic honors and gifts without seeming to relent about the recent raids. Ultimately, from the coups of their young warriors, the Taovayas extracted a "captain's uniform" and other "gear appropriate for [a chief]" for Guersec, a horse and gifts for each of the men in the Taovaya delegation sent to San Antonio, and annual gifts for the "body of the nation." Having pronounced Guersec "a person who had all the good qualifications of valor and affection for the Spaniards," Cabello also sent him gifts and an official confirmation stating his standing in Spanish eyes as "chief and governor of the nations of the Taboayazes to the end that he may lead and govern them in time of peace as well as in war" and asking that he "assemble his people to go out on campaigns against those who may be enemies of His Majesty." Again, military commitments defined the relationship between Spaniards and Taovayas.[38]

Only a month later, a Spanish military detachment escorting forty-nine representatives from Taovaya, Tawakoni, Iscani, and other Wichita bands homeward from San Antonio after a diplomatic visit had the chance to confirm in blood that military relationship when they discovered tracks of Comanche warriors along the way. The officer in charge, *alférez* (sublieutenant) Marcelo Valdés, quickly grasped the possibilities of diplomatic gain if they were to "apply all possible means to succeed in overtaking the enemy so that the Friendly Indians could see how the Spaniards could do their duty." After the Spanish and Wichita group found the Comanches and killed eight of the ten warriors, while losing only one soldier, the Wichita delegates declared themselves convinced that the "Spaniards were most valiant and very much their friends, since one of them had died defending them." In a final show of honor, Valdés turned over to the Wichita observers all the trophies taken, including five horses and "all the *chimales* [round leather shields], spears, arrows, and scalps that belonged to the enemy."[39]

In turn, Spanish officers interpreted as reciprocal honor the Wichita men's expressions of grief and mourning over Corporal Juan Casanova, who lost his life in the battle. At the battle site, Wichita warriors demonstrated "such sorrow," governor Cabello later wrote, "that it would have seemed the dead man was their own chief." Wichita leaders promptly dismissed the soldiers from their obligation to escort them farther in order that they could hurry home with the fallen man "so that his wife . . . might mourn him." In a further gesture greatly impressing Spanish officials and civilians alike, one of the Wichita chiefs sent a warrior to attend Casanova's funeral in San Antonio, where in mourning on behalf of Wichitas, he cut his hair, as he would have for his own brother, and reputedly wept more than the soldier's own relatives.[40]

Newly committed Wichita and Spanish allies now decided that if their brotherhood was to succeed, they had to turn Comanches from competitors into kin as well. Wichita negotiations with Spaniards had caused friction with their former allies and trading partners, and they wanted their Comanche brothers back. The Spaniards, as always, hoped simply for peace. As Caddo leaders had helped Spaniards achieve an accord with Wichitas, now Wichita men would take the lead as male mediators whose own past relations of honor with Comanches might get Spaniards safely into Comanchería under their escort. Spanish efforts to reestablish standing among Wichitas had also gained them new interpreters to aid in this new endeavor. Two Frenchmen and one Spaniard who had been living among Taovayas went to San Antonio with the Wichita party to celebrate Guersec's inauguration. By the spring of 1785, Spanish officials had pardoned the three men—Alfonso Rey, Pedro Vial, and José Mariano Valdés—for their unlicensed residence among Indians. They then agreed to live at San Antonio de Béxar and commit their skills as, respectively, blacksmith, medical practitioner, and interpreter to the community and presidio. The serendipitous arrival in San Antonio of Francisco Xavier Chaves (the escaped captive who identified the Wichita youths as the authors of San Antonio's mysterious horse thefts) also proved valuable to Spanish officials. Chaves had been captured near Albuquerque, New Mexico, as a young boy, had been adopted by a Comanche mother to replace a son she had lost, and then had been sold to the Taovayas years later, after her death severed his Comanche connection. In the summer of 1784, he had accompanied the young Taovaya warriors on their raiding coups but then escaped to present himself at the San Antonio de Béxar presidio. Although he had spent much of his youth among Taovayas, he still retained enough knowledge of Comanche language and culture to aid Cabello. Taovaya chiefs Guersec and Eschas would now try to get Vial and Chaves a hearing with Comanche leaders so they could plead a case for Spanish diplomacy.[41]

The daunting question, however, remained whether or not Comanche leaders had reason to respond to joint Taovaya-Spanish overtures. For the preceding fifteen years, they had watched as their former Wichita allies had drawn closer to Spaniards in Texas without gaining much in exchange. Eastern bands of Comanches who had traded horses, mules, and captives to Wichitas in exchange for their agricultural products and French armaments had equally reliable trading partners in Pawnees on the Northern Plains and in western Comanche peoples who alternately traded with or raided Spanish and Pueblo communities in northern New Mexico. With so many economic options, Comanches had no need to pursue peace and trade instead of war and raids in Texas. As long as horses and mules gained in raids supplemented their growing pastoral herds and markets remained for the products of their bison hunting, they had little inclination to accommodate San Antonio officials desperate for conciliation.

In the 1780s, however, environmental and demographic upheavals tempered Comanche viewpoints. A severe drought across the Southwest in the late 1770s hindered agricultural production in many of the communities on which western Comanches relied for subsistence products and reduced grazing lands upon which the bison they hunted and the horses they raised depended. At the same time, both western and eastern Comanche bands suffered their first devastating smallpox outbreaks in a series of epidemics between 1778 and 1781 that ravaged Spanish and Indian settlements across Louisiana, Texas, New Mexico, and the Southern Plains. Demographic losses compounded a period of limited trade resources to give Comanches a new sense of vulnerability. For the first time, they confronted increasing dependence on factors and people beyond their own control. To ensure their continued socioeconomic strength, they sought new commercial and political opportunities in both Texas and New Mexico.[42]

There were peaceful moments between Spanish and Comanche peoples in Texas between 1769 and 1785, but those moments had been fleeting and always framed by a violent context from which Spaniards seemed incapable, and Comanches unwilling, to extricate themselves. The negotiations that had first brought Wichita leaders to San Antonio de Béxar in 1772 had also marked the first peaceful visit by a Comanche leader, principal chief Evea, who accompanied Wichita allies to the Spanish settlement with five hundred of his own people. But intervening Comanche raids on Spanish horse herds and Spanish deportation of captive Comanche women had derailed all possibility of a truce (as will be seen in Chapter 6). At that point, neither Comanche leading men nor Spanish officials could separate their politics from warfare.[43]

When the French trader J. Gaignard had visited Taovaya settlements along the Red River in October 1773, Comanches periodically met him there as well and expressed pleasure at seeing him. Yet, like the Wichitas, they stressed that their friendliness rested in his identity as a Frenchman and that "they would listen to the word of the French." Gaignard eventually met with Evea himself but primarily took away from the meeting a sense of awe at the display of Comanche power. The number of people who came in Evea's party so impressed the Frenchman that he thought that the Comanche leader had brought with him "the whole nation." Gaignard did try to stress French-Spanish unity and, in supplication to the Comanche leader, asked Evea to "forbid the young men to make war on the Spaniards," now that Spaniards and French "are one." To "open Comanche ears and hearts to peace," Gaignard presented Evea with a Spanish flag to signal amity, a blanket to cover the blood spilt between them, knives to straighten the crooked trail of their relations, and tobacco to be smoked by the young men "so that war may be at an end." "Charmed" to have the flag, Evea proclaimed his intention "to place it over his cabin, that all the Naytanes [Comanches] might see it." Nevertheless, peaceful encounters would be few and far between as long as raids gained Comanches far more than trade ever would. Even the viceroy at one point had to admit his admiration for warriors who could raid the presidial herds at San Antonio de Béxar "so adroitly that to their satisfaction and pleasure, they were able to choose the best horses for themselves."[44]

Another passing moment of diplomatic opportunity to appeal to Comanche bonds of camaraderie and "brotherhood" had come in 1778, but Spanish bungling instead pushed Spanish-Comanche détente from raids to war. Decisions by the 1777–78 *junta de guerras* finally enabled plans for a joint Norteño-Spanish campaign against Apaches. Spaniards hoped not only to mollify estranged Wichita leaders but also to persuade Comanches that an alliance with Spaniards would be more profitable than enmity. With Comanches the clear "masters of the region" and Wichitas the "master-key of the north," Texas officials well knew that the welfare of the province would rise or fall upon their "alliance, companionship, aid, knowledge, and intrepidity."[45]

A military campaign would allow Spaniards to attain the respect and allegiance of Comanches, who "excel all the other nations in breeding, strength, valor, and gallantry." In effect, Spaniards had to prove their valor and honor to these indomitable warriors if they were to enjoy their alliance. "Whenever they [Comanche men] go to the aid of any warlike tribe," Mézières had explained in 1777, male comrades "are given the name *Techan*, similar in meaning to *comilito* of the Romans, and comrade in our language, and there results at once among those who use it a sort of kinship, a very firm union of interests, a complete sharing of common injuries, and a deep-seated opinion that the violator of so sacred a pact will receive the punishment which the supreme being has ready for liars." To approach such Comanche men, Mézières had called upon the aid of a young Comanche warrior who had been wounded in battle and captured, and whom both Ripperdá and Mézières had come to "look upon more as a son." They sent the young man home carrying Spanish diplomatic overtures to Comanche leaders.[46]

Subsequent events, however, went so horribly awry that the Comanches ended up with only a need to exact vengeance in exchange for Spanish dishonor. In response to the Natchitoches official's invitation to meet, a party of Comanche warriors led by chief Evea's son had traveled to the new Spanish town of Bucareli in search of Mézières after not finding him at the Taovaya villages (where his message had told them to expect him). They camped outside town and released their horses to graze. They had not yet approached the settlement or discovered that Mézières had departed that very day, when Bucareli citizens attacked them. The Spaniards killed several warriors and forced the rest to withdraw. In his subsequent denunciation of the townspeople, Mézières decried their knee-jerk hostility, arguing that the Comanche men's actions—turning their horses loose and sitting down to rest—"did not give them the appearance of enemies." All the Spanish settlers had seen, though, was a party of Comanche men, and as Mézières angrily recorded, "without first asking the important questions of who they were, what they were seeking, and where they were going . . . by which conference and calmness it is probable that a disastrous attack would have been averted and our moderation and prudence established—they opened fire, killed several Indians, wounded others, put the rest to flight, and despoiled them of their horses." The Spanish men's violence brought the wrath of Comanche warriors down upon the province for the next seven years.[47]

Raids and counterattacks intensified in concert as Comanche war parties avenged the sullied honor of their fallen comrades. They first focused their ire on Bucareli itself, in October 1778 taking 240 horses in a raid meant to lure pursuers into an ambush precisely where the Spaniards had attacked Evea's son. Another raid netted 202 horses. One family fled with such speed they left a fire burning in a fireplace that burnt down their house, spread to surrounding structures, and razed half the settlement. It didn't matter, because everyone had left for the safety and sanctuary of neighboring Caddo and Wichita villages. All too soon, Comanche targets expanded to the San Antonio area, where for a time Spaniards and Comanche men seemed locked in a violent one-upmanship that would allow no other rivals.[48]

Warriors and soldiers alike seemed to view their struggles as referendums on their national and individual honor. Comanches lost no opportunity to flaunt their dominance over Spaniards. After a battle that pitched a small, poorly armed presidial force against Comanches with superior numbers and weapons, warriors wearing the coats of killed soldiers rode by San Antonio to alert the fort of their fallen comrades. Upon arrival at the battle site, Spaniards found six men set around a tree, all scalped and some missing noses and fingers, with sticks propped in their eyes to keep them open—open to their unmanning? Spanish victories, on the other hand, were far fewer, and commanders often bemoaned the difficulty of dividing up the belongings of one or two fallen Comanches into trophies for more than seventy soldiers. Thus, imagine their delight when an assembled force of Spanish soldiers, citizens, and mission residents surprised a group of Comanche warriors near the Guadalupe River and killed nine or ten Comanche men, counting as their coup a gun, three spears, eight many-feathered headdresses, several bows, quivers, and arrows, an English ax, and most notably a feathered halberd taken from a chief. Tellingly, when Apache warriors traveled to San Antonio hoping to buy some of

Comanches of western Texas "dressed as when they are going to war." One wears a feathered head-dress and the other a buffalo-hide cap; their faces are painted red and their chests and arms with black stripes; and they are armed with long-shafted lances with sharp metal heads, a bow and a quiver of arrows, and shields, one feathered and the other painted rawhide. Watercolor by Lino Sánchez y Tapia after the original sketch by Jean Louis Berlandier, a French botanist who traveled through Texas as a member of a Mexican boundary and scientific expedition in the years 1828–31. Courtesy of the Gilcrease Museum, Tulsa, Oklahoma.

these trophies, Governor Cabello flatly refused, telling them to overcome cowardice and achieve their own victories if they wished trophies of Comanches. In this way, Cabello used trophies taken from a feared foe to castigate Apaches as failed allies as compared with their "valiant" Comanche enemies, while also bolstering Spanish valor for having, at least momentarily, won a victory over that enemy. Neither Spanish nor Comanche valor was for trade or purchase in that high-stakes warfare.[49]

Another exchange in 1780 crystallized the high costs of the dueling Spanish-Comanche animosity at both provincial and individual levels. That year, Governor Cabello presented Comanche men with an irresistible opportunity for both profit and coup: a herd of two thousand cattle to be sent from Texas to Louisiana to supply Spanish forces fighting in the American Revolution. Setting up encampments in the woods between the Guadalupe and Colorado Rivers—an area so rough and impenetrable to all but Comanches that it was called the "Monte del Diábolo" (Devil's Mountain)—Comanche men established a semipermanent base from which to launch raids on both ranches and any supply trains daring the roads throughout the San Antonio region. As the raids mounted, so too did the humiliations, especially as each strike ended when retaliatory Spanish parties, one after another, pulled up short at the Guadalupe without the strength or courage to cross into a zone of Comanche control. At the sight of Comanche warriors, one unit abandoned horses and arms in their rush to flee—a disgrace that led Cabello to indict the leading officer on formal charges for "cowardice." Another presidial commander, Marcelo Valdés, tried to persuade one group of ninety-one soldiers, settlers, and mission Indians to continue by promising to find a small enough group of Comanche men to beat in order to salve Spanish pride. He actually sent a patrol up and down the Guadalupe looking for likely opponents. The plan failed miserably, though, when word arrived that, while they had been patrolling, Comanches had routed the first one thousand head of cattle Cabello had purchased from multiple mission ranches. In the wake of such devastation, no one in San Antonio would risk the loss of more cattle or endanger their own personal safety while driving them. Thanks to the Comanches' power—and their imperative to avenge warriors' deaths—the American Revolution would proceed without Spanish aid from Texas.[50]

Then Comanches proceeded to shut down the province itself. The "many trails and signs" of the raiders who seemed to strike at will across the province inspired terror among Spanish officials and settlers. Comanches put their mark on the landscape as the boundaries of Spanish territory shrank in comparison. Presidial officers charted a route circumscribing a semicircle around the west, north, and east sides of San Antonio, about twelve miles out from town, along which soldiers patrolled several times a day. Daily they returned with reports that they had "found no grove or gully unmarked by numerous vestiges of Comanche encampments"—footprints, bonfires, smoke, and the trails made by horses, mules, and people. A siege mentality at San Antonio led Governor Cabello to order a variety of precautions against false alarms and undue attention from "hostiles." There was, he proclaimed, to be no firing of guns, no barking of dogs, no children playing, and particularly, no women in the streets making disorderly noises—this after the screams of one woman had brought men running from all over, only to find a domestic dispute, not a Comanche raid, in progress. In a petition to the governor, the San Antonio *ayuntamiento* (municipal council) expressed the "great consternation" gripping the province. "In sum," they wrote, "this province is in such deplorable circumstance that there is not a scrap of meat left to eat, a pound of butter cannot be found for any amount of money, much less a candle to light one's way withal; furthermore, within four days there will be no firewood left to burn: the hostiles will give us no respite. If this war continues for two more months—and it is obvious that it will continue until the enemy destroys everyone—the few persons that might remain will die of hunger."[51]

As they had years before with Apaches, Spanish imaginations read their powerlessness before the Comanches as impotence that would lead to bloody emasculation. Reports to Mexico City repeatedly pleaded for aid, emphasizing that Comanches were overrunning the region and that if they decided to put an end to the province, it would be impossible to stop them. Hasinais visiting San Antonio tried to explain to Cabello that Comanche warriors "will not leave until they avenge themselves sufficiently by taking many horses." Yet, when Cabello impressed upon Commandant General Teodoro de Croix the fatal danger Comanches posed to Spanish Texas, he warned him that the warriors' goals were not simply to take horses, because "when they have no cattle and horses to fatten their greed, they will do so by coming to kill us in our own homes, to sate their natural animosity." Accusing Comanche warriors of every violent act "as has been invented by tyranny, hatred and rancor," Cabello argued that after they killed Spaniards who resisted them, they mutilated them "by cutting off small pieces and wetting inside the ill-fated cadaver the spears of as many of their own as have been [killed]."[52]

Superior Comanche military power threatened not only Spanish limbs and lives—the dread of being unable "to prevent the mutilation of any of [the province's] members"—but also Spanish honor when they found themselves "impotent" in the face of the Indian warriors' domination. Because Spanish honor derived from men's ability to fulfill their patriarchal roles as defenders of dependents, their inability to protect Spanish women and children especially suggested Spanish emasculation. Imagined violence against women cluttered reports of potential Comanche domination. The commandant general's response offered little balm for diminished male honor. In recognition that the "incessant attacks of the Comanche" had paralyzed the province to the point that "not a foot of land is free from hostility," Teodoro de Croix could only conclude that "If they continue with the same steadfastness, the desolation of the province will be consequent, irremediable and immediate, and . . . very few vassals of the king may remain to contemplate this misfortune." At this point, Croix saw only two possible courses open to the Spaniards there: abandon Texas entirely or, as he proposed, incorporate all settlements, forts, and missions into one or two key areas in order to concentrate their feeble defensive capabilities. The best they could hope for was a "respectable defensive war."[53]

Yet, that anticipated final destruction never occurred. Unbeknownst to Spanish officials, a particularly virulent smallpox epidemic that had swept through the San Antonio region in late 1780 had traveled, probably with raiders, back to Comanche settlements. Smallpox that had broken out in western Louisiana and eastern Texas in 1777 and 1778 may have also worked its way across the Southern Plains to Comanche villages through their trade networks. In San Antonio, nothing had been seen or heard that winter but "the tolling of bells and the sight of burials," and one can only imagine the even worse devastation within Comanchería. Only one report reached San Antonio five years later, when a Spanish and Wichita party visiting an eastern Comanche village along the Red River learned from chiefs Camisa de Hierro (Iron Shirt) and Cabeza Rapada (Shaved Head) that their rancherías had lost two-thirds of their population. Though smallpox had wreaked havoc, later Spanish observers still estimated the village population to include at least two thousand warriors and an equal number of women and children. Losses likely were not felt equally by all Comanche bands, particularly those farther west, since the expansion of Comanchería and the rise of Comanche power on the Southern Plains had not yet reached their peak.[54]

It was a few years later, in 1785, that Wichita leaders Guersec and Eschas—trusted by both Spaniards and Comanches as men of valor and standing—finally assumed the challenge of ending hostilities between their old and new allies. And as they put into motion efforts to contact principal Comanche men, the rituals and language at every step in the meetings during that summer would be framed in terms of male honor. The highly ritualized political processes that ensued communicated the difficulty of the task at hand.

Before they could proceed, Guersec and Eschas had to seek the approval of their warriors. Thus, each summoned the men, both young and old, from neighboring Taovaya and Wichita settlements on either side of the Red River. In long speeches, each leader explained the proposed trip to Comanche rancherías to mediate "a solid peace between that nation and the Capitán Grande of San Antonio." With such language they identified Cabello as a respected military leader with a status analogous to that of their own headmen and as a representative of the community of San Antonio (defining the town as a polity similar to Wichita and Comanche residential settlements). Pointing out that this peace would involve Wichitas as well as Comanches and Spaniards, Guersec and Eschas argued that all were to be friends "so that they might live and let live, one with another, and forgive the killings, and thefts of horses that had occurred among them all, including in this friendship their brothers, the Taguacanes [Tawakonis] and Izcanis and Flechazos." To emphasize the potential benefits, they reminded their warriors of the hospitality and gifts (that is, arms and ammunition) that would be forthcoming from such relationships. After listening carefully to all that their leaders had to say, the gathered Taovaya and Wichita warriors accepted the two men's counsel, saying they "were very content that the said peace might take place." As a ritual seal of approval, the mass of warriors then rose from their seats and "gave so many whoops that it seemed that the sky might fall or that all of the ranchería would sink from the clamor," according to Spanish observers.[55]

Now that they had the warriors' sanction, Guersec and Eschas could take the next step—a requisite parley with individual Comanches prior to approaching Comanche rancherías. As Spanish agents Pedro Vial and Francisco Xavier Chaves waited and watched, the two Wichita leaders sent a party of Taovaya and Wichita warriors to seek out possible Comanche contacts. Finding a Comanche *capitán* tracking Osage horse raiders, they gave him the message from Guersec and Eschas. Responding to the invitation, the *capitán* "came with all of his people" to the Taovaya village. Comanche headmen, like their Wichita counterparts, led by consensus, so the accompaniment of "all of his people" allowed them to hear and judge the words of Guersec and Eschas for themselves. All responded favorably after hearing of Wichita and Spanish intentions, and Vial as well as Guersec and Eschas furthered Comanche goodwill by presenting many gifts to the *capitán* and his people. Finally, the journey into Comanchería could begin, and Wichitas, Comanches, and Spaniards all set out "in the greatest brotherhood."[56]

After seven days of travel, the Comanche *capitán* declared that they had reached a point from which he needed to go ahead with his people to advise leaders at the first Comanche ranchería of their approach. Four days later, he finally returned to say that he had "overcome all the difficulties for entrance," and the ranchería's *capitán* was even then sending out arrows to all the other settlements and to all the principal chiefs to alert them of the new arrivals. The party continued and soon sighted the first of several very large settlements spread out across an open plain along the Red River. At that point, wearing Spanish regalia became for Guersec and Eschas another critical component to their role as intermediaries in these peace negotiations. The two chiefs carefully donned Spanish military uniforms and medals that would communicate to Comanche warriors that they came in honorable standing as comrades to Spaniards. Guersec and Eschas remained in the uniforms throughout their stay, providing a visual display of alliance with Spaniards until negotiations drew to a close. Vial and Chaves meanwhile unfurled the Spanish standard, marking their own identity and role in the diplomatic exchange. Choreographed Comanche ritual greeted them in turn. Two hundred warriors rode out in two files toward the visiting party and, upon reaching them, fired gun salutes while holding their military formation. Once Spanish and Wichita representatives responded with salutes of their own, the Comanche men either gave them their hand or embraced them. Thus, through well-established rituals did they establish a "good order" by which to enter the ranchería.[57]

The visit began with the requisite displays of hospitality. The ranchería's leader promptly took the entire party—Vial, Chaves, Guersec, Eschas, two Spanish servants, and the escort of twelve Taovaya and Wichita warriors—to a large bison-hide tent. With an abundance of bison and deer meat, fruits, and plant roots, Comanche hosts fed the Spaniards and the Wichita warriors while Comanche headmen conferred with Guersec and Eschas before receiving the Spanish delegation. The *capitán* whom they had met on the road explained that once all had assembled for councils, the Spaniards were not to leave the tent until they were called.[58]

As Comanche warriors, principal men, and chiefs poured in from surrounding rancherías, they periodically called upon Vial and Chaves to inquire why they were there. The assembly of Comanche leaders was an impressive one, including two principal chiefs, Camisa de Hierro and Cabeza Rapada, and ten *jefes*, or *capitanes chiquitos* (subchiefs), each one of whom in turn brought his own contingent of principal elders and young warriors. At individual meetings, Vial and Chaves strove to distribute gifts proportionally to each man's standing. As the gifts were received, the Comanche leaders listened carefully for any discrepancies between what the Spaniards had to say versus what they had already heard from Guersec and Eschas.[59]

Once the Comanche headmen had ascertained that they all "were telling them the same thing" without deceit, they sent *tlatoleros* (criers) to assemble their respective groups to hold councils of their own. For ten days, Guersec and Eschas then traveled from one to another of these gatherings to promote the "Capitán of San Antonio" as a man of honor and to promote the benefits that would accrue to those who took him as a friend. After "all of the eleven or twelve rancherías of which the *Cumanchería Oriental* is composed had met," then a principal council was called. Again, consensus ruled the fate of negotiations as men, women, and children, young and old, were called "so that they might hear from our own mouths the reason for our coming," recorded Vial.[60]

Led by Guersec and Eschas in their uniforms and medals, Vial and Chaves carried the Spanish flag hoisted on a tall pole into the council. There they found themselves encircled by what they estimated were seven hundred Comanches seated on the ground "as many as four deep," outside of which "were an infinity of young men, women, and children, who were standing." Camisa de Hierro and Cabeza Rapada introduced the two Spanish representatives and then directed them to a place in the circle alongside the principal Comanche men, a seating arrangement that included only men of standing. The two principal chiefs next shared a tobacco pipe with Vial, Chaves, Guersec, and Eschas before passing it among the ten *capitanes chiquitos,* until all the tobacco was smoked. Then and only then did they ask Vial to speak.[61]

Speaking in the Taovaya language (which most of the assembled Comanches understood), Pedro Vial used the knowledge of Comanche political categories he had gained while living and trading in the Wichita villages. He first established kin connections with Comanches for himself and Chaves and, more specifically, linked them to bonds of camaraderie and honor among Comanche men. Addressing the Comanche men as "Brothers," he pointed out that he and Chaves were not strangers and had been among them before, Chaves as a captive and Vial as a trader from the Arkansas post. Chaves, most importantly, had fought alongside their warriors in campaigns against Apaches. Shared male activities grounded bonds of friendship and camaraderie, and the experience of fighting together held particular significance for Comanche and Wichita warriors, as borne out by military relationships that they viewed as akin to brotherhood. Vial recalled how he had always enjoyed the kind hospitality of their villages, while Chaves had appreciated their good treatment when he lived among them. "Having adapted to the life among the Tavoayaces," Vial continued, "I, as well as my companion, have been found to be good and very truthful men." Past connections as kin and as military comrades would help to establish Vial's and Chaves's standing as honorable men, despite their current membership in the Spanish community at San Antonio.[62]

Vial next explained why Spaniards would make better allies than enemies, due to the status of Governor Cabello and the bravery of Spaniards in general. It was the reputation of the "Capitán Grande of San Antonio" (Cabello) as a "very brave" man, he testified, that had convinced Vial and Chaves to return to live among Spaniards, not simply that they were "of that nation." Upon their return to San Antonio, they had received much respect, "as if I were a brother of all of them." Comanche leaders could identify with the valiant and strong *capitán grande,* Vial implied, since he had "such a good heart and is such a good gentleman." Moreover, he told the Comanche warriors, the Spanish leader commanded soldiers so brave that they could "make incessant war against you." This peace overture did not come from Spanish fear, Vial insisted, because the *capitán grande* was ready to supply plenty of guns, powder, and shot to as many men as it would take "to kill all Cumanches that inflicted on him such injuries as they had done up to now." But, Vial asserted, that same gun, powder, and shot could just as easily be shared with them, because the Spanish leader accorded "good treatment" and "generous hospitality" to "his friends." Thus, the message from the *capitán grande* was, "if they wish to come to this presidio to talk with me, I will give them my hand and thenceforth have them as friends." What the Spanish leader most wanted was an alliance of equals, Vial claimed, a "brotherly peace" in which both sides forgave and forgot the killings they had committed against one another in the past. In other words, to describe Cabello, Vial went step by step through the standards by which any Comanche would measure an honorable man: bravery, strength, hospitality, and generosity.[63]

Last, Vial turned to what Spaniards had to offer as allies, advertising the hospitality, gifts, and trade that they could provide Comanches, once they accepted the governor's hand in alliance. Vial knew, he explained, that Comanches did not need the alliance of Spaniards, but he and Chaves worried that their Comanche friends were missing out on the diplomatic gifts and trade goods that by personal experience they had witnessed Taovayas, Tawakonis, Iscanis, Wichitas, and Flechazos enjoying. As proof of the *capitán grande*'s good heart (and as further promotion of Spanish goods available through peace), Vial reminded them of the gifts sent by the Spanish leader. If Comanches and Spaniards became "true friends," the Spanish governor not only would send traders to their villages "to provide all of the *treta* [traffic] that they need" in exchange for the hides and goods they could offer in return but also would host Comanche leaders every year at San Antonio with festivities and gifts. Turning to Guersec and Eschas, Vial pointed to their uniforms as proof that they could confirm "with their own mouths about the goods and comforts that came with Spanish friendship."[64]

Guersec also drew on the language of kinship to explain the economic grounds for their relationship with Spaniards. The *capitán grande* in San Antonio had taken on the role of "father" by supplying Wichitas with "guns, powder, shot, pots, axes, hoes, knives, etc." Spaniards had thereby earned the standing of "brothers" to the allied peoples of Taovaya, Tawakoni, Wichita, Iscani, and Flechazo settlements. Guersec stressed that they would like to have the benefit of "brotherhood" with both Spaniards and Comanches and so urged them too to gain the *capitán grande* of San Antonio as a "father," that is, as the supplier of material goods that "succor our needs."[65]

Though echoing the Caddos' and Wichitas' own diplomatic kin designations, Guersec tapped into the kin terminology of brotherhood with keen purpose, knowing its even greater significance in the language of Comanche diplomacy. At the individual level, Comanches recognized the closest relationships between men through an institution of formal friendship designated by the sibling terminology "brothers." Such relationships almost always arose when men shared battlefield experiences that pledged them to one another for life. Sodality groups and practices of male friendship among Comanche warriors often created stronger or more meaningful bonds than those of biological brotherhood. Military fraternities of men who had raided and fought together functioned as kin and prestige groups among male ranks who marked their membership with special insignia, decoration, dances, and songs. Kin obligation to avenge offenses committed against family members extended to such brotherhoods. This terminology thus carried resonance for military bonds of camaraderie and ensured that the bonds were between men of equal standing. Comanches demanded the same reciprocal behavior required by such kinship terms in alliances as well.[66]

Even if they became allies of Comanches, however, Spaniards would fall into a separate and more distant category of kinship. Although Vial and Guersec might call upon a language of kinship to frame their diplomatic mission and the relations they hoped to build between Spaniards and Comanches, they knew they must propose a different kind of "brotherhood." Within Comanche societies, status relationships among men were predicated upon rank and hierarchies that ensured kinship cooperation by strictly regimenting competition between individuals. Protocols encouraged solidarity and consensus, as seen in the requirement that Comanche men remove status markers found in dress and decoration to participate in council meetings. This practice did not extend to diplomatic meetings with representatives of other nations, where the display of military uniforms and banners and the order of seating arrangements and pipe smoking reinforced the status identity of Comanches and their visitors. In their negotiations then, Comanche men might speak of "meeting as brothers," but they meant that social controls internal to their culture informed their relations with outsiders without bringing those outsiders fully into Comanche ranks. Perhaps reflecting his understanding of Comanche custom, Pedro Vial recorded the pledges of affection he had given Comanche leaders—pledges that superseded political or national difference—by declaring, "The Spanish regarded them as brothers [even though] they were not like them."[67]

After all these public declarations, the mechanisms of Comanche politics of consensus went into motion. Headmen did not have the authority to act without extensive consultation and approval. Vial and Chaves retired to their tent, while the *tlatoleros* began soliciting all the respective groups' reactions and opinions and while *capitanes grandes* Camisa de Hierro and Cabeza Rapada held private councils again with Guersec and Eschas. It took meetings through the night to reach a concerted Comanche response, and then another public hearing was called. Vial and Chaves watched from their tent as the *tlatoleros* again directed all the people into the same seating order to hear the speeches their leaders would address to the visiting delegation. Comanche *capitanes* then led the Spaniards to the great circle to resume their seats. The pipe-smoking ceremony followed, and then Camisa de Hierro stood to speak. Addressing Vial and Chaves, he announced that he had found signs of the truth of their words, in that "you have not disquieted us, nor has the sun clouded, nor has the smoke from our pipe twisted." They would therefore forget "the killings that the Spaniards have committed against our fathers, sons, and brothers."[68]

Although Camisa de Hierro referred to Governor Cabello as "our Father the Capitán Grande," the Comanche leader nevertheless made it clear that his people's relationship with Spaniards would be one of "brothers." Comanche bilateral lineage (similar to Caddo and Wichita matrilineage) limited the role of fathers, and their extended families tended to form around two or more senior men who were often brothers, further superseding the authority of fathers within nuclear families. In this way, Camisa de Hierro declared a truce though not yet a peaceful alliance, pledging that "from now on, the war with our brothers the Spaniards has ended." In a not-so-insignificant side note, he expressed regret that two parties of warriors, one sent to raid the presidial herds at San Antonio de Béxar and La Bahía and the other to make war against Apaches, could not be recalled and so pointed out that their deeds must not be held against the agreement of peace currently being negotiated. Moreover, Camisa de Hierro's use of the kin terminology of "brotherhood" with Spaniards did not appear to carry the resonance it did *among* Comanches—that specifying the male bonds of "warrior partners." In other words, he did not seek Spanish assistance as allied warriors in campaigns against Apaches; he only requested they not interfere. All he asked of his Spanish brothers was greater access to the Apache enemies.[69]

Martial goals that had once set Comanches against Spaniards could now be advanced with the Europeans' assistance; the Comanche polity had finally found a use for Spaniards. Neither a promise of trade nor the end of Spanish military campaigns against them had persuaded Comanche listeners of Vial's and Guersec's words. Rather, Camisa de Hierro emphasized that Spaniards and Comanches shared a common enemy—Lipan Apaches—and if the *capitán grande* of San Antonio wished to make a "solid peace," then the condition they demanded of him was that he allow Comanche warriors passage through southern Texas and promise not to oppose them as they continued their war. In return, they would consult with their "comrades and brothers" to the west (who implicitly were not bound by this agreement any more than the treaties of western Comanches and New Mexicans had meant Spanish-Comanche peace in Texas) in order to negotiate free passage to Santa Fe for Spanish Texans. To test the diplomatic waters, Camisa de Hierro would send three *capitanes chiquitos*—Oxinicante, Taninchini, and Paruatuosacante—with their wives to accompany Vial and Chaves to San Antonio "to see what reception our Father, the Capitán Grande, accords us" and "to hear what our Father, the Capitán Grande, wants to tell them." Just as Guersec had done the year before, Camisa de Hierro and Cabeza Rapada did not go to meet with Cabello themselves but rather sent lower-ranking emissaries in their stead to assess the diplomatic situation in San Antonio. At the end of his speech, Camisa de Hierro called for his peoples' agreement by twirling one of the lengths of cloth given him as a diplomatic present by Vial.[70]

Three days later, the joint Spanish-Comanche party departed with Oxinicante, Taninchini, and Paruatuosacante at the lead, navigating Vial and Chaves through rugged woods and hills for the twelve days it took to reach San Antonio—clearly a route between Comanchería and the Spanish town known only to them. In San Antonio, Spanish protocol would seek to match the themes of military honor that had prevailed at the Red River rancherías. Upon arriving, Vial and Chaves left their Comanche guests in a house at the first entrance of the presidio and hastened to Cabello with reports that the Comanches were as "domesticated" and "humane" in their rancherías "as they had been fierce and inhuman in the campaign." They emphasized to the governor the need to match Comanche hospitality to preserve honor for guest and host. Cabello then summoned leading citizens to help him arrange lodging and gifts for the Comanche party, while he sent every soldier he could find to provide a formal escort for the visitors. Although the entire Béxar garrison did not equal in number the group of two hundred Comanche warriors who had greeted Vial and Guersec's party outside their rancherías two weeks before, Spanish soldiers did the best they could as they led Oxinicante, Taninchini, Paruatuosacante, and their wives through the streets of San Antonio. Spanish residents poured out of their homes to watch and welcome the cavalcade. During the days that followed, while the Comanche couples rested and Vial and Chaves spent long hours priming Cabello for the upcoming meetings, Cabello reported, "all the people here have been assiduous in bringing them fruits and sweets, and wherever they go, they have them enter their houses to give them something to eat and whatever they have."[71]

After the requisite preliminaries of hospitality, councils between Cabello, Oxinicante, Taninchini, and Paruatuosacante (with Vial and Chaves translating) began in earnest. The subject and language of diplomacy remained the highly masculine ones of warfare. Negotiations proceeded better than expected, considering that one of the *capitanes* chosen by Camisa de Hierro and Cabeza Rapada was the son of Evea, who had been ambushed at Bucareli in 1778 and whose strong reservations about Spanish

The military plaza at San Antonio de Béxar, c. 1857. Courtesy of the National Oceanic and Atmospheric Administration/Department of Commerce, Washington, D.C.

honor and trustworthiness had made him an ideal candidate, in the eyes of the two *capitanes grandes*, to put Cabello and the Spaniards of San Antonio to the test. Having been warned by Vial and Chaves, Cabello took special care in demonstrating his respect and generosity to this man.[72]

At the council table, the two sides formally agreed to pledges made at the Comanche rancherías—that hostilities would end, that they would "meet as brothers and good friends" whenever they encountered one another, and that they would recognize one another's friends and enemies as their own. In answer to Camisa de Hierro's requirements, Cabello happily agreed to allow Comanche warriors free passage all the way into Coahuila, asking only that they stop in at the presidio to alert Spaniards of their plans, report their progress, and, in doing so, allow the governor to show them hospitality and regularly renew their relations of peace. Cabello further pledged an annual presentation of gifts to Comanche leaders, together with a supply of traders to their rancherías—so that they would realize the "usefulness" of remaining friends with Spaniards. In exchange, he asked that they bar strangers from their lands. Because the governor had no leverage to push this point, however, the category of "strangers" necessarily excluded English and French traders who came to exchange goods for the hides Comanches hunted.[73]

Ritual celebrations of their first-ever peace agreement would have to await the summer, as the three Comanche representatives needed first to return home to inform all in their nation of what had been discussed. Then, they explained, Comanche leaders would wish to ratify the agreement by their own custom—with a "ceremony of having them and us open a large hole in the area facing their territories and bury in it mutually and similarly two live horses, two loaded rifles, two spears, two shields, and two bows with two quivers of arrows, all of which afterwards would be covered with the same earth by both parties, who would pass over the site from opposite sides to meet in the middle." Comanche and Spanish peoples would thereby pledge "that the war we have had is buried and that both one and the other may travel freely and securely—we to their rancherías and they to our settlements." Cabello acceded to their wishes with secret relief, as his stores of diplomatic gifts needed replenishing. They would meet again in six moons, and each side could use the time to make the requisite arrangements.[74]

Before the visitors left, however, Spanish officials recognized the new accord by giving the Comanche men diplomatic gifts that might symbolically and practically substitute for the future war trophies their new native allies were forgoing. To the governor, Pedro Vial suggested that Comanche leaders receive "the equivalent of what they might obtain through pillage, theft, and the raids which they carry out when at war." The war-related honors of men charged even peaceful Spanish-Comanche gift exchange. Thus, in San Antonio that fall, Oxinicante, Taninchini, and Paruatuosacante received captain's uniforms, medals, canes of office, and muskets. As a responding honor, the three *capitanes chiquitos* chose to wear the uniforms and carry a Spanish flag for their farewell rituals and speeches in the plaza in front of the governor's residence. Just as they might have worn a Spanish scalp on their belt to signal domination over an enemy, now they wore or displayed their gifts to mark themselves Spanish allies.[75]

With the aid of Wichita leaders, Comanche and Spanish warrior-diplomats thereby finally forged their first truce in the summer and fall of 1785. In a report to the commandant general two months later, Governor Domingo Cabello explained what he had learned from the process about the "extremely delicate nature" of the Comanche character. "It is essential," he argued, "that they be shown total love and be made to believe that one is quite satisfied with them." To keep them grateful, content, and confident of Spanish affection—and thus ensure peace, trade, and communication—the "greatest artfulness" was required of the governor. He not only had to "regale" them with gifts but also had to allow them to call him "father." Cabello wrote that he was now able to reconcile the "generous spirit" of Comanche men with their fierce warrior status, realizing that "when [Comanche warriors] have friendship, they are expressive and friends with their friends." His insistence that they would tolerate no rudeness and that they *must* be kept content with trade clarified what the terms would be—that is, Comanche terms of male camaraderie and kinship—on which Spanish peace and alliance with the most powerful of the Nations of the North would succeed or fail.[76]

Diplomatic accord between Spanish San Antonio and the Caddo, Comanche, and Wichita nations was rare in Texas until late in the century. Modes of communication were always complicated by previous hostility and violence. When peace was achieved, Spanish and Indian men precariously rested it upon ceremony and ritual meant to accommodate balances of power without compromising perceptions of male honor. Diplomatic nomenclature and gifts infused negotiations with a martial, masculine tone, transforming all contractual communication into that of fellow warriors, now allied as comrades and brothers. Not surprisingly, any violations of honor codes could lead them readily back to the battlefield.

Because these European and Indian men measured military, and thereby political, power through warrior numbers and ability, and because they defined hostile actions as masculine endeavor, Indian women's involvement in diplomacy, when it occurred, assumed a particular importance of its own. Peace did not reign at all times, but Spanish, Caddo, Wichita, and Comanche leaders did slowly work out rituals of reconciliation. A critical corollary to manly diplomatic efforts became women's role in expressing peace rather than hostility, and strength rather than aggression. Male-dominated negotiations on battlefields and in council houses might establish a truce, but customary practices involving women proved crucial to maintaining the peace agreements that followed. As captives, slaves, and emissaries, women emerged as official and unofficial diplomats during this period of often combustible diplomacy.

chapter six

Womanly "Captivation": Political Economies of Hostage Taking and Hospitality

Throughout Spanish efforts to make peace with Apaches, Wichitas, and Co-manches in the 1770s and 1780s, male rituals may have dominated diplomatic language and ceremony, but the material terms of negotiation more often than not revolved around women. In varying diplomatic strategies, women were sometimes pawns, sometimes agents. Just as Apache, Wichita, and Comanche political customs reflected the more martial air of former enemies seeking to become new allies, so too did women initially enter these exchanges by coercive and violent routes. Women's more active participation in intermarriage and hospitality rituals later reemerged in critical ways in different native groups' "practices of peace."

In their diplomacy with Spaniards, Comanche and Wichita men first turned to already established exchange networks of captive women that had developed out of their economic alliances with the French. Among Wichitas, Comanches, and Spaniards, however, such networks would be framed not as market ex-changes but as hostage exchanges within the politics of postbattle reparations. Because the political use of captives had been a continuous thread running throughout Spanish negotiations with Lipan Apaches previously, that experi-ence shaped the ways in which Spaniards responded to peace agreements initi-ated with Wichitas and Comanches. Captive exchange then developed directly out of past warfare. Women's appearance within subsequent diplomacy high-lights the periodic attempts of Spanish, Wichita, and Comanche men to trans-form transient truces into permanent peace.

Beginning in the 1760s, Wichita (and later Comanche) men searched for ways by which Texas Spaniards might replace Frenchmen as trading partners when Spanish authorities cut off licensed exchange networks into Louisiana in 1769. An essential ingredient of those networks had been female captives whom they had taken in war with native enemies and then traded for French arms and goods. Although Spanish horses, bison hides, deerskins, and bear fat had moved along French exchange networks to New Orleans and France, women tended to travel no farther than the households of European men living in Natchitoches and other western posts who desired domestic servants or sexual, and sometimes marital, partners. The continuing intimate and familial desires of European traders and hunters living in the hinterlands of Louisiana fueled a contraband version of that trade after 1769. But to supplement that market exchange, Comanche and Wichita men turned the Spanish trade prohibitions on their head, putting female captives to a new economic use by seeking profits from Spanish officials in Texas through what Spaniards preferred to call "ransom" or "redemption" payments.

That new form of exchange may have served native material needs, but from a Spanish perspective it could also be purely diplomatic. Unlike Spaniards' earlier hostilities with Apaches—when they sent their own forces to take Apache women and children captive—Spanish officials now sought to acquire captive Indian women through ransoming, with the purpose of using them as lures with which to draw the women's kin into political negotiation. Indeed, Spaniards could make diplomatic overtures to both the women's captors and the women's families. Notably, Spanish forces never risked the enmity of Wichita men with raids bent on capturing Wichita women. Because hostilities continued through the 1780s with Comanches, some Comanche women did fall prey to Spanish capture, although the military power of Comanche bands ensured that the much smaller and weaker presidial forces of Texas Spaniards managed to take only a very few.

The female sex of the majority of captives subject to such political exchanges still tapped into an association of women with peace. In the traffic itself, female captives became the bargaining chips by which male captors negotiated truce and alliance. As with the Apaches at midcentury, women also emerged as mediators, able to move back and forth between their own people and Spaniards when men from either group could not safely or successfully do so. Hence, the exchange of women— despite its violent and coercive origins—became a critical component in efforts to effect peace in the latter half of the century.

Spanish involvement in native systems of captive taking and exchange did not secure the peace with Wichitas in the 1760s and 1770s, but it did offer limited economic exchange when the Spanish viceroyalty dragged its bureaucratic feet in establishing the commercial trade demanded by Wichita alliances. Wichitas often found that it was captive Spanish women from New Mexico (whom they acquired through trade with, or raids on, the women's original native captors) who best garnered Spanish attention and Spanish ransom payments. Furthermore, redeeming captive Spanish women repeatedly smoothed over conflicts when the horse raiding of young Wichita men made peace a tricky proposition through the 1780s. Some of these women, though, appear to have remained to live among the Wichitas or in the nearby Spanish villa of Nacogdoches. As ties among Caddo, Wichita, Spanish, and French peoples increased at the local level in mixed neighborhoods and settlements in eastern Texas, the responsibilities of Caddo and Wichita women within their societies' systems of hospitality found new or renewed political currency in their diplomacy with Spaniards.

Meanwhile, Lipan Apaches, who had been shunted aside by Spanish officials seeking relations with their Norteño enemies, pursued a twofold strategy. They first tried to establish trade alliances with Caddoan and Tonkawan peoples to the east and then turned their attention to eliciting some limited form of defensive alliance with local Spaniards in San Antonio and La Bahía by settling their families nearby. Women stood at the center of both strategies. As the means to make amends for their former hostility, Lipan Apache leaders offered to return many of the captive women taken during earlier raids against Caddos and the loosely allied bands of Tonkawas, Bidais, Mayeyes, Akokisas, and Cocos living south and southwest of the Hasinais. Then Apaches forged new trade and military ties by uniting their own families with those of the Caddo and Tonkawa confederations through intermarriage.

Comanche women came to the political fore in Texas in the wake of the Spanish-Comanche peace treaty of 1785, playing powerful roles in the "practices of peace" by which Comanche men communicated and maintained ties of brotherhood with their new Spanish allies. The restoration or sale of female Indian captives periodically occurred in Comanche-Spanish exchanges as well (for both political and economic purposes), yet it was the presence of Comanche women in their bands' diplomatic and trade parties to San Antonio that truly served as the barometer of Comanche relations of peace. The presence or absence of women indicated Comanche leaders' estimation of their Spanish "brothers" at the time of meeting. Spaniards soon learned to reward the female members of delegations with gifts and services, recognizing their presence for what it was: signs of rapprochement.

The Spaniards' ability to navigate these different diplomatic customs and strategies varied with individual Spanish leaders and with the financial and administrative support of their viceregal superiors. Spanish mistakes could be read as insults by native leaders who, of course, continued to hold the balance of power. Indeed, the Spaniards' need for alliance with these bands—whether Caddos, Apaches, or Wichitas, whose economic strength waxed and waned, or Comanches, whose dominance had not yet even reached its peak—reflected their weak position in the region relative to their Indian peers. Such power differentials, in turn, demanded careful Spanish attention to native custom. Repeatedly, officials at all levels of gov-

ernment within Texas and the Interior Provinces directed that amity with Comanches, Wichitas, Apaches, and the "Friendly Nations" be secured at all cost.
The native terms by which friendship would be maintained put women squarely
at the heart of Spanish-Indian peace practices.

Unlike their Apache foes at midcentury, Wichita men were not seeking the return of
their own wives, daughters, sisters, and mothers when in the 1760s and 1770s they first
approached Spaniards in Texas with offers of female captive exchange. Such exchange
tended to be more an economic and political rather than personal negotiation for
Wichita leaders because Wichita women were not at risk of Spanish capture. Instead,
Wichitas held captive women primarily from raids and skirmishes with native enemies or purchased them through trade with Comanches. Unlike their Comanche
allies, Wichitas do not appear to have married many captive women or adopted many
captive children, particularly Spanish captives, into their families. They even distinguished captives from Wichita women with body decoration. The extensive tattooing
on women's faces, necks, chests, and breasts varied only slightly among Wichita
women living in the same community, indicating band as opposed to individual identification—differentiating them both from other native peoples and from the captives
held in their settlements. Wichita captive trade first developed in response to French
demand and continued in the 1770s and 1780s because of Spaniards' lucrative "redemption payments." The former garnered trade alliances with Caddos and Frenchmen, and the latter facilitated a new form of alliance with Spaniards. Because Wichita
men neither formed marital unions with their captives nor brokered unions between
their own women and the European men to whom they traded the captives, Wichita
exchanges of women remained entirely outside the bonds of kinship. Nevertheless,
they used both exchange systems to preserve the material and defensive security of
their families and the extended kin networks that tied Wichita bands together.[1]

That new political value first became attached to captive Indian women back
when Wichita-Spanish peace processes opened in the 1760s. Taking lessons learned
in French markets about European desires for enslaved women, Wichita diplomatic
overtures were made to Spaniards in the form of captive women. As a means of
furthering talks following fray José de Calahorra's visit to the Tawakoni-Iscani villages in 1760, Tawakoni warriors captured three Spanish women from Apaches who
had originally taken them hostage in New Mexico. Tawakoni leaders traveled to the
Nacogdoches mission to report their deed and in so doing emphasized that they had
rescued the women "for this purpose" and "for this end." During Calahorra's next
visit, Spaniards presented flags, armaments, and silver-mounted staffs of command
to Tawakoni chief El Flechado en la Cara and Iscani chief Llaso in return for custody

of the three captive women. Still more presents and goods then flowed into the stores of the two headmen after the exchange. By 1763, Calahorra's negotiation with Tawakonis and Iscanis ultimately netted the Spaniards a total of eleven or twelve ransomed captives, including a Christian Apache woman named Ysabel (all originally taken by Pelone Apaches). Two years later, even the much-heralded return of Lieutenant Antonio Treviño came with accompanying offers from Taovaya chief Eyasiquiche of far more female captives than the lone man.[2]

Building on these early gestures, the Taovayas' return of two Spanish women became just as important as the return of Parrilla's two cannons in 1770 when peace negotiations finally began in earnest (see Chapter 5). The 1770 overture was a rare case in which adoption and kinship complicated the political process. Natchitoches commander Athanase de Mézières reported that the two women had lived so long among Taovayas that they had married and borne children and thus were no longer "slaves" but "free." More important, despite the Taovaya leaders' offer, Mézières knew the men conditioned the return on the women's consent and doubted that they or their Wichita husbands would agree to tear apart their families. Not surprisingly, the following year, when the chief visited Tinhioüen's village again to leave a message regarding his wish for harmony with Spaniards, he did not bring the women. Rather, he left two "hostages," most likely Taovaya boys or young men, "in pledge of his promise," who would remain there until he returned from meeting with Mézières. In the final peace agreement, the return of Christian captives living in Wichita villages held equal place with stipulations of a cease-fire, restoration of Parrilla's cannons, military alliance, and diplomatic protocols, yet no record indicates that the women ever left the Taovaya villages.[3]

The story of one Wichita woman's redemption illustrates the power of native custom in Spanish-Indian diplomacy, Spanish need and desire to conform to Indian expectations, and the central importance women played in paving the way for peaceful relations. When several principal men from Kichai, Iscani, Tawakoni, and Taovaya bands journeyed to San Antonio to ratify the peace with Governor Juan María de Ripperdá in 1772, a principal Taovaya chief told Ripperdá that he had received word that his wife, who had been captured by Apaches a few months before, had been sold by her captors to a Spaniard in Coahuila. He saw in the Spaniards' desire for the Wichitas' alliance a new opportunity to regain his wife in circumstances where he himself could not, and he asked what the governor could do to effect her return. "She is so much esteemed by him," Ripperdá reported to the viceroy, "that he assures me that she is the only one he has ever had, or wishes to have until he dies, and, as she leaves him two little orphans, he begs for her as zealously as he considers her deliverance difficult."[4]

Ripperdá quickly realized how critical it would be for him to rescue the Taovaya woman, for if he did not, "all that we have attained and which is of so much importance would be lost." In other words, the success of the newly completed peace would rest upon the captive woman's return. A month later, Ripperdá could only exult in his good fortune in another letter to the viceroy, because "having very urgently requested from the governor of Coahuila the wife of the principal chief of the Tauayas [Taovayas], whom the Apaches captured and sold to the Spaniards of that province," she had been brought to San Antonio with a convoy of maize and was even then a guest in Ripperdá's home. He had had to buy her from a Spanish dealer, since she had already fallen prey to Spanish enslavement. More to the point, he reiterated "that she may be the key that shall open the way to our treaties."[5]

Ripperdá played host to the Taovaya woman for six months following her rescue, waiting for news of her release to travel via Natchitoches to the Taovaya villages. In February 1773, her husband finally arrived with eight warriors and a French trader to act as interpreter, and at last Ripperdá could write to the viceroy of the successful conclusion to the captive redemption. In March, the governor sent word that the happy husband as well as the entire Taovaya delegation was staying in Ripperdá's home and wished authorization to continue on to visit the viceroy, presumably in thanks for the woman's emancipation.[6]

At about the same time, Governor Ripperdá also resorted to more coercive measures in using captive women in negotiations with Comanches. Perhaps unsurprisingly, he bungled it badly. The governor initiated contact in 1772. In February, a detachment from the Béxar presidio returned to San Antonio with unheralded prizes: four Comanches, three women and one girl. Ripperdá already had three other Comanche women in his control who had been captured months before and who had been held so long in one of the San Antonio missions that all three had been baptized and two married off to mission Indian residents. As shortly became clear, however, these women desperately wanted to escape back to their own families. Because of their baptisms, the Spaniards would not return them to live in apostasy, but the governor decided that the four new captives could be put to diplomatic use. Since the Spanish government had recently completed new peace agreements with both Wichita and Caddo bands, he hoped for the first time to attract (or blackmail) Comanches to the negotiating table as well. With that intention, Ripperdá sent two of the women, under military escort, back to their village with political gifts to present to their chief, Evea. Meanwhile, he kept the other woman and the little girl as hostages.[7]

In response, seven Comanche warriors rode into San Antonio a month later, led by a woman carrying a cross and a white flag meant to secure their safe entrance into the Spanish town. Chief Evea and his leading men well knew that they had to put a woman at the head of that delegation. Hostilities had been the rule for too long for Spaniards to see a Comanche party composed only of men as boding anything but a fight. The woman leading the party was one of the female captives freed by Ripperdá and also the mother of the little girl still held hostage. Whatever Evea's wishes or intent, *she* came for her daughter. Others in the party included the hostage girl's father, the husband of the other hostage woman, and the brother of two of the three baptized Comanche women held in the missions. All together, everyone had a personal—kin—stake in this meeting.[8]

The group reunited with the two recent hostages, received more diplomatic gifts from Ripperdá, and upon departure, took their own form of ransom payment by making off with four hundred horses from the Béxar presidio herds. They also tried to liberate the three baptized Comanche women—together with their willing husbands, who apparently preferred a life among Comanches to whatever the mission had to offer. Spanish soldiers, however, stopped their escape. That one recaptured woman then tried to kill herself provides a painful glimpse at the level of despair and desperation faced by captives. The Comanche rescue party was itself not home free once it got away from the Spanish town. Apache warriors attacked them as they fled, killed seven men, captured half of the horses, three of the women and the little girl, and turned them back over to the Spaniards (probably for a ransom). The stalwart Comanche woman who had led the expedition managed to escape her Apache captors, but in her flight fell into the hands of still more Indian warriors from one of the San Antonio mission communities. They too returned her to Ripperdá's control. Spanish officials, angered at what they labeled Comanche "treachery" for using women to feign peace (with the cross and white flag), sent all the women to different forms of enslavement in Coahuila. Though Ripperdá briefly tried to persuade Viceroy Bucareli y Ursúa to consider "sending the women back to their people"— even the missionized ones, because of "how little faith they profess"—the viceroy categorically refused. Thus, the two married Comanche women from the mission were destined for Coahuila missions accompanied by their husbands, while the single woman and the mother and daughter suffered more punitive fates, most likely servitude or labor camps, at the hands of the governor of Coahuila.[9]

At first this story suggests Spanish power (at least to exact revenge), but the governor's rash actions caused far more problems for the relatively weak Spaniards. Comanche leaders were not yet done with Ripperdá, nor were they about to give up the fight for their female relatives. That summer, a number of them traveled to San Antonio in the company of allied Wichita chiefs to retrieve the women now in Coahuila. Chief Evea himself joined the conference. Ripperdá initially attempted to shame the

Comanche men by displaying the "false" white flag of truce carried earlier by the Comanche woman. His efforts fell on deaf ears. Though he claimed to the viceroy to have sent the men away empty-handed, Ripperdá found himself upstaged by the husband of one woman, who had come well prepared to wait out the governor in protest of his wife's enslavement. Either the warrior made quite an impression upon the besieged Ripperdá or the governor never had any intention of turning the formidable Comanche men away, because in the same letter where he bragged of cowing Evea with the "false" flag, he reported that he had advised the governor of Coahuila to ensure that the Comanche woman was not baptized, so that indeed she could be returned to her husband. The viceroy agreed with his decision, arguing that the "volubility" of the Comanche men over their women was proof that they would persevere until they got them back. Records fail to confirm whether she was indeed set free and returned to her family, but her redemption, if it even came, was certainly not sufficient to ease the Comanches' hostility and need to avenge the others who were lost.[10]

When Spanish officials acquired Comanche women to coerce peace with their bands, they were trying to forge an alliance through an act of hostility. Spanish captive diplomacy may have also resonated, negatively, with social controls internal to Comanche societies. Indeed, to these men, Spanish policies targeting their wives or female family members may have most resembled practices of "wife stealing," which were governed by codes of male competition. Though sometimes representing a woman's effort to escape an unwanted marriage, wife stealing put male honor to the test, and so competition for male rank within Comanche communities sometimes involved taking wives from husbands. A loss of reputation, influence, and privileges might follow, as others assumed a lack of ability on the victim's part that his male rivals, particularly the man who stole his wife, possessed. Moreover, in bride-service societies like those of the Comanches, nothing affected a man's social and political rank as much as the loss of a wife. Without her, a man also lost home, shelter, and the provision of services that allowed him to offer other men hospitality. A man had to take action in response or suffer disgrace. If wives could not be regained, warriors demanded compensation through damage payments in goods, horses, clothing, and guns. The importance of such an exchange lay not in the actual value of the articles but in the maintenance of honor. If indeed Comanche men interpreted Spanish actions within the terms of their own social controls, it is not surprising that Spaniards encountered men who came to San Antonio and refused to leave until they regained their wives or exacted revenge by raids and warfare.[11]

In the meantime, Natchitoches officials led by Mézières sought a way to maintain the slave markets for Apache women still being captured by Wichita and Comanche warriors, as a means of wooing them to the negotiating table. Spaniards were no strangers to the idea of enslaved Apaches, and with promises of continued exchange, Spanish officials could offer themselves as worthy replacements for the French traders so beloved by Wichitas. The cession of Louisiana from French to Spanish control had direct ramifications on the trade networks among Caddos, Wichitas, and Comanches. Not only had the new Spanish governor of Louisiana, Alexandro O'Reilly, enacted trade restrictions against Norteños; he had also extended official Spanish prohibitions against the enslavement and sale of Indians to Louisiana. Yet, if the Spanish government did not find another channel for the Wichitas' valuable traffic in women, others nearby would happily meet their needs. Taovayas, for example, pointed out that "they liked the French of the Arkansas River better than those of Natchitoches, since the latter wish nothing but deer skins, which they do not have, while those of the Arkansas River take horses, mules and slaves, by means of which they get what they need." The combination of Spanish law and contraband competition meant that Mézières faced an uphill road in creating a new outlet for the captives Wichita and Comanche men continued to take in battle.[12]

The Arkansas post and the region surrounding it remained a hotbed of illicit exchange networks, despite all the Spanish laws, and the extralegal activities there could bring harm as well as profit to Wichitas. In 1770, Mézières wrote to the Louisiana governor about men who had deserted from troops or ships or who had committed robbery, homicide, or rape and were known to be living on the Arkansas River "under the name of hunters." By taking their "pernicious customs" into these lands, they presented a problem to both the colony's domestic and diplomatic policies. "They live so forgetful of the laws," he wrote, "that it is easy to find persons who have not returned to Christian lands for ten, twenty, or thirty years, and who pass their scandalous lives in public concubinage with the captive Indian women whom for this purpose they purchase among the heathen, loaning those of whom they tire to others of less power, that they may labor in their service, giving them no other wage than the promise of quieting their lascivious passions." Despite the crude implication that Indian women's supposedly "lascivious" nature mitigated what was clearly abduction and rape, Mézières recognized the devastation rendered Wichita and Caddo communities by the Frenchmen's extralegal market in captive Indian women. The French "malefactors," he explained, used the lure of arms and ammunition to encourage Osage warriors living near them to attack and raid bands of Tawakonis, Iscanis, Kichais, and Taovayas "for the purpose of stealing women, whom [the Frenchmen] would buy to satisfy their brutal appetites; Indian children, to aid them in their hunting; horses, on which to hunt wild cattle; and mules, on

Tawakoni (Wichita) man and woman harvesting corn, illustrating the bounty of agricultural fields cultivated by Wichita women. Note the man's long-barreled gun laid nearby, indicating the ever-present danger of Osage raiders. Watercolor by Lino Sánchez y Tapia after the original sketch by José María Sánchez y Tapia, an artist-cartographer who traveled through Texas as a member of a Mexican boundary and scientific expedition in the years 1828–31. Courtesy of the Gilcrease Museum, Tulsa, Oklahoma.

which to carry the fat and the flesh." To treat with the Wichitas, Spaniards needed to balance the purchase of Wichita warriors' own captives with the protection of Wichita women from capture.[13]

To secure the Wichitas' alliance, Mézières argued that a critical element would be creating a market in San Antonio to which Wichitas could bring Apache captives taken in war. If Lipan Apaches could also be weakened through captive taking, then officials saw good reason to encourage it by keeping a market of some kind open for this trade. Unlike in New Mexico, where a traffic in captives took place within the context of *ferias* (trade fairs), similar commerce did not develop in Texas until after the 1790s, so Spaniards had to rely instead on the venue of diplomatic gift exchange to offer goods and horses to Comanches and Wichitas. Mézières wrote that it would be diplomatically savvy if "permission be given them to sell here the captives that they may bring, because their rescue will be an act of great humanity, as well as because it will serve to encourage such expeditions [against Apaches]." The phrasing of "rescue" and "act of great humanity" were no doubt a sop to Spanish authorities, casting the "sale" as redemption when, after all, Indian slavery was illegal. But sale it was, even if the proceeds went to the church, as he suggested, arguing that "it will be well to fix amicably a moderate price for each individual," so that "this sale will compensate the missions for the injurious losses which they have suffered from epidemics, war, and the incessant flight of the apostates, while it is a ransom certainly worthy of the favor of the All Powerful."[14]

Spanish officials recognized the opportunity both to negotiate an alliance with captors through the ransoming process itself and to obtain for themselves, by commercial rather than violent means, captive Indian women to be used in turn in diplomatic relations with the women's families. Suggesting the changed value captive women held for Spanish officialdom in the second half of the century, captives were no longer to be included among the "booty" of war apportioned among Spanish soldiers and civilians as servants and slaves. Such distribution of captives, as the marqués de Rubí first expressed in his 1768 *Dictamen*, "makes impossible their return, which would be capable by itself alone of winning the good will of some nations less cruel than the Apaches." The 1772 *Reglamento* followed Rubí's recommendations to draw a new distinction between captured Indian men and women, directing that men—"prisoners of war"—be sent to Mexico City, where the viceroy would "dispose of them as seems convenient," while women and children—"captives"—were "to be treated with gentleness, restoring them to their parents and families in order that they recognize that it is not hatred or self-interest but the administration of justice that motivates our laws."[15]

Spanish officials in Texas pursued these gendered tactics with a number of different Indian groups and were willing to ransom captives from Apaches as well. When Lipan warriors captured a woman and two boys in a 1779 revenge raid on a Tonkawa ranchería, the governor of Texas offered the warriors eight horses for the three captives. He wanted the boys because they "could become Christians by virtue of their youth," but his desire for the Tonkawa woman was purely political, since she could be restored to Tonkawa leaders as "proof of friendship." Interestingly, the Apache men refused, not because eight horses represented an unfair price, but because they did not want to become obligated to the governor by the exchange. They too measured the political benefit-versus-cost ratio of such transactions.[16]

Then the viceroyalty threw an unexpected wrench into the debate over how to create a market for the Apache women captured by Wichitas, while protecting Wichita women from Osage encroachments. The 1772 *Reglamento* that guided the realignment of military policy across the northern provinces ordered the abandonment of all missions and presidios in Texas, except for those at San Antonio and La

Bahía, in an effort to make the province more defensible. The directive encompassed the entire Spanish population living at the Los Adaes presidio and civil settlement as well as the three missions located among Nacogdoches, Adaes, and Ais bands. Caddo leaders responded with alarm. At a time when Osage, Choctaw, and Chicka- saw raids were on the rise, the removal of those settlers signaled the sundering of Spanish alliances with Caddos and Wichitas that had been affirmed only two years before. Hasinai *caddí* Bigotes postponed a campaign against Osage enemies in order to lead a large contingent of Caddos to meet with Spanish officials at Mission Nacogdoches in protest. Hasinai *caddí* Texita accompanied Spanish representatives from Los Adaes to Mexico City in the winter of 1773–74 to petition the viceroy for permission for the Spanish families to return. In meetings with Spanish officials, Caddo discourse pointedly emphasized not the loss of Los Adaes soldiers but specifi- cally that of the Spanish families of women and children, in explaining their anger.[17]

For Caddos, not merely a military alliance but a kin relationship was being broken. In 1768, when fray José de Solís had traveled through the Caddo and Spanish communities surrounding Los Adaes during an inspection of the missions there, the intertwined nature of Caddo and Spanish homesteads and the political significance of women within them was obvious. To visit a mission was to visit the surrounding Caddo hamlets, as families of Hasinais, Nasonis, Nacogdoches, Nabedaches, Ais, and Adaes with their *caddís* joined the resident Franciscan to greet the missionary's arrival. They did so not as congregants but as neighbors. Caddo women wearing paint, tattoos, and chamois dresses bordered with numerous beads from European trade held center stage in welcome parties, just as they had so many years before. The women brought "presents" of hens, chickens, and eggs for Solís, and he reciprocated with *piloncillo* (brown sugar candy), *pinole* (a beverage made from parched, ground corn mixed with sugar and water), and biscuits. At one village, a woman named Sanate Adíva had even assumed the responsibilities of a *caddí*, with *tanmas* (admin- istrative assistants) and *connas* (shaman priests) in her service.[18]

When fray Calahorra visited the Tawakoni villages in the 1760s, he too had been welcomed by groups of women and children and had been impressed by the hospi- tality of well-ordered settlements surrounded by bounteous fields. At the Taovaya villages in the 1770s, principal men greeted Antonio Treviño and Mézières as old friends and showed "the greatest pleasure at seeing and associating with the Span- iards from San Antonio for the first time" by "inviting the women and children to get acquainted with them." So prominent were women's labors in Wichita hospi- tality that Mézières could only conclude in a report to the commandant general that "Their government is democratic, not even excluding the women, in consideration of what they contribute to the welfare of the republic." If Spaniards now withdrew all their women and families from the region, could there be any greater betrayal of "brotherhood" for Caddo and Wichita men who viewed fraternal families as uniquely tied to one another?[19]

The Spanish government once again was poised to undermine something they had inadvertently done right in accordance with Caddo and Wichita kinship-based diplomacy. Despite his objections, Governor Ripperdá had no choice but to implement the royal edict. Meanwhile, local Spanish residents were equally distressed at the rupture to their kin associations. Many of the estimated five hundred settlers refused to relocate to San Antonio de Béxar. Thirty-five Adaesano families and an equal number near Nacogdoches fled "into the woods" or to sanctuary in nearby Caddo hamlets. Spanish settlers' actions clarify the contrast between top-down Spanish policy decided in Mexico City and the on-the-ground experience of Spaniards who understood better the nuances of native-controlled Texas.[20]

Other Spanish families left women and children among their native kin as a pledge that they would soon return, echoing symbolic Caddo acts at the beginning of the century. On the day of forced evacuation, for instance, twenty-four people stopped at El Lobanillo, the ranch of Antonio Gil Ibarvo's family since the 1730s, saying that they would go no further. Some claimed illness, while others claimed the need to care for the sick. Altogether this female-dominated group counted at least ten women, including Ibarvo's mother, sister, and sister-in-law. At the same time, consider what Caddos and Wichitas saw when the government's orders gave Spanish families only five days to pack their belongings and forced them to leave behind planted fields weeks before harvest time. Commander José González had to go door to door to harry families to leave, while women and children marched on foot and were forced to sell clothes, rosaries, and other personal treasures to buy food along the way—all resulting in the deaths of ten children and twenty adults during the march and thirty more after their arrival in San Antonio.[21]

In the wake of Caddo, Wichita, and Adaesano determination to keep their communities together, Spanish officials in 1774 approved the establishment of a new town, Nuestra Señora del Pilar de Bucareli, centrally located between San Antonio and various villages of Wichitas, Caddos, and Akokisas, but that lasted less than four years. Tellingly, when Bucareli settlers (125 men, 89 women, and 128 children) fled their homes in the aftermath of the 1778 Comanche revenge raids, they did not run to the better-garrisoned town of San Antonio; rather, they again led their wives and children to asylum among their Caddo neighbors. Nor did they wish to reestablish Bucareli. They preferred to remain among the Hasinai and Nacogdoches villages, using the Comanche attack as an excuse to move back home where they had wanted to be since the evacuation of Los Adaes—in the midst of Caddo hamlets, the Natchitoches post, and the trade and kin networks uniting them. And if they couldn't live there, they requested permission to move to Natchitoches. Athanase de Mézières's answer in the face of Spanish predicament and native sentiment was simple: more women. "In order to infuse courage into these [Bucareli] families," he suggested, "they should be strengthened by others from Los Adaes." In 1779, again, a new intercultural settlement arose, this time nestled among Caddo hamlets near the former site of the Nacogdoches mission, which gave the new town its name. Spanish officials sought to adopt in limited form the policies of licensed traders and gift giving previously practiced successfully by the French government. To do so, diplomatic relations with Caddos and Wichitas, based first in Natchitoches, extended to Nacogdoches using the contacts and expertise of French traders who came to live in the new settlement. Reflecting the importance of the new community in maintaining good relations with Caddo and Wichita allies, it became the seat of the new lieutenant governor of the province—Ibarvo would hold the post until 1791—with a large stone house immediately erected as the commissary for Indian trade.[22]

In a region where a captive exchange network had marked the economy for over sixty years, Nacogdoches not surprisingly became not only a symbol of continued intermingling of Spanish, Wichita, and Caddo communities but also a key site for the ransom and restoration of captives—especially when those captives were Spanish women and children from New Mexico. The trade even marked the landscape, with a nearby creek long called "Cautivo." It was often French traders at Nacogdoches, now Spanish citizens, who alerted Spanish officials to the presence of captives among Wichita bands and who led the diplomatic missions seeking to "redeem" those women and children. The number of traders with enslaved Indian consorts or freed wives also grew. Freed Apache slaves also remained in the area—one Apache man (enslaved as a boy) was even granted a subsistence allowance by the governor "to destroy any desire on his part to incorporate back into his [Apache] nation." Official censuses only hinted at the numbers, and sacramental records—though listing almost two hundred Indian women and children in the Natchitoches area over the century—also offer only a partial accounting. Nevertheless, by 1803, almost one-quarter of the native-born European population in the region counted Indian slaves among their ancestry, and 60 percent of that number claimed descent directly from an enslaved Indian parent or grandparent.[23]

The same exchange networks that had been sending Indian women and children to French slave markets in Louisiana in the first half of the century thereby remained in operation, but their endpoints were now increasingly in Texas. In 1774, for instance, news reached Governor Ripperdá that two youths, a Spanish girl and a mulatto boy, had traversed quite a distance through the captive exchange networks

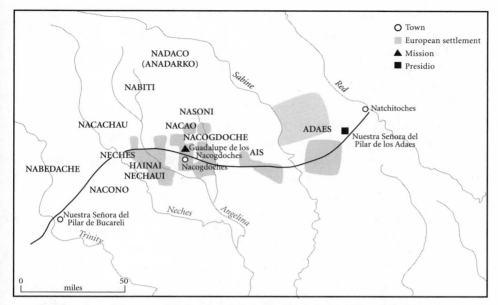

Spanish and French homesteads and settlements intermingled among Caddo hamlets by the mid-eighteenth century. Map drawn by Melissa Beaver.

crisscrossing New Mexico and Texas. They had first been captured by Apaches, had subsequently fallen into Comanche hands when taken by force from Apache warriors, and finally ended up in a Taovaya village after a Taovaya chief purchased them from the Comanches. Ripperdá tried to ensure that at least two more trips were added to their travels before they came to an end—transferring the children from Taovaya to Spanish hands in Nacogdoches and from San Antonio back to their New Mexico homes.[24]

The routes from New Mexico to Texas and Louisiana might not change, but the number of captive Spanish women and children traveling along it did. Spanish-Indian tensions, not only in Texas but also in New Mexico, made women of every sort, including Spanish, vulnerable to becoming diplomatic or economic pawns. Prior to the 1770s, Wichita and Caddo peoples had only occasionally ransomed Spanish women and children (gained originally from Comanches) through officials in Natchitoches, but in the 1770s and 1780s, records indicate a rise in the number of Spanish captives ransomed in Texas, perhaps reflecting their increasing value as a source of revenue in place of trade. Thus, during the very period when Comanches' looming presence kept Spaniards mentally and physically besieged in San Antonio, news of their capture of women continuously filtered into town—news that could not help but increase the level of fear, even as more peaceful relations with Wichitas made the return of some of those captured Spaniards possible for the first time. Strikingly, however, every captive was taken in New Mexico, not Texas. The seeming rise in the number of Spaniards held as captives by Comanches might frighten the populations in San Antonio, but they were not personally touched by these losses.[25]

The ransom received by some Taovayas from Nacogdoches trader José Guillermo Esperanza for a Spanish woman named Ana María Baca and her six- or eight-year-old son spoke to the profits to be gained in the diplomatic trade. For Ana María, they received "three fusils [muskets], three cloth *naquisas* [netted cloth], two blankets, four axes, three hoes, two *castetes* [?] with their pipe, one pound of vermillion, two pounds of beads, ten *belduques* [knives], twenty-five fusil stones [flints], eight steels [for striking flints], six ramrods, six awls, four fathoms of wool sash, and three hundred bullets with necessary powder." For Baca's small son, the Taovayas received a similar set of items. Notably, Taovayas were not the only ones who planned to profit from Ana María's captivity. A Nacogdoches lieutenant, Christóbel Hilario de Córdoba, to whom Esperanza had related his purchase, reported with outrage that Esperanza planned to take the woman and sell her in Natchitoches, "where there could not but be plenty of Frenchmen to purchase her and molest her, as is their custom, since she still is attractive." Córdoba forestalled the woman's sale into concubinage by taking her and her son into protective custody. Córdoba's intervention (which Spanish officials vehemently supported) suggested how aberrant it was that Ana María's Spanish identity had not excluded her from the category of women whom Esperanza felt he might acceptably sell into the sex trade. But perhaps this "Spanish" woman had developed a native-based identity—she might not have wanted to be redeemed—and that too would have imperiled her.[26]

She did not seem to fare much better at the hands of the Spanish government. When Governor Cabello began inquiries following her redemption, he received information suggesting that she had formed a union with a Taovaya man during her almost thirteen years in the Taovaya villages. Francisco Xavier Chaves, another former Taovaya captive who had become one of the governor's interpreters and emissaries to the Wichitas, told Cabello that Baca was twenty-eight years old, a native of Tomé, New Mexico, and had been captured at the age of fifteen, most likely by Comanches, and then sold to the Taovayas. Her age and time in captivity made it clear that her six- or eight-year-old son must have had a Taovaya father. Though Cabello made no observation concerning the mixed-blood identity of Ana María's son, in letters to the commandant general, he also made no mention of efforts to locate her family. His diffidence regarding reunification with her family was accompanied by the suggestive statement that "I have urged Captain Gil Ibarvo to take the greatest care not to let this woman be lost, as the aforementioned Chaves has informed me further that she is quite good looking." Did he perhaps think that her family would not welcome her return but that her beauty would offset her experience so that he or his lieutenant governor could marry her off to a resident in Nacogdoches or San Antonio?—making Cabello little better than Esperanza.[27]

As Wichitas had begun to realize the rewards of ransoming New Mexican women to officials in Texas, Spanish officials tried to increase their financial means to keep such captive diplomacy afloat. Authorities within the Comandancia General used stories like that of Ana María Baca to establish a new program for collecting alms that would help underwrite the expenses of such ransoms across the northern provinces. From the late medieval period in Spain, Spaniards had long maintained such institutionalized collections by both the church and the state in militarized regions. Alms for the ransom of captive women and children had once been one of the "compulsory bequests" made by Texas citizens in their wills, but by the 1770s they had disappeared. Unofficial, ad hoc ransoms of Spanish captives had begun in the 1770s in Nueva Vizcaya, but such efforts had quickly run up against financial exigencies. The concern was that presidial forces would "shrink from actively seeking to secure the ransom or exchange of prisoners" if there were no guarantee of reimbursement for costs incurred. Many captives had no known relatives or their families were too impoverished to assume the costs of either ransoms or reimbursements. Commandant General Teodoro de Croix therefore declared that "since the establishment of this undertaking . . . is of direct concern to humanity, to the Faith, and to the state," he would seek to create a fund to which the provinces under his command would make "pious contributions."[28]

Although Croix made no explicit connection between this order and the ransoms offered to Wichita bands in Texas, his 1781 report on the state of the northern provinces made clear his awareness that Norteños "are particularly sensitive over the failure of their barter with the Louisiana merchants in hides, riding horses, and captives, in exchange for guns, powder, balls, knives, mirrors, vermilion, and other trinkets"—a "form of commerce they call *treta*." His successors were far more pointed in making the connection. In 1784, Felipe de Neve's official *bando* (edict) "promoting the greater relief of the poor Christians that have the misfortune of groaning under the yoke of captivity which they suffer among the savage Indians," announced the questionable claim that 152 captives were held by "friendly heathens inhabiting the north of the province of Texas, between those of Louisiana and New Mexico." Among those mythic 152, the only captives whose identity demanded redemption were captive Spaniards or Christian Indians, according to Neve's order. Neve's successor, José Antonio Rengel, reiterated the belief in 152 captives, though he specified even more directly that they were all "in the power of the Taovayas."[29]

In 1780, alms gathering began anew in churches, but the "hand of Christian piety" soon proved insufficient, and Croix's successor, Felipe de Neve, ordered that church collections be supplemented by *cabildos* throughout the provinces, which were to appoint individuals to "beg for alms from house to house" on one feast day each month. Magistrates and civilian judges would do the same among the "most conspicuous and zealous persons" in their districts. It was not until 1784 that pressure from Neve actually resulted in any alms collection in Texas. In response to Neve's complaints that Texas officials had failed to contribute to the alms that Spanish law demanded all provinces collect for the ransoming of Christian captives, Governor Cabello explained simply that no captives from Texas had been taken and thus there was little local imperative to give to such a fund. Despite pressures from above, collections remained sluggish in the province. In 1784, for example, officials received 15 pesos and 4½ reales from residents of San Antonio, but nothing from La Bahía and Nacogdoches. The following year, total amounts rose to 35 pesos and 6 reales from San Antonio, 36 pesos and 4 reales from La Bahía, but a measly 6½ reales from Nacogdoches. In 1786, when only 12 pesos came from San Antonio, 20 pesos and 7 reales from La Bahía, and nothing from Nacogdoches, officials decided that downsizing collection responsibilities to a "single, appropriate individual" would be acceptable for the province's fund. The fund totaled only 105 pesos and 7½ reales by 1788, and no payments had been deducted from it, again suggesting the lack of local demand for such aid in Texas. Again, settlers appeared far more attuned to the real priorities of native diplomacy.[30]

Indeed, sentiments in local Spanish communities such as Nacogdoches and Natchitoches—which were closely related to neighboring Wichita settlements—apparently diverged the most from those of provincial authorities. Throughout the years, as alms were collected for the ransoming of captive women and children, the Nacogdoches community living nearest the villages of the Taovayas—where the majority of captives were supposedly held—contributed the least to the funds. Their lack of action in either contributing alms or seeking other remedies for the reputed captivity of Spaniards so near their settlement suggests they knew that such inflated numbers had little to do with reality and more to do with political rhetoric. It may also imply localized exchanges taking place beyond the eyes or ears of provincial officials.[31]

For Wichita men, meanwhile, it was the safety of their own wives and children that increasingly drove their diplomacy as the raids of Osages menaced their families and made trade supplies (or ransom payments) from Spaniards all the more critical to their defensive capabilities. To this end, Wichita leaders put women—their need for well-provisioned male defenders—to rhetorical use within Spanish-Wichita diplomatic and economic exchange. Kichai men, for instance, used women symbolically to emphasize their determination to defend their trade interests. In 1783, an expedition from Nacogdoches led by Antonio Gil Ibarvo visited a Kichai village to persuade the leaders there to limit commerce to only Spaniards in Nacogdoches. Ibarvo particularly desired to cut off their exchange with the Louisiana competition represented by Louis de Blanc and Bouet Laffitte, two Frenchmen based in Natchitoches. Kichai leaders calmly explained that the Frenchmen better served them, offering twice the Spanish rate of exchange for their deerskins and customarily honoring Kichai men with more generous hospitality. In response to Ibarvo's threat to arrest the French traders and take them off in shackles, enraged Kichai warriors said they would stop him by fighting until all was destroyed and all warriors dead. Even then, they continued, Spanish forces would not be done with them. At that point, Ibarvo "must also kill the women who would defend the French traders"; only then could he "take the traders and the children and bring them with them." The Kichai men thus used the specter of women fighting to convey the depth of their community's commitment to the defense of their trade interests and economies. Spanish soldiers would not only be met with a fight; they would have to become the killers of women to force their trade policies upon Kichai men.[32]

Spanish agents responded in kind, trying to strike fear in Wichita chiefs and warriors by countering with a threat of their own. Sent to meet with Wichita and Taovaya leaders about warriors' raids in the San Antonio area in response to Spanish trade failures, Pedro Vial warned the men, "If you Taovayas and Wichitas are among those who send their people to make trouble at San Antonio, there will be no one to save you from those who may harm you." Their raids, he continued, would prove to put not only warriors but also their women and children at risk. Vial asserted, "What you [must] wish is to see your villages destroyed and your families enslaved by other nations." The destruction—of a quite thorough nature—would not come at the hands of Spanish soldiers, however. All that Spanish officials had to do, Vial threatened, was cut off the supply of trade goods and firearms that enabled Wichita men to defend themselves. Then their Indian enemies "will steal your sons and your women, and you will not be able to go out to hunt to support your families, or to sleep in peace, and then the other nations that are friends of the Spaniards will hate you." In other words, the men would no longer be respected as men. To drive the point home that the warriors' actions put their women in danger equal to that faced by men on the battlefield, Vial added that "if you wish to make war on the Spaniards, it is not necessary for the men to go; send the women—which will be the same." He thus made more potent the Spanish threat by aiming it at Wichita women, but put the blame for any harm that might come to the women squarely on the shoulders of Wichita men. In the process, he defamed Wichita manhood for putting their women in danger.[33]

When such rhetoric did not work, Wichita leaders simply returned to the diplomatic use of captive women to gain leverage in negotiations. Thus did Taovaya chief Qui Te Sain offer five Spanish captives to Louisiana governor Bernardo de Gálvez as a means of getting material aid for his warriors who were struggling to hold off Osage onslaughts in 1780 with inferior weapons. In 1784, when newly elected Taovaya chief Guersec and his principal men endeavored to make amends for the horse raids of their young warriors, they sent four emissaries to San Antonio along with three European men who had been living among Taovayas for years. Guersec's seven representatives carried with them a message that Taovaya leaders were prepared to release into Spanish custody "all captive men and women who remained with them and would do so as soon as a trade thereof was arranged." One of the three European residents of the Taovaya village, Pedro Vial, carried with him proof of the captives living there: a six-year-old Apache child and an eighteen-year-old Spanish woman named María Teresa de los Santos he had purchased from Taovaya men before his departure. Only one of the girls garnered Cabello's concern, as the governor wrote simply, "the Apache received none of my attention, but the other one did because she was a Spaniard and a Christian." Cabello promptly gave Vial sixty pesos after being shown the list of goods that Vial had given the Taovayas for her; no amount was offered for the Apache girl, suggesting that she remained Vial's property. In addition to renewing Spanish obligations to distribute annual presents and supplies (as promised in earlier treaty agreements), Cabello added five hundred pesos worth of goods to the total as ransom payment for the captives—who were to be brought the following summer to Nacogdoches, where Taovayas, Wichitas, Iscanis, and Tawakonis would claim their annual supplies. Thus, Wichita leaders secured a "bonus" in addition to the renewal of trade goods. So was a story line set that played out again and again, as Spanish and Wichita leaders used female captives to heal breaches created by their respective failures of trade and horse raiding.[34]

Lipan Apaches too pursued new forms of peace from the 1770s onward, but they faced a much rougher path to that goal because official Spanish policies directed that Texas seek the alliance of Wichitas and Comanches to the detriment of Apaches during this period. Recommendations from the Comandancia General repeatedly swung back and forth between war and peace, in tune with the wavering state of the treasury and the military, both of which determined whether the forces that could be put in the field had any chance of survival, much less success. De facto peace policies came into being in localities like Texas before they were institutionalized at the level of the commandancy. So Apaches had to persuade Texas officials first, and changes in Apachería aided that process. By the 1770s and 1780s, eastern Apaches had splintered into so many small bands that they were making decisions almost on a family-by-family basis. In this context, Lipan leaders developed dual strategies, one seeking peace and alliance with Bidais, Hasinais, and Tonkawas that would open up Louisiana markets to their trade, the other returning to former plans to establish civil settlements and mission residence in or near San Antonio that might by extension gain them a defensive alliance with Spaniards. Both plans placed women at the heart of Apache diplomatic efforts.[35]

Spanish policy shifts inadvertently opened up opportunities on which Lipan leaders could capitalize. Once Caddo and Wichita peoples had negotiated peace agreements with Spaniards in San Antonio in the 1770s, their raids on Spanish herds and a steady supply of horses for the Louisiana trade diminished. They had both built extensive herds that their defensive and commercial needs demanded be maintained. As a result, their trade with native peoples in central Texas expanded. The constant debt or lack of supplies of resident trader José María Armant, whom Spanish officials stationed at Nacogdoches in the 1780s, by default strengthened the Caddos' ties to their native trading partners even further. Bidai allies with whom Hasinais had long shared ties through exchange and marriage had already established trade with Lipan Apaches by midcentury. French traders in turn had regularly visited Bidai rancherías along the Trinity River southwest of the Hasinai villages since the 1740s and by the 1770s had begun trading arms and ammunition in exchange for horses brought to the Bidais by Lipan Apaches. Thus, Bidai leaders represented crucial agents through which Lipan Apaches might seek inclusion in the kin ties the Bidais enjoyed with Hasinais. For Bidais and Hasinais alike, the Lipan Apaches could offer a new source of horses, while their trade contacts could bring Apaches their first chance to obtain French arms and ammunition.[36]

Apache overtures initially sought to open trade ties with offers of female captives taken earlier from Hasinai settlements—women whose return to their families might serve as gestures of conciliation. These gestures' meaning increased in the wake of epidemics that devastated Hasinai families in 1777. Captive women provided a unique avenue by which Apaches could put the bounty of past hostilities to work in the name of peace with their former Caddo enemies. Captive diplomacy among Apaches, Bidais, and Hasinais would have to be effected in the face of Spanish opposition, however. When Apache leaders first made diplomatic overtures to Hasinais via their Bidai allies in the late 1770s, they did so right under the nose of Spanish officials. The Spanish settlements of San Antonio and La Bahía proved ideal locations to make contact with visiting Hasinai leaders, who traveled there to maintain relations with Spanish officials and thus came within the reach of Apache leaders who could approach them within the neutral confines of the two presidios.

News reached the Lipan encampments in 1779 that Hasinai *caddí* Texita had arrived at La Bahía with a delegation to meet with Governor Cabello concerning the shortage of traders and trade goods being made available to their villages—the news likely coming via Bidais who also visited the presidio that week. Lipan chiefs El Joyoso, Josef Grande, Josef Chiquito, El Manco Roque, and Manteca Mucho promptly gathered an estimated six hundred men and women to travel there as well—signaling their peaceful intent by both the women in their party and the four Hasinai captives they brought with them to return to Texita. Unfortunately, Cabello received word of their approach and hurried the Hasinais' departure with false warnings that Apaches were coming with hostile purpose, sending a military escort of seven soldiers to ensure that the two groups did not meet. For Spaniards, only "disastrous results" could ensue from such a meeting, Cabello believed, fearing that such an alliance was sure to turn against Spaniards. Covering all his bases, Cabello similarly lied to Tonkawa leaders about Apache intentions a couple of months later in hopes of preventing their rapprochement as well.[37]

Apache leaders remained undaunted, however, and in the company of Bidais approached a small party of Hasinais visiting with Cabello at La Bahía the following year. Again, Cabello did everything he could to keep the two groups apart, this time barricading the Hasinai *caddí*, his wife, and two warriors in their quarters within the garrison to prevent contact. Yet, Lipan chief Chiquito and his men merely ignored the Spaniards and spoke through the door to the Hasinais, offering "to give them horses, arms, and *even women*" if they would go with them to another location to discuss peace and an alliance. Finding the two chiefs talking with one another thus, Cabello promptly expelled the Apache men from the presidio. Seeking to avert the "coalition" so desired by Apaches, Cabello tried to persuade the Hasinai leader and his wife that, once they were enticed away, the Lipan warriors secretly planned to kill them so that they could "dance many mitotes with their scalps."[38]

Events two years later indicated that Cabello had failed again and, more significantly, that the Lipan leaders' "enticements" through the door involved not only returning female Hasinai captives to their families but also uniting Lipan women in marriages with Hasinai men. Diplomatic doors could be opened with the return of captured women, and intermarriage could strengthen amity with kinship affiliation. Intermarriage, it seems, had become a crucial means of Caddo-Apache alliance.

When a Hasinai man and his wife from the Angelina village visited San Antonio in 1782, Cabello learned, much to his chagrin, that the woman was not a Hasinai but a *Lipana*. She had been captured by Taovayas in 1779 and sold to a French trader in Illinois before the Hasinai man rescued her from enslavement. Now married, he was bringing her to visit with her family and hold diplomatic parleys with Apache men; they only passed through San Antonio because it offered a good resting point along the way to the Apache encampments. Not so coincidentally, that fall Lipan, Mescalero, and Natage Apaches attended a huge trade fair held by Hasinais, Bidais, Mayeyes, Akokisas, and Tonkawas, where they traded 1,000 horses in exchange for 270 guns and ammunition. Despite continued attempts by Spaniards to keep these groups at odds, signs of alliance only grew along with increasing Hasinai and Tonkawa resistance to Spanish proposals for campaigns against Apaches. As native relations yet again developed far from possible Spanish surveillance—despite Spanish spies being sent to the trade fairs—officials took special note of the identity of women in diplomacy parties whenever they came to San Antonio and La Bahía. In 1784, they recorded the visit of yet another party of Hasinais, including a Lipan woman among the dignitaries' wives. An Apache woman named Teresa and her son seen at a Tonkawa village during another trade fair told them that intermarriages had also begun to link Lipan and Tonkawa communities together.[39]

From a Caddo standpoint, these unions were simply part of a long tradition of intermarriage as a means of forging alliances and, in concert with unions formed with Bidais, Mayeyes, Tonkawas, and other native groups of central Texas, helped replenish populations devastated by smallpox epidemics in the late 1770s. Newly brokered unions built on others with captive and enslaved Apache women and their descendants, whom the Wichitas and the Comanches had sold into Caddo territories in Texas and Louisiana throughout the century. Many of the European traders who bought and sold Apache captives and maintained their own unions (both licit and illicit) with Apache women may have also encouraged Hasinais to listen to Lipan peace and trade overtures late in the century. François Morvant, for instance, had lived as a resident trader among Caddos and later Wichitas with his Apache wife, Ana María, and their five children before moving his family to Nacogdoches in the last decades of the century. Marriage and baptism records testify to the presence of enslaved and free Apache women as concubines, wives, and mothers in Natchitoches and Nacogdoches well into the nineteenth century.[40]

These intertwined relationships mirrored a trade network that slowly emerged in the 1780s linking Natchitoches and another Louisiana outpost at Opelousas with Hasinais, Tonkawas, Bidais, Mayeyes, Atakapas, Akokisas, Cocos, and Apaches. Great trade fairs involving thousands of men, women, and children from these bands grew in number, bringing Apache family bands with horses and mules taken from Spanish settlements in Texas and Coahuila to trade for muskets, powder, and bullets. These native trade alliances held despite Spanish efforts to sever their ties—efforts that included cutting off annual gifts and supplies to the Caddos and their central Texas allies (now called the "Twenty-One Friendly Nations"), the assassination of Tonkawa chief El Mocho (an Apache who had been taken captive, adopted, and then assumed leadership among the Tonkawas, championing trade relations with Lipans), and the threat of assassination against his successor, El Gordo, if he did not cut off trade relations with Apaches. Yet, the kinship ties of intermarriage and the exchange of captive women and children had made Caddos, Bidais, and their allies "the most steadfast friends" with Lipans, friends who resented Spanish strategies that made them suffer.[41]

Relations between Spaniards and Lipans also gave proof of the disjuncture between official policy and life on the ground—even in San Antonio, under the very nose of diplomats such as Governor Cabello. Peaceful relations at the local level often gave the lie to official declarations of hostility between Apache and Spanish peoples of Texas. Indeed, Spanish policies vacillating between the desires for war at higher levels of the Spanish bureaucracy and the realities of friendships in San Antonio made diplomatic relations quite mercurial. Many a high-ranking official would have agreed with Commandant General Teodoro de Croix when he complained in 1781 that Apaches came to the negotiating table "overbearing and proud, and with hands bloody from victims, vassals of the king, whom they had sacrificed to their fury." Rather than showing appropriate humility, the warriors arrogantly "demanded food, presents, and gifts." For him and others in the Comandancia General, it took a royal order issued on February 20, 1779, temporarily halting the use of open war, to make them accept the need for negotiation. Croix tried his best, nevertheless, to restrict the use of diplomacy, directing that presents be given only "at suitable times so that [Apaches] may not be given cause for conceit or arrogance nor acquire our gifts as if we had been forced to give them," and they should be given only to those Apache men who "evidenced voluntary and real subjection." Such moments proved rare indeed. Yet, as Apache family bands in Texas turned to Spaniards for alliance and "protection," their actions could be framed by local officials as constituting these bands' acceptance of the commandancy general's new peace establishments (*establecimientos de paz*) policy. In hopes of ending the Apaches' raids and making them dependent on Spanish officials, the program in 1786 began offering them incentives—subsidies, goods, arms, and ammunition—if they agreed to settle near the watchful eye of presidios. They would be termed communities of "*Apaches de paz*."[42]

In the meantime in Texas, Apache warriors and Spanish soldiers and citizens who interacted on a daily basis knew better than remote officials what the daily exigencies were that brought their families together. At this local and more personal level, Spanish-Apache ties could be seen more clearly, especially as Apaches increasingly sought out civil settlements near Spanish presidios like Béxar, where the defense of their women and children could be joined with that of Spaniards. Now it was families and not just warriors whom Apaches wished to unite at such sites. Since midcentury, Spanish residents had been visiting Lipan rancherías regularly, staying for days to trade (illicitly) guns, ammunition, French tobacco, and other goods in exchange for mules, horses, bison hides, and deerskins. Through the exchanges, some Spaniards learned the Lipan language. Others gained friends with whom they shed tears over Apache loved ones who were lost to Comanche raids.[43]

By the 1770s, friendly sentiment toward Lipans was widespread in the San Antonio community. In 1779, when rumors reached San Antonio of a proposed Coahuila-based campaign against Lipan Apaches, Cabello reported that in contradiction to his own support of the plan, a majority of civilians in town were "very anxious about the harm which will befall their friends the Lipan Apaches," when soldiers and officers leaked the news to them. "For in spite of the injuries and damages suffered at the hands of these Indians," Cabello wrote, "so much affection is held for them, that I fear, and not without reason, that these people are capable of warning the Apaches of this news." That summer, Lipan chief El Joyoso visited the home of retired presidial captain Luis Antonio Menchaca to ask him where Spaniards in San Antonio stood vis-à-vis the situation in Coahuila. Menchaca, in the company of his Lipan friends, took the question directly to Governor Cabello. Before this gathering, Cabello agreed to support their permanent settlement in Texas under peace accords that would exchange defensive aid on the part of the Spaniards with the return of stolen horses and mules on the part of the Lipans. A month later, six hundred Apache men and women camped near San Antonio while their chiefs, El Joyoso, Josef Grande, Josef Chiquito, El Manco Roque, and Manteca Mucho, frustrated Cabello by their efforts to meet with Hasinai leaders. Yet, even then, Cabello had to admit that "these Indians were so human and were so admired by everyone here."[44]

Whereas the security of Apache women had once kept Apache men suspicious of Spaniards, now it had the power to bring them together—perhaps because both Apache and Spanish women now lived in the same locale around San Antonio. The bonds between Spanish soldiers and Apache warriors reflected their shared struggles to defend their families and communities, oftentimes side by side. During the marqués de Rubí's inspection of the Béxar presidio in 1767, a mustering of troops by Captain Menchaca had provided a startling sight for the marqués when the soldiers appeared in unofficial and rather unmilitary dress, each using handkerchiefs, lace, buttons, and gaudy ornaments to create his own individual colors and insignia—suggestive of the individual war dress and decoration of Lipan warriors alongside whom they had been fighting. The similarity of the Spaniards' dress to that of their native allies may have reached such a degree that it became a concern for higher authorities. In 1777, orders came down from the Comandancia General specifying the proper uniforms to be worn by the military on the northern frontier—from detailed description of the cut and color of coats and trousers to the two musketlike ornaments made of five threads of gold that might adorn their collars—as well as immediately prohibiting "bragging" on oval leather shields via "extravagant design." By regulation, only the name of the presidio, in medium letters, could appear on shields.[45]

Spanish-Apache friendships became multigenerational as time passed. Ten years after Captain Menchaca's soldiers had shocked Rubí with their native-inspired dress, Menchaca's son used his position as a powerful merchant and storekeeper in San Antonio to uphold his personal friendship with Lipan leaders, providing the Lipan men with food and goods for their wives and children, no matter what the official trade restrictions were. Thus, in 1779, when seven Lipan chiefs visited San Antonio, it was to his "very good friend" Luis Mariano Menchaca rather than to Governor Cabello that chief El Joyoso gave a ten-year-old captive Mayeye girl as a gift. The good faith shown by the San Antonio merchant did not merely help to supply Lipan families materially; Menchaca also was there at crucial moments to aid their safety and diplomacy. When one hundred Taovaya warriors came to the areas of San Antonio and La Bahía on a raiding spree for horses and Apaches in the summer of 1784, Menchaca quickly warned Lipan families and urged them to cut short a trip with other Apaches hunting for bison along the Guadalupe River. In 1786, after Tawakoni, Iscani, and Flechazo warriors attacked Lipan rancherías, San Antonio residents hastened to check on their Apache neighbors, only to find that the women, children, and elderly had been sent into the wilderness for safety while the men remained in such a state of mourning "that they [the Spaniards] hardly knew them, considering how humane and jovial they had been."[46]

As official Spanish-Apache relations soured in the wake of the Comanche peace, the personal power of individual male leaders first imperiled and then saved the situation by strategic use of the symbolism and reality of women's presence. Despite good relations between families of Lipan warriors and Spanish soldiers and citizens, in 1784 Governor Cabello joined his administrative peers in Coahuila and Chihuahua in declaring that Apaches deserved "no quarter" and encouraged Wichita and Comanche campaigns against Lipan bands. Four years earlier, when the small-pox epidemic swept through, this same man had said he hoped "that not a single Lipan Apache lives through it, for they are pernicious—despite their apparent peace-fulness and friendliness." In the same vein, following the Wichita raids on Lipan rancherías in 1786, Cabello used self-confessed "duplicity" and "tricks" in an at-tempt to set up chief Zapato Sas's bands for an ambush by forcing them to move away from the San Antonio vicinity and into the area of San Sabá—the site of the infamous 1758 Norteño attack. Promising Spanish military support and trade, but only if the Lipans told him where they would establish a permanent encampment, the governor then turned around and sent word to Comanche and Wichita warriors where to find them. Even as he schemed at their destruction, Cabello also demanded rituals of humiliation as "proof of peace" from Lipan leaders—nothing short of their surrender or military defeat would serve his purposes. In response, Lipan leaders washed their hands of Spanish officialdom, exasperated at the lack of respect shown them by Cabello. Precisely at the moment when a truce seemed impossible, though, Spanish and Apache leaders found new means of conciliation. A change in admin-istration at the end of 1786—with Governor Cabello replaced by Rafael Martínez Pacheco—ensured that the powder keg did not explode.[47]

Suddenly, Lipan leaders found their overtures about using a permanent mission and secular settlements to link their families more tightly with those of Spaniards welcomed by the new governor as well as by church and military leaders. Martínez Pacheco, a seasoned veteran of the Texas borderlands was a man Lipan headmen could trust. Apaches reenvisioned the mission-presidio complex at San Antonio as an ideal center from which to build a Spanish-Apache alliance. Martínez Pacheco agreed, reporting to his superiors that without a safe settlement for their families, the Apaches' subsistence would have to rely on horse and cattle raiding that in turn would hurt Spanish families. San Antonio's *cabildo* praised the permanent settle-ments arranged by Lipan leaders in conjunction with Governor Martínez Pacheco as a means of stopping the taking of *mesteñas* (wild, unbranded horses) and the illicit slaughtering of great numbers of domestic livestock and *orexanos* (wild, unbranded cattle) by Apache men seeking to feed their families. In an unusual twist, even Comanche leaders felt that such settlements would aid the peace, declaring they would attack Apaches only "as long as they do not find them settled in permanent towns with the Spanish." Finally, Lipan leaders could build upon ties of friendship and kinship with the San Antonio community and do so with the support of the Spanish administration.[48]

Relations of honor between individual Spanish and Lipan men proved strong enough to overcome Apaches' fears for the safety of their women and children. In 1787 soldiers from the Béxar presidio under the command of Lieutenant José Antonio Curbelo and *alférez* (sublieutenant) Manuel de Urrutia promptly went to the aid of families of Lipan Apaches moving from their gathering place at Arroyo del Atascoso to the town of San Antonio. Five chiefs, including Josef Chiquito and Zapato Sas, greeted them with "great affection as they had done on other occasions," expressed the wish that the Spaniards had given warning of their coming so that they could have ridden out to greet them properly with a delegation, and gratefully received the provisions of corn, biscuits, meat, candy, and tobacco brought for their women and children. In thanks for the promised escort, horses to carry their women and children, and the goodwill supplies, one of the leaders warmly welcomed them to his home "along with all the other Indians and children, amid great rejoicing." Evening prayers preceded a "great dance" lasting into the wee hours of the morning. Meanwhile, however, chief Casaca brought rumors from San Antonio that more soldiers were on the way to imprison and kill them, that other chiefs were even then imprisoned at the Béxar presidio, and that they would all be shackled and sent off to Veracruz and then to "some dwellings which were located in the middle of the ocean [Cuba], there to live out their days in labor," a warning that sent the women and children fleeing in tears. Seemingly, the Apaches' doubts had not all been put to rest, but after some hours, Curbelo, Urrutia, and the Lipan chiefs succeeded in calming everyone's ragged nerves.[49]

Ratifications of the new peace, embodied in a joint settlement, came in gendered form, much as they had at midcentury. Martínez Pacheco gave Lipan leaders gifts and supplies to aid in transporting their families to San Antonio, as well as recognizing chiefs with hats, flags, bridles, horses, and the services of an armorer to repair their rifles. The presence of Apache women within mission communities provided corollary female symbols of alliance. Lipan families already gathered at Mission San Antonio de Valero formed the primary link between independent Lipan rancherías and the Spanish community. Within two months, Martínez Pacheco could boast of the "first fruits of the harvest of the Lipan Apaches," citing the baptism of an Apache woman who was dying and wished to be "buried like the Spanish," as well as a captive Comanche woman who had accompanied Lipans into Mission Valero, who "asked to leave their midst and be baptized, in order to marry a Christian Indian from this presidio." Writing to his superiors with proof of Apache goodwill (and the success of his decision), Martínez Pacheco forwarded more success stories—all of women—with fray José Francisco López giving further evidence of such sincerity on the part of the Lipans congregated at Valero. The missionary also recorded the efforts of "heathen" parents to create ritual ties for their children within the Spanish community. Thus fray López recorded that a Lipan warrior named Santa Rosa and his wife, "She Whom They Saw with the Herbs," brought their daughter to him to be baptized as "María Manuela." In similar fashion, the missionary's baptismal entry for a Lipan boy named "Manuel Antonio" still identified his mother as "Tobacco" and his father as "He Who Fell Down," indicating their choice to remain unconverted even as they sought the recognition for their child. When the son of another Lipan couple died soon after his baptism, the child was given a "generous burial" by the parish priest that was attended by "all the important people" of the Spanish villa and presidio in an outpouring of support for their Lipan friends. Not only did Martínez Pacheco use the example of Apache women seeking baptism to win support for his diplomacy, he also rewarded the women themselves through the provision of supplies and gifts specifically designated for them—and by inference, their kin. The governor even purchased supplies of corn for the Apache mission community from the Hasinai villages, thereby perpetuating Lipan-Hasinai trade ties in a roundabout manner.[50]

In the first year of permanent settlement, Martínez Pacheco further conceived of a plan to have Lieutenant José Antonio Curbelo and *alférez* Manuel de Urrutia begin a cyclical pattern of living among the Lipan settlements for at least half of each month, in this way assuring the Apache families of the Spaniards' commitment to peace. In response, Lipan leaders and families greeted Urrutia every two weeks, expressing their joy in his company and their regret each time he had to leave. Rosters for the Béxar presidio through 1806 show up to twelve men regularly listed as "with the Lipanes," while officers such as Curbelo and Urrutia remained on permanent special assignment to the Lipan rancherías. These Spaniards formed lasting bonds with their Lipan compatriots and proved fiercely loyal whenever fabricated rumors of either Spanish duplicity or Apache violence threatened the peace. As they traveled back and forth between the Lipan and Spanish communities, the hospitality shown them by Lipan families bespoke the growing trust that developed the longer the Spanish men lived among them. The feelings were mutual, as Urrutia fondly described the "many good deeds which I have experienced among these people."[51]

Within this new context of trust and camaraderie, the loss and redemption of captive women and children linked Spanish and Apache peoples in new ways. When Apache rancherías suffered enemy raids, some Spaniards used diplomatic channels to effect the return of any captives taken. Thus, after Comanches attacked the ranchería of chief Cíbolo near San Sabá in 1787 and took a handful of women and children—including the sister of chief Agá—Lieutenant Curbelo filled the role of brother to his grief-stricken Lipan compatriots when the duty of escorting Comanche visitors out of San Antonio presented him with the opportunity to ransom a Lipan boy from his Comanche captors. Sadly, Curbelo never had the chance to return the boy to his family because the child fell ill and died on the way back to town; still, he consoled himself with the knowledge that the child had died having been baptized at his own request, saying "he wished to go with the God of the Spanish." His superiors tried to remind the lieutenant that they could not approve the "rescue of every heathen Indian, with which . . . we could be properly concerned"; Curbelo apparently had acted purely upon personal sentiment.[52]

It also became a weekly entry in the Béxar presidio log that *alférez* Urrutia arrived or departed in the company of Lipan chiefs with equal numbers of men and women coming to meet with the governor, receive gifts, and thus affirm their relations of honor. Urrutia and his men also shared in the Apaches' daily lives, escorting Lipan families when they went to trade horses in La Bahía, to hunt bison, to kill and butcher beef cattle, and to extract tame horses from *mesteña* herds as allowed by Commandant Juan de Ugalde's directives. If Urrutia was not in their ranchería at the moment they chose to pursue these trips, they simply rode to San Antonio to request his company. He and his men thus joined the group of men protecting the safe passage of Apache women and families in their travels. In honor of his inclusion within symbolic kin networks of their communities, Apache leaders such as Zapato Sas included Urrutia in the diplomatic envoy sent to parley with Ugalde when he traveled through the province in the summer of 1788. Clearly, the ties between Spanish and Lipan men had moved far beyond duty, to friendship and brotherhood —a transformation brought about by the intimate ties of shared kin-based community life. Spanish-Lipan relations offered a story of individual successes despite other regional and national failures across the northern provinces, as an insecure peace was found to be far preferable to incessant war for the Spanish and Apache families living as neighbors in south-central Texas.[53]

During this same period, Comanches were just beginning to employ their own "practices of peace" with Spaniards in Texas, following initial treaty negotiations in the fall of 1785. Comanche women and families predominated in Comanche leaders' expressions of alliance and reciprocity, though the political use of captive women never materialized as it had with the Wichitas. The respective peace treaties of 1785 and 1786 in Texas and New Mexico presented an interesting contrast between the needs and aims of Spanish and Comanche peoples in the two regions. In the meetings between Domingo Cabello and the three *capitanes chiquitos* in September 1785, one of the Spanish governor's stipulations was that eastern Comanches present Spanish captives for ransoming without offering them to any other nation— presumably in an attempt to curtail the exchange network that continued to send captive Spanish women and children to Wichita villages along the Red River. In contrast, although captives were sent from New Mexico, the peace agreements made there at the same time did not mention any requisite ransoms. One Comanche chief did return two captives "at no cost" as a goodwill gesture at meetings with the *alcalde mayor* of Taos, but when he compounded the gesture by also volunteering his own son and that of another leader as hostages, he was practicing a different kind of diplomatic ritual. Just as the chief informally cast captives and kin hostages in the same category, Spaniards' failure to mention the return of Spanish captives suggests that mechanisms were already in place in New Mexico for the exchange of such captives and were deemed sufficient within the terms of peace.[54]

Further emphasizing the contrast with New Mexico, treaty stipulations in Texas remained rhetorical; real ransoms of Spanish women held by Comanches occurred only occasionally and haphazardly, as individual opportunities presented themselves. Thus, in 1788, when Lieutenant Curbelo rescued the Apache boy from captivity while part of an official escort accompanying Comanches part of the way home, he also ransomed a young Spanish girl of fifteen or sixteen whom Martínez Pacheco had directed him to redeem during the trip (something the governor apparently had not been able to accomplish himself during the time the Comanche party stayed in San Antonio). Another time, during one of José Mares's trips through Comanchería to scout routes between San Antonio and Santa Fe, he managed to persuade chief Tociniqunita to accept eight horses in exchange for a female captive only after days of barter and negotiation, again at the instigation of Martínez Pacheco. Clearly, Texas officials could only pursue informal channels in their efforts to regain captive Spanish women and children—whatever treaties said, the balance of power rested firmly in Comanche hands. Spaniards' decreasing opportunities to ransom such women and children likely reflected social and economic transformations within Comanche societies as well. As the century drew to a close, Comanches increasingly adopted such captives into their families as a means of meeting rising labor demands, because their pastoral economy and trading networks continued to expand even while they lost people to smallpox. Captives then held far more labor value than any material reward from their sale, exchange, or ransom. Evea, the Comanche chief who had fought so valiantly with Governor Ripperdá for the return of his village's women in the 1770s, had two Lipan wives (both captured daughters of Apache chief Boruca) in the 1780s, signaling the shift from trade and ransom to adoption and marriage in the wake of the 1780 epidemic.[55]

Even if captive women did not emerge as might be expected in Spanish-Comanche diplomacy, Comanche women unexpectedly did. Strikingly for Comanches—whose familial, economic, and political hierarchies all confirmed male-dominated divisions of authority and allowed little public space for women in diplomacy—the very real presence of women played a decisive role in Comanche-Spanish relations once amity was achieved late in the 1780s. The importance that women would assume in these relations emerged over the months between the initial meeting of Governor Cabello and the three lower-ranking chiefs sent to San Antonio by Camisa de Hierro and Cabeza Rapada in the fall of 1785 and the ultimate ratification of peace agreements almost a year later. Within weeks of the delegation's departure in October, San Antonio was inundated with Comanche visitors, and the inclusion of women in almost every visiting party heralded a sea change in Comanche-Spanish politics in Texas. Initially, the presence of women among visiting Comanches signaled the peaceful intentions of parties whose approach to San Antonio might still be viewed as suspicious, while at the same time communicating a new Comanche trust in Spaniards that women could travel safely into their settlements.[56]

That said, two impetuous Comanche youths actually arrived before more senior men and women, seeking out their new Spanish friends for the first time, and their young age may have proven as significant as the gender of the visiting women in calming Spanish reactions to their approach. The boys arrived calling themselves the "brothers" of Spaniards and displaying diplomatic gifts from Spaniards as their passport to gain welcome to San Antonio. On December 9, 1785, the youths appeared outside of town, having been sent by the three *capitanes chiquitos* to inform Cabello that they and their wives had reached the first Comanche settlements and that reports of Spanish-Comanche negotiations were being received with pleasure.[57]

Outside the presidio, the two boys encountered six Spanish youths whose initial fears at the sight of Comanches on horseback, armed and painted, quickly gave way to relief when the two inquisitive visitors declared themselves "friends and brothers of the Spaniards," held out their hands, and tried to explain that they only wished to see the *capitán grande* of San Antonio for themselves. One wonders how all this was communicated beyond the customary goodwill evident in a handshake; surely there were some striking gestures and pantomimes of peace to accompany these words. Once two of the Spanish boys had been taken up on their horses by the Comanche youths, they all raced into town, shouting for all to hear that they were "friendly Comanches and brothers of the Spaniards," so that by the time they reached the door of Cabello's residence, quite a crowd had gathered. When Cabello too came out to see what all the commotion was about, he found himself taken up in "innumerable embraces" by the young men who displayed as their "credentials" a gun with a recognizable "fire-gilt shield" that the governor had given one of the *capitanes chiquitos* in October. When Pedro Vial and Francisco Xavier Chaves rushed up, they too exchanged the "most extreme expressions of joy" with the boys. During their seven-day stay, the "very rational and polite" young men found themselves fed and housed with translator André Courbière and entertained by the townspeople, particularly when they were taken to dances, where they "went wild with joy, admitting they had not thought the Spaniards were such a good people."[58]

A Comanche couple arrived two weeks later, also curious about their new allies, and they too first encountered a Spaniard outside of town who traveled with them into the settlement. The man not only brought his wife as a sign of peaceful intent but also wore a white scarf upon his head onto which he had painted a red cross (presumably modeled after the Burgundian flag). The cross, he hoped, would signal his identity as an ally of Spaniards and gain them entry to San Antonio. Perhaps as insurance, though, he also carried no gun but only a pike, a quiver of arrows with its bow, and a spear—an outfit Cabello deemed "so unarmed" that it elicited his respect for the man's daring to travel with so little to defend himself and his wife. The man responded that his lack of arms indicated that he trusted their safety among "brother" Spaniards. In his exchanges with the couple, Cabello further noted that the man and woman were "of very good appearance and presence," conveying to the governor both the high status they must enjoy within Comanche society and the fact that it was "indispensable to entertain them with the hospitality appropriate." They too found housing in Courbière's home, met with Cabello, received generosity from the San Antonio residents, and attended the town's bullfights and festivities in celebration of the feast of the Virgin of Guadalupe. The Virgin, whose image had once graced the banners of diplomatic expeditions into Indian lands, now presided over an entirely new scene of peaceful and hospitable European-Indian contacts.[59]

Visiting parties of Comanche men and women continued to grow in size and number. Just as one group would leave, another would arrive to take its place. In January of 1786, nineteen Comanche men and three women led by one of the three *capitanes chiquitos* arrived outside San Antonio, fired salutes to announce their arrival (as was customary when entering their rancherías), and by the time they approached the gates of the presidio and Cabello's residence, found themselves accompanied by numerous people celebrating their welcome. Perhaps as an advertisement of the goods from hunts and raids they had for trade, the visiting Comanches had brought chamois, bison hides—and two small captive Apache girls—to exchange for horses.[60]

Again and again, the governor marveled at the arrival of small parties of Comanche men and women, undaunted by the dangers that kept most Spaniards within the limits of the San Antonio villa. He periodically attempted to "warn them concerning the strange method of their coming in such small parties, exposing themselves to being found by the Lipans," while never grasping that it was he who

Comanches of western Texas "dressed as when they are at peace," likely drawn in San Antonio de Béxar. The presence of the woman and the baby in the cradleboard appear to be part of the presentation of peaceful intent. Watercolor by Lino Sánchez y Tapia after the original sketch by José María Sánchez y Tapia. Courtesy of the Gilcrease Museum, Tulsa, Oklahoma.

was the "stranger" to the world of Comanche dominion. The rather disgruntled governor seemed unable to appreciate fully the power of the nation with which he was now dealing—one whose women as well as men could travel with impunity between their rancherías and his capital.[61]

By March, the number of Comanche visits had persuaded Cabello to contract the building of a guest house on land neighboring the home of André Courbière. The structure would be designed with four large rooms so that Indian diplomats of different bands could stay there at the same time. In a further bow to Comanche custom (most likely at Courbière's suggestion), the site for the structure was selected not only for its close proximity to San Antonio's primary interpreter but also because it stood along the San Antonio River, a location that would allow the daily baths demanded by Comanche hygiene.[62]

Suddenly, however, the stream of visitors dissipated, and no Comanche was seen after April. The six-month time frame for treaty ratification came and went, and Cabello began to wonder, nervously, what was afoot. In late summer, Comanche women finally arrived to break the silence, bringing word that negotiations between Texas Spaniards and eastern Comanches must wait. Cabeza Rapada had died in battle against Mescalero Apaches along the Pecos River, Comanche rancherías were in deep mourning for his loss, and Camisa de Hierro had since departed to avenge his death, they explained. In the interim, Cabello attempted to impress the Co-manche women and the men who accompanied them with a show of the "boxes and bundles of goods" that he had designated to "regale" them and gave gifts to take with them on their journey home, where he hoped they would promote the benefits to be had at San Antonio.[63]

At the end of August, another delegation brought distinguished Comanche leaders —though not principal *capitanes*—to San Antonio for the promised parleys, celebra-tions, and gift exchange necessary to ratify formally the peace agreements discussed almost a year before. In his stead (again), Camisa de Hierro sent three chiefs—two from the October meetings, and the other his "most beloved" brother (though whether a comrade or actual affinal sibling remained unclear). Apparently, within Comanche hierarchy, the governor of Texas did not hold equal rank or weight to a man like Camisa de Hierro. The lower-ranking leaders came accompanied by nine-teen warriors and seventeen women, however—a well-balanced delegation accord-ing to gender.[64]

Yet, Cabello soon discovered that it was not only Cabeza Rapada's death but also his own failure to meet Comanche rules of diplomacy that had kept Comanche men and women away all summer. In meetings that extended over three weeks, the principal men castigated the Spanish governor because he had offered them no return for the numerous efforts so many of their men and women had made to travel to him. San Antonio residents and soldiers had housed, fed, entertained, and escorted their Comanche guests, but still Cabello's failure to reciprocate appropri-ately denied Comanche families and communities the opportunity to demonstrate hospitality and thereby maintain balance within the two peoples' fledgling relations of honor. Such relations were not fixed by a one-time agreement, but constantly measured and tested, and the obligations of reciprocity had to be faithfully culti-vated. In fact, the Comanche men explained, their visit to San Antonio was partly occasioned by the need to warn Cabello that young warriors might raid the settle-ment in response to this dishonor.[65]

The big presentation of gifts that Cabello had long planned also proved insuffi-cient. The three Comanche chiefs and the members of their accompanying party happily received muskets, gunpowder, bullets, and a multitude of other gifts. Yet, the governor made no mention of establishing trade with Comanches despite reports, whose import Cabello ignored, that while Comanches were conspicuously absent from San Antonio they were frequenting Taovaya towns for exchanges with Louisiana traders. Worse still, the gifts intended to recognize the standing of Comanche chiefs were riddled with errors. Cabello chose not to give them the "Medal of Merit" reserved for Camisa de Hierro, only showing it to them as a supposed enticement for the principal chief's own visit. Meanwhile, the customary military uniforms did not fit the tall frame of Camisa de Hierro's brother, and the headmen pointedly refused to accept silver-handled staffs of command and returned two previously given to them. By explanation, they told of elderly women at their rancherías who had experienced divinations warning them that "whenever they would break or lose their staff they would die." Giving gifts endowed with personal power could threaten the very relations they were meant to unite if the "medicine" of batons of office proved more hazardous than beneficial.[66]

Most important, though the governor gave cursory recognition to the women who accompanied Comanche delegates to diplomatic conferences by including them in gift distributions, he remained inattentive to the social and communal aspects of Comanche diplomacy. Relations of honor required balanced reciprocity and thereby required him to send representatives into Comanchería. Cabello wrote of his awareness that "it is necessary to treat them with great affection and consistency because they are of an extremely delicate nature and will not put up with any rudeness," but he fell short in discerning which actions would be most likely construed as rudeness by Comanche custom.[67] On the last day before the party's departure, Camisa de Hierro's brother returned to the subject, asking that Cabello send, along with all the gifts and supplies to be transported to Comanchería, several Spaniards who could visit their rancherías. Suggesting that a lengthy visit was desired by Comanches, the chief explained that the Spaniards could stay until Camisa de Hierro chose to go to San Antonio, at which point they could return in his company. Implicitly, he also made the visit a condition to be met before the principal chief would consider a trip of his own to the Spanish town. Cabello, however, would only say no, claiming that a debilitating lack of horses and finances made such a trip impossible.[68]

As with Lipan Apaches, Comanches' perspectives on Spanish leadership underwent a rapid shift once Rafael Martínez Pacheco assumed the governorship by January 1787—a shift easily measured in the sharp rise of Comanche women and families who converged on San Antonio once news reached them of the change of authority. After the last visit with Cabello in September, Comanches had not visited San Antonio at all, and Martínez Pacheco later reported to the commandant general that he had been told that their absence "was nothing other than their displeasure with my predecessor the last time they were at this capital just after the peace agreements." In the meantime, however, Pedro Vial had traveled through Comanchería to chart a route from San Antonio to Santa Fe with the aid of Comanches— providing at least one required return visit to Comanche rancherías. Martínez Pacheco went on to argue that the quality of trade goods and diplomatic gifts that he had found in the San Antonio stores had to improve, for "what is given to each one of the Indians and to their chiefs is not worth their trouble to come from so many leagues away with the enormous hardships they face and the dangers from their enemies." Already the new governor seemed more perceptive than his predecessor.[69]

In response, Comanche leaders arrived in increasing numbers and brought larger numbers of women and children with them. From Martínez Pacheco's tenure on, Comanche leaders replaced the one or two women who had previously accompanied parties to San Antonio with whole families and family bands in their traveling parties. The difference was striking. In October 1787, for instance, four chiefs— Soquina, Sojaís, Guaquanquan, and Cavellera de Baquera—along with ten principal men, thirty warriors, twenty-three women, and six children from eastern Comanche bands arrived in San Antonio. In January 1788, the governor recorded the arrival of twenty-two chiefs—seventeen of whom had never come to San Antonio before— along with thirty warriors, thirty-four women, and seven children. The seventeen new visitors came at the invitation of the other fifteen, "who told them about the good lodging and treatment they had received from Spaniards." Once in town, the Comanche men and women found the new hospitality house ready for their use. The guest house was always outfitted and supplied with corn, beef, dried meat, squash, tortillas, salt, sugar candy, firewood, candles, copper pots, barrels, basins, and "two men to attend them" as cooks and servants during their stay. Soldiers dispensed separate supplies upon their departure for the journey home. Monthly gift lists indicated that visitors received clothes, hats, shoes, cloth, blankets, ornaments, spurs, saddle trappings, bridles, ammunition, tobacco, horses, and the services of town merchants and artisans, most popularly the armorer, who offered to repair the Comanches' rifles. Texas Spaniards were getting much better at Comanche protocols and obligations of generosity.[70]

In return, Spanish expeditions into Comanchería sought out Comanche women's hospitality, designing their routes to pass through Comanche rancherías upon which they relied for food, shelter, and guidance. As Spaniards traveled between Comanche encampments, they were never alone, since men and women provided them with "an escort to accompany them to the place where the escort can be relieved by warriors and guides from another ranchería." During each stop, Spaniards

Comanche Village, Women Dressing Robes and Drying Meat, *by George Catlin, 1834–35. Courtesy of the Smithsonian American Art Museum, Washington, D.C.*

might share many rituals confirming honor with Comanche men, but women played crucial roles in the guidance and hospitality Spaniards enjoyed while visiting their communities. On his first trip back from San Antonio to Santa Fe in 1786–87, for example, when chief Soquina pledged to accompany Pedro Vial all the way from his ranchería to Santa Fe, the party quickly swelled to include Soquina, three other chiefs, two warriors, and all their wives. As they traveled, each Comanche encampment welcomed their arrival by raising a Spanish flag and providing food, lodging, smoking, care for horses, and long talks into the night. The ability of Comanche men to offer such hospitality relied on the labors and provisions of women. By the time José Mares arrived in San Antonio from Santa Fe later in the fall of 1787, chiefs Soquina, Sojaís, Guaquanquan, and Cavellera de Baquera, ten principal men, thirty-eight warriors, twenty-three women, and six children had chosen to join the escort party for the small, four-man Spanish expedition. In the end, Spaniards concluded, this kind of "hospitality shown to visitors" and "the valor they display which is admirable even in their women" equaled in importance the number of Comanche warriors and the extent of the lands they occupied in marking the Comanche nation as superior to all others.[71]

Once Comanche leaders refocused on taking advantage of the rapprochement with Spaniards, women came to San Antonio not merely to signal peace but in order to trade goods, receive gifts, and translate communications. The inclusion of women to "express friendship" became a particular source of material profit.[72] The ritual return from Spaniards for such female affirmations of Comanche amity came in the form of gifts, food, and other "necessities for their maintenance." Monthly logs and diaries of events maintained at Béxar through the 1810s recorded the daily arrivals of native visitors (with their number and sex carefully noted) coming "in the practice of peace" and requiring customary presentations of food and gifts.[73] Spanish hospitality customs that developed under Martínez Pacheco's direction benefited the San Antonio community as well, since he purchased many of the supplies and gifts within town, and the services called on the skills of tailors, armorers or blacksmiths, cooks, female tortilla makers, and interpreters. Rosters for the Béxar presidial company also listed men with permanent assignments each month to interpreter duties, "housing Indians," and escort units. At any time, one-quarter of the presidial force might be employed to accompany large parties of Comanche families much of the way home. More and more, the lists also detailed gifts and services specifically requested for or by Comanche women. Tailors received clothing orders from women as well as men—with forty-two ponchos made for women and their children who visited one winter, for example. In similar fashion to men who brought their rifles to be serviced, Comanche women brought for repair the "pots in which their meals are cooked."[74]

In return, Spanish residents traveled into Comanchería to share in bison hunts and *mesteña* roundups with Comanche families, exchanging goods to such an extent that Indian products became a staple of San Antonio trade to Saltillo. Trade extended to the Nacogdoches community as well, as when "the Indian María" along with her husband, Comanche chief Soquina, two principal men, seven warriors, thirty-two women, and twenty-two children rode into town seeking to sell bison hides. The tone of the Spanish report and the reference to María by name implied that Spaniards knew her as well as they did Soquina.[75]

One of the most fascinating symbolic reversals within Comanche-Spanish relations came when Spanish settlements in Texas became sanctuaries for eloping Comanche couples caught in domestic wife stealing. In 1788, for instance, Governor Martínez Pacheco recorded that three Comanche men and one woman appeared in San Antonio, and that one of the men, the youngest brother of principal chief Guacuanquacis, sought a safe haven because he had "stolen" the woman, and he and she feared "that those of their nation might kill them, as they are used and accustomed to doing to those who steal their women." Years later, another couple, one of whom was again the child of a high-ranking Comanche leader, rushed to the protection of the commander at the La Bahía presidio. This time, the daughter of chief Chihuahua had eloped with a young man and, after deciding to cut their visit short at the presidio, the pair effected a quick escape with the aid of three horses left hobbled nearby (much to the dismay of an unwitting Spanish accomplice). Social controls internal to their communities had so infused the meanings and obligations of diplomatic alliances that the children of Comanche leaders could appeal to their fathers' Spanish allies in securing aid from outside of Comanche society.[76]

Soldiers and warriors could broker a truce from the battlefield, but it took women to solidify and maintain a peace. Because hostility had defined the interactions between Spanish and native men in Texas, women often fell captive to one group or another and became bargaining chips for mediation. It is telling that the use of women in the latter half of the century predominated among Apaches, Wichitas, and Comanches who shared the most volatile relations with Spaniards. Native diplomats focused on the economic benefits to be gained through the ransoming of captured women, while Spanish captive diplomacy valued and manipulated hostage women for their political worth. In total, because they all learned to associate women with diplomacy, a signification of peace extended even to the exchange of captive women. In such a context, the willingness to send female family members into another's company and care served as a significant act of trust between men. Tying the fate of wives and children together in neighboring or joint settlements made real the gestures of symbolic alliance. Even as men of competing Spanish, Caddo, Wichita, Apache, and Comanche groups used women as figurative and literal currency in attempts to assert power vis-à-vis one another, they also forged bonds of alliance through women's marriage, mediation, and hospitality.

Conclusion

On the surface, it might seem that by the 1780s the signification of peace in the form of a woman had come a long way from the power invoked by the Virgin Mary's image on Spanish banners in the 1690s. Yet, in many ways, individual native systems of conveying peace through the presence of women, brokering alliance through networks of real and fictive kinship, and maintaining political and economic ties through joint family settlement varied little in their core functions over the century. Of course, the distinct cultural and political economies of Caddos, Cantonas, Payayas, Apaches, Wichitas, and Comanches had determined the spectrum of practices and beliefs governing those diplomatic systems. In their turn, Spaniards had read, understood, and responded to those controls in different ways, at different times, with different peoples—with resultant relations often riding upon their successes and failures in understanding the world of native politics to which they were beholden for peace.

If we scan across the North American continent in the eighteenth century, cross-cultural relations in Texas appear far different from those in other regions. To the west, Pueblos had allowed Spaniards to return to New Mexico following the short-lived success of their 1680 Revolt, and chastened missionaries and settlers tempered the religious and labor demands made on their Pueblo neighbors. Yet, Spanish enslavement and Indian captivity together created a vast network of human exchange that would disrupt innumerable families and bands while incorporating untold numbers into the servile underclass of Spanish society. In the western region of the Great Lakes, called the *pays d'en haut* by the French, Frenchmen had learned the rhythms of calumet ceremonies and the rhetoric of trade jargons in order to foster a mutually lucrative fur trade network with numerous Indian nations. With French settlement focused far to the east in the St. Lawrence valley, it would be primarily unlicensed traders known as *coureurs de bois* and a handful of Jesuits who infiltrated these regions to the west. Establishing claim to Louisiana, French traders and agents extended their networks to the south among the Choctaws, Caddos, Wichitas, and others.

Through commercial exchange, mutual accommodation and mutual dependence went hand in hand for Indian and French peoples. Meanwhile, along the Atlantic, the English had made little if any effort to learn native languages, ascertain native interests, or recognize native rights to the land. With steady immigration consisting increasingly of families, the English population grew rapidly, together with its demand for land and the force to take it. Having destroyed the littoral nations through a combination of deadly disease, fiery warfare, and ravaging slave raids, the English in the eighteenth century were turning their energies toward the more powerful interior nations of Iroquois, Shawnees, Creeks, and Cherokees. Such efforts eventually encouraged the establishment of an independent United States and the beginning of new policies to dispossess eastern-dwelling Indian peoples of their homes and lands by force and coercion. The often Anglo-centered narrative of conquest, colonization, and expansion in early America thus differs markedly from Spanish circumstances in Texas, where survival was contingent upon accommodating Indian nations with power greater than their own.[1]

The stories of Indian-Spanish relations across Texas and over the duration of the eighteenth century add up to quite a distinctive sum within the worlds of early North American historiography. Elsewhere, scholars have already found European discourses of discovery, exploration, conquest, and settlement to be gendered and sexualized with the projection into the "New World" of "Old World" notions of masculinity and femininity.[2] European structures of colonial authority in other regions of the Americas asserted dominion through cultural prescriptions and interventions into institutional and domestic life with different consequences for indigenous men and women. In seeking to understand these consequences of colonial expansion, scholars have studied changes in gendered valuation of labor, control of resources, political participation, and domains of status and authority.[3] All of these areas witnessed to some degree the power of Christian and commercial European influences to transform and sometimes derail native gender systems. Some of the most prolific scholarly debates have focused on the ways in which colonizers viewed and judged indigenous and enslaved peoples in gender-specific ways, in the process constructing categories of "white," "black," "Indian," "savage," and "race" through gender and sex differences.[4] Concepts such as hybridity and the categorization of unions between European men and Indian women as *métissage* and *mestizaje* and of their offspring as *métis* and *mestizo* further cast colonial relations as sexual exchange and mediation. These concepts, in turn, complicate distinctions of culture and race.[5]

Race would become as important in Texas as it already had become in Virginia, New Mexico, and Louisiana, but that would not happen until the nineteenth century. In eighteenth-century Texas, native concepts of gender cut across what in other areas of early America were European perceptions of racial difference because native institutions of kin-based social and political order predominated. The appearance of gendered standards and practices in political economies of gift giving and hospitality, alliances instituted in joint family settlements, honors and dishonors inherent in violence and war, exchanges of women through intermarriage, captivity and hostage taking, and political relationships conceived through fictive and real kinship marked the power of diverse Indian peoples and nations, each in their own way, to frame diplomatic negotiations by their own rules. It is not that race was not there—of course it was; it had become a central component of Spanish worldviews well before the eighteenth century—but gender prevailed over it, because native controls prevailed over those of Spaniards. The Spanish documentary record makes this clear: they did not get to call their own tune even in their own record books.

If Indian dominance was especially clear in Texas, it was likely not unique. Indian peoples throughout the Americas continued to exert power over their would-be European conquerors into the nineteenth century. The view from Texas should push us to interrogate the assumptions we bring to the reading and writing of European-Indian relations and the history of early America, which despite our best efforts are often still freighted with unspoken or unconscious presumptions of European technological superiority, Indian "primitivism," Indian resistance, and implicit, corresponding European dominance. To paraphrase David Weber, what many North Americans remember about Indian-Spanish relations begins and ends with the conquistadors—despite the fact that in the 1790s, independent Indians still controlled over half of Spanish America. Perhaps that might not seem unexpected, given that the Spanish government lost control of its finances, its vast bureaucracy, and its own subjects. Yet, we err similarly with the history of European-Indian relations across the continent. The story of early North America too often reduces to a preordained chronicle of the pre–United States. We are, after all, storytellers, and stories demand a narrative arc; surely the narrative of early America ends with the creation of the United States. In a form of "upstreaming," that framework inevitably misshapes and misdirects our reading of documents, events, and peoples in the sixteenth, seventeenth, eighteenth, and even nineteenth centuries. By the 1790s, much more than half of North America was in native hands. How can we possibly understand that world on its own terms—terms far removed from the assumptions that tell us that defeat was inevitable for Native Americans, whether by disease or war, and that the only sensible narrative arc is one of declension, albeit with notable interludes of noble last stands?[6]

In December of 1819, Juan Antonio Padilla painted a clear picture of the state of Spanish-Indian relations in Texas as Spanish rule drew to a close in Mexico. After an assessment of the position of each Indian nation in Texas, he concluded that the province of Texas remained "all under the domination of the barbarian." "Barbarians," or *indios bárbaros*, still meant independent Indians with commercial and military might. Moreover, "domination" did not necessarily mean war or hostility in clear-cut terms. From San Antonio southward, small Spanish settlements dotted the landscape like isolated islands in a vast sea over which Indians reigned, making them easy targets for raids. The peace treaties in Texas had the effect of encouraging mounted Apache and Comanche raiders to take aim at Coahuila and Nuevo León rather than at their Texas allies. Native powers thus still failed to see Spaniards as one united nation.[7]

Over the first two decades of the nineteenth century, reverberations of Mexico's War for Independence soon engulfed the province of Texas, leading to round after round of civil disturbances among royalists, rebels, and Anglo-American interlopers from the neighboring United States. When Spanish trade obligations fell apart because of disruptions in production and supply lines caused by the war, native groups often divided along family band lines, so that some remained friendly to Spanish interests while others returned to taking by force what they could no longer receive through peace policies. Those who stood by their Spanish allies and the Spanish Crown offered military aid against Anglo-American invaders and Mexican insurgents alike. In 1806, thirty-three Comanche chiefs and two hundred warriors pledged their assistance to Governor Antonio Cordero when Anglo-American soldiers stood poised on the Texas-Louisiana border ready to assert with force that U.S. boundary claims extended to the Rio Grande. Ties between Governor Cordero and Comanche chief Sargento grew so close that Sargento adopted Cordero's name to signal brotherhood. In 1810, Cordero lent official sanction and prestige to forty Comanche warriors under *capitán grande* Sargento's leadership by commissioning the men with Spanish military uniforms. Meanwhile, local Spaniards in the Nacogdoches area found sanctuary among Caddo neighbors and allies when insurrections turned against them. Once the war ended with Mexican independence in 1821, however, no matter which side they had favored, Caddo, Lipan, and Comanche leaders traveled at the invitation of Agustín de Iturbide to the Mexican capital in Monterrey to renew peace relations between their nations and the newly independent Mexico. Their dominion continued long after as well. Historian Andrés Reséndez points out that among the competing nations in nineteenth-century Texas, Comanchería defended its territorial boundaries better than did Mexico and maintained its sovereignty longer than did the Texas Republic.[8]

It was not until well into the nineteenth century that Anglo-Americans built up sufficient numbers and force to establish dominion and, in turn, to categorize all native peoples as a single, subordinate group to be either removed or exterminated— and even then they would do so primarily by the power of germs, not steel. As Anglo-Americans slowly expanded their grasp in the region, so too did they bring a new racial element to the foreground of the region's cross-cultural struggles, giving primacy to concepts and expressions of Anglo, Indian, and Hispanic "races." Almost another entire century would elapse, though, before Anglo-American dominance was firmly entrenched and native controls declined in Texas. As that process unfolded over the nineteenth century, idioms of cross-cultural relations changed so that gender continued to serve an important role, but simply as it structured notions of racial identity and hierarchy. Only then did gender assume the function most commonly associated with it in the colonial context—that of marking difference, of distinguishing the defiled from the sacred, and the barbarous from the civilized. Only then did gender supply a foundation for invidious hierarchies of difference and discourses of race. If that process was at no time simple, quick, or manifest, then surely it was not destiny.

notes

INTRODUCTION

1. Memorial of the College of Zacatecas to King Ferdinand VI, Jan. 15, 1750, in Leutenegger and Habig, *Texas Missions of the College of Zacatecas*, 54; Pedro de Rivera, "Diario y Derrotero" [Diary and Itinerary], in J. Jackson, *Imaginary Kingdom*, 41; report by Tomás Felipe Winthuysen, Aug. 19, 1744, Béxar Archives, Center for American History, University of Texas at Austin (hereafter cited as BA); strength reports and daily records of occurrences for the cavalry company of the royal presidio of San Antonio de Béxar for Jan. 1781, Mar. and Apr. 1783, BA; marqués de Rubí, Dictamen of Apr. 10, 1768, in J. Jackson, *Imaginary Kingdom*, 181–82. Historian Peter Gerhard argues that "In no other colonial gobierno [area ruled by a governor] of America was the Spanish presence so tenuous as in Texas. Uninterrupted Spanish settlement here lasted just over a century, and it was confined to a few frontier outposts surrounded by 'unreduced' and often hostile Indians. The area under control was not always the same, as missions and garrisons were founded, moved about, and abandoned." Gerhard, *North Frontier of New Spain*, 335–38.

2. In Rubí's plan, implemented in the royal "Regulations" of 1772, San Antonio de Béxar and La Bahía would be the only towns above the line of presidios, spread at one-hundred-mile intervals from the Gulf of Mexico to California, to mark the northern limits of Spanish dominion and defense. Marqués de Rubí, Dictamen of Apr. 10, 1768, in J. Jackson, *Imaginary Kingdom*, 181, 185, 195.

3. Morfi, *History of Texas*, 2:273; "Report of the Journey Made by Don Nicolás de Lafora in Company with Marqués de Rubí to Review the Interior Presidios," in Lafora, *Frontiers of New Spain*, 185–86.

4. Cabeza de Vaca, *Account*; Adorno, "Negotiation of Fear," 176; Wade, "Go-Between," 333, 339.

5. Chipman, *Spanish Texas*, 205–6; Tjarks, "Comparative Demographic Analysis of Texas." See Weber, *Spanish Frontier in North America*, 195, for comparison with the population of other provinces.

6. Teja, "Spanish Colonial Texas," 114, 120–23, "St. James at the Fair," and *San Antonio de Béxar*; J. Jackson, *Los Mesteños*; Weber, *Spanish Frontier in North America*, 192.

7. The work offering the best, indeed magisterial, narration of the cross-cultural relations of Spanish and Indian peoples in Texas (as well as New Mexico) during this period is John, *Storms Brewed in Other Men's Worlds*.

8. Richter in fact makes this statement to measure some improvement in perspectives on early America that in the past did not recognize the displacement and dispossession of Indian populations at European hands, instead seeing only a grand narrative of "civilization's" progressive spread across the continent. Richter, *Facing East from Indian Country*, 8. See also White, *Middle Ground*, ix, 52. James Axtell asserts that historians "must imaginatively ignore our knowledge of the denouement." Axtell, *Invasion Within*, 5.

9. Guy and Sheridan, "On Frontiers," 4, 15; Baretta and Markoff, "Civilization and Barbarism," 590; Merrill, "Cultural Creativity and Raiding Bands"; Slatta, "Spanish Colonial Military Strategy and Ideology"; K. Jones, "Comparative Raiding Economies." See also the critical response of Wunder and Hämäläinen, "Of Lethal Places and Lethal Essays," to Adelman and Aron, "From Borderlands to Borders."

10. Shoemaker, *Strange Likeness*, 4–8.

11. DeMallie, "Kinship," 307; Albers, "Symbiosis, Merger, and War," 98–99; Lévi-Strauss, *Elementary Structures of Kinship*. Studies that have explored kin-based political interactions between Indians and Europeans include G. Anderson, *Kinsmen of Another Kind*; Thorne, *Many Hands of My Relations*; and White, *Middle Ground*.

12. Shoemaker, "Categories," 51; Sabo, "Structure of Caddo Leadership," 163; DeMallie, "Kinship," 321–24, 328–30.

13. Interestingly, Tessie Liu persuasively argues for the links between racial thinking and kinship as principles of social organization if one considers how race can be a synonym for house, kindred, or family and how ideas of bloodlines and lineages stratified European societies. See Liu, "Race and Gender," and "Teaching the Differences." For racial categorizations in Spanish America, see Pagden, *Fall of Natural Man*; Mörner, *Race Mixture*; Cope, *Limits of Racial Domination*; R. Jackson, *Race, Caste, and Status*; Gutiérrez, *When Jesus Came*; and Estrada de Gerlero, "Representation of 'Heathen Indians.' "

14. Weber, "Bourbons and Bárbaros," 80, and *Bárbaros*, 15; Gradie, "Discovering the Chichimecas."

15. Shoemaker, *Strange Likeness*, 125–40, and "How Indians Got to Be Red"; Merrell, "Racial Education of the Catawbas"; Fur, " 'Some Women Are Wiser' "; Albers, "Symbiosis, Merger, and War"; Lévi-Strauss, *Elementary Structures of Kinship*; Donna J. Haraway, " 'Gender' for a Marxist Dictionary," in *Simians, Cyborgs, and Women*, 143; De Lauretis, "The Technology of Gender," in *Technologies of Gender*, 2–3; Scott, "Gender: A Useful Category of Historical Analysis"; Claassen and Joyce, *Women in Prehistory*; K. Brown, *Good Wives, Nasty Wenches*, 4.

16. Brooks, *Captives and Cousins*; Gutiérrez, "Honor Ideology," and *When Jesus Came*. Of significance most recently has been the recognition that no single honor code governed the values and relations of those societies, but rather there were (in the words of Steve Stern) "several overlapping yet distinct honor/shame codes in play at various levels of the color-class hierarchy." S. Stern, *Secret History of Gender*, 302. See also Johnson and Lipsett-Rivera, *Faces of Honor*; and Twinam, *Public Lives, Private Secrets*.

17. This diversity originated in a variety of linguistic stocks including Tunican, Caddoan,

Uto-Aztekan, Atakapan, and Athapaskan, while over six hundred named Indian groups appear in the documentary records of eighteenth-century Texas. Lipan Apache oral traditions record that they still communicated with Comanches through signs in the nineteenth century, after more than one hundred years of contact. Collins, "Named Indian Groups in Texas"; Opler, *Myths and Legends*, 237–38, 252–53. Similarly, George Kendall recorded that, upon encountering Wichitas in 1840, only two or three "had picked up a smattering of Spanish" and relied on signs and gestures to communicate with the Anglo-Americans of Kendall's expedition. Kendall, *Narrative of the Texan Santa Fé Expedition*, 170–71. Damián Massanet [Mazanet] to Carlos de Sigüenza, 1690, in Bolton, *Spanish Exploration in the Southwest*, 374; Solís, "Solís Diary of 1767," 26; strength report and record of daily occurrences of the cavalry company of the royal presidio of San Antonio de Béxar for Jan. 1781, BA.

18. Governor of Louisiana, Luis de Unzaga y Amezaga, to Athanase de Mézières, Nov. 29, 1770, and report by De Mézières of the expedition to Cadodachos, Oct. 29, 1770, in Bolton, *Athanase de Mézières*, 1:232, 210; Opler, *Myths and Legends*, 7. Many Indian groups in Texas maintained rules similar to that which Gordon Sayre termed "transparent signification," in which words had to be supported by actions for Europeans to gain native acceptance and trust. In a similar vein, Sayre argues that in much European writing can be found an assumption that human nature is the same for the French and the Indians—for example, beliefs that everyone is a bit vain, or desires status and respect, and that differences only appear in how societies express or structure that vanity, status, or respect. Sayre, *Les Sauvages Américains*, 177, 194, 267. For discussion of cross-cultural communication and interaction in forms other than language, see Dening, *Performances*; Todorov, *Conquest of America*; Lockhart, "Sightings"; MacGaffey, "Dialogues of the Deaf"; and Greenblatt, *New World Encounters*. See also Kertner, *Ritual, Politics, and Power*, 30.

19. Burkholder, "Honor and Honors in Colonial Spanish America"; Lourie, "Society Organized for War"; McAlister, "Social Structure and Social Change"; Alonso, *Thread of Blood*; S. Stern, *Secret History of Gender*, 151–64; Secoy, *Changing Military Patterns*; Newcomb, "Re-examination of the Causes"; Kavanagh, *Comanche Political History*; La Vere, *Caddo Chiefdoms*; C. Carter, *Caddo Indians*; G. Anderson, *Indian Southwest*.

PART I

1. The following reconstruction and those that will introduce Parts II and III are written in the spirit of Daniel Richter's call for historians to shift their perspectives in analyzing contacts and interactions between Indians and Europeans in early North America so that they, the historians, stand metaphorically in Indian country, looking over the shoulders of Indians at unfurling events to visualize those events as they might have appeared before Indian eyes and to understand how those eyes made sense of what they were seeing. Richter, *Facing East from Indian Country*, 11–12, 19–32, 36–39. As Richter points out, however, our ability to imagine this Indian perspective is limited by barriers of time and culture as well as the dearth of records left by Indians themselves. My reconstruction of events in 1686 relies

primarily upon the accounts written by three members of Sieur de la Salle's expedition, Recollect priest Father Anastase Douay, La Salle's older brother abbé Jean Cavelier, and Henri Joutel, who served as La Salle's post commander at Fort Saint Louis on the Texas coast. See Douay, "Narrative"; Cavelier, *Journal of Jean Cavelier*; and Joutel, *La Salle Expedition to Texas*. The reconstruction of the ways in which Caddos might have viewed and interpreted those events relies upon the works of a variety of historians, anthropologists, and archaeologists. See Swanton, *Source Material*; Wyckoff and Baugh, "Early Historic Hasinai Elites"; Magnaghi, "Changing Material Culture"; Sabo, "Reordering Their World," "Encounters and Images," and "Rituals of Encounter"; C. Carter, *Caddo Indians*; and La Vere, *Caddo Chiefdoms*.

2. Baugh, "Regional Polities and Socioeconomic Exchange"; Krieger, *Culture Complexes and Chronology*. When the remnants of the Hernando de Soto expedition, under the command of Luis de Moscoso after Soto's death, reached the lands of the Caddo, they found "some turquoises and cotton blankets which the Indians gave them to understand by signs were brought from the west." Clayton, Knight, and Moore, *De Soto Chronicles*, 1:148.

3. "Canneci" was the Caddoan name for Apaches, who were held as enemies by Jumanos and Caddos alike.

4. For one survivor's critique of La Salle's leadership, see translations of the records of Jean L'Archevêque's interrogations by Spanish officials in 1688, in O'Donnell, "La Salle's Occupation of Texas," 17. Another French survivor who lived among the Hasinais for three years, Pierre Talon, made implicit commentary on La Salle's failures as a leader, and he may have shared this vision with his adopted Indian kin. See Pierre Talon, "Voyage to the Mississippi through the Gulf of Mexico," in Weddle, Morkovsky, and Galloway, *La Salle, the Mississippi, and the Gulf*, 234.

5. The eleven communities making up the Hasinai confederacy were the Nacao, Nacachau, Nacono, Nechaui, Hainai, Neche, Nadaco (or Anadarko), Nabedache, Nabiti (or Namidish, or Nawidish), Nacogdoche, and the lower Nasoni. The Kadohadacho confederacy included two Kadohadacho communities, as well as those of the Nanatsoho, the upper Nasoni, and the upper Natchitoches. Lower Natchitoches, Ouachita, Yatasi, and Doustioni bands seem to have coalesced into the Natchitoches confederacy after 1700. Perttula, "Caddo Nation," 217–20; Swanton, *Source Material*, 7–14; La Vere, *Caddo Chiefdoms*, 34–35.

6. Espinosa, *Crónica de los Colegios*, 689.

7. Perttula, "Caddo Nation," 84–89; Sabo, "Structure of Caddo Leadership"; Swanton, *Source Material*, 16–25; La Vere, *Caddo Chiefdoms*, 1–14, 33–34.

8. Spaniards made various *entradas* into the region, beginning with that of Cabeza de Vaca and Estevanico, survivors of the sixteenth-century Narváez expedition, but only the remnants of the Soto expedition led by Moscoso in 1542 had met the Caddos previously. For sources and discussions of the Soto expedition, see Clayton, Knight, and Moore, *De Soto Chronicles*; Young and Hoffman, *Expedition of Hernando de Soto*; Milanich, *Hernando de Soto Expedition*; Strickland, "Moscoso's Journey through Texas"; and Woldert, "Expedition of Luis de Moscoso."

9. Douay, "Narrative," 232, 231.

10. Perttula, "Long-Term Effects," *"Caddo Nation,"* and "European Contact and Its Effects."

11. Weddle, *Wilderness Manhunt*, 5–14.

12. See Weddle, *Wilderness Manhunt*, for the story in detail.

13. N. Hickerson, *Jumanos*.

14. Posada, *Alonso de Posada Report*; "Itinerary of Juan Dominguez de Mendoza, 1684," in Bolton, *Spanish Exploration in the Southwest*, 320–43; Hackett, *Historical Documents*; Douay, "Narrative," 232–33; Cavelier, *Journal of Jean Cavelier*, 73; Bolton, "Spanish Occupation of Texas."

15. N. Hickerson, *Jumanos*, 120–45.

CHAPTER 1

1. Among the numerous Caddo bands, the Hasinais dominated the ethnographic observations made by the earliest Spanish and French expeditions to the region and, in turn, many current historical and anthropological studies of the Caddoan peoples. I will use "Caddo" when referring to the cultural group in general and will use "Hasinai" or other band affiliation when historical specificity requires it.

2. Descriptions of diplomatic visits by neighboring Indian peoples to Caddo villages— recorded by Spanish Franciscans living among the Caddos in the 1690s through 1720s— make clear that the ritual behaviors used by Caddos to greet and welcome European visitors were the same as those offered native visitors. See Espinosa, *Crónica de los Colegios*, 685, 714– 16; and fray Francisco Casañas de Jesús María to the viceroy of Mexico, Aug. 15, 1691, in Hatcher, "Descriptions of the Tejas," 301.

3. Sabo, "Reordering Their World," 26.

4. Sabo, "Structure of Caddo Leadership," 166.

5. Espinosa, *Crónica de los Colegios*, 695–96. For interpretation of the oral tradition, see Sabo, "Structure of Caddo Leadership," 162–63.

6. Sabo, "Structure of Caddo Leadership"; Wyckoff and Baugh, "Early Historic Hasinai Elites"; Rogers, "Dispersed Communities and Integrated Households."

7. Sabo, "Encounters and Images," 221.

8. In order to provide a picture of the ways in which face-to-face interactions served as exercises in communication beyond spoken language, this composite sketch of contact rituals is drawn from the following expedition records. I use descriptions from expedition journals dating from 1686 through 1722 for general details about ceremonies, but this chapter focuses primarily on the 1680s and 1690s. Where necessary for accuracy, I note when rituals, gifts, or actions changed in form or function over time. The sources for these early encounters are solely from European expedition journals, diaries, and records. Listed in chronological order of their arrival in Caddo lands, Spanish expedition sources include Chapa, *Texas and Northeastern Mexico*; accounts of Alonso de León, fray Damián Mazanet,

fray Isidro de Espinosa, and Juan Antonio de la Peña, in Hadley, Naylor, and Schuetz-Miller, *Presidio and Militia*; expedition records of Alonso de León and fray Damián Mazanet (cited as "Massanet"), in Bolton, *Spanish Exploration in the Southwest*; Foik, "Expedition of Don Domingo Terán"; Ramón, "Captain Don Domingo Ramón's Diary"; Casañas to the viceroy, Aug. 15, 1691, and fray Francisco Hidalgo to the viceroy, Nov. 4, 1716, in Hatcher, "Descriptions of the Tejas"; Espinosa, *Crónica de los Colegios*, 671–754; and Céliz, *Diary of the Alarcón Expedition*. French descriptions of first contact ceremonies in Texas come from Joutel, *La Salle Expedition to Texas*; accounts of Anastase Douay and Henri de Tonti, in Cox, *Journeys of Rene Robert Cavelier*; Cavelier, *Journal of Jean Cavelier*; "Talon Interrogations"; La Harpe, "Account of the Journey," and *Historical Journal of the Establishment*.

9. Espinosa, *Crónica de los Colegios*, 715.

10. Douay, "Narrative," 228; Espinosa, "Espinosa-Olivares-Aguirre Expedition," 9; Céliz, *Diary of the Alarcón Expedition*; and Peña, "Account of the 1720–1722 Entrada." Unfortunately, we do not know what roles the women of visiting parties played in diplomatic rituals in answer to their Caddo hostesses due to the failure of European observers like Espinosa to describe them—perhaps because the women's actions took place away from male view or because European bias led Spaniards and Frenchmen to deem the women's actions not significant enough to record.

11. Espinosa, "Diary of the 1716 Entrada," 8–10; Joutel, *La Salle Expedition to Texas*, 88, 90, 157, 162, 206.

12. Douay, "Narrative," 225, 228; Ramón, "Captain Don Domingo Ramón's Diary," 18, 20; Espinosa, "Diary of the 1716 Entrada," 8–10.

13. Céliz, *Diary of the Alarcón Expedition*, 66; Espinosa, "Diary of the 1716 Entrada," 378, 380; Joutel, *La Salle Expedition to Texas*, 92–93. Nor were Europeans above interpreting gestures to their own ends, investing ceremonies with meanings that better served their own purposes. In a moment of wishful thinking in 1721, for instance, the marqués de Aguayo "placed his hands over the heads of [Caddo] men, women and children which [he presumed] is the Indians' sign of pledging *obedience*." Peña, "Account of the 1720–1722 Entrada," 413. See also *Autos* of Alonso de León, May 18, 1688, in O'Donnell, "La Salle's Occupation of Texas," 7; Chapa, *Texas and Northeastern Mexico*, 117, 149; and fray Damián Massanet to don Carlos de Sigüenza, 1690, in Bolton, *Spanish Exploration in the Southwest*, 359.

14. La Harpe, "Account of the Journey," 526; Viceroy marqués de Valero to don Martín de Alarcón, Mar. 11, 1718, in Pichardo, *Pichardo's Treatise on the Limits*, 3:264; Joutel, *La Salle Expedition to Texas*, 162; Foik, "Expedition of Don Domingo Terán," 18; Foster and Jackson, "1693 Expedition of Gregorio de Salinas Varona," 305.

15. Benavides, *Benavides' Memorial of 1630*, *Memorial of Fray Alonso de Benavides*, and *Fray Alonso de Benavides' Revised Memorial*; Colahan, *Visions of Sor María de Agreda*.

16. Massanet to Sigüenza, 1690, in Bolton, *Spanish Exploration in the Southwest*, 354, 387; fray Damián Mazanet to Viceroy conde de Galve, Sept. 1690, in Hadley, Naylor, and Schuetz-Miller, *Presidio and Militia*, 332. Alonso de León and one of his officers, Juan

Bautista Chapa, also separately recorded that the *caddís* had told them of long-ago visits of a woman who appeared to the Caddos and gave them religious instruction, a story that De León and Chapa both interpreted as evidence of Agreda's visits. Alonso de León, "Testimonio de autos de las diligencias para la segunda entrada que se ha de ejecutar a la provincia de los Tejas y recorrer los parajes inmediatos a la bahía del Espíritu Santo," as cited in Seco Serrano, *Cartas de Sor María de Jesús*, xxxix n. 77. See also Chapa, *Texas and Northeastern Mexico*, 138. María de Jesús de Agreda's importance to the establishment of a Spanish missionary presence in Texas is further indicated by the 1718 naming of one of the east Texas missions, Nuestra Señora de la Purísima Concepción de Agreda, in her honor by the Spanish governor of Texas, Martín de Alarcón. Her significance to the history of missionary Texas was emphasized by Spanish historians writing in the eighteenth century. Two of the most prominent historians of the period who wrote in the 1770s and the 1780s, Antonio Bonilla and Juan Agustín Morfi, both credited Agreda as the figure most responsible for bringing missionaries to Texas by the end of the seventeenth century. Bonilla, "Bonilla's Brief Compendium," 17–18; Morfi, *Excerpts from the Memorias*, xi. See also Arricivita, *Apostolic Chronicle* 1:171, 353, 362, 364, 381–83. An eighteenth-century apocryphal story also asserted that the marqués de Valero, who as viceroy ordered the settlement of Texas in 1718, was inspired to do so by having read as a child Agreda's writings on her trips to the New World to catechize Indians there. Pichardo, *Pichardo's Treatise on the Limits*, 2:520–21. The influence of Agreda did not end with Spanish entry into Texas but continued to shape Spanish missionary work among Indians across the northern provinces of New Spain. Her biography of the Virgin Mary, titled *Mystical City of God*, appeared regularly in inventories of Texas missions—presumably a work widely consulted by missionaries for teachings and devotions about the Virgin. Fray Benito Fernández de Santa Ana, a Texas missionary, asserted that the Franciscans working in the missionary fields of New Spain's northern frontiers decided upon their method "in the enlightened and exalted spirit of Venerable María de Jesús de Agreda." Fernández de Santa Ana, "Memorial of Father Benito Fernández," 295. For sample inventories, see Leutenegger and Habig, *San José Papers*.

17. Casañas to the viceroy, Aug. 15, 1691, in Hatcher, "Descriptions of the Tejas," 296–97; Cavallero Macarti to Governor Angel de Martos y Navarrete, Nov. 17, 1763, Archivo San Francisco el Grande, vol. 27, Center for American History, University of Texas at Austin; Morfi, *History of Texas*, 1:88, and *Excerpts from the Memorias*, 6; G. Dorsey, *Traditions of the Caddo*; Newkumet and Meredith, *Hasinai*.

18. Terán de los Rios, itinerary and daily account, in Foik, "Expedition of Don Domingo Terán," 12; Peña, *Aguayo Expedition into Texas*, 81. According to tradition, the Virgin Mary appeared to St. James the Apostle when he traveled from Palestine to the city of Zaragoza (Spain) to establish a church and appoint bishops there. In a vision, Mary told James, "'I, son Diego, am your protector. . . . build me a church in my name . . . I shall work wonderful signs, especially to help those who in their necessity come to this place.'" She then left behind a carved wooden image of herself holding the baby Jesus and standing on a column. The cult of Our Lady of Pilar (the Pillar) arose around veneration of this image at

Zaragoza. She was named patron saint of the city in 1641 and patron saint of the kingdom of Aragon in 1678, and over the next century, a cathedral was built to house and venerate the image. María de Jesús de Agreda elaborated on the tradition even further in her life of the Virgin Mary, *Mystical City of God* (1680). Brading, *Mexican Phoenix*, 3, 38–40, 39 (for quote). The edition of the Peña diary cited here includes the final salutations and summary of accomplishments by the expedition that were omitted from the Hadley, Naylor, and Schuetz-Miller edition. The form and meaning of iconography surrounding the Virgin Mary in Spain, New Spain, and Latin America has undergone many transformations between the sixteenth and twenty-first centuries. For the history of this religious and cultural symbolism, see Poole, *Our Lady of Guadalupe*; Phelan, *Millennial Kingdom of the Franciscans*; and Warner, *Alone of All Her Sex*.

19. Remensnyder, "Virgin Mary and the Conversion"; Peña, *Aguayo Expedition into Texas*, 81; fray Miguel Santa Maria y Silva to Viceroy Antonio Bucareli y Ursúa, July 21, 1774, in Bolton, *Athanase de Mézières*, 1:77–78.

20. Espinosa, "Espinosa-Olivares-Aguirre Expedition," 10; Massanet to Sigüenza, 1690, in Bolton, *Spanish Exploration in the Southwest*, 380; Foik, "Expedition of Don Domingo Terán." As historian Mary Elizabeth Perry explains, for early modern Spanish society, "religious symbols functioned as a common language recognized by most people as representing widely held beliefs and attitudes." Perry, *Gender and Disorder*, 41. For further perspectives on the importance held by the royal standard among the Spanish, see Martin and Brewster, *Expedition into Texas of Fernando del Bosque*; "Itinerary of the De León Expedition of 1689," in Bolton, *Spanish Exploration in the Southwest*; Céliz, *Diary of the Alarcón Expedition*; Espinosa, "Diary of the 1716 Entrada"; Ramón, "Captain Don Domingo Ramón's Diary"; and Espinosa, *Crónica de los Colegios*.

21. Massanet to Sigüenza, 1690, in Bolton, *Spanish Exploration in the Southwest*, 379.

22. Because Louisiana and Texas never developed into a French missionary field, Indians of this region associated the imagery of the Virgin only with the Spanish. Douay, "Narrative," 234; Pichardo, *Pichardo's Treatise on the Limits*, 1:237; Solís, "Diary of a Visit of Inspection," 67. Fray Juan Agustín Morfi found the exchange significant enough to repeat in his history of the province, recording that "one neophyte of this [Ais] nation, after being well instructed in the catechism, had had explained to him the perfection of the Queen of Angels, and when the missionary hoped, as a result of the attention with which he had listened, to receive some expression of devotion, was surprised to see him coldly say, 'Well, I prefer Misura (meaning the Devil) to that woman which you praise.'" Morfi, *Excerpts from the Memorias*, 4.

23. "Talon Interrogations," 257; Foik, "Expedition of Don Domingo Terán," 5, 19 (for quote), 63. In 1690, a Hasinai *caddí* had sent a delegation made up of his brother, a nephew, and two other relatives to Mexico City in the company of the León expedition so that the four men might meet with the viceroy. Two turned back along the way due to illness, and one was killed "accidentally" in the town of Querétaro, so that only the *caddí*'s nephew (who would later be known as Bernardino and would become a *caddí* himself in the 1710s) met

with the viceroy. Bernardino then returned to Caddo lands in 1691 with the Terán de los Rios expedition and became one of the most vociferous supporters of the Spaniards' expulsion from Texas in 1693. It was the death in Querétaro that Terán was attempting to explain in this passage—the official instructions he had received from the viceroy included the directive that he assure Hasinai leaders that every effort had been made to bring the murderers to justice. Massanet to Sigüenza, 1690, in Bolton, *Spanish Exploration in the Southwest*, 382; "Itinerary of the De León Expedition of 1690," in ibid., 418; Alonso de León to Viceroy conde de Galve, July 12, 1690, in Hadley, Naylor, and Schuetz-Miller, *Presidio and Militia*, 323.

24. Espinosa, "Espinosa-Olivares-Aguirre Expedition," 8; fray Damián Mazanet, "Diary Kept by the Missionaries," in Foik, "Expedition of Don Domingo Terán," 57–58; Espinosa, *Crónica de los Colegios*, 685; Massanet to Sigüenza, 1690, in Bolton, *Spanish Exploration in the Southwest*, 364, 380.

25. Sabo, "Rituals of Encounter," 83–85.

26. Sabo, "Reordering Their World"; G. Dorsey, *Traditions of the Caddo*; Newkumet and Meredith, *Hasinai*; C. Carter, *Caddo Indians*, 162–63; Griffith, *Hasinai Indians of East Texas*, 97–98; Swanton, *Source Material*; Wyckoff and Baugh, "Early Historic Hasinai Elites." Europeans in the British and French regions of colonial America also used dress, body decoration, and objects of ritual exchange as markers of Indian identity. See Sayre, *Les Sauvages Américains*.

27. Casañas to the viceroy, Aug. 15, 1691, in Hatcher, "Descriptions of the Tejas," 218; Espinosa, *Crónica de los Colegios*, 715; La Harpe, "Account of the Journey," 380; Chapa, *Texas and Northeastern Mexico*, 153. French diplomat Luis Juchereau de St. Denis reportedly asserted that "to get along well with Spaniards, one had to heap honors upon them and show them much deference." Quoted in Pénicaut, *Fleur de Lys and Calumet*, 185. For European ritual and ceremony, see Muir, *Ritual in Early Modern Europe*; Wisch and Munshower, *Triumphal Celebrations and the Rituals of Statecraft*; Wilentz, *Rites of Power*; and Davis, *The Gift in Sixteenth-Century France*, 85–99, 161.

28. Wyckoff and Baugh, "Early Historic Hasinai Elites," 234–41; Sabo, "Structure of Caddo Leadership," and "Reordering Their World," 38–39; La Vere, *Caddo Chiefdoms*, 14–22. For theory and history regarding the relationship of male honor with battlefield accomplishments, military display, and public recognition in early modern Europe and New Spain, see Roper, *Oedipus and the Devil*, 107–24; Miller, *Humiliation and Other Essays*; Brandes, *Metaphors of Masculinity*; Bennassar, *Spanish Character*; and Lourie, "Society Organized for War." For studies of honor in colonial Latin America, see Burkholder, "Honor and Honors in Colonial Spanish America"; S. Stern, *Secret History of Gender*; Gutiérrez, *When Jesus Came*; and Brooks, *Captives and Cousins*.

29. Espinosa, "Diary of the 1716 Entrada," 368, 370, 376, 378, 381; Terán de los Rios, itinerary and daily account, in Foik, "Expedition of Don Domingo Terán," 10–11, 18–19; Chapa, *Texas and Northeastern Mexico*, 150; Joutel, *La Salle Expedition to Texas*, 206; Douay, "Narrative," 231; Griffith, *Hasinai Indians of East Texas*, 81–84; Swanton, *Source Material*,

140–48. The Ramón expedition, for instance, marked its departures and returns from presidios in northern Mexico with elaborate fanfare, greeted by resident officials who "came out to receive us in two lines, and we returned the courtesy by saluting with our bows and arrows." Ramón, "Captain Don Domingo Ramón's Diary," 7, 10.

30. Joutel, *La Salle Expedition to Texas*, 206; Massanet to Sigüenza, 1690, in Bolton, *Spanish Exploration in the Southwest*, 380; Céliz, *Diary of the Alarcón Expedition*, 77; Peña, "Account of the 1720–1722 Entrada," 420–21.

31. Douay, "Narrative," 232; itinerary of Juan Dominguez de Mendoza, 1684, in Bolton, *Spanish Exploration in the Southwest*, 331; Espinosa, *Crónica de los Colegios*, 715; Gregory, "Eighteenth-Century Caddoan Archaeology," 280; Magnaghi, "Changing Material Culture"; Pagès, *Travels Round the World*, 74–75.

32. Interestingly, the riding contests had been primarily between the Spaniards and three Frenchmen who traveled with them—making political competitions personal ones as well. Ramón, "Captain Don Domingo Ramón's Diary," 10; W. Foster, *Spanish Expeditions into Texas*, 115. See also Peña, "Account of the 1720–1722 Entrada," 413–14, 420–29, 447; and Morfi, *History of Texas*, 1:203.

33. Joutel, *La Salle Expedition to Texas*, 204–5.

34. Bolton, *Hasinais*, 131; Espinosa, "Espinosa-Olivares-Aguirre Expedition," 8; Cavelier, *Journal of Jean Cavelier*, 91, 103; Aguayo to Casafuerte, n.d., in Pichardo, *Pichardo's Treatise on the Limits*, 1:247.

35. Casañas to the viceroy, Aug. 15, 1691, in Hatcher, "Descriptions of the Tejas," 213; Morfi, *Excerpts from the Memorias*, 32, 46; Espinosa, *Crónica de los Colegios*, 708; Douay, "Narrative," 231; C. Carter, *Caddo Indians*, 162–63; Griffith, *Hasinai Indians of East Texas*, 97–98; Swanton, *Source Material*, 140–48; Magnaghi, "Changing Material Culture."

36. Bolton, *Hasinais*, 123–24; "Itinerary of the De León Expedition of 1689," in Bolton, *Spanish Exploration in the Southwest*, 403; Cavelier, *Journal of Jean Cavelier*, 73.

37. Casañas to the viceroy, Aug. 15, 1691, in Hatcher, "Descriptions of the Tejas," 213; Joutel, *La Salle Expedition to Texas*, 206; Chapa, *Texas and Northeastern Mexico*, 137; Espinosa, *Crónica de los Colegios*, 697, 701–2, 714; Morfi, *Excerpts from the Memorias*, 46.

38. Espinosa, *Crónica de los Colegios*, 713; Terán de los Rios, itinerary and daily account, in Foik, "Expedition of Don Domingo Terán," 14, 15; Joutel, *La Salle Expedition to Texas*, 210; Hidalgo to the viceroy, Nov. 4, 1716, and Casañas to the viceroy, Aug. 15, 1691, in Hatcher, "Descriptions of the Tejas," 57, 213–14, 217, 285. In contrast to native women's body decoration, men's tattoos did not appear to inspire revulsion or denigration in European observers but simply their recognition as status markers.

39. Peña, "Account of the 1720–1722 Entrada," 403.

40. Wyckoff and Baugh, "Early Historic Hasinai Elites," 234–37; Sabo, "Structure of Caddo Leadership," 169; La Vere, *Caddo Chiefdoms*, 14–18; Casañas to the viceroy, Aug. 15, 1691, in Hatcher, "Descriptions of the Tejas," 215–18.

41. Massanet to Sigüenza, 1690, and "Itinerary of the De León Expedition of 1690," in Bolton, *Spanish Exploration in the Southwest*, 377, 378, 379, 381, 415, 416; Casañas to the

viceroy, Aug. 15, 1691, in Hatcher, "Descriptions of the Tejas," 217; Terán de los Rios, itinerary and daily account, in Foik, "Expedition of Don Domingo Terán," 33, 34–35; Chapa, *Texas and Northeastern Mexico*, 149, 150; Espinosa, "Diary of the 1716 Entrada," 381; Ramón, "Captain Don Domingo Ramón's Diary"; Espinosa, *Crónica de los Colegios*, 685, 716; Céliz, *Diary of the Alarcón Expedition*, 74, 75.

42. Wyckoff and Baugh, "Early Historic Hasinai Elites," 246–48; Sabo, "Structure of Caddo Leadership," 169; Massanet to Sigüenza, 1690, in Bolton, *Spanish Exploration in the Southwest*, 377–79.

43. Wyckoff and Baugh, "Early Historic Hasinai Elites," 243; Sabo, "Structure of Caddo Leadership," 169–71; Terán de los Rios, itinerary and daily account, in Foik, "Expedition of Don Domingo Terán," 19, 33–34.

44. Swanton, *Source Material*, 158; Espinosa, "Diary of the 1716 Entrada," 381, 382; Peña, "Account of the 1720–1722 Entrada," 415–16; Ramón, "Captain Don Domingo Ramón's Diary," 20; Céliz, *Diary of the Alarcón Expedition*; Espinosa, *Crónica de los Colegios*, 685; Casañas to the viceroy, Aug. 15, 1691, in Hatcher, "Descriptions of the Tejas," 212; La Harpe, "Account of the Journey," 255–56, 372–74, 377, 383, 385, 528–29; Pénicaut, *Fleur de Lys and Calumet*, 150.

45. Jean Cavelier was La Salle's brother and one of those survivors who finally made it to Illinois posts in 1687. Henri de Tonti, "Memoir Sent in 1693," in Cox, *Journeys of Rene Robert Cavelier*, 1:46; Joutel, *La Salle Expedition to Texas*, 92–93, 243–44, 254–55.

46. Céliz, *Diary of the Alarcón Expedition*, 74.

47. Espinosa, *Crónica de los Colegios*, 716; Céliz, *Diary of the Alarcón Expedition*, 76, 78; La Harpe, "Account of the Journey," 258–59, 384.

48. Joutel, *La Salle Expedition to Texas*, 154–55; Céliz, *Diary of the Alarcón Expedition*, 75; La Harpe, "Account of the Journey," 528–29.

49. Peña, "Account of the 1720–1722 Entrada," 415, 421; Espinosa, *Crónica de los Colegios*, 714; Céliz, *Diary of the Alarcón Expedition*, 78; "Itinerary of the De León Expedition of 1690," in Bolton, *Spanish Exploration in the Southwest*, 415; Ramón, "Captain Don Domingo Ramón's Diary," 18, 20–21; Joutel, *La Salle Expedition to Texas*; Sabo, "Reordering Their World," 29–32, and "Structure of Caddo Leadership," 169. The French trader Jean-Baptiste Bénard de la Harpe concluded much the same about the Wichitas, the other major horticultural Indian bands in Texas. Wichita women, he wrote, "carry gallantry still further than the men." "During our sojourn at their villages," he explained, "they [the women] did not cease to bring us dishes of beans and corn, prepared with the marrow of buffalo and some smoked meat; they strived even to surpass one another at bringing better foods." La Harpe, "Account of the Journey," 532–33. Europeans who later took up residence among Caddos found the mark of a woman's honor within the ranks of matrilineal clans was the hospitality offered by her household. Fray Isidro de Espinosa asserted that Hasinai women "are so provident that as soon as a guest arrives at their home, no matter what the time of day, they put a large bowl of food (which was prepared in abundance that morning) into his hands." Espinosa, "Diary of the 1716 Entrada," 381.

50. La Harpe, "Account of the Journey," 255, 256, 385; "Instructions Given by the Superior Government to Be Observed in the Expedition to the Province of Texas," Jan. 23, 1691, in Foik, "Expedition of Don Domingo Terán," 5.

51. La Harpe, "Account of the Journey," 532, 255; Hidalgo to the viceroy, Nov. 4, 1716, in Hatcher, "Descriptions of the Tejas," 57; Ramón, "Captain Don Domingo Ramón's Diary," 21. Studies of the meanings of gift exchange in non-Western cultures include Mauss, *Gift*; Sahlins, *Stone Age Economics*; and Lévi-Strauss, *Elementary Structures of Kinship*. For the importance of exchange and reciprocity in Caddo societies, see La Vere, *Caddo Chiefdoms*. For Spanish and French societies, see Gutiérrez, *When Jesus Came*; Davis, *The Gift in Sixteenth-Century France*; S. Stern, *Secret History of Gender*; and Sayre, *Les Sauvages Américains*.

52. Alonso de León to Viceroy conde de Galve, July 12, 1690, in Hadley, Naylor, and Schuetz-Miller, *Presidio and Militia*, 322; Ramón, "Captain Don Domingo Ramón's Diary," 21; Peña, "Account of the 1720–1722 Entrada," 413, 414, 415, 417, 419, 422, 423, 427; and Céliz, *Diary of the Alarcón Expedition*. A *quexquémil* was a triangular garment that hung to the waist and was worn by women of some Indian peoples native to Mexico. With Apaches moving into Texas from the west, Comanches and Wichitas moving from the Northern Plains, and Osage pressures from the east, Caddos faced increasing competition for hunting and trading territories on several fronts in the early eighteenth century. The possession of guns, however, did not mark a shift to warfare, but only an additional weapon for deployment. In 1691, fray Francisco Casañas de Jesús María noted that, at Hasinai feasts honoring their ancestors' past victories, lower-ranking chiefs or captains honored the grand *xinesí* by presenting him with bows and arrows as highly valued goods. Casañas to the viceroy, Aug. 15, 1691, in Hatcher, "Descriptions of the Tejas," 301; Massanet to Sigüenza, 1690, in Bolton, *Spanish Exploration in the Southwest*, 376.

53. Casañas to the viceroy, Aug. 15, 1691, in Hatcher, "Descriptions of the Tejas," 213.

54. Peña, "Account of the 1720–1722 Entrada," 415, 417, 419, 422, 423; "Itinerary of the De León Expedition of 1690," in Bolton, *Spanish Exploration in the Southwest*, 416; Terán de los Rios, itinerary and daily account, in Foik, "Expedition of Don Domingo Terán," 19, 34; Céliz, *Diary of the Alarcón Expedition*, 57–58, 86; Morfi, *History of Texas*, 1:206.

55. Fray Damián Mazanet to Viceroy conde de Galve, June 14, 1693, in Hadley, Naylor, and Schuetz-Miller, *Presidio and Militia*, 344.

56. Casañas to the viceroy, Aug. 15, 1691, in Hatcher, "Descriptions of the Tejas," 292–95, 301; Mazanet to conde de Galve, June 14, 1693, Feb. 17, 1694, in Hadley, Naylor, and Schuetz-Miller, *Presidio and Militia*, 344, 353.

57. Mazanet to conde de Galve, June 14, 1693, Feb. 17, 1694, in Hadley, Naylor, and Schuetz-Miller, *Presidio and Militia*, 345, 346–47.

58. Casañas to the viceroy, Aug. 15, 1691, in Hatcher, "Descriptions of the Tejas," 294–99; Perttula, *"Caddo Nation,"* 70–89, and "European Contact and Its Effects." Fray Francisco Hidalgo reported that the belief that baptism might kill them remained strong among

the Hasinais in 1716. The spread of European diseases would prove to batter the Caddos throughout the eighteenth century, with an epidemic occurring roughly every sixteen years, reducing their population by 90 percent between 1691 and 1816. Hidalgo to the viceroy, Nov. 4, 1716, in Hatcher, "Descriptions of the Tejas," 56.

59. Casañas to the viceroy, Aug. 15, 1691, in Hatcher, "Descriptions of the Tejas," 288–89, 299.

60. For discussion of conceptions of female honor in Spain and Spanish America, see Perry, *Gender and Disorder*; Gutiérrez, *When Jesus Came*; Lavrin, *Sexuality and Marriage*; and Seed, *To Love, Honor, and Obey*. For European readings of Indian gender, see Perdue, "Columbus Meets Pocahontas"; and K. Brown, "Anglo-Algonquian Gender Frontier."

61. Espinosa, *Crónica de los Colegios*, 691, 707–8. For the fusion of political, social, and religious authority within Caddo society and analysis of this rite in particular, see Sabo, "Structure of Caddo Leadership," 171.

62. Casañas to the viceroy, Aug. 15, 1691, in Hatcher, "Descriptions of the Tejas," 291. For male prestige dependent upon women's labor in a bride-service system, see Collier, *Marriage and Inequality in Classless Societies*.

63. Body decoration held greater importance for women than for men in signifying band affiliation, since it served to distinguish them from the female captives whom many groups held. Mardith K. Schuetz suggests that Hasinai body tattoos not only marked tribal identification but also reflected age, sex, and accomplishments. Schuetz, "Commentaries on the Interrogations: Ethnological Data," in Weddle, Morkovsky, and Galloway, *La Salle, the Mississippi, and the Gulf*, 259–74.

64. Casañas to the viceroy, Aug. 15, 1691, in Hatcher, "Descriptions of the Tejas," 285; Espinosa, *Crónica de los Colegios*, 714; Solís, "Solís Diary of 1767," 13.

65. Joutel, *La Salle Expedition to Texas*, 88; Douay, "Narrative," 225, 228.

66. Casañas to the viceroy, Aug. 15, 1691, in Hatcher, "Descriptions of the Tejas," 284; Espinosa, *Crónica de los Colegios*, 698, 701. St. Denis's statement seems to indicate that some Frenchmen recognized Hasinai distinctions between marital unions (which were monogamous and required fidelity) and premarital sexual relations, which were not taboo but acceptable to Hasinais (and, by the by, to most Frenchmen and Spaniards not of an elite class). St. Denis, "St. Denis's Declaration," 178–79.

67. Massanet to Sigüenza, 1690, in Bolton, *Spanish Exploration in the Southwest*, 382, 385–87.

68. Chapa, *Texas and Northeastern Mexico*, 152, 151; Massanet to Sigüenza, 1690, in Bolton, *Spanish Exploration in the Southwest*, 383; fray Damián Mazanet to the viceroy, Sept. 1690, in Hadley, Naylor, and Schuetz-Miller, *Presidio and Militia*, 336–37. Alonso de León claimed to have tried to avoid just such violence, writing to the viceroy that he stationed very few soldiers at the mission encampments to protect against Apache raids "because of the harm that they might do as bachelors." This decision was likely not a voluntary one, as he wrote that it "was in consideration of the Indian governor's [*caddí*'s] initial objection to the

soldiers . . . because they might molest the women of his settlement." Alonso de León to Viceroy conde de Galve, July 12, 1690, in Hadley, Naylor, and Schuetz-Miller, *Presidio and Militia*, 322–23.

69. "Instructions Given by the Superior Government to Be Observed in the Expedition to the Province of Texas," Jan. 23, 1691, in Foik, "Expedition of Don Domingo Terán," 6.

70. Fray Damián Massanet to Viceroy conde de Galve, c. Jan. 1692, in Pichardo, *Pichardo's Treatise on the Limits*, 3:172–76; Espinosa, *Crónica de los Colegios*, 679.

71. Fray Damián Mazanet, comisario de los Tejas, to conde de Galve, viceroy of New Spain, June 14, 1693, in Hadley, Naylor, and Schuetz-Miller, *Presidio and Militia*, 343, 346, 347. Hasinai men began this campaign, killing horses and cattle, as early as 1691—animals given them by Spanish commanders seeking to support missions they imagined were populated by Hasinai neophytes—as reflected in reports to Spanish officials coming not only from the letters of dismayed missionaries but also from information supplied by Jumano leader Juan Sabeata. Terán de los Rios, itinerary and daily account, and Mazanet, "Diary Kept by the Missionaries," in Foik, "Expedition of Don Domingo Terán," 19, 28, 59.

72. Mazanet to conde de Galve, Feb. 17, 1694, in Hadley, Naylor, and Schuetz-Miller, *Presidio and Militia*, 352–54.

73. Ibid. Interestingly, as Mazanet's party fled the region, four soldiers deserted, two of whom he believed to be no loss since they were "irresponsible people who had left the hand of God and given themselves over to vice with the Indian women." Given his directness in identifying earlier incidents as rape, this reference seems to suggest something less violent, and perhaps even consensual. Because it is unlikely that Mazanet would have allowed any of the soldiers he had accused of rape to remain at the missions (especially since he could have sent them home with either the Terán or Salinas expeditions), it is possible that these deserters may have formed real relationships with Hasinai women—though if so, they were clearly not enough to offset Hasinai leaders' desires to rid themselves of the Spaniards. Or it may be that, by this point, Mazanet's disillusionment with Caddo peoples who refused his attempts to teach them Christianity had led him to blame Hasinai women for the rapes, believing their supposed "savage" lasciviousness enticed Spanish men to criminal deeds.

CHAPTER 2

1. Sabo, "Indians and Spaniards in Arkansas," 197, and "Structure of Caddo Leadership."

2. "Talon Interrogations"; Sayre, *Les Sauvages Américains*, 14, 266; Schmitt and Schmitt, *Wichita Kinship*, 23.

3. Weddle, "La Salle's Survivors," 427–29; "Talon Interrogations," 220–23, 240.

4. "Talon Interrogations," 229, 240, 257.

5. Ibid., 238, 253, 239.

6. Ibid., 251.

7. Joutel, *La Salle Expedition to Texas*, 207. Another Frenchman, Jean Géry, found a home and adoption into male ranks among Indian peoples farther west, only to be discovered and

captured at a ranchería twenty leagues north of the Rio Grande by Alonso de León in 1687. For translations of the Spanish depositions regarding the discovery of Géry, see O'Donnell, "La Salle's Occupation of Texas"; and Weddle, *Wilderness Manhunt*.

8. Joutel, *La Salle Expedition to Texas*, 210–11, 213. For discussion of the meaning of tattoos among the Caddos, see Mardith K. Schuetz, "Commentaries on the Interrogations: Ethnological Data," in Weddle, Morkovsky, and Galloway, *La Salle, the Mississippi, and the Gulf*, 267–68.

9. Joutel, *La Salle Expedition to Texas*, 231, 236, 219–21; "Itinerary of the De León Expedition of 1689," in Bolton, *Spanish Exploration in the Southwest*, 402, 403. For translations of the Spanish depositions of Grollet and L'Archevêque, see O'Donnell, "La Salle's Occupation of Texas," 25.

10. Joutel, *La Salle Expedition to Texas*, 236–37. Matrilocal residence meant that households were organized around extended family related through women, usually including the female head of a clan, her daughters, and the daughters' husbands and children.

11. Ibid., 210, 222; "Talon Interrogations," 253.

12. Bossu, *Travels in the Interior of North America*, 67; Joutel, *La Salle Expedition to Texas*, 212, 214, 227, 235–36. The veracity of Bossu's account should not be accepted without question, since many believe he never actually traveled in North America and that his writings are fiction cannibalized from others' accounts; but in that case, it could be the story of someone else who met the son.

13. Joutel, *La Salle Expedition to Texas*, 210, 212, 226, 227, 229.

14. Ibid., 214.

15. Ibid., 231, 220; Douay, "Narrative," 1:232. Abbé Jean Cavelier, the older brother of La Salle, also wrote of having women offered to him, though his account seems highly exaggerated and gives weight to the critiques of Jean Delanglez, the editor and translator of Cavelier's journal, and other scholars about its accuracy and reliability, given that he wrote many years after the events he described and, purposely or not, bungled chronology to the point that Delanglez suggests that he made up events that could not have occurred. Cavelier claimed that Indian men "led us to a beautiful cabin outside the village, where they brought us some fifty of the most beautiful girls of the village" and that the Frenchmen elicited "horrible cries" from the Indians when they, the Frenchmen, "fled from the persecutions of these prostitutes." Cavelier, *Journal of Jean Cavelier*, 91. For Delanglez's critique, see ibid., 5, 7–8, 25–26.

16. Hackett, *Historical Documents*, 1:233–89.

17. Jean L'Archevêque was a member of the second party to visit the Caddos in 1687 but chose to remain among the Hasinais when the rest continued on to Canada. For translation of the interrogation of Pierre Meunier in Mexico City, see Appendix A of Joutel, *La Salle Expedition to Texas*, 283–89. For details of the Frenchmen's discovery and capture by Spaniards, see fray Damián Massanet to don Carlos de Sigüenza, 1690, "Itinerary of the De León Expedition of 1689," and "Itinerary of the De León Expedition of 1690," in Bolton, *Spanish Exploration in the Southwest*; and Foik, "Expedition of Don Domingo Terán." Spanish

authorities apparently feared the men could take back useful information about Spanish territory if they were allowed to return to France, so their final destinations in New Mexico were not necessarily of their own choosing. Weddle, *Wilderness Manhunt*, 235–37, and "La Salle's Survivors."

18. The journal of Bienville's expedition is included in Le Moyne d'Iberville, *Iberville's Gulf Journals*. Wedel, *La Harpe's 1719 Post*; Usner, *Indians, Settlers, and Slaves*; Lauber, *Indian Slavery in Colonial Times*, 75; "Talon Interrogations," 256.

19. Charlevoix, *History and General Description of New France*, 4:32–38; Usner, *Indians, Settlers, and Slaves*.

20. D. Hickerson, "Historical Processes, Epidemic Disease"; La Harpe, "Account of the Journey," 253–54; Morfi, *Excerpts from the Memorias*, 2–3, 4–5, 7–9, and *History of Texas*, 1:79–92.

21. Guillaume Thomas François Raynal, *Histoire philosophique et politique, des etablissements et du commerce des Européans dans les deux Indes . . .* , 7 vols. (Amsterdam, 1772–74), cited in Pichardo, *Pichardo's Treatise on the Limits*, 1:258; Zitomersky, "Form and Function of French–Native American Relations." This dual French and native settlement pattern differs from that found in French Canada, which Zitomersky characterizes as dual "regions" of settlement in which the French developed concentrated French establishments in one central area while leaving native areas in the continental interior relatively free of French settlement except for limited military forts, trading posts, and mission stations.

22. Fray Francisco Casañas de Jesús María to the viceroy of Mexico, Aug. 15, 1691, in Hatcher, "Descriptions of the Tejas," 283; Espinosa, *Crónica de los Colegios*, 701; Swanton, *Source Material*; Parsons, *Notes on the Caddo*; La Vere, *Caddo Chiefdoms*.

23. Collier, *Marriage and Inequality in Classless Societies*, 22, 23.

24. Usner, *Indians, Settlers, and Slaves*, 255; Athanase de Mézières to Bernard de Gálvez, Sept. 14, 1777, and Mézières to the viceroy, Feb. 20, 1778, in Bolton, *Athanase de Mézières*, 2:146, 176.

25. Bridges and De Ville, "Natchitoches and the Trail"; Mills, *Natchitoches, 1729–1803*, entries 13, 128, 148, 168, 207, 350 for Derbanne; entries 126, 208, 215, 340, 342, 348, 454, esp. 1000 for Guedon; Nardini, *My Historic Natchitoches*, 39, 41, 61; General Commissioner Jean Baptiste Duclos to Minister of Marine and Colonies, Jérôme de Pontchartrain, Oct. 12, 1713, in Rowland and Sanders, *Mississippi Provincial Archives*, 2:144; Bolton, *Texas in the Middle Eighteenth Century*, 37–38. Spanish Franciscans established a mission, Nuestra Señora de los Dolores de los Ais, among the Ais in 1716.

26. Mills, *Natchitoches, 1729–1803*, entries 9, 40, 41, 119, 455, 732, 773 for Brevel; entries 2255, 2641, 2837, 2932, 3096 for Prudhomme and Le Court; De Ville, *Marriage Contracts of Natchitoches*, entries 45, 54; Mills, *Natchitoches, 1800–1826*, and *Natchitoches Colonials*; Maduell, *Census Tables for the French Colony*; Mills and Mills, *Tales of Old Natchitoches*, 19–22. The names of other women of different Caddo nations, predominantly the Natchitoches, appear in sacramental records of the baptism of children of unnamed fathers. Mills, *Natchitoches, 1729–1803*, entries 2826, 2827, 2998, and *Natchitoches, 1800–1826*, entries 138, 139, 407,

408, 1211, 1237, 1238, 1575; Nardini, *My Historic Natchitoches*, 108. In a Spanish investigative report concerning the first peace conference with the Wichitas, Alexis Grappe emerged as one of the "Frenchmen who have been established [in the nation of the Kadohadachos] for many years," who kept Caddos well-supplied with arms and ammunition, and who was, reputedly, "the one who commands them [the Kadohadachos]." "Depositions relative to the Expedition to Cadodachos," Oct. 30–31, 1770, and fray Miguel Santa Maria y Silva to the viceroy, July 21, 1774, in Bolton, *Athanase de Mézières*, 1:222–26 (see also 144, 148, 157, 158), 2:74, 75.

27. Wright, *Only Land They Knew*; Trudel, *L'Esclavage au Canada Français*; Usner, "From African Captivity to American Slavery"; McGowan, "Planters without Slaves"; G. Hall, *Africans in Colonial Louisiana*; Din, *Spaniards, Planters, and Slaves*, 3–17.

28. Giraud, *History of French Louisiana*, 2:129; Spear, "Colonial Intimacies"; Brasseaux, "Administration of Slave Regulations," and "Moral Climate of French Colonial Louisiana"; O'Neill, *Church and State in French Colonial Louisiana*; Allain, "Manon Lescaut et Ses Consoeurs"; Mills, *Natchitoches, 1729–1803*; Bolton, *Athanase de Mézières*, 1:48, 64, 90, 91, 162, 168, 2:76; D. Lee, "Indian Slavery in Lower Louisiana," 87, 92.

29. Webb and Gregory, *Caddo Indians of Louisiana*; Gregory, "Eighteenth-Century Caddoan Archaeology"; D. Lee, "Indian Slavery in Lower Louisiana"; La Vere, *Caddo Chiefdoms*; D. Hickerson, "Trade, Mediation, and Political Status." For reciprocity and the relationships it reflected or created in premodern societies, see Albers, "Symbiosis, Merger, and War."

30. Kerlérec, "Projet de paix et d'alliance avec les Cannecis." Historian James F. Brooks argues that the captivity and later adoption and marriage of captive native women in the New Mexico hinterlands represented a violent extreme of practices of exogamous exchange of women in precapitalist societies by which "mutual obligations of reciprocity are established between kindreds, bands, and societies." Brooks, " 'This Evil Extends Especially,' " 281. See also Brooks, *Captives and Cousins*, 177–97.

31. Casañas to the viceroy, Aug. 15, 1691, in Hatcher, "Descriptions of the Tejas," 208; *auditor de guerra*, marqués de Altamira, "*Informe*," June 20, 1774, in Pichardo, *Pichardo's Treatise on the Limits*, 1:220; Espinosa, "Diary of the 1716 Entrada"; Ramón, "Captain Don Domingo Ramón's Diary."

32. Céliz, *Diary of the Alarcón Expedition*, 83; fray Antonio Margil de Jesús to Viceroy marqués de Valero, June 23, 1722, in Margil de Jesús, *Nothingness Itself*, 283; Espinosa, *Crónica de los Colegios*, 723.

33. Governor Jacinto de Barrios y Jáuregui to Viceroy conde de Revilla Gigedo, Nov. 8, 1750, Apr. 17, 1753, in Pichardo, *Pichardo's Treatise on the Limits*, 4:16, 67; *Autos* of Alonso de León, May 18, 1688, in O'Donnell, "La Salle's Occupation of Texas," 6; "Itinerary of the De León Expedition of 1689," in Bolton, *Spanish Exploration in the Southwest*, 390. Spaniards long cited French customs of intermarriage to explain their seeming advantages in colonial competitions with the Spanish. When discussing their problems having to do with the French, Spanish officials in Texas referenced historians of Spanish Florida, such as Andreas González Barcia, who argued that the French in sixteenth-century Florida similarly "had

had time to cultivate the friendship of the *caciques*, by whose daughters and relatives they themselves had children." Andreas González Barcia, *Ensayo Cronológico para la Historia General de la Florida* (Madrid, 1723), cited in Pichardo, *Pichardo's Treatise on the Limits*, 1:240.

34. Barrios y Jáuregui to Revilla Gigedo, Apr. 17, 1753, and auditor Domingo Valcárcel to Revilla Gigedo, Sept. 25, 1753, in *Pichardo's Treatise on the Limits*, 4:67, 98, 234 (for quote); 1:264. In steadfast defense of the noble savage ideal, one French observer of Louisiana and Texas, Pierre Marie François Pagès, also concluded that Indians learned their depravity from Frenchmen who had "communicated the impurities of their immoral lives to several families among this simple race of men." Pagès, *Travels Round the World*, 68–69.

35. Gutiérrez, *When Jesus Came*, 284–92; Carrasco, "Indian-Spanish Marriages"; Socolow, *Women of Colonial Latin America*, 33–39; Powers, "Conquering Discourses of 'Sexual Conquest,' " 19, and *Women in the Crucible of Conquest*, 89–92.

36. Espinosa, "Diary of the 1716 Entrada," 379–82; Ramón, "Captain Don Domingo Ramón's Diary," 19–21.

37. Peña, "Account of the 1720–1722 Entrada," 405, 413, 416–17, 420; Page du Pratz, *History of Louisiana*, 150.

38. Judge Advocate General Juan de Oliván Rebolledo to Viceroy marqués de Valero, Dec. 24, 1717, and royal attorney to the viceroy, July 2, 1719, BA; marqués de Valero to Martín de Alarcón, Mar. 11, 1718, in Pichardo, *Pichardo's Treatise on the Limits*, 3:264; royal attorney to the viceroy, July 3, 1719, BA; Juan de Oliván Rebolledo, "Comments on Instructions Given Don Domingo Terán and Suggestions for the Founding of Settlements and Missions at the Spring of San Antonio, the Bay of Espíritu Santo, and among the Asinais and Cadodaches," c. 1718, BA; marqués de San Miguel de Aguayo to Viceroy marqués de Casafuerte, n.d., in Pichardo, *Pichardo's Treatise on the Limits*, 2:103.

39. Fray Damián Mazanet to Viceroy conde de Galve, Sept. 1690, in Hadley, Naylor, and Schuetz-Miller, *Presidio and Militia*, 337.

40. C. Castañeda, *Our Catholic Heritage in Texas*, 2:124; Oliván Rebolledo to the viceroy, Dec. 24, 1717, July 2, 1719, BA; Oliván Rebolledo to the viceroy, Dec. 1717, BA.

41. *Autos* of Alonso de León, May 18, 1688, in O'Donnell, "La Salle's Occupation of Texas"; fray Damián Massanet to don Carlos de Sigüenza, 1690, and "Itinerary of the De León Expedition of 1689," in Bolton, *Spanish Exploration in the Southwest*, 355, 366, 390; "Orders of Viceroy conde de Revilla Gigedo," Feb. 10, 1751, investigations by governor of Texas, Pedro del Barrio Junco y Espriella, Oct. 1, 1751, Señor Fiscal Andreu to Revilla Gigedo, Mar. 1, 1752, and opinion of marqués de Altamira, Sept. 13, 1752, in Pichardo, *Pichardo's Treatise on the Limits*, 4:4, 8–10, 23, 30, 35 (see also 321–22); St. Denis, "St. Denis's Declaration," 181–82; fray Francisco Hidalgo to Viceroy marqués de Valero, Apr. 18, 1718, in Pichardo, *Pichardo's Treatise on the Limits*, 4:314–15.

42. Juan de Oliván Rebolledo to the king, Apr. 28, 1718, with accompanying documents, BA; C. Carter, *Caddo Indians*, 157. Caddos would continue to count upon the presence of wives and families as a guarantee of French trade, in defiance of Spanish opposition as the

century wore on. At midcentury, for instance, a Hasinai *caddí* stressed to Spanish captain Joachín de Orobio y Basterra his pleasure that French traders continued to build homes for their families, because by that act he knew the traders planned to settle permanently in his lands and stay year-round, even through the winters. Investigation of report of French settlements in Texas by Captain Joachín de Orobio y Basterra, Jan. 12, 1746, BA.

43. Ramón, "Captain Don Domingo Ramón's Diary," 8–9; Espinosa, "Diary of the 1716 Entrada," 366; Peña, "Account of the 1720–1722 Entrada," 415, 430; Céliz, *Diary of the Alarcón Expedition*, 43; Teja, *San Antonio de Béxar*, 17–18.

44. Fray Francisco Hidalgo to the viceroy, Nov. 4, 1716, in Hatcher, "Descriptions of the Tejas," 55; Espinosa, *Crónica de los Colegios*, 695–97; fray Damián Mazanet to Viceroy conde de Galve, Feb. 17, 1694, in Hadley, Naylor, and Schuetz-Miller, *Presidio and Militia*, 346.

45. Sabo, "Structure of Caddo Leadership," 168.

46. Joutel, *La Salle Expedition to Texas*, 160; Espinosa, *Crónica de los Colegios*, 690; Sabo, "Structure of Caddo Leadership," 168.

47. Massanet to Sigüenza, 1690, in Bolton, *Spanish Exploration in the Southwest*, 379–80; Espinosa, "Diary of the 1716 Entrada," 382–84; Ramón, "Captain Don Domingo Ramón's Diary," 22.

48. Espinosa, *Crónica de los Colegios*, 716; Céliz, *Diary of the Alarcón Expedition*, 74–76, 78.

49. Peña, "Account of the 1720–1722 Entrada," 418–29.

50. Ibid., 418–29, 419 (for quote).

51. Espinosa, "Diary of the 1716 Entrada," 382; Peña, "Account of the 1720–1722 Entrada," 426; Céliz, *Diary of the Alarcón Expedition*, 73.

52. The "Guatsas" mentioned by Mazanet were perhaps Guapites (or Coapites). Fray Damián Mazanet, comisario de los Tejas, to conde de Galve, viceroy of New Spain, June 14, 1693, in Hadley, Naylor, and Schuetz-Miller, *Presidio and Militia*, 346; Casañas to the viceroy, Aug. 15, 1691, in Hatcher, "Descriptions of the Tejas," 296; Espinosa, *Crónica de los Colegios*, 703.

53. Casañas to the viceroy, Aug. 15, 1691, in Hatcher, "Descriptions of the Tejas," 216; Gutiérrez, *When Jesus Came*, 63.

54. Hidalgo to the viceroy, Nov. 4, 1716, in Hatcher, "Descriptions of the Tejas," 56–57, 61; Espinosa, *Crónica de los Colegios*, 691; Habig, *Alamo Chain of Missions*, 196.

55. Pichardo, *Pichardo's Treatise on the Limits*, 1:261; fray Antonio Margil de Jesús to Viceroy marqués de Valero, June 23, 1722, in Margil de Jesús, *Nothingness Itself*, 282. The mythology of the Caddos emphasized strict gendered divisions of labor, lines that could not be crossed by men or women without ill effects. G. Dorsey, *Traditions of the Caddo*.

56. Margil de Jesús to marqués de Valero, Feb. 13, 1718, and July 2, 1719, in Pichardo, *Pichardo's Treatise on the Limits*, 4:131–36, esp. 135; José González to Governor Manuel de Sandoval, quoted in Carlos de Franquis Benites de Lugo to marqués de Torreblanca, Aug. 26, 1739, BA. A letter from fray Francisco Vallejo, also quoted in the letter, makes the same plea for aid for the soldiers and their families.

57. Espinosa, *Crónica de los Colegios*, 715; Sabo, "Structure of Caddo Leadership," 171.

58. Fray Ignacio Antonio Ciprián to fray Juan Antonio Abasolo, Oct. 27, 1749, Archivo San Francisco el Grande, vol. 5, transcripts, Center for American History, University of Texas at Austin; Memorial of the College of Zacatecas to King Ferdinand VI, Jan. 15, 1750, in Leutenegger, *Texas Missions of the College of Zacatecas*, 51.

59. Pedro de Rivera, "Diario y Derrotero" [Diary and Itinerary], in J. Jackson, *Imaginary Kingdom*; Naylor and Polzer, *Pedro de Rivera*; report by Tomás Felipe Winthuysen, Aug. 19, 1744, and *residencia* of Prudencio de Orobio y Basterra held by Tomás Felipe Winthuysen, Feb. 1, 1741, BA.

60. Gregory, "Eighteenth-Century Caddoan Archaeology," 15; Albers, "Symbiosis, Merger, and War," 100–103.

61. Leutenegger, *Texas Missions of the College of Zacatecas*, 27, 49–50; Gregory, "Eighteenth-Century Caddoan Archaeology," 46–69, 147–48; Surrey, *Commerce of Louisiana during the French Régime*, 412–14.

62. Itinerary of inspection conducted by Pedro de Rivera, 1724–28, in Naylor and Polzer, *Pedro de Rivera*, 83, 85, 157–58; Espinosa, *Crónica de los Colegios*, 747; Morfi, *History of Texas*, 2:259.

63. Corbin, "Spanish-Indian Interaction"; Gregory, "Eighteenth-Century Caddoan Archaeology," 235–36; Gregory and McCorkle, *Historical and Archaeological Background*, 20–35; Bolton, *Texas in the Middle Eighteenth Century*, 39–40; Weber, *Spanish Frontier in North America*, 173–76.

64. Lafora, *Frontiers of New Spain*, 166; Leutenegger, *Texas Missions of the College of Zacatecas*, 24–26, 48, 50–52, 54, 59; Espinosa, *Crónica de los Colegios*, 748. Spanish missionaries regularly appear in the sacramental registers for Natchitoches through midcentury. See Mills, *Natchitoches, 1729–1803*; D'Antoni, *Natchitoches Registers*, 11, 17, 43, 47, 50, 52, 59, 60, 64; and Solís, "Diary of a Visit of Inspection," 65, 66.

65. Bolton, *Texas in the Middle Eighteenth Century*, 40; Giraud, *History of French Louisiana*, 5:384–86, 426–27; Nardini, *My Historic Natchitoches*, 49; Juan Antonio Bustillo y Ceballos to the viceroy, Nov. 26, 1731, Nacogdoches Archives, Texas State Library and Archives, Austin.

66. Mills, *Natchitoches, 1729–1803*, entries 13, 168 for Derbanne; entries 16, 332, 406, 464, 485, 490, 671, 731, 860, 1011 for Marie des Neges de St. Denis; marriage petition of Manuel Antonio de Soto Bermúdez and María de Neges de St. Denis, May 20, 1754, BA; fray Francisco Ballejo to Governor Manuel de Sandoval, Aug. 29, 1736, and José González to Sandoval, Aug. 29, 1736, in Pichardo, *Pichardo's Treatise on the Limits*, 3:484–85, 489–90; D'Antoni, *Natchitoches Registers*; Nardini, *My Historic Natchitoches*, 59, 61, 68.

PART II

1. This reconstruction of events in April of 1709 relies on the account left by fray Isidro de Espinosa of the expedition he, fray Antonio de Olivares, and Captain Pedro de Aguirre

pursued with fourteen soldiers from the Mission of San Juan Bautista and the Presidio of Rio Grande del Norte in Coahuila. See Espinosa, "Espinosa-Olivares-Aguirre Expedition." William Foster's *Spanish Expeditions into Texas* offers valuable analysis of routes, maps, and geography covered by the expedition, and Robert Weddle's *San Juan Bautista* covers in minute detail Spanish actions based in northern Coahuila that affected events in Texas. For the native peoples involved in the interactions, I rely primarily upon Newcomb, "Historic Indians of Central Texas"; and Campbell, *Indians of Southern Texas and Northeastern Mexico*, particularly the essay "Espinosa, Olivares, and the Colorado River Indians, 1709." For sources on José de Urrutia, see González, "Legend of Joseph de Urrutia"; Dunn, "Apache Relations in Texas," 239; and Juan de Oliván Rebolledo to the viceroy, July 18, 1733, BA. Fray Damián Mazanet reported that when the Spaniards were hounded out of Caddo lands in 1693, they found refuge among Cantonas for a brief while, at which point four soldiers— Nicolás Rodelo, Francisco González, Marcos Juan, and José de Urrutia—deserted. All but Urrutia turned up within a couple of months at the Presidio of San Juan Bautista in Coahuila. Fray Damián Mazanet to Viceroy conde de Galve, Feb. 17, 1694, in Hadley, Naylor, and Schuetz-Miller, *Presidio and Militia*, 354–55.

2. Wade, *Native Americans*, 22, 152–58.

3. Fray Benito Fernández de Santa Ana to fray Pedro del Barco, Feb. 20, 1740, in Leutenegger, "Two Franciscan Documents," 202.

4. Wade, *Native Americans*; Sheridan, "Social Control and Native Territoriality"; G. Anderson, *Indian Southwest*, 67–104; Campbell, *Indians of Southern Texas and Northeastern Mexico*, 39–59, 71–77.

5. Wade, *Native Americans*, 56.

6. Foik, "Expedition of Don Domingo Terán," 49.

7. Espinosa, "Diary of the 1716 Entrada," 377–78.

8. Céliz, *Diary of the Alarcón Expedition*, 51.

9. *La Conquistadora* was an image of the Virgin Mary associated with Hernán Cortés's conquest of Mexico, during which the Virgin was believed to have appeared in battle and to have helped bring about Spanish victory by blowing dust into the eyes of the Indians who opposed Cortés's forces. This representation was most associated with "Our Lady of Los Remedios," an image of the Virgin Mary with which Cortés reputedly had replaced Aztec idols on the altar of the great temple at Tenochtitlan. She thus became a "holy conqueror" and "captain of the Christian armies," earning the popular title *La Conquistadora* in association with the Spanish conquerors. In similar spirit, Spaniards in New Mexico had an image of the Virgin, *Nuestra Señora de la Conquista*, also popularly referred to as *La Conquistadora*, whose wooden statue was preserved during the Pueblo Revolt of 1680 and returned to the province with the Spanish reconquest in 1693. Later, in the Mexican War for Independence, Los Remedios's image became tied to royalist forces as either *La Conquistadora* or *La Gachupina* (one who came with the conquerors from Spain, "Gachupín" being a derogatory term for peninsular Spaniards), while the Virgin of Guadalupe was taken up by rebel forces

as *La Criolla* (a Spaniard native to/born in the Americas). Brading, *Mexican Phoenix*, 41, 46–47, 50, 71, 76–77; Weber, *Spanish Frontier in North America*, 139–40; Poole, *Our Lady of Guadalupe*, 3, 24–25, 109.

10. Reff, *Disease, Depopulation, and Cultural Change*; Gerhard, *North Frontier of New Spain*.

11. Gerhard, *North Frontier of New Spain*, 328, 344–48.

12. Campbell, *Payaya Indians of Southern Texas*, 5.

13. For the logs of the De León/Mazanet (1690), Salinas Verona (1693), Terán de los Rios/Mazanet (1691), Ramón/Espinosa (1716), Alarcón (1718–19), and Aguayo (1720–22) expeditions, see the sources cited in Chapter 1, note 8. See also Campbell, *Indians of Southern Texas and Northeastern Mexico*.

14. Newcomb, "Historic Indians of Central Texas"; Prikryl, "Fiction and Fact about the Titskanwatits."

15. Hester, "Texas and Northeastern Mexico," 194. For an introduction to the debates of archaeologists, anthropologists, and historians engaged in disentangling the cultural complexities of native peoples and identities in southern Texas, see ibid.; Hester, "Perspectives on the Material Culture"; Campbell, *Indians of Southern Texas and Northeastern Mexico*, 39–59, 71–77, 79–93; and Wade, *Native Americans*. For the most current synthesis of historical and archaeological work to date on Coahuilteco speakers, their links to the San Antonio missions, and their present-day descendants' efforts to receive federal recognition, see Thoms et al., *Reassessing Cultural Extinction*. For models of merger and cooperation among native peoples, see Albers, "Symbiosis, Merger, and War," esp. 112–17; and White, *Middle Ground*.

16. Aten, *Indians of the Upper Texas Coast*; Ricklis, *Karankawa Indians of Texas*.

CHAPTER 3

1. Fray Benito Fernández de Santa Ana to fray Pedro del Barco, Feb. 20, 1740, in Leutenegger and Habig, *San José Papers*, 1:53.

2. Hinojosa, "Friars and Indians"; C. Castañeda, *Our Catholic Heritage in Texas*; fray Mariano de los Dolores y Viana to Viceroy conde de Revilla Gigedo, Jan. 12, 1752, in Dolores y Viana, *Letters and Memorials*, 138. See also Dolores y Viana to Governor Barrios of Texas, Colonel Parrilla, and Governor Martos y Navarrete, Feb. 6, 1759, in ibid., 311–12.

3. As Gary Anderson argues, missions became a place for "native ethnogenesis and cultural reinvention." G. Anderson, *Indian Southwest*, 67. Schuetz, "Indians of the San Antonio Missions," 116–231.

4. Fernández de Santa Ana to del Barco, Feb. 20, 1740, in Leutenegger and Habig, *San José Papers*, 1:53.

5. Pedro de Rivera, "Diario y Derrotero" [Diary and Itinerary], in J. Jackson, *Imaginary Kingdom*, 29–30, 42; Naylor and Polzer, *Pedro de Rivera*, 86, 160–61; Peña, "Account of the 1720–1722 Entrada," 409; Teja, *San Antonio de Béxar*, 18.

6. The Payayas offer a unique snapshot of native use of mission settlements. Because the

missions were established in the midst of traditional Payaya ranges, Payayas quickly became the largest ethnic group within the San Antonio community, numbering an identifiable total of 184 between 1719 and 1789 (though fewer than 50 were present in any given year). Of the five Spanish mission communities eventually established in San Antonio, Payayas clearly considered Valero their home village and entered no others. At the same time, however, comparison of baptism, marriage, and burial records indicates that though many Payayas accepted baptism and agreed to marriage sacraments, they did not choose to be buried in mission cemeteries, suggesting their preference for burial at traditional native sites. Many others continued to live independently in different settlements scattered across Texas and Coahuila, as individuals and families moved back and forth between independent rancherías and mission settlements. Campbell, *Payaya Indians of Southern Texas*, 11–14.

7. Céliz, *Diary of the Alarcón Expedition*, 86.

8. Fray Antonio Margil de Jesús to marqués de San Miguel de Aguayo, Dec. 26, 1719, in Margil de Jesús, *Nothingness Itself*, 268; fray Antonio Olivares et al., "Oposición a la fundación de la Mission de San José del río de San Antonio," Feb. 23, 1720, in Leutenegger and Habig, *San José Papers*, 1:20–26.

9. Report of Captain Juan Valdéz, Mar. 13, 1720, in Leutenegger and Habig, *San José Papers*, 1:27–42.

10. Céliz, *Diary of the Alarcón Expedition*, 86; Schuetz, "Indians of the San Antonio Missions," 337–41.

11. Peña, "Account of the 1720–1722 Entrada," 405–6, 409, 412–14.

12. Ibid, 433–34.

13. Aten, *Indians of the Upper Texas Coast*, 68; Ricklis, *Karankawa Indians of Texas*, 138–40.

14. Schuetz, "Indians of the San Antonio Missions," 254–67, 277, 294; Governor Jacinto de Barrios y Jáuregui, "Informe del gobernador sobre la misíon de San José," May 28, 1758, in Leutenegger and Habig, *San José Papers*, 1:131; Leutenegger, *Inventory of the Mission*, 29–30, and *Guidelines for a Texas Mission*, 31; Decree of Commandant General Pedro de Nava, Apr. 10, 1794, in Leutenegger and Habig, *San José Papers*, 2:101.

15. Schuetz, "Professional Artisans in the Hispanic Southwest," 19–20; Teja, "Forgotten Founders," 34–35; Schuetz, "Indians of the San Antonio Missions," 71, 244; T. N. Campbell, "Coahuiltecans and Their Neighbors," in *Indians of Southern Texas and Northeastern Mexico*, 49, 51; Salinas, *Indians of the Rio Grande Delta*, 121–22; Ricklis, *Karankawa Indians of Texas*, 4; Peña, "Account of the 1720–1722 Entrada," 432; Teja, *San Antonio de Béxar*, 44–47.

16. Report of fray Ignacio Antonio Ciprián to fray Juan Antonio Abasolo, Oct. 27, 1749, in Leutenegger and Habig, *San José Papers*, 1:97; J. Clark, *Mission San José y San Miguel*, 24; report of the status of the Texas missions, Mar. 6, 1762, in Dolores y Viana, *Letters and Memorials*, 333; Scurlock and Fox, *Archeological Investigation of Mission Concepción*, 12; Schuetz, "Historical Outline of Mission," 8, and "Indians of the San Antonio Missions," 71, 245; Ricklis, "Spanish Colonial Missions," 134; K. Gilmore, *Mission Rosario*, 2:15, 80.

17. Schuetz, "Professional Artisans in the Hispanic Southwest," 24, 26–27, 35–36; K. Gilmore, *Mission Rosario*, 2:24, 82.

18. Salinas, *Indians of the Rio Grande Delta*, 70; Campbell and Campbell, *Indian Groups Associated with Spanish Missions*; Schuetz, "Indians of the San Antonio Missions," 49–50, 58–60, 335, 337–41, 352.

19. Fray Jaudenes to Manuel Muñoz, Oct. 13, 1791, in Nunley, "Translation of Spanish Documents," 71; K. Gilmore, "Indians of Mission Rosario" [1984], 176–77; J. Clark, *Mission San José y San Miguel*, 27; Campbell and Campbell, *Indian Groups Associated with Spanish Missions*, 40–41; Schuetz, "Indians of the San Antonio Missions," 357–58; Arricivita, *Apostolic Chronicle*, 2:3–5.

20. Fray José Francisco López to fray Rafael José Verger, May 5, 1789, in Dabbs, "Texas Missions in 1785," 15; summary of military events at the presidios of San Antonio de Béxar and La Bahía during the month of Feb. 1784, BA; Rosalind Z. Rock, "Los Habitantes: A History of Texas' Mission San Juan de Capistrano and Its People," unpublished manuscript cited in Thoms et al., *Reassessing Cultural Extinction*, 34–35, 91; Schuetz, "Historical Outline of Mission," 4; census report, fray Jesús Garavito to captain of La Bahía presidio, Juan Bautista de Elguezábal, June 30, 1797, and census of Rosario, Oct. 23, 1796, cited in Oberste, *History of Refugio Mission*, 210, 366; K. Gilmore, "Indians of Mission Rosario" [1984], 177; fray Vallejo to Antonio Cordero, Dec. 13, 1806, in Nunley, "Translation of Spanish Documents," 85.

21. Fray Antonio Margil de Jesús and fray Isidro Felix de Espinosa to Reverend Fr. Procurator, fray Mathías Sáenz de San Antonio, July 24, 1724, in Margil de Jesús, *Nothingness Itself*, 304; fray Benito Fernández de Santa Ana to fray Miguel Sevillano de Paredes, Aug. 8, 1737, in Fernández de Santa Ana, *Letters and Memorials*, 27; Fernández de Santa Ana to del Barco, Feb. 20, 1740, in Leutenegger and Habig, *San José Papers*, 1:56; opinion of Pedro de Rivera contained within decree of Viceroy marqués de Casafuerte, July 1, 1730, BA.

22. Fray Miguel Sevillano de Paredes, "Transsumpto de vn Memorial que por parte de este collegio se remitio al Rey en el Consejo Real de Indias estaño de 1729 en 12 de Nob^e," Dunn Transcripts, 1716–1749, Archivo del Colegio de la Santa Cruz de Querétaro, Center for American History, University of Texas at Austin; Leutenegger, *Inventory of the Mission*, 29; Bolton, *Texas in the Middle Eighteenth Century*, 142–48; Rubí, "Itinerario de Señor Marqués de Rubí," in J. Jackson, *Imaginary Kingdom*, 122, 124, 131, 134.

23. Céliz, *Diary of the Alarcón Expedition*, 67. Espíritu Santo was moved twice and reestablished for other Indian groups, notably Aranamas and Tamiques. Ricklis, *Karankawa Indians of Texas*, 153; Rubí, "Itinerario de Señor Marqués de Rubí," 141; Oberste, *History of Refugio Mission*, 123–25.

24. Ricklis, *Karankawa Indians of Texas*, 162–67, and "Aboriginal Karankawan Adaptation," 231–35; fray José Francisco Mariano Garza to Manuel Muñoz, July 21, 1793, as translated in Oberste, *History of Refugio Mission*, 85; see also 71, 76, 84, 98, 123, 180, 190, 209–10, 222–26; K. Gilmore, "Indians of Mission Rosario" [1984], 164, 183, 187, and "Indians of Mission Rosario" [1989], 239–40; Ricklis, "Spanish Colonial Missions"; DeFrance, "Zooarcheological Evidence of Colonial Culture Change"; K. Gilmore, *Mission Rosario*, 2:155–59.

25. Gerhard, *North Frontier of New Spain*; Reff, *Disease, Depopulation, and Culture Change*.

26. Schuetz, "Indians of the San Antonio Missions," 141–50, 161–66. In 1772, the mean age at Capistrano was 25.7, at Espada 26.1, at Concepción 25.4, and at Valero 28.0. Schuetz, "Indians of the San Antonio Missions," 127–29, 173, 221–23.

27. Fray José Francisco López, "Report and Account That the Father President of the Missions in the Province of Texas or New Philippines Sends to the Most Illustrious Señor Fray Rafael José Verger," May 5, 1789, in Dabbs, "Texas Missions in 1785," 6, 7.

28. Juan de Oliván Rebolledo to the viceroy, July 18, 1733, BA.

29. McDonald, Hindes, and Gilmore, "Marqués de Aguayo's Report," 62.

30. Barrios y Jáuregui, "Informe del gobernador sobre la misíon de San José," May 28, 1758, in Leutenegger and Habig, *San José Papers*, 1:131–32; Morfi, *History of Texas*, 1:93–95, 97; fray José de Solís, report on Mission San José, 1768, in Leutenegger and Habig, *San José Papers*, 1:148.

31. Morfi, *History of Texas*, 1:93–94; Leutenegger, *Inventory of the Mission*, 33; report of the status of the Texas missions, Mar. 6, 1762, in Dolores y Viana, *Letters and Memorials*, 333, 336–40; Habig, *Alamo Chain of Missions*, 139.

32. Fray Mariano de los Dolores y Viana to Viceroy conde de Revilla Gigedo, Jan. 12, 1752, in Dolores y Viana, *Letters and Memorials*, 138. See also Dolores y Viana to Governor Barrios of Texas, Colonel Parrilla, and Governor Martos y Navarrete, Feb. 6, 1759, in ibid., 311–12. Decree of Commandant General Pedro de Nava, Apr. 10, 1794, in Leutenegger and Habig, *San José Papers*, 2:95–96.

33. Report of Captain Juan Valdéz, Mar. 13, 1720, in Leutenegger and Habig, *San José Papers*, 1:33; Paredes, "Transsumpto de vn Memorial," Dunn Transcripts, 1716–1749, University of Texas at Austin.

34. Leutenegger, *Guidelines for a Texas Mission*, 38. For a general summary and description of Spanish mission systems of labor, see Schuetz, "Indians of the San Antonio Missions," chap. 5. For a missionary's idealized picture of what the San José mission accomplished along lines of appropriate divisions of labor, see Solís, "Solís Diary of 1767," 21. For gender ideals in Spain and New Spain, see Perry, *Gender and Disorder*; and Gutiérrez, *When Jesus Came*.

35. Leutenegger, *Guidelines for a Texas Mission*, 38; Francisco de Tovar to Hugo O'Conór, Aug. 4, 1768, BA.

36. Leutenegger and Habig, *San José Papers*, 1:132; report of the status of the Texas missions, Mar. 6, 1762, in Dolores y Viana, *Letters and Memorials*, 346; Almaráz, *Inventory of the Rio Grande Missions*, 33; Oberste, *History of Refugio Mission*, 43; fray Joseph Francisco Mariano Garza, "Memoria de lo que pro ahora se juzga precisamente necesario para la nueva fundacion del Refugio," Nov. 6, 1794, Dunn Transcripts, 1790–1793, Archivo General de Indias, Audiencia de Guadalajara, Catholic Archives of Texas, Austin; Leutenegger, *Guidelines for a Texas Mission*, 20–22; Schuetz, "Indians of the San Antonio Missions," 268.

37. Leutenegger, *Guidelines for a Texas Mission*, 10, 17–39, 41–45; report of the status of the Texas missions, Mar. 6, 1762, in Dolores y Viana, *Letters and Memorials*, 327–54; Leutenegger, *Inventory of the Mission*; Tomás Felipe Winthuysen to Viceroy conde de Fuenclara,

Aug. 19, 1744, BA; Ricklis, *Karankawa Indians of Texas*, 154; Morfi, *History of Texas*, 1:93–95; Schuetz, "Indians of the San Antonio Missions," 269–80.

38. Petition of Benito Fernández de Santa Ana to Governor Francisco García Larios, Sept. 9, 1748, in Fernández de Santa Ana, *Letters and Memorials*, 79; Leutenegger, *Inventory of the Mission*, 33; Schuetz, "Indians of the San Antonio Missions," 242–43; Weddle, *San Juan Bautista*, 64; report of the status of the Texas missions, Mar. 6, 1762, in Dolores y Viana, *Letters and Memorials*, 346. Dolores y Viana also writes of the Indians running away from work to "their old way of living in the wilderness" in his 1739 letter to Viceroy Archbishop Juan Antonio de Vizarrón, in ibid., 29–30. Captain Toribio de Urrutia to the viceroy, Dec. 17, 1740, in Leutenegger and Habig, *San José Papers*, 1:83.

39. "Were you lazy?" was also a constant refrain in fray Bartholomé García's Spanish-Coahuilteco *Manual para administrar los santos sacramentos* (Manual for the Administration of the Holy Sacraments) in questioning failures to confess, to do penance, or to attend mass. Dolores y Viana to Vizarrón, 1739, in Dolores y Viana, *Letters and Memorials*, 29; report of the status of the Texas missions, Mar. 6, 1762, in ibid., 346; Paredes, "Transsumpto de vn Memorial," Dunn Transcripts, 1716–1749, University of Texas at Austin; fray Manuel de Silva, "Inventory of the Goods Belonging to This Mission Espiritu Santo," Nov. 27, 1783, in "Texas Missions of the Coastal Bend: Espiritu Santo, Rosario, Refugio," trans. William H. Oberste, typescript, 1980, William H. Oberste Papers, Catholic Archives of Texas, Austin.

40. Schuetz, "Indians of the San Antonio Missions," 241; petition of Fernández de Santa Ana to García Larios, Sept. 9, 1748, in Fernández de Santa Ana, *Letters and Memorials*, 81.

41. Silva, "Inventory of the Goods," Oberste Papers, Catholic Archives of Texas; Jennifer L. Logan, "Archaeology," in Thoms et al., *Reassessing Cultural Extinction*, 109–11; Ricklis, *Karankawa Indians of Texas*, 154; Aten, *Indians of the Upper Texas Coast*, 69; Solís, "Diary of a Visit of Inspection," 52.

42. Report of fray Ignacio Antonio Ciprián, Oct. 27, 1749, in Leutenegger and Habig, *Texas Missions of the College of Zacatecas*, 22; Schuetz, "Indians of the San Antonio Missions," 209, 246; T. N. Campbell, "Indians of the San Antonio Missions," in *Indians of Southern Texas and Northeastern Mexico*, 83; J. Clark, *Mission San José y San Miguel*, 138; Leutenegger, *Guidelines for a Texas Mission*, 49 (for quote); Scurlock and Fox, *Archeological Investigation of Mission Concepción*, 39–49; Cargill and Hard, "Assessing Native American Mobility."

43. Leutenegger, *Guidelines for a Texas Mission*, 53–54; J. Clark, *Mission San José y San Miguel*, 139; Oberste, *History of Refugio Mission*, 124, 182–83, 229–30; fray Antonio Garavito to Juan Elguezábal, interim commander at Presidio La Bahía, Mar. 25, 1798, as translated in Ricklis, *Karankawa Indians of Texas*, 161; Ricklis, "Spanish Colonial Missions," 134–35; Francisco Viana to Governor Antonio Cordero, Nov. 16, 1805, BA.

44. Salinas, *Indians of the Rio Grande Delta*, 125–26; K. Gilmore, *Mission Rosario*, 1:67, 2:82, 99–105; Hester et al., *From the Gulf to the Rio Grande*; Ricklis, "Spanish Colonial Missions," 133, 157–58, 165; Fox, "Indians at Rancho de las Cabras"; Lohse, "Lithics from the San Antonio de Valero Mission"; Schuetz, *History and Archeology of Mission*, 2:69–73. In analyzing lithic

assemblages among excavation findings at Mission San Antonio de Valero, Jon C. Lohse found a combination of Perdiz arrow points (which are characteristic of native technologies in south Texas) and Guerrero arrow points (which are characteristic of native technologies in northern Mexico) as well as a combination of archaic and historic artifacts, and he argues that it suggests both the northward spread of native technologies from Mexico into Texas as a result of the mixing of native peoples from those regions (pre– and post–Spanish contact) and the continued movement of Indians between native and mission settlements.

45. K. Gilmore, *Mission Rosario*, 1:67–69, 2:117–120; Ricklis, "Spanish Colonial Missions"; Schuetz, *History and Archeology of Mission*, 2:44–46, 62–68; Scurlock and Fox, *Archeological Investigation of Mission Concepción*, 129, 136–37; fray Antonio de Olivares to the viceroy, Oct. 1716, in Leutenegger, "Two Franciscan Documents," 198; Hester, *Digging into South Texas Prehistory*, 125–26, and "Perspectives on the Material Culture," 223–24; LeRoy Johnson, *Life and Times of Toyah-Culture Folk*; Aten et al., *Excavations at the Harris County Boys' School Cemetery*, 104.

46. Moorhead, *Presidio*; Faulk and Faulk, *Defenders of Empire*.

47. Aten, *Indians of the Upper Texas Coast*, 68; Newcomb, "Karankawa"; K. Gilmore, "Indians of Mission Rosario" [1984]; Bolton, *Athanase de Mézières*, 1:267, 332, 2:30, 40, 43, 44, 62, 299; Morfi, *History of Texas*, 1:97; Schuetz, "Indians of the San Antonio Missions," 273–74; Solís, "Solís Diary of 1767," 15, 17, 20, 38, 39; report of fray Juan de Dios María Camberos, 1758, cited in K. Gilmore, *Mission Rosario*, 2:5.

48. Fray Mariano de los Dolores y Viana to acting mayor of San Fernando, Juan Joseph de Montes de Oca, Oct. 8, 1745, in Dolores y Viana, *Letters and Memorials*, 47–48; Arricivita, *Apostolic Chronicle*, 2:35; Dunn, "Apache Relations in Texas," 252.

49. Petition de fray Benito Fernández de Santa Ana al señor auditor, Feb. 20, 1750, in Porrúa Turanzas, *Documentos para la historia*, 209; Allen, "Parrilla Expedition to the Red River"; Arricivita, *Apostolic Chronicle*, 2:12–13, 21; Starnes, *San Gabriel Missions*, 29–30.

50. Tomás Felipe Winthuysen to Viceroy conde de Fuenclara, Aug. 19, 1744, BA; Lafora, *Frontiers of New Spain*, 160. As commandant inspector of the internal presidios, Hugo O'Conor made similar arguments in a report ten years later. See O'Conor, *Defenses of Northern New Spain*, 57–58. Roque de Medina to Hugo O'Conor, Mar. 8, 1774, Luis Antonio Menchaca to O'Conor, Mar. 9, 1774, O'Conor to Rafael Martínez Pacheco, Apr. 20, 1774, Martínez Pacheco to O'Conor, Apr. 20, 1774, and O'Conor to Viceroy Antonio María de Bucareli y Ursúa, Apr. 20, 1774, in Bolton, *Athanase de Mézières*, 2:33, 40, 42, 43–44, 46; Bucareli y Ursúa to Governor Juan María, Barón de Ripperdá, Feb. 21, 1776, BA.

51. Santa María, *Relación Histórica de la Colonia*, 97; Schuetz, "Indians of the San Antonio Missions," 70–80; K. Gilmore, "Indians of Mission Rosario" [1984], 187; Aten, *Indians of the Upper Texas Coast*, 69, 81–82.

52. Report of the status of the Texas missions, Mar. 6, 1762, in Dolores y Viana, *Letters and Memorials*, 342; Solís, "Solís Diary of 1767," 12; Morfi, *Excerpts from the Memorias*, 45. For discussion of early modern Spanish ideas of "barbarism" as they were applied to Indians of the New World and associated with the bestial world, see Pagden, *Fall of Natural Man*, esp.

chap. 2. For comparison with battles over gender and sexuality in Spanish missions in other northern provinces, see Deeds, "Double Jeopardy"; Hurtado, *Intimate Frontiers*, 1–19; and Hackel, *Children of Coyote*, 182–227.

53. Perry, *Gender and Disorder*, 6–8; Lavrin, "Sexuality in Colonial Mexico"; Gutiérrez, *When Jesus Came*; Spurling, "Honor, Sexuality, and the Catholic Church"; Perdue, "Columbus Meets Pocahontas," 7–13; Fur, " 'Some Women Are Wiser,' " 92–95.

54. Perry, *Gender and Disorder*, 48; Salinas, *Indians of the Rio Grande Delta*, 123; Gatschet, *Karankawa Indians*, 60–61; fray José Francisco Mariano Garza to Manuel Muñoz, May 17, 1793, cited in Oberste, *History of Refugio Mission*, 78; Schuetz, "Indians of the San Antonio Missions," 60–63, 240–41.

55. Espinosa, "Espinosa-Olivares-Aguirre Expedition," 12; Morfi, *History of Texas*, 2:174; Olivares to the viceroy, Oct. 1716, in Leutenegger, "Two Franciscan Documents," 198.

56. Paredes, "Transsumpto de vn Memorial," Dunn Transcripts, 1716–1749, University of Texas at Austin; Leutenegger, *Guidelines for a Texas Mission*, 24–30; Silva, "Inventory of the Goods," Oberste Papers, Catholic Archives of Texas; Leutenegger, *Inventory of the Mission*, 29–31; fray Ildefonso Marmolejo, "Inventory of the Mission San José and the Increase Gained during the Year and Ten Months since It Is in My Care," Oct. 14, 1755, and accounts of supplies for 1792 and 1793 for Mission San José, in Leutenegger and Habig, *San José Papers*, 1:125, 2:12–58; Schuetz, "Indians of the San Antonio Missions," 240; Olivares to the viceroy, Oct. 1716, in Leutenegger, "Two Franciscan Documents," 197–98; Barrios y Jáuregui, "Informe del gobernador sobre la misíon de San José," May 28, 1758, in Leutenegger and Habig, *San José Papers*, 1:131.

57. Solís, "Diary of a Visit of Inspection," 40–41, 47, 52; Olivares to the viceroy, Oct. 1716, in Leutenegger, "Two Franciscan Documents," 199; Schuetz, "Indians of the San Antonio Missions," 95–96; Dolores y Viana to Captain Toribio de Urrutia, Sept. 25, 1749, in Dolores y Viana, *Letters and Memorials*, 86; Leutenegger, *Guidelines for a Texas Mission*, 41; Morfi, *History of Texas*, 1:97.

58. García, *Manual para administrar los santos sacramentos*.

59. Ibid.; Schuetz, "Indians of the San Antonio Missions," 235, 282.

60. Rafael Martínez Pacheco to Commandant General Juan de Ugalde, Jan. 6, 1788, BA; Hackel, *Children of Coyote*, 189–203.

61. Decree of Commandant General Pedro de Nava, Apr. 10, 1794, in Leutenegger and Habig, *San José Papers*, 2:96; Dolores y Viana to Vizarrón, 1739, in Dolores y Viana, *Letters and Memorials*, 22; report of the status of the Texas missions, Mar. 6, 1762, in ibid., 347.

62. *Fiscal* Areche, recommendation to the viceroy, July 13, 1772, BA. For discussions of various aspects of patriarchal ideology in New Spanish societies, see Lavrin, *Sexuality and Marriage*; Seed, *To Love, Honor, and Obey*; Gutiérrez, *When Jesus Came*; Warner, *Alone of All Her Sex*, 179–90; Espinosa, *Crónica de los Colegios*, 773; and Juan Cortés, diary of the Bahía presidio for April, Apr. 30, 1797, cited in Oberste, *History of Refugio Mission*, 205.

63. These are just three of six refrains. "As the Father, So the Son," in Margil de Jesús, *Nothingness Itself*, 315–16.

64. Schuetz, "Indians of the San Antonio Missions," 121; Campbell, *Payaya Indians of Southern Texas*, 13–14; K. Gilmore, "Indians of Mission Rosario" [1984], 169; Johnson and Campbell, "Sanan," 204–6. For comparison with other areas of North America, see Mintz and Wolf, "Analysis of Ritual Co-Parenthood"; and Sleeper-Smith, *Indian Women and French Men*, 43–44.

65. García, *Manual para administrar los santos sacramentos*; "Hymn to Our Lady, Assumed into Heaven," and "The Alabado Hymn of Praise," in Margil de Jesús, *Nothingness Itself*, 317–22; Solís, "Diary of a Visit of Inspection," 40; Leutenegger, *Inventory of the Mission*, 25–26; report of the status of the Texas missions, Mar. 6, 1762, in Dolores y Viana, *Letters and Memorials*, 331.

66. Schuetz, "Indians of the San Antonio Missions," 331–32; Céliz, *Diary of the Alarcón Expedition*, 86. The biblical law of levirate was an injunction dictating that if a married man died without children, it was the duty of his brother or other male near relative to marry the widow, and that a son born of that union would assume the dead man's name and thus perpetuate his lineage, honor, and inheritance. See Deuteronomy 25:5–10, Ruth 2:20, 3:2, 9–13, 4:1–11; Genesis 38; Matthew 22:23–33. Report of fray Ignacio Antonio Ciprián, Oct. 27, 1749, in Leutenegger and Habig, *Texas Missions of the College of Zacatecas*, 21, 23; report of the status of the Texas missions, Mar. 6, 1762, in Dolores y Viana, *Letters and Memorials*, 342; *residencia* of Governor Juan Antonio de Bustillo y Ceballos conducted by Governor Manuel de Sandoval, July 8, 1733, BA; Fernández de Santa Ana to del Barco, Feb. 20, 1740, in Leutenegger and Habig, *San José Papers*, 1:57.

67. Burial numbers also lagged behind those of baptisms (about two-fifths to three-fourths as many), suggesting that a number of people chose not to spend their lives at the missions. Report of fray Ignacio Antonio Ciprián, Oct. 27, 1749, in Leutenegger and Habig, *Texas Missions of the College of Zacatecas*, 25; Aten, *Indians of the Upper Texas Coast*, 69; Newcomb, "Karankawa," 365; fray Francisco Xavier Ortiz, "Razón de la Visita de los Misiones de San Xavier y de las de San Antonio de Valero en la Prov. y Governación de Texas, Masio de 1756," cited in Habig, *Alamo Chain of Missions*, 55, 133, 168, 212; report of the status of the Texas missions, Mar. 6, 1762, in Dolores y Viana, *Letters and Memorials*, 330, 334–35, 336, 338; Barrios y Jáuregui, "Informe del gobernador sobre la misión de San José," May 28, 1758, in Leutenegger and Habig, *San José Papers*, 1:130–31; Solís, "Diary of a Visit of Inspection," 47, 53; Leutenegger, *Inventory of the Mission*; 1772 *inventario* for Concepción, cited in Scurlock and Fox, *Archeological Investigation of Mission Concepción*, 8; 1772 *inventario* for Capistrano, cited in Schuetz, "Historical Outline of Mission," 5; baptismal, marriage, and burial records for Missions San Francisco Solano, San Antonio de Valero, and Nuestra Señora de la Purísima Concepción de Acuña, photostat copies, n.d., Catholic Archives of Texas, Austin. For similar comparative analysis of marriage and baptism records, see Cline, "Spiritual Conquest Reexamined"; and Nutini, "Polygyny in a Tlaxcalan Community."

68. Captain Manuel Espadas to Governor Rafael Martínez Pacheco, Apr. 9, 1790, in Oberste, *History of Refugio Mission*, 108; K. Gilmore, "Indians of Mission Rosario" [1984], 178; *residencia* of Governor Bustillo conducted by Governor Sandoval, July 8, 1733, BA.

69. Ricklis, *Karankawa Indians of Texas*, 23, 141–42; Salinas, *Indians of the Rio Grande Delta*; Campbell and Campbell, *Indian Groups Associated with Spanish Missions*.

70. Fray José Francisco López to fray Rafael José Verger, May 5, 1789, in Dabbs, "Texas Missions in 1785," 18; Schuetz, "Indians of the San Antonio Missions," 352–54.

71. Leutenegger, *Inventory of the Mission*, 21, 25–26; Fernández de Santa Ana to del Barco, Feb. 20, 1740, in Leutenegger and Habig, *San José Papers*, 1:59; Jennifer L. Logan, "Linguistics," in Thoms et al., *Reassessing Cultural Extinction*, 95–100; López to Verger, May 5, 1789, in Dabbs, "Texas Missions in 1785," 16. The eighteen groups were: Alazapas, Borrados, Chayopins, Manos de Perro, Mescales, Orejónes, Pacaos, Pacoas, Pacuaches, Pajalats, Pamaques, Pampopas, Pausanes, Piguiques, Sanipaos, Tacames, Tilijaes, and Venados. García, *Manual para administrar los santos sacramentos*. In 1732, Gabriel Vergera also compiled a dictionary for the Coahuilteco language spoken by Pajalats living along the Rio Grande and at Mission Concepción, and a second manual for the catechism written at San Bernardo mission on the Rio Grande in the Pacuache (Paguache) dialect has been lost. Schuetz, "Indians of the San Antonio Missions," 43–44.

72. Petition of Fernández de Santa Ana to García Larios, Sept. 9, 1748, in Fernández de Santa Ana, *Letters and Memorials*, 93; baptismal record, vol. 2, 1807–28, at Mission of Our Lady of Refuge (de la Bahía), Oberste Papers, Catholic Archives of Texas.

73. Campbell, *Payaya Indians of Southern Texas*, 13–14; Campbell and Campbell, *Indian Groups Associated with Spanish Missions*, 68; Johnson and Campbell, "Sanan," 204–6.

74. Rosalind Z. Rock, "Los Habitantes: A History of Texas' Mission San Juan de Capistrano and Its People," unpublished manuscript cited in Thoms, *Reassessing Cultural Extinction*, 33, 79; Dabbs, "Texas Missions in 1785," 6; Elguezábal, "Description of Texas in 1803," 514; Tjarks, "Comparative Demographic Analysis of Texas," 317; conde de la Sierra Gorda to the viceroy, Sept. 27, 1792, Saltillo Archives, Center for American History, University of Texas at Austin; López, "Report on the San Antonio Missions," 490; Leutenegger, *Inventory of the Mission*, 25–26; inventory of the material possessions of Mission San José, 1794, in Leutenegger and Habig, *San José Papers*, 2:92–140; "Register of Persons in This Pueblo of San Antonio Valero," Dec. 31, 1804, BA; censuses of Mission San José and Mission of La Purísima Concep[ció]n de Acuña, Jan. 1805, BA; Schuetz, "Indians of the San Antonio Missions," 182–205.

75. Pichardo, *Pichardo's Treatise on the Limits*, 4:144; Solís, "Solís Diary of 1767," 11.

76. Memorial from the government of the *villa* of San Fernando and the Royal Presidio of San Antonio de Béxar to Governor Martínez Pacheco, regarding the people's right to the *mesteña* horses and cattle of Texas, San Fernando de Béxar, 1787, BA.

CHAPTER 4

1. Rubí, "Itinerario de Señor Marqués de Rubí," in J. Jackson, *Imaginary Kingdom*, 106–11, 181; Lafora, *Frontiers of New Spain*, 146–48.

2. Fray Damián Mazanet, "Diary Kept by the Missionaries," in Foik, "Expedition of Don

Domingo Terán," 58; Juan de Oliván Rebolledo to the viceroy, 1719, and commission issued by Viceroy marqués de Valero to Juan de Oliván Rebolledo, June 3, 1719, BA.

3. Opler, "Kinship Systems," *Myths and Legends*, and *Lipan and Mescalero Apache*; Schilz, *Lipan Apaches in Texas*; Sjoberg, "Lipan Apache Culture in Historical Perspective"; Griffen, *Culture Change and Shifting Populations*; Gunnerson, "Plains Apache Archaeology," and "Introduction to Plains Apache Archeology." For raiding economies, see Albers, "Symbiosis, Merger, and War," 108–10, 122–26; Merrill, "Cultural Creativity and Raiding Bands," 145; and K. Jones, "Comparative Raiding Economies," 100.

4. Opler, "Lipan Apache," "Kinship Systems," and *Myths and Legends*.

5. Minutes and resolutions of the third *junta de guerra*, held in Chihuahua, June 9–15, 1778, BA.

6. Opler, "Kinship Systems," and *Myths and Legends*, 13–37.

7. Dunn, "Apache Relations in Texas"; Wade, *Native Americans*, 161; Bernardo de Gálvez, "Notes and Reflections on the War with the Apache Indians," in John, "Cautionary Exercise in Apache Historiography," 304. John identifies the author as Gálvez in a later article, "Bernardo de Gálvez on the Apache Frontier."

8. Schuetz, "Indians of the San Antonio Missions," 160; fray Benito Fernández de Santa Ana to Viceroy Archbishop Juan Antonio de Vizarrón, June 30, 1737, in Fernández de Santa Ana, *Letters and Memorials*, 26–27; report of fray Ignacio Antonio Ciprián, Oct. 27, 1749, in Leutenegger and Habig, *Texas Missions of the College of Zacatecas*, 21–22; B. Gálvez, "Notes and Reflections," 304. For a later period that indicates the same predominance of men among those killed in raids on San Antonio, see list of the men and women killed by Indians, from 1813 to 1820, San Fernando church listings, Béxar County Archives, microfilm roll 63, #821, transcription in Adolph Casias Herrera Papers, Daughters of the Republic of Texas Library at the Alamo, San Antonio.

9. Poole, "'War by Fire and Blood,'" 119–20, 122, 126; Cuello, "Persistence of Indian Slavery," 687. For thoroughgoing analysis of how such rhetoric and policy played out in another northern province, Chihuahua, see Alonso, *Thread of Blood*.

10. The history of Spain, like that of the rest of western Europe, has involved warfare characterized by long-term sieges of settlements and raids aimed at capturing booty, livestock, and enemy prisoners of both sexes. Intermittent wars, coastal raiders, and pirates in the western Mediterranean made captivity a constant in the region's societies from antiquity into the nineteenth century. In the expansion and colonial settlement of Reconquest Spain, the participation of women in establishing permanent settlements was vital to the stabilization of the conquest but came at a high cost, since life in war-torn territories held particular hazards for women and demanded special precautions on the part of Spanish towns for women's defense. That hazard was captivity, and Spanish society viewed as abhorrent the potential risk of sex, whether coercive or not, between Muslim men and Christian women. See Brodman, *Ransoming Captives in Crusader Spain*; Dillard, *Daughters of the Reconquest*; Rodriguez, "Financing a Captive's Ransom"; Brooks, *Captives and Cousins*, 19–26; Alonso, *Thread of Blood*, 37; and Opler, *Myths and Legends*, 222–29.

11. Letter of marqués de Aguayo, Feb. 1725, cited in Dunn, "Apache Relations in Texas," 206.

12. Fray Francisco Hidalgo to Fr. Guardian Isidro de Espinosa, Nov. 3, 1723, in R. Carter, *Tarnished Halo*, 153; Dunn, "Apache Relations in Texas," 207, 208.

13. Arricivita, *Apostolic Chronicle*, 2:27; see also 1:292; Hidalgo to Espinosa, Nov. 3, 1723, in R. Carter, *Tarnished Halo*, 154–55.

14. Hidalgo to Espinosa, Nov. 3, 1723, in R. Carter, *Tarnished Halo*, 155; Arricivita, *Apostolic Chronicle*, 2:28; Dunn, "Apache Relations in Texas," 210.

15. Hidalgo to Espinosa, Nov. 3, 1723, in R. Carter, *Tarnished Halo*, 157; Arricivita, *Apostolic Chronicle*, 2:27–28; Pichardo, *Pichardo's Treatise on the Limits*, 1:247, 2:463, 3:411; Dunn, "Apache Relations in Texas," 212 n. 1.

16. Testimonies of Mateo Perez, Vicente Alvarez Travieso, and José de Urrutia in proceedings concerning the infidelity of the Apaches, June 28, 1738, BA; Dunn, "Apache Relations in Texas," 246.

17. Order of Governor Prudencio de Orobio y Basterra, Feb. 16, 1739, proceedings concerning the infidelity of the Apaches, June 28, 1738, and proceedings for the *residencia* of Prudencio de Orobio y Basterra, Feb. 1–Aug. 21, 1741, BA; Benito Fernández de Santa Ana to Viceroy Archbishop Juan Antonio de Vizarrón, Nov. 24, 1739, in Fernández de Santa Ana, *Letters and Memorials*, 32.

18. Moorhead, "Spanish Deportation of Hostile Apaches," 210–11, 215, 217, 219.

19. Memorial from the government of the *villa* of San Fernando and the Royal Presidio of San Antonio de Béxar to Governor Martínez Pacheco, regarding the people's right to the *mesteña* horses and cattle of Texas, San Fernando de Béxar, 1787, BA.

20. Fray Benito Fernández de Santa Ana to fray Pedro del Barco, Feb. 20, 1740, in Leutenegger and Habig, *San José Papers*, 1:64; baptisms, Mar. 12, 1745, San Fernando Cathedral Archives, cited in Teja, *San Antonio de Béxar*, 123, 194 nn. 18, 19. Yet, unlike the large *genízaro* (detribalized and enslaved Indian) population that grew steadily in New Mexico, the women and children held in bondage in Texas remained few in number, reflecting the weaker strength and force of Spaniards in Texas and the lack of trade with Plains Indians like Comanches, who often sold their own Apache captives in New Mexico markets. See Hinojosa and Fox, "Indians and Their Culture," 109–10; and Teja, *San Antonio de Béxar*, 122–23. For New Mexico, see Gutiérrez, *When Jesus Came*, 112–13, 149–56, 171–90, 199; and Brooks, *Captives and Cousins*, 6, 8, 121–42.

21. Kavanagh, *Comanche Political History*, 30; Thomas, *Anza's 1779 Comanche Campaign*, 29. Conversely, punishments for Spanish soldiers who "behaved abjectly before the enemy" took the form of ritual humiliation in which the guilty men were "made to parade publicly, with distaffs and other women's trappings." Wichita mythology spoke of punishing a failed warrior by making him assume the dress and occupations of a woman. If a Comanche war chief retreated from the battlefield, he lost his war bonnet and, once stripped of the markers of warrior identity, "men hailed him as 'elder sister.'" B. Gálvez, "Notes and Reflections,"

313. See also G. Dorsey, *Mythology of the Wichita*, 244; and Hoebel, *Political Organization and Law-Ways*, 35.

22. Antonio Valverde y Cosío's expedition diary, 1719, in Thomas, *After Coronado*, 132. David Weber cited this exchange in his *Spanish Frontier in North America* and originally translated the insult as calling the Spaniards "women." Later, he shared an updated translation through a personal communication—a translation he had gained from translator Victoria Schussheim, who suggested that in the eighteenth century the term "*crica*" designated female sex organs (what in modern Spanish would be "*coño*"), thus making the 1719 insult the equivalent of "*mujeres coñudas*." Weber, *Spanish Frontier in North America*, 168, 426 n. 97. For extensive use of Spanish references to honor, see the correspondence and reports of Athanase de Mézières, in Bolton, *Athanase de Mézières*, 1:140–41, 150, 180, 194, 218, 303, 312, 338, 349, 350, 2:45, 47, 51, 164, 178, 212, 274, 275, 289, 291; Opler, *Myths and Legends*, 243; and O'Conor, report to Teodoro de Croix, July 22, 1777, in *Defenses of Northern New Spain*, 48, 59, 65, 86.

23. Testimony of Captain Nicolás Flores y Valdéz, cited in Dunn, "Apache Relations in Texas," 217; fray Miguel Sevillano de Paredes, "Transsumpto de vn Memorial que por parte de este collegio se remitio al Rey en el Consejo Real de Indias estaño de 1729 en 12 de Nobᵉ," Dunn Transcripts, 1716–1749, Archivo del Colegio de la Santa Cruz de Querétaro, Center for American History, University of Texas at Austin.

24. Arricivita, *Apostolic Chronicle*, 2:31–33; Juan Antonio Pérez de Almazán to His Excellency the marqués de Casafuerte, Dec. 1, 1731, in Simpson and Nathan, *San Sabá Papers*, xv; Dunn, "Apache Relations in Texas," 225–30.

25. Arricivita, *Apostolic Chronicle*, 2:32.

26. Domingo Cabello, *Informe*, Sept. 30, 1784, Provincias Internas, vol. 64, pt. 1, Archivo General de México, Center for American History, University of Texas at Austin (hereafter cited as AGM-UT); Arricivita, *Apostolic Chronicle*, 2:32–33; report of Captain Juan Antonio de Bustillo y Ceballos, Jan. 31, 1733, cited in Dunn, "Apache Relations in Texas," 232–34.

27. Dunn, "Apache Relations in Texas," 238; proceedings concerning the infidelity of the Apaches, June 28, 1738, BA; Fernández de Santa Ana to Vizarrón, June 30, 1737, and Fernández de Santa Ana to fray Miguel Sevillano de Paredes, Aug. 8, 1737, in Fernández de Santa Ana, *Letters and Memorials*, 26–27, 30.

28. Petition of the garrison of San Antonio de Béjar to Governor Bustillo, Dec. 24, 1732, in Simpson and Nathan, *San Sabá Papers*, xvii; Arricivita, *Apostolic Chronicle*, 2:32; testimonies of Vicente Alvarez Travieso, Asencio del Razo, and Ignacio Lorenzo de Armas in Governor Prudencio de Orobio y Basterra's proceedings concerning the infidelity of the Apaches, June 25, 1738, BA; Bonilla, "Bonilla's Brief Compendium," 42, 43; Morfi, *History of Texas*, 2:293; statement of fray Gabriel de Vergara, Apr. 15, 1733, cited in Dunn, "Apache Relations in Texas," 237.

29. Fray Benito Fernández de Santa Ana to Viceroy conde de Revilla Gigedo, Feb. 23, 1750, in Hadley, Naylor, and Schuetz-Miller, *Presidio and Militia*, 484; Fernández de Santa Ana to

fray guardian Alonso Giraldo de Terreros, Feb. 2, 1746, in Fernández de Santa Ana, *Letters and Memorials*, 62–63.

30. Letters of Fray Benito Fernández de Santa Ana to Viceroy conde de Fuenclara, May 16, 1745, to Giraldo de Terreros, Dec. 4, 1745, to Captain Toribio de Urrutia, Feb. 1, 1746, to Giraldo de Terreros, Feb. 2, 1746, and to Viceroy conde de Revilla Gigedo, Feb. 23, 1750, in Fernández de Santa Ana, *Letters and Memorials*, 50, 54, 55–56, 58, 60, 63, 165; Arricivita, *Apostolic Chronicle*, 2:35–36, 39–40; John, *Storms Brewed in Other Men's Worlds*, 276.

31. Fernández de Santa Ana to Terreros, Feb. 2, 1746, and Fernández de Santa Ana to Urrutia, Feb. 1, 1746, in Fernández de Santa Ana, *Letters and Memorials*, 57, 61, 66; Fernández de Santa Ana to Revilla Gigedo, Feb. 23, 1750, in Hadley, Naylor, and Schuetz-Miller, *Presidio and Militia*, 483, 485, 486; Arricivita, *Apostolic Chronicle*, 2:35–36, 40; fray Mariano de los Dolores y Viana to Governor Pedro del Barrio y Espriella, Nov. 25, 1749, in Dolores y Viana, *Letters and Memorials*, 95–97; petition by Francisco José de Arocha, n.d., affidavit of don Francisco Manuel Polanco, Oct. 19, 1750, receipt for two Apache Indian girls received from Governor Pedro del Barrio y Espriella by Toribio de Urrutia, June 23, 1750, appeal to governor from the *cabildo, justicia*, and *regimiento* of San Fernando, June 25, 1750, and statement of Governor Pedro del Barrio y Espriella, July 28, 1750, in the case documents of the *Cabildo of San Fernando vs. Antonio Rodriguez Mederos*, July 19, 1749–Jan. 15, 1751, BA.

32. Cabello, *Informe*, Sept. 30, 1784, AGM-UT; Dunn, "Apache Relations in Texas," 261–62.

33. Fernández de Santa Ana to Revilla Gigedo, Feb. 23, 1750, in Hadley, Naylor, and Schuetz-Miller, *Presidio and Militia*, 486; Schuetz, "Indians of the San Antonio Missions," 345–46 (for baptism record); Arricivita, *Apostolic Chronicle*, 2:41–45 (44 for first quote, 41 for second quote); fray Mariano de los Dolores y Viana to Captain Toribio de Urrutia, Sept. 25, Nov. 29, 1749, and Dolores y Viana to Viceroy conde de Revilla Gigedo, Oct. 8, 1750, in Dolores y Viana, *Letters and Memorials*, 84–86, 99, 133.

34. Fernández de Santa Ana to Revilla Gigedo, Feb. 23, 1750, in Hadley, Naylor, and Schuetz-Miller, *Presidio and Militia*, 485, 486–87.

35. Schuetz, "Indians of the San Antonio Missions," 334, 345, 349–52; Leutenegger, *Inventory of the Mission*, 26; Dolores y Viana to Urrutia and Lieutenant Joseph Eca y Músquiz, Sept. 17, 1750, and Dolores y Viana to Revilla Gigedo, Oct. 8, 1750, in Dolores y Viana, *Letters and Memorials*, 120, 123–24, 132–33.

36. Dolores y Viana to Lieutenant Commander José Joaquin de Eca y Músquiz, Sept. 10, 1750, in Dolores y Viana, *Letters and Memorials*, 115–17; Jacinto de Barrios y Jáuregui to Viceroy conde de Revilla Gigedo, Apr. 17, 1753, in Pichardo, *Pichardo's Treatise on the Limits*, 4:65.

37. Fernández de Santa Ana to Revilla Gigedo, Feb. 23, 1750, in Hadley, Naylor, and Schuetz-Miller, *Presidio and Militia*, 489.

38. Fernández de Santa Ana to Terreros, Feb. 2, 1746, in Fernández de Santa Ana, *Letters and Memorials*, 61. An expedition led by Juan de Ulibarri found religious medals among

Apache men that they had preserved as spiritual sources, not of Christian salvation, but of Spanish military valor. When Ulibarri asked the warriors why they wore the crosses, medallions, and rosaries taken off Spanish dead, they responded simply that they had learned from long commerce with Spaniards that "because they [Spaniards] wore crosses and rosaries and images of saints, that they are very valiant." "The Diary of Juan de Ulibarri to El Cuartelejo, 1706," in Thomas, *After Coronado*, 72.

39. K. Gilmore, *Documentary and Archeological Investigation*, 36, 48, 49; Tunnell and Newcomb, *Lipan Apache Mission*, 18–22, 58–60; Fernández de Santa Ana to Revilla Gigedo, Feb. 23, 1750, in Hadley, Naylor, and Schuetz-Miller, *Presidio and Militia*, 488; Arricivita, *Apostolic Chronicle*, 2:47–48, 57; fray Francisco Manuel Arroyo, "Relacion de los Sacrilegos . . . en los Confines de los Texas en el Rio de San Sabá," ca. 1758, and fray Alonso Giraldo Terreros, inventory of supplies purchased in Mexico for the Mission Santa Cruz de San Sabá, Nov. 1757, in Hindes et al., *Rediscovery of Santa Cruz de San Sabá*, 12, 72–77; Dunn, "Apache Mission on the San Sabá River," 397; Simpson and Nathan, *San Sabá Papers*, 78; Weddle, *San Sabá Mission*.

40. Arricivita, *Apostolic Chronicle*, 2:59, 60–61.

41. Ibid., 2:60–61.

42. Ibid., 2:61–63.

43. Years later, fray Juan Domingo Arricivita wrote with hindsight that "as he [Chief Casa Blanca] had only seven hundred warriors to protect over two thousand, including women, children, and old men, and two thousand seven hundred head of stock, if he waited for his enemies there [at San Sabá], who were more numerous and had the advantage of firearms, the slaughter this would inflict would be frightful and would exterminate them completely." Arricivita, *Apostolic Chronicle*, 2:63–65. See José Cortés, *Views from the Apache Frontier*, 57, 77–78; and Opler, "Lipan Apache Death Complex."

44. Deposition of Sergeant Joseph Antonio Flores, Mar. 21, 1758, in Simpson and Nathan, *San Sabá Papers*, 58.

45. Depositions of Andrés de Villareal, Mar. 22, 1758, and Juan Leal, Mar. 22, 1758, in ibid., 68, 73.

46. Depositions of Juan Leal and Father Miguel de Molina, Mar. 22, 1758, in ibid., 74, 87; John, *Storms Brewed in Other Men's Worlds*, 290–303.

47. Deposition of Sergeant Joseph Antonio Flores, Mar. 21, 1758, minutes of Colonel Parrilla's interrogation of Lieutenant Juan Galván and various noncommissioned officers and soldiers, Mar. 22, 1758, deposition of Andrés de Villareal, Mar. 22, 1758, and petition presented to Colonel Parrilla by members of the garrison of San Luis de las Amarillas, Apr. 2, 1758, in Simpson and Nathan, *San Sabá Papers*, 48–50, 53–54, 64, 71, 107. Dolores y Viana later credited the two Apaches with saving the lives of two of the children and one of the women by helping them as they fled. Arricivita, *Apostolic Chronicle*, 2:70.

48. Depositions of Leal and Father Molina, in Simpson and Nathan, *San Sabá Papers*, 74, 85.

49. Deposition of Sergeant Flores, in ibid., 56; Romero de Terreros, "Destruction of the San Sabá Apache Mission"; Morfi, *History of Texas*, 2:382; Bolton, *Texas in the Middle Eighteenth Century*, 87; Weddle, *San Sabá Mission*, 82–89; Moorhead, *Presidio*, 171.

50. Depositions of Sergeant Flores, Villareal, and Leal, in Simpson and Nathan, *San Sabá Papers*, 53, 69, 74.

51. The severed head from the statue is listed among materials salvaged from the ruins and sent to Mission San Juan Bautista on the Rio Grande. Almaráz, *Inventory of the Rio Grande Missions*, 37; Hindes et al., *Rediscovery of Santa Cruz de San Sabá*, 13; Morfi, *History of Texas*, 2:383; Dunn, "Apache Mission on the San Sabá River," 411; Chipman, *Spanish Texas*, 287 n. 51; depositions of Sergeant Flores, Leal, and Father Molina, in Simpson and Nathan, *San Sabá Papers*, 56, 73–74, 89; Morfi, *History of Texas*, 2:384; Arricivita, *Apostolic Chronicle*, 2:68. Another incident involving the beating deaths of Spaniards is found in 1784, when Taovaya warriors beat two settlers to death during a raid. Governor of Texas, Domingo Cabello, to Commandant General Felipe de Neve, July 20, 1784, BA. Though eight dead is most often cited by scholars as the total killed in the attack, Juan M. Romero de Terreros suggests that subsequent accounts indicate that three others died later from wounds, making for an eventual total of eleven, not counting a reputed seventeen dead among the Comanches and their allies. Romero de Terreros, "Destruction of the San Sabá Apache Mission."

52. G. Dorsey, *Mythology of the Wichita*, 7; Wallace and Hoebel, *Comanches*, 246.

53. Hoebel, *Political Organization and Law-Ways*, 21; Athanase de Mézières, investigation of the murder of two Tuacana Indians, Aug. 1775, in Bolton, *Athanase de Mézières*, 2:117–19; Latin phrase translated in Athanase de Mézières to the governor of Louisiana, Luis Unzaga y Amezaga, Aug. 20, 1772, in ibid., 1:337–38; Bolton, *Hasinais*, 80.

54. G. Dorsey, *Mythology of the Wichita*, 7, 22, 34, 244; Opler, *Myths and Legends*, 223, 249; Sjoberg, "Culture of the Tonkawa," 292; Barnard, "Comanche and His Literature," 128; Gelo, "Comanche Belief and Ritual," 32–33, 120; "Talon Interrogations," 239; fray Francisco Casañas de Jesús María to the viceroy of Mexico, Aug. 15, 1691, and fray Francisco Hidalgo to the viceroy, Nov. 4, 1716, in Hatcher, "Descriptions of the Tejas," 217, 57; G. Dorsey, *Traditions of the Caddo*, 54–55; Espinosa, *Crónica de los Colegios*, 696, 710; Athanase de Mézières to the viceroy, Feb. 20, 1778, in Bolton, *Athanase de Mézières*, 2:175; Colonel Diego Ortiz Parrilla to fray José García, guardian of the College of San Fernando, Apr. 8, 1758, in Hadley, Naylor, and Schuetz-Miller, *Presidio and Militia*, 513.

55. For similar treatment of Spaniards by Aztec warriors, see Clendinnen, " 'Fierce and Unnatural Cruelty,' " 84.

56. Depositions of Father Molina, Leal, and Ensign Juan Cortinas, Mar. 27, 1758, and Colonel Parrilla to marqués de las Amarillas, Apr. 8, 1758, in Simpson and Nathan, *San Sabá Papers*, 76, 86, 118, 138–39.

57. Deposition of Villareal, and Parrilla to the viceroy, Apr. 8, 1758, in ibid., 71, 145.

58. Petition presented to Colonel Parrilla, Apr. 2, 1758, depositions of Sergeant Tomás de Ogeda, Mar. 27, 1758, and Sergeant Domingo Castelo, Mar. 27, 1758, and Parrilla to the viceroy, Apr. 8, 1758, in ibid., 107–15, 136; Arricivita, *Apostolic Chronicle*, 2:72.

59. Arricivita, *Apostolic Chronicle*, 2:70–73.

60. Schuetz, "Indians of the San Antonio Missions," 164; Weddle, *San Sabá Mission*, 137; Arricivita, *Apostolic Chronicle*, 2:74; Colonel Diego Ortiz Parrilla, *Consulta*, Nov. 18, 1759, cited in Tunnell and Newcomb, *Lipan Apache Mission*, 162; John, *Storms Brewed in Other Men's Worlds*, 303; Allen, "Parrilla Expedition to the Red River."

61. Fray Diego Jiménez and Manuel Antonio Cuevas to the viceroy, Jan. 24, 1763, in Arricivita, *Apostolic Chronicle*, 2:76, 81.

62. Arricivita, *Apostolic Chronicle*, 2:76; Felipe de Rábago de Terán, *Auto*, Dec. 31, 1761, and fray Diego Jiménez to Rábago y Terán, Oct. 8, 1762, Historia, vol. 84, Hackett Transcripts, AGM-UT.

63. Fray Diego Jiménez to the Father Guardian of the Council of the Holy Cross, Nov. 23, 1761, in Morfi, *History of Texas*, 2:399; Arricivita, *Apostolic Chronicle*, 2:77–79; Felipe Rábago y Terán, *Auto*, Jan. 23, 1762, as translated in Tunnell and Newcomb, *Lipan Apache Mission*, 166, 169; Wade, *Native Americans*, 195.

64. Tunnell and Newcomb, *Lipan Apache Mission*, 8, 31, 33, 162; Rubí, "Itinerario de Señor Marqués de Rubí," in J. Jackson, *Imaginary Kingdom*, 111; Arricivita, *Apostolic Chronicle*, 2:83; K. Gilmore, *Documentary and Archeological Investigation*, 14–15, 17, fig. 2b; Weddle, *San Sabá Mission*, 154–55.

65. Fray Diego Jiménez and fray Manuel Antonio de Cuevas to the señor auditor of the viceroy, Feb. 25, 1763, Dunn Transcripts, 1748–1763, Archivo General de Indias, Audiencia de México, Catholic Archives of Texas, Austin; Tunnell and Newcomb, *Lipan Apache Mission*, 168–71.

66. Arricivita, *Apostolic Chronicle*, 2:85, 86–87.

67. Ibid., 2:87; *Autos* of Felipe Rábago y Terán, Feb. 28, Mar. 18, Apr. 20, 22, 1767, cited in Tunnell and Newcomb, *Lipan Apache Mission*, 173–74.

68. Arricivita, *Apostolic Chronicle*, 2:86. The majority of burials found at San Lorenzo were those of women and children. Jiménez and Cuevas to the señor auditor, Feb. 25, 1763, Dunn Transcripts, 1748–1763, Catholic Archives of Texas; fray Diego Jiménez, report on the state of the missions from Oct. 1758 to Dec. 1767, Historia, vol. 20, AGM-UT; baptismal register of the Mission San Lorenzo de la Santa Cruz, in Almaráz, *Inventory of the Rio Grande Missions*, 45; Tunnell and Newcomb, *Lipan Apache Mission*, 18–22, 39–48, 114–25.

69. Jiménez, report on the state of the missions, AGM-UT; Jiménez and Cuevas to the señor auditor, Feb. 25, 1763, Dunn Transcripts, 1748–1763, Catholic Archives of Texas; Arricivita, *Apostolic Chronicle*, 2:82; fray Diego Jiménez to the Reverend Commissary, Oct. 28, 1762, in Morfi, *History of Texas*, 2:401.

70. For a shifting sense of the parameters of Apachería, see Solís, "Diary of a Visit of Inspection," 36–37. Turpin, "Iconography of Contact," 288; Kirkland and Newcomb, *Rock Art of Texas Indians*, 108 (for quote).

71. Title 10 of the *Reglamento*, in Brinckerhoff and Faulk, *Lancers for the King*, 33; Rubí, Dictamen of Apr. 10, 1768, in J. Jackson, *Imaginary Kingdom*, 180–81; report of the status of the Texas missions, Mar. 6, 1762, in Dolores y Viana, *Letters and Memorials*, 350.

72. Arricivita, *Apostolic Chronicle*, 2:24; minutes and resolutions of the third *junta de guerra*, held in Chihuahua, June 9–15, 1778, BA; councils of war held at Monclova (Dec. 11, 1777) and San Antonio (Jan. 5, 1778) to consider frontier Indian matters, in Bolton, *Athanase de Mézières*, 2:147–70.

PART III

1. Fray José de Calahorra y Sanz [Sáenz], "Diary of the Journey," Oct. 24, 1760, in Johnson and Jelks, "Tawakoni-Yscani Village."

2. The reconstruction of events comes from Pedro de Sierra to Governor Angel de Martos y Navarrete, Mar. 20, 1765, Calahorra to Governor Martos y Navarrete, July 16, 1765, statement of Calahorra, July 30, 1765, and testimony of Antonio Treviño before Governor Martos y Navarrete, July 13, 1765, BA. Treviño was called to testify to Martos y Navarrete about the details of his capture and about all he had observed during his time in the fortified Taovaya villages.

3. Though rare (most adult men captured in battle were destined for torture and death rather than adoption), this was not an altogether unheard-of decision on the part of a native leader. Jean Louis Berlandier, who was sent to Texas in the 1820s by the Mexican government to observe the region and its native inhabitants, wrote, "Sometimes in battle, when an enemy defends himself with courage and attracts attention for his bravery, the Comanches will try to capture him without harming him." "They offer him hospitality," he continued, "in order, they say, to perpetuate the race of a warrior, and they offer him women." In fact, if he was willing, they would readily adopt the prisoner into their band. José Francisco Ruíz, who lived among the Comanches for eight years and was Berlandier's main informant, explained that captured warriors were those respected for their courage, and they were "allowed rights and privileges after they join in a battle with the tribe, and particularly if they distinguish themselves in the campaign." Berlandier, *Indians of Texas in 1830*, 64; Ruíz, *Report on the Indian Tribes*, 15.

4. Calahorra to Governor Martos y Navarrete, July 16, 1765, statement of Calahorra, July 30, 1765, and testimony of Treviño, July 13, 1765, BA.

5. This description of the mission is based on the observations of Nicolás de Lafora and fray José de Solís, who both toured the area in 1767, the former with the marqués de Rubí's inspection of the defensive capabilities of the northern provinces, and the latter on an inspection tour of the missions administered by the mission college of Nuestra Señora de Guadalupe de Zacatecas. Lafora, *Frontiers of New Spain*, 166; Solís, "Diary of a Visit of Inspection," 69.

6. Calahorra to Governor Martos y Navarrete, July 16, 1765, statement of Calahorra, July 30, 1765, and testimony of Treviño, July 13, 1765, BA; Morfi, *Excerpts from the Memorias*, 11–12.

7. Having won Wichita warriors' high regard by his valor, the Spaniard, Antonio Treviño, became an oft-used emissary and diplomat representing Spanish officials in their relations with Taovayas and other Wichita bands. When he traveled with Athanase de Mézières in

1778 to visit these various bands, Taovaya men demonstrated their continued respect and attachment to Treviño, greeting him and those who accompanied him with great joy and carrying him upon their shoulders in an honorable welcome to their villages. The soldier-turned-diplomat proved so successful in the negotiations that Mézières recommended Treviño for promotion. For Treviño's later service as a mediator among the Wichitas, see reports of Mézières in Bolton, *Athanase de Mézières*, 2:199, 205, 215, 322.

8. Rubí, "Itinerario de Señor Marqués de Rubí," and Dictamen of Apr. 10, 1768, in J. Jackson, *Imaginary Kingdom*, 129–30, 130 n. 83, 195; Lafora, *Frontiers of New Spain*, 167.

9. Calahorra, "Diary of the Journey," Oct. 24, 1760, 411–14; Calahorra to Governor Martos y Navarrete, June 6, Aug. 20, 1763, BA.

10. Testimony of Treviño, July 13, 1765, BA.

11. Newcomb and Field, "Ethnohistoric Investigation of the Wichita Indians"; Mildred Mott Wedel, "The Wichita Indians in the Arkansas River Basin," in Ubelaker and Viola, *Plains Indian Studies*; Newcomb, *People Called Wichita*; John, "Wichita Migration Tale"; Vehik, "Cultural Continuity and Discontinuity," and "Wichita Culture History."

12. Kavanagh, *Comanche Political History*; M. Foster, *Being Comanche*; Betty, *Comanche Society before the Reservation*; Shimkin, "Shoshone-Comanche Origins and Migrations."

13. "Official Relation by the Lieutenant-Governor of Natchitoches to the Captain-General of Luisiana concerning the Expedition Which, by Order of His Lordship, He Made to Cadodachos to Treat with the Hostile Tribes Whose Chiefs Met in That Village," Oct. 29, 1770, in Bolton, *Athanase de Mézières*, 1:218–19.

14. Fray Mariano de los Dolores y Viana to Colonel Diego Ortiz Parrilla, Dec. 28, 1759, in Dolores y Viana, *Letters and Memorials*, 317–18.

15. For estimates of the Indian population and the number of warriors, see report of Dn. Athanacio de Mézières, captain of infantry, to Colonel Barón de Ripperdá, July 4, 1772, and report of the *junta de guerra* at San Antonio de Béxar, Jan. 5, 1778, in Bolton, *Athanase de Mézières*, 1:284–310, 2:165–66. During his 1766–68 inspection tour, the marqués de Rubí noted 50 soldiers at La Bahía, 22 at San Antonio de Béxar, 100 at San Sabá, and 60 at Los Adaes. In his "Dictamen," he proposed that following the extinction of San Sabá and Los Adaes, the two remaining presidios, La Bahía and San Antonio de Béxar, have garrisons of 50 and 80, respectively. In 1781, Teodoro de Croix proposed increasing those forces to 63 at La Bahía and 100 at San Antonio de Béxar. Lafora, *Frontiers of New Spain*, 151, 160, 167, 177; Rubí, Dictamen of Apr. 10, 1768, in J. Jackson, *Imaginary Kingdom*, 184; Teodoro de Croix, "General Report of 1781," in Thomas, *Teodoro de Croix and the Northern Frontier*, 78.

16. Morfi, *History of Texas*, 1:92–93; Croix, "General Report of 1781," 77.

17. Rubí, Dictamen of Apr. 10, 1768, in J. Jackson, *Imaginary Kingdom*, 182–83; Weber, *Spanish Frontier in North America*, 237–42.

18. Rubí, Dictamen of Apr. 10, 1768, in J. Jackson, *Imaginary Kingdom*, 181–82.

19. Alexandro O'Reilly, proclamation, Dec. 7, 1769, in Kinnaird, *Spain in the Mississippi Valley*, 2:126–27; Bolton, *Athanase de Mézières*, 1:136, 152, 168; Usner, *Indians, Settlers, and Slaves*, 133–34.

1. Kavanagh, *Comanche Political History*, 28–62; M. Foster, *Being Comanche*, 60–64; Comanche Field Notes, 1933, E. Adamson Hoebel Papers, series 5, American Philosophical Society, Philadelphia; report of Dn. Athanacio de Mézières, captain of infantry, to Colonel Barón de Ripperdá, July 4, 1772, in Bolton, *Athanase de Mézières*, 1:295 (for quote); Sibley, "Historical Sketches of the Several Indian Tribes," 1:721; La Vere, *Caddo Chiefdoms*, 43, 62, 109–16; and Sabo, "Reordering Their World," 36–39. Six years later, Mézières reiterated his point in a report to the commandant general of the Interior Provinces, writing that Wichita men "devote themselves wholly to the chase and to warfare. By the first they become rich, by the second famous. They come to be petty chiefs among their people, not by the prowess of their fathers, but by their own. To this is added the thought that in proportion to their achievements they will gain for themselves happiness in the next life." Athanase de Mézières to Teodoro de Croix, Apr. 18, 1778, in Bolton, *Athanase de Mézières*, 2:203.

2. Faulk, *Last Years of Spanish Texas*, 22–37; Chipman and Joseph, *Notable Men and Women*, 150–225; Arricivita, *Apostolic Chronicle*, 1:18, 71, 145, 279, 293; Weber, *Spanish Frontier in North America*, 198–235.

3. Kavanagh, *Comanche Political History*, 28–39; José Cortés, *Views from the Apache Frontier*, 56–57, 62, 69; Griffen, *Apaches at War and Peace*, 6–7; Chipman and Joseph, *Notable Men and Women*, 150–77, 202–25.

4. Writ from the *cabildo* of the *villa* of San Fernando de Béxar to Governor Angel de Martos y Navarrete, Aug. 1762, BA.

5. Juan Antonio Padilla, "Report on the Barbarous Indians of the Province of Texas," Dec. 27, 1819, in Hatcher, "Texas in 1820," 56; Mézières to Croix, Apr. 19 1778, in Bolton, *Athanase de Mézières*, 2:212; O'Conor, *Defenses of Northern New Spain*, 91–93; Teodoro de Croix, "General Report of 1781," in Thomas, *Teodoro de Croix and the Northern Frontier*, 79; Mézières to the viceroy, Feb. 20, 1778, in Bolton, *Athanase de Mézières*, 2:179.

6. O'Conor, *Defenses of Northern New Spain*, 56; Lafora, *Frontiers of New Spain*, 184; Gregory and McCorkle, *Historical and Archaeological Background*, 16–17; Chipman, *Spanish Texas*, 179. As early as 1744, Governor Winthuysen had tried to convince Viceroy conde de Fuenclara that neither the governor of the province nor a large garrison were needed in Los Adaes and should instead be moved to San Antonio de Béxar, identifying only the French (not Apaches) as a possible threat to the post. See Tomás Felipe Winthuysen to Viceroy conde de Fuenclara, Aug. 19, 1744, BA.

7. List of the effects which should be given to the three Indian nations of the Post of Natchitoches, Jan. 22, 1770, contract of [merchant] Juan Piseros with De Mézières, Feb. 3, 1770, and instructions for the traders of the Caddo and Yatasi nations, Feb. 4, 1770, in Bolton, *Athanase de Mézières*, 1:132–34, 143–46, 148–50; Sabo, "Reordering Their World," 39–40; Solís, "Diary of a Visit of Inspection," 70.

8. Agreement made with the Indian nations in assembly, Apr. 21, 1770, in Bolton, *Athanase de Mézières*, 1:157–58.

9. Ibid.

10. "Official Relation by the Lieutenant-Governor of Natchitoches to the Captain-General of Luisiana concerning the Expedition Which, by Order of His Lordship, He Made to Cadodachos to Treat with the Hostile Tribes Whose Chiefs Met in That Village," Oct. 29, 1770, in Bolton, *Athanase de Mézières*, 1:208; La Vere, *Caddo Chiefdoms*, 118.

11. Articles of peace granted to the Taouaïazés Indians, Oct. 27, 1771, and governor of Louisiana, Antonio de Ulloa, to commandant inspector of presidios, Hugo O'Conor, 1768, in Bolton, *Athanase de Mézières*, 1:256–60, 128–29; La Vere, *Caddo Chiefdoms*, 71–72, 117.

12. Mézières to governor of Louisiana, Luis Unzaga y Amezaga, May 15, 1770, and Unzaga y Amezaga to Mézières, June 1, 1770, in Bolton, *Athanase de Mézières*, 1:160–63, 171–73.

13. Mézières to Unzaga y Amezaga, May 20, Sept. 27, 1770, and "Official Relation," Oct. 29, 1770, in ibid., 1:199, 205, 209.

14. Natchitoches post commandant Macarti to Texas governor Angel de Martos y Navarrete, Sept. 10, 1763, BA; "Official Relation," Oct. 29, 1770, in Bolton, *Athanase de Mézières*, 1:209–11.

15. "Official Relation," Oct. 29, 1770, and fray Miguel Santa María y Silva to Viceroy Antonio María de Bucareli y Ursúa, July 21, 1774, in Bolton, *Athanase de Mézières*, 1:211–12, 2:73, 71. In depositions taken immediately after the expedition, however, two Spanish soldiers, Sergeant Domingo Chirinos and Christobal Carbaxal, make no mention of such exclusion or indifference toward the Spaniards present, though in general they believed that "the Indians failed to make any true sign of peace." "Depositions of Sergeant Domingo Chirinos and Christobal Carbaxal relative to the Expedition to Cadodachos," Oct. 30–31, 1770, in ibid., 1:220–27.

16. Mézières had been planning to make this demand for quite a time, since the second quote regarding the intentions behind his demand that they go to San Antonio comes from a letter he wrote to the governor of Louisiana the previous May. Mézières to Unzaga y Amezaga, May 21, 1770, and "Official Relation," Oct. 29, 1770, in ibid., 1:199, 210, 212–14.

17. Report by Athanase de Mézières to Luis Unzaga y Amezaga on the expedition to Cadodachos, Oct. 29, 1770, Unzaga y Amezaga to Mézières, Nov. 29, 1770, Mézières to Unzaga y Amezaga, Mar. 14, 20, 1771, and Unzaga y Amezaga to Mézières, Apr. 6, 1771, in ibid., 1:220, 232–33, 245–46, 248.

18. Mézières to Unzaga y Amezaga, July 3, 1771, governor of Texas, Juan María, Baron de Ripperdá, to Unzaga y Amezaga, Dec. 31, 1771, in ibid., 1:249–51, 264, 265.

19. Mézières to Unzaga y Amezaga, Feb. 1, May 20, 1770, in ibid., 1:140–42, 199–200. Later, the Wichitas redeemed trophies taken by others. In 1774 and again in 1779, Tawakoni warriors attacked Comanches and redeemed from them Spanish scalps. Tawakonis had sworn "to treat as their enemies those who are ours," explained Mézières, and the repossession of the scalps won words of praise. Recovery of the scalps—labeled an "atrocious trophy of barbarism" by Spaniards—further cemented the Tawakoni warriors' valorous reputation. Mézières praised the deed as symbolic of the Tawakoni nation's "zeal and bravery," while Commandant General Teodoro de Croix interpreted it as "proof of faithful friendship."

Mézières to Unzaga y Amezaga, Dec. 16, 1774, Mézières to Commandant General Teodoro de Croix, Aug. 23, 1779, and Commandant General Croix to José de Gálvez, minister of the Indies, May 23, 1780, in ibid., 2:115, 261, 310.

20. Articles of peace granted to the Taouaïazés Indians, Oct. 27, 1771, in ibid., 1:256–60. In 1778, for instance, Mézières made a personal diplomatic pilgrimage through Wichita settlements and asked, as a "father," that Wichita warriors "invite, incite, and force" Comanches to Spanish friendship, adding that he counted on Wichita warriors as defenders of the peace "to have the axe raised, not letting it fall to give blows, but to prevent them." Mézières to Bernardo de Gálvez, Sept. 13, 1779, in ibid., 2:275.

21. Ripperdá to Unzaga y Amezaga, Dec. 31, 1771, and Ripperdá to Mézières, Oct. 7, 1771, in ibid., 1:266, 255–56.

22. Barón de Ripperdá, certification of the treaty with the Taovayas, Apr. 27, 1772; report of Dn. Athanacio de Mézières, captain of infantry, to Colonel Barón de Ripperdá, July 4, 1772, and Ripperdá to the viceroy, July 5, 1772, in ibid., 1:260, 299, 320–22. Tawakoni men also referred to Mézières as the "Painted Chief," implying that he too had gone through a similar ceremony of incorporation. The "paint," a niece in France explained, was in the form of serpents tattooed on his legs and floral designs on his chest as male status markers earned while he lived among natives as a young man. Caroline Stéphanie Félicité Ducrest, Comtesse de Genlis, *Memoires inedits de madame la comtesse de Genlis*, as cited in Mills, "(De) Mézières-Trichel-Grappe," 34, 72 n. 210; Chipman and Joseph, *Notable Men and Women*, 153. In a similar spirit, as late as 1792, the grandson of St. Denis, Louis de Blanc, invited Caddo warriors to join Natchitoches soldiers in battle by sending around a "drawing of a painted leg" as a symbol of his grandfather's titled rank as "Big Leg" among their communities. Luis de Blanc to Barón de Carondelet, Apr. 16, 1792, in Kinnaird, *Spain in the Mississippi Valley*, 3:26. For similar ceremonies fifty years before with Frenchmen, see La Harpe, "Account of the Journey."

23. G. Dorsey, *Mythology of the Wichita*, 8, 284; Wallace and Hoebel, *Comanches*, 272–75; Kavanagh, *Comanche Political History*; fray Francisco Casañas de Jesús María to the viceroy of Mexico, Aug. 15, 1691, in Hatcher, "Descriptions of the Tejas," 217; La Harpe, "Account of the Journey," 259; auditor Domingo Valcárcel to the viceroy, Sept. 25, 1753, in Pichardo, *Pichardo's Treatise on the Limits*, 4:98. Apache men of repute, similarly to those of other nations, added special designations such as "*Jasquié*," meaning "valiant," to their names. Cordero, "Cordero's Description of the Apache—1796," 341; Merino, "Views from a Desk in Chihuahua," 155.

24. Mézières to Croix, May 24, Sept. 13, 1779, instructions for the traders of the Cadaux D'Acquioux and Hiatasses nations, Feb. 4, 1770, and "Official Relation," Oct. 29, 1770, in Bolton, *Athanase de Mézières*, 2:254, 275–76, 1:206–20, 148–51, 209–10; appointment of the Taboayaz chief, Feb. 14, 1785, BA.

25. Galloway, " 'Chief Who Is Your Father.' " For discussions of kinship systems and their significance to political and social organization within these societies, see G. Dorsey, *Mythology of the Wichita*; Schmitt and Schmitt, *Wichita Kinship*; Newcomb, *People Called*

Wichita, and *Indians of Texas*; Parsons, *Notes on the Caddo*; D. Hickerson, "Historical Processes, Epidemic Disease"; and Swanton, *Source Material*.

26. Qui Te Sain, chief of the village of the Taovayas, to Bernardo de Gálvez, Nov. 4, 1780, in Kinnaird, *Spain in the Mississippi Valley*, 1:392.

27. Albers, "Symbiosis, Merger, and War," 111–12; "Official Relation," Oct. 29, 1770, in Bolton, *Athanase de Mézières*, 1:209–10; see also 2:210, 270; Johnson and Jelks, "Tawakoni-Yscani Village," 414–15; Opler, *Myths and Legends*, 245; Morfi, *Excerpts from the Memorias*, 6; Parsons, *Notes on the Caddo*, 28; G. Dorsey, *Mythology of the Wichita*; Schmitt and Schmitt, *Wichita Kinship*; Newcomb, *People Called Wichita*; Gladwin, "Comanche Kin Behavior"; Wallace and Hoebel, *Comanches*; M. Foster, *Being Comanche*; Kavanagh, *Comanche Political History*.

28. Albers, "Symbiosis, Merger, and War," 108.

29. Report of Dn. Athanacio de Mézières, July 4, 1772, Ripperdá to Viceroy Antonio María de Bucareli y Ursúa, July 5, 1772, and Mézières to Bucareli y Ursúa, July 16, 1772, in Bolton, *Athanase de Mézières*, 1:289, 297, 299–300, 302, 303, 311, 323–26, 328.

30. Bucareli y Ursúa to Ripperdá, Dec. 9, 1772, Ripperdá to Bucareli y Ursúa, Mar. 30, 1773, and Bucareli y Ursúa to Ripperdá, May 8, 1774, BA. In this last letter, the viceroy listed at least six different orders in which he barred the gun trade. John, *Storms Brewed in Other Men's Worlds*, 463; report of Dn. Athanacio de Mézières, July 4, 1772, J. Gaignard, journal of an expedition up the Red River, 1773–74, and Ripperdá to Croix, Apr. 27, 1777, in Bolton, *Athanase de Mézières*, 1:301–2, 2:89, 127; Bolton, "Spanish Abandonment and Re-Occupation of East Texas," 94, 97.

31. J. Gaignard to Louisiana governor Luis de Unzaga y Amezaga, Jan. 4, 1774, and Gaignard, journal of an expedition, in Bolton, *Athanase de Mézières*, 2:81–82, 84–86.

32. Gaignard, journal of an expedition, in Bolton, *Athanase de Mézières*, 2:87–100.

33. Qui Te Sain to Bernardo de Gálvez, Nov. 4, 1780, in Kinnaird, *Spain in the Mississippi Valley*, 1:392.

34. Antonio Gil Ybarbo [Ibarvo] to Gálvez, Nov. 1, 1780, in ibid., 1:390–91; La Vere, *Caddo Chiefdoms*, 123–24.

35. Grappe, "Expedition to the Kichai," 75–76.

36. Domingo Cabello to Felipe de Neve, June 20, July 20, 1784, BA; John, *Storms Brewed in Other Men's Worlds*, 647–51.

37. Cabello to Croix, Sept. 17, Oct. 12, 1780, and Cabello to Neve, June 20, July 20, 1784, BA.

38. Appointment of the Taboayaz chief, Feb. 14, 1785, and Cabello to Commandant General José Antonio Rengel, Feb. 18, 1785, BA.

39. Cabello to Rengel, Apr. 7, 1785, BA.

40. Ibid.; Schmitt, "Wichita Death Customs," 201.

41. Cabello to Rengel, Feb. 17, May 19, 1785, BA; John, "Francisco Xavier Chaves."

42. Kavanagh, *Comanche Political History*, 126–31; Brooks, *Captives and Cousins*, 68–72; Betty, *Comanche Society before the Reservation*, 29, 96–120.

43. Ripperdá to the viceroy, July 4, 5, 1772, in Bolton, *Athanase de Mézières*, 1:314–15, 321–22.

44. Gaignard, journal of an expedition, in Bolton, *Athanase de Mézières*, 2:88, 91, 93–94; Bucareli y Ursúa to Ripperdá, May 8, 1774, BA.

45. Mézières to Gálvez, Sept. 14, 1777, and plan for a campaign against the Apaches, Feb. 7, 1778, in Bolton, *Athanase de Mézières*, 2:182, 206.

46. Mézières to Gálvez, Sept. 14, 1777, plan for a campaign, Feb. 7, 1778, and Mézières to Croix, Apr. 18, 19, 1778, in ibid., 2:146 (for first quote), 179, 181–82, 200 (for second quote), 206, 213.

47. Mézières to Croix, Nov. 15, 1778, in ibid., 2:232–33; John, *Storms Brewed in Other Men's Worlds*, 523–24.

48. Cabello to Croix, Feb. 10, 11, 1779, and Croix to Cabello, May 14, 1779, BA; Croix, "General Report of 1781," 77, 86; Bolton, "Spanish Abandonment and Re-Occupation of East Texas," 127–28.

49. A halberd is a weapon combining an ax and a pike mounted on a six-foot handle. Cabello to Croix, Feb. 12, July 17, 1780, BA; strength reports of the cavalry company of the royal presidio of San Antonio de Béxar, Dec. 31, 1780, Feb. 28, 1781, BA.

50. Cabello to Croix, July 4, 10, 17, Aug. 17, Oct. 20, 1780, BA.

51. For descriptions of surveillance routes, see strength reports and daily records of occurrences at the presidio of San Antonio de Béxar, Dec. 1780, Jan., Feb. 1781, BA. These reports continued through the decade. Vasconcelos, *Journal of a Texas Missionary*, 16–20; *expediente* concerning precautions to be taken in view of the threat of hostile Indians, Apr. 2–23, 1781, BA; petition from the *ayuntamiento* [town council] of San Fernando de Béxar to Governor Domingo Cabello, 1781, BA. "*Expediente*" is a record-keeping term used by the Spanish government for a bundle of documents pertaining to the same topic.

52. Cabello to Croix, Aug. 17, Sept. 16, 19, Oct. 20, Nov. 1, 1780, BA.

53. Cabello to Croix, Oct. 20, 1780, BA; Croix, "General Report of 1781," 74, 75, 77, 79, 83–87.

54. Cabello to Croix, Oct. 20, Nov. 20, 1780, BA; Mézières to Croix, Nov. 15, 1778, in Bolton, *Athanase de Mézières*, 2:231–32; La Vere, *Caddo Chiefdoms*, 78; Vial and Chaves, "Inside the Comanchería," 37–38, 49; Kavanagh, *Comanche Political History*, 93, 95, 98, 102.

55. Vial and Chaves, "Inside the Comanchería," 33–34.

56. Ibid., 34–35.

57. Ibid., 36.

58. Ibid.

59. "List of Goods and Effects That Have Been Provided to Pedro Vial and Francisco Xavier Chaves," June 17, 1785, BA; Vial and Chaves, "Inside the Comanchería," 37–38.

60. Vial and Chaves, "Inside the Comanchería," 38.

61. Ibid., 38–39.

62. Ibid., 39–40. For other firsthand testimony indicating that "brotherhood" was a relationship Comanches had shared with European men in the eighteenth century, see the testimonies of Luis Febre, Pedro Satren (or Latren), and Joseph Miguel Riballo to the governor of New Mexico, Tomás Vélez Cachupín, 1749–50, and Declaration of Felipe de

Sandoval, Mar. 1, 1750, in Pichardo, *Pichardo's Treatise on the Limits*, 3:298–324. After arriving in Taos, New Mexico, in the company of Comanches, the three Frenchmen, Febre, Satren, and Riballo (and later the Spaniard Felipe de Sandoval), were all brought before the governor to be questioned about what Spanish officials considered their illegal activities of living and trading among "hostile" Wichitas and Comanches and, by extension, whether those activities reflected French imperial goals that might menace New Spain's northern provinces. The interrogations of the four men also sought as much information as possible about Wichita and Comanche bands that, by themselves or as allies of the French, represented a threat to the Spaniards.

63. Vial and Chaves, "Inside the Comanchería," 39–42. For discussion of the qualities of leadership valued in Comanche society, see Kavanagh, *Comanche Political History*, 28–36, 43.

64. Vial and Chaves, "Inside the Comanchería," 39–44.

65. Ibid., 44.

66. Hoebel, "Comanche and Hɜkandika Shoshone Relationship Systems," 448; Kavanagh, *Comanche Political History*, 40, 48; Gelo, "On a New Interpretation of Comanche Social Organization"; Kardiner, "Analysis of Comanche Culture"; Comanche Field Notes, 1933, E. Adamson Hoebel Papers, American Philosophical Society; Wallace and Hoebel, *Comanches*, 272–75; Neighbors, "Na-ü-ni, or Comanches of Texas," 131.

67. Pedro Vial, "Diary of Pedro Vial, Béxar to Santa Fe," Oct. 4, 1786–May 26, 1787, in Loomis and Nasatir, *Pedro Vial and the Roads to Santa Fe*, 279; see also 272. Thomas Gladwin, in discussing Comanche kin behavior, wrote, "A person will never use a special relationship term toward another unless this other reciprocates by using an appropriate term toward the first." While Gladwin's analysis focused on internal social relations among the Comanches, one may suppose that with the use of kin terminology in diplomacy, Comanches brought to the practice similar expectations of usage and behavior. He does report that "The closer terms of kinship . . . are also extended in their application to non-related or little-known people toward whom one wishes to show friendliness or respect. . . . With the selection of terms there is, apparently, a selection of behavior patterns also, always followed consistently by both parties involved." Gladwin, "Comanche Kin Behavior," 80. See also Betty, *Comanche Society before the Reservation*, 13–45.

68. Vial and Chaves, "Inside the Comanchería," 44–45.

69. Ibid.; Hoebel, "Comanche and Hɜkandika Shoshone Relationship Systems," 447.

70. Vial and Chaves, "Inside the Comanchería," 39–46. The names of the three delegates are found in "An Account of the Events Which Have Occurred in the Provinces of New Mexico concerning Peace Conceded to the Comanche Nation and Their Reconciliation with the Utes, since November 17 of Last Year [1785] and July 15 of the Current [1786]," in Thomas, *Forgotten Frontiers*, 320. See also Kavanagh, *Comanche Political History*, 106.

71. Vial and Chaves, "Inside the Comanchería," 48; Domingo Cabello to José Antonio Rengel, Oct. 3, 1785, BA.

72. Cabello to Rengel, Nov. 25, 1785, BA.

73. Ibid.; "Treaty with the Eastern Comanches," Oct. 1785, in Simmons, *Border Comanches*, 21–22.

74. Cabello to Rengel, Nov. 25, 1785, BA.

75. Pedro Vial and Francisco Xavier Chaves, "Diary of Trip from San Antonio to the Comanche Villages to Treat for Peace," Nov. 15, 1785, in Kavanagh, *Comanche Political History*, 103; Cabello to Rengel, Nov. 25, 1785, BA.

76. "Replies Given by the Governor of the Province of Texas to Questions Put to Him by the Lord Commandant General of the Interior [Provinces] in an Official Letter of the 27th of January, 1786, concerning Various Circumstances of the Eastern Cumanche Indians," Apr. 30, 1786, and Cabello to Rengel, draft, Feb. 20, 1786, BA.

CHAPTER 6

1. Parker, "Manners, Customs, and History," 683; Wissler, *North American Indians of the Plains*, 148; G. Dorsey, *Mythology of the Wichita*, 3.

2. Marqués de Cruillas to Governor Angel de Martos y Navarrete, Oct. 1, 1762, testimony of Antonio Gallardo, May 10, 1763, testimony of Joaquín Cadena, May 11, 1763, fray José Calahorra y Sáenz to Martos y Navarrete, June 6, 1763, examination of witnesses of the third trip of fray Calahorra to the Tehuacanas (especially the testimonies of Pedro de Sierra and Antonio Gallardo), Oct. 24, 1763, Calahorra to Martos y Navarrete, June 6, 1763, July 16, 1765, and statement of Calahorra, July 30, 1765, BA. These documents are contained within the bundled *expediente* headed "Documents concerning settlement of the Tehuacana and Yscani Indians into missions, Oct. 1, 1762–Nov. 15, 1763" (though Calahorra's letter on July 16 and statement on July 30, 1765, are within the later *expediente*, "Proceedings concerning the restoration of Antonio Treviño to his presidio, Mar. 20–Aug. 26, 1765"), BA. In addition to fray Calahorra, the soldiers who had accompanied him to the Tawakoni and Iscani villages in the early 1760s and witnessed his meetings with leaders there were asked to testify about what they had heard and observed. Martos y Navarrete to Commandant Macarti, Nov. 5, 1763, in Pichardo, *Pichardo's Treatise on the Limits*, 4:334–36; Johnson and Jelks, "Tawakoni-Yscani Village"; F. Smith, *Wichita Indians*, 37.

3. "Official Relation by the Lieutenant-Governor of Natchitoches to the Captain-General of Luisiana concerning the Expedition Which, by Order of His Lordship, He Made to Cadodachos to Treat with the Hostile Tribes Whose Chiefs Met in That Village," Oct. 29, 1770, Athanase de Mézières to the governor of Louisiana, Luis Unzaga y Amezaga, July 3, 1771, and treaty with the Taovayas, Oct. 27, 1771, in Bolton, *Athanase de Mézières*, 1:216, 251, 256–59.

4. Barón de Ripperdá to Viceroy Antonio María de Bucareli y Ursúa, July 5, 1772, in ibid., 1:322.

5. Ripperdá to Bucareli y Ursúa, July 5, Aug. 2, 1772, and Ripperdá to Unzaga y Amezaga, Sept. 8, 1772, in ibid., 1:322, 334–35, 348; Bucareli y Ursúa to Ripperdá, Dec. 9, 1772, BA.

6. Ripperdá to Bucareli y Ursúa, Mar. 30, 1773, and Bucareli y Ursúa to Ripperdá, Nov. 16, Dec. 9, 1772, May 25, 1773, BA.

7. Bucareli y Ursúa to Ripperdá, Mar. 24, Apr. 28, 1772, BA; Ripperdá to Unzaga y Amezaga, May 26, 1772, in Bolton, *Athanase de Mézières*, 1:273; John, *Storms Brewed in Other Men's Worlds*, 406.

8. Bucareli y Ursúa to Ripperdá, June 16, 1772, BA; Ripperdá to Unzaga y Amezaga, May 26, 1772, in Bolton, *Athanase de Mézières*, 1:274.

9. Bucareli y Ursúa to Ripperdá, June 16, 1772, BA; Ripperdá to Unzaga y Amezaga, May 26, 1772, in Bolton, *Athanase de Mézières*, 1:274.

10. Bucareli y Ursúa to Ripperdá, June 16, 1772, BA; Ripperdá to Bucareli y Ursúa, July 5, 1772, in Bolton, *Athanase de Mézières*, 1:321–22. It might seem likely that this Comanche warrior's wife was the woman who had headed the original rescue delegation, though Ripperdá made no mention of the daughter in his records of the Comanche man's protests. However, it might just as easily have been one of the three women held in the missions. Spanish missionaries would see little reason to recognize a prior union by Comanche custom—thus, unsanctified by the church—as an impediment to marriage to a mission neophyte, or they could just as easily have identified the third woman as "single" only because she had not been married in the church, as had the other two.

11. Scholars have made the most study of wife stealing in Comanche society. See Hoebel, *Political Organization and Law-Ways*, 49–65; Kardiner, "Analysis of Comanche Culture," 57, 60, 88; Collier, *Marriage and Inequality in Classless Societies*, 45–50; Kavanagh, *Comanche Political History*, 40; and Gladwin, "Comanche Kin Behavior." For historical accounts, see Ruíz, *Report on the Indian Tribes*, 14; and Berlandier, *Journey to Mexico*, 1:344.

12. Alexandro O'Reilly, proclamation, Dec. 7, 1769, in Kinnaird, *Spain in the Mississippi Valley*, 2:126–27; Bolton, *Athanase de Mézières*, 1:136, 152, 168, 2:95; Webre, "Problem of Indian Slavery in Spanish Louisiana"; Baade, "Law of Slavery in Spanish Luisiana."

13. Mézières to Unzaga y Amezaga, May 20, 1770, in Bolton, *Athanase de Mézières*, 1:166–69.

14. Mézières to Ripperdá, July 4, 1772, and Mézières to the viceroy, Feb. 20, 1778, in Bolton, *Athanase de Mézières*, 1:313, 2:185–86; John, "Nurturing the Peace," 351; Teja, "St. James at the Fair," 397. For a New Mexico trade comparison, see Frank, *From Settler to Citizen*, 14–21, 30–34; Gutiérrez, *When Jesus Came*, 151–55, 179–90; and Brooks, *Captives and Cousins*, 60–68, 125, 162–64.

15. Rubí, Dictamen of Apr. 10, 1768, in J. Jackson, *Imaginary Kingdom*, 205; Brinckerhoff and Faulk, *Lancers for the King*, 31–35. Distinctions existing in the law, however, often had little to do with practices on the ground, and the use of captive women and children for diplomatic gain did not ensure their welfare or ultimate freedom. Captive Indian women were never made exempt from punitive policies that sent them to labor camps and enslavement in Mexico City and Cuba. Ana María Alonso points out that 610 women and children, as compared with 55 men, made up the number of Apaches taken captive by forces of the Provincias Internas between 1786 and 1789. Alonso, *Thread of Blood*, 37. See also Archer, "Deportation of Barbarian Indians"; and Moorhead, "Spanish Deportation of Hostile Apaches."

16. Domingo Cabello to the commandant general of the Interior Provinces, Teodoro de Croix, Mar. 18, 1779, BA.

17. The missions were Nuestra Señora de Guadalupe de los Nacogdoches, San Miguel de Linares de los Adaes, and Nuestra Señora de los Dolores de los Ais. Bolton, "Spanish Abandonment and Re-Occupation of East Texas"; Ripperdá to Unzaga y Amezaga, Apr. 17, 1773, in Bolton, *Athanase de Mézières*, 2:30.

18. Solís, "Diary of a Visit of Inspection," 60–69; Gregory and McCorkle, *Historical and Archaeological Background*, 37.

19. Mézières to Croix, Apr. 18, 1778, in Bolton, *Athanase de Mézières*, 2:203. Women's contribution, Mézières continued, was found in the extensive nature of their labors: "The women tan, sew, and paint the skins, fence in the fields, care for the cornfields, harvest the crops, cut and fetch the fire-wood, prepare the food, build the houses, and rear the children, their constant care stopping at nothing that contributed to the comfort and pleasure of their husbands." See also Mézières to Croix, Apr. 7, 19, 1778, in ibid., 2:197, 205. Among Wichita men considered friends and thus brothers, "kinship behavior and terms were extended on the basis of this relationship to both families so that parents of a friend became 'father' and 'mother' and his siblings became 'brother' and 'sister.' " Schmitt and Schmitt, *Wichita Kinship*, 22.

20. Ripperdá to Unzaga y Amezaga, Apr. 15, 1773, in Bolton, *Athanase de Mézières*, 2:30; Bolton, "Spanish Abandonment and Re-Occupation of East Texas," 83–84, 86–87, 96, 102, 108–12, 119–20; F. Smith, *Caddo Indians*, 73.

21. Antonio Gil Ibarvo to Hugo O'Conor, Jan. 8, 1774, transcript, Historia, vol. 51, AGM-UT; Bolton, "Spanish Abandonment and Re-Occupation of East Texas," 86–88; Chipman and Joseph, *Notable Men and Women*, 192–94; Mézières to Croix, Mar. 18, Apr. 19, 1778, and Croix to José de Gálvez, Sept. 23, 1778, in Bolton, *Athanase de Mézières*, 2:188, 205, 227.

22. Croix to Governor Cabello, May 14, 1779, and opinion of auditor general of the Interior Provinces, Pedro Galindo y Navarro, Jan. 18, 1780, BA; Mézières to Croix, Aug. 23, 1779, and Croix to José de Gálvez, May 23, 1780, in Bolton, *Athanase de Mézières*, 2:261, 310; Bolton, "Spanish Abandonment and Re-Occupation of East Texas," 127–31; Chipman and Joseph, *Notable Men and Women*, 195–96.

23. Solís, "Diary of a Visit of Inspection," 66; Lafora, *Frontiers of New Spain*, 167; testimonies of Julien Besson, Louis Le Mathe, Mary Senes Brevel, Jean Baptiste Grappe, and François Grappe to John Sibley, Sept. 15–22, 1805, *American State Papers*, Class 1, *Foreign Relations*, vol. 2. Sibley, the U.S. agent stationed in Natchitoches in the early 1800s, asked Besson, Le Mathe, Brevel, and the Grappes—all residents who had lived in or near the settlement of Bayou Pierre since the days of French rule—to testify as to past Spanish-French boundary lines along the Red River. See also the *expediente* concerning the trial of José Antonio Ortiz, July 5–13, 1805, BA; Gregory, "Eighteenth-Century Caddoan Archaeology," 261–69; Gregory and McCorkle, *Historical and Archaeological Background*, 88–90; Croix to Ripperdá, Sept. 11, 1777, BA; Mills, "Social and Family Patterns," 238, *Natchitoches, 1800–1826, Natchitoches, 1729–1803*, and *Natchitoches Colonials*.

24. Bucareli y Ursúa to Ripperdá, July 26, 1775, BA; Harper, "Taovayas Indians, 1769–1779," 184.

25. Brooks, *Captives and Cousins*, 160–207.

26. Report of Christóbel Hilario de Córdoba, interim lieutenant at Nacogdoches, Aug. 26, 1786, and "Record of the Trade Goods Which José Guillermo Esperanza Gave to the Taboayaz Indians to Rescue a Captive Spanish Woman Named Ana María Baca, with a Separate List of Those Goods Paid Out for the Rescue of a Son of Hers," Aug. 26, 1786, BA.

27. "Official Relation," Oct. 29, 1770, in Bolton, *Athanase de Mézières*, 1:216; Cabello to Jacobo Ugarte y Loyola, Oct. 5, 1786, BA. James Brooks offers a definitive study of the widespread interpenetration of Spanish and native communities through captivity, adoption, and cultural exchange in New Mexico, in *Captives and Cousins*, 179–93.

28. Compulsory bequests included as well the Holy Church of Jerusalem, the Brotherhood of the Most Holy Sacrament, and orphan girls. See the wills of María Melián, Dec. 3, 1738, Juan Delgado, Oct. 20, 1745, and Domingo de la Cruz, Apr. 23, 1745, within the *cuaderno* (notebook) of the Notary Public and Secretary of the Municipal Council, *villa* of San Fernando, Mar. 22, 1738, BA; will of Mateo Pérez, n.d., ca. June 1747, BA; Croix to Cabello, June 8, 1780, in *expediente* concerning a program for the collection of alms with which to ransom Christian captives from the Indians, June 8, 1780–Aug. 9, 1784, BA; Brodman, "Military Redemptionism and the Castilian Conquest"; Rodriguez, "Financing a Captive's Ransom."

29. Teodoro de Croix, "General Report of 1781," in Thomas, *Teodoro de Croix and the Northern Frontier*, 76; *bando* of the Lord Commandant General, Felipe de Neve, May 8, 1784, and Rengel to Cabello, Apr. 30, 1785, BA.

30. *Bando* of the commandant general, Neve to Cabello, Apr. 28, 1784, and Cabello to Neve, May 8, Aug. 3, 1784, BA; Domingo Cabello, notice and record of money produced in the settlements of Texas through alms collected since the month of September of the year 1784, Dec. 31, 1784, Dec. 31, 1785, BA; "Proceedings Conducted in Order to Establish a Deposit for the Alms Collected in the Towns of the Presidio de Béxar, Villa of San Fernando, Presidio of La Bahía del Espíritu Santo, and Pueblo of Nacogdoches since the End of the Month of September 1784, . . . for the Ransom of Captives among the Savage Indians in Accordance with the Orders of the Lord Commandant General of These Internal Provinces, Issued June 7th of the Present Year, 1786," BA; Luis Mariano Menchaca, "Report and Account of the Funds Produced in the Settlements of Texas by the Alms Collected from January of 1786 . . . for the Ransom of Christian Captives Who Are among the Savage Indians," Jan. 28, 1788, BA.

31. Minutes and resolutions of the third *junta de guerra*, held in Chihuahua, June 9–15, 1778, BA.

32. Grappe, "Expedition to the Kichai," 75.

33. "Diary of Pedro Vial, Béxar to Santa Fe," Oct 4, 1786–May 26, 1787, in Loomis and Nasatir, *Pedro Vial and the Roads to Santa Fe*, 275–76.

34. Qui Te Sain, "Words of the Great Chief of the Village of the Taovayas Addressed to Their Father Don Bernardo de Gálvez," Nov. 4, 1780, in Kinnaird, *Spain in the Mississippi Valley*, 2:392; Domingo Cabello to José Antonio Rengel, Feb. 18, 20, Mar. 20, Apr. 1, 1785, BA;

Rengel to Cabello, Apr. 30, 1785, BA; Domingo Cabello, instructions to Antonio Gil Ybarbo, José María de Armant, and Andrés Benito Courbière, Apr. 4, 1785, BA.

35. See Weber, *Bárbaros*, 148–51, 156–59, for a brief summary. See also Griffen, *Apaches at War and Peace*, 61, 69; and Thomas, *Teodoro de Croix and the Northern Frontier*.

36. Gregory, "Eighteenth-Century Caddoan Archaeology," 70; Céliz, *Diary of the Alarcón Expedition*, 78; Solís, "Diary of a Visit of Inspection," 62; Ripperdá to Mézières, Oct. 7, 1771, declaration of Gorgoritos, Bidai chief, Dec. 21, 1770, Ripperdá to Unzaga y Amezaga, Dec. 31, 1771, report of Athanase de Mézières to Barón de Ripperdá, July 4, 1772, and Ripperdá to Bucareli y Ursúa, July 6, 1772, in Bolton, *Athanase de Mézières*, 1:255–56, 260–62, 266–67, 305, 328; La Vere, *Caddo Chiefdoms*, 80, 113.

37. Mézières to Croix, Nov. 15, 1778, in Bolton, *Athanase de Mézières*, 2:231–32; Cabello to Croix, Sept. 3, 1779, Croix to Cabello, Nov. 24, 1779, and Cabello to Croix, Nov. 30, 1779, BA; La Vere, *Caddo Chiefdoms*, 78–79.

38. Croix to Cabello, Nov. 24, 1779, Cabello to Croix, Aug. 17 (for quote), Nov. 30, 1780, BA; strength report and daily record of occurrences at the presidio of San Antonio de Béxar, June 1783, BA.

39. Strength reports and daily records of occurrences, Sept. 30, 1782, Sept. 30, 1783, BA; Cabello to Felipe de Neve, Mar. 20, Sept. 20, 1784, and Antonio Leal to Manuel Muñoz, July 10, 1794, BA; John, *Storms Brewed in Other Men's Worlds*, 635–36.

40. Mézières to the governor of Louisiana, Luis Unzaga y Amezaga, May 15, 1770, Unzaga y Amezaga to Mézières, June 1, 1770, José de la Peña to Unzaga y Amezaga, Sept. 14, 1772, and investigation of the murder of two Tuacana Indians, Aug. 1775, in Bolton, *Athanase de Mézières*, 1:102, 109, 160–63, 171–73, 2:21, 119; Tjarks, "Comparative Demographic Analysis of Texas," 324–26, 331, 335–37; La Vere, *Caddo Chiefdoms*, 80; Derrick and Wilson, "Effects of Epidemic Disease."

41. Croix to Cabello, Feb. 1, 1780, BA; Cabello to Pedro Piernas, Jan. 13, 1783, in Kinnaird, *Spain in the Mississippi Valley*, 3:69–70; Cabello to Neve, July 15, 1784, Cabello to José Antonio Rengel, Sept. 19, 1785, Jan. 25, 1786, Cabello's instructions to Ybarbo, Armant, and Courbière, Apr. 4, 1785, Jacobo Ugarte y Loyola to Cabello, Aug. 3, Oct. 5, Nov. 20, 1786, and Cabello to Ugarte y Loyola, June 26, July 3, Sept. 10, 1786, BA; La Vere, *Caddo Chiefdoms*, 58, 90.

42. Croix, "General Report of 1781," Oct. 30, 1781, in Thomas, *Teodoro de Croix and the Northern Frontier*, 43, 89, 97; Griffen, *Apaches at War and Peace*; Gálvez, *Instructions for Governing the Interior Provinces of New Spain*; Moorhead, *Apache Frontier*.

43. Petition and judicial proceedings against Sebastián Monjaras, Dec. 15, 1774, legal proceedings in the case of contraband tobacco from Natchitoches, Apr. 9, 1775, and criminal proceedings against Pedro Leal and Carlos Riojas for being engaged in unlawful trade, June 10, 1775, BA.

44. Cabello to Croix, May 14, 1779, Aug. 20, Sept. 3, 1779, June 17, 1780, BA.

45. Moorhead, *Presidio*, 185–89, 207; C. Castañeda, *Our Catholic Heritage in Texas*, 4:237–

38; order regarding uniforms of the presidial companies, July 21, 1777, and methods for administering the interests of the presidial and flying companies, Aug. 16, 1777, BA.

46. Cabello to Croix, Mar. 18, 1779, Cabello to Neve, June 20, 1784, Rafael Martínez Pacheco to Juan de Ugalde, Dec. 9, 1787, Cabello to Croix, June 17, 1780, strength report and daily record of occurrences, Feb. 1784, and Cabello to Jacobo Ugarte y Loyola, June 12, 1786, BA. For more on the influential Menchaca family, see Teja, *San Antonio de Béxar*, 27, 104, 113–16; and Chabot, *With the Makers of San Antonio*, 103–5.

47. Domingo Cabello, "*Informe*," Sept. 30, 1784, Provincias Internas, vol. 64, pt. 1, AGM-UT; Ugarte y Loyola to Cabello, Aug. 3, 1786, Cabello to Ugarte y Loyola, Sept. 11, 25, 1786, Martínez Pacheco to Ugalde, Sept. 29, 1787, and Cabello to Croix, Oct. 20, 1780, BA.

48. Martínez Pacheco to Ugalde, Dec. 29, 1786, Sept. 29, Dec. 9, 1787, Jan. 7, 1788, fray José Raphael Oliva to Martínez Pacheco, Feb. 11, 1787, Martínez Pacheco to Oliva, Feb. 14, 1787, memorial from the government of the *villa* of San Fernando and the Royal Presidio of San Antonio de Béxar to Governor Martínez Pacheco, regarding the people's right to the *mesteña* horses and cattle of Texas, 1787, and Martínez Pacheco to Ugarte y Loyola, Oct. 12, 1787, BA.

49. Ugarte y Loyola to Martínez Pacheco, Feb. 1, 1787, "Report on the Gifts and Food Provided to the Lipan Indians from December 27 of the Proximate Past Year of 1786 up to Today, February 1787," BA.

50. Ugarte y Loyola to Martínez Pacheco, Feb. 1, 1787, "Report on the Gifts and Food Provided . . . February 1787," Martínez Pacheco to Ugarte y Loyola, Mar. 10, 1787, report of fray José Francisco López, Oct. 15, 1787, Martínez Pacheco to Ugalde, Sept. 29, 1787, Mar. 31, 1788, report on expenditures made on the Lipan Indians between Feb. 24 and Apr., 1787, and report on expenditures made for the Lipan Indians who live in the mission village of San Antonio Valero, May 1–June 30, 1787, BA.

51. *Expedientes* containing copies of correspondence between Martínez Pacheco and Lieutenant Curbelo, Sept. 19–25, 1787, and Sept. 21–28, 1787, and Martínez Pacheco to Ugalde, Sept. 29, 1787, BA. For the first and last troop assignments to the Lipan villages, see summary of the inspection passed on the cavalry company of the royal presidio of San Antonio de Béxar, May, June, July 1787, and report showing the total number of troops and assignments in the province of Texas, June 26, 1806, BA.

52. Martínez Pacheco to Ugalde, Dec. 9, 21, 1787, Jan. 7, Feb. 16, 1788, and Ugalde to Martínez Pacheco, Feb. 29, 1787, BA.

53. Martínez Pacheco to Ugalde, Dec. 9, 1787, May 29, July 6, 1788, logs of the events taking place at the presidio of San Antonio de Béxar pertaining to the Department of War, compiled from what occurred during the months of Sept., Nov., Dec. 1788, and Jan. 1789, strength reports and daily records of occurrences at the presidio of San Antonio de Béxar for 1789 onward, BA; San José book of burials, fray José Manuel Pedrajo to Governor Manuel Muñoz, May 8, 1791, Lieutenant Bernardo Fernández to Muñoz, May 9, 1791, Pedrajo to Muñoz, June 8, 1791, and Fernández to Muñoz, June 10, 1791, in Leutenegger and

Habig, *San José Papers*, 1:203, 263–68, 273–76; fray José Mariano Roxo to Muñoz, Nov. 29, 1791, Commandant General Pedro de Nava to Muñoz, July 4, 1793, and fray José Mariano de Cardenas to Muñoz, Jan. 14, 1799, in ibid., 2:5–6, 225–27.

54. Cabello to José Antonio Rengel, Nov. 25, 1785, and summary of occurrences in New Mexico concerning the peace with the western Comanches from the 12th day of July 1785 when four hundred individuals from the said nation presented themselves at the Pueblo of Taos, Dec. 31, 1785, BA; Rivaya-Martínez, "Comanche-Spanish Treaty of 1786," 114–19; Brooks, *Captives and Cousins*, 74–79.

55. Martínez Pacheco to Ugalde, Feb. 16, 1788, BA; "Itinerary and Diary of José Mares, Béxar to Santa Fe," Jan. 18–Apr. 27, 1788, in Loomis and Nasatir, *Pedro Vial and the Roads to Santa Fe*, 307; Martínez Pacheco to Ugarte y Loyola, Mar. 10, 1787, BA; Brooks, *Captives and Cousins*, 60, 63, 160–91.

56. Cabello to Rengel, Dec. 9, 24, 1785, Jan. 10, 24, Feb. 20, Apr. 24, July 30, Aug. 31, Sept. 25, 1786, BA.

57. Cabello to Rengel, Dec. 9, 1785, BA.

58. Ibid.

59. Cabello to Rengel, Dec. 24, 1785, BA.

60. Cabello to Rengel, Jan. 10, 1786, and Rengel to Cabello, Feb. 27, 1786, BA.

61. Cabello to Rengel, Apr. 24, 1786, BA.

62. Cabello to Rengel, Mar. 14, Apr. 24, July 31, 1786, Ugarte y Loyola to Cabello, Sept. 28, 1786, and Cabello to Ugarte y Loyola, Dec. 2, 1786, BA.

63. Cabello to Ugarte y Loyola, July 16, July 30, Aug. 28, 1786, and strength reports and daily records of occurrences at the presidio of San Antonio de Béxar, July 1786, Aug. 1786, BA.

64. Strength reports and daily records of occurrences, Aug. 1786, and Cabello to Ugarte y Loyola, Sept. 11, 1786, BA.

65. Strength reports and daily records of occurrences, Aug. 1786, and Cabello to Ugarte y Loyola, Sept. 11, 1786, BA.

66. Cabello to Ugarte y Loyola, July 16, Sept. 24, 25, 1786, and Domingo Cabello, "Report of the Items Which Have Been Presented to 3 Chiefs of the Comanche Nation, and to 19 Indians and 9 Indian [Women] of the Same [Nation]," Sept. 25, 1786, BA; Kavanagh, *Comanche Political History*, 120.

67. Cabello to Ugarte y Loyola, Sept. 24, 1786, BA.

68. Ibid.

69. Martínez Pacheco to Ugalde, Sept. 29, 1787, "Testimony of the Certification Given by the Illustrious *cabildo, justicia y regimiento* of the Villa of San Fernando and the Royal Presidio of San Antonio de Béxar to the Interim Governor, don Raphael Martínez Pacheco, regarding the State of the Province of Texas on the 3rd of December of the Proximate Past Year, When He Took Command of It," Aug. 27–28, 1787, and Martínez Pacheco to Ugarte y Loyola, Oct. 15, 1787, BA.

70. Martínez Pacheco to Ugarte y Loyola, Oct. 12, 27, 1787, Jan. 7, 1788, and reports on the

gifts and food offered visitors from the Comanche Nation, Jan. 31, Mar. 31, Apr. 11, June 5, Oct. 21, Nov. 5, Dec. 14, 26, 1787, BA. This list only includes reports from Pacheco's first year in office, but such records continued through 1807.

71. Vial's expedition diary makes clear that Spaniards did not choose to travel by the shortest route but by "the route on which the settlements and villages of the Indians [Comanches] are located." "Diary of Pedro Vial, Béxar to Santa Fe," Oct. 4, 1786–May 26, 1787, in Loomis and Nasatir, *Pedro Vial and the Roads to Santa Fe*, 282–85; see also 323, 338, 472, 490–92, 498, 531; Morfi, *History of Texas*, 1:88–89; Martínez Pacheco to Ugarte y Loyola, Oct. 12, 1787, report of the gifts and food provided to Comanches, Oct. 21, 1787, and Martínez Pacheco to Ugalde, Jan. 18, 19, 21, 1788, BA; José Cortés, *Views from the Apache Frontier*, 82.

72. Governor of Texas, Rafael Martínez Pacheco, reports on expenditures, Apr. 30, Sept. 3, 1787, Martínez Pacheco to Ugalde, Sept. 17, 1787, Aug. 17, 1789, Juan José Curbelo, list of peaceable Indians visiting Béjar pesidio and receiving gifts and food, Mar. 31, 1805, and list of friendly Indians visiting Béxar and receiving gifts and food, Nov. 30, 1805, José Joaquín Ugarte, schedule of supplies for Indian presents on hand December 1804 and those issued during 1805 to friendly tribes of North and to Comanches [at Nacogdoches], Dec. 31, 1805, and Ugarte, inventory of goods given to Indians during 1806, Mar. 20, 1807, BA.

73. Reports of Governor Martínez Pacheco, Mar. 31, Sept. 3, 1787, June 30, 1789, and Martínez Pacheco to Ugalde, Sept. 17, 1787, Oct. 13, 1788, Mar. 2, Aug. 17, 1789, BA.

74. "Report on the Effects Purchased from the Individuals Listed in Each of the Entries Expressed Below, for Giving to the Indians," Oct. 20–21, 1787, May 14, 1788, BA; "Report on the Work Which I, Francisco Orendáin, Master Armorer of the Presidial Company of San Antonio de Béjar, Have Performed for the Indians Who Entered in Peace into This Province from January 1, 1789 to July 10, 1790," BA; Martínez Pacheco to Ugarte y Loyola, Oct. 27, 1787, BA; "Report on the Gifts and Food Provided to Three Comanche Indians Who Stayed at This Presidio on December 24, 1787, Four from the Same Nation Who Arrived the Same Day, Two Who Arrived on the 28th of the Said Month, Twenty-two Chiefs, Thirty Warriors, Thirty-three women, and Seven Children Who Arrived on the 29th of the Said Month, and Two More Who Arrived on the 13th of January of This Year, All of Whom Left on the 18th of Said Month," Feb. 29, 1788, BA.

75. Dionisio Valle, diary of events at Nacogdoches for June 1805, July 1, 1805, BA; Elizabeth A. H. John, "Independent Indians and the San Antonio Community," in Poyo and Hinojosa, *Tejano Origins*, 126, 129; John, "Nurturing the Peace."

76. Martínez Pacheco to Ugalde, Mar. 3, 1788, and Francisco Viana to the governor of Texas, Antonio Cordero, Jan. 24, 1806, BA.

CONCLUSION

1. Gutiérrez, *When Jesus Came*; Brooks, *Captives and Cousins*; Kessell, "Spaniards and Pueblos"; White, *Middle Ground*; Usner, *Indians, Settlers, and Slaves*; Calloway, *One Vast*

Winter Count; Merrell, *Indians' New World*; Richter, *Facing East from Indian Country*; Gallay, *Indian Slave Trade*.

2. Here, I am paraphrasing Louis Montrose, from his essay "Work of Gender in the Discourse of Discovery," 2. See also Zamora, "Gender and Discovery"; and Bucher, *Icon and Conquest*.

3. Perdue, *Cherokee Women*; Schroeder, Wood, and Haskett, *Indian Women of Early Mexico*; Shoemaker, *Negotiators of Change*, and "Rise or Fall of Iroquois Women"; K. Anderson, *Chain Her by One Foot*; A. Castañeda, "Sexual Violence in the Politics"; Devens, *Countering Colonization*; A. Klein, "Plains Truth"; Silverblatt, *Moon, Sun and Witches*.

4. Powers, *Women in the Crucible of Conquest*; Socolow, *Women of Colonial Latin America*; K. Brown, "Anglo-Algonquian Gender Frontier"; Perdue, "Columbus Meets Pocahontas"; K. Hall, *Things of Darkness*; Hendricks and Parker, *Women, "Race," and Writing*; McClintock, *Imperial Leather*; Mohanty, "Under Western Eyes"; K. Brown, *Good Wives, Nasty Wenches*; Morgan, *Laboring Women*.

5. Twinam, *Public Lives, Private Secrets*; Sleeper-Smith, *Indian Women and French Men*; Thorne, *Many Hands of My Relations*; J. Brown, *Strangers in Blood*; Van Kirk, *Many Tender Ties*; Peterson and Brown, *New Peoples*; Stoler, "Carnal Knowledge and Imperial Power," *Race and the Education of Desire*, and "Sexual Affronts and Racial Frontiers"; Young, *Colonial Desire*.

6. Weber, *Bárbaros*, 11.

7. Padilla, "Report on the Barbarous Indians of the Province of Texas," Dec. 27, 1819, in Hatcher, "Texas in 1820," 48–49, 54, 56, 57, 59, 60; Weber, *Bárbaros*, 15; Adams, "Embattled Borderland," and "At the Lion's Mouth"; Reséndez, *Changing National Identities at the Frontier*, 47.

8. John, "Nurturing the Peace," 354–55, 361–62; Kavanagh, *Comanche Political History*, 151, 196–98; Antonio Cordero to Commandant General Nemesio de Salcedo, June 16, 1806, Jan. 28, 1807, Mar. 31, 1807, BA; report of the Texas missions by fray Bernardino Vallejo, Feb. 11, 1815, in Leutenegger and Habig, *San José Papers*, 3:23–24; Reséndez, *Changing National Identities at the Frontier*, 49, 57–58.

bibliography

This work seeks to balance military and administrative records generated at provincial and imperial levels of Spanish government with ethnographic and archaeological studies of relevant Native American peoples. As listed below, a number of archival collections were consulted, but the Béxar Archives has proven the key source of Spanish primary documents. From 1717 through 1836, official documents dealing with administrative, legal, military, religious, and economic aspects of life in Texas were assembled in San Antonio de Béxar by the governments of New Spain and Mexico. Those documents are now housed, calendared, and in some part translated as one record collection titled the "Béxar Archives" at the Center for American History at the University of Texas at Austin. Moreover, Herbert E. Bolton, often viewed as the founder of Spanish borderlands history (the study of those regions of the United States that were once a part of New Spain), and generations of his students combed the state and church archives of Mexico and Spain for relevant documents to transcribe, microfilm, photocopy, and bring back to the United States. Several substantial collections of these documents are also held at the Center for American History. Additionally, an impressive array of Spanish primary accounts and documents has been published in translation—often with accompanying Spanish text and annotations—to encourage access and use by U.S. historians. This scholarship, what historian David J. Weber has informally referred to as the "Borderlands phenomena," began with Bolton's students but has grown into large-scale research programs, such as the Old Spanish Missions Research Library now housed at Our Lady of the Lake University and the Documentary Relations of the Southwest at the Office of Ethnohistorical Research of the Arizona State Museum at the University of Arizona. Though cited in their English forms, any documents that required interpretation for a particular turn of phrase or precise use and meaning of words has been consulted, when possible, in the original Spanish.

Challenges of a different nature arise in using European and Euroamerican documents to understand the actions, behaviors, expressions, and beliefs of Native Americans in the eighteenth century. Certainly, attention to the perspectives and attitudes of the European authors of such documents may help to filter out possible distortions and biases, but other kinds of sources are crucial to balancing, correcting, and aiding the interpretation of sources generated by Europeans about Native American peoples. As is true for all histories of American Indians before the early nineteenth century, primary sources providing Indian perspectives on interactions with Europeans are the most difficult (if not impossible) to find. Recognizing the gross inaccuracy of generalizations about Indians in the aggregate adds the further challenge of identifying and understanding differences among the many and diverse groups of Indian peoples who lived across the regions of present-day Texas and the Southern Plains. Ethnographic, anthropological, and archaeological works and available oral traditions, as well as the work of Native American scholars, have been consulted in an effort to construct a picture of Indian polities, cultures, practices of diplomacy and warfare, and concepts of kinship and gender both before and after European contact.

MANUSCRIPT COLLECTIONS

Austin, Texas
  Catholic Archives of Texas
    Archivo General de Indias
      Audiencia de Guadalajara
      Audiencia de México
    Spanish and Mexican Manuscript Collection
    William H. Oberste Papers
  Texas State Library and Archives
    Nacogdoches Archives
  University of Texas, Center for American History
    Archivo del Colegio de la Santa Cruz de Querétaro
    Archivo General de México
      Historia
      Provincias Internas
    Archivo San Francisco el Grande
    Béxar Archives
    Saltillo Archives
Philadelphia, Pennsylvania
  American Philosophical Society
    E. Adamson Hoebel Papers
    Elsie Clews Parsons Papers
    Harry Hoijer Papers
San Antonio, Texas
  The Daughters of the Republic of Texas Library at the Alamo
    Adolph Casias Herrera Papers

PRINTED PRIMARY SOURCES

Almaráz, Félix D., Jr., ed. and trans. *Inventory of the Rio Grande Missions, 1772: San Juan Bautista and San Bernardo.* San Antonio: Center for Archaeological Research, University of Texas at San Antonio, 1980.

Arricivita, Juan Domingo. *Apostolic Chronicle of Juan Domingo Arricivita: The Franciscan
　　Mission Frontier in the Eighteenth Century in Arizona, Texas, and the Californias.*
　　Translated by George P. Hammond and Agapito Rey. Revised translation by Vivian A.
　　Fisher. 2 vols. Berkeley, Calif.: Academy of American Franciscan History, 1996.
Benavides, Alonso de. *Benavides' Memorial of 1630.* Edited by Cyprian J. Lynch. Translated
　　by Peter P. Forrestal. Washington, D.C.: Academy of American Franciscan History,
　　1954.
——. *Fray Alonso de Benavides' Revised Memorial of 1634, with Numerous Supplementary
　　Documents Elaborately Annotated.* Edited and translated by Frederick W. Hodge,
　　George P. Hammond, and Agapito Rey. Albuquerque: University of New Mexico
　　Press, 1945.
——. *The Memorial of Fray Alonso de Benavides, 1630.* Edited by Frederick Webb Hodge
　　and Charles Fletcher Lummis. Translated by Mrs. Edward E. Ayer. Chicago: Privately
　　printed, 1916.
Benson, Nettie Lee, ed. and trans. "Bishop Marín de Porras and Texas." *Southwestern
　　Historical Quarterly* 51 (July 1947): 16–40.
——. "A Governor's Report on Texas in 1809." *Southwestern Historical Quarterly* 71 (April
　　1968): 603–16.
Berlandier, Jean Louis. *The Indians of Texas in 1830.* Edited by John C. Ewers. Translated by
　　Patricia R. Leclercq. Washington, D.C.: Smithsonian Institution Press, 1969.
——. *Journey to Mexico during the Years 1826 to 1834.* Edited by C. H. Muller and
　　Katherine K. Muller. Translated by Sheila M. Ohlendorf, Josette M. Bigelow, and
　　Mary M. Standifer. 2 vols. Austin: University of Texas Press for the Texas State
　　Historical Association and the Center for American History, 1980.
Bolton, Herbert E., ed. *Athanase de Mézières and the Louisiana-Texas Frontier, 1768–1780:
　　Documents Published for the First Time, from the Original Spanish and French
　　Manuscripts, Chiefly in the Archives of Mexico and Spain.* 2 vols. Cleveland: Arthur H.
　　Clark, 1914.
——. *Spanish Exploration in the Southwest, 1542–1706.* New York: Scribner's Sons, 1916.
Bonilla, Antonio. "Bonilla's Brief Compendium of the History of Texas, 1772." Translated
　　by Elizabeth Howard West. *Quarterly of the Texas State Historical Association* 8 (July
　　1904): 3–78.
Bossu, Jean-Bernard. *Travels in the Interior of North America, 1751–1762.* Translated by
　　Seymour Feiler. Norman: University of Oklahoma Press, 1962.
Bridges, Katherine, and Winston De Ville, eds. and trans. "Natchitoches and the Trail to
　　the Rio Grande: Two Early Eighteenth-Century Accounts by the Sieur Derbanne."
　　Louisiana History 8 (Summer 1967): 239–59.
Brinckerhoff, Sidney B., and Odie B. Faulk. *Lancers for the King: A Study of the Frontier
　　Military System of Northern New Spain, with a Translation of the Royal Regulations of
　　1772.* Phoenix: Arizona Historical Association, 1965.
Cabeza de Vaca, Alvar Núñez. *The Account: Alvar Núñez Cabeza de Vaca's Relación, an*

Annotated Translation. Translated by Martin A. Favata and José B. Fernández. Houston: Arte Público Press, 1993.

———. *Cabeza de Vaca's Adventures in the Unknown Interior of America.* Translated by Cyclone Covey. New York: Collier Books, 1961.

Cavelier, Jean. *The Journal of Jean Cavelier: The Account of a Survivor of La Salle's Texas Expedition, 1684–1688.* Translated by Jean Delanglez. Chicago: Institute of Jesuit History, 1938.

Céliz, Fray Francisco. *Diary of the Alarcón Expedition into Texas, 1718–1719.* Translated and edited by Fritz Leo Hoffmann. Los Angeles: Quivira Society, 1935.

Chapa, Juan Bautista. *Texas and Northeastern Mexico, 1630–1690.* Edited by William C. Foster. Translated by Ned F. Brierley. Austin: University of Texas Press, 1997.

Charlevoix, Pierre François Xavier de. *History and General Description of New France.* 1744. Translated by John Gilmary Shea. 6 vols. New York: Privately printed, 1872.

Clayton, Lawrence A., Vernon James Knight Jr., and Edward C. Moore, eds. *The De Soto Chronicles: The Expedition of Hernando de Soto to North America in 1539–1543.* 2 vols. Tuscaloosa: University of Alabama Press, 1993.

Cordero, Antonio. "Cordero's Description of the Apache—1796." Edited and translated by Daniel S. Matson and Albert H. Schroeder. *New Mexico Historical Review* 32 (1957): 335–56.

Cortés, José. *Views from the Apache Frontier: Report on the Northern Provinces of New Spain, by José Cortés, Lieutenant in the Royal Corps of Engineers, 1799.* Edited by Elizabeth A. H. John. Translated by John Wheat. Norman: University of Oklahoma Press, 1989.

Cox, Isaac Joslin, ed. *The Journeys of Rene Robert Cavelier, Sieur de la Salle.* 2 vols. New York: Allerton, 1922; New York: AMS Press, 1973.

Dabbs, J. Autrey, trans. "The Texas Missions in 1785." *Preliminary Studies of the Texas Catholic Historical Society* 3 (January 1940): 5–24.

D'Antoni, Blaise C., trans. *The Natchitoches Registers, 1734–1764.* Vol. 1, *Being a Compilation of Baptismal, Marriage, and Funeral Records of the Poste Saint Jean Baptiste de Natchitoches for the Years 1734–1764.* New Orleans: Privately printed, 1970.

De Ville, Winston, ed. and trans. *Marriage Contracts of Natchitoches, 1739–1803.* Nashville, Tenn.: Benson Printing, 1961.

Dolores y Viana, Fray Mariano de los. *Letters and Memorials of Fray Mariano de los Dolores y Viana, 1737–1762: Documents on the Missions of Texas from the Archives of the College of Querétaro.* Edited by Marion A. Habig. Translated by Benedict Leutenegger. San Antonio: Old Spanish Missions Historical Research Library at Our Lady of the Lake University, 1985.

Douay, Anastase. "Narrative of La Salle's Attempt to Ascend the Mississippi in 1687." In *The Journeys of Rene Robert Cavelier, Sieur de la Salle,* edited by Isaac Joslin Cox, 1:222–47. New York: Allerton, 1922; New York: AMS Press, 1973. All citations are to the 1973 edition.

Edman, Grace A., trans. "A Compilation of Royal Decrees in the Archivo General de la Nación Relating to Texas and Other Northern Provinces of New Spain, 1719–1799." M.A. thesis, University of Texas at Austin, 1930.

Elguezábal, Juan Bautista. "A Description of Texas in 1803." Edited and translated by Odie B. Faulk. *Southwestern Historical Quarterly* 66 (April 1963): 513–15.

Espinosa, Isidro de. *Crónica de los Colegios de Propaganda Fide de la Nueva España.* Edited by Lino Gómez Canedo. Washington, D.C.: Academy of American Franciscan History, 1964.

——. "Diary of the 1716 Entrada." In *The Presidio and Militia on the Northern Frontier of New Spain: A Documentary History,* edited by Diana Hadley, Thomas H. Naylor, and Mardith K. Schuetz-Miller, 2:365–97. Tucson: University of Arizona Press, 1997.

——. "The Espinosa-Olivares-Aguirre Expedition of 1709: Espinosa's Diary." Edited by Paul J. Foik. Translated by Gabriel Tous. *Preliminary Studies of the Texas Catholic Historical Society* 1 (March 1930): 1–14.

——. "Ramón Expedition: Espinosa's Diary of 1716." Translated by Gabriel Tous. *Preliminary Studies of the Texas Catholic Historical Society* 1 (April 1930): 4–24.

Fernández de Santa Ana, Fray Benito. *Letters and Memorials of the Father Presidente Fray Benito Fernández de Santa Ana, 1736–1754: Documents on the Missions of Texas from the Archives of the College of Querétaro.* Edited by Marion A. Habig. Translated by Benedict Leutenegger. San Antonio: Old Spanish Missions Historical Research Library at Our Lady of the Lake University, 1981.

——. "Memorial of Father Benito Fernández concerning the Canary Islanders, 1741." Translated by Benedict Leutenegger. *Southwestern Historical Quarterly* 82 (January 1979): 265–96.

Flores, Dan L., ed. *Jefferson and Southwestern Exploration: The Freeman and Custis Accounts of the Red River Expedition of 1806.* Norman: University of Oklahoma Press, 1984.

——. *Journal of an Indian Trader: Anthony Glass and the Texas Trading Frontier, 1790–1810.* College Station: Texas A&M University Press, 1985.

Foik, Paul J., ed. "The Expedition of Don Domingo Terán de los Rios into Texas (1691–1692)." Translated by Mattie Austin Hatcher. *Preliminary Studies of the Texas Catholic Historical Society* 2 (January 1932): 3–67.

Foster, William C., and Jack Jackson, eds. "The 1693 Expedition of Gregorio de Salinas Varona to Sustain the Missionaries among the Tejas Indians." Translated by Ned F. Brierley. *Southwestern Historical Quarterly* 97 (October 1993): 264–311.

Gálvez, Bernardo de. *Instructions for Governing the Interior Provinces of New Spain, 1786.* Edited and translated by Donald E. Worcester. Berkeley, Calif.: Quivira Society, 1951.

García, Fr. Bartholomé. *Manual para administrar los santos sacramentos de penitencia, eucharistia, extrema-uncion y matrimonio.* Mexico: Imprenta de los herederos de Dona Maria de Rivera, 1760.

García Rejón, Manuel, comp. *Comanche Vocabulary, Trilingual Edition.* Translated by Daniel J. Gelo. Austin: University of Texas Press, 1995.

Gómez, Arthur R., ed. *Documentary Evidence for the Spanish Missions of Texas.* Spanish Borderlands Sourcebooks, no. 22. New York: Garland, 1991.

Gómez Canedo, Lino, ed. *Primeras exploraciones y poblamiento de Texas, 1686–1694.* Monterrey: Instituto Tecnológico y de Estudios Superiores de Monterrey, 1968; Monterrey: Editorial Porrua, 1988.

Grappe, François. "An Expedition to the Kichai: The Journal of François Grappe, September 24, 1783." Edited and translated by David La Vere and Katia Campbell. *Southwestern Historical Quarterly* 98 (July 1994): 58–78.

Hackett, Charles Wilson, ed. and trans. *Historical Documents Relating to New Mexico, Nueva Vizcaya, and Approaches Thereto, to 1773.* 3 vols. Washington, D.C.: Carnegie Institution of Washington, 1926–1937.

Hadley, Diana, Thomas H. Naylor, and Mardith K. Schuetz-Miller, eds. *The Presidio and Militia on the Northern Frontier of New Spain: A Documentary History.* Vol. 2, pt. 2, *The Central Corridor and the Texas Corridor, 1700–1765.* Tucson: University of Arizona Press, 1997.

Hatcher, Mattie A. "Texas in 1820." *Southwestern Historical Quarterly* 23 (July 1919): 47–68.

——, ed. and trans. "Descriptions of the Tejas or Asinai Indians, 1691–1722." *Southwestern Historical Quarterly* 30 (January 1927): 206–18, (April 1927): 283–304, 31 (July 1927): 50–62, (October 1927): 150–80.

Hoffmann, Fritz L., ed. and trans. "The Mezquía Diary of the Alarcón Expedition into Texas, 1718." *Southwestern Historical Quarterly* 41 (April 1938): 312–23.

Jackson, Jack, ed. *Imaginary Kingdom: Texas as Seen by the Rivera and Rubí Military Expeditions, 1727 and 1767.* Austin: Texas State Historical Association, 1995.

Joutel, Henri de. *The La Salle Expedition to Texas: The Journal of Henri Joutel, 1684–1687.* Edited by William C. Foster. Translated by Johanna S. Warren. Austin: University of Texas Press, 1998.

Kendall, George Wilkins. *Narrative of the Texan Santa Fé Expedition.* Chicago: Lakeside Press, 1929.

Kerlérec, Louis Billouart de. "Projet de paix et d'alliance avec les Cannecis et les avantages qui en peuvent résulter, envoyé par Kerlérec, gouverneur de la province de la Loüisianne, en 1753." In M. Le Baron Marc de Villiers du Terrage, "Un Mémoire Politique du XVIII Siécle Relatif au Texas," *Journal de la Société des Américanistes de Paris,* n.s., 3 (1906): 65–76.

Kinnaird, Lawrence. *Spain in the Mississippi Valley, 1765–1794.* 3 parts. Annual Report of the American Historical Association for the Year 1945, vols. 2–4. Washington, D.C.: Government Printing Office, 1946–49.

Lafora, Nicolás de. *The Frontiers of New Spain: Nicolás de Lafora's Description, 1766–1768.* Edited and translated by Lawrence Kinnaird. Berkeley, Calif.: Quivira Society, 1958.

La Harpe, Jean-Baptiste Bénard de. "Account of the Journey of Bénard de la Harpe: Discovery Made by Him of Several Nations Situated in the West." Translated by Ralph A. Smith. *Southwestern Historical Quarterly* 62 (July 1958): 75–86, (October 1958): 246–59, (January 1959): 371–85, (April 1959): 525–41.

——. *The Historical Journal of the Establishment of the French in Louisiana.* 1831. Edited by Glenn R. Conrad. Translated by Joan Cain and Virginia Koenig. Lafayette: University of Southern Louisiana Press, 1971.

Le Moyne d'Iberville, Pierre. *Iberville's Gulf Journals.* Translated and edited by Richebourg Gaillard McWilliams. Tuscaloosa: University of Alabama Press, 1981.

León, Alonso de. *Historia de Nuevo León, con noticias sobre Coahuila, Tejas y Nuevo Mexico.* Mexico City: Libreria de la Vda. de ch. Bouret, 1909.

Leutenegger, Benedict, ed. and trans. *Guidelines for a Texas Mission: Instructions for the Missionary of Mission Concepción in San Antonio (ca. 1760).* San Antonio: Old Spanish Missions Historical Research Library at San José Mission, 1976.

——. *Inventory of the Mission San Antonio de Valero: 1772.* Office of the State Archeologist, Special Report no. 23. Austin: Texas Historical Commission, 1977.

——. "Two Franciscan Documents on Early San Antonio, Texas." *The Americas* 25 (October 1968): 191–206.

——. *The Zacatecan Missionaries in Texas, 1716–1834: Excerpts from the* Libros de los Decretos *of the Missionary College of Zacatecas, 1707–1828.* Office of the State Archeologist Reports, no. 23. Austin: Texas Historical Survey Committee, 1973.

Leutenegger, Benedict, trans., and Marion A. Habig, ed. *The San José Papers: The Primary Sources for the History of Mission San José y San Miguel de Aguayo from Its Founding in 1720 to the Present.* 3 vols. San Antonio: Old Spanish Missions Historical Research Library at San José Mission, 1978–1983.

——. *The Texas Missions of the College of Zacatecas in 1749–1750: Report of Fr. Ignacio Antonio Ciprián, 1749, and Memorial of the College to the King, 1750.* San Antonio: Old Spanish Missions Historical Research Library at San José Mission, 1979.

Loomis, Noel M., and Abraham P. Nasatir. *Pedro Vial and the Roads to Santa Fe.* Norman: University of Oklahoma Press, 1967.

López, José Francisco. "Report on the San Antonio Missions in 1792." Edited by Marion A. Habig. Translated by Benedict Leutenegger. *Southwestern Historical Quarterly* 77 (April 1974): 487–98.

Maduell, Charles R. *The Census Tables for the French Colony of Louisiana from 1699 through 1732.* Baltimore: Genealogical Publishing, 1972.

Margil de Jesús, Antonio. *Nothingness Itself: Selected Writings of Ven. Fr. Antonio Margil, 1690–1724.* Edited by Marion A. Habig. Translated by Benedict Leutenegger. Chicago: Franciscan Herald Press, 1976.

Martin, George C., ed., and Betty B. Brewster, trans. *Expedition into Texas of Fernando del Bosque, Standard-Bearer of the King Don Carlos II in the Year 1675.* San Antonio: Norman Brock, 1947.

McDonald, David, Kay Hindes, and Kathleen Gilmore, eds. and trans. "The Marqués de Aguayo's Report to the King regarding His Expedition to Restore and Establish Missions and Presidios in Texas, 1720–1722." *Bulletin of the Texas Archeological Society* 70 (1999): 59–64.

Merino, Manuel. "Views from a Desk in Chihuahua: Manuel Merino's Report on Apaches and Neighboring Nations, c. 1804." Edited by Elizabeth A. H. John. Translated by John Wheat. *Southwestern Historical Quarterly* 95 (October 1991): 139–76.

Milanich, Jerald T., ed. *The Hernando de Soto Expedition.* New York: Garland, 1991.

Mills, Elizabeth Shown. "Natchitoches Baptisms, 1724–1776: A Supplement to Mills' Natchitoches, 1729–1803." *Natchitoches Genealogist* 7 (April 1983): 6–11.

———. *Natchitoches Colonials: Censuses, Military Rolls, and Tax Lists, 1722–1803.* Chicago: Adams Press, 1981.

———. *Natchitoches, 1800–1826: Translated Abstracts of Register Number Five of the Catholic Church Parish of St. François des Natchitoches in Louisiana.* New Orleans: Polyanthos, 1980.

———. *Natchitoches, 1729–1803: Abstracts of the Catholic Church Registers of the French and Spanish Post of St. Jean Baptiste des Natchitoches in Louisiana.* New Orleans: Polyanthos, 1977.

Morfi, Fray Agustín de. *Account of Disorders in New Mexico, 1778.* Edited and translated by Marc Simmons. Isleta: Historical Society of New Mexico, 1977.

———. *Excerpts from the Memorias for the History of the Province of Texas: Being a Translation of Those Parts of the Memorias Which Particularly Concern the Various Indians of the Province of Texas.* Translated by Frederick C. Chabot. Revised translation by Carlos Eduardo Castañeda. San Antonio: Naylor Printing, 1932.

———. *History of Texas, 1673–1779.* Translated and edited by Carlos E. Castañeda. 2 vols. Albuquerque: Quivira Society, 1935.

Naylor, Thomas H., and Charles W. Polzer, eds. and trans. *Pedro de Rivera and the Military Regulations for Northern New Spain, 1724–1729: A Documentary History of His Frontier Inspection and the* Reglamento de 1729. Tucson: University of Arizona Press, 1988.

———. *The Presidio and Militia on the Northern Frontier of New Spain, 1570–1700.* Tucson: University of Arizona Press, 1986.

Neighbors, Robert S. "The Na-ü-ni, or Comanches of Texas; Their Traits and Beliefs, and Their Divisions and Intertribal Relations." In *Information respecting the History, Condition, and Prospects of the Indian Tribes of the United States,* 5 vols., edited by Henry R. Schoolcraft, 5:125–34. Philadelphia: Lippincott, Grambo, 1855.

Nunley, Carol Elaine. "A Translation of Spanish Documents pertaining to Mission Nuestra Señora del Rosario." M.A. thesis, Texas Women's University, 1975.

O'Conor, Hugo. *The Defenses of Northern New Spain: Hugo O'Conor's Report to Teodoro de Croix, July 22, 1777.* Translated by Donald C. Cutter. Dallas: Southern Methodist University Press for the DeGolyer Library, 1994.

———. "The Interior Provinces of New Spain: The Report of Hugo O'Conor, January 30,

1776." Edited and translated by Mary Lou Moore and Delmar L. Beene. *Arizona and the West* 13 (1971): 265–82.

O'Donnell, Walter J., ed. and trans. "La Salle's Occupation of Texas." *Preliminary Studies of the Texas Catholic Historical Society* 3 (April 1936): 5–33.

Oliva, Fray José Rafael. *Management of the Missions in Texas: Fray José Rafael Oliva's Views concerning the Problem of the Temporalities in 1788*. Edited by Marion A. Habig. Translated by Benedict Leutenegger. San Antonio: Old Spanish Missions Historical Research Library at San José Mission, 1977.

Page du Pratz, Antoine Simon le. *The History of Louisiana, or of the Western Parts of Virginia and Carolina*. London: J. Becket, 1774; New Orleans: Pelican Press, 1947. All citations are to the 1947 edition.

Pagès, [Pierre Marie François] de. *Travels Round the World, in the Years 1767, 1768, 1769, 1770, 1771*. 2 vols. London: J. Murray, 1791.

Parker, William B. "Manners, Customs, and History of the Indians of South-Western Texas." In *Information respecting the History, Condition, and Prospects of the Indian Tribes of the United States*, 5 vols., edited by Henry R. Schoolcraft, 5:682–85. Philadelphia: Lippincott, Grambo, 1855.

Peña, Juan Antonio de la. "Account of the 1720–1722 Entrada." In *The Presidio and Militia on the Northern Frontier of New Spain: A Documentary History*, edited by Diana Hadley, Thomas H. Naylor, and Mardith K. Schuetz-Miller, 2:398–464. Tucson: University of Arizona Press, 1997.

——. *Aguayo Expedition into Texas, 1721: An Annotated Translation of the Five Versions of the Diary Kept by Br. Juan Antonio de la Peña*. Translated by Richard G. Santos. Austin: Jenkins Publishing, 1981.

Pénicaut, André. *Fleur de Lys and Calumet: Being the Pénicaut Narrative of French Adventure in Louisiana*. 1953. Translated by Richebourg Gaillard McWilliams. Tuscaloosa: University of Alabama Press, 1988.

Pichardo, Fray José Antonio. *Pichardo's Treatise on the Limits of Louisiana and Texas*. Edited and translated by Charles Wilson Hackett, 4 vols. Austin: University of Texas Press, 1931–46.

Porrúa Turanzas, José, ed. *Documentos para la historia eclesiástica y civil de la Provincia de Texas o Nuevas Philipinas, 1720–79*. Madrid: José Porrúa Turanzas, 1961.

Posada, Alonso de. *Alonso de Posada Report, 1686: A Description of the Area of the Present Southern United States in the Seventeenth Century*. Edited and translated by Alfred Barnaby Thomas. Pensacola, Fla.: Perdido Bay Press, 1982.

Ramón, Domingo. "Captain Don Domingo Ramón's Diary of His Expedition into Texas in 1716." Edited and translated by Paul J. Foik. *Preliminary Studies of the Texas Catholic Historical Society* 2 (April 1933): 3–23.

Reyes, Fray José Mariano. "New Documents on Father José Mariano Reyes." Translated by Benedict Leutenegger. *Southwestern Historical Quarterly* 71 (April 1968): 583–602.

Rowland, Dunbar, and Albert Godfrey Sanders, eds. *Mississippi Provincial Archives, French*

Dominion. 3 vols. Jackson: Press of the Mississippi Department of Archive and History, 1927–32.

Ruíz, Jose Francisco. *Report on the Indian Tribes of Texas in 1828.* Edited by John C. Ewers. Translated by Georgette Dorn. New Haven: Yale University Library, 1972.

St. Denis, Louis Juchereau de. "St. Denis's Declaration concerning Texas in 1717." Translated by Charmion Clair Shelby. *Southwestern Historical Quarterly* 26 (January 1923): 190–216.

Santa María, Fray Vicente de. *Relación Histórica de la Colonia del Nuevo Santander, y Costa del Seno Mexicano.* México City: Universidad Nacional Autónoma de México, Dirección General de Publicaciones, 1973.

Seco Serrano, Carlos, ed. *Cartas de Sor María de Jesús de Ágreda y de Felipe IV.* Biblioteca de Autores Españoles, no. 108. Madrid: Ediciones Atlas, 1958.

Sibley, John. "Historical Sketches of the Several Indian Tribes in Louisiana, South of the Arkansas River, and between the Mississippi and River Grande." *American State Papers,* Class 2, *Indian Affairs* (1806), 1:721–31.

Simmons, Marc, ed. *Border Comanches: Seven Spanish Colonial Documents, 1785–1819.* Santa Fe: Stagecoach Press, 1967.

Simpson, Lesley B., ed., and Paul D. Nathan, trans. *The San Sabá Papers: A Documentary Account of the Founding and Destruction of San Sabá Mission.* San Francisco: John Howell Books, 1959.

Solís, José de. "Diary of a Visit of Inspection of the Texas Missions Made by Fray Gaspar José de Solís in the Year 1767–1768." Translated by Margaret Kenney. *Southwestern Historical Quarterly* 35 (July 1931): 28–76.

———. "The Solís Diary of 1767." Translated by Peter P. Forrestal. *Preliminary Studies of the Texas Catholic Historical Society* 1 (March 1931): 3–42.

"The Talon Interrogations: Voyage to the Mississippi through the Gulf of Mexico." Translated by Ann Linda Bell. In *La Salle, the Mississippi, and the Gulf: Three Primary Documents,* edited by Robert S. Weddle, Mary Christine Morkovsky, and Patricia Galloway, 209–58. College Station: Texas A&M University Press, 1987.

Thomas, Alfred Barnaby. *Anza's 1779 Comanche Campaign.* Edited by Ronald E. Kessler. Monte Vista, Colo.: Ronald E. Kessler, 1994.

———. *Forgotten Frontiers: A Study of the Spanish Indian Policy of Don Juan Bautista de Anza, Governor of New Mexico, 1777–1787.* Norman: University of Oklahoma Press, 1932.

———. *Teodoro de Croix and the Northern Frontier of New Spain, 1776–1783, from the Original Documents in the Archives of the Indies, Seville.* Norman: University of Oklahoma Press, 1941.

———, ed. and trans. *After Coronado: Spanish Exploration Northeast of New Mexico, 1697–1727: Documents from the Archives of Spain, Mexico, and New Mexico.* Norman: University of Oklahoma Press, 1935.

Vasconcelos, Fray Mariano Antonio de. *Journal of a Texas Missionary, 1767–1802: Diario Historico of Fr. Cosme Lozano Narvais, Pen Name of Fr. Mariano Antonio de*

Vasconcelos. Translated by Benedict Leutenegger. San Antonio: Old Spanish Missions Historical Research Library at San José Mission, 1977.

Vial, Pedro, and Francisco Chaves. "Inside the Comanchería, 1785: The Diary of Pedro Vial and Francisco Chaves." Edited by Elizabeth A. H. John. Translated by Adán Benavides. *Southwestern Historical Quarterly* 91 (July 1994): 27–56.

Weddle, Robert S., Mary Christine Morkovsky, and Patricia Galloway, eds. *La Salle, the Mississippi, and the Gulf: Three Primary Documents.* College Station: Texas A&M University Press, 1987.

SECONDARY SOURCES

Adams, David B. "At the Lion's Mouth: San Miguel de Aguayo in the Defense of Nuevo León, 1686–1841." *Colonial Latin American Historical Review* 9 (Summer 2000): 325–46.

———. "Embattled Borderland: Northern Nuevo León and the Indios Bárbaros, 1686–1870." *Southwestern Historical Quarterly* 95 (October 1991): 205–20.

Adelman, Jeremy, and Stephen Aron. "From Borderlands to Borders: Empires, Nation-States, and the Peoples in between in North American History." *American Historical Review* 104 (June 1999): 818–41.

Adorno, Rolena. "Negotiation of Fear in Cabeza de Vaca's *Naufragios.*" *Representations* 33 (1991): 163–99.

Albers, Patricia C. "Symbiosis, Merger, and War: Contrasting Forms of Intertribal Relationship among Historic Plains Indians." In *The Political Economy of North American Indians,* edited by John H. Moore, 94–132. Norman: University of Oklahoma Press, 1993.

Albers, Patricia, and Beatrice Medicine, eds. *The Hidden Half: Studies of Plains Indian Women.* Lanham, Md.: University Press of America, 1983.

Alfaro, Juan. "The Spirit of the First Franciscan Missionaries in Texas." *U.S. Catholic Historian* 9 (1990): 49–66.

Allain, Mathé. "Manon Lescaut et Ses Consoeurs: Women in the Early French Period, 1700–1731." In *Proceedings of the Fifth Meeting of the French Colonial Historical Society,* edited by James J. Cooke, 18–26. Lanham, Md.: University Press of America, 1980.

Allen, Henry Easton. "The Parrilla Expedition to the Red River in 1759." *Southwestern Historical Quarterly* 43 (July 1939): 53–71.

Almaráz, Félix D., Jr. "Franciscan Evangelization in Spanish Frontier Texas: Apex of Social Contact, Conflict, and Confluence, 1751–1761." *Colonial Latin American Historical Review* 2 (Summer 1993): 253–87.

———. "Harmony, Discord, and Compromise in Spanish Colonial Texas: The Rio San Antonio Experience, 1691–1741." *New Mexico Historical Review* 67 (October 1992): 329–56.

Alonso, Ana María. *Thread of Blood: Colonialism, Revolution and Gender on Mexico's Northern Frontier.* Tucson: University of Arizona Press, 1995.

Anderson, Gary Clayton. *The Conquest of Texas: Ethnic Cleansing in the Promised Land, 1820–1875.* Norman: University of Oklahoma Press, 2005.

——. *The Indian Southwest, 1580–1830: Ethnogenesis and Reinvention.* Norman: University of Oklahoma Press, 1999.

——. *Kinsmen of Another Kind: Dakota-White Relations in the Upper Mississippi Valley, 1650–1862.* Lincoln: University of Nebraska Press, 1984.

Anderson, Karen. *Chain Her by One Foot: The Subjugation of Native Women in Seventeenth-Century New France.* New York: Routledge, 1991.

Archer, Christon I. "The Deportation of Barbarian Indians from the Internal Provinces of New Spain, 1789–1810." *The Americas* 29 (January 1973): 376–85.

Aten, Lawrence E. *Indians of the Upper Texas Coast.* New York: Academic Press, 1983.

Aten, Lawrence E., Charles K. Chandler, Al B. Wesolowsky, and Robert M. Malina. *Excavations at the Harris County Boys' School Cemetery: Analysis of Galveston Bay Area Mortuary Practices.* Edited by Harry J. Shafer and Thomas R. Hester. Texas Archeological Society, Special Publication no. 3. Dallas: Texas Archeological Society, 1976.

Axtell, James. *The Invasion Within: The Contest of Cultures in Colonial North America.* New York: Oxford University Press, 1985.

——. "Some Thoughts on the Ethnohistory of Missions." *Ethnohistory* 29 (1982): 35–41.

——. "Through Another Glass Darkly: Early Indian Views of Europeans." In *After Columbus: Essays in the Ethnohistory of Colonial North America,* 125–43. New York: Oxford University Press, 1988.

Baade, Hans W. "The Form of Marriage in Spanish North America." *Cornell Law Review* 61 (November 1975): 1–89.

——. "The Law of Slavery in Spanish Luisiana, 1769–1803." In *Louisiana's Legal Heritage,* edited by Edward F. Haas, 43–86. Pensacola, Fla.: Perdido Bay Press for the Louisiana State Museum, 1983.

Bailey, L. R. *Indian Slave Trade in the Southwest.* Los Angeles: Westernlore Press, 1966.

Baker, Vaughan, Amos Simpson, and Mathé Allain. "Le Mari est Seigneur: Marital Laws Governing Women in French Louisiana." In *Louisiana's Legal Heritage,* edited by Edward F. Haas, 7–17. Pensacola, Fla.: Perdido Bay Press for the Louisiana State Museum, 1983.

Bannon, John Francis. "The Mission as a Frontier Institution: Sixty Years of Interest and Research." *Western Historical Quarterly* 10 (July 1979): 304–22.

——. *The Spanish Borderlands Frontier, 1513–1821.* New York: Holt, Rinehart, and Winston, 1970.

Baretta, Silvio R. Duncan, and John Markoff. "Civilization and Barbarism: Cattle Frontiers in Latin America." *Comparative Studies in Society and History* 20 (1978): 587–620.

Barnard, Herwanna Becker. "The Comanche and His Literature with an Anthology of His Myths, Legends, Folktales, Oratory, Poetry, and Songs." M.A. thesis, University of Oklahoma, Norman, 1941.

Barnes, Thomas C., Thomas H. Naylor, and Charles W. Polzer. *Northern New Spain: A Research Guide.* Tucson: University of Arizona Press, 1981.

Baugh, Timothy G. "Regional Polities and Socioeconomic Exchange: Caddoan and Puebloan Interaction." In *The Native History of the Caddo: Their Place in Southeastern Archeology and Ethnohistory,* edited by Timothy K. Perttula and James E. Bruseth, 145–58. Studies in Archeology, no. 30. Austin: Texas Archeological Research Laboratory, University of Texas at Austin, 1998.

Beezley, William H., Cheryl English Martin, and William E. French, eds. *Rituals of Rule, Rituals of Resistance: Public Celebrations and Popular Culture in Mexico.* Wilmington, Del.: Scholarly Resources, 1994.

Bell, Duran. "Defining Marriage and Legitimacy." *Current Anthropology* 38 (April 1997): 237–53.

Bennassar, Bartolomé. *The Spanish Character: Attitudes and Mentalities from the Sixteenth to the Nineteenth Century.* Translated by Benjamin Keen. Los Angeles: University of California Press, 1975.

Betty, Gerald. *Comanche Society before the Reservation.* College Station: Texas A&M University Press, 2002.

Bolton, Herbert E. "The Beginnings of Mission Nuestra Señora del Refugio." *Southwestern Historical Quarterly* 19 (April 1916): 400–404.

———. "The Founding of Mission Rosario: A Chapter in the History of the Gulf Coast." *Quarterly of the Texas State Historical Association* 10 (October 1906): 113–39.

———. "The Founding of the Missions on the San Gabriel River, 1745–1749." *Southwestern Historical Quarterly* 17 (April 1914): 323–78.

———. *The Hasinais: Southern Caddoans as Seen by the Earliest Europeans.* Edited by Russell M. Magnaghi. Norman: University of Oklahoma Press, 1987.

———. "The Jumano Indians in Texas, 1650–1771." *Quarterly of the Texas State Historical Association* 15 (July 1911): 66–84.

———. "The Mission as a Frontier Institution in the Spanish American Colonies." In *Bolton and the Spanish Borderlands,* edited by John Francis Bannon, 187–211. Norman: University of Oklahoma Press, 1964.

———. "The Native Tribes about the East Texas Missions." *Quarterly of the Texas State Historical Association* 11 (April 1908): 249–76.

———. "The Spanish Abandonment and Re-Occupation of East Texas, 1773–1779." *Quarterly of the Texas State Historical Association* 9 (October 1905): 67–137.

———. "Spanish Activities on the Lower Trinity River, 1746–1771." *Southwestern Historical Quarterly* 16 (April 1913): 339–77.

———. "The Spanish Occupation of Texas, 1519–1690." *Southwestern Historical Quarterly* 16 (July 1912): 1–26.

———. *Texas in the Middle Eighteenth Century: Studies in Spanish Colonial History and Administration.* Berkeley: University of California Press, 1915; Austin: University of Texas Press, 1970. All citations are to the 1970 edition.

Boxer, Charles R. *Mary and Misogyny: Women in Iberian Expansion Overseas, 1415–1815; Some Facts, Fancies and Personalities.* London: Duckworth, 1975.

Brading, D. A. *Mexican Phoenix: Our Lady of Guadalupe; Image and Tradition across Five Centuries.* New York: Cambridge University Press, 2001.

Brandes, Stanley. *Metaphors of Masculinity: Sex and Status in Andalusian Folklore.* Philadelphia: University of Pennsylvania Press, 1980.

Brasseaux, Carl A. "The Administration of Slave Regulations in French Louisiana, 1724–1766." *Louisiana History* 21 (Spring 1980): 139–58.

——. "The Moral Climate of French Colonial Louisiana, 1699–1763." *Louisiana History* 27 (Winter 1986): 27–41.

Brodman, James William. "Military Redemptionism and the Castilian Conquest, 1180–1250." *Military Affairs* 44 (February 1980): 24–27.

——. *Ransoming Captives in Crusader Spain: The Order of Merced on the Christian-Islamic Frontier.* Philadelphia: University of Pennsylvania Press, 1986.

Brooks, James F. *Captives and Cousins: Slavery, Kinship, and Community in the Southwest Borderlands.* Chapel Hill: University of North Carolina Press for the Institute of Early American History and Culture, 2002.

——. " 'Lest We Go in Search of Relief to Our Lands and Our Nation': Customary Justice and Colonial Law in the New Mexico Borderlands, 1680–1821." In *The Many Legalities of Early America*, edited by Christopher L. Tomlins and Bruce H. Mann, 150–80. Chapel Hill: University of North Carolina Press for the Institute of Early American History and Culture, 2001.

——. " 'This Evil Extends Especially . . . to the Feminine Sex': Negotiating Captivity in the New Mexico Borderlands." *Feminist Studies* 22 (Summer 1996): 279–309.

Brown, Jennifer S. H. *Strangers in Blood: Fur Trade Company Families in Indian Country.* Vancouver: University of British Columbia Press, 1980.

Brown, Kathleen M. "The Anglo-Algonquian Gender Frontier." In *Negotiators of Change: Historical Perspectives on Native American Women*, edited by Nancy Shoemaker, 26–48. New York: Routledge, 1995.

——. "Brave New Worlds: Women's and Gender History." *William and Mary Quarterly*, 3rd ser., 50 (April 1993): 311–28.

——. *Good Wives, Nasty Wenches, and Anxious Patriarchs: Gender, Race, and Power in Colonial Virginia.* Chapel Hill: University of North Carolina Press for the Institute of Early American History and Culture, 1996.

Bucher, Bernadette. *Icon and Conquest: A Structural Analysis of the Illustrations of de Bry's Great Voyages.* Chicago: University of Chicago Press, 1981.

Buller, Galen M. "Comanche Oral Narratives." Ph.D. diss., University of Nebraska, Lincoln, 1977.

Burkholder, Mark A. "Honor and Honors in Colonial Spanish America." In *The Faces of Honor: Sex, Shame, and Violence in Colonial Latin America*, edited by Lyman L.

Johnson and Sonya Lipsett-Rivera, 18–44. Albuquerque: University of New Mexico Press, 1998.

Burton, Helen Sophie. "Family and Economy in Frontier Louisiana: Colonial Natchitoches, 1714–1803." Ph.D. diss., Texas Christian University, Fort Worth, 2002.

Calloway, Colin G. *One Vast Winter Count: The Native American West before Lewis and Clark.* Lincoln: University of Nebraska Press, 2003.

Campbell, T. N. *The Indians of Southern Texas and Northeastern Mexico: Selected Writings of Thomas Nolan Campbell.* Austin: Texas Archeological Research Laboratory, University of Texas at Austin, 1988.

———. *The Payaya Indians of Southern Texas.* San Antonio: Southern Texas Archaeological Association, 1975.

Campbell, T. N., and T. J. Campbell. *Indian Groups Associated with Spanish Missions of the San Antonio Missions National Historical Park.* Special Report no. 19. San Antonio: Center for Archaeological Research, University of Texas at San Antonio, 1985.

Cargill, Diane A., and Robert J. Hard. "Assessing Native American Mobility versus Permanency at Mission San Juan de Capistrano through the Use of Stable Isotope Analysis." *Bulletin of the Texas Archeological Society* 70 (1999): 197–213.

Carrasco, Pedro. "Indian-Spanish Marriages in the First Century of the Colony." In *Indian Women of Early Mexico*, edited by Susan Schroeder, Stephanie Wood, and Robert Haskett, 87–103. Norman: University of Oklahoma Press, 1997.

Carter, Cecile Elkins. *Caddo Indians: Where We Come From.* Norman: University of Oklahoma Press, 1995.

Carter, Robert F. *The Tarnished Halo: The Story of Padre Francisco Hidalgo.* Chicago: Franciscan Herald Press, 1973.

Castañeda, Antonia I. "Sexual Violence in the Politics and Policies of Conquest: Amerindian Women and the Spanish Conquest of Alta California." In *Building with Our Hands: New Directions in Chicana Studies*, edited by Adela de la Torre and Beatríz M. Pesquera, 15–33. Los Angeles: University of California Press, 1993.

———. "Women of Color and the Rewriting of Western History: The Discourse, Politics, and Decolonization of History." *Pacific Historical Review* 53 (1992): 501–33.

Castañeda, Carlos E. "Earliest Catholic Activities in Texas." *Catholic Historical Review* 17 (1931–32): 278–95.

———. "Myths and Customs of the Tejas Indians." In *Southwestern Lore*, edited by J. Frank Dobie, 167–74. Publications of the Texas Folk-Lore Society, no. 9. Dallas: Southwest Press for the Texas Folk-Lore Society, 1931.

———. *Our Catholic Heritage in Texas, 1519–1936.* 7 vols. Austin: Von Boeckmann-Jones, 1936–58; New York: Arno Press, 1976. All citations are to the 1976 edition.

Chabot, Frederick C. *Indians and Missions.* San Antonio: Naylor Printing, 1930.

———. *Mission La Puríssima Concepción.* San Antonio: Naylor Printing, 1935.

———. *With the Makers of San Antonio.* San Antonio: Artes Graficas, 1937.

Chipman, Donald E. *Spanish Texas, 1519–1821.* Austin: University of Texas Press, 1992.

Chipman, Donald E., and Harriett Denise Joseph. *Notable Men and Women of Spanish Texas.* Austin: University of Texas Press, 1999.

Claassen, Cheryl, and Rosemary A. Joyce, eds. *Women in Prehistory: North America and Mesoamerica.* Philadelphia: University of Pennsylvania Press, 1997.

Clark, John W., Jr. *Mission San José y San Miguel de Aguayo Archeological Investigations, December 1974.* Austin: Texas Historical Commission, 1978.

Clark, Robert Carlton. *The Beginnings of Texas, 1684–1718.* 1907. Philadelphia: Porcupine Press, 1976.

———. "Louis Juchereau de Saint Denis and the Re-establishment of the Tejas Missions." *Southwestern Historical Quarterly* 6 (July 1902): 1–26.

Clendinnen, Inga. *Aztecs: An Interpretation.* New York: Cambridge University Press, 1991.

———. "The Cost of Courage in Aztec Society." *Past and Present* 107 (May 1985): 44–89.

———. "Disciplining the Indians: Franciscan Ideology and Missionary Violence in Sixteenth-Century Yucatán." *Past and Present* 94 (February 1982): 27–48.

———. " 'Fierce and Unnatural Cruelty': Cortes and the Conquest of Mexico." *Representations* 33 (Winter 1991): 65–100.

Cline, Sarah. "The Spiritual Conquest Reexamined: Baptism and Christian Marriage in Early Sixteenth-Century Mexico." *Hispanic American Historical Review* 73 (August 1993): 453–80.

Colahan, Clark. *The Visions of Sor María de Agreda: Writing, Knowledge, and Power.* Tucson: University of Arizona Press, 1994.

Collier, Jane Fishburne. *Marriage and Inequality in Classless Societies.* Stanford: Stanford University Press, 1988.

Collier, Jane Fishburne, and Sylvia Junko Yanagisako. *Gender and Kinship: Essays toward a Unified Analysis.* Stanford: Stanford University Press, 1987.

Collins, Michael B. "Named Indian Groups in Texas: A Guide to Entries in the New Handbook of Texas." *Bulletin of the Texas Archeological Society* 70 (1999): 7–16.

Connell, R. W. *Masculinities.* Berkeley: University of California Press, 1995.

Coopwood, Bethel. "Notes on the History of La Bahía del Espíritu Santo." *Quarterly of the Texas State Historical Association* 2 (October 1898): 162–69.

Cope, R. Douglas. *The Limits of Racial Domination: Plebeian Society in Colonial Mexico City, 1660–1720.* Madison: University of Wisconsin Press, 1994.

Corbin, James E. "Spanish-Indian Interaction on the Eastern Frontier of Texas." In *Archaeological and Historical Perspectives on the Spanish Borderlands West,* edited by David Hurst Thomas, 269–75. Vol. 1 of *Columbian Consequences.* Washington, D.C.: Smithsonian Institution Press, 1989.

Cuello, José. "Beyond the 'Borderlands' Is the North of Colonial Mexico: A Latin-Americanist Perspective to the Study of the Mexican North and the United States Southwest." In *Proceedings of the Pacific Coast Council on Latin American Studies,* edited by Kristyna P. Demaree, 9:1–24. San Diego: San Diego State University Press, 1982.

——. "The Persistence of Indian Slavery and Encomienda in the Northeast of Colonial Mexico, 1577–1723." *Journal of Social History* 21 (Summer 1988): 683–700.

Curcio-Nagy, Linda A. "Native Icon to City Protectress to Royal Patroness: Ritual, Political Symbolism and the Virgin of Remedies." *The Americas* 52 (January 1996): 367–91.

Curtis, Edward S. "The Comanche." In *The North American Indian: Being a Series of Volumes Picturing and Describing the Indians of the United States, the Dominion of Canada, and Alaska*, 20 vols., edited by Frederick Webb Hodge, 19:181–98. New York: Johnson Reprint, 1930.

——. "The Wichita." In *The North American Indian: Being a Series of Volumes Picturing and Describing the Indians of the United States, the Dominion of Canada, and Alaska*, 20 vols., edited by Frederick Webb Hodge, 19:35–106. New York: Johnson Reprint, 1930.

D'abbadie Soto, Enrique. *Fray Damián de Massanet (del Colegio Apostólico de la Santa Cruz de Querétaro) y la conjura francesa*. Querétaro: Archivo Histórico del Estado, 1994.

Davis, Natalie Zemon. *The Gift in Sixteenth-Century France*. Madison: University of Wisconsin Press, 2000.

——. "Iroquois Women, European Women." In *Women, "Race," and Writing in the Early Modern Period*, edited by Margo Hendricks and Patricia Parker, 243–58. New York: Routledge, 1994.

Deagan, Kathleen A. "*Mestizaje* in Colonial St. Augustine." *Ethnohistory* 20 (Winter 1973): 55–65.

——. "Spanish-Indian Interaction in Sixteenth-Century Florida and Hispaniola." In *Cultures in Contact: The Impact of European Contacts on Native American Cultural Institutions, A.D. 1000–1800*, edited by William W. Fitzhugh, 281–318. Washington, D.C.: Smithsonian Institution Press, 1985.

Deeds, Susan M. *Defiance and Deference in Mexico's Colonial North: Indians under Spanish Rule in Nueva Vizcaya*. Austin: University of Texas Press, 2003.

——. "Double Jeopardy: Indian Women in Jesuit Missions of Nueva Vizcaya." In *Indian Women of Early Mexico*, edited by Susan Schroeder, Stephanie Wood, and Robert Haskett, 255–72. Norman: University of Oklahoma Press, 1997.

DeFrance, Susan D. "Zooarcheological Evidence of Colonial Culture Change: A Comparison of Two Locations of Mission Espíritu Santo de Zuñiga and Mission Nuestra Señora del Rosario, Texas." *Bulletin of the Texas Archeological Society* 70 (1999): 169–88.

Delanglez, Jean, S.J. *The French Jesuits in Lower Louisiana (1700–1763)*. Washington, D.C.: Catholic University of America, 1935.

De Lauretis, Teresa. *Technologies of Gender: Essays on Theory, Film, and Fiction*. Bloomington: Indiana University Press, 1987.

DeMallie, Raymond J. *Comanche Treaties: Historical Background*. Washington, D.C.: Institute for the Development of Indian Law, 1977.

——. "Kinship: The Foundation for Native American Society." In *Studying Native America:*

Problems and Prospects, edited by Russell Thornton, 306–56. Madison: University of Wisconsin Press, 1998.

Dening, Greg. *Performances.* Chicago: University of Chicago Press, 1996.

——. "Towards an Anthropology of Performance in Encounters in Place." In *Pacific History: Papers from the 8th Pacific History Association Conference,* edited by Donald H. Rubinstein, 3–6. Mangilao: University of Guam Press and Micronesian Area Research Center, 1990.

Derrick, Sharon McCormick, and Diane E. Wilson. "The Effects of Epidemic Disease on Caddo Demographic Structure." *Bulletin of the Texas Archeological Society* 72 (2001): 91–103.

Devens, Carol. *Countering Colonization: Native American Women and Great Lakes Missions, 1630–1900.* Los Angeles: University of California Press, 1992.

Di Leonardo, Micaela, ed. *Gender at the Crossroads of Knowledge: Feminist Anthropology in the Postmodern Era.* Los Angeles: University of California Press, 1991.

Dillard, Heath. *Daughters of the Reconquest: Women in Castilian Town Society, 1100–1300.* New York: Cambridge University Press, 1984.

Din, Gilbert C. *Spaniards, Planters, and Slaves: The Spanish Regulation of Slavery in Louisiana, 1763–1803.* College Station: Texas A&M University Press, 1999.

Din, Gilbert C., and A. P. Nasatir. *The Imperial Osages: Spanish-Indian Diplomacy in the Mississippi Valley.* Norman: University of Oklahoma Press, 1983.

Donahue, William H. "Mary of Agreda and the Southwest United States." *The Americas* 9 (January 1953): 291–314.

Dorsey, George A. "Caddo Customs of Childhood." *Journal of American Folk-Lore* 18 (July–September 1905): 226–28.

——. *The Mythology of the Wichita.* Washington, D.C.: Carnegie Institution of Washington, 1904.

——. *Traditions of the Caddo.* Washington, D.C.: Carnegie Institution of Washington, 1905.

Dorsey, Peter A. "Going to School with Savages: Authorship and Authority among the Jesuits of New France." *William and Mary Quarterly,* 3rd ser., 55 (July 1998): 399–420.

Douglas, Mary. *Natural Symbols: Explorations in Cosmology.* London: Barrie and Jenkins, 1973.

——. *Purity and Danger.* New York: Praeger, 1966.

Ducille, Anne. "Othered Matters: Reconceptualizing Dominance and Difference in the History of Sexuality in America." *Journal of the History of Sexuality* 1 (1990): 102–27.

Dunn, William Edward. "The Apache Mission on the San Sabá River: Its Founding and Failure." *Southwestern Historical Quarterly* 17 (April 1914): 379–414.

——. "Apache Relations in Texas, 1718–1750." *Quarterly of the Texas State Historical Association* 14 (January 1911): 198–274.

——. "The Founding of Nuestra Señora del Refugio, the Last Spanish Mission in Texas." *Southwestern Historical Quarterly* 25 (January 1922): 174–84.

——. "Missionary Activities among the Eastern Apaches previous to the Founding of the

San Sabá Mission." *Quarterly of the Texas State Historical Association* 15 (January 1912): 186–200.

———. "Spanish Reaction against the French Advance toward New Mexico, 1717–1727." *Mississippi Valley Historical Review* 2 (December 1915): 348–62.

Early, Ann M. "The Caddos of the Transmississippi South." In *Indians of the Greater Southeast: Historical Archaeology and Ethnohistory*, edited by Bonnie G. McEwan, 122–41. Gainesville: University Press of Florida, 2000.

Elam, Earl Henry. "The History of the Wichita Indian Confederacy to 1868." Ph.D. diss., Texas Tech University, 1971.

Estrada de Gerlero, Elena Isabel. "The Representation of 'Heathen Indians' in Mexican Casta Painting." In *New World Orders: Casta Painting and Colonial Latin America*, edited by Ilona Katzew, 42–57. New York: Americas Society Art Gallery, 1996.

Ewers, John C. "The Influence of Epidemics on the Indian Populations and Cultures of Texas." *Plains Anthropologist* 98 (1973): 104–15.

———. "Symbols of Chiefly Authority in Spanish Louisiana." In *The Spanish in the Mississippi Valley, 1762–1804*, edited by John Francis McDermott, 272–84. Urbana: University of Illinois Press, 1972.

———. "Women's Roles in Plains Indian Warfare." In *Plains Indian History and Culture: Essays on Continuity and Change*, 191–204. Norman: University of Oklahoma Press, 1997.

Faulk, Odie B. "The Comanche Invasion of Texas, 1743–1836." *Great Plains Journal* 9 (Fall 1969): 10–50.

———. *The Last Years of Spanish Texas, 1778–1821*. London: Mouton, 1964.

Faulk, Odie B., and Laura E. Faulk. *Defenders of Empire: Presidial Soldiers on the Northern Frontier of New Spain*. Albuquerque: Museum of Albuquerque, 1987.

Ferguson, R. Brian, and Neil L. Whitehead, eds. *War in the Tribal Zone: Expanding States and Indigenous Warfare*. Santa Fe: School of American Research Press, 1992.

Fields, Barbara J. "Ideology and Race in American History." In *Region, Race, and Reconstruction: Essays in Honor of C. Vann Woodward*, edited by J. Morgan Kousser and James M. McPherson, 143–77. New York: Oxford University Press, 1982.

Flores, Dan. "Bison Ecology and Bison Diplomacy: The Southern Plains from 1800 to 1850." *Journal of American History* 78 (September 1991): 465–85.

———. *Caprock Canyonlands: Journeys into the Heart of the Southern Plains*. Austin: University of Texas Press, 1990.

———. *Horizontal Yellow: Nature and History in the Near Southwest*. Albuquerque: University of New Mexico Press, 1999.

Folmer, Henri. "De Bourgmont's Expedition to the Padoucas in 1724, the First French Approach to Colorado." *Colorado Magazine* 14 (July 1937): 121–28.

———. *Franco-Spanish Rivalry in North America, 1524–1763*. Glendale, Calif.: Arthur H. Clark, 1953.

Forbes, Jack D. *Apache, Navaho, and Spaniard*. Norman: University of Oklahoma Press, 1960.

Ford, Ramona. "Native American Women: Changing Statues, Changing Interpretations." In *Writing the Range: Race, Class, and Culture in the Women's West*, edited by Elizabeth Jameson and Susan Armitage, 42–68. Norman: University of Oklahoma Press, 1997.

Forêt, Michael James. "Red over White: Indians, Deserters, and French Colonial Louisiana." In *Proceedings of the Seventeenth Meeting of the French Colonial Historical Society, Chicago, May 1991*, edited by Patricia Galloway, 79–89. New York: University Press of America, 1993.

Foster, Morris W. *Being Comanche: A Social History of an American Indian Community.* Tucson: University of Arizona Press, 1991.

Foster, William C. *Spanish Expeditions into Texas, 1689–1768.* Austin: University of Texas Press, 1995.

Foucault, Michel. *The Order of Things: An Archaeology of the Human Sciences.* New York: Random House, 1970.

Fox, Anne A. "The Indians at Rancho de las Cabras." In *Archaeological and Historical Perspectives on the Spanish Borderlands West*, edited by David Hurst Thomas, 259–67. Vol. 1 of *Columbian Consequences*. Washington, D.C.: Smithsonian Institution Press, 1989.

Frank, Ross. *From Settler to Citizen: New Mexican Economic Development and the Creation of Vecino Society, 1750–1820.* Los Angeles: University of California Press, 2000.

Fur, Gunlög. *A Nation of Women: Delaware Gender Relations and Colonial Encounters.* Philadelphia: University of Pennsylvania Press, forthcoming.

———. " 'Some Women Are Wiser than Some Men': Gender and Native American History." In *Clearing a Path: Theorizing the Past in Native American Studies*, edited by Nancy Shoemaker, 75–103. New York: Routledge, 2002.

———. "Women's Authority and the Anomalies of Vision in Delaware Experiences of Colonial Encounters." International Seminar on the History of the Atlantic World, 1500–1800, Working Paper no. 98-08. Cambridge: Harvard University, 1998.

Gallay, Alan. *The Indian Slave Trade: The Rise of the English Empire in the American South, 1670–1717.* New Haven: Yale University Press, 2002.

Galloway, Patricia. " 'The Chief Who Is Your Father': Choctaw and French Views of the Diplomatic Relation." In *Powhatan's Mantle: Indians in the Colonial Southeast*, edited by Peter H. Wood, Gregory A. Waselkov, and M. Thomas Hatley, 254–78. Lincoln: University of Nebraska Press, 1989.

Gatschet, Albert S. *The Karankawa Indians: The Coast People of Texas.* Archaeological and Ethnological Papers of the Peabody Museum, Harvard University, no. 1. Cambridge: Peabody Museum of American Archaeology and Ethnology, 1891.

Gelo, Daniel Joseph. "Comanche Belief and Ritual." Ph.D. diss., Rutgers University, 1986.

———. "On a New Interpretation of Comanche Social Organization." *Current Anthropology* 28 (August–October 1987): 551–55.

Gerhard, Peter. *The North Frontier of New Spain*. Norman: University of Oklahoma Press, 1982.

Gilmore, David D. *Manhood in the Making: Cultural Concepts of Masculinity*. New Haven: Yale University Press, 1990.

Gilmore, Kathleen Kirk. "Caddoan Interaction in the Neches Valley, Texas." Ph.D. diss., Southern Methodist University, 1973. Available from *Reprints in Anthropology*, vol. 27. Lincoln, Neb.: J & L Reprint, 1983.

——. *Documentary and Archeological Investigation of Presidio San Luis de Amarillas and Mission Santa Cruz de San Sabá, Menard County, Texas: A Preliminary Report*. Austin: State Building Commission, Archeological Program, 1967.

——. "French, Spanish, and Indian Interaction in Colonial Texas." *Bulletin of the Texas Archeological Society* 63 (1992): 123–33.

——. "The Indians of Mission Rosario." In *The Scope of Historical Archaeology: Essays in Honor of John L. Cotter*, edited by David G. Orr and Daniel G. Crozier, 163–91. Philadelphia: Laboratory of Anthropology, Temple University, 1984.

——. "The Indians of Mission Rosario: From the Books and from the Ground." In *Archaeological and Historical Perspectives on the Spanish Borderlands West*, edited by David Hurst Thomas, 231–43. Vol. 1 of *Columbian Consequences*. Washington, D.C.: Smithsonian Institution Press, 1989.

——. *Mission Rosario: Archaeological Investigations, 1973 and 1974*. Archaeological Report no. 14, pts. 1 and 2. Austin: Texas Parks and Wildlife Department, Parks Division, Historic Sites and Restoration Branch, 1973–74.

——. *The San Xavier Missions: A Study in Historical Site Identification*. Texas State Building Commission, Archeological Program Report no. 16. Austin: Texas State Building Commission, 1969.

——. "Treachery and Tragedy in the Texas Wilderness: The Adventures of Jean L'Archeveque in Texas (a Member of La Salle's Colony)." *Bulletin of the Texas Archeological Society* 69 (1998): 35–46.

Giraud, Marcel. *A History of French Louisiana*. Translated by Brian Pearce. 2 vols. 1958. Baton Rouge: Louisiana State University Press, 1993. All citations are to the 1993 edition.

Gladwin, Thomas. "Comanche Kin Behavior." *American Anthropologist* 50 (1948): 73–94.

Goddard, Ives. "The Languages of South Texas and the Lower Rio Grande." In *The Languages of Native America: Historical and Comparative Assessment*, edited by Lyle Campbell and Marianne Mithun, 353–89. Austin: University of Texas Press, 1979.

González, Anibal. "The Legend of Joseph de Urrutia." *Sayersville Historical Association Bulletin* 6 (Summer 1985): 14–19.

Gradie, Charlotte M. "Discovering the Chichimecas." *The Americas* 51 (July 1994): 67–88.

Grafton, Anthony. *New Worlds, Ancient Texts: The Power of Tradition and the Shock of Discovery*. Cambridge: Belknap Press of Harvard University Press, 1992.

Greenblatt, Stephen. *Marvelous Possessions: The Wonder of the New World.* Oxford: Clarendon Press, 1991.

——, ed. *New World Encounters.* Los Angeles: University of California Press, 1993.

Gregory, Hiram Ford. "Eighteenth-Century Caddoan Archaeology: A Study in Models and Interpretation." Ph.D. diss., Southern Methodist University, 1973.

——, ed. *The Southern Caddo: An Anthology.* New York: Garland, 1986.

Gregory, Hiram F., Jay C. Blaine, and Sheila Morrison. *Excavations, 1981–82: Presidio de Nuestra Señora del Pilar de los Adaes.* Natchitoches, La.: Northwestern State University, Williamson Museum, 1982.

Gregory, Hiram F., and Aubra Lee. *Excavations: Presidio de Nuestra Señora del Pilar de los Adaes.* Natchitoches, La.: Northwestern State University, Williamson Museum, 1984.

Gregory, Hiram F., and James L. McCorkle Jr. *Historical and Archaeological Background of Los Adaes State Commemorative Area, Natchitoches Parish, Louisiana, 1980–1981.* Report prepared for the Louisiana State Division of Culture, Tourism and Recreation. Natchitoches, La.: Northwestern State University, 1981.

Griffen, William B. *Apaches at War and Peace: The Janos Presidio, 1750–1858.* Albuquerque: University of New Mexico Press, 1988.

——. *Culture Change and Shifting Populations in Central Northern Mexico.* Tucson: University of Arizona Press, 1969.

Griffith, William Joyce. *The Hasinai Indians of East Texas as Seen by Europeans, 1687–1772.* Middle American Research Institute, Philological and Documentary Studies, vol. 2. New Orleans: Tulane University Press, 1954.

Grinnell, George Bird. "Who Were the Padouca?" *American Anthropologist* 22 (July–September 1920): 248–60.

Gunnerson, James H. "An Introduction to Plains Apache Archeology—The Dismal River Aspect." Bureau of American Ethnology, Bulletin 173. *Smithsonian Institution Anthropological Papers,* no. 58 (1960): 131–260.

——. "Plains Apache Archaeology: A Review." *Plains Anthropologist* 13 (August 1968): 167–89.

Gutiérrez, Ramón A. "A Gendered History of the Conquest of America: A View from New Mexico." In *Gender Rhetorics: Postures of Dominance and Submission in History,* edited by Richard C. Trexler, 47–63. Binghamton, N.Y.: Medieval and Renaissance Texts and Studies, 1994.

——. "Honor Ideology, Marriage Negotiation, and Class-Gender Domination in New Mexico, 1690–1846." *Latin American Perspectives* 12 (Winter 1985): 81–104.

——. *When Jesus Came, the Cornmothers Went Away: Marriage, Sexuality and Power in New Mexico, 1500–1846.* Stanford: Stanford University Press, 1991.

Guy, Donna J., and Thomas E. Sheridan. "On Frontiers: The Northern and Southern Edges of the Spanish Empire in the Americas." In *Contested Ground: Comparative Frontiers on the Northern and Southern Edges of the Spanish Empire,* edited by Donna J. Guy and Thomas E. Sheridan, 3–15. Tucson: University of Arizona Press, 1998.

——, eds. *Contested Ground: Comparative Frontiers on the Northern and Southern Edges of the Spanish Empire.* Tucson: University of Arizona Press, 1998.

Haas, Edward F., ed. *Louisiana's Legal Heritage.* Pensacola, Fla.: Perdido Bay Press for the Louisiana State Museum, 1983.

Haas, Jonathan, ed. *The Anthropology of War.* New York: Cambridge University Press, 1990.

Habig, Marion A. *The Alamo Chain of Missions: A History of San Antonio's Five Old Missions.* Chicago: Franciscan Herald Press, 1968.

——. *The Alamo Mission: San Antonio de Valero, 1718–1793.* Chicago: Franciscan Herald Press, 1977.

——. "Mission San José y San Miguel de Aguayo, 1720–1824." *Southwestern Historical Quarterly* 71 (April 1968): 496–516.

——. *San Antonio's Mission San José.* San Antonio: Naylor Printing, 1968.

Hackel, Steven W. *Children of Coyote, Missionaries of Saint Francis: Indian-Spanish Relations in Colonial California, 1769–1850.* Chapel Hill: University of North Carolina Press for the Institute of Early American History and Culture, 2005.

——. "The Staff of Leadership: Indian Authority in the Missions of Alta California." *William and Mary Quarterly*, 3rd ser., 54 (April 1997): 347–76.

Hall, Gwendolyn Midlo. *Africans in Colonial Louisiana: The Development of Afro-Creole Culture in the Eighteenth Century.* Baton Rouge: Louisiana State University Press, 1992.

Hall, Jacquelyn Dowd. " 'The Mind That Burns in Each Body': Women, Rape, and Racial Violence." In *Powers of Desire: The Politics of Sexuality*, edited by Ann Snitow, Christine Stansell, and Sharon Thompson, 328–49. New York: Monthly Review Press, 1983.

Hall, Kim F. *Things of Darkness: Economies of Race and Gender in Early Modern England.* Ithaca, N.Y.: Cornell University Press, 1995.

Hall, Thomas D. *Social Change in the Southwest, 1350–1880.* Lawrence: University Press of Kansas, 1989.

Hämäläinen, Pekka. "The Western Comanche Trade Center: Rethinking the Plains Indian Trade System." *Western Historical Quarterly* 29 (Winter 1998): 485–513.

Haraway, Donna J. *Simians, Cyborgs, and Women: The Reinvention of Nature.* New York: Routledge, 1991.

Harby, Mrs. Lee C. "The Tejas: Their Habits, Government, and Superstitions." In *Annual Report of the American Historical Association for the Year 1894*, 63–82. Washington, D.C., 1895.

Harper, Elizabeth Ann. "The Taovayas Indians in Frontier Trade and Diplomacy, 1719–1768." *Chronicles of Oklahoma* 31 (Autumn 1953): 268–89.

——. "The Taovayas Indians in Frontier Trade and Diplomacy, 1779–1835." *Panhandle-Plains Historical Review* 26 (1953): 41–72.

——. "The Taovayas Indians in Frontier Trade and Diplomacy, 1769–1779." *Southwestern Historical Quarterly* 57 (October 1953): 181–201.

Hatcher, Mattie Austin. "Myths of the Tejas Indians." In *Texas and Southwestern Lore*, edited by J. Frank Dobie, 107–18. Publications of the Texas Folk-Lore Society, no. 6. Austin: Texas Folk-Lore Society, 1927.

Heflin, Eugene. "The Oashuns or Dances of the Caddo." *Bulletin of the Oklahoma Anthropological Society* 1 (March 1953): 39–42.

Hendricks, Margo, and Patricia Parker, eds. *Women, "Race," and Writing in the Early Modern Period*. New York: Routledge, 1994.

Hester, Thomas R. *Digging into South Texas Prehistory*. San Antonio: Crown, 1980.

——. "Perspectives on the Material Culture of the Mission Indians of the Texas-Northeastern Mexico Borderlands." In *Archaeological and Historical Perspectives on the Spanish Borderlands West*, edited by David Hurst Thomas, 213–29. Vol. 1 of *Columbian Consequences*. Washington, D.C.: Smithsonian Institution Press, 1989.

——. "Texas and Northeastern Mexico: An Overview." In *Archaeological and Historical Perspectives on the Spanish Borderlands West*, edited by David Hurst Thomas, 191–211. Vol. 1 of *Columbian Consequences*. Washington, D.C.: Smithsonian Institution Press, 1989.

——, ed. *Ethnology of the Texas Indians*. Spanish Borderlands Sourcebooks, no. 7. New York: Garland, 1991.

Hester, Thomas R., et al. *From the Gulf to the Rio Grande: Human Adaptation in Central, South, and Lower Pecos Texas*. San Antonio: Center for Archaeological Research, University of Texas at San Antonio, 1989.

Hickerson, Daniel A. "Hasinai-European Interaction, 1694–1715." *East Texas Historical Journal* 34 (1996): 3–16.

——. "Historical Processes, Epidemic Disease, and the Formation of the Hasinai Confederacy." *Ethnohistory* 44 (Winter 1997): 31–52.

——. "Trade, Mediation, and Political Status in the Hasinai Confederacy." *Research in Economic Anthropology* 17 (1996): 149–68.

Hickerson, Nancy Parrott. *The Jumanos: Hunters and Traders of the South Plains*. Austin: University of Texas Press, 1994.

Hindes, V. Kay, Mark R. Wolf, Grant D. Hall, and Kathleen Kirk Gilmore. *The Rediscovery of Santa Cruz de San Sabá: A Mission for the Apache in Spanish Texas*. Spanish documents translated by Philip A. Dennis. San Sabá Regional Survey Report no. 1, Archaeology Laboratory, Texas Tech University. N.p.: Texas Historical Foundation and Texas Tech University, 1995.

Hinojosa, Gilberto M. "Friars and Indians: Toward a Perspective of Cultural Interaction in the San Antonio Mission." *U.S. Catholic Historian* 9 (Spring 1990): 7–26.

Hinojosa, Gilberto M., and Anne A. Fox. "Indians and Their Culture in San Fernando de Béxar." In *Tejano Origins in Eighteenth-Century San Antonio*, edited by Gerald E. Poyo and Gilberto M. Hinojosa, 105–20. Austin: University of Texas Press for the University of Texas Institute of Texan Cultures at San Antonio, 1991.

Hoch-Smith, Judith, and Anita Spring, eds. *Women in Ritual and Symbolic Roles.* New York: Plenum Press, 1978.

Hoebel, E. Adamson. "Comanche and Hᴈkandika Shoshone Relationship Systems." *American Anthropologist* 41 (July–September 1939): 440–57.

——. *The Political Organization and Law-Ways of the Comanche Indians.* Memoirs of the American Anthropological Association, no. 54. Menasha, Wisc.: American Anthropological Association, 1940.

Hoijer, Harry. "The History and Customs of the Lipan, as Told by Augustina Zuazua." *Linguistics* 161 (1975): 5–38.

Holmes, Jack D. L. "Do It! Don't Do It! Spanish Laws on Sex and Marriage." In *Louisiana's Legal Heritage*, edited by Edward F. Haas, 19–42. Pensacola, Fla.: Perdido Bay Press for the Louisiana State Museum, 1983.

Horn, Rebecca, and Eric A. Hindraker. "Translating Christianity in the Colonial Americas." Paper presented at the annual meeting of the Organization of American Historians, Memphis, Tennessee, April 2003.

Hoyt, Cathryn A. "Material Culture of the Spanish Explorers." *Bulletin of the Texas Archeological Society* 63 (1992): 7–26.

Hurtado, Albert L. *Indian Survival on the California Frontier.* New Haven: Yale University Press, 1988.

——. *Intimate Frontiers: Sex, Gender, and Culture in Old California.* Albuquerque: University of New Mexico Press, 1999.

Hymes, Dell. *Language in Culture and Society: A Reader in Linguistics and Anthropology.* New York: Harper and Row, 1964.

Jackson, Jack. *Los Mesteños: Spanish Ranching in Texas, 1721–1821.* College Station: Texas A&M University Press, 1986.

——. *Shooting the Sun: Cartographic Results of Military Activities in Texas, 1689–1829.* 2 vols. Austin: Book Club of Texas, 1998.

Jackson, Robert H. *Race, Caste, and Status: Indians in Colonial Spanish America.* Albuquerque: University of New Mexico Press, 1999.

Jaenen, Cornelius J. "Conceptual Frameworks for French Views of America and Amerindians." *French Colonial Studies* 2 (1978): 1–22.

——. "The Role of Presents in French-Amerindian Trade." In *Explorations in Canadian Economic History: Essays in Honour of Irene M. Spry*, edited by Duncan Cameron, 231–50. Ottawa: University of Ottawa Press, 1985.

John, Elizabeth A. H. "Bernardo de Gálvez on the Apache Frontier: A Cautionary Note for Gringo Historians." *Journal of Arizona History* 29 (Winter 1988): 427–30.

——. "A Case Study in the Interdependence of Archeology and History: The Spanish Fort Sites on the Red River." *Bulletin of the Texas Archeological Society* 63 (1992): 197–209.

——. "A Cautionary Exercise in Apache Historiography." *Journal of Arizona History* 25 (Autumn 1984): 301–15.

——. "Francisco Xavier Chaves: Soldier-Interpreter." In *The Human Tradition in Texas*, edited by Ty Cashion and Jesús F. de la Teja, 21–33. Wilmington, Del.: Scholarly Resources, 2001.

——. "Nurturing the Peace: Spanish and Comanche Cooperation in the Early Nineteenth Century." *New Mexico Historical Review* 59 (October 1984): 345–69.

——. *Storms Brewed in Other Men's Worlds: The Confrontation of Indians, Spanish, and French in the Southwest, 1540–1795*. College Station: Texas A&M University Press, 1975.

——. "A Wichita Migration Tale." *American Indian Quarterly* 7 (Fall 1983): 57–63.

Johnson, LeRoy. *The Life and Times of Toyah-Culture Folk: As Seen from the Buckhollow Encampment, Site 41KM16, of Kimble County, Texas*. Austin: Texas Department of Transportation and Texas Historical Commission, 1994.

Johnson, LeRoy, and T. N. Campbell. "Sanan: Traces of a Previously Unknown Aboriginal Language in Colonial Coahuila and Texas." *Plains Anthropologist* 37 (August 1992): 185–212.

Johnson, Leroy, Jr., and Edward B. Jelks, eds. and trans. "The Tawakoni-Yscani Village, 1760: A Study in Archeological Site Identification." *Texas Journal of Science* 10 (December 1958): 405–22.

Johnson, Lyman L., and Sonya Lipsett-Rivera, eds. *The Faces of Honor: Sex, Shame, and Violence in Colonial Latin America*. Albuquerque: University of New Mexico Press, 1998.

Johnson, Walter. "On Agency." *Journal of Social History* 37 (2003): 113–24.

Jones, David E. *Sanapia: Comanche Medicine Woman*. New York: Holt, Rinehart and Winston, 1973.

Jones, Kristine L. "Comparative Raiding Economies: North and South." In *Contested Ground: Comparative Frontiers on the Northern and Southern Edges of the Spanish Empire*, edited by Donna J. Guy and Thomas E. Sheridan, 97–114. Tucson: University of Arizona Press, 1998.

Jones, Oakah L., Jr. *Los Paisanos: Spanish Settlers on the Northern Frontier of New Spain*. Norman: University of Oklahoma Press, 1979.

——. "Rescue and Ransom of Spanish Captives from the *Indios Bárbaros* on the Northern Frontier of New Spain." *Colonial Latin American Historical Review* 4 (Spring 1995): 129–48.

Kardiner, Abram. "Analysis of Comanche Culture." In *The Psychological Frontiers of Society*, 81–100. New York: Columbia University Press, 1959.

Kavanagh, Thomas W. *Comanche Political History: An Ethnohistorical Perspective, 1706–1875*. Lincoln: University of Nebraska Press, 1996.

Kelley, J. Charles. "Juan Sabeata and Diffusion in Aboriginal Texas." *American Anthropologist* 57 (October 1955): 981–95.

Kendrick, T. D. *Mary of Ágreda: The Life and Legend of a Spanish Nun*. London: Routledge and Kegan Paul, 1967.

Kertner, David I. *Ritual, Politics, and Power*. New Haven: Yale University Press, 1988.

Kessell, John L. "Spaniards and Pueblos: From Crusading Intolerance to Pragmatic Accommodation." In *Archaeological and Historical Perspectives on the Spanish Borderlands West*, edited by David Hurst Thomas, 127–38. Vol. 1 of *Columbian Consequences*. Washington, D.C.: Smithsonian Institution Press, 1989.

Kicza, John E. "Dealing with Foreigners: A Comparative Essay regarding Initial Expectations and Interactions between Native Societies and the English in North America and the Spanish in Mexico." *Colonial Latin American Historical Review* 3 (Fall 1994): 381–97.

Kidwell, Clara Sue. "Indian Women as Cultural Mediators." *Ethnohistory* 39 (Spring 1992): 97–107.

Kinnaird, Lawrence. "Spanish Treaties with Indian Tribes." *Western Historical Quarterly* 10 (January 1979): 39–48.

Kirkland, Forrest, and W. W. Newcomb Jr. *The Rock Art of Texas Indians*. Austin: University of Texas Press, 1967.

Klein, Alan M. "The Plains Truth: The Impact of Colonialism on Indian Women." *Dialectical Anthropology* 7 (1983): 299–313.

Klein, Cecelia F. "Fighting with Femininity: Gender and War in Aztec Mexico." In *Gender Rhetorics: Postures of Dominance and Submission in History*, edited by Richard C. Trexler, 107–46. Binghamton, N.Y.: Medieval and Renaissance Texts and Studies, 1994.

Krieger, Alex D. *Culture Complexes and Chronology in Northern Texas, with Extension of Puebloan Datings to the Mississippi Valley*. University of Texas Publication, no. 4640. Austin: University of Texas, 1946.

Krippner-Martínez, James. "The Politics of Conquest: An Interpretation of the *Relación de Michoacán.*" *The Americas* 47 (October 1990): 177–97.

Kupperman, Karen Ordahl. *Indians and English: Facing Off in Early America*. Ithaca, N.Y.: Cornell University Press, 2000.

——, ed. *America in European Consciousness, 1493–1750*. Chapel Hill: University of North Carolina Press for the Institute of Early American History and Culture, 1995.

Laqueur, Thomas. *Making Sex: Body and Gender from the Greeks to Freud*. Cambridge: Harvard University Press, 1990.

Lauber, Almon Wheeler. *Indian Slavery in Colonial Times within the Present Limits of the United States*. Studies in History, Economics and Public Law, no. 54. New York: Columbia University, 1913.

La Vere, David. *The Caddo Chiefdoms: Caddo Economies and Politics, 700–1835*. Lincoln: University of Nebraska Press, 1998.

——. "Friendly Persuasions: Gifts and Reciprocity in Comanche-Euroamerican Relations." *Chronicles of Oklahoma* 71 (Fall 1993): 322–37.

Lavrin, Asunción. "Sexuality in Colonial Mexico: A Church Dilemma." In *Sexuality and Marriage in Colonial Latin America*, edited by Asunción Lavrin, 47–95. Lincoln: University of Nebraska Press, 1989.

———, ed. *Sexuality and Marriage in Colonial Latin America*. Lincoln: University of Nebraska Press, 1989.

Lee, Aubra Lane. "Fusils, Paint, and Pelts: An Examination of Natchitoches-Based Indian Trade in the Spanish Period, 1766–1791." M.A. thesis, Northwestern State University, Natchitoches, 1990.

Lee, Dayna Bowker. "Indian Slavery in Lower Louisiana during the Colonial Period, 1699–1803." M.A. thesis, Northwestern State University, Natchitoches, 1989.

Lerner, Gerda. *The Creation of Patriarchy*. New York: Oxford University Press, 1986.

Lesser, Alexander. "Caddoan Kinship Systems." *Nebraska History* 60 (1979): 260–71.

Lévi-Strauss, Claude. *The Elementary Structures of Kinship*. Edited by Rodney Needham. Translated by James Harle Bell and John Richard von Sturmer. Rev. ed. Boston: Beacon Press, 1969.

Liu, Tessie P. "Race and Gender in the Politics of Group Formation: A Comment on Notions of Multiculturalism." *Frontiers* 12, no. 2 (1991): 155–65.

———. "Teaching the Differences among Women from a Historical Perspective: Rethinking Race and Gender as Social Categories." *Women's Studies International Forum* 14 (1991): 265–76.

Lockhart, James. "Sightings: Initial Nahua Reactions to Spanish Culture." In *Implicit Understandings: Observing, Reporting, and Reflecting on the Encounters between Europeans and Other Peoples in the Early Modern Era*, edited by Stuart B. Schwartz, 218–48. New York: Cambridge University Press, 1994.

Lohse, Jon C. "Lithics from the San Antonio de Valero Mission: Analysis of Materials from 1979 Excavations at the Alamo." *Bulletin of the Texas Archeological Society* 70 (1999): 266–79.

Lourie, Elena. "A Society Organized for War: Medieval Spain." *Past and Present* 35 (December 1966): 54–76.

MacCormack, Sabine. "Limits of Understanding: Perceptions of Greco-Roman and Amerindian Paganism in Early Modern Europe." In *America in European Consciousness, 1493–1750*, edited by Karen Ordahl Kupperman, 79–129. Chapel Hill: University of North Carolina Press for the Institute of Early American History and Culture, 1995.

MacGaffey, Wyatt. "Dialogues of the Deaf: Europeans on the Atlantic Coast of Africa." In *Implicit Understandings: Observing, Reporting, and Reflecting on the Encounters between Europeans and Other Peoples in the Early Modern Era*, edited by Stuart B. Schwartz, 249–67. New York: Cambridge University Press, 1994.

Magnaghi, Russell M. "Changing Material Culture and the Hasinai of East Texas." *Southern Studies* 20 (Winter 1981): 412–26.

———. "The Indian Slave Trader: The Comanche, a Case Study." Ph.D. diss., St. Louis University, 1970.

Marriott, Alice, and Carol K. Rachlin, eds. *Plains Indian Mythology*. New York: Thomas Y. Crowell, 1975.

Martin, Cheryl English. *Governance and Society in Colonial Mexico: Chihuahua in the Eighteenth Century*. Stanford: Stanford University Press, 1996.

Martin, George Castor, comp. *The Indian Tribes of the Mission Nuestra Señora del Refugio*. San Antonio: Wendell Potter, 1936.

Mauss, Marcel. "Body Techniques." Translated by Ben Brewster. In *Sociology and Psychology: Essays*, 95–123. Boston: Routledge and Kegan Paul, 1979.

——. *The Gift: The Form and Reason for Exchange in Archaic Societies*. 1924. Translated by W. D. Halls. New York: W. W. Norton, 1954.

McAlister, L. N. "Social Structure and Social Change in New Spain." *Hispanic American Historical Review* 43 (1963): 349–70.

McClintock, Anne. *Imperial Leather: Race, Gender and Sexuality in the Colonial Contest*. New York: Routledge, 1995.

McGowan, James T. "Planters without Slaves: Origins of a New World Labor System." *Southern Studies* 16 (Spring 1977): 5–26.

Merrell, James H. *The Indians' New World: Catawbas and Their Neighbors from European Contact through the Era of Removal*. Chapel Hill: University of North Carolina Press for the Institute of Early American History and Culture, 1989.

——. "The Racial Education of the Catawbas." *Journal of Southern History* 50 (1984): 363–84.

Merrill, William L. "Cultural Creativity and Raiding Bands in Eighteenth-Century Northern New Spain." In *Violence, Resistance, and Survival in the Americas: Native Americans and the Legacy of Conquest*, edited by William B. Taylor and Franklin Pease, G.Y., 124–52. Washington, D.C.: Smithsonian Institution Press, 1994.

Miller, William Ian. *Humiliation and Other Essays on Honor, Social Discomfort and Violence*. Ithaca, N.Y.: Cornell University Press, 1993.

Mills, Elizabeth Shown. "(De) Mézières-Trichel-Grappe: A Study of a Tri-Caste Lineage in the Old South." *Genealogist* 6 (Spring 1985): 4–84.

——. "Social and Family Patterns on the Colonial Louisiana Frontier." *Sociological Specturm* 2 (July–December 1982): 233–48.

Mills, Elizabeth Shown, and Gary B. Mills. *Tales of Old Natchitoches*. Cane River Creole Series, no. 3. Natchitoches, La.: Association for the Preservation of Historic Natchitoches, 1978.

Mintz, Sidney W., and Eric R. Wolf. "An Analysis of Ritual Co-Parenthood (Compadrazgo)." *Southwestern Journal of Anthropology* 6 (Winter 1950): 341–68.

Mitchell, Pablo. *Coyote Nation: Sexuality, Race, and Conquest in Modernizing New Mexico, 1880–1920*. Chicago: University of Chicago Press, 2005.

Mohanty, Chandra. "Under Western Eyes: Feminist Scholarship and Colonial Discourses." *Boundary 2: A Journal of Post-Modern Literature and Culture* 12–13 (Spring–Fall 1984): 333–58.

Montrose, Louis. "The Work of Gender in the Discourse of Discovery." *Representations* 33 (Winter 1991): 1–41.

Moorhead, Max L. *The Apache Frontier: Jacobo Ugarte and Spanish-Indian Relations in Northern New Spain, 1769–1791.* Norman: University of Oklahoma Press, 1968.

———. *The Presidio: Bastion of the Spanish Borderlands.* Norman: University of Oklahoma Press, 1975.

———. "Spanish Deportation of Hostile Apaches: The Policy and the Practice." *Arizona and the West* 17 (Autumn 1975): 205–20.

Morgan, Jennifer L. *Laboring Women: Reproduction and Gender in New World Slavery.* Philadelphia: University of Pennsylvania Press, 2004.

Mörner, Magnus. *Race Mixture in the History of Latin America.* Boston: Little, Brown, 1967.

Morris, Wayne. "The Wichita Exchange: Trade on Oklahoma's Fur Frontier, 1719–1812." *Great Plains Journal* 9 (Spring 1970): 79–84.

Muir, Edward. *Ritual in Early Modern Europe.* New York: Cambridge University Press, 1997.

Nardini, Louis Raphael. *My Historic Natchitoches and Its Environment.* Natchitoches, La.: Nardini Publishing, 1963.

Nasatir, Abraham P. *Borderland in Retreat: From Spanish Louisiana to the Far Southwest.* Albuquerque: University of New Mexico Press, 1976.

Nelson, Al B. "Campaigning in the Big Bend of the Rio Grande in 1787." *Southwestern Historical Quarterly* 39 (January 1936): 200–227.

———. "Juan de Ugalde and Picax-Ande Ins-Tinsle, 1787–1788." *Southwestern Historical Quarterly* 43 (April 1940): 438–64.

Newcomb, W. W., Jr. "Historic Indians of Central Texas." *Bulletin of the Texas Archeological Society* 64 (1993): 1–63.

———. *The Indians of Texas: From Prehistoric to Modern Times.* Austin: University of Texas Press, 1961.

———. "Karankawa." In *Southwest*, edited by Alfonso Ortiz, 359–67. Vol. 10 of *Handbook of North American Indians*, edited by William C. Sturtevant. Washington, D.C.: Smithsonian Institution Press, 1983.

———. *The People Called Wichita.* Phoenix: Indian Tribal Series, 1977.

———. "A Re-examination of the Causes of Plains Warfare." *American Anthropologist* 52 (July–August 1950): 317–30.

Newcomb, W. W., and T. N. Campbell. "Southern Plains Ethnohistory: A Re-examination of the Escanjaques, Ahijados, and Cuitoas." In *Pathways to Plains Prehistory: Anthropological Perspectives of Plains Natives and Their Pasts; Papers in Honor of Robert E. Bell*, edited by Don G. Wyckoff and Jack L. Hofman, 29–43. Memoirs of the Oklahoma Anthropological Society, no. 3. Duncan, Okla.: Cross Timbers Press, 1982.

Newcomb, W. W., Jr., and W. T. Field. "An Ethnohistoric Investigation of the Wichita Indians in the Southern Plains." In *Wichita Indian Archaeology and Ethnology: A Pilot Study*, edited by Robert E. Bell, Edward B. Jelks, and W. W. Newcomb, 271–434. New York: Garland, 1974.

Newkumet, Vynola Beaver, and Howard L. Meredith. *Hasinai: A Traditional History of the Caddo Confederacy*. College Station: Texas A&M University Press, 1988.

Nutini, Hugo. "Polygyny in a Tlaxcalan Community." *Ethnology* 4 (1965): 123–47.

Oberste, William H. *History of Refugio Mission*. Refugio, Tex.: Refugio Timely Remarks, 1942.

O'Neill, Charles Edward. *Church and State in French Colonial Louisiana: Policy and Politics to 1732*. New Haven: Yale University Press, 1966.

Opler, Morris Edward. "Cause and Effect in Apachean Agriculture, Division of Labor, Residence Patterns, and Girls' Puberty Rites." *American Anthropologist* 74 (October 1972): 1133–51.

——. "The Kinship Systems of the Southern Athabaskan-Speaking Tribes." *American Anthropologist* 38 (1936): 620–33.

——. *Lipan and Mescalero Apache in Texas*. New York: Garland, 1974.

——. "Lipan Apache." In *Plains*, edited by Raymond J. DeMallie, 941–52. Vol. 13 of *Handbook of North American Indians*, edited by William C. Sturtevant. Washington, D.C.: Smithsonian Institution Press, 1984.

——. "The Lipan Apache Death Complex and Its Extensions." *Southwestern Journal of Anthropology* 1 (Spring 1945): 122–41.

——. *Myths and Legends of the Lipan Apache Indians*. New York: American Folk-Lore Society, 1940.

O'Rourke, Thomas. *The Franciscan Missions in Texas, 1690–1793*. Studies in American Church History, vol. 5. Washington, D.C.: Catholic University of America, 1927; New York: AMS Press, 1974.

Pagden, Anthony. *The Fall of Natural Man: The American Indian and the Origins of Comparative Ethnology*. New York: Cambridge University Press, 1994.

Parsons, Elsie Clews. *Notes on the Caddo*. Memoirs of the American Anthropological Association, no. 57. Menasha, Wisc.: American Anthropological Association, 1941.

Pascoe, Peggy. "Gender, Race, and Intercultural Relations: The Case of Interracial Marriage." *Frontiers* 12 (1991): 5–18.

Perdue, Theda. *Cherokee Women: Gender and Culture Change, 1700–1835*. Lincoln: University of Nebraska Press, 1998.

——. "Columbus Meets Pocahontas in the American South." *Southern Cultures* 3 (1997): 4–21.

Perry, Mary Elizabeth. *Gender and Disorder in Early Modern Seville*. Princeton, N.J.: Princeton University Press, 1990.

Perttula, Timothy K. *"The Caddo Nation": Archaeological and Ethnohistoric Perspectives*. Austin: University of Texas Press, 1992.

——. "European Contact and Its Effects on Aboriginal Caddoan Populations between A.D. 1520 and A.D. 1680." In *The Spanish Borderlands in Pan-American Perspective*, edited by David Hurst Thomas, 501–18. Vol. 3 of *Columbian Consequences*. Washington, D.C.: Smithsonian Institution Press, 1991.

——. "French and Spanish Colonial Trade Policies and the Fur Trade among the Caddoan Indians of the Trans-Mississippi South." In *The Fur Trade Revisited: Selected Papers of the Sixth North American Fur Trade Conference, Mackinac Island, Michigan, 1991*, edited by Jennifer S. H. Brown, W. J. Eccles, and Donald P. Heldman, 71–91. East Lansing: Michigan State University Press and Mackinac State Historic Parks, 1994.

——. "Kee-Oh-Na-Wah'-Wah: The Effects of European Contact on the Caddoan Indians of Texas, Louisiana, Arkansas, and Oklahoma." In *Ethnohistory and Archaeology: Approaches to Postcontact Change in the Americas*, edited by J. Daniel Rogers and Samuel M. Wilson, 89–109. New York: Plenum Press, 1993.

——. "The Long-Term Effects of the De Soto Entrada on Aboriginal Caddoan Populations." In *The Expedition of Hernando de Soto West of the Mississippi, 1541–1543: Proceedings of the De Soto Symposia, 1988 and 1990*, edited by Gloria A. Young and Michael P. Hoffman, 237–53. Fayetteville: University of Arkansas Press, 1993.

Peterson, Jacqueline, and Jennifer Brown, eds. *The New Peoples: Being and Becoming Métis in North America*. Winnepeg: University of Manitoba Press, 1985.

Phares, Ross. *Cavalier in the Wilderness: The Story of the Explorer and Trader Louis Juchereau de St. Denis*. Baton Rouge: Louisiana State University Press, 1952.

Phelan, John Leddy. *The Millennial Kingdom of the Franciscans in the New World*. Rev. 2nd ed. Berkeley: University of California Press, 1970.

Pitt-Rivers, Julian. "Honour and Social Status." In *Honour and Shame: The Values of Mediterranean Society*, edited by J. G. Peristiany, 21–77. Chicago: University of Chicago Press, 1966.

Poll, Carolyn Garrett. "Reservation Policy and the Economic Position of Wichita Women." *Great Plains Quarterly* 8 (Summer 1988): 158–71.

Poole, Stafford. *Our Lady of Guadalupe: The Origins and Sources of a Mexican National Symbol, 1531–1797*. Tucson: University of Arizona Press, 1995.

——. "Some Observations on Mission Methods and Native Reactions in Sixteenth-Century New Spain." *The Americas* 50 (January 1994): 337–49.

——. " 'War by Fire and Blood': The Church and the Chichimecas, 1585." *The Americas* 22 (October 1965): 115–37.

Powers, Karen Vieira. "Conquering Discourses of 'Sexual Conquest': Of Women, Language, and *Mestizaje*." *Colonial Latin American Review* 11 (2002): 7–32.

——. *Women in the Crucible of Conquest: The Gendered Genesis of Spanish American Society, 1500–1600*. Albuquerque: University of New Mexico Press, 2005.

Poyo, Gerald E., ed. *Tejano Journey, 1770–1850*. Austin: University of Texas Press, 1996.

Poyo, Gerald E., and Gilberto M. Hinojosa. "Spanish Texas and Borderlands Historiography in Transition: Implications for United States History." *Journal of American History* 75 (1988): 393–416.

——, eds. *Tejano Origins in Eighteenth-Century San Antonio*. Austin: University of Texas Press for the University of Texas Institute of Texan Cultures at San Antonio, 1991.

Prikryl, Daniel J. "Fiction and Fact about the Titskanwatits, or Tonkawa, of East Central Texas." *Bulletin of the Texas Archeological Society* 72 (2001): 63–72.

Radding, Cynthia. *Wandering Peoples: Colonialism, Ethnic Spaces, and Ecological Frontiers in Northwestern Mexico, 1700–1850.* Durham, N.C.: Duke University Press, 1997.

Ratcliffe, Sam D. "'*Escenas de Martirio*': Notes on The Destruction of Mission San Sabá." *Southwestern Historical Quarterly* 94 (April 1991): 506–34.

Ray, Verne F. *Ethnohistorical Analysis of Documents Relating to the Apache Indians of Texas.* New York: Garland, 1974.

Reff, Daniel T. *Disease, Depopulation, and Cultural Change in Northwestern New Spain, 1518–1764.* Salt Lake City: University of Utah Press, 1991.

Reiter, Rayna R., ed. *Toward an Anthropology of Women.* New York: Monthly Review Press, 1975.

Remensnyder, Amy. "The Virgin Mary and the Conversion of Sacred Space on Spanish Frontiers (ca. 1000–ca. 1550)." Paper presented at the Latin American History Workshop, Princeton University, 1997.

Reséndez, Andrés. *Changing National Identities at the Frontier: Texas and New Mexico, 1800–1850.* New York: Cambridge University Press, 2005.

Ricard, Robert. *The Spiritual Conquest of Mexico: An Essay on the Apostalate and the Evangelizing Methods of the Mendicant Orders of New Spain, 1523–1572.* Translated by Leslie Byrd Simpson. Berkeley: University of California Press, 1966.

Richter, Daniel K. *Facing East from Indian Country: A Native History of Early America.* Cambridge: Harvard University Press, 2001.

——. *The Ordeal of the Longhouse: The Peoples of the Iroquois League in the Era of European Colonization.* Chapel Hill: University of North Carolina Press for the Institute of Early American History and Culture, 1992.

Ricklis, Robert A. "Aboriginal Karankawan Adaptation and Colonial Period Acculturation: Archeological and Ethnohistorical Evidence." *Bulletin of the Texas Archeological Society* 63 (1992): 211–43.

——. *The Karankawa Indians of Texas: An Ecological Study of Cultural Tradition and Change.* Austin: University of Texas Press, 1996.

——. "The Spanish Colonial Missions of Espíritu Santo (41GD1) and Nuestra Señora del Rosario (41GD2), Goliad, Texas: Exploring Patterns of Ethnicity, Interaction, and Acculturation." *Bulletin of the Texas Archeological Society* 70 (1999): 133–68.

Riley, Carroll L. "Early Spanish-Indian Communication in the Greater Southwest." *New Mexico Historical Review* 46 (October 1971): 285–314.

Rivaya-Martínez, Joaquín. "The Comanche-Spanish Treaty of 1786 in Ethnohistorical Perspective." M.A. thesis, University of California at Los Angeles, 2001.

Rodriguez, Jarbel. "Financing a Captive's Ransom in Late Medieval Aragon." *Medieval Encounters: Jewish, Christian, and Muslim Culture in Confluence and Dialogue* 9 (2003): 164–81.

Rogers, J. Daniel. "Dispersed Communities and Integrated Households: A Perspective from Spiro and the Arkansas Basin." In *Mississippian Communities and Households*, edited by J. Daniel Rogers and Bruce D. Smith, 81–98. Tuscaloosa: University of Alabama Press, 1995.

Rohrbaugh, Charles L. "An Hypothesis for the Origin of the Kichai." In *Pathways to Plains Prehistory: Anthropological Perspectives of Plains Natives and Their Pasts; Papers in Honor of Robert E. Bell*, edited by Don G. Wyckoff and Jack L. Hofman, 51–63. Memoirs of the Oklahoma Anthropological Society, no. 3. Duncan, Okla.: Cross Timbers Press, 1982.

Romero de Terreros, Juan M. "The Destruction of the San Sabá Apache Mission: A Discussion of the Casualties." *The Americas* 60 (April 2004): 617–27.

Roper, Lyndal. *Oedipus and the Devil: Witchcraft, Sexuality, and Religion in Early Modern Europe*. New York: Routledge, 1994.

Rosaldo, Michelle Zimbalist, and Louise Lamphere, eds. *Woman, Culture, and Society*. Stanford: Stanford University Press, 1974.

Rubin, Gayle. "The Traffic in Women: Notes on the 'Political Economy of Sex.' " In *Toward an Anthropology of Women*, edited by Rayna R. Reiter, 157–210. New York: Monthly Review Press, 1975.

Rushforth, Brett. " 'A Little Flesh We Offer You': The Origins of Indian Slavery in New France." *William and Mary Quarterly*, 3rd ser., 60 (October 2003): 777–808.

Sabo, George. "Encounters and Images: European Contact and the Caddo Indians." *Historical Reflections/Reflexions Historiques* 21 (Spring 1995): 217–42.

——. "Indians and Spaniards in Arkansas: Symbolic Action in the Sixteenth Century." In *The Expedition of Hernando de Soto West of the Mississippi, 1541–1543: Proceedings of the De Soto Symposia, 1988 and 1990*, edited by Gloria A. Young and Michael P. Hoffman, 192–209. Fayetteville: University of Arkansas Press, 1993.

——. "Reordering Their World: A Caddoan Ethnohistory." In *Visions and Revisions: Ethnohistoric Perspectives on Southern Cultures*, edited by George Sabo and William M. Schneider, 25–47. Athens: University of Georgia Press, 1987.

——. "Rituals of Encounter: Interpreting Native American Views of European Explorers." In *Cultural Encounters in the Early South: Indians and Europeans in Arkansas*, edited by Jeannie Whayne, 76–87. Fayetteville: University of Arkansas Press, 1995.

——. "The Structure of Caddo Leadership in the Colonial Era." In *The Native History of the Caddo: Their Place in Southeastern Archeology and Ethnohistory*, edited by Timothy K. Perttula and James E. Bruseth, 159–74. Studies in Archeology, no. 30. Austin: Texas Archeological Research Laboratory, University of Texas at Austin, 1998.

Sahlins, Marshall. *Stone Age Economics*. Chicago: Aldine, 1972.

Salinas, Martín. *Indians of the Rio Grande Delta: Their Role in the History of Southern Texas and Northeastern Mexico*. Austin: University of Texas Press, 1990.

San Antonio in the Eighteenth Century. San Antonio: San Antonio Bicentennial Heritage Committee, 1976.

Sayre, Gordon M. *Les Sauvages Américains: Representations of Native Americans in French and English Colonial Literature*. Chapel Hill: University of North Carolina Press, 1997.

——. "Native American Sexuality in the Eyes of the Beholders, 1535–1710." In *Sex and Sexuality in Early America*, edited by Merril D. Smith, 35–54. New York: New York University Press, 1998.

Scarry, Elaine. *The Body in Pain: The Making and Unmaking of the World*. New York: Oxford University Press, 1985.

Schaedel, Richard P. "The Karankawa of the Texas Gulf Coast." *Southwestern Journal of Anthropology* 5 (Summer 1949): 117–37.

Schilz, Thomas F. *Lipan Apaches in Texas*. Southwestern Studies, no. 83. El Paso: Texas Western Press, 1987.

Schilz, Thomas Frank, and Donald E. Worcester. "The Spread of Firearms among the Indian Tribes on the Northern Frontier of New Spain." *American Indian Quarterly* 11 (Winter 1987): 1–10.

Schmitt, Karl. "Wichita Death Customs." *Chronicles of Oklahoma* 30 (Summer 1952): 200–206.

Schmitt, Karl, and Iva Osanai Schmitt. *Wichita Kinship, Past and Present*. Norman, Okla.: University Book Exchange, n.d.

Schneider, Jane. "Of Vigilance and Virgins: Honor, Shame and Access to Resources in Mediterranean Societies." *Ethnology* 10 (January 1971): 1–24.

Schroeder, Susan, ed. *Native Resistance and the Pax Colonial in New Spain*. Lincoln: University of Nebraska Press, 1998.

Schroeder, Susan, Stephanie Wood, and Robert Haskett, eds. *Indian Women of Early Mexico*. Norman: University of Oklahoma Press, 1997.

Schuetz, Mardith K. "An Historical Outline of Mission San Juan de Capistrano." *La Tierra: Journal of the Southern Texas Archaeological Association* 7 (1980): 3–15.

——. *Historic Background of the Mission San Antonio de Valero*. Austin: State Building Commission, Archeological Program, 1966.

——. *The History and Archeology of Mission San Juan Capistrano, San Antonio, Texas*. 2 vols. Austin: State Building Commission, Archeological Program, 1968–69.

——. "The Indians of the San Antonio Missions, 1718–1821." Ph.D. diss., University of Texas at Austin, 1980.

——. "Professional Artisans in the Hispanic Southwest: The Churches of San Antonio, Texas." *The Americas* 40 (July 1983): 17–71.

Schwartz, Stuart B., ed. *Implicit Understandings: Observing, Reporting, and Reflecting on the Encounters between Europeans and Other Peoples in the Early Modern Era*. New York: Cambridge University Press, 1994.

Scott, Joan W. "Gender: A Useful Category of Historical Analysis." *American Historical Review* 91 (1986): 1053–75.

Scurlock, Dan, and Daniel E. Fox. *An Archeological Investigation of Mission Concepción, San Antonio, Texas*. Austin: Texas Historical Commission, 1977.

Secoy, Frank Raymond. *Changing Military Patterns on the Great Plains (17th Century through Early 19th Century)*. Monographs of the American Ethnological Society, no. 21. Locust Valley, N.Y.: J. J. Augustin, 1953.

——. "The Identity of the 'Padouca': An Ethnohistorical Analysis." *American Anthropologist* 53 (1951): 525–42.

Seed, Patricia. *Ceremonies of Possession in Europe's Conquest of the New World, 1492–1640*. New York: Cambridge University Press, 1995.

——. "Taking Possession and Reading Texts: Establishing the Authority of Overseas Empires." In *Early Images of the Americas: Transfer and Invention*, edited by Jerry M. Williams and Robert E. Lewis, 111–47. Tucson: University of Arizona Press, 1993.

——. *To Love, Honor, and Obey in Colonial Mexico: Conflicts over Marriage Choice, 1574–1821*. Stanford: Stanford University Press, 1988.

Sheridan, Cecilia. "Social Control and Native Territoriality in Northeastern New Spain." In *Choice, Persuasion, and Coercion: Social Control on Spain's North American Frontiers*, edited by Jesús F. de la Teja and Ross Frank, 128–41. Albuquerque: University of New Mexico Press, 2005.

Shimkin, D. B. "Shoshone-Comanche Origins and Migrations." *Proceedings of the Sixth Pacific Science Congress of the Pacific Science Association* 4 (1940): 17–25.

Shoemaker, Nancy. "Categories." In *Clearing a Path: Theorizing the Past in Native American Studies*, edited by Nancy Shoemaker, 51–74. New York: Routledge, 2001.

——. "How Indians Got to Be Red." *American Historical Review* 102 (1997): 625–44.

——. "The Rise or Fall of Iroquois Women." *Journal of Women's History* 2 (Winter 1991): 39–57.

——. *A Strange Likeness: Becoming Red and White in Eighteenth-Century North America*. New York: Oxford University Press, 2004.

——, ed. *Clearing a Path: Theorizing the Past in Native American Studies*. New York: Routledge, 2001.

——. *Negotiators of Change: Historical Perspectives on Native American Women*. New York: Routledge, 1995.

Sibley, John. "Vocabulary of the Caddo Language." *American Naturalist* 13 (1879): 787–90. Reprinted in *The Southern Caddo: An Anthology*, edited by Hiram F. Gregory. New York: Garland, 1986.

Silverblatt, Irene. *Moon, Sun, and Witches: Gender Ideologies and Class in Inca and Colonial Peru*. Princeton, N.J.: Princeton University Press, 1987.

Sjoberg, Andreé F. "The Culture of the Tonkawa, a Texas Indian Tribe." *Texas Journal of Science* 5 (September 1953): 280–304.

——. "Lipan Apache Culture in Historical Perspective." *Southwestern Journal of Anthropology* 9 (Spring 1953): 76–98.

Skeels, Lydia L. M. *An Ethnohistorical Survey of Texas Indians*. Archeological Report, no. 22. Austin: Texas Historical Survey Committee, 1972.

Slatta, Richard W. "Spanish Colonial Military Strategy and Ideology." In *Contested Ground:*

Comparative Frontiers on the Northern and Southern Edges of the Spanish Empire, edited by Donna J. Guy and Thomas E. Sheridan, 83–96. Tucson: University of Arizona Press, 1998.

Sleeper-Smith, Susan. *Indian Women and French Men: Rethinking Cultural Encounter in the Western Great Lakes*. Amherst: University of Massachusetts Press, 2001.

Smedley, Audrey. *Race in North America: Origin and Evolution of a Worldview*. 2nd ed. Boulder, Colo.: Westview Press, 1999.

Smith, F. Todd. *The Caddo Indians: Tribes at the Convergence of Empires, 1542–1854*. College Station: Texas A&M University Press, 1995.

——. *The Wichita Indians: Traders of Texas and the Southern Plains, 1540–1845*. College Station: Texas A&M University Press, 2000.

Smith, James E. "The Vinson Site: A Norteño Focus Indian Village in Limestone County, Texas." *Bulletin of the Texas Archeological Society* 64 (1993): 65–162.

Smith, Merril D., ed. *Sex and Sexuality in Early America*. New York: New York University Press, 1998.

Smits, David D. "The 'Squaw Drudge': A Prime Index of Savagism." *Ethnohistory* 29 (1982): 281–306.

Snow, David H., ed. *The Native American and Spanish Colonial Experience in the Greater Southwest*. 2 vols. New York: Garland, 1992.

Socolow, Susan Migden. *The Women of Colonial Latin America*. New York: Cambridge University Press, 2000.

Spear, Jennifer. "Colonial Intimacies: Legislating Sex in French Louisiana." *William and Mary Quarterly*, 3rd ser., 60 (January 2003): 75–98.

——. " 'They Need Wives': Métissage and the Regulation of Sexuality in French Louisiana, 1699–1730." In *Sex, Love, Race: Crossing Boundaries in North American History*, edited by Martha Hodes, 35–59. New York: New York University Press, 1999.

Spicer, Edward H. *Cycles of Conquest: The Impact of Spain, Mexico, and the United States on the Indians of the Southwest, 1533–1960*. Tucson: University of Arizona Press, 1962.

Spielmann, Katherine A., ed. *Farmers, Hunters, and Colonists: Interaction between the Southwest and the Southern Plains*. Tucson: University of Arizona Press, 1991.

Spurling, Geoffrey. "Honor, Sexuality, and the Catholic Church: The Sins of Dr. González, Cathedral Canon." In *The Faces of Honor: Sex, Shame, and Violence in Colonial Latin America*, edited by Lyman L. Johnson and Sonya Lipsett-Rivera, 45–67. Albuquerque: University of New Mexico Press, 1998.

Starnes, Gary B. *The San Gabriel Missions, 1746–1756*. Madrid: Spanish Ministry of Foreign Affairs, 1969.

Steck, Francis Borgia. "Forerunners of Captain de León's Expedition to Texas, 1670–1675." *Southwestern Historical Quarterly* 36 (July 1932): 1–28.

Stern, Peter. "The White Indians of the Southwest." *Journal of the Southwest* 33 (Autumn 1991): 262–81.

Stern, Steve J. "Paradigms of Conquest: History, Historiography, and Politics." Quincentenary supplement, *Journal of Latin American Studies* 24 (1992): 1–34.

———. *The Secret History of Gender: Women, Men, and Power in Late Colonial Mexico.* Chapel Hill: University of North Carolina Press, 1995.

Stoler, Anne Laura. "Carnal Knowledge and Imperial Power: Gender, Race, and Morality in Colonial Asia." In *Gender at the Crossroads of Knowledge: Feminist Anthropology in the Postmodern Era,* edited by Micaela di Leonardo, 51–101. Los Angeles: University of California Press, 1991.

———. *Race and the Education of Desire: Foucault's* History of Sexuality *and the Colonial Order of Things.* Durham, N.C.: Duke University Press, 1995.

———. "Sexual Affronts and Racial Frontiers: European Identities and the Cultural Politics of Exclusion in Colonial Southeast Asia." *Comparative Studies in Society and History* 34 (1992): 514–51.

Strickland, Rex W. "Moscoso's Journey through Texas." *Southwestern Historical Quarterly* 46 (October 1942): 109–37.

Surrey, N. M. Miller. *The Commerce of Louisiana during the French Régime, 1699–1763.* Studies in History, Economics, and Public Law, no. 71. New York: Columbia University, 1916.

Swagerty, William R. "Spanish-Indian Relations, 1531–1821." In *Scholars and the Indian Experience: Critical Reviews of Recent Writing in the Social Sciences,* edited by William R. Swagerty, 36–78. Bloomington: Indiana University Press, 1984.

Swanton, John R. "The Caddo Social Organization and Its Possible Historical Significance." *Journal of the Washington Academy of Sciences* 21 (May 4, 1931): 203–6.

———. *The Indians of the Southeastern United States.* Smithsonian Institution, Bureau of American Ethnology, Bulletin 137. Washington, D.C.: Smithsonian Institution, 1946.

———. "Mythology of the Indians of Louisiana and the Texas Coast." *Journal of American Folk-Lore* 20 (1907): 285–90.

———. *Source Material on the History and Ethnology of the Caddo Indians.* Smithsonian Institution, Bureau of American Ethnology, Bulletin 132. Washington, D.C.: Smithsonian Institution, 1942.

Taylor, William B. "The Virgin of Guadalupe in New Spain: An Inquiry into the Social History of Marian Devotion." *American Ethnologist* 14 (1987): 9–33.

Teja, Jesús F. de la. "Forgotten Founders: The Military Settlers of Eighteenth-Century San Antonio de Béxar." In *Tejano Origins in Eighteenth-Century San Antonio,* edited by Gerald E. Poyo and Gilberto M. Hinojosa, 27–38. Austin: University of Texas Press for the University of Texas Institute of Texan Cultures at San Antonio, 1991.

———. "Indians, Soldiers, and Canary Islanders: The Making of a Texas Frontier Community." *Locus: An Historical Journal of Regional Perspectives on National Topics* 3 (Fall 1990): 81–96.

———. *San Antonio de Béxar: A Community on New Spain's Northern Frontier.* Albuquerque: University of New Mexico Press, 1995.

——. "Spanish Colonial Texas." In *New Views of Borderlands History*, edited by Robert H. Jackson, 107–30. Albuquerque: University of New Mexico Press, 1998.

——. "St. James at the Fair: Religious Ceremony, Civic Boosterism, and Commercial Development on the Colonial Mexican Frontier." *The Americas* 57 (January 2001): 395–416.

Teja, Jesús F. de la, and Ross Frank. *Choice, Persuasion, and Coercion: Social Control on Spain's North American Frontiers.* Albuquerque: University of New Mexico Press, 2005.

TePaske, John J. "French, Spanish, and English Indian Policy on the Gulf Coast, 1513–1763: A Comparison." In *Spain and Her Rivals on the Gulf Coast*, edited by Ernest F. Dibble and Earle W. Newton, 9–39. Pensacola, Fla.: Historic Pensacola Preservation Board, 1971.

Thomas, David Hurst, ed. *Columbian Consequences.* 3 vols. Washington, D.C.: Smithsonian Institution Press, 1989–91.

Thoms, Alston V., et al., eds. *Reassessing Cultural Extinction: Change and Survival at Mission San Juan Capistrano, Texas.* San Antonio: San Antonio Missions National Historical Park, National Park Service; College Station: Center for Ecological Archaeology, Texas A&M University, 2001.

Thorne, Tanis C. *The Many Hands of My Relations: French and Indians on the Lower Missouri.* Columbia: University of Missouri Press, 1996.

Thurman, Melburn D. "A New Interpretation of Comanche Social Organization." *Current Anthropology* 23 (October 1982): 578–79.

Tjarks, Alicia Vidaurreta. "Comparative Demographic Analysis of Texas, 1777–1793." *Southwestern Historical Quarterly* 77 (1974): 291–338.

Todorov, Tzvetan. *The Conquest of America: The Question of the Other.* New York: Harper and Row, 1984.

Torre, Adela de la, and Beatríz M. Pesquera, eds. *Building with Our Hands: New Directions in Chicana Studies.* Los Angeles: University of California Press, 1993.

Trexler, Richard C. *Sex and Conquest: Gendered Violence, Political Order, and the European Conquest of the Americas.* Ithaca, N.Y.: Cornell University Press, 1995.

——, ed. *Gender Rhetorics: Postures of Dominance and Submission in History.* Binghamton, N.Y.: Medieval and Renaissance Texts and Studies, 1994.

Trigger, Bruce G. "Early Native North American Responses to European Contact: Romantic versus Rationalistic Interpretations." *Journal of American History* 77 (March 1991): 1195–1215.

Troike, Rudolph C. "Notes on Coahuiltecan Ethnography." *Bulletin of the Texas Archeological Society* 32 (1961): 57–63.

Trudel, Marcel. *L'Esclavage au Canada Français: Histoire et Conditions de L'Esclavage.* Québec: Les Presses Universitaires Laval, 1960.

Tunnell, Curtis D., and W. W. Newcomb Jr. *A Lipan Apache Mission: San Lorenzo de la Santa Cruz, 1762–1771.* Texas Memorial Museum, Bulletin no. 14. Austin: University of Texas at Austin, 1969.

Turgeon, Laurier. "The Tale of the Kettle: Odyssey of an Intercultural Object." *Ethnohistory* 44 (1997): 1–29.

Turpin, Solveig A. "The Iconography of Contact: Spanish Influences in the Rock Art of the Middle Rio Grande." In *Archaeological and Historical Perspectives on the Spanish Borderlands West*, edited by David Hurst Thomas, 277–99. Vol. 1 of *Columbian Consequences*. Washington, D.C.: Smithsonian Institution Press, 1989.

Twinam, Ann. *Public Lives, Private Secrets: Gender, Honor, Sexuality, and Illegitimacy in Colonial Spanish America*. Stanford: Stanford University Press, 1999.

Ubelaker, Douglas H., and Herman J. Viola, eds. *Plains Indian Studies: A Collection of Essays in Honor of John C. Ewers and Waldo R. Wedel*. Washington, D.C.: Smithsonian Institution Press, 1982.

Usner, Daniel H., Jr. "From African Captivity to American Slavery: The Introduction of Black Laborers to Colonial Louisiana." *Louisiana History* 20 (Winter 1979): 25–48.

——. *Indians, Settlers, and Slaves in a Frontier Exchange Economy: The Lower Mississippi Valley before 1783*. Chapel Hill: University of North Carolina Press for the Institute of Early American History and Culture, 1992.

Van Kirk, Sylvia. *Many Tender Ties: Women in Fur Trade Society, 1670–1870*. Norman: University of Oklahoma Press, 1980.

Vansina, Jan. *Oral Tradition as History*. Madison: University of Wisconsin Press, 1985.

Vehik, Susan C. "Cultural Continuity and Discontinuity in the Southern Prairies and Cross Timbers." In *Plains Indians, A.D. 500–1500: The Archaeological Past of Historic Groups*, edited by Karl H. Schlesier, 239–63. Norman: University of Oklahoma Press, 1994.

——. "Wichita Culture History." *Plains Anthropologist* 37 (November 1992): 311–32.

Wade, Maria F. "Go-Between: The Roles of Native American Women and Alvar Núñez Cabeza de Vaca in Southern Texas in the 16th Century." *Journal of American Folklore* 112 (Summer 1999): 332–42.

——. *The Native Americans of the Texas Edwards Plateau, 1582–1799*. Austin: University of Texas Press, 2003.

Wallace, Ernest, and E. Adamson Hoebel. *The Comanches: Lords of the South Plains*. Norman: University of Oklahoma Press, 1952.

Warner, Marina. *Alone of All Her Sex: The Myth and the Cult of the Virgin Mary*. New York: Vintage Books, 1976.

Webb, Clarence H., and Hiram F. Gregory. *The Caddo Indians of Louisiana*. 2nd ed. Louisiana Archeological Survey and Antiquities Commission, Anthropological Study no. 2. Baton Rouge: Department of Culture, Recreation, and Tourism, 1986.

Weber, David J. *Bárbaros: Spaniards and Their Savages in the Age of Enlightenment*. New Haven: Yale University Press, 2005.

——. "Blood of Martyrs, Blood of Indians: Toward a More Balanced View of Spanish Missions in Seventeenth-Century North America." In *Archaeological and Historical Perspectives on the Spanish Borderlands East*, edited by David Hurst Thomas, 429–

48. Vol. 2 of *Columbian Consequences*. Washington, D.C.: Smithsonian Institution Press, 1990.

———. "Bourbons and Bárbaros: Center and Periphery in the Reshaping of Spanish Indian Policy." In *Negotiated Empires: Centers and Peripheries in the Americas, 1500–1820*, edited by Christine Daniels and Michael V. Kennedy, 79–103. New York: Routledge, 2002.

———. *The Spanish Frontier in North America*. New Haven: Yale University Press, 1992.

———, ed. *The Idea of Spanish Borderlands*. Spanish Borderlands Sourcebooks, no. 1. New York: Garland, 1991.

———. *New Spain's Far Northern Frontier: Essays on Spain in the American West*. Albuquerque: University of New Mexico Press, 1979.

Weber, David J., and Jane M. Rausch, eds. *Where Cultures Meet: Frontiers in Latin American History*. Wilmington, Del.: Scholarly Resources, 1994.

Webre, Stephen. "The Problem of Indian Slavery in Spanish Louisiana, 1769–1803." *Louisiana History* 25 (Spring 1984): 117–35.

Weddle, Robert S. "La Salle's Survivors." *Southwestern Historical Quarterly* 75 (April 1972): 413–33.

———. *San Juan Bautista: Gateway to Spanish Texas*. Austin: University of Texas Press, 1968.

———. *The San Sabá Mission: Spanish Pivot in Texas*. Austin: University of Texas Press, 1964.

———. *Wilderness Manhunt: The Spanish Search for La Salle*. Austin: University of Texas Press, 1973.

Wedel, Mildred Mott. *The Deer Creek Site, Oklahoma: A Wichita Village Sometimes Called Ferdinandina; An Ethnohistorian's View*. Oklahoma Historical Society, Series in Anthropology, no. 5. Oklahoma City: Oklahoma Historical Society, 1981.

———. *La Harpe's 1719 Post on Red River and Nearby Caddo Settlements*. Texas Memorial Museum, Bulletin 30. Austin: University of Texas at Austin, 1978.

———. *The Wichita Indians, 1541–1750: Ethnohistorical Essays*. Reprints in Anthropology, no. 38. Lincoln, Neb.: J & L Reprint, 1988.

———. "The Wichita Indians in the Arkansas River Basin." In *Plains Indian Studies: A Collection of Essays in Honor of John C. Ewers and Waldo R. Wedel*, edited by Douglas H. Ubelaker and Herman J. Viola, 118–34. Washington, D.C.: Smithsonian Institution Press, 1982.

Weist, Katherine M. "Plains Indian Women: An Assessment." In *Anthropology on the Great Plains*, edited by W. Raymond Wood and Margot Liberty, 255–71. Lincoln: University of Nebraska Press, 1980.

White, Richard. *The Middle Ground: Indians, Empires, and Republic in the Great Lakes Region, 1650–1815*. New York: Cambridge University Press, 1991.

———. "The Winning of the West: The Expansion of the Western Sioux in the Eighteenth and Nineteenth Centuries." *Journal of American History* 65 (September 1978): 319–43.

Whitehead, Neil L. "Tribes Make States and States Make Tribes: Warfare and the Creation of Colonial Tribes and States in Northeastern South America." In *War in the Tribal Zone: Expanding States and Indigenous Warfare*, edited by R. Brian Ferguson and Neil L. Whitehead, 127–50. Santa Fe: School of American Research Press, 1992.

Wilentz, Sean, ed. *Rites of Power: Symbolism, Ritual, and Politics since the Middle Ages.* Philadelphia: University of Pennsylvania Press, 1985.

Wisch, Barbara, and Susan Scott Munshower, eds. *Triumphal Celebrations and the Rituals of Statecraft.* Vol. 1 of *"All the World's a Stage . . .": Art and Pageantry in the Renaissance and Baroque.* 2 vols. Papers in Art History from the Pennsylvania State University, no. 6. University Park: Department of Art History, Pennsylvania State University, 1990.

Wissler, Clark. *North American Indians of the Plains.* New York: American Museum of Natural History, 1948.

Woldert, Albert. "The Expedition of Luis de Moscoso in Texas in 1542." *Southwestern Historical Quarterly* 46 (October 1942): 158–66.

Wood, Peter H. "La Salle: Discovery of a Lost Explorer." *American Historical Review* 89 (April 1984): 294–323.

Wood, Stephanie. "Sexual Violence in the Conquest of the Americas." In *Sex and Sexuality in Early America,* edited by Merril D. Smith, 9–34. New York: New York University Press, 1998.

Wright, J. Leitch. *The Only Land They Knew: The Tragic Story of the American Indian in the Old South.* New York: Free Press, 1981.

Wunder, John R., and Pekka Hämäläinen. "Of Lethal Places and Lethal Essays." *American Historical Review* 104 (October 1999): 1229–34.

Wyckoff, Don G., and Timothy G. Baugh. "Early Historic Hasinai Elites: A Model for the Material Culture of Governing Elites." *Mid-Continental Journal of Anthropology* 5 (1980): 225–88.

Yanagisako, Sylvia Junko, and Jane Fishburne Collier. "Toward a Unified Analysis of Gender and Kinship." In *Gender and Kinship: Essays toward a Unified Analysis,* edited by Jane Fishburne Collier and Sylvia Junko Yanagisako, 14–50. Stanford: Stanford University Press, 1987.

Young, Gloria A., and Michael P. Hoffman, eds. *The Expedition of Hernando de Soto West of the Mississippi, 1541–1543: Proceedings of the De Soto Symposia, 1988 and 1990.* Fayetteville: University of Arkansas Press, 1993.

Young, Robert J. C. *Colonial Desire: Hybridity in Theory, Culture and Race.* New York: Routledge, 1995.

Zamora, Margarite. "Gender and Discovery." In *Reading Columbus,* 152–79. Berkeley: University of California Press, 1993.

Zavala, Adina de. "Religious Beliefs of the Tejas or Hasanias Indians." Publications of the Folk-Lore Society of Texas, no. 1, edited by Stith Thompson, 39–43. Austin: Folk-Lore Society of Texas, 1916.

Zitomersky, Joseph. "The Form and Function of French–Native American Relations in Early Eighteenth-Century French Colonial Louisiana." In *Proceedings of the Fifteenth Meeting of the French Colonial Historical Society, Martinique and Guadaloupe, May 1989,* edited by Patricia Galloway, 154–77. New York: University Press of America, 1992.

El Cañón, 159, 190–94, 202, 206, 216
El Gran Cabezón (Apache chief), 189, 190
El Joyoso (Apache chief), 268, 271, 272
El Lumen (Apache chief), 193–94
El Turnio (Apache chief), 190, 194
Enslavement, Indian: in French Louisiana, 80,
    84–86, 255–56, 260, 269; and Spanish deporta-
    tion, 169–70, 174, 175, 189, 230, 253, 254, 257,
    274, 339 (n. 15); Spanish laws regarding, 165,
    170, 255, 256–57, 339 (n. 15); in Spanish New
    Mexico, 11, 170, 256, 287, 309 (n. 30), 324
    (n. 20); and Spanish slave raiding, 110, 115,
    161–62, 163, 165–75; in Spanish Texas, 165–76,
    189, 193, 257, 260, 324 (n. 20). *See also* Cap-
    tivity; Women—captive
Ervipiames, 114, 116, 124–26, 129, 133, 160; and
    Mission San Francisco Xavier de Nájera, 126,
    132
Eschas (Taovaya [Wichita] chief), 229, 236–41
Espinosa, fray Isidro de: among Caddos, 20, 33,
    45, 48, 64, 82, 92, 94, 95, 102; and San Antonio
    missions, 131, 149, 152; and 1709 expedition, 34,
    39, 46, 109–12, 113, 116
Evea (Comanche chief), 230, 231, 232, 243, 252,
    253, 254, 277
Eyasiquiche (Taovaya [Wichita] chief), 197–201,
    206, 251

Family. *See* Kinship
Fernández de Santa Ana, fray Benito, 113, 119, 122,
    132, 156, 165, 170, 173, 177
Firearms: among Caddos, 44–45, 56, 75, 77, 90,
    103, 104, 161, 177, 212, 221, 269–70, 304 (n. 52);
    among Comanches, 161, 180–81, 182, 187, 189,
    203, 206, 213, 240, 281, 285; lack of among
    Apaches, 160, 172, 224, 267, 269–70; in mis-
    sions, 136–37, 144–45, 146; Spanish prohibi-
    tions regarding, 203, 208, 213, 222–23; among
    Wichitas, 161, 180–81, 182, 187, 189, 203, 206,
    213, 221, 222, 223, 224, 240
Flechazos. *See* Wichitas
Franciscans: and Apaches, 166–67, 170, 173, 175,
    176, 177–80, 188, 189–91, 192–94; and Caddos,
    59–60, 71, 87, 95, 99–103, 106–7, 304 (n. 58);
    306 (n. 73); and central and south Texas native
    populations, 119–58; and disease, 59–60, 100;
    and martyrdom, 180, 183–84, 208; methods of,
    120–21; native interpretations of, 99–103; and

sexuality and marriage, 63–64, 100–101, 104,
    120, 147–55, 306 (n. 73). *See also* Diplomatic
    conventions: and religious symbolism;
    Missions
Frenchmen: adopted by Caddos, 72–79, 90–91;
    and Apache slaves, 84–86, 247–48, 269; associ-
    ated with Norteño dominance, 181, 186–88,
    189, 195, 202; and Caddo diplomacy, 17–20,
    22–56 passim, 58, 70, 71, 209, 220; as deserters
    and survivors of La Salle's expedition, 72–75,
    76, 77, 79, 80, 92; employed by Spanish offi-
    cials, 208, 209, 213, 222, 223–24, 227, 229, 260,
    279; lack of trade with Apaches, 86, 161; trade
    with Caddos, 73, 79, 80, 83, 86, 103, 104, 161,
    215–16; trade with central Texas natives, 133,
    267, 269–70; trade with Comanches and
    Wichitas, 161, 203, 206, 222, 224–26, 230, 247–
    48, 252, 263, 265, 282; trade with Spaniards,
    89–90, 93, 105–6

Gaignard, J., 223–24, 230–31
García, fray Bartholomé, 150–51, 156, 318 (n. 39)
Gender: defined, 9, 10–11; and race, 2, 13, 288,
    289, 291. *See also* Manhood; Womanhood;
    Women
Gift exchange. *See* Diplomatic conventions—
    gift-giving
Gil Ibarvo, Antonio, 225–26, 259, 260, 263, 265
González, José (commander of Los Adaes pre-
    sidio), 103, 108, 259
Grande Terre, Jeanne de la, 84, 108
Grande Terre, Marie Anne de la, 84, 213
Grappe, Alexis, 84, 213, 216, 309 (n. 26)
Guedon, Jacques, 83, 84, 213
Guersec (Taovaya [Wichita] chief), 227–28, 229,
    236–41, 266
Guns. *See* Firearms

Hasinais: confederacy, 24, 296 (n. 5); and Fran-
    ciscans, 59–60, 71, 87, 95, 99–103, 106–7, 304
    (n. 58), 306 (n. 73); origin stories, 37; and
    Spanish expulsion in 1693, 59, 64–67, 87, 111,
    112, 305 (n. 68), 306 (n. 71). *See also* Caddos
Hidalgo, fray Francisco, 49, 56, 90, 93, 102
Horses: among Apaches, 160–61, 267, 269–70;
    among Caddos, 45, 66, 80, 267; among
    Comanches, 201, 202, 229; as focus of raids,
    66–67, 161, 180, 188, 196, 201, 206, 216, 223,

Savagery, Spanish constructs of, 9; as heathenism mixed with French moral corruption, 88, 310 (n. 34); in missions, 121, 148, 150, 154, 158; toward opponents in raids and warfare, 164, 165, 173, 187–88, 194–95, 203

Settlement as alliance, 286, 287; with Apaches, 175, 178, 179, 190, 192, 249, 267, 270, 271–76; with Caddos, 70, 92, 93, 94–108, 258–60; with central and south Texas natives, 112–13, 115, 155, 158, 160; as *establecimientos de paz*, 270; with Wichitas, 222. *See also* Mission-presidio complexes

Sexual unions. *See* Cross-cultural unions

Slavery. *See* Enslavement, Indian

Soldiers, Spanish: as fighters, 171, 172, 173, 177, 186–87, 188, 232, 234; as mission guards, overseers, or defenders, 58, 61, 65, 140, 146, 190–91, 192–94; numbers of, in Texas, 94, 99, 122, 144, 331 (n. 15); as residents in missions, 157; as settlers, 92–93, 103, 105–6, 122, 211; violence of, 64–67, 92, 305 (n. 68), 306 (n. 73)

Solís, fray José de, 11; among Caddos, 41, 258; and missions, 142, 144–45, 148

Soquina (Comanche chief), 283, 284, 285

Sulujams, 123–24, 128, 138–39

Tacames, 128, 131

Talon, Pierre, 41, 72–75, 77, 79, 80, 92, 296 (n. 4)

Taovayas, 231, 272; as allies of Comanches, 230, 282; captives among, 251, 261, 262, 264, 269; diplomacy with Spaniards, 197–99, 215, 217–18, 219, 220–21, 223–24, 227–29, 251–52, 255, 258, 265–66; Red River settlement of, 200–201, 202; as Spanish-Comanche mediators, 236–41; among Wichita allies, 201, 217, 221, 222. *See also* Wichitas

Tattoos: as identity marker, 46, 75, 250, 305 (n. 63); misinterpreted as sign of sexuality, 63, 150; as sign of adoption, 73, 74, 75, 76, 78, 334 (n. 22); as status marker, 48, 63, 149, 219, 302 (n. 38)

Tawakonis, 202, 272; as allies of Caddos, 146, 197; diplomacy with Spaniards, 200, 215, 217, 219, 222, 227, 228, 250–51, 258, 333 (n. 19); among Wichita allies, 201, 221, 237, 240, 255, 266. *See also* Wichitas

Terán de los Rios, Domingo: among Caddos, 41, 48, 50, 52, 58, 65–66; expedition of (1691–92), 39, 300 (n. 23)

Texas, province of, 2–3, 5–6, 293 (n. 1); origin of name *Tejas*, 2, 20

Texita (Hasinai *caddí*), 258, 268

Tilpacopals, 129, 156

Tinhioüen (Kadohadacho *caddí*), 212, 213, 214, 215, 217, 226, 251

Tonkawas, 73, 161, 257; as Apache allies, 249, 267, 268, 269, 270; at missions, 120, 131, 132; among Norteños, 146, 175, 180, 181, 185, 191, 202; at Ranchería Grande, 116

Tonti, Henri, 22, 53, 58

Treviño, Antonio, 198–201, 223, 251, 258, 330 (n. 7)

Tusonibis, 46, 109, 110, 113

Urrutia, José de, 110, 168, 313 (n. 1)

Urrutia, Toribio de, 141, 156, 174

Vial, Pedro, 229, 237–43, 265–66, 278, 283, 284

Virgin Mary: and Caddo diplomacy, 31, 35, 38–42, 43, 57, 61, 90, 91, 287, 300 (n. 22); and Comanche and Wichita diplomacy, 215, 279; iconography of, 299 (n. 18), 313 (n. 9); in missions, 136, 152, 153–54; and Ranchería Grande diplomacy, 110, 111, 113–14

Warfare: and mutilation, 163, 166, 170–71, 173, 183, 185, 192, 228, 232, 235; native conventions of, 86, 171–72, 173–74, 181–86, 222, 227, 231; rhetoric of, 162, 164–65, 170, 171, 181, 183, 187–88, 216, 217, 230, 235–36, 245, 265–66, 270; and Spanish ideas of "just war," 165; and trophy-taking, 48–49, 170–71, 183–84, 185, 192, 218, 228, 232–33, 245, 251, 326 (n. 38), 333 (n. 19); and violence, 164, 166, 173, 183–86, 191–92, 194, 232

Wichitas, 116, 185, 197–99, 221; alliance with Comanches, 197, 236–41; diplomacy with Spaniards, 197–201, 215–29, 231, 250–52, 254–66; economy of, 181, 197, 200, 201, 203, 206; enmity with Apaches, 207, 216, 224, 227, 272–73; kinship, 198, 201, 220–21, 259, 340 (n. 19); migration to Texas, 197, 201; in Norteño alliance, 175, 180–81, 202, 203, 206, 207; political organization and rank of, 201, 207–8, 219, 236–37, 332 (n. 1); raids on Spaniards, 145, 146, 180, 188, 191–92, 222, 248, 265–66; as Spanish-Comanche mediators, 228–29, 236–41, 243,